THEGREENGUIDE
Poland

Wawel Cathedral, Kraków © haulu/iStockphoto

General Manager	Cynthia Clayton Ochterbeck

THEGREENGUIDE **POLAND**

Editorial Manager	Jonathan P. Gilbert
Principal Writer	Dennis McEvoy
Production Manager	Natasha G. George
Cartography	Stephane Anton, Thierry LeMasson
Photo Editor	Yoshimi Kanazawa
Photo Researcher	Claudia Tate
Proofreaders	Jane Donovan, Alison Coupe
Interior Design	Chris Bell
Cover Design	Chris Bell, Christelle Le Déan
Layout	Michelin Apa Publications Ltd., Alison Rayner
Cover Layout	Michelin Apa Publications Ltd.
Contact Us	The Green Guide
	Michelin Maps and Guides
	One Parkway South
	Greenville, SC 29615, USA
	www.michelintravel.com
	Michelin Maps and Guides
	Hannay House
	39 Clarendon Road
	Watford, Herts WD17 1JA, UK
	✆01923 205240
	www.ViaMichelin.com
	travelpubsales@uk.michelin.com
Special Sales	For information regarding bulk sales, customized editions and premium sales, please contact our Customer Service Departments:
	USA 1-800-432-6277
	UK 01923 205240
	Canada 1-800-361-8236

HOW TO USE THIS GUIDE

PLANNING YOUR TRIP

The blue-tabbed PLANNING YOUR TRIP section gives you **ideas for your trip** and **practical information** to help you organize it. You'll find tours, a host of outdoor activities, a calendar of events, information on shopping, sightseeing, kids' activities and more.

INTRODUCTION

The orange-tabbed INTRODUCTION section explores Poland's **Nature** and geology. The **History** section spans from first settlement to modern EU nation. The **Art and Culture** section covers architecture, art, literature and music, while **The Country Today** delves into modern Poland.

DISCOVERING

The green-tabbed DISCOVERING section features Principal Sights by region, featuring the most interesting local **Sights**, **Walking Tours**, nearby **Excursions**, and detailed **Driving Tours**. Admission prices shown are normally for a single adult.

ADDRESSES

We've selected the best hotels, restaurants, cafes, shops, nightlife and entertainment to fit all budgets. See the Legend on the cover flap for an explanation of the price categories. See the back of the guide for an index of hotels and restaurants.

Sidebars

Throughout the guide you will find blue, orange and green-colored text boxes with lively anecdotes, detailed history and background information.

😊 A Bit of Advice 😊

Green advice boxes found in this guide contain practical tips and handy information relevant to your visit or to a sight in the Discovering section.

STAR RATINGS★★★

Michelin has given star ratings for more than 100 years. If you're pressed for time, we recommend you visit the ★★★ or ★★ sights first:

★★★ **Highly recommended**
★★ **Recommended**
★ **Interesting**

MAPS

- 😊 Principal Sights map.
- 😊 Region maps.
- 😊 Maps for major cities and villages.
- 😊 Local tour maps.

All maps in this guide are oriented north, unless otherwise indicated by a directional arrow. The term "Local Map" refers to a map within the chapter or Tourism Region. A complete list of the maps found in the guide appears at the back of this book.

PLANNING YOUR TRIP

A. Galy / MICHELIN

INTRODUCTION TO POLAND

CONTENTS

DISCOVERING POLAND

Welcome to Poland

Poland's location in the centre of Europe, between East and West, has placed the country at the heart of many of Europe's cataclysms and upheavals. Beyond the associations and implications of this strategic position between Germany and Russia, the country is a great unknown for most foreign visitors. Sandy beaches await along the Baltic coast, Alpine mountains guard the southern border, and unspoilt forests and lakes dot the landscape in the northeast. But the pride of Poland is old royal Kraków, with its great town square, ancient university, and Wawel Castle.

WARSAW, MASOVIA, LUBLIN PLATEAU (pp104–155)

Warsaw is the best place to appreciate Poland's triumph over 20C misfortunes, in a buzzing capital city that sets the pace for the rest of the country. Lublin and Kazimierz Dolny boast beautiful monuments and a relaxed air, as if time has been stopped, while Łódź is waking from its economic doldrums and restoring its 19C architectural splendour.

WARMINA, MASURIA AND PODLASIE (pp156–189)

A land of thick forests and crystal lakes, this area offers an escape from urban excess. This is the most unspoilt region of Poland, with no large cities, but instead secluded national parks, the most impressive of which are the Białowieża forests, where kings and tsars once hunted, and bison still live. The Masurian Lake District offers endless outdoor activities in summer and Warmia has its Teutonic heritage.

KRAKÓW AREA (pp190–241)

The gem here is of course Kraków, unscathed during the last war and beautifully restored after the neglect of the communist years. Just out of town are the remarkable Wieliczka Salt mines, a monument to Polish industry and ingenuity. A haunting and terrible reminder of World War II's impact on Poland is at Auschwitz, where so many of Europe's Jews were brutally murdered. A potent symbol of Poland's Catholic faith can be seen in Częstochowa, home to the venerated Black Madonna icon.

Rynek Główny, Main Market Square,Kraków

Sopot wooden pier and beach in Pomerania

© Tom_u/Dreamstime.com

LITTLE POLAND AND THE CARPATHIANS *(pp242–289)*

Spectacular soaring mountain peaks and splendid timber architecture, this is a very picturesque region alive with assorted folk customs. Zakopane offers rustic relaxation in alpine surroundings; small historic cities such as Tarnów and Sandomierz boast architectural gems and small town hospitality. Sanok has one of the best *skansens* (open air museums) in all of Poland, and southeast Poland is scattered with timber churches.

SILESIA AND THE SUDETEN *(pp290–319)*

Silesia's capital Wrocław is a great surprise to many, with its lively grand town square and university making it one of the most vibrant cities in Poland. More wonderful surprises await the visitor in Jawor and Świdnica, where two spectacular Protestant timber churches have survived all of the region's wars. Skiing and hiking are also within reach, along the Czech border in the Karkonosze Mountains, plus quaint spa towns nestle within the region's mountainous western section.

GREATER POLAND *(pp320–347)*

Some of the most ancient settlements in Poland are located in Greater Poland: Biskupin's fortified villlage documents Poland's prehistory whereas the cathedrals of Poznań and Gniezno played crucial roles in the formative years of the Polish state. The region also boasts Toruń, the birth place of Copernicus, a city that still has much of its architecture preserved from the great astronomer's day.

POMERANIA *(pp348–383)*

The Polish seaside is lined with sandy beaches and pine forests, while guarding the outlet of the Vistula River is the mightly old city of Gdańsk. The splendour of Gdańsk's monuments is testament to the city's former economic power as a seaport and banking centre. For nightlife and relaxation, Sopot is Poland's premier seaside resort offering swanky hotels and elegant cafés. Malbork is where the presence of the Teutonic Knights is best appreciated. They left their mark all over northern Poland, with severe brick Gothic churches and castles, but none can match the grandeur of the Order's former headquarters.

Roundabout in Warsaw City
© Nlek/Dreamstime.com

Michelin Driving Tours

Read on to explore the areas highlighted on the inside front cover map.

GDAŃSK AND THE BALTIC COAST

Allow one week to visit the region in depth.

Discover the Tri-City *(Trójmiasto)*, which includes **Gdańsk**, **Sopot** and **Gdynia**. Extending over a distance of more than 35km, this urban collective is easily accessible by public transport. Take time to stroll along the streets of the former Danzig, an ancient Hanseatic city razed to the ground during the war and magnificently rebuilt to its former glory. Two days will enable you to visit the whole town. Escape for a day to Sopot, the seaside resort, to stroll along the promenade and meander through the town. Gdynia, a port built to provide Poland with an outlet to the sea when Gdańsk was a German port, features an architectural heritage dating from the 1920s–1930s. Discover another aspect of the coastal fringe by exploring the **Hel peninsula**, a long strip of land between only 100m and 300m wide, where pine trees grow on sandy soil. You can find accommodation along the whole peninsula, or you can choose to sleep in the old fishing port of Hel at the tip. Bathing enthusiasts will appreciate the choice of swimming either in the Baltic sea on the north side of the peninsula or along the calmer bay on the south side. Eat some fresh flounder along the coast and expect to receive it with two forks, which is how the locals expect it to be eaten. Driving west from Hel, the coast extends towards the German border, offering more stretches of beach. In **Łeba**, a fashionable seaside resort, you will find several fine beaches. Here, you can cycle or ramble through the **Słowiński nature park**, famous for its shifting sand dunes gaining ground yearly on the pine forest. Extending inland from Gdańsk is the **Kashubian Switzerland** or Little Pomeranian Switzerland *(Szwajcaria Kaszubska)*. The Kashubian influence, deeply marked by traditions, can be felt around the towns of **Kartuzy** and **Chmielno**.

Finally, reserve one whole day for a visit to the famous huge **Malbork Castle** (southeast of Gdańsk), the jewel in the crown of the Teutonic Knights' architecture.

TORUŃ AND GREATER POLAND: THE ORIGINS OF THE POLISH STATE

Allow four days to a week to discover the region which saw the birth of the Polish State.

Toruń has a well-preserved Old Town and offers visitors an occasion to walk among Gothic brick buildings that have been on the UNESCO World Heritage Site list since 1997. Stroll around the Rynek (market square), with its imposing town hall, along the banks of the Wisła. The Hanseatic city is best toured on foot and, after a day viewing all the sights, you can have a peaceful night within the ramparts. Devote half a day to a visit to **Chełmno**, a small, but prosperous town during the golden age of the Hanseatic League, surrounded by well-preserved fortifications, situated

Jetty at Sopot

C. Hervé-Bazin / MICHELIN

35km from Toruń. From **Chełmno** you can head for Poznań, located 143km southwest. On the way, stop by the interactive archaeological site/museum of **Biskupin**, known as the Polish Pompei, and get an insight into life in Poland during the neolithic period. Slightly further on, **Gniezno** boasts a sanctuary dedicated to St Adalbert, whose life is recalled through the low-reliefs of a huge bronze door. Between Gniezno and Poznań, the **Ostrów Lednicki** archaeological reserve offers the possibility of seeing the remains of the palace of the first Polish sovereign on an island in Lake Lednica.

Poznań is a lively city with a long-standing tradition of trade fairs and students. It boasts one of the finest and largest *Ryneks* in the country. Surrounding the imposing town hall are the Baroque and Classical façades of houses which were restored after the last war. Take time to discover the narrow streets and numerous churches. Two days are advised in order to get a feel of the town. Devote one day to a tour of the nearby **castles of Kórnik** and **Rogalin**. If you have some time left, go to **Kalisz**, presumed to be the oldest town in Poland, and 15km further, visit **Gołuchów Castle Museum** nestling in a lovely park with oak trees boasting circumferences of 5m. **Antonin Hunting Palace** is 37km from the castle.

A WEEK THROUGH "YESTERDAY'S" EUROPE

From the time she joined the European Union, Poland has been its eastern 'rampart'! As Ukraine has embarked on a political and economic programme of modernisation, the situation in Belarus is much less straightforward.
Both countries played a role in the development of Polish culture which still bears their imprint. Indeed, populations of Ukrainian and Belarusian origin live in the eastern regions of Poland, perpetuating their

Basilica in Święta Lipka

F. Soreau / MICHELIN

traditions and folklore and sometimes also their political memory.
Białystok, **Lublin**, **Zamość** and **Przemyśl** are examples of such blending of influences. The main interest of these towns, in addition to the rich architectural heritage found in and around them, lies in the imprint of their mixed culture: Jewish influence in Lublin, Orthodox in Białystok, Graeco-Catholic in Przemyśl, military in Zamość. Exploring these towns offers the opportunity to step back in time and rediscover Europe as it was before the 20C conflicts.

MASURIA

Allow three days to discover the region; if you wish to enjoy nature to the full, you will need longer.
From the spring to the beginning of autumn is the best time to discover Masuria. In winter, thick snow cover and biting cold offer the possibility of enjoying cross-country skiing, fishing through a hole in the ice and ice-yachting.
Reszel, a small, welcoming Gothic town, hosts an interesting 14C castle along with other Gothic structures, and is only 6km northwest of **Święta Lipka**, where one can visit a beautiful late-Baroque church and sanctuary – one of the most popular places of pilgrimage in Poland. The organ is stunning and worth listening to

when played. Another 26km to the east, **Kętrzyn** is the site of one of the castles of the Teutonic Knights and a good base from which to visit the **Wolf's Lair**, Adolph Hitler's general headquarters, from where he supervised military operations in the East. The site is now a fortified ghost town on the edge of the **Masurian lakeland** extending eastwards and known as "The Land of a Thousand Lakes". In summer, the ports of **Giżycko**, **Węgorzewo** and **Mikołajki** attract a crowd of yachting enthusiasts who enjoy sailing on the lakes, some of which are now nature reserves. The surrounding forests are crisscrossed by renowned hiking trails. Continuing eastwards for about 70km leads you to the far reaches of Poland. Still relatively unexplored by tourists, these regions boast lakes and dense forests around the towns of **Suwałki** and **Augustów**. Starting from the latter, there are fascinating canoeing itineraries along the canal of the same name.

WROCŁAW AND THE SUDETEN

Allow one week; more if you plan to go rambling.
Wrocław is full of surprises. A tour of the capital of Lower Silesia will take at least two or three days. You will need time to explore the Rynek, lined with splendidly restored houses, to stroll along the bustling streets, enlivened by the sizeable student population, and to stroll along the banks of the Oder. Ostrów Tumski, former island, site of where **Wrocław** first began and religious centre for the **Wrocław** Archdiocese, has a beautifully maintained cathedral and several churches. Parks and open spaces will give you a chance to take a break and children will love the zoo which became famous all over the country through a television programme. According to the amount of time at your disposal and what you fancy, you will have the opportunity of heading for the Karkonosze region and of discovering the town of

Jelenia Góra and the ski resort of **Karpacz**. Rambling and the discovery of nature are activities on offer less than 100km from Wrocław. Stop on the way to visit the wooden churches of **Jawor** and **Świdnica**, listed by UNESCO. 80km south of Wrocław, the **Kłodzko area** offers rambles in the heart of the Table Mountains, with their jagged landscapes. The Bear Cave and the network of tunnels of Kłodzko Fortress will take you deep underground. End your round tour with a visit to **Paczków**, a town sometimes referred to as the Polish Carcassonne (a fortified town in southern France). A 350km round tour starting from Wrocław will enable you, over four days, to see all these sites and even make a detour to the peaceful towns of **Opole** and **Brzeg**; the area surrounding the latter boasts ten wooden churches containing rediscovered 14C frescoes.

FORMER EASTERN PRUSSIA – ELBLĄG AND OLSZTYN

Allow three or four days at least to get an overall view, but you will need one week to explore it thoroughly.
Slightly set back from the Baltic coast, **Elbląg** is a fine Hanseatic town, rebuilt in traditional style with modern architectural touches. A visit to the renowned gallery of contemporary art is recommended.
The town is the starting point for boat trips on the **Elbląg Canal**, which offers exciting hydroengineering attractions: dams, locks, safety gates and slipways along 80km of the canal. One can see boats pulled up onto the land and hoisted on rails. The trip to Ostróda lasts 11 hours, but it is possible to halve the journey's time by disembarking at Miłomłyn. Just 15km northeast of Elbląg, the town of **Frombork** has based its tourist trade on its association with Copernicus, who was a canon of the cathedral and is buried inside. Visit the impressive fortified cathedral towering above the Wiślany laguna: in fine weather, the Russian town of Kaliningrad can

be seen from the top of the tower. 60km southeast of Elbląg, **Olsztyn**, a little-known but pleasant town spread across several hills and boasting many parks, makes a good overnight stop. Do not miss the medieval castle. End the round tour in **Lidzbark Warmiński**, a town dominated by one of the most spectacular Gothic castles and once the residence of the bishops of Warmia.

CARPATHIANS AND TATRAS
Allow at least one week.
It is possible to travel through the Polish mountains in a week, from **Zakopane** to **Sanok**, along a 400km-long itinerary, taking time for the occasional ramble.
From Zakopane south of Kraków to Sanok at the south-eastern end of the country, Poland looks like a mountainous region: small mountains like the Beskid (East or West), Alpine areas such as the Tatras around Zakopane and smaller, rolling mountains like the Bieszczady. These regions all retain their strong traditions, both in architecture and in folk arts and crafts. Rambling paths, which often lead through the heart of nature parks, are well marked and open to all levels of difficulty. When you visit these mountain ranges, you will be able to see the Slovakian border on a clear day. The Tatra Mountains extend well into Slovak territory and if you sail down the Dunajec Gorge in the Pienini, you will have a Polish cliff on one side and a Slovak one on the other!

LITTLE POLAND AND WOODEN CHURCHES
Allow one week along the small roads of the South.
All over Little Poland, you will see brown panels with the words *"Szlak Architektury Drewnianej"* signalling some remarkable wooden monument. Most of the time it is a church. The most famous churches, on UNESCO's World Heritage List, are **Lipnica Murowana**, **Binarowa**, **Sękowa** or **Dębno**. Villages situated southeast of Kraków, towards **Nowy Sącz** and **Gorlice**, boast wooden churches built between the 15C and 19C, which have withstood the ravages of time. Located beyond the administrative boundaries, the **West Beskid** and the **Bieszczady** also contain treasures waiting to be discovered. Visitors who don't have that much time are advised to go on a tour of regionally known wooden churches and Orthodox structures often referred to as *cerkiew*. Lists of some of these churches are often held at the local Tourist Information offices.

When and Where to Go

Poland enjoys a continental climate tempered by an oceanic influence along the coastal areas. Each season is attractive for specific reasons. **Summers** tend to be hot and sunny, but cool temperatures and rains are not uncommon.

The average daily temperature is 25°C, but with recent global trends, it has often risen above 30°C, particularly inland, where winds are less prominent and temperatures can rise more easily. The tourist season reaches its peak in July and August when tourists and Polish holiday-makers converge towards the same places. Sailing is a major activity in the Masurian lake region from May to the end of August whereas mountainous regions and nature parks attract rambling enthusiasts. It is also during this period when tourist activities are in full swing (festivals, organised activities in the *skansens*, etc). It is essential to make reservations in advance and to bear in mind that the cost of accommodation is higher

Malbork Castle in the winter

W. Buss / MICHELIN

(high-season prices) than at any other time of the year.

Spring and **autumn** are undeniably the most pleasant seasons to visit Poland: the weather is mild, days are fairly long, tourist crowds manageable and the seasons are ideal periods for sport and other outdoor activities. In spring, the awakening of nature is spectacular throughout the country; it is the ideal time to discover the many national parks. In May, the park of Kórnik Castle, south of Poznań, boasts splendid magnolias in full bloom. In autumn, Polish forests are bedecked with an infinite variety of colours ranging from green to bright red, through a whole palette of yellows. And, from the second fortnight in September, one can hear stags bellowing during the rut.

Winters are cold and dry over most of the country but damp near the Baltic; warm clothing and rain gear are essential. Temperatures oscillate around 0°C except in January and February, the coldest months of the year, when the average temperature sinks to a few degrees below zero. Snow covers the major part of the country, but is not so abundant in coastal areas. In the mountains, snow cover is generally excellent from January through to March, and winter sports enthusiasts can indulge in skiing and snowshoeing.

In Masuria, this is also the time when ice-yachting competitions take place. Winter can also be the ideal season for visiting museums and enjoying Christmas markets in many of the larger town squares.

CITY TOURS

Warsaw and Kraków are exceptionally fine destinations for a weekend. Their international airports put them within easy reach. By prolonging the weekend by one or two days, you will also be able to enjoy the cities' immediate surroundings.

WARSAW

Allow at least three days in order to make the most of the town.

Poland's capital has been undergoing constant change for several years. Skyscrapers stand next to buildings erected during the Communist period. Traces of the old régime are still noticeable in some people's attitudes and in the architectural heritage, but 'Western lifestyle' has taken firm root to confirm Warsaw's status as a thriving European capital. Tour the Old Town and admire the splendid way in which it was rebuilt after the last war. Stroll through the streets lined with 17C and 18C houses. Visit the Historical Museum and, from the castle, go south along Krakowskie Przedmieście, part of the Royal Way which used to lead to the sovereigns' summer residence in the Łazienki Park. In the centre, the Palace of Culture is Warsaw's symbol and one can enjoy a fine panoramic view of the city from the top. Walk across Plac Piłsudskiego and pay homage to the Tomb of the Unknown Soldier before entering the Saxon Gardens. The north of the town bears traces of the Jewish district decimated by the Nazis. Visit the Nożyk Synagogue to stand in silent remembrance before the remains of the ghetto wall. A visit to the Jewish Historical Institute and the Jewish cemetery, one of the largest in Europe, will fully inform you of the history of this community.

A short way out of town, at the western exit, the Kampinos nature park is the ideal place to escape the hustle and bustle of the town for both locals and visitors.

Travelling 130km southeast of the capital, you find **Kazimierz Dolny**, on the banks of the Wisła, a scenic town built entirely in Renaissance style and well worth a day trip.

KRAKÓW

Spend a minimum of three days exploring the city of Kraków.

It is a bustling medieval city, one of the rare towns in Poland to have come out of World War II unscathed. If you don't have much time, restrict yourself to the historic centre around the Rynek and the Cloth Hall, to the buildings of the famous Jagiellonian University and to the visit of the Wawel, the Polish kings' pantheon, which includes the Castle and its Cathedral. Spend at least one evening in the Jewish district of Kazimierz. If you can spend longer in the town or perhaps a brief first stay gave you a taste for more, you can devote a week to the discovery of the city's museums and monuments, and enjoy the atmosphere of its streets to the full. Kraków is best toured on foot, in particular the Old Town, surrounded by the Planty Garden Ring and the Kazimierz quarter.

Excursions from Kraków include the sprawling **Wieliczka** salt mine in the south and the memorial and museum of **Auschwitz-Birkenau**.

For each of these excursions, allow an hour to an hour and a half for the journey and a whole day for the visit. Nearer town, the suburban site of **Zwierzyniec** offers fine rambles in a rustic setting dotted with ancient mounds, and 10km east of Kraków, you can visit **Nowa Huta**, a communist town built from scratch near a village which still retains its Cistercian monastery as well as a modern church, the Ark. Only 15km to the northwest, you will find the impressive **Ojców National Park**,

Sites on UNESCO's World Heritage List

- Kraków's historic centre *(1978)*
- The Wieliczka salt mines *(1978)*
- Auschwitz Concentration Camp *(1979)*
- Białowieża Forest *(1979)*
- Warsaw's historic centre *(1980)*
- The Old Town of Zamość *(1992)*
- The castle of the Teutonic Order at Malbork *(1997)*
- The medieval city of Toruń *(1997)*
- Kalwaria Zebrzydowska: mannerist architectural ensemble and landscape pilgrimage park *(1999)*
- The churches of peace in Jawor and Świdnica *(2001)*
- Wooden churches in the south of Little Poland *(2003)*
- The Muskau Park/Park Murzakowski *(2004)*
- Centennial Hall, Wrocław *(2006)*

where limestone rocks create rugged landscapes with steep-cut dips.

ACROSS THE BORDER

Being surrounded by as many as seven different countries, Poland offers a wide choice of excursions across her borders. In 2007, Poland along with the Czech Republic, Slovakia and Lithuainia joined the Schengen area, which meant that border posts were removed between these neighbouring countries. Make sure you hold the necessary documents, and eventually visas. In some countries, you will need the international Green Card for your vehicle. Make enquiries before leaving, as requirements differ considerably. If you rent a car, ask the hiring company to confirm that you are allowed to cross the border with the vehicle.

IN UKRAINE

EU nationals do not need a visa. Even though the country may not always be readily accessible on account of its political history and of its culture, a weekend excursion

Lwow, Ukraina

A. Galy / MICHELIN

to **Lwow** *(300km east of Kraków)* is recommended. The town is accessible by a regular bus service or by car. Bear in mind that the border is a real border where problems can still arise from time to time. Situated 80km further on, Lwow is the capital of western Ukraine, therefore of the Carpathians. The majority of the population speaks Ukrainian and most Ukrainians are practising Graeco-Catholics. They were at the origin of the Orange Revolution which swept away the last leaders having risen to power with the help of the ex-USSR. Lwow is on UNESCO's World Heritage List. Surprisingly spared by the Nazi occupation forces and by the Soviet power, Lwow is a mixture of Jewish, Armenian and Polish culture. Its architectural heritage, both religious and secular, its many icon and painting museums and its parks located in the town centre make it a great weekend destination. The youth of this university town is enthusiastically open to the world and foreigners from Western Europe are very welcome. We advise you to go through a travel agency (or your hotel) for buses from Kraków, Przemyśl, Lublin, Zamość (Zamojski Hotel) or Ustrzyki Dolne. Enquire at their Tourist Offices (*see practical pages*).

IN SLOVAKIA

A simple identity card (or passport) is necessary to cross the border.
From Zakopane situated in the Tatras (border crossing of Łysa Polana south of Zakopane or Chynze in the north),

from the Pienini (border crossing of Piwniczna), or from Barwinek in the Beskid, south of Krosno, the **Slovak Tatras** are easily accessible. Apart from the exceptional natural environment, it is pleasant to cross the border and encounter a different cultural atmosphere. The great number of Gypsies on the roads and their camps and villages are, of course, not tourist sights, but they confer to the region its undeniable character. The most interesting town for an excursion of a few hours or a couple of days is **Bardejów**. It is a Gothic and Renaissance city on UNESCO's list. The surrounding area boasts many wooden churches, similar to those seen in Poland. The village of Medzilaborce, 100km east of Bardejów, and close to the Polish border at Barwinek, houses the **Warhol Family Museum of Modern Art**. And indeed, the parents of the founder of pop art, who emigrated to the US in 1913, were natives of a mountain village close to Medzilaborce. Besides documents connected with his family, the museum houses original works by the artist, some of which are from New York's Andy Warhol Foundation for the Visual Arts.

IN RUSSIA

A visa is essential and you will need a letter of invitation or a hotel reservation (see www.russianvisa.org for more information). Caution and vigilance should be applied because Kaliningrad is not always safe.
From Poland, there are two ways of entering Russia or, more precisely, the **Kaliningrad enclave**. One way is from Gdynia, the port of Gdańsk, from where boats sail towards Kaliningrad. The other consists of crossing the border 90km north of Olsztyn via road 51. Kaliningrad is then 40km away. The most remarkable German monument left in the former Königsberg, destroyed by the raids of the British army and then by the assaults of the Red army, is the

red-brick Gothic cathedral. The town houses the grave of Emmanuel Kant, who was born and taught in this town.

IN BELARUS

A visa is essential to cross the border.
From Białystok, you can reach the town of **Hrodna**, also known as Grodno, 83km away. This well-preserved city, which has a population of 300,000, is famous for its historic architectural heritage and, above all, for its 12C wooden church and the Cathedral of St Francis Xavier.
Further south, on the Polish border, the town of **Brest** is renowned for its fortress, where the Russians withstood German attacks in 1941. 60km north of the town, you will be able to explore the Belarusian side of the Białowieski primeval forest, known there under the name of **Belavezhskaya Puscha**.

IN LITHUANIA

EU nationals should carry a passport to enter Lithuania.
Vilnius lies 70km from the Polish border. Allow at least two days for an excursion starting from Suwałki or Augustów. Situated at the confluence of the Vilnia and the Neris, the town was almost entirely rebuilt after World War II. It is nevertheless a splendid

Baroque city, on UNESCO's World Heritage List, with the full flavour of the Baltic States.

IN THE CZECH REPUBLIC

An identity card (or a passport) is all EU nationals and Swiss citizens need to enter the Czech Republic.
In winter, snow makes it difficult to cross the border in areas located along the mountain ranges. Indeed, passes are often closed at this time of year.
Prague, accessible via the E65 and E67 highways from Jelenia Góra and Kłodzko, lies only 100km from the Polish border. Allow at least two days for this excursion. if you are short of time, then you might prefer to stay on the Czech side of the mountains which the Republic shares with Poland.

IN GERMANY

An identity card (or a passport) is sufficient for EU nationals.
If you go through Wrocław or the Sudeten, you will see that **Berlin** is closer than Warsaw; 350km separate Wrocław from the German capital. Roads are in good condition. Do not hesitate to take two days from your schedule in order to soak up the Berlin atmosphere and visit the museums.

What to See and Do

OUTDOOR FUN
Local and regional Tourist Offices publish literature and will answer enquiries about activities that can be enjoyed in their region.
To find some suggestions, look up the Address Books in the Discovering section of this guide for shops, sports, recreation and more.

BOAT TRIPS

All lakes and rivers of a reasonable size lend themselves to boat trips. Private companies organise cruises

sometimes lasting several hours, from the simple nautical trip to the elaborate themed excursion.
For instance, Lake Wigry in **Podlasie** offers ideal conditions for the discovery of its hidden treasures.
On the **Masurian Lakes**, boat trips take visitors on a tour of nature reserves and small sanctuary islands where a multitude of protected birds find refuge. One can take a boat trip through canals in the north and in the south, in **Bieszczady**, several boat excursions on Poland's largest manmade lake, Solina, are on offer.
In **Toruń** and **Wrocław**, excursions on the river offer a new insight into the wealth of history and architecture.

CANOEING AND KAYAKING

The northeast of the country is the most suitable region for this kind of activity, in particular the River Krutynia, which flows through a vast forest south of the Masurian Lakes, and along the renowned course of the Czarna Hańcza prolonged, via an impressive series of locks, by the Augustów Canal. Elsewhere, the rivers Dewęca and Drawa in the Brodnica region welcome canoeing enthusiasts. South of Kraków, it is possible to canoe down the Dunajec and Bobr mountain streams. It's a little more demanding than paddling along peaceful rivers, but wonderfully stimulating.

♦ **Polish Canoe Federation (PZK)**
Ul. Ciołka 17, 01-445 Warsaw.
☎022 837 14 70 and 837 40 59.
www.pzkaj.pl.

CYCLING

Cycling and rambling are great options for discovering Poland with its choice of cycle and walking paths. Many towns suggest discovery trails in surrounding areas, very often in collaboration with bike-hire companies. For instance, the Tourist Office in Poznań publishes a map of the many itineraries starting from the town centre and linking Kórnik and Rogalin castles or running along the footpaths of the Greater Poland National Park. *It is not advisable to cycle in large cities unless there are designated cycle lanes.*

♦ **Polish Cycling Federation (PZK)**
Ul. Andrzeja 1, 05-800 Pruszków
☎022 430 34 00. www.pzkol.pl.

FISHING

Fishing is a year-round activity. In winter, frozen lakes lend themselves to fishing through a hole in the ice, in particular in the Masurian Lakeland, where perch is the most common fish, closely followed by eels. Next to Pomerania, this is the most renowned fishing region. Fishing for trout in the tumultuous mountain streams of the Bieszczady is also a sought-after activity. Salmon, on the other hand, is plentiful at the mouth of rivers and the Baltic offers almost 500km of coastline suitable for sea-fishing, the prize catch being cod. In Poland, one must hold a licence in order to be allowed to practise fishing, whether sea-fishing or fresh-water fishing.

♦ **Polish Fishing Association (PZW)**
Ul. Twarda 42, 00-831 Warsaw,
☎022 620 89 66. www.pzw.org.pl
will be able to tell you how to obtain a licence.

GUIDED TOURS

In towns, tours are usually scheduled by either the **PTTK**, or privately run tour agencies. PTTK *(Polskie Towarzystwo Turystyczno-Krajoznawcze)* includes polyglot guides who propose personalised guided tours, based on what you feel you'd like and how much time

Folk dancers

W. Buss / MICHELIN

you have. PTTK excels in providing information for natural areas and heritage sites. In addition, each fairly important town proposes discovery trails; apply to Tourist Offices. In Warsaw, for example, there is a special itinerary for discovering the Old Town, the Royal Way, the Wilanów Palace and the main monuments. Another trail is devoted to Jewish heritage. In Toruń, boat trips along the River Wisła offer a discovery of the town from the river that brought it wealth during its heyday.

Refuge in the Tatra Mountains

© Piotr Rydzkowski/iStockphoto

HUNTING

Polish forests are rich in various kinds of game. It is possible to hunt deer *(September–February)*, roe-deer *(May–September)*, wild boar *(April–February)*, hare *(October–January)* and even partridge *(September–October)*. The best hunting grounds are to be found in the northeast of the country, as well as in the Bieszczady region. Roe-deer live mainly in Masuria, Pomerania and Greater Poland, where Prince Antoni Radziwiłł, a keen hunter, had a sumptuous wooden hunting palace built. Deer can be found in the majority of Poland's forests.

◆ **Polish Hunting Association (PZŁ)**
Ul. Nowy Świat 35, 00-029 Warsaw.
℘022 826 20 51. www.pzlow.pl.

ICE-YACHTING

in winter, when lakes and rivers are caught under a thick cover of ice, yachting enthusiasts always find a way to practise their favourite sport. Ice-yachting has become more popular in Poland, especially since she is a competitive leader in both world and European ice-yachting championships. It is practised mainly in the northeast, on the lakes and canals of Masuria, Warmia and Pomerania. The small town of Mikołajki gathers a great number of ice-yachting enthusiasts.

MOUNTAINEERING

Apart from climbing walls found throughout the country, the southern border is the main part of Poland where one can practise mountain climbing. In the Tatras, for instance, Zakopane is the ideal base from which to set out on an expedition. Guides and equipment available on location.

◆ **Polish Mountaineering Federation (PZA)**
Ul. Noakowskiego 10/12, 00-666 Warsaw. ℘022 875 85 05. www.pza.org.pl.

RAMBLING

Forests, mountains and nature parks abound which is why the Polish countryside lends itself beautifully to walking. Tracks and footpaths are plentiful and well marked. In each region, you will find a selection of maps detailing a choice of itineraries. Sometimes journey times are indicated on the maps, and the different sights you will see on the way are described so that you can make the most of your visit to a given region. The Polish authorities, particularly in the case of nature parks and protected areas, are making tremendous efforts to mark and maintain trails. If you can afford the time, do not hesitate to explore the countryside on foot to see some beautiful vistas from atop a mountain.

HORSE RIDING

Horse riding is a popular activity in Poland, which can be practised as part of a package tour or through private riding centres and holiday farms.

Riding across the Bieszczady National Park is a sought-after experience, as are riding tours along the Baltic beaches. It is, of course, possible to make longer tours, in particular along the 250km-long Transjurassic track linking the Kraków area to Częstochowa. In the Beskid and the Bieszczady, enthusiasts can enjoy riding small mountain horses known as Hutsuls (Huculy).

- ◆ **Polish Equestrian Federation (PZJ)**
  Ul. Lektykarska 29, 01-687 Warsaw.
  ✆ 022 639 32 40. www.pzj.pl.

SAILING

The ideal region for sailing enthusiasts is, without a doubt, Masuria. Lakes Śniardwy and Mamry, one of the largest in Poland, offer fine sailing opportunities. An important network linking lakes, canals and rivers makes it possible to sail over distances of nearly 200km. The main ports are Giżycko, Węgorzewo and Mikołajki. Sailing is also a popular activity on the Baltic Sea, in the bay of Gdańsk and around the Hel peninsula. For beginners, the Szczecin laguna is ideal as there are calm waters around the Trzebież marina. From there, it is possible to reach the island of Wolin, a former Viking colony and now a nature park.

- ◆ **Polish Sailing Federation (PZŻ)**
  Ul. Chocimska 14, 00-791 Warsaw.
  ✆ 022 541 63 40. www.pya.org.pl

SEA BATHING

With over 600km of coastline along the Baltic Sea, Poland offers a large number of beaches backed by cliffs, lagunas, or those that extend along estuaries. In Western Pomerania, sea bathing takes place around Szczecin, but the Gdańsk region has the greatest number and variety of beaches. Sopot, with its long promenade, is a great favourite. A little further north, Łeba is somewhat similar. Other appealing resorts include Kołobrzeg, Międzyzdroje, Darłowo and Ustka. Finally, the sand strip of the Hel peninsula offers a long stretch of beaches dotted with fishing villages. Bear in mind that the water on the side of the Baltic Sea is a little cold, but can be quite invigorating!

SKIING

Polish ski resorts have gained a good reputation throughout Europe over the past few years. Snow cover is significant and of good quality between November and April, but the best skiing season usually only extends from January to March; landscapes are charming and prices very affordable. Cross-country skiing, Alpine skiing and snowboarding are the main activities, but snowshoeing tours and sleigh rides are also very popular and affordable.

Zakopane, in the heart of the Tatras, is Poland's winter sports capital and a must for skiing enthusiasts. Well

Sailing is a popular sport in Poland

© Andrzej Puchta/iStockphoto

provided with runs and ski-lifts, it offers the possibility of skiing at an altitude of over 2,000m. Among other nearby resorts worth visiting is Bukowina Tatrzańska. Skiing is also one of the Beskid's major activities; the town of Szczyrk, for example, has an altitude of 811m, with peaks several hundred metres higher. In the Sudeten, the resort of Szklarska Poręba, on the slopes of Mount Szrenica, boasts a run which is lit at night. The ski runs of nearby Karpacz are on the slopes of Mount Kopa. The one downside to skiing in Poland is the tendency for anarchy to occur in the queue (or lack of any type of queue) for the lifts/T-bars. This can make reaching the lift slow.

Cross-country skiing forms part of the activities on offer in high-altitude resorts but also in the valleys of the Tatras and in the Beskid. Near Szklarska Poręba, in the Sudeten, the annual Piast race takes place in January. It is possible to practise cross-country skiing in the picturesque wooded area of Suwłaki or the Masurian Lakes, situated in the low-lying areas of the country's northeastern region.

More information is available on the website www.skiing-poland.com.

SLEIGH RACING

This Polish tradition normally takes place at carnival time in the Tatra and Beskid Mountains. However, soon after the first snowfalls, horse-drawn sleighs can be found across the country.

WILDLIFE WATCHING

Wolves still roam the forests in the Suwłaki region, while beavers colonise the numerous lakes. You can hear stags bellowing in Augustów Forest or in the Bieszczady Mountains. The Masurian Lakes are dotted with islands that are all sanctuaries for protected bird species. You can spot storks in both the north and south of the country, which is a treat for many visitors. In the Białystok region, the

---

Tour of Polish Towns by Train

If you are mainly interested in Polish towns, why not tour the country over two weeks comfortably settled in first-class velvet-covered seats or, if your budget objects, in second-class seats covered in imitation leather? Travelling by train is not expensive, it is also pleasant and you are always taken to the very heart of cities: from Warsaw to Gdańsk via Malbork, from Gdańsk to Toruń, Poznań and then Wrocław. From Wroclaw to Kraków and from the latter back to Warsaw, you will have the opportunity to see a great deal of the country's cultural wealth. And, to help organise your trip, visit the Polish railways website: www.pkp.pl.

Białowieza nature park offers visitors the rare privilege of meeting Europe's last bisons. The Biebrza Marshes are also superb for spotting wildlife, particularly birds and rare plants.

SPAS

Poland has over 30 natural spa centres open year-round. The various thermal springs provide treatments suitable for a range of complaints. The most widespread means of treatment are mineral baths, mud baths, drinking mineral water, inhaling and hydrotherapy. Most of these spas are located in either the north or south of the country, with a few in the centre, including a spa in Konstancin, outside Warsaw.

To view a map of where these spas are in Poland, visit www.sanatoria.com.pl. The Kłodzko region boasts four spas: Duszniki Zdrój, Kudowa Zdrój, Polanica Zdrój and Lądek Zdrój. All kinds of illnesses are treated there, from respiratory complaints to skin conditions and rheumatism.

In the Beskid, Krynica and Ustroń specialise in the treatment of metabolic disorders, including obesity. Other spas, situated at the foot of mountains, include Polańczyk, in the Bieszczady region, Iwonicz Zdrôj, near the Carpathians, Rabka, between Kraków and Zakopane, and Cieplice Zdrój, close to Jelenia Góra in Silesia. One can soak in the waters in Ciechocinek, 24km southeast of Toruń. The town of Inowrocław, 36km southwest of Toruń, has its own treatment centre.

A special mention should go to the **Sanatorium in Wieliczka**, south of Kraków, for originality, because it uses the facilities of the impressive salt mines which gives the local water such unusual properties.

ACTIVITIES FOR KIDS

Poland is a child-friendly place due to people's tolerance and their warm and open approach to children.

Many restaurants and cafés welcome children and offer, if not high chairs, then the option of smaller portions. Children will enjoy the open-air festivals, as well as some of the annual events, including The Great Dragon Parade (June) and the Kraków Nativity Scene *(szopka)* Competition.

In this guide, sights of particular interest to children are indicated with a symbol. Some attractions may offer discount fees for children; these are indicated in the opening times information of the sight.

SHOPPING
OPENING TIMES

Shops are usually open from 10am to 6pm from Monday to Friday, with shorter hours on Saturday. In major towns, some shops selling food and alcohol remain open late at night and sometimes 24hr/day. In all Polish towns you will find small kiosks, often indicated by a big **RUCH** sign, where you will be able to buy anything and everything: postcards, sweets, cigarettes and newspapers.

PRODUCTS

Amber is plentiful In the north of the country, along the Baltic and in Masuria; necklaces, pendants and

Souvenir stand

C. Hervé-Bazin / MICHELIN

earrings make lovely gifts. In view of the development of synthetic amber, caution is recommended and it is best to go to official dealers. You will find the finest items in Gdańsk. In rural regions, particularly mountainous areas, there are interesting **textiles** to be bought, both for clothing and decorative purposes. Keep an eye out for **contemporary designers** whose work is often quite imaginative. Travel souvenirs include fine **art books**, which will remind you of the sites and monuments you visited, glassware and wood carvings. And last but not least are Polish **posters**, whether political or cultural.

You will need special permission to take any work of art or book dating from before 1945 out of the country.

FOOD AND DRINK

There is a wide choice of great food and drink in Poland. **Vodka** tops the list for alcohol. There are varieties for every taste, from the bison herb drink *(żubrówka)* to more austere or sweeter varieties. Polish **beer** also has its share of devotees. **Charcuterie** is popular, in particular sausages and smoked ham. The mountainous regions offer different **cheeses**, including the tasty **oscypek** that has a delicate smokey flavour. Toruń, famous for **pierniki**, is the capital of gingerbread.

SIGHTSEEING
ADMISSION TIMES

Opening times of museums *(usually closed on Monday)* and other tourist sites mentioned in this guide were recorded on location. In reality, opening hours are less than reliable, and even unpredictable, particularly off-season and in more remote areas. Be patient and do not hesitate to ring the doorbell or knock at the door: it can happen that a keeper will eventually let you in and allow you to see a hidden collection.

MUSEUMS

Museums are often closed on Mondays. Admission costs between 5 and 20 PLN *(without a guide)*. Some museums only accept groups by prior appointment. For those that are located outside towns, allow the cost of parking in addition to admission charges. Explanations are often, but not always, in English. Plan your visits carefully, as museums usually close around 3 to 4pm.

Taking photographs is usually forbidden; some museums allow photography against payment of an additional charge of about 20 PLN.

NATURE PARKS

Rambling in Poland's beautiful countryside is easy. The wealth of natural sites and the determination to preserve this unique heritage led to the opening of no fewer than 23 nature parks throughout the country: many environments and ecosystems are represented. There has been a genuine effort to develop and enhance these areas; running through each of them are marked paths and discovery trails intended to make ramblers aware of the unique natural wealth of each site.

The **Góry Stołowe National Park** (est. 1993) has a fantastic landscape providing a superb setting for rambles, as in the Karkonosze, where paths running along the mountain slopes offer the opportunity of seeing ibex once imported from Corsica. In the northeasterly located **Wigierski Park** (est. 1989), lakes and forests abound. Well-kept marked paths make it possible for ramblers to encounter beavers, the symbol of the region. About 24km to the northwest of Kraków, bats living in caves are the mascot of the tiny **Ojców National Park** (est. 1956). Here, the limestone strata carved by erosion forms spectacular landscapes through which paths wend their way past castles perched on high ground and churches by the waterside. The seaside is just as fascinating with the **Słowiński National Park** and its strange shifting dunes, some of which reach 30m high. The **Białowieża National Park**, bordering Belarus and Poland, boasts the oldest primeval forest in Europe, home to around 800 wisent (European bison) and the village of Białowieża.

Adam Mickiewicz

For Poles, Mickiewicz embodied Polishness, Romanticism and Patriotism (though he's also the national poet of Lithuania). It is agreed that Mickiewicz's three masterpieces are *Dziady Part III*, *Księgi narodu polskiego i pielgrzymstwa (The Books of the Polish Nation and Pilgrimage)* – both first published in 1832 – and *Pan Tadeusz* (1834), an epic poem that all Polish students are required to read and memorise excerpts from. A filmed version was directed by Andrzej Wajda in 1999, proving that Mickiewicz's message of Christian philosophy and Romanticism is still relevant in Poland. He called Poland the "Christ of Nations" because of the country's martyrdom and struggle for independence in the 19C. In another well-known work, *Do Matki Polki (To a Polish Mother)*, he sarcastically suggests that Polish children should be given chains, rather than toys to play with, to prepare them for the injustice ahead for those born into an enslaved, occupied nation.

BOOKS
HISTORY AND REFERENCE

A Concise History of Poland.
Jerzy Lukowski and Hubert Zawadzki. *(2001).* This book, full of maps and illustrations, covers Polish society from medieval times to the present day; with an interesting focus on how Poland was altered by, and responded to, 45 years of communism.

Napoleon's Campaign in Poland 1806–1807. Francis Loraine Petre. *(2004).* A serious analytical study of military war and a wonderful overview of Napoleon's army confronting some of its most worthy opponents.

The Spring Will be Ours: Poland and the Poles from Occupation to Freedom. Andrzej Paczkowski. *(2003).* This is the first English-language book to focus on the turbulent half-century in Poland that began in 1939 with the outbreak of World War II. It offers an analysis of contemporary Polish history.

God's Playground. Norman Davies. *(2005).* Davies' treatment of Polish history is even-handed and fair as he presents an overview of the many facets of Poland. His historical books are renowned and respected in Poland.

Polish Customs, Traditions & Folklore. Sophie Hodorowicz. *(1996).* A wonderful introduction to an array of Polish traditions, covering religious holidays as well as secular activities.

FOR YOUNG READERS

Poland. Sean McCollum. *(1999).* Friendly text and design presents the country's landscape and describes in easy-to-understand language its main ethnic and cultural features. Full-colour photos, simple sidebars, a pronunciation guide, further reading list and index complete the presentation.

How to Draw Poland's Sights and Symbols. Melody S. Mis. (2004). This fun art-instruction book helps children draw simple objects such as the Polish flag, as well as major monuments (Malbork Castle) to engage the young traveller. There is also a 'fact list', time line and glossary.

FICTION

Contemporary Writers of Poland. Danuta Błaszak. *(2005).* This anthology presents contemporary writers of Poland, including two Nobel Prize winners, Czesław Milosz and Władysława Szymborska; it consists of two parts: poetry and short stories.

The Street of Crocodiles. Bruno Schulz. *(1992).* Collection of beautifully crafted short stories replete with descriptions of main streets and landmarks, as well as images of the inhabitants of Drohobych. Schulz was also a painter, though many of his works have been lost. On November 19, 1942, the writer and artist was shot by the Gestapo in the streets of Drohobych.

Ferdydurke. Witold Gombrowicz. *(2000).* A masterpiece of European modernism, first published in 1937, this novel was banned first by the Nazis and then by the Communists. Humorous and absurdist, although perhaps no longer so subversive, this book is a treasure trove of rebellion.

The Painted Bird. Jerzy Kosiński. *(1965).* A powerful book of surreal scenes; the nightmarish world of a child adrift in remote villages, faced with the hostility and cruelty of Polish peasants.

The Tin Drum. Günter Grass. (1997). A classic book (and film) with Gdańsk as background and under siege during World War II.

The Captive Mind. Czesław Miłosz. *(1953).* A superb exploration into ways of thinking and creativity, by Nobel Prize winner Miłosz.

FILMS

Człowiek z Marmuru (Man of Marble). Andrzej Wajda. *(1976).* This film is set in the 1970s as a young filmmaker wishes to find out more about the life of a bricklayer who was a symbol of the Socialist regime in the 1950s and 60s, when newly built industrialised centres, such as *Nowa Huta* (New Steelworks), were proud examples of concrete socio-realism and the celebration of industry.

Człowiek z Żelaza (Iron Man). Andrzej Wajda. *(1981).* Another Wajda classic and a Cannes Festival winner, this film focuses on the Solidarity movement in Gdańsk and contains a lot of factual footage and anecdotes; the film was produced during a time of relative cultural lenience in Poland.

Nóż w Wodzie (Knife in the Water). Roman Polański. *(1962).* Nominated Best Foreign Film at the Academy Awards in 1963, this was Polanski's first full-length film; it blends beautiful images, a wonderful soundtrack and tension into a story involving only three people. The film was shot in the Masurian Lakeland.

Rejs (The Cruise). Marek Piwowski. *(1970).* Full of nuances and references poking fun at an absurd socialist/communist system, this film works on the premise of being a weekend trip along the Wisla River, but turns out to be a comedy of errors; a favoured Polish cult film classic.

Dekalog (The Decalogue). Krzysztof Kieślowski. *(1988).* This was originally a series for TV consisting of ten one-hour films based on each of the Ten Commandments. The films are open to interpretation and are full of symbolism.

Miś (Teddy Bear). Stanisław Bareja. *(1981).* A comedic romp with a man, nicknamed 'miś' who needs to get to London in order to ensure his ex-wife doesn't steal his money from a bank account. The joy in the film is the comedy in both the script and sight gags as well as how crazy it might have been to procure a passport and leave the country during the socialist regime.

Wesele (The Wedding). Wojciech Smarzowski. *(2004).* An absurd and comic modern wedding in a rural part of Poland.

Ogniem i Mieczem (With Fire and Sword). Jerzy Hoffman. *(1999).* Based on an epic novel by Henryk Sienkiewicz, this film brings history, love and war to life as it tracks a 17C story of war between Poland and Ukraine.

Nóż w Wodzie *(Knife in the Water)* by Roman Polański (1962)

Calendar of Events

Poland has an array of festive events celebrating various types of music, culture and traditions. Many of the main ones are listed below but there are so many festivals taking place every year that it may be helpful to see a list of events for the current year on the following website: www.culture.pl.

JANUARY
Gdańsk – Polish Dance Festival www.klubzak.com.pl.

FEBRUARY
Warsaw – Poster Bienniale biannual. www.postermuseum.pl/en/biennale.
Toruń – Jazz Od Nowa Festival www.jazz.umk.pl.

MARCH
Wrocław – Przeglad Piosenki Aktorskiej (Singing Actors' Festival). www.um.wroc.pl.
Poznań – Jazz Festival www.poznan.pl.
Toruń – Klamra Theatre Festival www.visittorun.pl.

EASTER
Kalwaria Zebrzydowska – Passion Play.
Kraków – Rękawka festivities Tuesday after Easter.
Kraków – Misteria Paschalia Sacred Music Festival www.misteriapaschalia.pl.
Warsaw –International Beethoven Festival. www.beethoven.org.pl.

APRIL
Kraków – International Jazz Festival www.krakow-info.com.
Wrocław – Jazz nad Odra Festival www.um.wroc.pl.
Toruń – Toruński Festiwal Nauki i Sztuki– Toruń Festival of Science and Art. www.visittorun.pl.

MAY
Kraków – Film Festival. www.kff.com.pl.
Zakopane – Country Fair
Częstochowa – Queen of Poland's Feast. 3 May.
Kraków – Photography Month Festival. www.photomonth.com.

JUNE
Kraków – The Great Dragon Parade early June; www.cracowonline.com/events.php.
Kraków/Kazimierz – Festival of Jewish Culture. June/July. www.jewishfestival.pl.

Gdańsk FETA –International Festival of Open Air and Street Theatre

© Dariusz Kuzminski/Dreamstime.com

Kraków – International Short Film Festival.
Wrocław – Wrocław Non Stop. end of the month. www.wroclaw-life.com.
Opole – Polish Song Festival end of the month.
Poznań – Malta International Theatre Festival www.poznan-life.com.
Toruń – Song of Songs Festival www.songofsongs.pl.
Gdańsk – International Festival of Organ Music. until the end of August. www.en.gdansk.gda.pl.

JULY

Kraków – Street Theatre International Festival. teatrkto.pl.
Kraków – Summer Jazz Festival www.cracjazz.com.
Zamość – International Folk Festival.
Toruń – Music and Architecture Summer Festival. late June–late August. www.visittorun.pl.
Gdańsk – Northern Peoples Folklore Festival.
Gdańsk – 'Baltic Sail': International Regattas. www.gdansk-online.eu.
Gdańsk FETA – International Festival of Open Air and Street Theatre www.plama.art.pl.

AUGUST

Krynica – Jan Kiepura European Festival. www.kiepurafestival.pl.
Zakopane – Mountain Folk Festival last week in August. www.zakopane-life.com.
Częstochowa – Feast of the Częstochowa Virgin. 26 August.
Kraków – Music in Old Kraków Festival. www.krakow-info.com.
Kudowa Zdrój – International Music Festival.
Duszniki Zdrój – Chopin Festival www.chopin.festival.pl.
Gdańsk – Shakespeare Festival www.shakespearefestival.pl.
Gdańsk – St Dominic's Fair (3 weeks of outdoor events and open-air market; started 700 years ago.

Reconstructions and historical pageants

The Poles love reconstructions of major episodes in their history. At the prehistoric site of Biskupin, an archaeological festival takes place every year during the third week in September. In Gniew, in Pomerania and in Gołub-Dobrzyń, near Toruń, medieval tournaments are re-enacted. In Frombork Castle, the siege of 1410 is re-enacted at the end of July each year.

Jarosław – Song of Our Roots Early Music Festival. www.festiwal. jaroslaw.pl.

SEPTEMBER

Częstochowa – Harvest Festival 1st Sunday in September.
Zawoja – Folk Song and Dance End of the month.
Wrocław – Wratislawia Cantans www.wratislaviacantans.pl.
Kłodzko – Theatre Festival.
Kraków – Sacrum Profanum Music Festival. www.sacrum profanum.com.
Gdańsk – Gdynia Film Festival http://eng.fpff.pl.

OCTOBER

Kraków – Unsound New Music Festival. www.unsound.pl/en.
Warsaw –Jazz Jamboree Festival www.jazz-jamboree.pl.
Warsaw – International Film Festival Warszawa Film Fest; www.wff.pl.

NOVEMBER

Kraków – Andrzejki (St Andrew's Day). Night of 29–30 November.

DECEMBER

Poznań – International 'Masks' Theatre Festival. First weekend in December. http://visitpoznan.info.
Kraków – Szopki Krakowskie – Kraków Nativity Scene Competition.

Know Before You Go

USEFUL WEBSITES

www.poland.gov.pl

A font of Polish information covering history, culture, economy, tourist information and tips for business travellers. You can check the exchange rate, catch up on the latest regional news, listen to Polish radio and plan your trip to Poland, all within just a few clicks.

www.poland.com

Offers information and advertising related to travel and business in Poland. There are special offers for hotels, rental cars and package tours, a forum and a section on Polish culture.

www.cie.gov.pl

European Information Centre – Information on Poland in the European Union.

www.mkidn.gov.pl

Ministry of Culture and Heritage.

www.instytutksiazki.pl

Cultural news.

www.culture.pl

Everything from biographies of Polish cultural figures to museums and recent exhibits.

INTERNATIONAL TOURIST OFFICES

- **Polish National Tourist Office, London**
  Level 3, Westgate House, West Gate, London W5 1YY.
  ℘(44) 0870 0675 010 *(brochure line)*. www.visitpoland.org.

- **Polish National Tourist Office, New York**
  5 Marine View Plaza, Suite 208 Hoboken, NJ 07030.
  ℘(1) 201 420 9910
  www.poland.travel/en-us.

LOCAL TOURIST OFFICES
TOURIST OFFICES

Every town wanting to promote its cultural heritage has a Tourist Office with English-speaking staff. Available literature is of good quality and includes sight and tour brochures, detailed rambling maps and various regionally produced flyers.

PTTK (Polskie Towarzystwo Turystyczno Krajoznawcze)

The Polish Association for promoting tourism has a vast network of offices in the country's major cities. For decades now, it has been looking after footpaths and river courses as well as a few regional museums specialising in nature. www.pttk.pl

ASSOCIATIONS
UK

The Polish community outside Poland amounts to 40 million and is the second largest diaspora in the world, next to that of China. There are about two million Poles living in the UK. The Polish Cultural Institute is a non-profit organisation associated with the Polish Ministry of Foreign Affairs, dedicated to promoting Polish culture in Britain.

The aim of the Institute is to bring contemporary Polish culture to a wider British audience through programmes featuring art, film, theatre, music and literature. As well as holding events in the beautiful English Heritage building in the heart of London's West End, they also take their events to venues around the UK.

- **Polish Cultural Institute**
  52/53 Poland St, London W1F 7LX.
  ℘(44) 203 206 2004.
  www.polishculture.org.uk.

US

Polish traditions are certainly alive and well in the US, particularly around Chicago, where many immigrants settled. The Polish Cultural Institute in New York is a diplomatic mission of the Ministry of Foreign Affairs of the Republic of Poland and promotes Polish cultural activities in the US and helps to develop social outreach programmes.

- ♦ **Polish Cultural Institute**
  350 Fifth Avenue Suite 4621
  New York, NY 10118
  ☎(1) 212 239 7300.
  www.polishculture-nyc.org.

- ♦ **www.polskiinternet.com**
  P.O. Box 56099, Chicago,
  IL 60656-0099, USA.
  ☎(1) 773 544 8809.
  www.polskiinternet.com.

Created in Chicago in 1998 to promote all Polish and Poland-related web sites on the internet. Their goal is to promote Polish Culture and Heritage and to help Poles around the world connect with their fellow countrymen for social and/or business purposes. Most visitors and featured websites are from the USA, but other countires are represented. This is one of the largest directories of Polish associations available online.

INTERNATIONAL VISITORS
EMBASSIES AND CONSULATES

Embassy of the Republic of Poland, London
47 Portland Place London W1B 1JH. ☎(44) 0207 291 3520. www.polishembassy.co.uk.

Embassy of the Republic of Poland, Ontario
443 Daly Avenue, Ottawa, Ontario K1N 6H3. ☎(1) 613 789 0468. www.ottawa.polemb.net.

Embassy of the Republic of Poland, Washington, DC
2640 16th Street, NW Washington, DC 20009. ☎(1) 202 234 3800. www.polandembassy.org.

Consulate of Poland, New York
233 Madison Avenue, New York, NY 10016. ☎(1) 212 561 8160. www.polishconsulateny.org.

ENTRY REQUIREMENTS
Identity Card, Passport
Nationals of countries within the EU need only a national identity card, or passport. Nationals of other countries must be in possession of a valid national passport.

Visa
No visa is required for nationals of any of the EU countries or of one of the countries having signed an agreement with Poland (including Switzerland).

CUSTOMS REGULATIONS

Exporting certain items of historical, artisitic or cultural value may be prohibited or subject to particular regulations – so be careful if you are keen to buy antiques. It is strictly forbidden to carry weapons, drugs or dangerous products. If you are found to have a high quota of alcohol and tobacco, you may be asked to prove it is for personal consumption.
Residents of EU Member States are allowed to bring home 10 litres of alcohol, 90 litres of wine, 110 litres of beer and 200 cigarettes.
US residents may bring back $800 worth of items duty free, as accompanied baggage. Keep your receipts with you. One litre of alcoholic beverages may be included in your exemption if you are 21 years old. The exemption includes not more than 200 cigarettes and 100 cigars. Tourists can recover VAT (a 22% tax in Poland) on purchases over 200 PLN. The simplest way is to make any large purchases in a store with a 'tax free' offer advertised (*keep your passport and return ticket handy*).

PETS

The shipment of cats and dogs to Poland is permitted upon receipt of an official veterinary certificate by border authorities, subject to conditions. The relevant form may be obtained from Polish consulate or embassy websites (*see left*). When travelling within the EU with your pet check that the microchip can be read before you go and make sure that the paperwork for your pet is in order.

Under the Pet Travel Scheme (PETS), dogs, cats and ferrets may enter/re-enter participating countries (e.g. UK) without quarantine as long as they meet the rules. Check www.defra.gov.uk for more information.

HEALTH
BRITISH TRAVELLERS

During a temporary stay in Poland, **British and Irish citizens** are entitled to emergency medical treatment on the same terms as Polish nationals upon production of a **European Health Insurance Card (EHIC)** issued in the UK before leaving the country. The EHIC is available free of charge from post offices, by calling the UK's Department of Health ☎0845 606 2030 or visiting https://www.ehic.org.uk/Internet/home.do (Ireland: *www.ehic.ie*). The EHIC is not a substitute for medical and travel insurance; you will find further information about health insurance in Poland at *www.nfz.gov.pl/ue*. Travellers from **outside the European Union** should ask their travel agent or insurance agent about medical coverage abroad.

US TRAVELLERS

If an American citizen becomes seriously ill or injured abroad, a US consular officer can assist in locating appropriate medical services and informing family or friends. If necessary, a consular officer can also assist in the transfer of funds from the United States. However, payment of hospital and other expenses is the responsibility of the traveller.

Before going abroad, learn what medical services your health insurance will cover overseas.

If your health insurance policy provides coverage outside the United States, carry both your insurance policy identity card as proof of such insurance and a claim form. Although many health insurance companies will pay "customary and reasonable" hospital costs abroad, very few will pay for your medical evacuation back to the United States. Medical evacuation can easily cost $10,000 and upwards, depending on your location and medical condition.

The Social Security Medicare program does not provide coverage for hospital or medical costs outside the US. Senior citizens may wish to contact the American Association of Retired Persons for information about foreign medical care coverage with Medicare supplement plans.

Any medication being carried overseas should be left in the original containers and clearly labelled.

The booklet *Health Information for International Travel* may be obtained through the Superintendent of Documents, US Government Printing Office, Washington, DC 20402.

For detailed information on physicians abroad, the authoritative reference is *The Official ABMS Directory of Board Certified Medical Specialists*, published for the American Board of Medical Specialists and its certifying member boards. This publication should be available in your local library. US embassies and consulates abroad maintain lists of hospitals and physicians. Major credit card companies can also provide the names of local doctors and hospitals abroad. Hotels can provide information about local medical services.

PHARMACIES

There is little difference between Polish and other European pharmacies. The same medicines are available and the staff will often speak English. Most large towns have 24/7 chemists.

ACCESSIBILITY

Anything built from the 1990s onwards is likley to be wheelchair friendly. Modern buses, hotels and some InterCity trains are accessible. Sadly, older, unrenovated museums are likely to have too many steps, as will basement venues in Old Town town centres. There's not much braille used for interpreting either.

Getting There and Getting Around

BY PLANE

Low-cost European short-haul airlines have made flying the the most practical and cost-effective way of travelling to Poland for most visitors.

AIRLINES

LOT, the national airline *(www.lot. com)* offers domestic and international service. Other airlines that offer budget flights within Poland as well as from various points throughout the European Union include: **Wizzair** *(www.wizzair.com)*, **easyJet** *(www.easyjet.com)* and **Ryan Air** (www.ryanair.com). Flight time to Warsaw from London is two and a half hours, time between Warsaw and New York is 8.5 hours.

BY TRAIN

It's easy to travel from the UK to Poland by train. Cities with direct routes into Poland include Vienna, Berlin, Prague and Moscow. A good website to check on Intercity trains within the country and to various other countries is www.intercity. pl. Travel in Poland is included on both InterRail *(www.interrailnet.com)* and Eurail *(www.eurail.com)* passes. The Polish State Railways **PKP** (Polskie Koleje Państwowe, *www.pkp.pl*) network includes over 25 000km of lines, making most places in Poland accessible by train. **Express trains**, **Intercity** and **Eurocity** operate long-distance routes, directly linking major cities.

😊 **Useful rail words** 😊

główny: central station (useful information since all major towns have several stations).
tor: track
peron: platform

😊 **Go by rail** 😊

pkp.com.pl – The rail company's official site is useful for planning train travel inside Poland, with schedules and routes.

Their timetables are marked in red with an R next to the time.
'Fast trains' are in fact rather slow since they stop more often than express trains. They are also marked in red. As for **normal trains**, they can be *really* slow! All trains offer the choice between first and second class. First-class carriages on 'normal' trains are few but more exist on the more modern Intercity (IC) locomotives. All stations have a left-luggage office; allow 8 PLN per day. Don't forget night trains for long journeys, but it is sometimes essential to reserve couchettes a long time in advance.

BY COACH/BUS

Coach travel from London to Warsaw takes approximately 27 hours. In the UK, you can call the **National Express** dedicated booking line ☎08717 818 178, the Disabled Persons Travel Helpline ☎08717 818 179, the textphone line for customers who are deaf or hard of hearing ☎0121 455 0086. www.nationalexpress.com.
Eurolines has a far-reaching network, and its website www.eurolines.com has information on their pass offer for low-cost travel between Europe's classic cities: 15 or 30 days' unlimited coach travel between 40 cities.
You can pre-book your first journey and for all other journeys, book as you travel. Trains are a better choice over long distances, but buses, although slower, are often the only means of reaching remote places, particularly in mountainous regions or rural areas. A few private companies operate services between large towns. Bus terminals are often situated near railway stations and sometimes share the same ticket office. Private companies usually have their own

terminal. Information for the State company **PKS** *(www.pks.warszawa. pl)* offers a comprehensive website providing timetables and destinations leaving from Warsaw. PKS is a national company, but for travel information leaving from a particular city, one must replace 'warszawa' with, for example, 'Łódź or 'Kraków'.

BY CAR

Do not forget the car registration papers, but the International Insurance Green Card is no longer required now that Poland is a member of the EU. However, Swiss nationals and non-EU citizens are still required to have one with them; if they don't, they run the risk of being fined several thousand Zlotys. It is possible to acquire one at the border posts before entering Poland.

MAIN MOTORWAYS LEADING TO POLAND

Michelin Motoring Atlas Europe gives itineraries for driving to Poland from anywhere in Europe. Poland has borders with Germany, the Czech Republic, Slovakia, Ukraine, Belarus, Lithuania and Russia. Below are the main highways leading into Poland:
E 28: German border, Kokbaskowo, Szczecin, Koszalin, Słupsk, Gdynia, Gdańsk.
E 30: German border, Świecko, Poznań, Konin, Warsaw, Siedlce, Biała Podlaska, Terspol, Belarusian border.
E 36: German border, Olszyna.
E 40: German border, Zgorzelec, Wrocław, Opole, Kraków, Rzeszów, Przemyśl, Medyka, Ukrainian border.
E 67: Czech border, Słone, Kudowa Zdrój, Wrocław, Piotrków Trybunalski, Warsaw.
E 75: Czech border, Cieszyn, Bielsko-Biała, Katowice, Czestochowa, Lódź, Toruń, Gdańsk.
E 77: Slovak border, Chyżne, Kraków, Kielce, Warsaw, Ostróda, Elblag, Gdańsk.
E 462: Czech border, Cieszyn, Bielsko-Biała, Wadowice.

BORDER POSTS OPEN 24H/DAY

With Ukraine
Medyka, Korczowa, Hrebenne, Dorohusk, Zosin, Krościenko.

With Belarus
Terespol, Koroszczyn, Sławatycze, Kuźnica, Białostocka, Połowce, Bobrowniki.

With Russia
Gołdap, Gronowo, Bezledy.

INTERNET ROUTE PLANNING

You can obtain personalised itineraries, addresses of hotels and restaurants, as well as practical and sightseeing information about places on the way through Michelin's route-planning service:
www.viamichelin.com.

DRIVING LICENCE

In order to drive in Poland, you must have either a valid passport and an international driving licence, or a driving licence from another EU country. The Green Card is no longer necessary since Poland is now a member of the EU.

CAR HIRE

Renting a car in Poland will cost between 100 and 400 PLN per day depending on the model and agreement. It is possible to drive a rented vehicle through the neighbouring countries, but you must check the company's policy on whether cars are allowed into Russia, Belarus and Ukraine. Most companies will agree, for an additional fee, to allow you to return the car to the agency in another city. Large international companies are all represented in Poland but there are also more modest private companies that are likely to be cheaper but may not offer such a flexible or English-speaking service.

Avis
www.avis.pl
Reservations office within Poland:
☎0801 1 200 10

Warsaw: *in the centre* ☏*022 630 73 16*
Okęcie Airport: ☏*022 650 48 72*
Gdańsk: ☏*058 300 60 05*
Poznań: ☏*061 849 23 35*
Wrocław: ☏*071 372 35 67*
Bydgoszcz: ☏*052 375 38 08*
Kraków: ☏*012 629 61 08*
Katowice: ☏*032 257 20 70*

Budget
www.budget.com.pl
Central reservation: ☏*022 650 40 62*
Kraków: ☏*012 637 00 89*
Gdańsk: ☏*058 305 61 55*

Europcar
www.europcar.com.pl
Warsaw Okęcie Airport*:*
☏*022 650 44 52*
Kraków: ☏*012 633 77 73*
Gdańsk : ☏*058 341 98 43*

Hertz
www.hertz.com.pl
Central reservation*:* ☏*022 500 16 20*
Warsaw Okęcie Airport: ☏*022 650 28 96*
Gdańsk: ☏*058 349 48 08*
Katowice: ☏*032 284 51 03*
Kraków: ☏*012 285 50 84*
Łódź: ☏*042 686 60 01*
Olsztyn: ☏*089 532 12 38*
Poznań: ☏*061 868 41 77*

National
www.nationalcar.com.pl
Warsaw Okęcie Airport*:*
☏*022 868 75 74*
Kraków: ☏*0505 761 461*
Gdańsk: ☏*0665 301 706*

POLISH CAR HIRE COMPANIES:
Local Rent A Car
www.lrc.com.pl
Office in Warsaw: ☏*022 826 71 00;*

GE-CAR
Warsaw *Okęcie Airport:* ☏*022 650 33 85*

Joka Rent a Car
www.joka.com.pl
Kraków: ☏*012 429 66 30*
Warsaw: ☏*022 636 63 93*
Gdańsk: ☏*058 320 56 45*

Express Rent a Car
www.express.pl ☏**012 1 97 79**
Express has competitive rates and provides cars to Gdańsk, Warsaw, Kraków and Katowice airports.

ROAD CONDITIONS

The road network is well developed, but surfaces vary from smooth new motorways to uneven single tracks and single-lane throughways. Sections of motorway, marked with the letter E followed by a figure, lead out of many of the urban areas including Warsaw, Wrocław, Gdańsk and Kraków. There are a few main roadways running along a north–south axis and a big motorway running from west to east, linking the German border and Kraków *(via Wrocław and Katowice)*.

The rest of the network is in a steady state of renovation; the areas in need of most work are the narrow two-lane main roads that have either potholes or long trenches caused by the mixture of the weight of lorries and expanding asphalt due to extreme hot and cold weather. Such roads are becoming less of a feature on the network.

Overtaking is commonplace and can be quite alarming for drivers used to more than one lane. As a result, expect to see cars coming towards you on your side of the road as they aim to overpass. Lorries and farm vehicles often slow traffic down, which is why the bolder drivers make what appear to be reckless moves, but are usually done out of necessity to save time. If the roads you need to take are smaller, don't base the number of kilometres in a distance to calculate your journey time; for example, the distance between Warsaw and the Masurian Lakes (around 240km) is a 4hr drive.

In winter, snow cover blocks the passes linking Poland with the Czech Republic and with Slovakia. In isolated regions such as Podlasie, many roads also become impassable.

DISTANCE BETWEEN THE MAIN TOWNS

	Białistok	Kraków	Gdańsk	Łodź	Lublin	Olsztyn	Poznań	Warsaw	Wrocław
Białistok	–	490	4132	367	260	227	503	193	539
Kraków	490	–	597	242	295	508	450	296	275
Gdańsk	413	597	–	357	506	268	313	345	448
Łodź	367	242	357	–	261	315	221	139	208
Lublin	260	295	506	261	–	373	477	166	433
Olsztyn	227	508	268	315	373	–	330	218	466
Poznań	503	450	313	221	477	330	–	312	168
Warsaw	193	296	345	139	146	218	312	–	352
Wrocław	539	275	448	208	433	466	168	352	–

MAPS AND PLANS

Michelin Map 720 Poland, on a scale of 1:700,000, gives an excellent view of the whole country.

HIGHWAY CODE

Traffic in Poland drives on the right. The Polish highway code is similar to codes currently used in the rest of Europe. Indeed, road signs are international. Right of way is indicated by road signs but in town bear in mind that right of way must be given to trams at all times.

SPEED LIMITS

- 50km/hr in built-up areas.
- 90km/hr on other roads.
- 100km/hr on dual carriageways
- 130km/hr on motorways.

Vehicles towing a caravan must not exceed 70km/hr.

LIGHTS

The law states that headlights must always be dipped.

SAFETY PRECAUTIONS

Wearing a seat belt is compulsory. Children under 12 must sit in a safety seat. Drivers must not use hand-held mobile phones, but may use headsets and other hands-free devices to make and receive calls.

All vehicles must be equipped with a first-aid kit, replacement bulb and a warning triangle. In built-up areas, you must comply with the injunctions of police officers in uniform or civilian clothes. Outside built-up areas, you must comply with injunctions of police officers in uniform or in civilian clothes if they are standing near a police car. Minimum driving age is 17 years old.

ROAD SIGNS

Road signs are similar to those used in the rest of Europe although there are a few specific panels essentially concerning built-up areas. The road sign marking the entrance to a built-up area features the outline of a

Pedestrian crossing

B. Brillon / MICHELIN

town. Crossed by a red line, the same panel indicates the end of the built-up area. A road sign featuring a little girl holding a balloon means that children are often crossing at that spot.

DRINKING AND DRIVING

The law takes a zero tolerance stance on drinking and driving on the road. Any intake of alcohol, even the slightest, by the driver of a vehicle can lead to a hefty fine and an arrest. When it reaches 0.5mg/litre of alcohol in the blood, the simple breach of the law becomes a criminal offence and the offender runs the risk of being sent to prison for up to two years with immediate effect.

PARKING

Most towns are now equipped with parking ticket machines. In smaller towns, a municipal employee sells parking tickets. His presence guarantees the safety of your vehicle but if you have to park overnight, choose an enclosed guarded car park. These car parks are located often on the edge of town centres (at least 30 PLN per night).

FINES

The penalty for failing to observe any of the highway code rules is a fine ranging from 100 to 500 PLN. Points taken from driving licences is an additional penalty that applies in some cases and, in view of agreements between Poland and countries that also use this system, foreign offenders in theory run the risk of having points taken from their own licence.

FUEL

Poland has numerous petrol stations belonging either to Polish companies such as CNG and Orlen, or to internationally known organisations like Shell. Most petrol outlets located on main roads are open 24hr a day. Others are open from 6am to 8pm or even 10pm. All types of fuel are available. 94-octane petrol is marked

in yellow, whereas 95 and 98-octane unleaded petrol is marked in green. Also on sale is unleaded U95 petrol intended for cars without a catalytic converter, as well as diesel. Allow about 4.47 PLN for a litre of petrol and about 3.7 PLN for a litre of diesel.

BREAKDOWN

The **Starter** patrol offers roadside assistance to those who subscribe to the service (_061 831 98 25; www. starter24.pl)_. If you have a treakdown, you can call the 24/7 call centre on _0600 222 222_.
The **Polish Automobile and Motorway Federation (PZM)** also provides roadside breakdown service. Within a 50km radius of main towns, a simple phone call (_022 1 9637 national assistance; www.sospzmot. pl)_ will enable you to benefit from the federation's free breakdown service if you have an AIT (Alliance Internationale de Tourisme) card or are a member of a motoring club affiliated to the Fédération Internationale de l'Automobile (FIA).

BY PUBLIC TRANSPORT

In large towns, you will usually have the choice between tram, bus or metro _(in Warsaw only)_. Tickets can be bought in RUCH kiosks and in hotels. There are travel cards for one day, one week and one month. Information is available from Tourist Offices.

BY TAXI

Taxi ranks are indicated by a panel "Taxi". A higher rate applies to journeys taken on Saturdays, Sundays, at night between 10pm and 6am, and beyond urban areas. The first kilometre costs approximately 6 PLN, thereafter the charge is 2.5 PLN per kilometre. In Warsaw and Kraków, taxis waiting outside stations and at the airport are likely to charge more. In all Polish towns, you can ring for a taxi. Calling for a taxi tends to be cheaper than if you get one on the street.
 Always _use registered taxis and make sure that the meter is working_.

Where to Stay and Eat

WHERE TO STAY

There are many accommodation options in Poland and prices vary widely, from wonderfully inexpensive to prohibitively costly (often found in major cities).

FARM HOLIDAYS

Agricultural Tourism
(Agroturystyka) – This is a more recent tourist development offering visitors the option to live 'closer to the land' by offering either the chance to help with work on the farm or simply to enjoy organically produced food harvested from an adjacent farm. In some instances this term is used rather slimly and the only 'earthy' aspect of the 'agro' experience is the fact that horse riding is on offer.

PRIVATE ROOMS

Getting a private room is similar to the concept of a very basic bed and breakfast, in some cases without the breakfast. Whether they are in towns or in the country, private rooms are indicated by panels marked **Noclegi** (night) or **Pokoje** (room).

GUEST HOUSES

Guest houses vary in comfort and luxury but are often a great compromise between the sparcity of a private room and potentially higher costs and large size of big hotels. They are often called either **hotelik** or **pensjonat**.

CAMPSITES

The network of campsites operated by the PFCC (197 in all) covers the whole country. Campsites are open from 1 May or 1 June to 15 or 30 September.

♦ **Polish Federation of Camping & Caravaning (PFCC)**
  Ul. Grochowska 331.
  ☏ 022 810 60 50.
  www.pfcc.eu

WEBSITES

www.discover-poland.pl
A good website showing hotel offers and discounts in various Polish cities.

www.hotelsinpoland.com
Good selection of various types of hotel throughout the country.

www.staypoland.com
A good site for accommodations and tours.

Hotel Gołębiewski in Mikołajki, Masurian Lake District

© Polish National Tourist Office

www.polhotels.com
This site lists an assortment of deals on hotels and apartments throughout Poland and also lists several car hire companies.

www.hotelspoland.com
A site that focuses on an array of accommodation and specialises in good discounts.

www.warsawshotel.com
Renting an apartment can be an interesting alternative to staying in a hotel and allows you the freedom to prepare your own food and/or save money for families or groups of friends.

HOTELS

There are hotels of all categories, for all tastes and at all prices. The number of hotels has been increasing over the past few years. Hotels dating from the Communist period have not all disappeared. Some of them were restored and adapted to a more modern and pleasant level of comfort, others, now becoming rare, still boast the atmosphere of bygone days: huge marble halls, brown wallpaper or wall-to-wall carpet, neon lights, outdated furniture and beds. It can be a real journey back in time! However, over the past several years, modern establishments have sprung up, particularly in some town centres undergoing full renovation programmes. From five-star hotels (with all business facilities and spas) and charming guest houses to clean budget hostels, the choice is wide enough to suit most needs.

♦ **Polish Tourist Board Reservation System**
www.polska.travel.en

Orbis Hotel Group runs the largest hotel network in Poland. Its members include Sofitel, Ibis and Mercure. To make reservations at Orbis Group hotels: *0801 606 606, +48 502 805 805. www.orbis.pl.*

☺ Useful Tip ☺

In towns, most hotels propose lower tarifs during weekends. It is not necessary to pack products like soap or shampoo; most establishments consider that they owe it to their reputation to provide these for customers.

BOUTIQUE HOTELS

The market for, and availability of, small luxury hotels, is beginning to grow. On offer, for example, are former granaries magnificently restored in Toruń, Reszel Castle or the Antonin hunting lodge in Greater Poland.

BUDGET ACCOMMODATION

Several options of budget accommodation are available through organisations such as youth hostels, pensions, tourism centres and private room associations.
You can book a place in a youth hostel by contacting:

♦ **Polish Youth Hostel Federation (PTSM)**
Ul. Chocimska 28,
00-791 Warsaw *022 849 81 28.*
www.ptsm.org.pl.

In some towns, **student hostels** welcome visitors in summer and during university holidays, particularly in Warsaw, Kraków, Wrocław, Poznań and Gdańsk.

WHERE TO EAT

Eating well will not cost you a lot in Poland, where restaurants are plentiful and varied.

MIECZNY BARS

The **Bar Mleczny** ("milk bar") is a real Polish institution and a legacy from the Communist era, operating as self-service establishments. They attract students, those on modest budgets and those looking for traditional Polish food without the fanfare. One can eat well for around 15 PLN, where helpings are often copious. The menu

Outdoor eating, Poznań

R. Mattes / MICHELIN

is not hard to decipher, since dishes are usually visible behind the counter.

RESTAURANTS

Restaurants targeting tourists, where the décor is often over-the-top and/ or full of lace doillies and fake flowers, tend to be mediocre. It's best to look for places that offer real Polish specialities or typical dishes from Poland's neighbours such as Ukraine. Besides classic restaurants, there are pizzerias, chain restaurants , coffee and tea houses, bistros and establishments that offer *Karczma* (inn) or *Chłopskie Jadło* ('peasant' kitchen). These last two options serve Polish food in large portions and have a rustic atmosphere. They are great places to go after a day of activity or during the winter.

Opening Times

Restaurants are usually open without a break from 11am or noon to 10pm. Some of them specify that they are open "until the last customer goes". The Poles tend to have dinner around 7pm, so the last customer could be leaving around 9.30pm, but this isn't the case in the larger cities.
Mealtimes in Poland are, traditionally, the following: **Breakfast** is copious (eggs, sliced meats, bread, dairy products) and enables one to hold out for a good part of the day. Towards midday, Poles have a very light snack, but the second meal, which could be compared to **lunch**, is only taken at the end of the working day, around 4pm. The third, lighter meal, **dinner**, is taken around 7pm. People in large cities do not observe these meal times and dinner is often taken fairly late at night.

Menu

In more modest establishments, the menu in Polish may be difficult to decipher, which gives one an opportunity to have a potentially unusual but interesting culinary experience. However, many places do offer menus in English. You may find that some menus show the weight, in grammes, in which a particular item will be charged and served.
This is useful to know because, for example, a piece of fish might seem inexpensive, but the menu may only be showing the price of its first 100gms and you may be served a piece that is actually over 200gms.

The Bill

Although one can have a generous and tasty meal in a milk bar for ten złotys, a meal in a more traditional establishment costs between 30 and 70 PLN. In a highly rated restaurant, the bill can vary from 100 to 1,000 PLN, wine included. Tips are not included; it is recommended to leave an additional ten per cent.

Basic Information

BUSINESS HOURS

Traditionally, business hours in Poland were from 7am–3pm, but the common hours now are, generally, Monday–Friday 8.30am–5pm, Saturday 9am–1pm with operations closed on a Sunday. Please note that these hours are not the same for shopping, which include Sunday hours in shopping centres which are often open until 8pm on most days.

COMMUNICATIONS
TELEPHONE

To make a call from a public telephone booth, you must buy phone cards of 25, 50 or 100 units in kiosks or at the reception desk of some hotels. Keep in mind that many of the public phone booths are not maintained as well as they used to be, due to the ubiquitous mobile phone.

Calling Poland from Abroad

Dial the international access code (usually 00) then 48 (country code), followed by the area code (omitting the initial 0) and the number of the person you are calling.

Phoning Abroad from Poland

for the UK, dial 00 then 44 followed by the area code (omitting the initial 0) and the number.

Country codes

Ireland: 📞 00 + 353
Canada: 📞 00 + 1
USA: 📞 00 + 1
Australia: 📞 00 + 61
New Zealand: 📞 00 + 64

Local and National Calls

Due to recent changes, calls dialled both within a region and between two regions must include the area code including the initial 0.

Some area codes:

Warsaw: 022
Gdańsk: 058
Kraków: 012

MOBILE/CELL PHONES

Poland uses the GSM network, which also covers the rest of Europe. The GSM cover is efficient over the whole of the country. Before going, ask your phone company to activate your international access. Bear in mind, however, that all calls (including incoming calls) will be charged at the rate of international calls, even if you are calling someone in Poland. An alternative to such hefty costs is to ensure that your phone is unblocked (this can be done through your provider or in most independent mobile phone shops) and to purchase a Polish SIM card on a pay-as-you-go tariff. SIM cards are easy to purchase and names of suppliers include Orange, Tak-Tak and Play.

INTERNET

There are plenty of internet cafés throughout Poland. Allow 4 PLN for a one-hour connection. Wi-Fi hotspots are often available in hotel lobbies, public squares and numerous cafés.

DISCOUNTS

Discounted tickets are referred to as **ulgowy**. Seniors qualify at age 60 and children are considered as such, usually, between 4–15. Children under 4 travel free on public transport and from ages 4–10, they travel half price. Students, people under 26 and teachers can also benefit from discounts on entrance fees to sites and museums as well as travel if they show either an International Student/Youth or Teacher Card, which can all be obtained from STA travel outlets (www.statravel.co.uk). Various cities, including Warsaw and Kraków, offer all tourists the opportunity to buy special cards that offer free transport, free and/or discounted rates to museums, sites, recreational facilities and certain restaurants.

ELECTRICITY

Polish plugs provide standard continental sockets with 220-volt current. There is always a plug-in hotel rooms for a laptop or a mobile (cell) phone charger.

EMERGENCIES

The numbers indicated below should be kept at hand. Telephone operators do not always speak English and, if you can't make yourself understood, try, as a last resort, to get in touch with your embassy.

Police
  *℘*997, *℘*112 from a mobile
Fire brigade
  *℘*998 *(free)*
Medical emergency
  *℘*999 *(free)*

Polish doctors are competent whatever the establishment, but public hospitals are run on a much tighter budget than private ones. The equipment is usually less efficient and there are an insufficient number of beds.
See 'Health' under KNOW BEFORE YOU GO.

Tourist Emergency Helpline
  *℘*0800 200 300 *(free)*,
  *℘*0608 599 999 *(charged)*.
The tourist emergency helpline functions from the end of June to the end of September and operates In English, German and Russian.

MAIL/POST

Post offices are generally open weekdays from 8am to 7pm, and on Saturday mornings. A *Poczta Główna* (main post office) is centrally located and some are open 24/7.
Stamps can be bought in post offices or in kiosks *(RUCH)*.
To send a letter to an EU country you need *(at time of writing)* a 2.40 PLN stamp; to the US, 2.50 PLN. EMS-Pocztex courier service can be used from any Post Office in town.
Allow roughly a week for mail to reach Britain or the US.
Postal codes in Poland have five figures. Large towns may have more than one code. For example, in Warsaw, the codes begin with 00-033.

MONEY
CURRENCY

The Polish unit of currency is the Złoty (which means 'golden').
The local abbreviation is Zł and the international one is PLN.
One Złoty is divided into 100 Groszy. There are notes of 10, 20, 50, 100 and 200 Złotys and coins of 1, 2, 5, 10, 20, 50 groszy and 1, 2, 5 Złotys.
For the sake of convenience and the fact that there is no guarantee that the taxi driver or small merchant will have (or wish) to give you his/her change, have small change handy as well as low-denomination notes. The Euro is sometimes accepted, but this is unpredictable, so be sure to have local currency at hand.

EXCHANGE

Exchanging money on the black market is illegal. There are bureaux de change **(Kantor)** everywhere: in Post Offices, large hotels, airports and shopping streets. Bureaux de Change only exchange cash, not traveller's cheques. Opening times vary; when they are not open 24hr a day, they usually work from 9am–6pm during the week and until noon on Saturday. Commission is not charged.
The following are some exchange rates at time of writing:
4.10 PLN to one **Euro**
4.86 PLN to one **British Pound**
3.18 PLN to one **US Dollar**
The current exchange rate is available daily on the Polish National Bank website: *www.nbp.pl*.

BANKS

Banks are generally open from Monday to Friday 9am–5pm and on Saturdays from 9am–1pm.

Postal Codes

At the beginning of all practical pages for each town in the guide, you will find the postal code and phone code of the town and region. **Poland's country code is *℘*48.**

Warsaw Tourist Card

The **Warsaw Tourist Card**, enables visitors to benefit from free public transport, free entry to museums or reduced rates at restaurants, museums, recreational facilities, other tourist sites, car rentals and boutiques. Cards can be for 24 hours or three days. Available at Warsaw tourist offices.

TRAVELLER'S CHEQUES

Traveller's cheques offer a reliable means of insuring against theft although they are becoming more difficult to exchange and your exchange rate may be better if you draw cash directly from an ATM.

ATMS/CASH DISPENSERS

They are available in the main streets of most town centres, in railway stations, airports and shopping centres. Instructions are in English, German and sometimes French.

CREDIT CARDS

Major bank cards are accepted in most parts of the country. Credit cards are accepted without difficulty in large hotels and restaurants, but be prepared to pay in cash in smaller, more modest, establishments.
In case of loss or theft, dial:
℘022 515 31 50 or ℘0515 30 00.

PRICES

Staying in Poland should not break the bank, assuming you plan neither to stay in five-star hotels each night, nor eat at fancy restaurants on a regular basis. For a comfortable double room, you should allow a minimum of 250 to 300 PLN per night in Warsaw and other large towns, 160 to 205 PLN in a lesser establishment. A room in a B&B costs around 100 PLN.
Meal in a restaurant: this varies according to the nature and standard of the establishment. Allow between 6 and 35 PLN for a dish and 15 to 100 PLN for a meal. Most travellers will find prices in Poland very reasonable. Food and accommodation prices aren't prohibitive, and you can get some bargains for handmade items. The areas where you may find that

prices are more than they should be are fuel, electronic equipment and many brand-name sporting goods and related equipment.

PUBLIC HOLIDAYS

January 1	New Year
Sunday and Monday	Easter
1 May	Labour Day
3 May	Constitution Day
Thursday; variable	Corpus Christi
15 August	Assumption Feast
1 November	All Saints' Day
11 November	Independence Day
25 and 26 December	Christmas

INTERNATIONAL STUDENT CARD

Students and teachers will find the International Student or Faculty Identity Card (ISIC) very useful to obtain discounts for travel and museum entry fees.
Additional information from:

♦ **STA Travel – UK** Call Centre open Mon–Fri 9am–8pm, Sat 9.30am–6pm, Sun 10am–5pm. Over 60 offices around the country. ℘(44) 0871 2300 040. www.statravel.co.uk

♦ **STA Travel – US** Call Centre open daily 24/7. ℘(1) 800 781 4040 www.statravel.com

SMOKING

Smoking is prevalent throughout Poland and only a few official smoking bans have been initiated in public spaces. For example, in some cities smoking has been banned at bus and tram stops. That said, smokers may be puffing on borrowed time, as the idea

Train Timetable

to pass legislation to ban smoking in more public areas has been debated. Many restaurants have smoking and non-smoking areas, and bars and clubs will often have a no-smoking policy at the bar, but the distinction of smoke/no smoke is fuzzy. Encouraging news for non-smokers is that some restaurant and café owners have taken the bold step to ban smoking in their establishments altogether, which may start a trend.

TIME
Winter: GMT + 1; summer: GMT + 2. Poland is always one hour ahead of Britain. Official time changes occur on the same date throughout Europe: the last Sunday in October and the last Sunday in March.

TIPPING
Tips are not included and it is recommended to leave an additional 10% or 15% if you're feeling particularly generous. Porter and valet services should be tipped according to the task and taxi drivers are often given 10%. Tipping a tour guide is acceptable and the amount is at the discretion of the client.

SOCIAL ETIQUETTE
No matter how much Polish society changes, there are a few social traditions that are likely to persist: give odd amounts of flowers and try not to kiss or shake hands over a threshold, as it's considered to be bad luck. You may find that men of a certain age continue to kiss the hands of women on greeting them, but this is a custom likely to fade away with each new generation of males. If invited over to a Pole's home for dinner be sure to bring a small gift: a bottle of wine or some chocolates. Avoid giving chrysanthemums as they are reserved for funerals. The Polish language is very formal and normally people who do not know each other well use honorific titles when addressing someone who is not a good friend or family member. So if you know a bit of Polish or pick some up while visiting Poland, be sure to use the *Pan/Pani* forms plus the surnames when speaking to people with whom you aren't on close terms.

Historically, Poland has always had close links with western European culture, but for 45 years following World War II Poland was under Soviet domination. Poles are not very fond of the term *eastern Europe*, which really only became a common expression during the Cold War, so it's better to say that Poland is in *central* Europe.

CONVERSION TABLES

Weights and Measures

1 kilogram (kg)	**2.2 pounds (lb)**	**2.2 pounds**	*To convert*
6.35 kilograms	14 pounds	1 stone (st)	*kilograms*
0.45 kilograms	16 ounces (oz)	16 ounces	*to pounds,*
1 metric ton (tn)	**1.1 tons**	**1.1 tons**	*multiply by 2.2*
1 litre (l)	**2.11 pints (pt)**	**1.76 pints**	*To convert litres*
3.79 litres	1 gallon (gal)	0.83 gallon	*to gallons, multiply*
4.55 litres	1.20 gallon	1 gallon	*by 0.26 (US)*
			or 0.22 (UK)
1 hectare (ha)	**2.47 acres**	**2.47 acres**	*To convert*
1 sq kilometre	**0.38 sq. miles**	**0.38 sq. miles**	*hectares to*
(km²)	**(sq mi)**		*acres, multiply*
			by 2.4
1 centimetre (cm)	**0.39 inches (in)**	**0.39 inches**	*To convert metres*
1 metre (m)	**3.28 feet (ft) or 39.37 inches**		*to feet, multiply*
	or 1.09 yards (yd)		*by 3.28; for*
			kilometres to miles,
1 kilometre (km)	**0.62 miles (mi)**	**0.62 miles**	*multiply by 0.6*

Clothing

Women					Men			
	35	4	2½			40	7½	7
	36	5	3½			41	8½	8
	37	6	4½			42	9½	9
Shoes	38	7	5½		Shoes	43	10½	10
	39	8	6½			44	11½	11
	40	9	7½			45	12½	12
	41	10	8½			46	13½	13
	36	6	8			46	36	36
	38	8	10			48	38	38
Dresses	40	10	12		Suits	50	40	40
& suits	42	12	14			52	42	42
	44	14	16			54	44	44
	46	16	18			56	46	48
	36	6	30			37	14½	14½
	38	8	32			38	15	15
Blouses &	40	10	34		Shirts	39	15½	15½
sweaters	42	12	36			40	15¾	15¾
	44	14	38			41	16	16
	46	16	40			42	16½	16½

Sizes often vary depending on the designer. These equivalents are given for guidance only.

Speed

KPH	10	30	50	70	80	90	100	110	120	130
MPH	6	19	31	43	50	56	62	68	75	81

Temperature

Celsius (°C)	0°	5°	10°	15°	20°	25°	30°	40°	60°	80°	100°
Fahrenheit (°F)	32°	41°	50°	59°	68°	77°	86°	104°	140°	176°	212°

To convert Celsius into Fahrenheit, multiply °C by 9, divide by 5, and add 32.
To convert Fahrenheit into Celsius, subtract 32 from °F, multiply by 5, and divide by 9.
NB: Conversion factors on this page are approximate.

Kazimierz Dolny on the Wisła
A. Galy / MICHELIN

The Country Today

Since 1989, Poland has been faced with a gigantic task: moving from a state-controlled economic system and an authoritarian government to a market economy and political democracy. This "metamorphosis" could not be achieved without radically changing society, mentalities and traditions. So, how far has Poland gone down this road?

DEMOCRACY IN POLAND
LARGE, HOMOGENEOUS, YOUTHFUL POPULATION

With **38.1 million inhabitants**, Poland represents 8.4% of the EU population. However, since 1999 the Polish population has been slowly decreasing. This is due to a lower birth rate; to a death rate which is still fairly high (over 8%); and to a negative migration balance (many Poles leave to find work in other EU countries).

Poles form around 97% of the country's population, the remainder consisting essentially of Germans, Ukrainians and Belarusians. The Polish population is one of the youngest in Europe, even though it is gradually getting older. People over 65 represent only 13% of the population and over one third of the total number of inhabitants is under 25. Life expectancy is three years less than the EU average, with pollution, overtaking tobacco, excessive alcohol intake, and the deteriorating health service cited as the main cause.

RAPID ECONOMIC TRANSITION

In 1989, the country's economic situation was alarming: hyper-inflation (700%), enormous debts, an obsolete, inefficient industry and backward agriculture. The **state-controlled system** which had been the rule for over forty years, had prevented the Poles, at least partially, from adjusting to the changing world. As early as 1990, the Minister of Finance, L. Balcerowicz, imposed **"radical remedies"** on the country in order to launch it into the market economy. These reforms continued to be implemented in spite of a slower process of privatisation between 1993 and 1997 due to a leftist party in power. The return of Balcerowicz as Minister of Finance in 1997–2000 attests to the people's will to continue his policy of reforms: massive privatisations, development of the free market rules, radical decrease of public debts and inflation, convertibility and reinforcement of the złoty, creation of the Warsaw stock exchange, income tax levied on individuals and a value-added tax (VAT). The aim was simple: maintain a **6–7% growth** in order to reduce the gap between Poland and EU countries. This vigorous policy paid off: the GNP increased by 42% between 1990 and 2002 and inflation is now stabilised around 2–3%. Although it reached 5.8% in 2006, the economic growth rate has been slowing down, in particular because of the unfavourable economic climate in the EU. It was mainly the two million small and medium-sized businesses created in the trade and services sector (food and computing stores, clothes shops, car dealers) which helped boost the Polish economy and employment. They employ 55% of the working population and produce a third of the GNP. However, they have to compete with foreign hypermarkets (LeClerc, Auchan, Carrefour, Ikea Decathlon, Leroy Merlin). In fact, foreign buyouts focused mainly on the most lucrative sectors: alcohol (Polmos bought by Bacardi and Pernod-Ricard), telecommunications (TPSA bought by France Télécom).

Three examples illustrating foreign investment and the creation of factories by large companies are: **Michelin** in the field of tyres, Dell in computing and the much earlier case of Fiat established before 1939. The private sector now generates 80% of the economic activity even though the public sector still employs a quarter of the working population. In spite of this, tricky problems are plentiful. **Agriculture** employs almost a quarter of the working population (on small plots averaging 6ha) and only produces

4% of the GNP. At least half of the two million farms will disappear during the coming years and the others will have to be radically modernised. Other difficulties arise from the **coal mines**, which are showing a loss and are in debt, and from the steel industry, which requires heavy investments as well as massive lay-offs.

INSTITUTIONAL AND ADMINISTRATIVE REFORMS

In 1997, Poland acquired a new **Constitution**, the previous one dating from 1952. Today, Poland's institutions are similar to those of France. Executive power is in the hands of a **President, elected by universal suffrage** for a five-year term *(renewable once)*, who has a right of veto in Parliament. Legislative power belongs to **two houses**, elected by direct universal suffrage for four years, the Diet (460 members elected by revised proportional representation, which gives a bonus to the largest parties) and the Senate (100 members elected by majority vote). In 1998 a reform of administrative autonomy introduced a third degree of decentralisation (districts or *powiaty*) and the number of regions (*województwo*) was reduced from 49 to 16.

DIFFICULT LEGACY OF THE OPPOSITION

Democratisation saw the emergence of a great number of **short-lived parties.** There is a proverb that says: "where four Poles are gathered, there are already five political parties". Among the main parties, the oldest are those on the Left, in particular the **SLD** (Democratic Left Alliance), formed from the ruins of the former Communist party. Samoobrona (Self-Defence), the populist agrarian party led by A. Lepper, which caught the public's attention, claims to be situated on the extreme left. The anti-Communist movement extended, after 1989, from the centre to the extreme right. The **intellectual, democratic trend** was represented by different parties in succession, including the Freedom Union (UW), whose main representatives were T. Mazowiecki, B. Geremek, L. Balcerowicz. **The liberal trend** is led by the **PO**, Civic Platform, founded in 2001 by men such as D. Tusk and J. Rokita. The conservative and Christian-Democrat trend is represented by **PiS** (Law and Justice, also founded in 2001) Jarosław Kaczyński (the twin brother of the former late President Lech Kaczyński) and Kazimierz Marcinkiewicz. Finally, the League of Polish Families (LPR) is an ultra-Catholic, nationalist and anti-European party.

CHANGES IN POWER AND "COHABITATION"

In 1989–90, the right wing held the Presidency (L. Wałęsa) and Parliament. In September 1993, the legislative elections brought the victory of the left wing, taking advantage of the population's discontent linked with the rapid social and economic reforms. This first

To purge or not to purge?

The compromise reached during the "Round Table" talks in 1989 provided for a peaceful transition from the Communist system to democracy and excluded a purge of the Civil Service. The second left/right co-habitation even implemented a process of general redemption which culminated in 2004–05, when L. Wałęsa agreed to meet W. Jaruzelski on a television set and when the leader of Solidarność and President A. Kwaśniewski invited each other to official and even private functions. And yet, for a few years now, the question of the purge or "lustration" has become fashionable again. Poland has not, until now, made the Communist archives public, unlike other eastern European countries. However, in February 2005, after the release on the Internet of a list of 240,000 names, the debate was reopened within Polish society and the nationalist right "purged" one of its war horses.

change in power, shared at the time by other eastern European countries, was marked by a short cohabitation; in November 1995, L. Wałęsa was beaten at the presidential election by A. Kwaśniewski, a former Communist of the SLD, re-elected on the first ballot in October 2000. The period 1997–2001 was in turn marked by a left/right power-sharing, known as "cohabitation", ending in September 2001 when the legislative elections were won by a left-wing coalition. But the political climate turned sour with a split of the governmental coalition in March 2003, scandals linked with corruption and increasing unpopularity of the Prime Minister, who was replaced in May 2004. In September and October 2005, the legislative and presidential elections led to the second change in power: the right wing came back and the left wing was crushed. However, the high level of abstention (between 50 and 60%) confirmed the politicians' representation crisis. Then on April 10, 2010 the conservative President Lech Kaczyński was killed in a tragic plane crash in Russia. A couple of years earlier his twin, Jarosław, had lost his position as Prime Minister. He then decided to run for president in July 2010 when new elections were called for after the shocking death of the President, but he lost to Bronisław Komorowski, from the more liberal PO party.

RADICALLY TRANSFORMED SOCIETY

Poland's **GNP** per inhabitant is less than half the EU average and the IDH, which measures the level achieved in terms of life expectancy, education and income per inhabitant, ranks the country 36th in the world. The average salary is around 500€ net per month (200€ for the guaranteed minimum wage), but this average is distorted by very high salaries, in particular in Warsaw, where they are twice as high as anywhere else. **Unemployment** is still a serious national issue, but has been improving, affecting 1.9 million people (12% of the working population) including 85% who do not get unemployment benefits (benefits

are only paid for six months and are in the region of 150€ per month). Young people under 25 and those over 45 who have no diplomas are worst off. About 30% of the total income of households comes from State assistance. However, budget restrictions and price increases make life difficult for the most underprivileged who think their country has moved from the era of full wallets and empty shops to that of full shops and empty wallets. In spite of the evident emergence of the middle classes in large towns, Poland still functions on **two levels**: there are those who were able to follow the modern economic movement and the others. Health and education are also on two different planes: private establishments, which have very high fees, and public establishments, forced by budget restrictions to be less well equipped and understaffed. The pension reform (the country has 9.5 million pensioners) is underway, combining some capitalisation with the present share-out system, but many elderly people are obliged to have financial help from their children. One of the consequences of these difficulties is the existence of a black market economy which is believed to represent over a quarter of the GNP and to involve over one million people who do not declare their work and their income although they sometimes receive social benefits.

FRANCO-POLISH FRIENDSHIP

In 1991, the presidents of both republics, L. Wałęsa and F. Mitterrand signed a treaty of friendship and solidarity between the two countries, the term "solidarity" in fact having never been used before in diplomatic language. In 2004, the Polish Season in France, Nowa Polska, enabled French and Polish people to celebrate and rediscover the history of a close and unusual relationship between the two peoples, who never fought each other, a very rare example in European history. This closeness is symbolised by the love stories of Marie-Louise de Gonzague and Władysław IV, Marie d'Arquien (Marysieńka) and Jan III Sobieski, Maria Leszczyńska and Louis XV,

Maria Walewska and Napoleon Bonaparte, George Sand and Chopin, Mme Hanska and Honoré de Balzac, Maria Skłodowska and Pierre Curie or, more recently, Sophie Marceau and Andrzej Żuławski. It may be a known fact that the Polish borrowed many words from the French (à propos, vis-à-vis, cul-de-sac, dossier, *en face, enfant terrible, passe-partout, calembour*, fondue, *pruderie, fiole, abat-jour, paysage, gendarmerie, garde-robe*) but the reverse is also true: riding (*calèche, cravache*), pastries (*baba*, meringue), clothes *(chapskas)*, not forgetting dances such as *mazurkas*, polkas and *polonaises*.

POLAND IN THE EU
BETWEEN THE EU AND THE US?

As early as 1994, Poland clearly showed its economic inclination towards the EU and its military inclination towards the US: the country applied for EU membership and, at the same time, joined NATO's "Partnership for Peace Agreement". In May 1997, Poland was invited into the **Atlantic Alliance** (in fact, full membership became official on 12 March 1999) and in December, the country's application for EU membership was accepted. In Copenhagen in 2002, Poland was one of the ten countries designated to join the EU (membership came into effect on 1 May 2004). In 2003, there was a hardening of West European opinion following Poland's decision to support the US intervention in Iraq and to buy F-16 planes rather than French Mirages or Swedish Gripen. However, the referendum on EU membership in June 2003 was a success in Poland: 77.4% of the population voted "yes", but the Poles rejected the project of European constitution in favour of the Nice Treaty (2000), which gave them more bargaining power. The European Parliament election in June 2004 was marked by a record abstention rate (almost 80%) and nearly half the new Polish members of the European Parliament can be said to be Euro-sceptics. However, the success of Poland's entry into the EU is gradually gaining the approval of the most reticent: farmers, who were

very pessimistic two years ago, had to admit that direct European subsidies were flooding in at the rate of 55 euros per ha (nearly 1.5 billion euros paid to 1.4 million farmers representing 85% of all farmers) and that exports of farm produce (milk, sugar beet, meat, cheese, butter) had increased by over 40% since membership came into force. Today, the EU is Poland's main trading partner (70% of exports and 60% of imports) and it brings into the country three-fifths of foreign capitals. Poland could, within a few years, join the euro zone but no date has yet been fixed since the country's budget deficit (nearly 6% of the GNP) is higher than the European limits. As for the opening of the labour market, it depends on bilateral agreements: the United Kingdom, Ireland, Spain, Holland, Norway, Italy, Sweden and Switzerland are, for the moment, the only countries to have signed full open labour agreements with Poland. Partially open labour agreements, based on quotas for specific professions, are signed with Belgium, France and Germany. Over a million Poles, with both highly skilled or manual labour backgrounds, have left Poland since its entry in the EU to search for better wages.

Polonia

Poland has, for the past century, had a strong emigration tradition, the most important waves of emigrants taking place between 1900 and 1918 and after 1945. Nearly 15 million Poles or persons of Polish origin live abroad. They form "Polonia", so dear to the heart of the Poles in the "old country" since almost every family has relatives abroad.

Nearly ten million of them live in the US (particularly in Chicago), almost 2 million live in Russia and in the former Soviet republics, 1.5 million in Germany and 1 million in France. There are also Polish minorities in Canada, Brazil, Australia and the UK.

An education system undergoing sweeping reforms

Poland has, since the 1990s, become aware of the necessity of reforming its education system: the adult population included only 7 per cent graduates and differences between regions were important, in particular between town and country. Responsibility for the school network was transferred to local authorities, teacher training was developed, school-leaving age was raised to 18, levels were modified to match European and American systems (development of nursery schools, creation of colleges or *gimnazjums*, and of vocational schools). In 2005, the school-leaving certificate *(matura)* became a national exam, less dependent on the appreciation of individual establishments, which should, in the future, enable pupils to enter a higher-education establishment without having to take an entrance exam.

In 1989, only 10 per cent of the 19–24 age group undertook higher-education studies, today their number has risen to 40 per cent, even though half of them only attend weekend or evening classes *(paying)* because they have another activity during the week or the day. But the 5.6 per cent of the GNP that the State spends on education (the OECD's average) are still insufficient in view of the country's demographic pattern. One of the consequences of this situation is the flourishing of private establishments. The majority of nursery schools and two-thirds of higher-education providers are now private. In towns, advertisements for fee-paying language tuition abound.

DIFFICULT RELATIONS WITH THE NEIGHBOURS

In November 1990, Poland signed a German-Polish friendship and good neighbourly agreement, guaranteeing the inviolability of the borders and the rights of the German minority in Poland. In August 1991, the meeting of the Polish, German and French foreign-affairs ministers marked the timid beginning of a trilateral cooperation known as the **Weimar Triangle**. In addition, four **Euro-regions** are developing on the western border. However, the memory of the atrocities perpetrated by the Nazis is still very present in the minds of the Poles and when Berlin speaks of the dramatic situation endured by six million Germans "displaced" in 1945 or the possible compensations their descendants could claim, feelings run high. The recent gas pipeline project between Russia and Germany, which by-passes Poland, was also the source of heated arguments. Since Poland partly depends on Russia for its oil, she must humour V. Putin in spite of serious disagreements. The diplomatic crisis between Poland and Belarus in 2005, close to Moscow, shows that relations between these countries are not yet normalised. It is no longer the case with **Ukraine**: the Poles were the staunchest supporters of the "Orange Revolution" (2004–5) which led the pro-Western side to power to the great displeasure of Moscow. There are still many Poles living around L'viv and economic relations between the two countries are important. Warsaw has stepped up security checks along this border to be ready to join the Schengen area, but her visa policy is very supple. Three Euro-regions were set up on the eastern border. To the south, Poland founded in February 1991, together with Hungary and Czechoslovakia, a group known as **Visegrad** to reinforce the positions of the three partners in the processus of European integration. Seven Euro-regions were created on the southern border. To the north, Poland is a member of the Council of Baltic States and a Euro-region was created.

THE IMPORTANCE OF THE CHURCH

With around **95% of Catholics**, including over 60% who practise their religion, Poland is one of the few countries of Europe where faith is so important. Attendance at the 15,000 churches and chapels is still high and Sunday Mass gathers church-goers of all ages. Every year on 15 August, 4–5 million pilgrims go to Częstochowa to pray in front of the icon of the Black Virgin, the protector and patron saint of Poland. The number of marriages remains high (marriage in church is recognised by the law) and the average age for a first marriage is around 27 (against 30 in the EU). There are differences of opinion about the place of religion in the State (in particular on the question of abortion, the concordat and sexual education in public schools). Some people today object to what they consider an excessive involvement of the church in political affairs or to the verbal faux pas of certain Catholic fundamentalists who can be heard on Radio Maryja, on the Trwam television channel or who express their ideas in the *Nasz Dziennik* daily newspaper.

SOLIDARITY AND FAMILY TRADITIONS

The Poles can at first appear slightly cold or obsequious to a European from the West; this is mainly due to variations in social behaviour. In Poland, you would rarely greet someone you meet but don't know, yet you would use several polite phrases when introduced. This is when you can really discover the extent of the Poles' hospitality: a Pole will do everything he can to help you if you are in difficulty. From the dark hours of their history, the Poles have retained an acute sense of duty towards themselves and their family but also towards others and towards their nation. Family ties are particularly strong, especially since the shortage and high cost of housing often compels several generations to live under the same roof, even though the divorce rate is rising. Houses and apartments are often still blessed on 6 January and the first letters of the name of the Three Kings are then written with chalk on the doors. Respect between generations is very high, although misunderstandings sometimes arise between those who spent most of their life under the Communist régime (the over-45s), those who lived during both periods (the 30-somethings) and the young, who were born after the mid-1980s.

Religious feasts offer the opportunity of gathering the whole family and often friends as well. **Weekends** are also privileged moments for the Poles who recharge their batteries in the country (barbecues on lake shores during the fine season, mountain activities in winter). Contrary to what happens on working days, when meal times are disturbed, weekends make it possible to enjoy the five traditional meals: breakfast at 9am, a second "breakfast" at midday, then lunch at 3pm, dinner at 5pm and supper at 8pm. The main meal takes place in the middle of the afternoon *(obiad)* and usually includes soup, a main course with meat and crudités and sometimes a cake for dessert, served with tea or a fruit tea *(kompot)*, even vodka or wine on special occasions.

Jasna Gora sanctuary in Częstochowa, home of the Black Virgin

© Polish National Tourist Office

POPULATION

With an average of 122 inhabitants per sq km, the Polish population is unequally spread throughout the territory. The north of the country is sparsely populated, in contrast with the **Warsaw** metropolitan area *(pop. 2.3 million)* and the industrial region of Upper Silesia (the **Katowice** conurbation has reached 3.5 million inhabitants!). Poland was originally a rural country but today 65% of its population lives in **urban areas** and there are more than 40 towns, with over 100,000 inhabitants. In addition to the two urban regions already mentioned, there are three other large concentrations of slightly over one million inhabitants each: **Kraków**, Poland's former capital on the River Wisła, **Łódź**, the large textile city, and **Gdańsk-Gdynia-Sopot**, known as the "3-Cities", with two ports on the Baltic.

The Polish population is also concentrated in other large towns such as **Wrocław, on the Oder** *(pop. 640,000)*, an important centre of metallurgy as well as of the chemical and food processing industries, **Poznań**, on the River Warta *(pop. 570,000)*, one of the country's oldest towns, **Szczecin**, a major port on the Baltic *(pop. 413,000)*, Bydgoszcz *(pop. 369,000)*, a large industrial city in the Lower Wisła Valley, **Lublin** *(pop. 356,000)* specialising in consumer goods and **Białystok** *(pop. 292,000)*, Poland's second most important textile centre.

Smoked cheese from Oscypek

A. Galy / MICHELIN

FOOD AND DRINK

Copious and rich in calories, Polish cuisine has skilfully appropriated the various influences of the populations who occupied the country over the centuries. The Baltic, the numerous lakes and rivers, the mountain ranges and the great plains provide each region with its specific products.

SOUPS

Any good meal starts with soup and with Poland having as wide a choice of soups as France has of cheeses, you will be offered mushroom soup, sorel soup, sauerkraut soup or crayfish soup served with a varied selection of ravioli or meatballs. The most common soups on the menus of restaurants or private homes are:

Barszcz, which belongs to the history of cuisine. In the old days, country people prepared this soup from sour fruit picked in forests. Later, beetroot replaced these berries. The sour taste was preserved by adding fermented beetroot juice (**kwas**), lemon or vinegar.

Żurek, or white *barszcz*, which is just as popular, is a soup made from fermented rye flour juice served with sausage.

And finally **flaki po warszawsku** or **Warsaw-style tripe**, which is a mixture of shin of beef and tripe seasoned with paprika, ginger and nutmeg.

MEAT

Whether grilled, coated in breadcrumbs, or covered with onions or prunes, **pork** is the Poles' favourite meat.

Poultry follows closely. Polish-style chicken, stuffed with breadcrumbs, egg and parsley, and duck stuffed with pieces of apple and soaked in red wine while cooking, are the two most famous poultry recipes.

The many wild areas and dense forests offer a choice of **game**. Hare, wild boar and roe-deer are particularly appreciated by hunters' families or by those who know where to find this kind of meat. As for **partridge**, once it has been stuffed with bread soaked in milk, currants and juniper, it reminds young generations that, in centuries gone by, royal and feudal hunts always ended with gargantuan feasts.

Beef is not so well liked, except for **steak tartare**, the origin of which goes back to the times when Mongol horsemen invaded central Europe, stocking a supply of raw meat under their saddles.

FISH

Polish cuisine is privileged in being able to use only choice fish or very tasty ones: **sturgeon** from the Baltic, **pike** from pure freshwater streams, or **pikeperch** from the lakes. **Carp**, which is probably the most commonly found fish on restaurant menus year-round, becomes a traditional festive dish on Christmas eve in homes all over Poland. As for **herring**, it is a popular cheap dish and laid out in small rolls stuffed with cucumber and hard-boiled egg or marinated in a mixture of oil and onions. Herring and vodka go very well together.

POLISH TRILOGY

Pierogi are small, crescent-shaped ravioli made from a simple dough consisting of flour, water, eggs and salt. This forms the base of a large number or creative variations. Among the most common are the Russian-style *pierogi* filled with white cheese, onions and potatoes, others being stuffed with mushrooms and cabbage. As a dessert, pierogi are filled with fruit: cherries, strawberries or blueberries.

Marinated cucumbers *(ogórki kiszone)* are eaten throughout the meal. As an appetiser with beer, as a first course or a main course with other vegetables. The cucumbers are picked before they are ripe and look more like gherkins. Pickled in brine made with cherry, vine and oak leaves, dill, coriander and a spoonful of white vinegar and brandy, they are believed to reduce the effect of vodka.

Cabbage is used in many ways, raw and cooked, but it is also the essential ingredient for a dish unanimously appreciated by Polish gourmets: *bigos*. Served as a first course or as a meal in itself, this kind of Polish-style sauerkraut is a mixture of several types of cabbage, pork, mutton or veal, game, mushrooms and

Roasted Pork Knuckle
© ShyMan/iStockphoto

even prunes, seasoned with many spices such as hot pepper from Jamaica, cardamom or nutmeg, and Madeira wine.

REGIONAL CUISINE

In Masuria and Warmia, forests and lakes are an inexhaustible source of high-quality products such as **fish dumplings** or pikeperch served with **crayfish tails**. More unusual are goose or duck's-blood soup *(czernina z golcami)*, and **Masurian gingerbread** *(piernik)* flavoured with chicory.

Anyone interested in drawing up a list of all the recipes based on **potatoes** should definitely go to Poland. Potato croquettes, mashed potato, potato noodles, potato soup, potato salad... potatoes are everywhere! More original

Pierogi
© ShyMan/iStockphoto

are **onions stuffed with mushrooms** (*gały cebulowe*).

The high number of miners in need of sustaining food and the proximity of Germany, Austria and the Czech Republic had a significant influence on Silesian cuisine. Specialities include the following: **Silesian noodles** made from potatoes; **krupniok**, made from offal, buckwheat flour and blood; **Silesian stuffed roll**, consisting of a slice of beef seasoned with mustard and stuffed with bacon, sausages and cucumbers pickled in salt.

The Polish court, for a long time based in Kraków, made it a point of honour to have a variety of European dishes on the menu. **Hungarian goulash**, **Vienna schnitzel** or **Russian-style pierogi** are quite at home in Little Poland.

Oscypek, a smoked cheese made from ewe's milk in shepherds' huts and **bryndza**, another cheese made from ewe's milk but unsmoked, are the tasty ambassadors of the Podhale region. Oscypek is on sale on the pavements of Zakopane. Cut into slices, covered with dill and heated in an oven for a few minutes, it goes very well with brandy. **Charcuterie** from Kurpie, a small region situated between Masovia and Podlasie, is renowned for its smoking technique using **juniper wood**. Juniper also flavours a local beer that is reputed to give credence to the toast, "To your health!" Except in the region along the border with Germany, around Zielona Góra, Polish wine-growing is nonexistent.

History

Since the Middle Ages Poland has ranked among the great European states. It had its heyday in the 16C when it became a centre of Renaissance art and of religious peace. However, the nobility, powerless to deal with the decline of the major trade routes, handed the country over to her powerful neighbours. Poland ceased to exist as an independent country between 1795 and 1918, yet it was during this period that the stateless nation took shape. After 1945, the country, by then ethnically homogeneous, stood up to the USSR through the Church and the working class yearning for the end of socialism. Differences in the 20C led some observers in the west to think there was "another Europe", but the entry of Poland into the EU in 2004 served as a reminder that her history fully shares in the major events that shaped the continent's political landscape.

ORIGINS AND THE SLAVS

The oldest traces of mining activity on Polish soil go back to 3,500 BC. Krzemi-

onki Opatowskie, near Kielce, is one of the world's best-preserved flint- quarrying sites. The sandy subsoil covering a major part of the country prevented the first settlers from establishing structures that could have left traces still visible today. The best known sites were preserved in mud and silt which covered them over after they were abandoned. The first town mentioned in written records was situated in **Greater Poland**: Kalisz was quoted in the 2C AD as being a trading port on the **amber route**, between the Baltic and the Mediterranean. The Poznań region seems to have been an important stopover along this trade route. And it was here that the Slavonic tribe of the **Polanie** settled around the 6C; later they gave their name and her first kings to their country.
See BISKUPIN (550 BC).

CHRISTIAN KINGS AND CONQUERORS (10C and 11C)

The 10C and 11C saw periods of intense struggle in the region between Western and Eastern Christians. Whereas the great majority of Slavonic leaders opted for Byzantium, the **Piast** dynasty of the Polanie joined Rome in order to halt the expansionist intentions of the Holy German Empire. Prince Mieszko was christened in Gniezno and his son **Bolesław** was crowned as the first king of Poland by the Pope in 1025. Strengthened by their Roman support, the two men managed to conquer vast territories (Pomerania, Silesia, Little Poland). In AD 1000, the borders of the kingdom were already those of present-day Poland. Many missionaries Christianised the region. These events created a bond between Poland and the Latin world. The Spaniard Ibrahim ibn Yaqub and the Frenchman Gallus Anonymus left detailed descriptions of their visit to Piast country.

♿ See t*he Romanesque doorway of Gniezno and Wrocław cathedrals.*

POLITICAL DISRUPTION AND ECONOMIC EXPANSION (12C and 13C)

During the 12C and 13C, rivalry between heirs to the crown and feudal division of land left Poland wide open to invasion. Faced with incursions by the **Teutonic Knights** and the **Mongols** or **Tatars**, the Piast kings chose to transfer their capital to Kraków. Following the invasions, which left whole territories deserted, Polish princes welcomed German and Dutch settlers and allowed them to retain their legal and fiscal structures, well adapted to a trade-based economy. Many Jews, persecuted in Western Europe, also found refuge here. The arrival of these people resulted in urban and commercial expansion. Thousands of villages and scores of towns were created and granted liberties and privileges (Wrocław in 1242, Poznań in 1253, Kraków in 1257). Many monasteries were built, in particular by the Cistercians who brought with them their know-how in farming.

♿ *See Malbork Castle, Cistercian abbeys at Trzebnica, Lubiąż and Wąchock.*

KAZIMIERZ THE GREAT (1333-1370)

The last king of the Piast dynasty, **Kazimierz III**, appropriately known as "the Great", accomplished many things: he unified the kingdom and strengthened the State, he welcomed immigrants, in particular Jews, he built churches and fortresses, he encouraged the development of towns (the towns of Kazimierz Dolny and Kazimierz, now a district of Kraków, are named after him). Kraków, in fact, became an important European centre: its **university** (1364) was one of the first in Europe. One should not therefore be surprised by what Jan Długosz, the first Polish historian, wrote around 1470: "Kazimierz received a country built of wood and left it built of bricks".

♿ *The Collegium Maius in Kraków, the town hall in Wrocław, castles in the Polish Jura, the medieval cities of Paczków and Kwidzyń, Gothic cathedrals in Kraków, Gniezno and Poznań, churches in Chełmno.*

Biskupin Museum

W. Buss / MICHELIN

UNION WITH LITHUANIA

Kazimierz having no legal heir, the great Polish lords decided to join in matrimony one of their queens and a still pagan Lithuanian duke. The union between the two states was then sealed for four centuries and the new **Jagiellonian dynasty** took charge of a huge territory able to face the threatening Teutonic Knights. The task was completed in 1410 with the resounding victory at **Grunwald** (Tannenberg) and at the end of the **Thirteen Years' War** (1454–66), when Poland recovered the city of Gdańsk. The country then stretched from the Black Sea to the Baltic and included part of Ukraine and Belarus, being thus the largest European State.

 See the Russo-Byzantine frescoes in Lublin, wooden churches in the Pieniny and the Carpathian foothills, Gothic monuments in Toruń and Gdańsk, Pelplin Cathedral.

GOLDEN AGE (16C)

Poland's Golden Age came in the 16C. The Baltic towns, liberated once and for all from Prussian domination, could form associations with the wealthy merchant cities of the **Hanseatic League**. In 1569, The Lublin Union enabled Poland and Lithuania to have one single Diet (or Parliament) and the same sovereign. The country's economy prospered, thanks to a dynamic middle-class, a large number of peasants and a powerful nobility. The **"Nihil Novi"** constitution (1505) forbade the monarch to take important decisions without the Diet's agreement. It was these magnates and the urban élite who opened Poland to the influence of humanism (symbolised by the astronomer **Copernicus**), of the Renaissance and of the Reformation. The **Renaissance** first flourished in Kraków, at the Jagiellonian Court, where King Sigismund, a patron of the arts, commissioned the construction of a new chapel for the royal castle from two Italian artists, Francesco Fiorentino and Bartolomeo Berecci. Important Polish towns had sumptuous town halls (ratusz) built: the Poznań town hall, the largest in the country, was built by Giovanni

Battista Quadro. Others were erected in Tarnów (Giovanni Maria Padovano) and Chełmno. In 1581, Bernardo Morando began the construction of Zamość, the pearl of the Polish Renaissance, also known as "the Padua of the North". The magnates' castles and palaces were also commissioned from Italian artists: Santi Gucci for Baranów, Galeazzo Appiani for Krasiczyn, Matteo Trapola for Łańcut and Nowy Wiśnicz, the Parra Brothers and Bernardo Neurone for Brzeg. At the end of the century and at the beginning of the next century, the city of Gdańsk, then the country's largest town, called on the best **Flemish architects and artists**: the Van den Block family, Johan Voigt, Anton van Opberghen. The **Reformation** met with a certain success as the élite wished to oppose the monarch and to seize the clergy's estates. As early as 1564, the Jesuits, who were Catholic agents of the Counter-Reformation, arrived in Poland with the aim of founding a number of colleges. However, whereas Europe was torn apart by the wars of religion, Poland appeared like an oasis of peace and a refuge for heretics. In 1573, one year after the St Bartholomew massacre, the Warsaw Confederation proclaimed that all religions were equal. The development of Protestantism, based on the reading of holy texts in the national language, was accompanied by the emergence of Polish, which gradually replaced Latin. At the end of the 16C, Russian first names were given a Polish flavour and finally disappeared. Prompted by the development of printing, the national literature expanded.

 See the Wawel Royal Castle and Sigismund's Chapel, town halls in Poznań, Tarnów and Chełmno, Zamość's ideal city, the castles and palaces of Baranów, Krasiczyn, Łańcut, Nowy Wiśnicz and Brzeg, the town centres of Gdańsk and Kazimierz Dolny.

A KING UNDER SUPERVISION AND A DIVIDED NOBILITY (17C)

Like the Piasts before them, the **Jagiellonians** left the annals of history through lack of heirs. Worried about the

TERRITORIAL EVOLUTION OF POLAND

0   250   500 km

————— Actual Polish Border

992
The Poland of the Piasts

1370
Poland at the death of
Casimir the Great

1771
Poland Before
Partition

1815
"Congress Poland"
of the Russian Empire

1923
Poland after World War I

1945
Territories under
Polish Administration

hostile intentions of their neighbours, Polish aristocrats decided to elect their new king themselves and did not rule out foreigners. However, each election gave rise to intrigues between the magnates and foreign powers. Between 1587 and 1668, Poland was governed by a Catholic branch of the **Swedish Vasa** dynasty who, at the very beginning of the 17C, decided to transfer the

Polish capital from Kraków to **Warsaw**. With the help of the Jesuits, the Vasa undertook to convert the country and its neighbours to Catholicism. Polish patriotism then became mixed with religious fanaticism and this was the cause of constant bad relations with the neighbours. There were successive wars against the Swedish Protestants, the Moslem Turks and Tatars and the Orthodox Russians and Ukrainians. After the terrible Swedish invasion of 1655–60, nicknamed "deluge", the country lay waste and the population, depleted by the Black Death, was reduced by a third. Polish art of that time is heavily marked by the macabre and the need for atonement. There was a sudden abundance of miraculous Virgins, dances of death, hermitages and calvaries. The magnates adapted palaces, churches and monasteries to the **Baroque** style. These edifices are full of portraits of aristocrats sporting long Turkish-style caftans and wearing a long moustache and a feathered bonnet over a partly shaved head. The term **"Sarmatism"** derived from the name of the nobility's mythical ancestors, describes the cultural specificity of this megalomaniac class shutting itself off from the rest of the world. The aristocracy dealt a second fatal blow to the kingdom in 1652 by demanding that decisions taken by the Diet be unanimous (**"liberum veto"**). The fact that **King Jan III Sobieski** was acknow-

ledged as the saviour of Christendom after he liberated a Vienna besieged by the Turks, did not empower him to halt the country's political decline. The last scuttling of Poland's independence took place in 1717, when the aristocrats granted Russia a say in their privileges: Poland then became in reality a **Russian protectorate**.

See the skulls chapels at Kudowa and Czerma, the hermitages in Wigry Park, Baroque monasteries at Częstochowa, Święta Lipka and Legnickie Pole, Warsaw's royal castle, the palaces of Wilanów, Ujazdów, Nieborów, Kielce, Białystok and Ujazd.

THE LAST POLISH KING: (1764–95)

In 1764, Prussia and Russia imposed their candidate to the crown, the Pole **Stanisław August Poniatowski**. This open-minded aristocrat, influenced by the spirit of the Enlightenment, chose as his second name that of the first Roman Emperor in order to show that he intended to reform the archaic structures of the State. However, his country was the object of negotiations between Prussia, Russia and Austria. During the first Partition in 1772, the three states seized about a third of the territory. In spite of this, Poniatowski invited to his court the greatest painters and sculptors of the time. Thus **Canaletto** could paint views of Warsaw which were very useful when

Łańcut Castle

the town had to be rebuilt after 1945. The King succeeded in persuading the Diet to adopt a liberal constitution. But Russia, considering the "revolutionary spirit" was gaining ground in the country, chose to send her army supported by the Polish nobility who were in favour of the Ancien Régime. In 1793, the second **Partition** further reduced the size of the country, and in 1795, after the national insurrection led by Tadeusz Kościuszko failed, the **third Partition** effectively wiped Poland from the European map for the next 123 years.

See the Łazienki Palace, The Arkadia Park.

A BRIEF NAPOLEONIC HOPE

After the disappearance of the Polish State, Paris became the main refuge of political exiles. France being at war with Austria, **General J. H. Dąbrowski** obtained from the Directoire in 1796 the permission to organise the first **"Polish legions"** with Polish soldiers captured by the Austrian army in the hope of liberating the country. "March, march, Dąbrowski, from Italy to Poland […], Poland is not dead as long as we live" are the words of their song, written by J. Wybicki, which later became the national anthem. The legions fought several battles but were finally sent to Saint-Domingue in 1802 to crush the black population's rebellion; the first consul, Bonaparte, was not yet ready to sacrifice the fragile European balance to further the Polish cause. Subsequently, there was a divide among the Poles between those who advocated cooperation with Russia (Adam Czartoryski) and those who favoured support from western powers. This opposition lasted for decades and influenced the country's destiny on many occasions.

In 1806–7, Napoleon, recently crowned Emperor of the French and at war with Prussia, triggered a Polish uprising in the territories occupied by the Prussians. The land taken from Poland by Prussia then formed the **Grand Duchy of Warsaw**, granted a constitution and the Napoleonic code in 1807–8. In 1809, the Polish army led by **Prince**

The Constitution of 3 May 1791

From 1775 onwards, a powerful nationalist movement was formed in Poland. Inspired by the French Revolution and the work of the Constituent Assembly, these patriots aimed to abolish the elected monarchy and the "liberum veto", grant more rights to the Third Estate, assert national sovereignty and find a balance between the power of the legislators, of the government and of the judges. On 3 May 1791, the Diet adopted this Constitution in spite of hostile reactions. It followed the American example (17 September 1787) and preceded the French (3 September 1791). Poland's National Day is now held on 3 May.

Poniatowski, took part in the victory against Austria, who had to cede to the Duchy the major part of the territories she occupied (including Kraków). Urged by the Poles to restore a real kingdom, Napoleon led them to expect, in 1811, that their independence would depend on the outcome of his war with Russia. However, in spite of the strong mobilisation of Polish soldiers and civilians, the disaster in Russia sealed the political fate of the Duchy, from then on occupied by the Tsar's troops.

CRUSHED REBELLIONS AND INTENSE EMIGRATION

In 1815, the Congress of Vienna which shared out the remains of Napoleon's Empire, became in fact a fourth Partition of Poland. A Polish kingdom or "Congress Kingdom of Poland" was officially created, but the tsar was declared king. The Congress then shared the remainder of the territory between Poland's three neighbours. In the annexed provinces, Prussians and Russians rapidly set up a policy of integration and encouraged a sometimes massive influx of settlers. The **autonomous republic of Kraków** alone could carry on with its political

Lwów and Wilno

Marshal Piłsudski compared Poland to a pretzel, empty in the centre but full on the edges. In 1918, he did his utmost to see that the northern and eastern territories were returned to Poland, however these were definitively lost in 1939. Among these border regions, the Lithuanian Vilnius (Wilno) and the Ukrainian L'viv (Lwów) are still dear to the heart of the Poles. The two towns which became Polish in the 14C long shared in the country's main historic events, even after the partitions: while Vilnius welcomed the poets Mickiewicz and Słowacki and became the cradle of Polish Romanticism, L'viv experienced political autonomy as the main town of Galicia.

and cultural activities: it became a refuge for the Polish nation. Nationalist **insurrections** took place in Poland in 1830 (November insurrection), 1846, 1848 (the Peoples' Spring throughout Europe), 1861, 1863 (January insurrection) and 1905 (following the first Russian revolution), but they did not lead to anything. The result, each time, was an intensified Russification and Germanisation. After each of these insurrections, waves of political refugees left their homeland. As early as 1830, over 5,000 Poles went into exile in France; they included the poet **Mickiewicz**, the composer **Chopin** and the politician **Adam Czartoryski**: their fame explains why this exodus was known as the **"Great Emigration"**.

THE INDUSTRIAL REVOLUTION

Despite what is generally believed, the Polish population of the late 19C is not exclusively made up of farmers. Although Władysław Reymont was awarded the Nobel Prize in Literature for his novel entitled *Peasants*, he also penned a work called *The Land of Great Promise*, in which the town of **Łódź** appears like a tower of Babel of the textile industry.

Łódź once had a large population of Jews and Germans and due to its association with fabric and factories, it claims to be the Polish Manchester (in England).
See the industrial architectural ensembles in Łódź.

A DIFFICULT INDEPENDENCE

Between 1905 and 1914, the political troubles which shook Europe rekindled the Poles' hopes for independence. However, when the First World War started, Poles who were recruited by the Russians had to fight their brothers of the Polish legions integrated into the Austro-Hungarian army and led by **Joseph Piłsudski** (1867–1935). It was he who proclaimed the independent republic on **11 November 1918**. Postwar treaties granted Poland several territories including the famous **"Danzig Corridor"** as well as the richest part of Silesia. But the Entente did not succeed in agreeing on the eastern borders: the project of the English minister Curzon was not unanimously endorsed. Russia and Poland therefore decided to fight it out. During the battle which took place near Warsaw in August 1920, known as the **"Miracle of the Wisła"**, Poland, with the help of French General Weygand, repelled the enemy and regained its historic territories of Belarus and Ukraine. But the country found it very difficult to manage its newly acquired independence: the numerous minorities demanded rights, political parties tore each other apart and a financial crisis shook the economy. Between 1919 and 1930, 495,000 Poles settled in France, essentially in the coal mining region of the Nord-Pas-de-Calais. To boost the economy, in 1924 the Diet launched the construction of the port of Gdynia. In May 1926, following a coup d'état, Piłsudski was first elected Minister of War before gradually gaining total control of the government at the end of the 1920s and beginning of the 1930s, when the world economic crisis hit the country. His programme was based on the **"sanacja"**, the "cleaning up" of the State; but this meant the internment of opponents. Poland also signed pacts of non-agression with the USSR and later with Germany. However, as early as March 1939, Hitler demanded that Poland give up Danzig and grant Germany important rights over the corridor.

GERMAN-SOVIET INVASION (1939–41)

On 1 September 1939, at 4.45am, the battleship *Schleswig-Holstein* fired its heavy guns at **Westerplatte**, a Polish enclave in the port of Gdańsk, while German tanks crossed the border. Prior to the invasion, Germany had secretly signed a pact with the USSR anticipating a partition of the country. On 17 September, Soviet troops in turn invaded Poland. The country could not fight back without western help; Germany and the USSR shared the land and thousands of Poles were imprisoned, deported to the Reich (almost 1 million) and the goulags of the Arctic and of Kazakhstan (over 1 million) or murdered by the Soviet secret police. Meanwhile, a government in exile, led by **General Sikorski**, was formed, at first in Angers then in London, after the French defeat in June 1940. In June 1941, there was a turning point, when Hitler threw his army across Polish territory to attack the USSR. Following a meeting in London between Sikorski and a Soviet representative, 75,000 Polish soldiers were liberated from the goulags and General Anders was asked to organise this newly formed army corps.

👁️*See the Wolf's Lair in Kętrzyn*

GHETTOS AND DEATH CAMPS

It is important to stress the difference between the fate of non-Jewish Poles and that of Jewish Poles. As early as October 1939, the German governor of Poland explained that "Poland would be treated as a colony: the Poles will become the slaves of the Great Reich". All those who refused to submit, in particular the élite, were sent to concentration camps or labour camps: Stutthof *(near Gdańsk)*, Auschwitz, Gross-Rosen *(near Wrocław)*, Majdanek *(near Lublin)* and Płaszów *(near Kraków)*. As for Jewish Poles, they were treated differently. At first, they were parked in **ghettos**; there were 400 in Poland alone, the most important being in Warsaw, Łódź, Kraków, Białystok, Lublin, Częstochowa, Kielce, Tarnów, Radom and Włocławek. Then, from the autumn of 1941, when the Nazis decided to implement the "final solution", it was in Poland that the **death camps** were set up. The reason behind this decision was that the country had a greater number of Jews and it was far enough to avoid arousing the curiosity of the German population. Therefore, between November 1941 and June 1942, the Nazis transformed Auschwitz and Majdanek into death camps and created five more death factories: Chełmno (Kulmhof), Bełżec, Birkenau (Auschwitz II), Sobibór and Treblinka. Around **2,700,000** people perished in those six camps. On 19 April 1943, rather than wait passively to be transferred to

The Katyń Tragedy

Stalin personally hated Poland. For him, the country was the Germans' gateway into Russia. In his own words, taming Poland was tantamount to trying to "saddle a pig". On 5 March 1940, Stalin ordered his secret police, the NKVD, to murder 25,700 Polish prisoners, including 15,000 officers and non-commisioned officers who represented the cream of the national intelligentsia. These executions are a symbol of Soviet cruelty and love of deceit: 200 people were killed every night by a German bullet in the back of the head. On 13 April 1943, the Germans discovered the mass grave in Katyń, near Smoleńsk (another two are located in Tver and Kharkov); but the Soviets always denied responsibility. It was only on 14 October 1992 that Boris Yeltsin acknowledged the facts in front of Lech Wałęsa, yet many Russians continue to deny them.

Poland and the Jews

Raising the subject of the Jews in Poland can be tricky. The Poles' dominant feeling is one of deep injustice: how can they be considered anti-Semitic when the country was the main refuge of European Jews and the Polish institutions never took part in the persecution and subsequent extermination of the Jews? In dealing with this sensitive question and differing opinions, clichés and historical over-simplifications usually dominate any debate: the anti-Polish side, including in particular American and European Jews, hold against Poland the waves of anti-semitism of the period between 1930 and 1960, when the Jews were used as scapegoats to justify the country's successive humiliations. The Poles, on the other hand, defend themselves, with E. Wiesel's support, by reminding their detractors that, during the war, even if all Jews were victims, all victims were not Jewish and that, in spite of the fact that helping a Jew was immediately punishable by death, a few thousand Jews were saved by Poles, in particular by the Żegota organisation (6,600 Poles have been honoured as "Righteous among the nations" by Israel). In fact, Poland is only beginning to come out of a phase of suppression, of refusing to see the difference and of a kind of "competition between victims". Since the discovery of the Kielce pogrom (4 July 1946) in 1996 and of Jedwabne (10 July 1941) in 2000, Polish historians have been courageously working in depth and they no longer hesitate to shed light on shady areas of their national history. Tourist offices are planning itineraries "in the footsteps of the Jews" and a large Museum of the History of Polish Jews is due to open in 2012 in Warsaw (www.jewishmuseum. org.pl).

See the Jewish districts in Kraków, Warsaw, Łódź, Wrocław, Lublin, Sandomierz, Kielce and Lesko, cemeteries in Tarnów, Szydłowiec, Chęciny and Leżajsk, synagogues in Łańcut, Zamość, Nowy Sącz, Tykocin, Bobowa, Sejny, Szydłów, Włodawa and Pińczów.

the camps and murdered, the Jews of the **Warsaw Ghetto** chose to rebel, although they knew it was hopeless. It took the Germans three weeks of fierce fighting to crush the rebellion.

It is impossible to convey in a few lines the reality of the ghettos and death camps in Poland. Various first-hand accounts are available: life in the Warsaw Ghetto (A. Czerniakow, M. Edelman, J. Korczak, H. Seidman, E. Ringelblum, M. Halter, W. Szpilman) or in the Łódź Ghetto (D. Sierakowiak, A. Cytryn) and in Auschwitz (Rudolf Hoess, Elie Wiesel, Martin Gray, Primo Levi, Rudolf Vrba, Jo Wajsblat), not forgetting films such as the (9-hour-long!) *Shoah* (1985) by C. Lanzmann, *Night and Fog* (1955) by A. Resnais and *The Pianist* (2002) by R. Polański based on W. Szpilman's autobiography.

See the Auschwitz and Majdanek death camps, the Treblinka Memorial, monuments connected with ghettos in Warsaw, Kraków and Łódź, Emanuel Ringelblum' Archives in the Warsaw Institute of Jewish History.

RESISTANCE MOVEMENTS AND WARSAW UPRISING: (August–October 1944)

Throughout the war, French and Polish officers worked together at deciphering messages sent by enemy troops (Enigma Code device). Polish troops took an active part in the Italy landings (Anders at Monte Cassino) and in Normandy. The Polish Government in London was involved in the creation of a **clandestine State** in Poland, something unique in Europe, with its own army, schools, press and justice. The Poles' great uprising against German occupation began in Warsaw on **1 August 1944**. In order to prevent the advancing Red Army from taking control of the country, the **Inland Forces (AK)** decided to attack. There followed street-by-street fighting

Birkenau camp, Auschwitz II

© Rafa Francis/Dreamstime.com

throughout the capital actively supported by the majority of the population. But the shortage of weapons and **Stalin**'s decision to refuse to help the insurgents forced them to surrender on **2 October**. The fighting, which lasted 63 days cost the lives of 18,000 AK soldiers and 150 to 200,000 civilians. The Germans razed 70% of the town after evacuating the population.

The number of Polish victims of the Second World War is considerable: to the **2.9 million Polish Jews** (88% of their population) who disappeared are to be added around **2 million people**, including 1.5 million due to the Nazi occupation and 500,000 due to the Soviet occupation, not forgetting the **50,000 Polish Tziganes (Gypsies)** (67% of their total population). In all, 15% of the country's population perished. The ruins of Warsaw fell into the hands of the Red Army in January 1945. It is then that the national liberation committee, formed in Lublin by the Communists, became the self-proclaimed provisional government of Poland. At the **Yalta Conference** held in the early part of 1945, the British and American governments obtained from the Soviets the assurance that free elections would be organised. However, this conference took place at a time when the Allies needed the help of the Soviets; Stalin could therefore impose his will.
See the Warsaw Rising Museum.

POPULATION MOVEMENT

Although the Curzon line was officially accepted in the east (it partly followed the course of the River Bug), the western border along the Oder-Neisse was not officially recognised for fear of violent German reactions. Thus Ukraine and Belarus gained territories from Poland who, in turn, recovered territories inhabited by **6 million Germans**. What occurred therefore was an East-West shift of population.

In the west, there was a real colonisation of the **"recovered territories"**; the number of private farms went up to 3 million, without a care for the consequences this splitting up would have on crop yields. In the east, millions of Poles had to leave the "lost territories", although 2 million chose to stay in the USSR. Those population transfers meant a real tragedy for the millions of people, not counting the few thousand Poles who left France and Belgium to settle in the recovered territories, the vast majority of those who settled in the west came from the lost territories; they travelled 600km and, on arrival, settled in a farm just abandoned by a German family.

The new Poland was built on an ethnically homogeneous territory, all the more so as most of the Jews who survived the war left the country between 1947 and 1950.

RUSSIAN REQUISITION (1947–56)

During the legislative elections of January 1947, denounced as non-democratic by Western powers, the Socialist-Communist coalition won 85% of the votes; they decided to merge to form the **PZPR** (Polish United Workers' Party). **W. Gomułka**, who wished Poland to follow her own road to socialism, was brushed aside in favour of **B. Bierut**. The satellisation of the country was underway: the **Kominform**, the consultative body of the different Communist parties was created in Szklarska Poręba, in Poland, in September 1947.

In 1949, Soviet Marshal K. Rokossovski was nominated Polish Minister of War. The **Palace of Culture and Science**, built in Warsaw between 1952 and 1955, was the symbol of this forced friendship between the Russian and the Polish people. It was in Warsaw that was signed in May 1955 the famous **Warsaw Pact** between the USSR and the popular democracies, intended to be the counterpart of NATO. On the economic front, forced industrialisation was launched together with the nationalisation of several thousand businesses; but the collectivisation of agriculture was a failure and later had to be abandoned. The PZPR governed the PRL, Poland's Popular Republic, in a totalitarian fashion with considerable help from the secret police and Soviet "advisers". **Repression** did not only concern political opponents such as soldiers of the AK or Catholic priests (**Cardinal Wyszyński** was imprisoned in 1953), but also the Party's rebellious civil servants. *See Warsaw's Historical Museum, the Nowa Huta industrial complex.*

UPRISINGS AND DASHED HOPES

In February 1956, hope was revived in Poland when **Khrushchev** denounced Stalin's crimes. After the **Poznań Uprisings**, the Party chose to call **Gomułka** back. However, from 1962, Polish leaders adopted a hard line once more. In order to stifle the student protest of March 1968, the government launched an **anti-Semitic campaign**: over half the 25,000 Jews still living in Poland went into exile. On 8 September 1968, a Pole – Ryszard Siwiec – immolated himself in Warsaw during a public event in protest against Warsaw Pact aggression in Czechoslovakia and Polish participation. Serious economic problems led the government to modify its foreign policy, particularly in order to obtain economic and technological aid from the prosperous Federal Republic of Germany, ready to officially recognise the Oder-Neisse line in exchange for emigration being granted to Germans residing in Poland.

On 7 December, **Willy Brandt** went to Warsaw to sign this agreement and symbolically stood in silent remembrance on the site of the former Warsaw ghetto. That same month, demonstrations took place in Gdańsk, Gdynia, Szczecin and Elbląg. Gomułka was replaced by **E. Gierek**, a former miner who lived in France and Belgium and wished to modernise the economy by borrowing from the West. The Poles lived in euphoria for assets were flooding into the country., but the injection of huge sums into an economy already weakened by the oil crisis only increased the country's indebtedness. In 1976, inflation was at 60%, strikes paralysed the country and new riots shook Radom and Ursus near Warsaw, where the famous tractors used in Communist countries were made. In 1978, the election of **Karol Wojtyła** as pope and his visit to Poland the following year encouraged the Poles to seek intellectual and political freedom.

GREAT FIGURES
NICOLAUS COPERNICUS (1473–1543)

A true Renaissance mind, Copernicus studied in Poland and in Italy, and obtained a doctorate in canon law in 1503. A mathematician, translator, economist, doctor of medicine and cartographer, he is known above all for his work as an astronomer. Thirty six years of research enabled him to show that although it is true that the Moon is a satellite of the Earth, the Earth's axis is

not fixed. Shattering the medieval vision of the world that placed man at the centre of the universe, the ideas of Nicolaus Copernicus had a considerable philosophical impact and sparked off violent reactions lasting for more than 200 years. His main work, *De revolutionibus orbium coelestium*, was probably written around 1520 (original manuscript kept in Kraków's Jagiellonian Library). It was published for the first time in 1543, a few days before the death of its author, in the Protestant town of Nuremberg.
See Toruń and Frombork.

FRÉDÉRIC CHOPIN (1810–49)

Born in Żelazowa Wola of a French father settled in Poland, Frédéric Chopin composed music before he could even read. At the age of 20, he decided to leave Warsaw and never returned to his native country. It is in Nohant, in the estate of his mistress and muse George Sand, that he composed the major part of his most remarkable works. Although Chopin is acknowledged as one of the fathers of Romanticism, his music is very personal, featuring harmonies well ahead of their time and sounds characteristic of Polish folklore. His repertoire is centred round the piano but he was the first composer to make piano music artistically autonomous by using chords, arpeggios, keys and scales not as a setting but as a real musical colour.

Suffering from tuberculosis, he died in Paris and is buried in the Père Lachaise cemetery. His heart is set into a wall of the nave of the Holy Cross Church in Warsaw. The major part of his work is kept in Poland at the Frédéric Chopin Society and at the National Library. The international Chopin Competition takes place in Poland every five years.
See the residences of Żelazowa Wola and Antonin, Ostrogoski Palace and the monument in Łazienki Park in Warsaw.

MARII CURIE-SKŁODOWSKA (1867–1934)

Maria Skłodowska was born in Warsaw and began her studies by following clandestine lectures in occupied Poland. In 1891, she left for France to obtain a doctorate. After discovering an article by the physicist H. Becquerel about mysterious rays emitted by uranium, Skłodowska began a programme of research about this still-unnamed phenomenon. She was the first woman to defend her thesis at the Sorbonne and later to hold her own chair there. Thus she paved the way for other women in the field of Science. Holding a degree in mathematics and in physics, she was also the first person to be awarded two Nobel prizes: the Nobel Prize in Physics in 1903, jointly with her husband Pierre (who died the following year) and Becquerel, for the discovery of radioactivity, and the Nobel Prize in Chemistry in 1911 for the discovery of radium (later used to treat cancer) and polonium (given that name as a tribute to her country). She died of Leukemia caused by that same radium. Her ashes and those of her husband Pierre, were transferred to the Panthéon in Paris in 1995.
See the Curie Museum in Warsaw.

JOHN PAUL II (1920–2005)

Karol Wojtyła was born in Wadowice, near Kraków. His youth was marred by the death of his mother and brother. While he was studying humanities at the philosophy faculty in Kraków, he discovered he had a passion for the theatre and for writing. It was during World War II that his vocation was revealed to him: in 1942, after the death of his father, he entered the clandestine seminary in Kraków and was ordained priest in 1946. He became a bishop in 1958 and Paul VI nominated him Archbishop of Kraków five years later, then Cardinal in 1967. The years 1960–70 turned him into one of the main instigators of the collapse of Communism; by tricking the Communist régime and sometimes standing up to it, he succeeded for instance in having a church built in the vast workers' complex of Nowa Huta. The choice of Karol Wojtyła, on 16 October 1978, as the first non-Italian pope for over 400 years, was no accident. His first words "Don't be afraid, open your countries' frontiers, and economic and political systems"

Political Figures

Stanisław Leszczyński (1677–1766) – Philosopher-king of Poland, known as the Beneficent, exiled and subsequently Duke of Lorraine.

Maria Leszczyńska (1703–68) – Daughter of the above, wife of Louis XV and a patron of science in Poland.

Tadeusz Kościuszko
© GeorgiosArt/iStockphoto

Tadeusz Kościuszko (1746–1817) – Hero of the War of Independence in the US and of the 1794 Uprising.

Jan Henryk Dąbrowski (1755–1818) – General, founder of the Polish Legions who gave his name to the national anthem.

Józef Poniatowski (1763–1813) – Prince, loyal to Napoleon who made him Marshal of France; died heroically at the battle of Leipzig and his name is inscribed on the Arc de Triomphe in Paris.

Adam Czartoryski (1770–1861) – Prince and politician, who became his country's unofficial ambassador at the Hôtel Lambert in Paris.

Maria Walewska (1789–1817) – Napoleon's mistress, who symbolised Polish women in the eyes of many Frenchmen.

Jarosław Dąbrowski (1836–71) – One of the leaders of the January insurrection and then of the Paris Commune.

Józef Piłsudski (1867–1935) – Major figure of European history, in particular in 1920 when he halted the Red Army.

Władysław Sikorski (1881–1943) – Head of the Polish Government in exile, he died in a mysterious plane accident.

Ubu (1896) – Imaginary tyrant of Poland, a country situated "nowhere" by Alfred Jarry.

Tadeusz Mazowiecki (1927–) – One of the founding members of Solidarność, very close to the Pope, first non-Communist head of government in Eastern Europe.

Zbigniew Brzeziński (1928–) – Jimmy Carter's adviser, who played a major role in East-West relations.

Ryszard Kukliński (1930–2004) – Member of the Polish army's High Command and important CIA spy.

Bronisław Geremek (1932–2008) – Major intellectual, committed on the side of Solidarność then to the construction of the European Community.

Lech Kaczyński (1949–2010) – Conservative President of Poland killed in plane crash with other government officials near Smolensk, Russia 10 April 2010.

Aleksander Kwaśniewski (1954–) – First ex-Communist President, freely elected.

The Polish Ex-Pat (2004–) – Symbol of the latest wave of Polish mass emigration and Polish "brain drain" into other EU countries, as the political and economic situation in Poland strives to find equilibrium.

sounded like a signal to the Poles. His visits to Poland in 1979, 1983 and 1987 were increasingly triumphant. He was venerated not to say adored by almost all the Poles and his death on 2 April 2005 gave rise to huge ceremonies throughout the country.

LECH WAŁĘSA (1943–)

Lech Wałęsa was born in 1943 in Popowo, in a province annexed by Germany at the time. After driving agricultural machines, he got a job as a shipyard electrician, taking part in strikes from 1970 onwards and rapidly becoming a charismatic leader capable of gathering around him hundreds of workers. In 1980, Wałęsa led the strike at the Gdańsk shipyard and founded the trade union **Solidarność**. He wanted to act the "Gandhi way" on a long-term basis, in a non-violent fashion inspired by Christian charity. The Pope, who supported him, received him in January 1981. Invited by the French trade unions and the non-Communist Left, he made a triumphant visit to Paris in October 1981. Arrested on 13 December 1981, he was released in November 1982 and placed under house arrest. In June 1983, he had another meeting with the Pope and in October he received the Nobel Peace Prize. In May and August 1988, he resumed his role as leader during a new wave of strikes in Gdańsk, but in view of the government's violent reaction, he called for the fighting to stop. In December 1988, he was allowed to go to France where, together with A. Sakharov, he was received with great honours by F. Mitterrand. Later, he took part in negotiations with the Communist authorities, which led on 5 April 1989 to the **Round Table Agreement**. The next day, Jaruzelski met Wałęsa, whom he had not seen since 1981. Yet another visit by Wałęsa to Rome showed the many sceptical Poles that the Pope approved this careful march towards a semi-democracy. In 1990, he was elected President of the Republic. However, having fallen out with his former Solidarność allies, confronted with the difficult economic transition and the rise in unemployment, he became painfully aware of his isolation, in particular during the cohabitation with the Left between September 1993 and November 1995. Beaten by a former Communist at the presidential election of 1995, he was humiliated at the 2000 election (barely 1 per cent of the votes).

MAZUREK DĄBROWSKIEGO

The **Polish National Anthem** is set to a lively Mazurka. The patriotic hymn was written shortly after the country lost its independence and was divided up between Austria, Russia and Prussia. The author of the *Song of the Polish Legions in Italy* – as the anthem was originally called – was Józef Wybicki.

Billboards welcoming Pope John Paul II in Gdańsk in 1999

F. Soreau / MICHELIN

He composed it in July 1795, in Reggio di Emilia, Italy, as the Polish legions, led by General Jan Henryk Dąbrowski were marching out to support Napoleon's army.

After the failure of the final effort to save Poand during the Kościuszko Uprising in 1794, many Poles emigrated to France in the hope that one good turn would deserve another and Napoleon Bonaparte would support the restoration of Poland as an independent state.

The Tsarist and Prussian governments banned the song in 1815 (after the defeat of Napoleon) and again in 1860. Yet it continued to serve rebellious Poles: against the Russians (1830, 1863); during the 1848 Spring of the Nations; as the anthem of the student union (Zwiazek Burszow, 1816–30). The students sang: "March, march, the youth/ go first as it should be/ following your leadership/ we will become a nation again."

At the end of the 19C, the song was modified to suit the context of the times ("March, March, the Poles, to fight and to work"). Dąbrowski was replaced by other military leaders, as current events required.

Finally, in 1926, "Dąbrowski's Mazurka" was officially recognised as the Polish national anthem. The title was listed for the first time in the Constitution of the Polish People's Republic in 1976: the Sejm approved the official text and music of the anthem in 1980.

MILESTONES OF POLAND'S HISTORY

966 — Conversion of Mieszko to Christianism

1309 — Teutonic State around Marlbork

1386 — Marriage of Jagiello of Lituania and Hedwig of Poland

15 July 1410 — Teutonic Knights defeated at Grunwald

28 January 1573 — Eternal peace between religions proclaimed by the "Warsaw Confederation"

1596 — Capital transferred to Warsaw

1683 — Ottomans stopped in front of Vienna by Jan III Sobieski

3 May 1791 — First liberal Constitution in Europe

1794 — Kościuszko Uprising against the three occupying countries

24 October 1795 — Third Partition and disappearance of Poland

1807 — Grand Duchy of Warsaw formed by Napoleon

1815 — "Congress Kingdom of Poland" in the hands of the Tsar

29 November 1830 — November Uprising

22 January 1863 — January Uprising

11 November 1918 — Independence of Poland

15 August 1920 – "Miracle of the Wisła" enabling Poland to push Russia back

12 May 1926 – Piłsudski in power after a coup d'état

1–17 September 1939 – Soviet-German invasion

19 April–20 May 1943 – Warsaw Ghetto Uprising

May 1944 – Monte Cassino victory in Italy

1 August–2 October 1944 – Warsaw Uprising

January 1947 – Large Communist victory after rigged elections

June 1956 – Poznań riots

March 1968 – Persecution of intellectuals and anti-semitic purge

14–18 December 1970 — Workers riots in Gdańsk, Gdynia, Elbląg and Szczecin

16 October 1978 — Election of Karol Wojtyła as Pope

August 1980 — New workers riots in the Baltic shipyards

31 August 1980 — Gdańsk agreement between Solidarność and the government

12–13 December 1981 — Martial law decreed by General Jaruzelski

5 April 1989 — Round Table Agreement between Communists and Solidarność
September 1989 — T. Mazowiecki, first non-Communist head of government
12 March 1999 — Poland joins NATO.
1 May 2004 — Poland joins the EU.
25 September 2005 — Lech Kaczyński, PiS party, elected President of Poland.

14 July 2006 — Lech's twin brother, Jarosław, PiS, designated Prime Minister.
November 2007 — Donald Tusk (pro-EU Civic Platform) becomes Prime Minister.
10 April 2010 — President Lech Kaczyński killed in plane crash near Smolensk, Russia.

Art and Architecture

Poland, a nation at the crossroads of East and West, has evolved over its history into a unique and distinctive culture. Polish nationality has maintained its unity and strength through art rather than politics, since the country was twice erased from the map of Europe. Many authors and artists in exile were steadfast in keeping the country alive through their works. After the 1918 reunification, nationalist cultural movements gave way to the exuberanceof the avant-garde. Artistic expression was then plunged deep into one of history's darkest moments; the trauma of the Holocaust and the censure of Soviet rule.

ORIGINS
Many civilisations passed through the vast plains of Poland, leaving traces found in archaeological excavations. Prominent among them were the **cythians** with their animal-style décor and the **armatians** (4C) with their strongly geometric art from the steppes.

ROMANESQUE TO BAROQUE
ROMANESQUE ART
After the conversion of Prince Mieszko I to Christianism in 966, Poland entered the sphere of western art. Religious stone architecture was introduced. Pre-Romanesque forms of architecture, drawing their inspiration from Bohemia, can be seen in the Church of SS Felix and Adauctus on Wawel, in Poznań Cathedral and in the Piasts' castles in Ostrów Lednicki, Giecz and Premyśl.

There are few traces left of the first churches, which were small rotundas *(Cieszyn)* and of the first 10C and 11C cathedrals, except for the second crypt (St Leonard) of Wawel Cathedral and St Andrew's Church in Kraków, which looks like a fortress-church, with its complex combination of towers and galleries *(Westwerk)*. This tendancy to fortification is evident in the churches of Opatów, Płock and Tum.

From the mid-12C, Romanesque architecture flourished in the ornamentation of **doorways** (Tum, St Mary Magdalene of Wrocław), of façades (the Church of the Hospitallers in Zagość) and rare carved pillars in Strzelno.

The remarquable mid-12C **bronze doors** intended for Płock Cathedral (today in Novgorod) as well as those in Gniezno are inspired by Mosan art.

Also dating from this period are a few miniatures and some extraordinary items of silver and goldwork.

The Cistercian Transition
During the years when the Cistercian Order was extending its zone of influence, between 1140 and 1300, 25 monasteries of various origins were created. Mainly established in Little Poland bet-

ween the Oder and the Wisła (Jędrzejów, Sulejów, Wąchock, abbey of Mogiła near Kraków), and in Silesia (in Trzebnica, the introduction of openwork windows heralds the late-Gothic style), Cistercian architecture is better preserved there than in Greater Poland where, being rarer, it disappeared or was considerably remodelled during the Baroque period. The Cistercians, initiating the transition from the Romanesque to the Gothic styles, introduced elements of Gothic architecture with semicircular arches and ribbed vaulting at the beginning of the 13C.

In Pomerania, Cistercians, who were dependent on German and Danish communities (Kołbacz, Oliwa), adapted the Gothic style of Western Europe to a brick-based architecture, followed in this way by the Franciscan and Dominican mendicant orders who also built brick monasteries such as the Dominican church in Sandomierz (1226), considered to be Poland's first brick-built church.

GOTHIC ART

Setting itself apart, Silesia developed its own regional school of Gothic architecture best represented by the basilicas of Strzegom and Wrocław (St Elizabeth's and St Mary Magdalene's churches) before coming under the influence of the Parler, a family of 14C architects from Germany who constructed many famous works across Europe.

Gothic Art in the North

The north of the country saw a flourishing of **"Backsteingotik"**, a German expression used to refer to brick-built Gothic edifices, characteristic of Poland and Northern Germany. The Teutonic Order erected vast castles on a square plan, the most important of which, situated in **Malbork**, was like a fortress-monastery, similar to the strongholds of Syria and Palestine. This northern Gothic featured massive walls and elaborately decorated gables as illustrated by Frombork Cathedral, Orneta Church, Toruń Cathedral and Lidzbark Warmiński Castle, as well as by churches boasting naves of equal height such as the Basilica of Our Lady in Gdańsk. Pelplin Cathedral offered the first example of English-style star vaulting.

Gothic Art in Towns

In the mid-14C, the influence of the monasteries was gradually replaced by that of the Crown, represented by the builder-king, **Kazimierz The Great**, who is said to "have found Poland built of wood and left it built of stone". New powers granted to towns based on urban charters (prawo miejskie) promoted a new kind of layout featuring a vast central market square (rynek) dominated by a town hall (ratusz) and a parish church (kościół farny); the finest example of this town planning is undeniably Kraków, which symbolises the power of

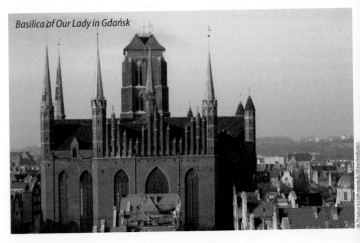

Basilica of Our Lady in Gdańsk

Gothic Military Architecture

Malbork: Teutonic castle (14C)

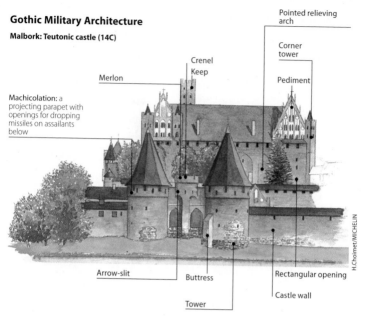

Pointed relieving arch

Corner tower

Crenel
Keep

Pediment

Merlon

Machicolation: a projecting parapet with openings for dropping missiles on assailants below

Arrow-slit

Buttress

Rectangular opening

Castle wall

Tower

H.Choimet/MICHELIN

the local middle class. Throughout the kingdom of Poland, large basilicas such as the cathedrals in Kraków, Gniezno, Poznań and Wrocław were erected on the foundations of existing buildings, some 50 castles (Ojców, Będzin, Olsztyn, Ogrodzieniec) were built and almost as many churches including, in particular, the three-naved collegiate church in Sandomierz, boasting fan and star vaulting, and the twin-naved Wiślica Church. The Church of the Holy Cross in Kraków spreads its star vaulting over a single central pillar with a palm-like capital. In the 14C, at the time of the accession to the throne of the Jagiellons, the **Flamboyant Gothic** style, with its ribbed vaulting and elongated pointed arches, its profusion of windows and of decoration and the emphasis on vertical lines met with a growing success which spread throughout the provinces.

Gothic Sculpture

The oldest wooden sculptures date from the 12C and 13C, and at the beginning of the 15C, the Virgin and Child became one of the favourite themes of Polish sculpture, under Italian influence. The Krużlowa Madonna, attributed to an artist from Little Poland, is the most famous and characteristic example of the "delicate style". It was also during this period that **Gothic altarpieces** acquired their definitive shape, featuring a vertical triptych with moving panels surrounding a carved centrepiece. With **Veit Stoss**, who worked in Kraków during the last quarter of the 15C, Polish sculpture found a new lease of life. His altarpiece of the Dormition of the Virgin in **St Mary's Church** in Kraków and the tomb of King Kazimierz Jagiello in Wawel Cathedral inspired artists until the middle of the 16C, even though new trends born, of the Italian Renaissance were already spreading.

At the same time, Poland was exposed to the influence of masters from Russia, as attested by the Byzantine-style frescoes decorating the Collegiate Cathedral of Sandomierz and those adorning the Holy Trinity Chapel in Lublin, dating from 1418.

THE RENAISSANCE

Sigismund I (married Bona Sforza d'Aragon, an Italian) invited Italian artists to Wawel thus bringing to Poland the more decorative art of the Renaissance. Between 1507 and 1532, while Germany, Bohemia, Masovia and Pod-

Flamboyant Gothic Architecture

Wrocław Town Hall (2nd half of the 13C, remodelled in late Gothic style)

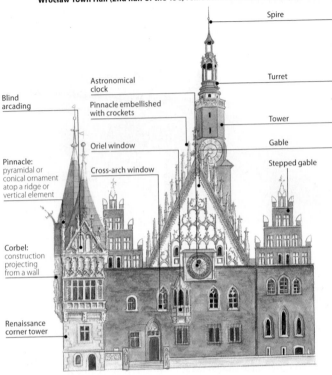

Spire

Turret

Tower

Gable

Stepped gable

Astronomical clock

Pinnacle embellished with crockets

Blind arcading

Oriel window

Cross-arch window

Pinnacle: pyramidal or conical ornament atop a ridge or vertical element

Corbel: construction projecting from a wall

Renaissance corner tower

H.Choimet/MICHELIN

lasie remained loyal to the late-Gothic style, the royal castle on Wawel Hill was transformed under the influence of Florentine architecture, as shown by the fine main courtyard surrounded by three superimposed arcaded galleries, and the coffered ceiling of the Audience Hall, otherwise still basically Gothic. Supervised in turn by **Francesco** from Florence, **Bartolommeo Berecci** and then **Benedykt** from Sandomierz, these remodellings prompted the kingdom's wealthy magnates to want to compete, which is what they did in Little Poland in the middle of the 16C in the palaces of Krzyżtopór, Krasiczyn or even Baranów, near Sandomierz, known as the little Wawel. Although it only borrowed a few decorative elements from the Renaissance style, religious architecture owed to Bartolommeo Berecci one of the masterpieces of the Polish golden age

(*Złoty Wiek*): the famous Sigismund Chapel added onto the side of Wawel Cathedral, on which many constructions were modelled.

The most flourishing towns at the height of their power built sumptuous town halls (*ratusz*) often surmounted by a crenellated tower, such as the Poznań town hall erected by Giovanni Battista Quadro. The lower part of the roofs of many buildings were enhanced by decorated attics. Threatened by a Turkish invasion, towns surrounded themselves with brick-and-earth fortifications, such as the extremely well-preserved Barbican in Kraków, dating from the 15C. A whole city, Zamość, built from 1579 onwards, was designed by one single Italian architect, **Bernardo Morando**, along the lines of a Renaissance-style town-planning project, although Eastern influences appeared in the middle of the 17C

Renaissance Architecture

Kraków: The Cloth Hall (16C, remodelled in neo-Gothic style in the late 19C)

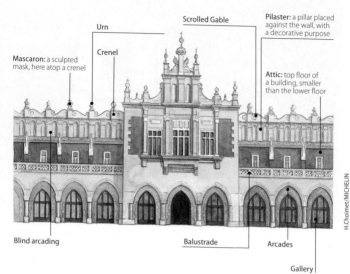

Urn

Scrolled Gable

Pilaster: a pillar placed against the wall, with a decorative purpose

Crenel

Mascaron: a sculpted mask, here atop a crenel

Attic: top floor of a building, smaller than the lower floor

Blind arcading

Balustrade

Arcades

Gallery

H.Choimet/MICHELIN

Renaissance Architecture remodelled as Baroque in the 18C

Zamość Town Hall

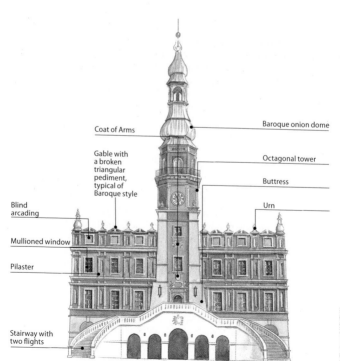

Coat of Arms

Baroque onion dome

Gable with a broken triangular pediment, typical of Baroque style

Octagonal tower

Buttress

Blind arcading

Urn

Mullioned window

Pilaster

Stairway with two flights

H.Choimet/MICHELIN

Poznań town hall

© Tomasz Jabloński/Dreamstime.com

with a group of Armenian houses. Most prominent in Gdańsk and in the Hanseatic cities, the **Dutch Mannerist style** was promoted by Anton van Opbergen, the architect of the Old Town Hall, by Abraham and Wilhem van den Blocke, and by the painter Hans Vredemann de Vries.

The sculptors **Santi Gucci**, **Gian Maria Padovano** and **Jan Michałowicz**, who worked on magnificent funerary monuments, intended for the royal family and the nobility, and on the decoration of many other monuments, rank among the most talented artists of their time. Finally, the painter-monk Stanisław Samostrzelnik from Mogiła Monastery produced important mural paintings.

THE BAROQUE STYLE

The Renaissance period undeniably bore the imprint of the **Jagiellonian royal dynasty**, but from the beginning of the Baroque period, the dominant influence was that of the Vasa royal dynasty, **Sigismund III** (1597–1632) who transferred the capital from Kraków to Warsaw in 1596 and his son Ladisław IV (1632–48). Coinciding with the arrival of the Jesuits in Poland, the Baroque style became the official style of the Counter Reformation, which made its first appearance in the Church of

SS Peter and Paul in Kraków. Designed as a scaled-down version of the Roman church of Il Gesu de Vignola, without aisles, designed on the Latin Cross plan, with a dome soaring above the crossing, it was the work of the Italian architect **Giovanni Trevano**, whereas the interior decoration (intended to hide the brickwork) was made by the stucco artist **Baltazar Fontana**. Having arrived in Poland around 1665, the Dutch architect **Tylman van Gameren**, who designed the Krasiński Palace in Warsaw and St Anne's Church in Kraków, softened with a touch of Classicism the exuberance of the initial Italian style. Other fine examples of pure Baroque style are to be found in the Jesuit Church in Poznań and in the Church of the Nuns of the Holy Sacrament in Warsaw, boasting elegant façades; on the other hand, the town of Gdańsk was not particularly marked, apart from the Royal Chapel, by the architectural style of the Counter Reformation. At the time architects generally tended to remodel old edifices in the Baroque style. Indeed, the Gothic interior of many a church was enhanced by Baroque decorative elements and enriched with marbles and stuccos.

Built at the beginning of the 18C, the **Rococo** bishop's palace in Kielce, decorated by **Antoni Frączkiewicz**, showed

Baroque Jesuit Architecture

Kraków: Church of SS Peter and Paul

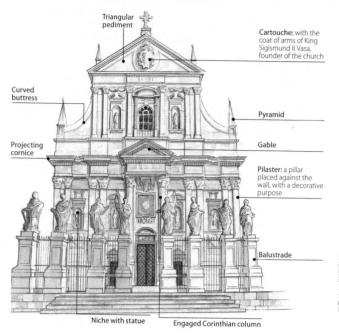

Triangular pediment

Cartouche: with the coat of arms of King Sigismund II Vasa, founder of the church

Curved buttress

Pyramid

Projecting cornice

Gable

Pilaster: a pillar placed against the wall, with a decorative purpose

Balustrade

Niche with statue

Engaged Corinthian column

H.Choimer/MICHELIN

Dutch Mannerist Architecture

Gdánsk: Golden House

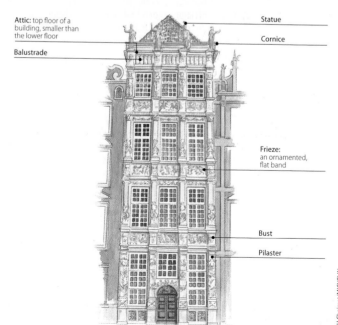

Attic: top floor of a building, smaller than the lower floor

Statue

Cornice

Balustrade

Frieze: an ornamented, flat band

Bust

Pilaster

H.Choimer/MICHELIN

a French influence which, strengthened by the bonds uniting the Polish and French courts, became more and more prominent. At the same time, following the victory against the Turks in 1683, the Eastern influence could be seen in the minor decorative arts. It was the period when **"Sarmatism"** *(Sarmatyzm)* was fashionable; this concept of another age, returning to a strange "East/West" blend, was favoured by Polish aristocrats who wished to rediscover, through the splendour of ceremonies and the magnificence of costumes, décor and weapons, the virtues and military glory of their Sarmatian ancestors. Associated with costume, the so-called Sarmatian portrait, introduced at the end of the 16C, remained fashionable until the 18C. Another type of typically Polish production also fashionable at that time were the portraits used to decorate coffins *(portret trumienny)*.

This was also the period when important royal art collections were assembled and interest for the arts resulted in the acquisition of works by Rubens in particular (he made portraits of the first two Vasa kings), or by masters of Dutch painting. Daniel Schultz from Gdańsk trained in Holland, then became the official painter of the royal family, while the Venetian Tommaso Dolabella adapted Italian Mannerism to religious and historical subjects.

ENLIGHTENMENT TO THE 20C
ROYAL PATRON OF THE ARTS

The Age of the Enlightenment brought with it a more international artistic period than Sarmatism had been, with its specifically Polish character in spite of the Oriental influence. King Stanisław August Poniatowski, a dedicated patron of the arts, great connoisseur of French culture and enthusiastic art collector, attracted to his court a number of foreign artists, in particular from Italy and France. In charge of the remodelling and furnishing of the interior of the royal castle in early classicist style were the French architect Victor Louis (1731–1800) and the Italian Dominico Merlini

(1731–97), who became the King's first architect after Jacob Fontana.

The Italian painter **Marcello Bacciarelli** (1731–1818), the King's main artistic adviser, settled in Warsaw in 1766 to take charge of the artists working at the Royal Castle. His task was, more specifically, to decorate the ceilings of the rooms of the new Łazienki summer royal residence, built jointly by an architect from Dresden, Jan Chrystian Kamsetzer, and by Merlini. Another eminent artist staying at the Polish court was Bernardo Bellotto, known as **Canaletto the Younger** (1720–80), who painted renowned *vedute* (townscapes with characters), just like his famous uncle. French artist **André Le Brun** (1737–1811), a disciple of Pigalle, was in charge of the royal sculpture studio while the painter **Jean-Pierre Norblin de la Gourdaine** (1745–1830), a protégé of Prince Czartoryski, introduced Poland to genre painting and battle scenes, a theme later developed by his pupil **Aleksander Orłowski** (1777–1832).

With the 1795 Partition and the end of the monarchy, the "styl Stanisławowski" was taken up by the Polish nobility, who commissioned many palaces to be built or rebuilt in Palladian, Neoclassical style or in Romantic, neo-Gothic style.

During the 19C, the division of the country between the three great neighbouring powers strengthened Austro-Hungarian, Prussian and Russian architectural influences – for instance in Warsaw, where late Neoclassicism recalls St Petersburg.

PAINTING AND NATIONALISM

Antoni Brodowski (1784–1832), who studied in Paris, was Poland's most outstanding Neoclassicist painter, whereas **Piotr Michałowski** (1800–55) is considered the country's greatest Romantic painter. Often compared to Géricault, this famous artist, who specialised in painting horses, also admired the Napoleonic period, which he illustrated through many paintings. Inspired by Cervantes' *Don Quixote*, he made many portraits of working-class people in the vein of Daumier.

King Stefan Báthory (1533-86) at Pskov acknowledging the victory of the Polish army in 1581 after a six month long siege, *(1872) by Jan Matejko*

Sharing his time between Vienna and Paris, **Henryk Rodakowski** (1823–94) was a great society portrait painter and an exponent of the realist style, admired in particular by Eugène Delacroix and Théophile Gautier.

Since the court no longer governed public and artistic life, the second half of the 19C saw many artists go into exile. While Prussian Poland went through an enforced Germanisation process and, following the 1863 insurrection, tsarist repression became fierce (Austro-Hungarian Galicia enjoyed relative freedom after 1861), some Polish artists turned to subjects and symbols of a national nature, art thus becoming a substitute for politics.

A great master of Polish historical painting, **Jan Matejko** (1838–93), founder of the "Kraków School", had many pupils (the most talented later rejected his style), and devoted his entire output to the "awakening of his enslaved nation's conscience". His huge compositions, overcrowded with characters, illustrate the great periods of Polish history. Deeply concerned with the preservation of his native Kraków's artistic heritage, he took part in the interior decoration of St Mary's Church. The lithographs of young **Artur Grottger** (1837–67) are inspired by the same themes.

The main exponent of realism in landscape painting, **Józef Chełmoński** (1846–1914), left contemplative works illustrating peasant or daily-life scenes. On the other hand, his contemporary, **Witold Pruszkowski** (1846–96), was a precursor of symbolism.

Particularly concerned with light, **Aleksander Gierymski** (1850–1901) produced genre scenes which can be classified as pre-Impressionist painting. Fascinated by Paul Gauguin (1848–1903), **Władysław Ślewiński** (1854–1918), who spent a major part of his life in Britanny, had strong links with the Pont-Aven School and influenced Stanisław Wyspiański and Józef Mehoffer.

Characterised by a blend of symbolism and realism, the work of **Jacek Malczewski** (1854–1929), a pupil of Matejko, stands apart. Painted in ever brighter colours, his eccentric self-portraits (featuring some surrealist elements) magnify the personality of an artist who is also affected by the thwarted destiny of his country. The National Museum in Poznań houses the major part of his work.

Another pupil of Matejko, **Maurycy Gottlieb** (1856–79), of Jewish origin, tried during his brief life to reconcile the Jewish and Christian traditions in an original way.

At first close to Impressionism, which he discovered in Paris, **Władysław Podkowiński** (1866–95) left few works, yet his *Madness*, exhibited in 1894, influenced by the emerging symbolist movement, was the talk of artistic circles. His friend **Józef Pankiewicz** (1866–1940), was the main exponent of French Impressionism in Poland before adhering to symbolism.

The excellent portrait-painter **Olga Boznańska** (1865–1907), known for her subtle range of colours, settled in Paris in 1894 and became one of the main exponents of post-Impressionism. In a more sombre vein, **Witold Wojtkiewicz** (1879–1909), who died prematurely in Warsaw, left a few most original Expressionist works, often featuring morbid and grotesque imaginary elements.

SYNTHESIS OF THE ARTS: YOUNG POLAND

Founded in Kraków in 1898, the Young Poland movement (*Młoda Polska*) was a blend of several pre-existing artistic trends (Impressionism, naturalism, symbolism, Expressionism) which gathered multifaceted talents. Marked by a return to Romanticism, repressed by the positivist period and tinged with new-found spirituality, it was one of the expressions of decorative Art Nouveau (*Secesja*).

A versatile creator, **Stanisław Wyspiański** (1869–1907), born into a

The Strange Garden (*1903*) by Józef Mehoffer

© World Illustrated/Photoshot

family of artists from Kraków, was considered the father of modernism. Before he devoted the last ten years of his life to the theatre, he produced graphic works, mainly pastels, including intimist canvases such as portraits or landscapes, as well as monumental projects such as the polychromes decorating Kraków's Franciscan Church and, above all, the magnificent stained-glass windows he made for the same church. Although he was a pupil of Matejko and later worked with him, his works betray the influence of the Viennese Secession, of French Art Nouveau (through a stylised rendering of plants) and even of Japanese art. His friend, the artist **Józef Mehoffer** (1869–1946), excelled in the decorative arts and became famous for the stained-glass windows which he made for the collegiate church in Fribourg (Switzerland) and which bear the mark of Art Nouveau. His painting is imbued with a unique feeling of intense delight and happiness.

Having also studied in Kraków, **Włodzimierz Tetmajer** (1862–1923) devoted his expressive, colourful art to the peasantry. **Wojcieh Weiss** (1875–1950), highly influenced by Przybyszewski's writings, produced amazing Expressionist paintings at the turn of the 20C, before returning to a more traditional style.

Having the same name as his famous son, **Stanisław Witkiewicz** (1851–1915) is essentially known as an art critic and theorist through his anthology *Our Art and Criticism* (1871), which influenced many a young artist. He also invented the so-called **Zakopane Style**, inspired by popular art from mountainous areas. Strongly influenced by Rodin during his stay in Paris between 1914 and 1922, **Xavery Dunikowski** (1875–1964) was THE great Polish sculptor whose style incorporated Cubist fragmentation and subsequently evolved considerably.

Also worth mentioning is **Bolesław Biegas** (1877–1954), who settled in Paris in 1902 and whose sculptures (also influenced by Rodin) and paintings are essentially symbolist.

THE PRECURSORS OF MODERN ART

After Poland recovered its independence in 1918, defending the national culture became a secondary issue and there was a blossoming of more radical artistic movements comparable to those of Western Europe. Led by a few exceptional figureheads, the Polish avant-garde showed a desire to experiment in the midst of a riot of artistic expression. The art magazine **Zwrotnica** founded by **Tadeusz Peiper** (1891–1961) was used as a forum for theoretical debate by the Polish avant-garde in the 1920s.

Exiled in Paris, **Tadeusz Makowski** (1882–1932), who was mainly influenced by Gauguin and Polish popular art, was probably the first to take into consideration the advent of Cubism, but it was above all in the work of **bigniew Pronaszko** (1885–1958) that the first Cubist elements were to be found. Combining Futurism and Cubism, **Tytus Czyżewski** (1880–1945) initiated a trend in Kraków in 1915, which was at first described as Polish Expressionism but soon evolved towards a more formal radicalism whose exponents adopted in 1918 the name "Formists" *(Formiści)*, while a dissident group from Warsaw, founded by the painter Eugene Zak, adopted the name "Rytm" in 1922. Prolonging this trend, the eminent logician **Léon Chwistek** (1884–1944) devised a theory, known as "Zonism" *(Stresfizm)*, about unity of form and colour.

More or less connected with this movement are the graphic works of the multidisciplinary artist **Stanisław Ignacy Witkiewicz** (1885–1939), known as **Witkacy**, initiator of naturalism and founder of the "Pure Form" theory. In addition to complex theoretical essays about art, he created his "Firma Portretowa" in 1924, of which he was the only member and for which he portrayed his contemporaries in a twisted and psychologically arbitrary way. He ranks among the best-known 20C Polish painters and his contribution in the field of photography was also substantial. The graphic works produced by **Bruno Schulz** as an illustrator, consisting of strange drawings, can be associated with this Expressionist trend.

More inclined towards internationalism than the Formists who aim to define a national art, are the founders of the Expressionist group Bunt (Revolt), centred around the magazine *Zdrój*, published in Poznań and including **Stanisław Kubicki** (1899–1934), who later drew nearer to German activism. Close to the Bunt group, the group of Jewish artists **Jung Idysz**, including Jankel Adler, was based in Łódź.

COLORISTS OF THE "PARIS COMMITTEE"

Art became diversified during the interwar period which gave rise to many schools and different trends, sometimes radically opposed.

For many Polish artists, during the first decades of the 20C Paris represented the hub of modernism in art. In order to quench their "thirst for modernity", which drove them to reject academicism still in force in Poland, a handful of young Polish artists arrived in Paris in 1924 and settled there for six years, founding the **"Paris Committee"** *(Komitet Paryski)*. Subscribing to a post-Impressionist and fauvist line advocating the dominance of colour, these pupils of Pankiewicz called themselves *"kapists"* or "KP" from the name of their leader **Józef Czapski** (1896–1993), a symbolic figure of contemporary Polish history, who settled permanently in France after the war. One of the rare officers to have survived the Katyń massacre, he repeatedly denounced, in several works, the crimes perpetrated

Kisling of Montparnasse

Born in a Jewish family from Kraków in 1891, **Moïse Kisling** was the pupil of Pankiewicz before he settled in France in 1910 and became one of the typical exponents of the Paris school.

by the Soviets. Another two founders of the Paris Committee were **Zygmunt Waliszewski** (1897–1936) and **Jan Cybis** (1897–1972). In Poland, a prize named after the latter is now awarded to a work in the artistic field.

The influence of the colorists, who were of no interest to the avant-garde, in Polish art teaching during the postwar period was important and long lasting.

CONSTRUCTIVIST INFLUENCE

From 1924 onwards, a new trend which had already appeared in Moscow and Berlin, **Constructivism**, entered Warsaw's artistic scene. Castigating the academic colorist trend of the kapists, the exponents of Constructivism advocated a radical break in order to retain pure form only, without any content whatsoever. Inspired by Soviet art and the Suprematism of Malevitch, whom they welcomed in Warsaw in 1927, they rejected all nationalist elements.

The father of Polish abstraction, **Henryk Stażewski** (1894–1988) ranks among the pioneers of the avant-garde of the 1920s and 1930s. He was the main exponent of Constructivism and, from the 1960s onwards, devoted himself to the rigour of geometric abstraction. Co-founder of the Communist group Blok in 1924, then a member of Praesens (founded by the architect S. Syrkus) from 1926 on, he later joined the a r *(artyści rewolucyjni)* and during the 1930s, exhibited as part of the Parisian groups Cercle and Carré, and Abstraction-Création. Linked to the latter, **Maria Nicz-Borowiak** (1896–1944) was also a major exponent of Polish Constructivism, as was **Mieczysław Szczuka** (1898–1927), theoretician and editor of the magazine *Blok*, close to the sculptress **Teresa Żarnower** (1895–1950).

Founder in 1929 of the avant-garde group **"a r"** (revolutionary artists), **Władysław Strzemiński** (1893–1952) initiated the first modern-art gallery inaugurated in February 1931 in the industrial city of Łódź, which aimed to mount one of the first permanent art exhibitions showing works by the world's avant-garde. He distanced

himself from Malevitch and Tatlin by developing his theory of "Unizm" from 1927 onwards and applied to his own painting the principles of "space-and-time rhythms". His wife **Katarzyna Kobro** (1898–1951), a sculptor formed in Moscow as he was, adapted the simple juxtaposition of area to spatial works. Connected with the Praesens Group, **Kazimir Podsadecki** (1904–70) distinguished himself in the use of the "Functionalist" photomontage technique. Theoretician of "mecanofacture", then initiator of the Blok Group before going to France in 1928, **Henryk Berlewi** (1894–1967) is considered one of the precursors of Op Art or Optical Art. Before he perfected his **"facto realism",** the painter **Marek Włodarski** (1903–60) joined the Artes Group, created in Lvov in 1929, who later moved on to the committed realist trend of Socialist-realism.

POSTWAR CONTEMPORARY ART

With the establishment of Communism, artists became employees of the State and closely dependent on the Ministry of Culture's sponsorship, a situation which continued into the 1980s. The painter of the Autodidacte Group **Andrzej Wróblewski** (1927–57) used his method *"neo barbaryczna"* to further the edification of Socialism. The same applies to **Maria Jarema** (1908–58), co-founder of the Kraków Group with Henryk Wiciński (1908–43), who later moved on to abstraction before collaborating with Kantor. A member of the communist group "Phrygian Cap", **Bronisław Wojciech Linke** (1906–62) combined satire and surrealism. The ZPAP, Union of Polish Artists, decided in June 1949 in Katowice to adopt Social Realism which ended in 1955. The end of the Soviet internationalist style gave rise to many new trends, such as the **55 Group** exhibiting their "visual metaphors" in the Krzywe Koło (Twisted Circle) Gallery in Warsaw or the **Grupa Krakowska II** of **Tadeusz Brzozowski** (1918–87), hostile to any form of aestheticism. The 1960s inau-

Memento Mori

Born in France in 1931, the artist **Roman Opałka** went back to live and study in Poland between 1935 and 1979 (he was deported to Germany in 1940). According to an anecdote, the fact that his wife waited for a long time in a Warsaw hotel in 1965 prompted him to conceive his project of formal painting: the passing of one's own lifetime comprehending "art as life", a subtle metaphysical reflection on time and the infinitely small.

He then began to give concrete expression to the countdown of his own existence by painting white numbers lined up on a black background, on canvases with identical measurements based on his own size (196 x 135cm). Prolonging this long line of numbers from painting to painting, he got to one million in 1972 and then added 1 per cent of white to the black background on each new canvas, which became greyer and greyer until the numbers and the background became one.

At the same time, he started recording his voice in 1972 and took a picture of his face at the end of each working day. All these details formed part of a global project which will be finalised with the death and therefore the last canvas of the artist. As he is now nearing the 6 millions, how many numbers separate him from the end of his human life and of his work completed at last?

gurated a period of diversity featuring all the western trends of Modernism. A "total artist" according to his own definition, **Tadeusz Kantor** (1915–90), who belonged to the Grupa Krakowska, began his informal period in 1948 by organising an avant-garde art exhibition around his *Metamorphoses*. His first medium, painting, gave him a decisive experience which led him to object to human representation and to adhere to the idea of the Fine Arts borrowing forms of action, of "performance art" and happenings, the first of which took place in 1965 in the **Foksal Gallery** in Warsaw, founded by artist **Włodzimierz Borowski** (1930).

A remarkable creator of modern tapestry when she started out, **Magdalena Abakanowicz** (1930) became one of the artists best represented in the world's main museums with her outdoor monumental sculptures.

Noteworthy artists also include **Jonasz Stern** (1904–88), who devoted himself to "painting matter" and incorporated in his paintings organic waste, and **Władysław Hasior** (1928–2000), who studied in Zakopane and produced amazingly poetic assemblages. Also worth mentioning are the technical experiments around the human body

of **Alina Szapocznikow** (1926–73) or the church polychromes of Orthodox artist **Jerzy Nowosielski** (1923), as well as the "wild expression" canvases of **Leon Tarasewicz** (1957), not forgetting the works of conceptualist artists **Ryszard Winiarski** (1936–2006) or **Roman Opałka** (b. 1931). Zdzisław Beksiński, Józef Szajna, Edward Dwurnik, Kazimierz Mikulski, Jerzy Beres, Jan Lebestein, Zbigniew Makowski, Krzysztof Wodiczko and Jarosław Kozłowski are also important figures on the 20C Polish artistic scene and there are always many artists ready to take over from their predecessors.

Finally, one should not omit, in the field of popular art, the painters **Eugeniusz Mucha** (1927) and **Nikifor** (1895–1968), a self-taught artist who has been compared to Henri Rousseau, known as *"le Douanier"* (toll-inspector).

POLISH POSTERS

Being the preferred support of political and cultural life (theatre, cinema, opera, jazz, circus), **poster painting**, which evolved from graphic art of the Art Nouveau and Constructivist periods, flourished in Poland towards the end of the 1950s. Propaganda posters, marked by Soviet realism, were closely

Pioneer of Geometric Abstract Art

Born in Kiev, Ukraine, in 1879, the Russian painter and writer, father of the white square on a white background (1917), **Kazimir Malevitch**, had Polish parents who were deported to Ukraine following an insurrection against Russian occupation. This was also the case of the legendary dancer and choreographer Vaslav Fomitch Nijinski, who was christened in Warsaw in 1890 with the Polish name Wacław Niżyński. He was also subjected to the Russian integration process, but always considered himself a son of Poland.

subjected to controls and censorship, but cultural posters, although also commissioned by the state, enjoyed the relative cultural liberation which followed the events of October 1956. Free from advertising constraints, "outside commercialisation", the popular art of poster painting was represented by talented graphic artists who managed to main-

tain a certain level of independence and artistic integrity, rejecting the aesthetic dogmas of Socialist realism. The production, which attests a real avant-garde creativity, rapidly led critics and art historians to speak of a Polish school of poster painting whose main exponents, acknowledged abroad, were in the 1960s, Jan Lenica (1928–2001), also a cartoon film maker, Roman Cieślewicz (1930–96), Tadeusz Trepkowski, Henryk Tomaszewski, Waldemar Świerzy, Jan Młodożeniec, Franciszek Starowiejski. The new generation includes Maciej Buszewicz, Jacek Staniszewski and Michał Batory, who has lived in France since 1987 and now works on posters for such theatres as the Théâtre de la Colline and the Théâtre de Chaillot.

In 1966, the first **Biennial International Poster Festival** took place in Warsaw and, in 1968, an annexe of the National Museum dedicated to this "street art" was created within the Wilanów Palace, near Warsaw.

Also worth mentioning is the Triennial International Engraving Festival which has, since 1966, been exhibiting the work of Kraków's famous school of engraving.

"Pax Sovietica" Polish Solidarity Movement Poster (1980)

PAX SOVIETICA

Literature and Drama

INSPIRED LITERATURE

It appears that the oldest-known sentence expressed in Polish came from a chronicle from the Henryków monastery in Silesia some time after AD 1270. Insignificant and spoken by a Polish peasant, it was taken down by a German Cistercian monk. In fact, until the 16C, Polish literature – owing to the importance assumed by the Church – was in Latin and reserved for the élite, as attested by the Annales Poloniae, historical chronicles by the Jesuit **Jan Długosz** (1415–80). The first book in Polish was printed in 1513 and, although the Protestant **Mikołaj Rej** (1509–69) is usually seen as the father of Polish literature, it is considered that popular language first flourished with the poet **Jan Kochanowski** (1532–86) and that the national language established its pedigree with the Jesuit preacher **Piotr Skarga** (1536–1612).

Associated with the Counter Reformation are the works of **Wacław Potocki** (1621–96) and **Samuel Twardowski** (1600–61), an exponent of the elegiac form, who drew his inspiration from Spanish sources. **Jan Chryzostom Pasek** (1636–1701), who wrote famous Memoirs still appreciated today, comes through his incredible war adventures as an extraordinary storyteller and swashbuckler, prefiguring the Polish historical novel. **King Jan III Sobieski** (1674–96), another battlefield regular, leaves a first-class account in the form of correspondence addressed to his French-born wife Mariette. 18C Polish literature generally drew its inspiration from 17C French authors, as illustrated in the moralising drama of Franciszek Bohomolec (1720–84). The Age of Enlightenment produced the "Prince of Poets", Prince-Bishop of Warmia (from 1766) and then Archbishop of Gniezno (from 1795), **Ignacy Krasicki** (1735801), a talented moralist, satirist, playwright and novelist.

A COUNTRY TORN APART... EXILED POETS

Following the partitions of Poland in 1795 and then again in 1815, the tsarist oppression, imposed by the absolute ruler Nicholas I, supplied Polish Romanticism with an exceptionally fertile compost for its development. The "Great Emigration", which followed the repressed insurrection of November 1830, gave a voice to the conscience of three great poets for whom literature, intended to convey patriotic feelings, became the only means of expression capable of safeguarding the national identity.

Adam Mickiewicz (1798–1855) is the most famous national bard of that period. Born in Lithuania, he was forced into a triumphant exile as early as 1823. and never saw his beloved country again. An idealist both in morals and in politics, he left a vast epic poem *Pan Tadeusz* and one of the sacred plays of the Polish drama repertoire, *Ancestors*.

Juliusz Słowacki (1809–49), the archetypal Romantic melancholiac, left a varied production marked by the mystical impulses of a man who saw himself as a spiritual guide. In response to *Ancestors*, he also wrote a Romantic drama on the theme of the insurrection, *Kordian*. His patriotic poetry, becoming more and more exuberant, drifted, at the end of his life, towards Messianic symbolism. Buried in Montmorency's Polish cemetery, his remains were transferred in 1927 to Wawel Cathedral, as those of Mickiewicz had been in 1890.

Zygmunt Krasiński (1812–59) was born in France and wrote in both languages. He is essentially known as the author of a social drama, *The Non-Divine Comedy*, on the theme of the silk-workers' uprising in Lyons in the 1830s, which ranked him as the most universal writer of the Romantic generation. He also left a colossal amount of correspondence.

POSITIVIST LITERATURE

The failure of the January 1863 insurrection resulted in the emergence of the positivist period, marked by realist trends, as well as social and political transformations, which led to the ultimate consecration of prose.

Representative of the historical novel, the works of prolific writer **Józef Ignacy Kraszewski** (18127), strongly inspired by French authors, find a perfect equivalent in Marejko's paintings. Although **Józef Korzeniowski** (1797–1863) was probably the best exponent of the realist novel, it is the name of **Henryk Sienkiewicz** (1846–1916) that is still remembered today. Famous author of the best-seller *Quo Vadis*, an epic novel about the beginnings of Christianity in ancient Rome, translated into 100 languages, this workaholic is mainly known in Poland for his historical *Trilogy*, for which he was awarded the Nobel Prize in 1905. Another positivist figure is **Bolesław Prus** (1845–1912) who, under the pen name of Aleksander Głowaski, wrote *The Doll*, one of the most famous Polish social novels. The first great female literary figure, **Eliza Orzeszkowa** (1841–1910) depicted with benevolence, in a populist vein, the world of ordinary people in the Polish provinces. **Adam Asnyk** (1838–97) and **Maria Konopnicka** (1842–1910) rank among the best poets of this generation.

"YOUNG POLAND" RENEWAL

In reaction to the realist trend came the modernist Young Poland *(Młoda Polska)* movement, which is today considered a period of the national history in its own right. The expression, which first came about in 1898, refers to the neo-Romantic movement, which maintained that art as a creator of worth was an object of veneration and creators alone were capable of achieving national renewal. The advent of this movement caused a change in sensitivity and style which affected all the arts.

An advocate of bohemian life and of Satanic literature, for ever in search of the "bare soul", **Stanisław Przybyszewski** (1868–1927) is considered a precursor of that movement. Following a long stay in Berlin, where he met Strindberg and Munch, he settled in Kraków and

gathered the new trends under the banner of *Moderna*, centred on the magazine *Życie (Life)*. An independent and original artist, he durably influenced a good deal of writers and artists.

Stanisław Wyspiański (1869–1907) stands as a significant figure of the movement, not only in the field of pictorial art, but also drama, with his famous play *The Wedding*, a tragi-comic parable about the fate of Poland, which renewed drama and revolution.

The main prose writers include **Wacłav Berent** (1873–1940), **Stefan Żeromski** (1864–1925), described as the "conscience of Polish literature", and above all, **Władysław Reymont** (1867–1925), whose huge four-volume epic novel entitled *Peasants* is considered a national saga, for which its author was awarded the Nobel Prize in Literature in 1924.

"THREE MUSKETEERS": GOMBROWICZ, SCHULZ AND WITKACY

The interwar period saw the emergence of three exceptional literary figures whose talents have now been recognised. In a country henceforth liberated from the patriotic ideal necessary to form a nation, their intellectual quest turned to new paths. Self-appointed by Gombrowicz himself, these "three musketeers" were three marginal artists who, each in his own way, furthered the cause of the Polish literary avant-garde. **Stanisław Ignacy Witkiewicz**, known as **Witkacy** (1885–1939), a fascinating figure of modern literature, was first and foremost an artist with many talents. The son of an interesting painter, art critic and theoretician, this indomitable individualist, based in Zakopane, initiated a theory of art reflecting a metaphysical obsession for "pure form". His parodic dramas *(difficult to translate and incomprehensible to many)*, which illustrate the search for pure drama, made him a precursor of the 1950s theatre of the absurd. His doomwatch theory, his anxiety about the future of our European civilisation and his prophecy of the loss of the individual led him to commit

Dedykacya (Self-portrait) (1921), by Bruno Schulz

© Interfoto/Alamy

suicide in September 1939, when Poland was invaded by the Nazis.

Bruno Schulz (1892–1942), whose talent is gradually being recognised, was a Jewish writer (and illustrator) born in Galicia (now Ukraine) whose exuberant style and sensual sensitivity were unequalled. His unusual literary output included two sets of short stories, *Street of Crocodiles* and *Under the Sign of the Hourglass*, in which he evokes his childhood in an enigmatic style. He died tragically, shot down in the street by a bullet in the head fired by an SS officer.

Wishing to distance himself from the vicissitudes of History, **Witold Gombrowicz** (1904–69) left Poland for good in 1939 and settled first in Argentina, then in France. His corrosive and deeply pessimistic works include his audacious first novel, *Ferdydurke*, which depicts a man shaped from the outside, unauthentic, caught in a vice-like conflict between maturity and immaturity and condemned to "never be himself". His other famous novel, *Pornography*, which places eroticism at the centre of his work, expresses the paradoxical immature liking of humanity for imperfection and youth.

LITERATURE IN THE POSTWAR YEARS

The worldwide catastrophy, which had been forecast by many intellectuals, left Poland – with the German occupation and the extermination of the Jews – deplete of her intellectual élite. Yet from this chaos emerged the amazingly mature verse of the young poet **Krzysztof Kamil Baczyński** (1921–44), killed in action during the Warsaw Uprising. During the immediate postwar period, writers pledged themselves to the new régime and placed their hatred of Nazism at the service of the new government. Under the influence of Stalinism, the country's cultural policy adopted a harder line and some writers (Władysław Broniewski) became fully implicated. Faced with such a dilemma, Tadeusz Borowski committed suicide in 1951, and Czesław Miłosz fled and went on to analyse in *The Captive Mind* the process of collective paranoia which threatened intellectuals at that time. Several important texts by exiled writers, gathered round the periodical *Kultura*, were published at the Paris Literary Institute by **Jerzy Giedroyć** (1906–2000) an important intellectual figure of the Polish emigration. Yet Polish writers were

85

among the first within the Communist block to stand up against ideological conformism and to reject the dogma of Socialist Realism, starting with two novels by **Leon Kruczkowski** (1900–62) *Revenge* and *The Germans*.

Using the theme of war, **Jerzy Andrzejewski** (1909–83) was one of the first **writers** to free himself from Communist power. Less of a protester, **Jarosław Iwaszkiewicz** (1894–1980) left a rich and varied **production**. **Tadeusz Konwicki** (b. 1926), also a filmmaker, was at first in favour of the Communist power but in two of his novels he recalls how he progressively distanced himself. Before settling in Paris in 1972, **Jewish author Adolf Rudnicki** (1912–90) witnessed the tragedy that Poland's Jewish population lived through.

POLISH SCHOOL OF POETRY

A major figure of postwar Polish literature, the poet and essayist **Czesław Miłosz** (1911–2004), awarded the Nobel Prize in Literature in 1980, had a long literary career that began before he went into exile in France and later in the US. His works include, in particular, a History of Polish Literature.

Poland's latest Nobel Prize in Literature was awarded in 1996 to the poet from Kraków, **Wisława Szymborska** (b. 1923), who writes in a pithy, pared down style. Other important poets include **Tadeusz Różewicz** (b. 1921) and **Zbigniew Herbert** (1924–98) with his *Mr Cogito*, the Polish double of Paul Valéry's Monsieur Teste. The playwright and novelist **Sławomir Mrożek** (b. 1930), who emigrated to France in 1963, writes satirical, burlesque stories and mocking plays inspired by the theatre of the absurd.

The field of science fiction boasts the most translated of Polish writers, **Stanisław Lem** (1921–2006), whose novel *Solaris* (1961) was successively adapted for the screen by Andreï Tarkowski, then Steven Soderbergh. More recently, international critics have welcomed the work of two reporters, **Hanna Krall** and **Ryszard Kapuściński**, who wrote the remarkable *The Shadow of the Sun* about Africa.

POLISH THEATRE

Traditionally dominated by the experimental National Theatre in Warsaw and the more conservative Old Theatre in Kraków, drama is a living art in Poland. The term "theatre" may seem too narrow to describe the work of the independent and permanently avant-garde artist that **Tadeusz Kantor** (19150) was. In 1955, he founded Kraków's Cricot 2 Theatre, named after the prewar literary café mainly popular with painters, where he imposed his own vision of the world, away from officially approved ideologies, through an informal but brutally radical theatre, aiming to destroy all form. In 1963, he imposed his "zero theatre", which conveyed the absolute discrepancy between text and dramatic art. After his show, *The Dead Class* in 1975, he developed his "Theatre of Death". Anecdote, plot and action were reduced to nothing; there was no more performance, no illustration of the play, no expression from the actors who were neutralised, just Kantor, ever present on stage, like a conductor, surrounded by objects, machines, packaging and dummies.

Another important figure of Polish drama was **Jerzy Grotowski** (1933–99), with his Laboratory Theatre in Wrocław, extended by the Garzienice Centre of Theatrical Research, where **Włodzimierz Staniewski** developed his "theatre ecology". More recently, **Krystian Lupa** (b. 1943) has been one of the most respected and influential Polish directors, since 1980 associated with the *Teatr Stary* in Kraków.

Wojtek Pszoniak, Jerzy Radziwiłowicz, Jerzy Stuhr and Andrzej Seweryn are world-famous Polish actors.

Polish Cinema

POLISH CINEMATOGRAPH PIONEERS

The first Polish cinematographic show took place on 14 November 1895 in Kraków but it was only in 1908 that a French filmmaker from the Pathé Frères company, Joseph-Louis Mundviller, made – under the pseudonym Jerzy Meyer – the first Polish fiction film: *Anthony, for the First Time in Warsaw*. Yet, as early as 1894, Kazimierz Prózyński tested a camera called "pleograph", and in 1898, Bolesław Matuszewski published the first Polish theory of the cinema in his brochure entitled *A New Source of History*. Instantly popular, the cinema developed steadily until the country became independent in 1918, with a production of about 30 films a year, During the following decade, which witnessed the début of one of Poland's first great academic film directors, Aleksander Ford, the national output slackened in favour of foreign productions, in particular French films, before being obliterated by the great world conflict which caused many actors and technicians to leave the country.

FROM STATE CINEMA TO EMANCIPATION

After the war, three films contributed to the renewal of Polish cinema now under State control. In 1947, *Forbidden Songs* by Leonard Buczkowski (one of Poland's greatest box-office successes) then in 1948, *Truth has no Frontiers* by A Ford and *The Last Stage* by Wanda Jakubowska, depict war and its consequences without any pretence, just before the brutal Stalinisation that took place between 1949 and 1953 and the generalisation of a clearly propagandist cinema. In the mid-1950s, as the Socialist Realist trend led to an artistic deadlock, it was severely questioned by a new generation of filmmakers, mostly trained at the cinema school created in 1948 in Łodź, who more or less succeeded in avoiding ideological demands and making it increasingly difficult for the Communist power to appropriate them politically. The double success of Andrzej Wajda's film *Kanał* at the 1957 Cannes Festival, then of *Mother Joan of the Angels* by Jerzy Kawalerowicz (1922) at the 1961 Festival, both films winning the Jury's Special Prize, confirmed the existence of this original Polish New Wave, which some saw as the precursors of other European new waves.

POLISH SCHOOL OF CINEMA

A symbolic figure of this *nowa fala*, **Jerzy Skolimowski** (1936) began his career by making very personal films, including *Distinguishing Features, none* (1964), *Walk-over* (1965) and *The Barrier*

Andrzej Wajda on the set of his film, Les Possédes (The Possessed) in 1987

© Catherine Cabrol/Kipa/Corbis

(1966), before embarking, under pressure from the censorship, on a more chaotic and not always convincing international career, which however includes the noteworthy *Deep End* (1970) and *The Shout* (1978).

Andrzej Munk (1921–61), undoubtedly one of the most talented filmmakers, made *Eroïca* in 1957 and *Luck to Spare* in 1960, two films in a short career of just four films, marked by scepticism and above all irony, and featuring characters engulfed by the great flood of history.

Walerian Borowczyk (1923–2006), who started out as a master of cartoons, was the first filmmaker to emigrate to France in 1959 (thus setting an example); he later specialised in erotic films, from the ambitious *Immoral Tales* (1974) to the more commercial and depressing *Emmanuelle 5* (1987).

Andrzej Wajda (b. 1926), noticed in the 1960s for his stylistic hesitations and questionable themes, convincingly came back in 1977 with the highly political *Man of Marble* and again in 1981 with *Man of Iron*, awarded the Palme d'Or in Cannes. The following year in France, he made a memorable *Danton* with Gérard Depardieu and Wojciech Pszoniak in the key roles. With over 30 films to his credit (in 2007, his film about the Katyń massacres was nominated for an Oscar), the so-called father of Polish cinema receives award after award, including an Oscar for the whole of his work. He had the honour of becoming a member of the Institut de France and to assume political responsibilities in Poland at the time of Lech Wałęsa's Presidency.

Other noteworthy figures of Polish cinema include **Wojciech Has** (1925–2000) who made *Farewell* in 1958, then *The Hour-Glass Sanatorium* based on a collection of stories by Bruno Schulz in 1972, and **Kazimierz Kutz** (b. 1929), author in 1960 of *Nobody Calls*, followed a year later by *Panic in a Train*.

CINEMA OF MORAL ANXIETY

Belonging to a generation of filmmakers anxious to free themselves from the traumas of the war, or at least decided to deal with them less directly, **Krzysztof Zanussi** (b. 1939) made his mark in 1969 with his very first film, *The Crystal Structure*, as the leader of a new trend in which one can detect the social criticism of a political system relying on corruption. Consistently producing from abroad films in the same stylistic vein known as "moral anxiety", this filmmaker, often accused of being too intellectuel, questions us about faith in one of his films, *Life as a Sexually Transmissible Terminal Disease* (2000). Undermined by the emigration of its main protagonists, Polish cinema made in Poland, which hardly existed in the mid-1980s, showed signs of dying until **Krzysztof Kieslowski** (1941–96) gave

Irène Jacob in The Double Life of Veronique *(1991) by Krzysztof Kieslowski*

© Sidéral/Canal +, photo: United Archives GmbH/Alamy

it a creative impulse and a new lease of life. He became famous through his cycle entitled *Decalogue* (1988–89), a remarkable series of ten films of about an hour each, produced for television and illustrating a modern application of the Ten Commandments. His last films, *The Double Life of Veronique* (1991) and the trilogy *Three Colours* (1993–94), both French co-productions, met with significant success, no doubt amplified by the participation of French actresses Irène Jacob, Julie Delpy and Juliette Binoche. Filip Bajon (b. 1947) with *Aria for an Athlete* (1979), Agnieszka Holland (b. 1948) with *Provincial Actors* (1979) and *Europa, Europa* (1990), Wojciech Marczewski (b. 1944) with *Escape of the Freedom Cinema* (1990) and more recently Krzysztof Krauze (b. 1953) and Robert Gliński (b. 1952) today share and prolong the same creative vein.

The unclassifiable filmmaker **Andrzej Żuławski** (b. 1940) only made two films in Poland: *Third Part of the Night* in 1970 and two years later, *The Devil*, banned by the board of censors. He then went on to make films in France and produced tormented, even hysterical films rarely acclaimed by critics and often unintelligible to the public. His film *Szamanka*, which marked a return to Poland in 1996, was no exception to the rule.

CINEMA OF NEW-FOUND FREEDOM

After the collapse of Communism and the progression towards a market economy, the very nature of film producing changed and forced most filmmakers to look for financing outside Poland, even if the State continued to invest in some prestigious projects such as the Polish-American co-production *Schindler's List* (1993) by Steven Spielberg, filmed in Kazimierz, Kraków's former Jewish district. The new generation also called on their illustrious elders for epic films inspired by the classics of Polish literature: Andrzej Wajda (b. 1926), for instance, adapted in 1999 the famous poem by Adam Mickiewicz, *Pan Tadeusz*, and Kawalerowicz (1922–2007) undertook in 2001 to adapt for the screen the

An international filmmaker

Born in Paris in 1933, Roman Polanski graduated in 1959 from the Cinema School in Lódź, then, in 1963, his first feature film, *Knife in the Water*, written in collaboration with Skolimowski, was nominated for the Oscar of the best foreign film. This was the only feature film he made in Poland before chosing to emigrate. Abroad, he made multi-genre films, often acclaimed by critics and public alike; he adapted *The Tenant* (1976), a novel by a writer of Polish origin, Roland Topor, then went on to make several remarkable films, reaching the top of his career with the success of *The Pianist*, filmed in Poland in 2001, winner of many awards.

no-less famous novel *Quo Vadis?* New directors confirmed during the 1990s include Andrzej Kondratiuk (1936), Janusz Kijowski (1939), the actor Jerzy Stuhr (1947), who turned director, and Jan Jakub Kolski (1956), whose adaptation of Gombrowicz's famous novel, *Pornography*, came out in a few French cinemas in 2005. The writer/director/artist Lech Majewski's (b. 1953) *The Garden of Earthly Delights* is an interesting exploration of art and death in Venice. While most recently, Bartek Konopka's (b. 1972) unusual documentary *Rabbit à la Berlin* (2009), about the thousands of rabbits that lived safely in the no man's land between the Berlin Wall was nominated for an Oscar in 2010.

Finally, it is worth mentioning the excellent production, during the period 1957–70, of **Polish cartoons** by filmmakers such as Jan Lenica (b. 1928), Walerian Borowczyk (1923–2006), Witold Giersz (b. 1927), who enjoyed a worldwide reputation, as well as the still strong Polish tradition of documentary filmmaking, illustrated by Marcel Łoziński (b. 1940), following in the steps of Kazimierz Karabasz (b. 1930), author of the famous *Musicians* (1960).

Music

A highly musical nation, Poland can proudly claim to be the native country of a genius: Chopin, an eminently national yet at the same time universal composer. A "tree" to be reckoned with, that hides a precious "wood" of contemporary music.

FROM THE ORIGINS TO ROMANTICISM

The first music pieces, kept in the national archives, date from the 11C, but the Polish school of Gregorian then polyphonic chant developed under the Piasts and later under the **Jagiellonians** with, in particular, Nicolaus of Radom in the 15C and, in the 16C, Nicolaus Gomólka, who marked the climax of Renaissance music. They were not followed by any original first-class composer and one can safely say that Polish classical music was born during the Romantic period.

An endearing figure of Romantic music, **Frédéric Chopin** (1810–1849), born to a Polish mother and a French father, both of them musicians, arrived in Paris in 1831. Apart from a few orchestral and chamber-music compositions, he essentially wrote for solo piano, having since childhood been a virtuoso of that instrument. He composed in an inexhaustible variety of styles (preludes, nocturnes, waltzes, polonaises, mazurkas). Drawing his inspiration from the depth of human feelings and from Polish folklore, he produced, from his close collaboration with his piano, some of the finest pages of Western music. As an ultimate symbol for this composer, whose soul was both exalted and tormented and whom George Sand called "this dear corpse", his body is buried in the Père Lachaise cemetery, while his heart lies in the Church of the Holy Cross in Warsaw. Eclipsed by Chopin's creative shadow, his near contemporary **Stanisław Moniuszko** (18192), who composed cantatas and lieder (based on texts from the great national poets), is considered, on account of his *Halka* and *The Enchanted Manor* as the true father of Poland's modern national opera, even though the first Polish operas (Italian opera was introduced in Warsaw in 1628) were written by Maciej Kamieński (1734821) and Jan Stefani (1746826). A childhood friend of Chopin, **Oskar Kolberg** (18140), who studied Poland's musical folklore, is considered a pioneer in the field of Polish ethnomusicology.

The virtuoso violinist **Henryk Wieniawski** (1835880) gave his name (as Chopin did for the piano in Warsaw) to a famous Polish festival which takes place every five years in Poznań.

THE NEGLECTED 20C "CHOPIN"

Comparable to Bartok in Hungary or Janaček in Czechoslovakia, **Karol Szymanowski** (1882937) was the main architect of the renewal of 20C Polish music. Co-founder with Karłowicz, Fitelberg, Różycki and Szeluto of the neo-Romantic group "Young Poland",

Chopin Playing the Piano in Prince Radziwill's Salon *(1887)*

© The Art Gallery Collection/Alamy

which tried to imitate the progressive trends of Western Europe, in 1927 he initiated the creation of the Association of young Polish musicians, who flocked to be trained in France, in particular by Nadia Boulanger. His whole work, deeply rooted in various fields of culture and nourished by a rich travel experience, can be divided into three periods: romantic, impressionist (with a touch of orientalism, for instance in *Myths* op.30) and Polish. For the last one, he searched for the national musical roots, which were secondary in his previous works but now formed the base of his musical structure. His ballet *Harnasie (The Bandits)*, influenced by folk music from the Tatras, was created in Paris in 1936. Essentially vocal, his last compositions, include masterpieces like his opera *King Roger* (1926), based on a libretto by Iwaszkiewicz and his *Stabat Mater* (1929). Although his works are still rarely recorded and need to be discovered, there is no doubt that he opened the way for a whole generation of musicians and established the trends of contemporary Polish music.

THE WAYS OF THE CONTEMPORARY AVANT-GARDE

From the 1960s, Poland was undoubtedly held as an avant-garde country in the field of contemporary music. Yet one could not speak of a Polish national school because composers came from very varied backgrounds and worked from different angles. After strictly academic beginnings, **Witold Lutosławski** (1913–94) drew his inspiration from folk music before approaching dodecaphonism and experimenting with random devices as in his *Venetian Games* and his *2nd Symphony*, probably his best composition. In 1970, his cello concerto was created in London by Mstislav Rostropowitch. Less well known, **Tadeusz Baird** (1928–81), Kazimierz Serocki (1922–81) and Jan Krenz (b. 1926) formed the 49 Group with the intention of composing serial music of a high artistic standard but more accessible to the listener. The first two co-founded the War-

saw Autumn Festival of contemporary music still acclaimed today. The name of **Andrej Panufnik** (1914–91) is rather more associated with sound experiments. **Krzysztof Penderecki** (b. 1933) is the most famous contemporary Polish composer. His complex musical language is mainly based on musical colour. A master of choral music, he excels in religious compositions. *Dies Irae* and *Passion According to St Luke* rank among his most famous works. He also composed a mystical opera, *The Devils of Loudun* (1967), but in the 1980s returned to more traditional, Neoclassical forms. His exact contemporary, also inclined towards spiritual quests, **Henrik Mikołaj Górecki** (b. 1933) composes deeply mystical music such as the famous and peaceful *3rd Symphony* known as the *Symphony of Sorrowful Songs*. His two quartets, composed for the Kronos Quartet, are equally remarkable.

OTHER MUSICIANS

An exponent of minimalist music, **Wojciech Kilar** (b. 1932) is also a great composer of film music, in particular for Polanski, for whom he wrote the soundtrack for *The Pianist*. Other noteworthy composers include **Jan A. P. Kaczmarek** and **Zbigniew Preisner**, official and much-appreciated composer of the sound tracks of Kieślowski's last films. Poland also boasts great virtuosi in the field of classical music, such as the tenor Jan Kiepura (1902–1966), the pianist Arthur Rubinstein (1886–1982), a great friend of Szymanowski, the harpsichord player Wanda Landowska (1879–1959) and Witold Malcuzynski. Ignacy Jan Paderewski (1860–1941) should be added to the list: the virtuoso pianist and politician became Prime Minister of the first independent government of the new Poland in 1919.

Internationally known Polish **jazz musicians** include the trumpet player Tomasz Stańko (b. 1942), the saxophonist Zbigniew Namysłowski (b. 1939), the singer Urszula Dudziak (b. 1943) and the legendary pianist Krzysztof Komeda (19319), who wrote the soundtracks to Polanski's first films.

Folk Arts and Traditions

Pictures circulated by the media between the postwar period and the 1980s gave a grey and dull account of Polish society. Although the political context was bound to lead to this kind of conclusion, greyness and dullness are not among the original values of Polish culture. Popular arts and folklore, which have come back into the limelight since the opening-up of the country to the world, are full of colour and life. A yearning for bygone days, imagined as better than the present, which often shows through festivals and costumes, is not a Polish specificity. It is common to many countries deeply attached to their cultural and religious roots!

IN SPITE OF HISTORY

Anybody visiting Poland will be surprised by the diversity and endurance of traditions. Whether pagan, religious or, by some mystery, a blend of both, regional cultural features are countless. The Poles' attachment to their roots is all the more intense since the 20C tried its best to destroy them. Marxism never approved of what could involve spirituality and recall the memory of Poland before the Communist era. And yet, as soon as the régime collapsed, stables and barns released the memories and rituals of former times. The Polish diaspora, spread throughout the world, contributes to maintain the country's cultural identity by financing all kinds of associations. Those who emigrated always made a point of organising nostalgic reunions, thus keeping alive regional customs and rites. Aware of the attraction this wealth of traditional folklore has on foreigners, each region tries to regulate the succession of events.

Handicraft, traditional music festivals, folk dancing and religious celebrations actively contribute to perfect the colourful festive image that the country wishes to promote. The Festival of Baltic Fishermen, the Festival of Silesian miners, the Beskid Transhumance Festival, the great Easter pilgrimages and the historic reconstructions are excellent resources for discovering some of Poland's traditions.

TRADITIONAL ARCHITECTURE
SKANSENS

Like many central European countries, Poland boasts numerous *skansens*. *Skansen*, a word of Scandinavian origin, refers to an outdoor ethnographic

Workers farmstead cottage in open-air ethnographic museum, Chorzow, Silesia

© Tomasz Bidermann/Dreamstime.com

museum gathering together buildings illustrating a region's architectural traditions. *Skansens* are often laid out in vast parks and include churches, farms, mills, manor houses or simple apiaries. Most of the buildings date from the 17C to the 19C. They are not replicas but authentic dwellings or places of worship carefully taken apart and moved from their original site, then re-assembled by master craftsmen. Visitors can walk into the dark rooms of farmhouses and look at farming implements or objects of daily life. They can see how the most modest rural homes were suitably equipped to be self-sufficient. Churches, often consecrated, where religious services are still held, are often richer than in towns, for they are looked after by the curators and watched, mostly by elderly people who earn an additional income by working for a few hours in the *skansen*. One can easily get the impression of walking through a village of the past. Farm animals roam around, adding to the convivial atmosphere. Organisers of festivals or traditional feasts regularly stage these events in *skansens*.

TRADITIONAL HOUSING, BETWEEN WOOD AND BRICK

It is no accident that *skansens* first appeared in the cold regions of Sweden and now flourish in central European countries such as Poland. They offer the best solution (apart from books) for preserving a nation's rural heritage. It is a fact that traditional materials used by people living along the Baltic coast, in the plains of Masovia or in the Tatras mountains did not withstand the test of time. Wood, which always formed the basis of constructions, could, unfortunately, stand up neither to snow and variations in temperature between winter and summer, nor to assorted invaders who overran the country, torch in hand. It is in the southern and eastern parts of Poland that the tradition of wooden architecture remains the strongest. From the Opole region to Podlasie via the Podhale and Little Poland, there are many wooden farms, villas and churches. In the Zakopane area, wooden constructions are still being built according to aesthetic criteria dating from the end of the 19C. In the heart of Little Poland, wooden houses are often whitewashed, then painted in bright colours, in particular, blue. In all these regions, roofs are covered with shingles or sometimes thatched. Further north, in Greater Poland or in Pomerania, and east, in Silesia and in the Łódź area, brick replaced wood with the advent of Gothic architecture. Castles, churches and large monuments in towns were often only built during the brick period. As for stone-building, which reached its peak all over Europe during the Romanesque period, there is practically no trace of it left since Poland did not really exist then and therefore few architectural ensembles were built at the end of the Middle Ages. Stone only came back in fashion during the Renaissance. It was thanks to the Italian, French or Northern European architects, who were invited by Polish sovereigns to design their castles or cities, that it again became a sought-after building material.

There are a few regional specificities such as granite houses in the villages of the Biebrza Valley or half-timbered buildings, dating from the 16C to the 20C, in the vicinity of Swołowo or Kluki on the Baltic coast.

TRADITIONAL CRAFTS

In Poland, as in many other countries, it is often difficult to tell the difference between regional handicraft, illustrating a tradition, and a simple souvenir. Anachronic "Russian dolls" are on offer next to jewellery made with amber from the Baltic or Podhale glass icons. There are impressive amounts of handicrafts on offer at markets, galleries and on the parking areas of major tourist sites. And yet, during the long Communist period, popular artistic expression, often connected with religious beliefs, was not encouraged. One must conclude that handicrafts, like folk dancing and regional costumes were so dear to the hearts of the Poles that they could not do without them. The growing tourist industry will certainly not stop the expansion of these crafts. Raw materials such as wood, wool or leather form the basis of traditional crafts. In all the markets one finds legions of **wooden boxes** carved with geometric or floral motifs. Clothes made from **wool** dyed with natural colouring agents are a reminder that the Polish climate can be harsh. Even though **tobacco pouches** and **pottery** are closely linked with Kashubia, **lace** with Little Poland, straw mats and furniture with Podlasie, the expanding tourist trade places less importance on regional product differences. Fortunately, a few crafts have retained their specific niche.

WYCINANKIORPAPERCUT-OUTS

In the 19C, peasant women made decorative paper cut-outs using knives and scissors intended for shearing sheep. The technique later improved until the *Wycinanki* became real paper lace decorations adorning walls and windows; they illustrate symbolic shapes such as moons, stars, arabesques or flowers. Offered to friends, the Wycinanki are also essential elements of religious festivals. The Kurpie region, between Masovia and Podlasie, the Łowicz area and Masovia as a whole are strongly attached to the Wycinanki heritage.

PISANKA OR DECORATED EGG

Another tradition requiring know-how and precision is that of the *Pisanka* or decorated egg. Once a pagan tradition, it became an Easter symbol celebrating the Resurrection of Christ just like the awakening of nature. These eggs can be found in many shops all over the country, but the tradition originates from the Carpathian regions. The Łemko populations from Ukraine or Slovakia, the Hutsul from the Romanian Carpathians and the Poles close to Belarusian culture are the initiators of this technique. Eggs are decorated with drawings made with beeswax and dipped in several coloured liquids. Strong heat then eliminates the coats of wax, revealing three or four colour motifs which draw their inspiration from various sources,

including religious symbols, geometric shapes and, only rarely, human figures. The eggs are sometimes made of wood and decorated with rough floral motifs.

GLASS PAINTING

Extremely popular since the 18C, paintings on glass were, owing to their low cost, intended for a rural or mountain clientele. Many can still be found today in Little Poland. Themes used are sacred or profane. Glass icons can be seen in many houses, churches and even cemeteries, as in Zakopane's old cemetery. Representations of Mary and Jesus are probably the most frequent. This technique has hardly changed. The support is a piece of window glass on which the artist paints a mirror image of his subject. He first draws the outline in gouache, then fills in the motifs with colours.

AMBER FROM THE BALTIC

Although amber is sold all over the country, it remains the symbol of the Baltic. This resin, fossilised some 40 million years ago, and offered by the sea, is the raw material that contemporary designers continue to cut. Workshops in Gdańsk, Warsaw and large towns turn this "gold of the North" into jewellery, lamps, medals or clocks.

Amber

A. Gely / MICHELIN

FESTIVALS AND FEASTS
DANCING, COSTUMES AND FESTIVALS

Polish folk-dancing troupes go all over the world to present shows organised like military parades. The warm colours and the dynamism of the young artists

Folk dancers

A. Galy / MICHELIN

charm their audiences. If they have so much success on the international stage, it is because Polish folklore is extremely rich and varied. In the 19C, Oskar Kolberg, a learned man, drew up a repertoire of the country's music, songs and dances, taking care to note regional differences. His study is still used as reference.

The **Mazurka**, a dance in triple time, of which Chopin was the main exponent with a contribution of some50 piano pieces, is one of the most popular dances in Poland and one of the best known throughout the world. It has emigrated to Russia, the US, Sweden and France. Composers as different as Ravel, Debussy or Tchaikowski have drawn their inspiration from it.

A few other dances, either in their classical or folk version, belong to the country's cultural heritage, including the **Polonaise**, the Kujawiak or the Krakowiak. As the name implies, the latter is one of the leading folk dances of Little Poland. All of them liven up summer festivals and family banquets in traditional inns.

Most Poles find it quite natural to belong to a folk group or to attend the numerous festivals dedicated to regional songs and dances. Caring deeply for one's roots and showing it openly is common in all age groups. The impressive quantity of summer events, during which all the generations celebrate their cultural background together, therefore comes as no surprise. Women wearing headscarfs, yellow, blue or green silk blouses and full skirts walk onto the stage, eager to dance. They are accompanied by men wearing sleeveless jackets and peacock feathers on their hats. If you do not have the opportunity to attend one of these festivals, just switch the television on. Many of the regional networks enjoy broadcasting such events.

Religious festivals

The faith and conviction of Polish Catholics, although shaken by the postwar Communist régimes, continue to influence the life of the country. The consumer society, which has been pouring in since the 1990s, and the spiritual disengagement which affects many European countries do not seem to make an impression on the devout. In addition to Sunday Mass, religious feasts are fervently celebrated.

CHRISTMAS CELEBRATIONS

As in many countries, Christmas in Poland brings families together, whatever their religious convictions. A visit from Father Christmas or St Nicholas is perfectly compatible with the celebration of the birth of Christ. The most fervent observe a short period of fasting before giving in to the temptation of the 12 ritual dishes on the evening of

24 December (Wigilia). Strict observance of the tradition requires abstaining from meat, but carp and pike are on the menu in many homes in addition to mushroom soup, pierogi (a speciality similar to ravioli) or stuffed cabbage. For dessert, there are pastries made with white cheese and dried fruit (sernik), and cakes with poppy seeds (makowiec). Then at last it is time for presents! Later on the guests go to church to hear the midnight Mass (Pasterka). The congregation sing Christmas carols, while marvelling at an elaborate nativity scene.

The Kraków Cribs

Even though all churches in Poland have cribs (szopki), in Kraków, a real event is organised around the "manger in Bethlehem". Every year at the beginning of December, artists exhibit their cribs at the foot of Adam Mickiewicz's statue. For over 60 years now, this competition has gathered together between 130 and 150 cribs, sometimes as tall as a man. They must all draw their inspiration from Kraków's architecture and include some of the town's legendary figures. Jesus can therefore be next to the dragon or the trumpet player playing the Hejnał. After celebrating the winner, the Historical Museum takes charge of the works.

Puppets and Winter Disguise

At Christmas time in the regions of the Beskid, Kraków, Lublin and Rzeszów, some villages uphold the tradition of the collection. Children carrying a star and a crib go from house to house, wishing people happiness in exchange for sweets; they are accompanied by a puppet depicting a Tzigane (Gypsy), a devil, death or a bison. The Museum of Lublin Castle exhibits puppets of that kind. The origin of this parade is the story of King Herod ordering the "Massacre of the Innocents".

NEW YEAR AND CARNIVAL

The New Year and **Carnival** celebrations also offer the opportunity of parading in the company of puppets and masks. Tziganes, Jews, devils, bears or beggars are the characters most often represented. Today these popular events have almost disappeared.

EASTER

This is the second most important celebration. On Palm Sunday, homes are decorated with willow branches covered with white catkins while most Poles paint very elaborate decorative motifs on eggs, which are then blessed in church on Holy Saturday with other food stuff (including a small lamb made of cake or sugar) which will be eaten the next day after Mass. Easter Monday (Smigus-Dyngus) is marked by massive spraying of water in the streets for luck.

ALL SAINTS' DAY

On this family occasion and National Holiday, Polish cemeteries are lit with thousands of candles and gravestones are cleaned and visited.

Kraków Cribs, exhibition at the foot of Adam Mickiewicz's statue

Polish Easter eggs

© fotohmmm/iStockphoto

MILITARY LEGENDS
THE LAJKONIK

The richly clothed Tatar chief (the *Khan*) parading on his horse is known by all visitors to Kraków's Market Square. This legend goes back to 1287, when the Tatars invaded the town. One night, the inhabitants of the village of Zwierzyniec summoned up their courage and attacked the Tatar camp, killing the Khan. The brave deed continues to be celebrated in Kraków. An actor, disguised as the Khan, walks around the Cloth Hall, thus perpetuating the tradition. In addition, every year in June, on the last day of the Corpus Christi week, a grand costumed procession makes its way from Zwierzyniec to the Market Square.

The *Lajkonik* walks along the streets in search of a few złotys, gently beating those who contribute; according to modern legend, fortune will smile on them later. As for the mayor of the town, it costs him a few glasses of wine!

THE BROHERHOOD OF THE ROOSTER

The Brotherhood of the Rooster is 700 years old. Archers, crossbowmen and arquebusiers used their skills to protect their villages and strongholds. These occasional warriors were not soldiers but tradesmen, bourgeois or craftsmen and they belonged to a Brotherhood which adopted the rooster, symbolising night watching, as its emblem. Kraków continues to celebrate the descendants of these brave marksmen.

On the first Monday after the eight days of the Corpus Christi Feast, the members of the present-day Brotherhood of the Rooster parade in medieval costume and challenge each other in friendly fashion during great competitions... by aiming at wooden roosters.

KULIG, A WINTER GAME

The *kulig* in its original form has ceased. Although some people are trying to make it fashionable again, it is impossible to imagine that it could regain its former craze. The *kulig* was a game reserved for wealthy aristocrats wishing to relax and amuse themselves during the Christmas festivities or around Ash Wednesday. It consisted of a cavalcade of horse-drawn carts filled with jolly fellows, who went across the countryside from manor to manor. They danced, ate and drank a lot until they didn't feel the cold anymore. Some were disguised as priests, others as *Tziganes* (Gypsies) or Jews.

The 20C put a stop to this somewhat excessive amusement, but the principle seems to be coming back with the help of tourists and the advent of a well-off young generation.

Nature

Poland's landscape sweeps down from the mountain ranges in the south through a varied landscape of wooded plains, forests, innumerable lakes, protected marshes and shifting sand dunes. The primeval forest in Białowieża is unique in Europe, while the lakes and mountains attract visitors from all over the world, keen to explore areas that were once privy only to natives and those in neighbouring countries. The marshes and lakes in particular foster a huge variety of exceptional flora and fauna.

LANDSCAPES

Poland extends 650km from north to south and 690km from east to west, covering an area of 312,700sq km, which makes it the **ninth largest country in Europe**. The imaginary lines linking the northernmost and southernmost points of the continent (North Cape in Norway and Cape Matapan in Greece) and its east and west boundaries (Central Ural in Russia and Cabo da Roca in Portugal) intersect near Warsaw, which places Poland at the **centre of Europe**. The general shape of the country is somewhat rounded, with a strip of land, the Hel Peninsula (34km long for an average width of 500m), jutting out into the sea. The country has over

3,000km of borders to which should be added 694km of coastline along the Baltic. It is bordered to the north by Russia over a distance of 210km (Kaliningrad region), to the east by Lithuania (103km), Belarus (416km) and Ukraine (529km), to the south by Slovakia (540km) and the Czech Republic (790km) and to the west by Germany (467km).

NATURAL AREAS

Poland is essentially a region of **lowlands**, forming part of the great north European plain. Indeed, the word "Pole" means "field" and "plain" in Polish. The average altitude is 173m and 91% of the territory lies below 300m. The southern part of the country alone is mountainous but the highest point does not rise above 2,500m. Poland's topography features five main natural regions: the sandy Baltic coastline and lakeland in the north, the great central plain, the plateaux and the foothills bordering the various mountain ranges in the south. The oldest massifs (the **Sudeten**) date from the Paleozoic era whereas the higher **Carpathian range** consists of younger Alpine-type mountains from the Tertiary era. The largest human concentrations in the country are settled in the areas where the Hercynian bedrock is rich in coal, lignite, copper, sulphur, zinc, lead and rock salt **(Silesia)**. During the Quarternary period, the great Scandinavian ice sheet (inlandsis) advanced

Tatras Mountains

across the plain and reached the foot of these mountains. The fertile silts (loess) deposited in front of the ice cap ensured the agricultural wealth of the Lublin plateaus, of Little Poland and of Lower Silesia around Wrocław. As the **inlandsis** receded, a process which ended only some 10,000 years ago, it carved the landscapes of Masuria and of Pomerania, forming an array of **lakes** and wooded **morainic hills** characterised by infertile podzolic soils. The ice sheet considerably disrupted the draining of the land and the course of the country's two great rivers. The **Wisła** or **Vistula** (1,087km) and the **Oder** or **Odra** (912km) drain northwards across most of the country before flowing into the Baltic. But their course sometimes veers at right angles and follows an east-west direction. The Wisła runs right across the centre of Poland and flows into the Gulf of Gdańsk. Its main tributary is the River Bug (730km), which acts as an eastern border along part of its course. The Oder has its source in the Czech Republic and forms a natural western border with Germany. Its main tributary is the Warta (753km). These rivers already feature the same characteristics as Russian rivers: they are frozen in winter and swell dramatically in spring when the snow melts. However, they are navigable during part of the year and well connected with one another by canals.

THE COASTAL PLAIN ALONG THE BALTIC

The Polish coastal fringe, between 40 and 100km wide, stretches along the Baltic, forming a fairly straight, sandy low-lying zone. Extending over a distance of 694km, it is only indented to the west by the Gulf of Szczecin (Oder Delta and Bay of Pomerania) and to the east by the Gulf of Gdańsk (Wisła Delta). The landscapes feature long **sandy beaches** (very crowded in summer) lined by dunes and forests of conifers. During the Tertiary period, the resin from these trees became fossilised in the form of **amber,** sometimes trapping insects or pieces of plants. The amazing brightness of amber led ancient peoples to

believe that it resulted from sun rays being solidified in the waves and later thrown back onto the beach. Amber, used for making jewellery and ornaments, was at the origin of a flourishing trade which reached its peak during the 2C AD. **Gdańsk** is still today the world's amber capital, a metropolitan hot spot and an important shipbuilding centre. The coastline features several natural treasures, among them the Słowiński National Park (on UNESCO's List of World Biosphere Reserves), where one can ramble among huge **shifting dunes** up to 30m high and by a few shallow coastal lakes. On the other hand, water in the Baltic is **five times less salted** than the North Sea or the Atlantic. That is why the subaquatic fauna is scarce (few molluscs and jellyfish). Large cetaceans (whales) are also rare because of the shortage of food, the relative shallowness of the sea, the total absence of tidal movements and the difficulty of going through the Danish Straits leading to the high seas.

THE LAKE REGION: POMERANIA AND MASURIA

The north of Poland is an area of low hills (200 to 300m) dotted with lakes. **Pomerania** extends from the German border (Oder) to the Wisła Valley. Lying east of the river, **Masuria** stretches to the country's eastern border. This region of Poland features some 9,300 lakes with an area of over 1ha, in other words more than 1% of the country's total area. It offers a landscape which is **unique** in Europe. Pomerania boasts the greater number of lakes but the two largest lakes are situated in Masuria (Lake Śniardwy has an area of 114sq km, Lake Mamry 109sq km). Connected by canals and rivers, the lakes form vast waterways. Many people enjoy angling and **sailing**, particularly in Masuria, where the longest nautical course totals 91km! The area shelters a great variety of aquatic flora and fauna. Lake Łukajno is on the List of World Biosphere Reserves and one can get a glimpse of wild ducks, swans, herons, etc. Landscapes feature sparsely populated wooded hills. Rye, oats, potatoes and flax grow on the meagre soil, part of which is devoted to pastures. Apart from seasonal jobs during the summer, **unemployment** is very high in this region.

THE GREAT CENTRAL PLAIN

Central Poland consists of several vast plains, cut from east to west by wide valleys. West of the Wisła are the plains of **Greater Poland** (through which flows the Warta) and of Kujavia; to the east are the plains of **Masovia** (drained by the middle Wisła) and of **Podlasie**. Together they form landscapes of lowland offering little contrast. In fact, this central openland area extends from Berlin to Moscow and for centuries, men, traders, travellers, non to mention invaders, have passed through it. Located here is the cradle of the Polish State, Gniezno, as well as one of Poland's economic centres, **Poznań**, and of course the capital, **Warsaw**. Commercially, it is one of the country's most **dynamic** regions. The landscapes are monotonous as they are in all stone-free sandy lowlands. Birch and pine forests alternate with strips of open cultivated land. The **Kampinos** primeval forest, lying west of Warsaw, attracts visitors interested in World Biosphere Reserves; the meeting of the Wisła and of the Scandinavian inlandsis resulted in a unique landscape of sand dunes covered with vegetation and of marshland. The Polish plain gets little rain but the thick layer of sandy clay often accounts for insufficient drainage of the soil, which creates an environment of **marshland** and **peat bogs** (such as the amazing **Biebrza National Park**). Soils are on the whole mediocre, but they were improved in the west by 100 years of Prussian occupation, through intensive use of chemical fertilisers.

FOOTHILLS AND LOW PLATEAUX

The Wisła and Oder valleys run through relatively low plateaux: Silesia, Little Poland, Lublin plateau and western Galicia. This southern area features an exceptional combination of agricultural and mining resources. It was therefore natural that it should attract human settlements, with a high rural population density in the Rzeszów and Sandomierz basins, and enormous **urban concentrations** in Silesia and in the ancient trading and cultural cities of **Kraków, Lublin** and **Wrocław**. The industrial basin of **Upper Silesia** is renowned for its important reserves of coal around **Katowice**. However, the region is currently undergoing a complete **redevelopment** programme. The **Little Poland** plateau is dominated by an ancient Hercynian massif, the Holy Cross Mountains (the highest peak, Mount Łysica reaching 612m), prolonged northwards by the Częstochowa Jurassic plateau. This area is the oldest from a geological point of view. There are

Biebrza marshes

important mineral deposits. The undulating landscapes feature limestone ridges dotted with medieval castles (eagles' nests around Kraków). The **Galicia** plateau is marked by fertile valleys and rich pastures alternating with sterile sandy soils and marshland. The **Lublin** alluvial plateau, covered with loess and fertile deposits, is one of Poland's main wheat-producing regions.

THE SUDETEN AND CARPATHIAN MOUNTAINS

The southern mountain ranges are unquestionably the country's natural borders. They include the Sudeten to the west (border with the Czech Republic), and to the east part of the western Carpathians (border with Slovakia). Although this area represents less than 10 per cent of the country's territory, it nevertheless occupies an important place in the Poles' collective imagination, both as the source of the country's two main rivers and as a holiday and recreation area rich in traditions. It is therefore Poland's top **tourist region**. Lying to the southwest of the country, the **Sudeten** stretch over a distance of 250km and the highest peak, Mount Śnieżka, summits at 1,602m. These mountains offer many spa and ski resorts, as well as impressive nature parks, including the Table Mountains (Góry stołowe), and the Giant Mountains (Karkonosze), a granite range where moufflons (small wild sheep) gambol over natural rock formations with shapes appearing to be sunflowers, horses' heads, and pilgrims.

To the southeast, the Carpathian fringe includes the **High Tatras** (Tatry), the **Beskid** (Beskidy), the Pieniny and the Bieszczady. Mount Rysy, south of Kraków, reaches 2,499m and is the highest peak of the High Tatras and throughout Poland. Winter sports resorts such as **Zakopane** are very popular and the Tatras National Park welcomes over 2 million visitors every year. Scattered over the park's territory are some 30 lakes filled with crystal-clear water, the most famous being Morskie Oko, the "Eye of the Sea" (covering 35ha and 51m deep) and many mountain

National Parks

Poland boasts 23 national parks (covering around 3,150sq km) and 1,368 nature reserves, some of them with unique fauna and flora. The most famous is the **Białowieża Park**, one of Europe's only two parks to be both on the list of World Biosphere Reserves and on UNESCO's World Heritage List. It represents the last area of the huge primeval forest which used to cover most European plains one thousand years ago. In all, nine national parks are on the list of World Biosphere Reserves: four mountain parks two forest parks, one lakeland park, one coastal park and one marshland park.

streams sometimes featuring spectacular waterfalls (Wielka Siklawa, 70m high). In springtime, fields known as "hale" are covered with thousands of crocuses. Many caves can also be visited. The **Beskid** is the country's second highest mountain range, peaking at 1,725m (Mount Babia Góra). In the **Pieniny National Park**'s limestone mountains, mountain rafts go down the Dunajec Gorge, which in places, looks like a deep grand canyon.

Poland's last Carpathian mountain range, the **Bieszczady**, culminating at 1,343m (Mount Tarnica), is particularly wild and sparsely populated. High pasture areas, called *połoniny*, are exceptionally beautiful. This park and those of the Giant Mountains, the Tatras and the Beskid, are listed by UNESCO as part of the Cultural and Natural World Heritage categories.

CLIMATE

Poland enjoys a **temperate climate**, featuring well-defined seasons and in particular **cold, dry winters** and **hot, rainy summers**. However, the climate can vary significantly from one year to the next. Apart from the specific mountain climate, which applies to the south of the country, the climate over the rest of the country marks a **transition** between the oceanic and continental influences. The great North European plain is an area where masses of humid air from the Atlantic or the North Sea come into contact with dry air from the inland regions of the Eurasian continent. Consequently, there are temperature variations from west to east and from north to south. The main characteristics of Poland's climate are **unstable weather conditions** and a frequent cloud cover; there are only between 30 and 50 clear days in a year. Dominant influences come from the west during the summer months (rainfall is two to three times more abundant than in winter and the average temperature is around 18°C) and from the east in winter (average temperature -3°C), particularly in December and January (the coldest month). The hottest month is July, when the average temperature is between 16 and 19°C. Warm days with temperatures of at least 25°C, ideal for tourism, can be expected in Poland from May until September ("golden autumn"). Their number increases as one moves away from the sea and closer to the mountains. In general, the northwest of Poland, close to the Baltic sea, enjoys a predominantly temperate oceanic climate with damp snowy winters and cool summers (sea breeze) with alternating periods of rain and sunshine. In the eastern part of the country, continental influences are more obvious, with harsh winters lasting over four months and drier summers. The main characteristic of mountainous areas is the presence of **snow** for the major part of the year. In the Sudeten, snow falls during 120 days and in the Tatras this can be extended to 145 days. In the Tatras Mountains one can sometimes experience the *foehn*, a violent wind, fairly warm and dry, called *halny* in Polish.

FLORA

Poland may look like a largely agricultural country but 28% of its territory is covered with forests. They are planted with coniferous forest pines (70%), and the remainder comprised of a mixture of resinous spruce and fir, and deciduous oak, beech, hornbeam and birch. Although the major part of Poland's forested regions have been cleared to make way for farming activities, one can still see areas untouched by human activities: some 30 primeval forests extend over part of the territory. The gems of Polish flora include the ancient Rogalin **oaks**, hundreds of which grow in the large forest situated near Poznań. Famous for their longevity, the oldest (over 700 years) have all got a name, Bartek, Chrobry, Lech, Czech and Rus, and are the heroes of many legends. Giant trees up to 50m high grow in the **Białowieża Primeval Forest**. In view of the absence of natural barriers that would limit plant migration, most species are transitory (apart from a

Environmental Issues

In Poland, "ecologically disastrous" zones concern 11% of the country's total area and 36% of the population. Poland has to face a high level of **air pollution** caused by the release of toxic gases by factories powered by coal or lignite. Nearly three quarters of the country's trees are affected by **acid rain**. Forests in the southwest are particularly spoiled because winds carry polluting elements released by Poland but also by Germany and the Czech Republic. Poland must also face **water pollution** problems caused by the release of toxic products by industries, large urban areas and even agriculture. 4/5 of all main rivers and the Baltic coast are severely polluted. However, some progress has been made. **Pollution measurements** now fall in line with EU standards and there are many more sewage treatment plants and anti-pollution filters (factories and cars) than before. The safeguard of the environment is well on its way but it requires time and heavy investments.

few endemic species in the Carpathian Mountains). There are, for instance, some berries belonging to Eurasian species and North American such as cranberry *(żurawina)*, blackcurrant *(czarna porzeczka)* or blueberry *(jagoda)*, which the Poles like a lot. Mushrooms are plentiful on tables at the beginning and end of the summer. If you arrive at the right time, you'll have no problem filling a basket.

FAUNA

Local fauna is almost identical to that found in the rest of Europe. Among domestic animals, dogs and **horses** are particularly dear to the heart of the Poles. Moreover, horse riding is a great national tradition and Polish breeding of Arab horses is famous throughout the world. Animals in parks and gardens peacefully cohabit with the local population. Birds come willingly to an outstretched hand to peck at some seeds, or squirrels answer your call (*"Basia, Basia...,"* Polish people say) and grab the hazelnut or walnut you are holding out to them. From the point of view of variety and number of species, the animal world is considerably richer than the plant world. There are, in Poland, 93 species of mammal, 406 species of bird, nine species of reptile, 18 species of batrachian and 55 species of fish. **White storks** hold a special place within the bird population. Poland is called the paradise of storks: a quarter of the European population of storks nests here because the birds find many places to build their nests and clean areas rich in food. The Poles are particularly fond of this creature and from March onwards, they look up to the sky and wait for the familiar clatter. Bird-watchers also have their own paradise: the **Biebrza marshes**, where 263 bird species can be spotted in these marshes during the brooding season, as well as during the migration period. The valley is one of the last places in Europe where aquatic and marshland birds can live, because most marshes on the European continent were drained. This prime environment is also very much

Lynx

© Polish National Tourist Office

appreciated by birds of prey, resulting in the highest number of different species (25) in Europe. In these marshy areas, one also meets **elk**, the most powerful members of the Cervidae family, and **beavers**. Another peatbog park on the list of World Biosphere Reserves is the **Polesie National Park**, east of Lublin. The national emblem of Poland is traditionally the **white-tailed eagle**, the country's largest bird of prey. A very small number nest in the north of the country, mainly on the Island of Wolin (this national park is also renowned for its cormorants and otters) and along the Baltic coast. Another interesting sight is the Nietoperek **bat reserve** in Greater Poland, which consists of a huge bunker built by the Germans between 1925 and 1941, where a few thousand bats hibernate every year. Poland also offers an impressive mammalian spectacle: **bisons**, the largest European animals are protected in several national parks, including the Białowieża National Park, where there are over 250 specimens. All thoroughbred bison born in Polish nature reserves are given names starting with the syllable *"Po"*, for example "Poranek" or "Pomruk". The high mountains in the south of the country shelter a particularly rich fauna. The most interesting wild species are **chamois**, **moufflons**, **deer**, **marmots** and **royal eagles**. Other large mammals are equally protected in Poland: **brown bears**, **wolves**, **lynx**, and **wild cats**.

Tatra mountains
© A.Olej -K.Kobus/TRAVELPHOTO/Polish National Tourist Office

WARSAW, MASOVIA, LUBLIN PLATEAU

As the capital of Poland, it is natural that Warsaw is the largest, richest, most dynamic city in the country, but because of its tumultuous history, Warsaw is also a fascinating testament to the will of the Polish nation to persevere and reinvent itself. Unlike other Polish cities, Warsaw doesn't have an obvious centre: the Old Town was splendidly rebuilt, but it's not where most Varsovians work or spend their free time. To overcome this, the city decided recently to renovate part of the Royal Way, Ul. Krakowskie Przedmieście, and turn this into a pedestrian mall on weekends. This has been quite successful and is an excellent example of the city's perpetual transformation.

Highlights

1 View from the observation deck of the **Palace of Culture and Science** in Warsaw (p123)

2 Enjoying a drink at an outdoor café on **Kazimierz Dolny's town square** (p142)

3 The frescoes of the **Gothic Chapel** in Lublin (p147)

4 Exploring the streets of an "ideal city" in **Zamość** (p151)

Past and Present

Another city that is reinventing itself is Łódź: once an economic powerhouse as evidenced by the city's magnificent palaces and magnate residences, the city fell on hard times when most of the textile factories closed down after the collapse of communism.

Now investors and artists are taking advantage of the great potential of the abandoned factories and warehouses and converting them into clubs, galler-ies, and shopping centres. Heading east from the capital, the pace of life slows down and the best place for a relaxing weekend away from the regions' large cities is the historically important Kazimierz Dolny. This charming town has inspired many a Polish painter with its Renaissance façades and hilltop views of the Vistula River.

Lublin is the largest city in Poland east of the Vistula River, a major university town, and an poignant reminder of Jewish culture in pre-war Poland. The city's Old Town is quieter, more contemplative than other such quarters in Poland, with fewer tourists and more locals still living on the atmospheric streets.

The city of Zamość is one of those special places that didn't develop slowly and organically, rather it was built from scratch as an "ideal city".

Thankfully, the city didn't suffer during the Swedish invasions of the 17C, and even though thousands of residents perished during World War II at the hands of the Nazis, the city remains a Renaissance planned town.

Castle Square, Warsaw

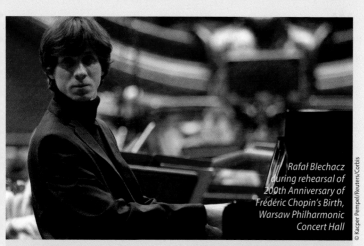

Rafał Blechacz during rehearsal of 200th Anniversary of Frédéric Chopin's Birth, Warsaw Philharmonic Concert Hall

Polish Pianists

2010 in Poland was the year of Chopin as it was the 200th anniversary of the great Romantic composer's birth. Chopin was also a revered virtuoso in his day, and since Chopin's time Poland has produced many more piano greats. There was even a time when one of Poland's most famous "exports" was virtuoso pianists: Ignacy Jan Paderewski (1860–1941) at the beginning of the 20C was the most highly paid and sought after pianist in the world and a great exponent of Chopin's music. In addition to being a great showman at the keyboard he also composed and represented Poland

Frédéric Chopin

internationally as prime minister after World War I and was known as a great orator who spoke seven languages. Leopold Godowsky (1870–1938) was revered by fellow pianists but was considered at his best when playing at home for himself or for friends. Some of his best known works are re-workings Chopin's études. Josef Hofmann (1876–1957), along with Vladimir Horowitz (1903–89), was considered by many to be the greatest technician of the piano of the 20C. Rachmaninoff considered him the top pianist of his day and dedicated his own 3rd piano concerto to Hofmann. Unfortunately later in life he was troubled by alcoholism and so recordings cannot do him justice. Artur Rubinstein (1887–1982), born into a Jewish family in Łódź, was famous for his technique, his interpretations of Chopin's music, and for his enormous memory and ability to play well into his 80s. Władysław Szpilman's (1911–2000) piano career has been overshadowed by the success of Roman Polański's film *The Pianist*, which was based on Szpilman's World War II memoirs. In 2005, a fresh, young Polish pianist Rafał Blechacz (b. 1985) took on the torch of representing the Polish musical tradition when he won the the 15th Frédéric Chopin International Competition.

This prestigious event is held every five years in Warsaw, so perhaps another young romantic Pole will channel the spirit of Chopin and repeat Blechacz' success in the future...

Warsaw★★★
Warszawa

Described by the writer Witold Gombrowicz as "the place where Eastern and Western cultures are abolished", Warsaw looks like no other European town. The city is a martyr of World War II, which literally reduced it to ashes. Today it is an odd mixture of reconstructed prewar districts and Baroque edifices, of concrete Stalinist blocks and striking modern buildings. This urban anarchism tends to baffle visitors and locals alike: nevertheless, it reflects the unique personality of this unusual capital, the showcase of Poland's past sufferings and ambitions for the future.

A BIT OF HISTORY
Origins

Warsaw entered history relatively late: although evidence of a first settlement dates from the 10C, it was only at the end of the 13C that the new city was built on the hill where the royal castle now stands. After it became the capital of the duchy of Masovia in 1413, the town expanded rapidly, both economically and culturally. When the duchy was incorporated into the Kingdom of Poland in 1526, on the death of the last Masovian prince, Warsaw became the obvious choice as the seat of political power of the new kingdom established in 1569 by the **Treaty of Lublin** joining Lithuania and Poland. The Diet (legislative assembly) immediately decided to have its headquarters here, in part because Warsaw was ideally located between Kraków in the south, and Vilnius in the north. Shortly thereafter, in 1573, Warsaw was for the first time the chosen venue for the coronation of King Sigismund III, who, after his castle was destroyed by fire, finally agreed to the centralisation of royal power and officially transferred the capital from Kraków to Warsaw in 1596. Despite this, most royal coronations and funerals continued to take place in Kraków.

▶ **Population:** 1,714,446.

Michelin Map: Map of Poland A2 – Województwo of Masovia.

Info: Ul. Krakowskie Przedmieście 15/17. ✆474 11 42 31. www.warsawtour.pl.

Location: Warsaw is 294km from Kraków and 343km from Gdánsk. The Wisła flows through the city, with the reconstructed old districts: the Old Town and the New Town lying on the west bank, to the north. Further south is the business centre, based near the Palace of Culture and Science, the main train station and an array of glass office buildings. The old residential districts of Żoliborz in the north and Mokotów (south) are greener, and Ujazdowski and Łazienki parks, both in the south, offer lots of trees. The Royal Way, the city's main thoroughfare, forms a northsouth axis from the Old Town down to Wilanów Palace. Across the river is Praga, the only district that escaped destruction during the war, which is now slowly gentrifying and attracting many artists.

Parking: Pay and Display as well as secure parking throughout the centre.

Don't Miss: The Old Town, the Palace of Culture and Science, the Łazienki Park, the Jewish memorials.

Kids: The Fotoplastikon, the zoo and numerous parks.

Timing: Allow 2 days to see the main sights, 3 days to add a themed tour (*see box overleaf*).

GETTING THERE

BY AIR – **Okecie Frédéric Chopin Airport** *(Port Lotniczy Okęcie im. Frederyka Chopina)* – *Ul. Żwigry i Wigury 1.* ✆*022 650 42 20.* www.lotnisko-chopina.pl. Warsaw Airport, situated 10km from the town centre, handles all domestic and international flights. To reach the town centre you can drive, take a taxi or bus: Bus 175 goes to the City Centre, runs every 15min and takes 30–45min. Tickets – *bilet normalny* 2,80 PLN – available at the Ruch kiosk in the arrivals hall. Extra ticket compulsory for each large piece of luggage. Taxis queue up at the terminal exits *(journey to the centre 30/40 PLN)*. Beware: don't accept taxis offered in the terminal; they are either illegal or expensive and not insured.

BY RAIL – **Central Railway Station (Dworzec PKP Warszawa Centralna)** – *Al. Jerozolimskie 54.* ✆*0221 94 36.* www.pkp.com.pl. Regular and Inter-City train services to every Polish town as well as to the capitals of neighbouring countries. Take bus 127 to get to the centre of town.

BY BUS – **Bus stations** – The Central Station **(Dworzec Centralny PKS Warszawa Zachodnia)** *Al. Jerozolimskie 144.* Handles the main part of the international as well as the domestic traffic within Poland.

GETTING AROUND

PUBLIC TRANSPORT – Warsaw boasts an extensive public transport network Info: ✆*022 94 84.* www.ztm.waw.pl.

Trams are recommended for further journeys in or out of the town centre *(daily 5am–11pm).*

Buses are best for the Royal Way *(daily 5am–11pm; Night buses 11pm–5am for twice the cost of a day ticket).* The **metro** *(daily 5am–0.15am)* is one northsouth line; east-west line is under construction.

Tickets – **single ticket** (*bilet jednorazowy*, 2.80≈PLN valid for one journey on one type of transport only), **daily ticket** (*bilet dobowy* – valid 24hr from the time it is stamped, on all modes of transport 9≈PLN), **3-day ticket** (*bilet trzydniowy* 13≈PLN– valid 72hr from the time it is stamped, on all modes of transport), **weekly ticket** (*bilet tygodniowy* 32 PLN). Children under 4 and people over 70 travel free. 50% concession for students with an **ISIC card**. Tickets can be bought from Ruch kiosks, post offices and, occassionally, on the bus with a surcharge. Frequent controls *(on-the-spot cash fines for non-residents)*. Journey description and the timetable are posted at the stops.

TAXIS – Taxis can be picked up at taxi ranks or reserved by phone (from a mobile, dial 22 before the number) – MPT (✆*919* – Service for disabled travellers) and WA-WA (✆*96 44*) have English-speaking operators. Be sure to avoid illegal taxis; legal taxis have their company name and phone number marked on the roof; fares are also marked on back passenger window.

VEHICLE HIRE – There are many hire companies at the airport, including: AVIS, ✆*572 65 65,* www.avis.pl (friendly branch in the town centre, in the Marrott Hotel).
HERTZ, ✆*500 16 20,* www.hertz.com.pl.
24hr/day breakdown service – Polish Motoring Association ✆*96 37.*
24h supervised car parks Old Town: *Ul.Senatorska 3*; centre: *Marc Pol (in front of the Palace of Culture).*
BIKE HIRE – Warsaw by Bike – *Ul.Stawki 19.* ✆*502 586 586.* www.warsawbybike.pl.

Warsaw underground entrance

© Polish National Tourist Office

PRACTICAL INFORMATION

Phone code – *022.*

Postal code – *begins with 00-033.*

Tourist Information Point (Punkt Informacji Turystycznej) – *94 31. www.warsawtour.pl.* These branches offer friendly, informative and efficient service in English.

Central Railway Station *(Dworzec PKP Warszawa Centralna – main hall). Al. Jerozolimskie 54 – Open May–Sept daily 8am–8pm. Oct–Apr 8am–7pm.*

Ul. Krakowskie Przedmieście – *Open May–Sept daily 9am–8pm. Oct– Apr 9am–6pm.*

Okęcie Airport (Terminal 1) – *Open May–Sept daily 8am–8pm. Oct– Apr 8am–6pm.*

Police – *997 (112 from a mobile phone). Ul. Wilcza 21. 022 603 70 55.*

Hospital and clinics – LIM Medical Centre: *Al. Jerozolimskie 65/79 (part of the Marriott Building). Open Mon–Fri 7am–9pm, Sat 8am–4pm. 022 458 70 00. www.cmlim.pl.*

Duodent (dental surgery) – *Ul. Nowolipki 21. Open Mon–Fri 8am–8pm. 838 82 68. www.duodent.com.pl.*

24hr/day pharmacy (Apteka) Central Station *(Dworzec Warszawa Centralna) al. Jerozolimskie 54. 825 13 72.*

Post office (Poczta) – There are many post offices, in particular at the airport, in the Central Station and in the *rynek* (square) of the Old Town *(open Mon–Fri 8am–8pm, Sat 8am–1pm).* Central post office: *Ul. Świętokrzyska 31/33 (open 24hr/day). www.poczta-polska.pl.*

Telephone – Public phone booths are everywhere but many aren't maintained due to the ubiquitous mobile phone. Magnetic cards for sale in post offices and RUCH kiosks.

ATMs (Bankomat) – There are many cash dispensers throughout the city and airport. It is very easy to withdraw cash 24hr/day.

Banks – Pekao-SA – *Plac Bankowy 2 (on the first floor of the Blue Tower) – Mon–Fri 8am–7pm, Sat 9am–4pm –*

It is possible to draw cash on presentation of a bank card and a passport (counter no. 9). The bank also exchanges American Express traveller's cheques.

Bureaux de change (Kantor) – There are many bureaux de change for changing money throughout the town; their rates are similar. Kantor Polski *(Ul. Wilcza 33)* and in the Central Station remain open 24hr/day.

Western Union (international money orders) – Bank BPH *(Ul. Krakowskie Przedmieście 1. Open Mon–Fri 8am–6pm).*

Internet cafés

Casablanca – *Ul. Krakowskie Przedmieście 4/6. Open Mon–Fri 9am– 1am, Sat 10am–1am, Sun 10am– midnight 9 PLN/hr. 022 828 14 47.*

Cyber Café – *Ul. Żwirki i Wigury 1. 022 650 01 72. Open daily 7am–1am.* Note that you can access free Wi-Fi in the Rynek, Ul. Chmielna and Warsaw University Library.

Grocery stores – You can find independent food stores throughout the city centre; further out, as well as in shopping centres, there are several supermarket chains including LeClerc, Real, Tesco and Auchan.

Laundromat – There is one self-service laundry located a bit outside of the city centre at *Ul. Księcia Janusza 23, Open daily 8am–9pm.* Free Wi-Fi while you wait.

International press – EMPIK *(Ul. Nowy Świat 15; open Mon–Sat 9am–10pm, Sun 11am–7pm)* – TRAFFIC Club *(Ul. Bracka 25; open Mon–Sat 10am–10pm, Sun 10am–7pm). 022 692 18 88*

WHERE TO GO

The **Warsaw Center of Tourist Information** *(Plac Zamkowy 1/13; open Mon–Fri 9am–6pm, Sat 10am– 6pm, Sun 11am–6pm; 022 635 18 81; www.wcit.waw.pl),* a privately run office, organises guided tours of the town in collaboration with **tour operators**. The classic tour includes

Royal Castle and column of King Sigismund III

R. Mattes / MICHELIN

Warsaw in three days

1st day – Start from Plac Zamkowy, then walk through the streets of the Old Town and of the New Town. After having lunch in this area, you can go back to Plac Zamkowy and from there walk down part of the Royal Way via Krakowskie Przedmieście and Nowy Świat, where you will find Holy Cross Church (Kościół Św. Krzyża), the Warsaw University (Uniwersytet Warszawski), and dozens of cafés and bars as this is the area where locals spend their free time.

2nd day – After exploring the Palace of Culture (Pałac Kultury i Nauki or PKiN) and the surrounding district, take a stroll through Ujazdowski and Łazienki parks, visit the Palace on the Water (Pałac na Wodzie) and the Chopin Monument, and visit Wilanów Palace (Pałac w Wilanowie).

3rd day – If you are interested in sights connected with Jewish culture, follow our itinerary through the former Ghetto, the Jewish cemetery, and visit the Warsaw Rising Museum. You can also explore the National Museum.

the Old Town, the Royal Way, the Wilanów Palace and the main monuments (Tomb of the Unknown Soldier, Ghetto Heroes Memorial, etc). The Tourist Information Points also offer advice on available tours.
*Consider buying the **Warsaw Card** *(available at Tourist Info Points)*, enabling free or discounted access to museums, restaurants and recreational facilities. Free public transport too!
No 180 bus – This line linking most of the capital's tourist sights offers visitors an overall view of Warsaw for the price of a single ticket *(daily 7am– 11pm)*. Stops at Rondo de Gaulle'a and all along the Royal Way.
Useful magazines and brochures – The following monthly magazines (in English) provide all the necessary information about Warsaw (including practical information, and entertainment, food and drink): *Warsaw in Your Pocket (www. inyourpocket.com/poland/warsaw), Warsaw Insider, The Visitor Warsaw Edition, New Poland Express, Welcome to Warsaw*. They are available in hotels and foreign-newspaper retailers.

Decline and the Golden Age

From the mid-17C to World War II, Poland and Warsaw entered into a period of incessant conflicts and wars. Between 1655 and 1658, the Swedes and the Transylvanians invaded the kingdom on three occasions and plundered the Polish capital. Ruined and robbed of its cultural assets, Warsaw continued to decline slowly until Saxon princes, under pressure from Russia and Austria, undertook to rebuild the town between 1697 and 1763. By creating the **"Saxon Axis"**, perpendicular to the Royal Way, and establishing their residence in its centre, they opened the way for a new era of urban planning characterised in particular by the construction of large vistas. **Stanisław II Poniatowski**, a young, forward-looking monarch and a great art lover, completed Warsaw's transformation into a modern urban centre and encouraged the construction of Baroque and later Classical edifices.

The second half of the 18C thus marked the "Golden Age" of Warsaw, by then the undisputed centre of the country's political, economic, commercial and industrial life as well as the centre of Polish Enlightenment. However, in 1795, following the third Partition of Poland, Warsaw was annexed by Prussia and lost its status as a political and artistic capital. It regained some of its influence during the interlude of the Grand Duchy of Warsaw (1806–15), which gave back to the Poles their own government and central administration, but the Congress of Vienna soon put the town under Russian control. The Russians' liberal attitude did not, however, hinder the economic and intellectual development of Warsaw and the first university was inaugurated in 1818. In 1831, the failure of the anti-Russian uprising led to severe reprisals: Warsaw was relegated to the rank of provincial town and its cultural and educational establishments were closed. It was only at the onset of World War I that Russian domination began to falter, giving way to the German army who occupied the town. Polish independence was only regained in 1918 and Warsaw became once more the capital of a free country.

Unfortunately, the people's hopes for a new lease of life and all the energy they poured into rebuilding their city were shattered at the outbreak of World War II.

World War II

In September 1939, Hitler invaded Poland and, within a few weeks, Warsaw was occupied by the German army. This marked the beginning of the darkest years of the town's history: its leaders were deported or imprisoned, educational establishments closed once more and, as early as 1940, the entire Jewish population was transferred to a **ghetto** area and subjected to

Old Town

© Kate Shephard/Shutterstock

repressive measures and starvation. When, at the beginning of the summer of 1944, Hitler's army began to pull back as Soviet troops moved forward, the **Polish resistance movement** organised an uprising in order to hasten the liberation of Warsaw. However, this heroic initiative proved to be a disaster: armed clashes, unsupported by the Russian allies, left 200,000 dead on the Polish side. Wild with rage and a desire for vengeance, Hitler ordered the systematic destruction of the Polish capital. At the end of the war, 850,000 Warsaw residents, i.e. two-thirds of the population, were either missing or dead. Reduced to ashes, Warsaw was no more than a name on the map of Europe.

City of Perpetual Change

For a while, one of the courses of action contemplated was to leave Warsaw in ruins, as a kind of open-air museum of the horrors of World War II. The idea was eventually abandoned and Warsaw was rebuilt. Since the collapse of the communist regime, the town has for the first time in its history, fully recovered the status of political, economic and cultural capital of Poland. The resurrection of Warsaw, a city in perpetual change, is a history lesson for the whole of humanity.

☙WALKING TOURS

1 OLD CITY DISTRICT Plan II

It is no doubt paradoxical to use the term "old districts" for a town practically razed to the ground and rebuilt. However, within those parameters, the Old Town (Stare Miasto) which used to include some medieval monuments, the New Town (Nowe Miasto) built in the 17C and 18C, the Theatre-Opera district (19C) and the Royal Way are all considered to be part of the Old Town.

OLD TOWN★★
(Stare Miasto)
Most of the Old Town is pedestrianised; it is possible to find parking space in the adjacent streets. ☙Allow 2hr for the area tour, half a day if you include a visit

to the museums. A good starting point for a tour of the Old Town is Plac Zamkowy (Castle Square) with the bronze column of King Sigismund III (1644) in its centre. From there, the tour continues along the colourful paved streets.

The Old Town forms one of Warsaw's finest architectural ensembles. Entirely destroyed, it was meticulously rebuilt after reproductions dating from the 18C, essentially with funds donated by the Polish diaspora and thanks to the tenacity of the voluntary work force. In 1982, this unprecedented undertaking earned the town a place on UNESCO's World Heritage List. The Old Town features a picturesque central market square (Rynek) surrounded by a grid-plan network of streets.

The Royal Castle★
(Zamek Królewski) B2
Plac Zamkowy4. ⏰Open Mon 11am–4pm, Tue–Sat 10am–6pm, Sun 11am–6pm; last admission 1hr before closing. ✆22/14 PLN, Sun free. ☙Guided tours by appointment in English, Mon–Sat, 100 PLN. Allow 2hr for the visit. ✆022 355 51 70. www.zamek-krolewski.pl.
Erected in the 14C, then remodelled in Baroque style, the Royal Castle was the home of the dukes of Masovia and of the kings of Poland before becoming the seat of Parliament and then, from 1918 onwards, the official residence of the President of the Republic. After the war, the communist authorities were not in favour of its reconstruction, which was finally undertaken in 1971 under pressure from the country's intellectual élite. Although the building is a replica, most of the castle's paintings and furniture, taken to a safe place at the beginning of the war, are originals.

The visit of the castle is divided into two itineraries. Route 1 covers the Court Rooms, the Parliamentary Rooms and the apartment of Prince Stanisław as well as the room containing frescoes by the famous romantic painter Jan Matejko. Route 2 leads through the apartments of King Stanisław August Poniatowski and the Great Apartment, including the Marble Room and the National Hall. On Mondays, only one Route is offered.

St John's Cathedral★
(Archikatedra Św. Jana) B2
Ul. Świętojańska 8.

Built in Gothic style at the end of the 13C, this is Warsaw's oldest church. The cathedral contains the Renaissance tombs of the last Masovian princes and a 16C Crucifix with real hair on Christ's head. In addition, the crypt houses the ashes of famous Poles, such as Henryk Sienkewicz, awarded the Nobel Prize in Literature in 1905, and pianist Ignacy Paderewski.

Dziekania Street, on the right of the cathedral, leads to the pretty triangular Kanonia Place, lined with **houses** which once belonged to the **canons** of the Warsaw Chapter. Note in the centre a bronze **bell** dating from 1646, damaged during its construction. The amazing little passageway situated before Jezuicka Street leads to the Gnojna Góra terrace, from which one can quietly admire the River Wisła.

The Rynek★★
(Rynek Starego Miasta) B1

Lined with colourful multi-storeyed houses of Renaissance and Baroque inspiration, the Rynek was, until the middle of the 19C, the administrative, commercial and cultural centre of Warsaw, staging fairs and festivities as well as public executions. Today, some of the best traditional restaurants in the capital are located here and the numerous outdoor cafés offer a pleasant break in fine weather.

At no. 20 stands the **Adam Mickiewicz Literature Museum** (Muzeum Mickiewicza; ◑open Mon, Tue, Fri 10am–3pm, Wed, Thu 11am–6pm, Sun except third Sun of the month 11am–5pm; last admission 30min before closing; ⊜6 PLN; ℘022 831 40 61; www.muzeumliteratury.pl) Essentially devoted to Adam Mickiewicz, the 19C cult Romantic writer, author of Pan Tadeusz, a jewel of Polish literature, this museum also stages usually very interesting temporary

exhibitions about Polish literature from the 18C to the 20C.

Some of the façades lining the north side of the square are those of the **Historical Museum of Warsaw★**

WARSAW
map I

0   500 m

(Muzeum historyczne starej Warszawy; *Rynek n°28; English-speaking guides available for 20 PLN; ☎ 022 635 16 25; www.mhw.pl*). The museum covers all the aspects of Warsaw's life from its foundation until 1990. Don't miss the short documentary film recounting the systematic destruction of the town by the Nazis in 1944 *(English version at noon)*.

FROM THE MARKET SQUARE TO THE NEW TOWN A-B1

The tour of the town continues through Nowomiejska and Szeroki Dunaj Streets, which offer a glimpse of the Old Town's backyards, then on to Piwna Street. Lined with jeweller's, bookstalls and antique shops, it also boasts **St Martin's Church**★ (Kościól Św. Marcina).

This 14C Gothic edifice featuring a Baroque interior is a favourite of newlyweds, who are congratulated by family and friends in the arcaded courtyard after the religious ceremony. Note also that Adam Jarzębski, the king's musician and 17C author of the first guidebook of Warsaw, written in verse (!) is buried inside. The tour of the Old Town would not be complete without a detour via Podwale, along which the brick **ramparts** were rebuilt in order to restore its original charm. The open path surrounding the walls is lined with commemorative plaques placed there as a tribute to foreigners who at some time supported the Polish cause, such as the French poet Alfred de Vigny. The **Monument of the Little Insurgent** (Pomnik Małego Powstańca) is undoubtedly the most poignant memorial along Podwale: with enormous helmet on his head and rifle in hand, he pays tribute to the children who died during the Warsaw Uprising. Following the ramparts, which feature on the north side the statue of Wars and Sawa, the lovers who founded the town, stands the **Barbican** (Barbakan). Originally a point of entry and defence of the city, it now attracts traditional local artists and marks the transition between the Old Town and the New Town.

The New Town★
(Nowe Miasto) A-B1
This small but elegant district, created in the 15C and integrated into the municipality of Warsaw in the 18C, features a specifically peaceful atmosphere.

Freta Street B1
Freta Street is lined with galleries, cafés and places of worship and one should try to get a glimpse of the courtyards

and parks hidden behind the façades. **No. 16** is the birthplace of Marie Skłodowska-Curie, twice awarded the Nobel Prize for her discovery of radium

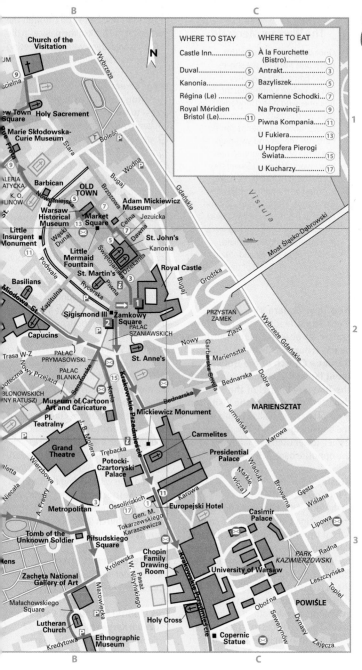

WHERE TO STAY

Castle Inn.................. ③
Duval........................ ⑤
Kanonia.................... ⑦
Régina (Le) .... ⑨
Royal Méridien
Bristol (Le)............ ⑪

WHERE TO EAT

À la Fourchette
(Bistro)................... ①
Antrakt..................... ③
Bazyliszek................ ⑤
Kamienne Schodki... ⑦
Na Prowincji............ ⑨
Piwna Kompania...... ⑪
U Fukiera................. ⑬
U Hopfera Pierogi
Świata................... ⑮
U Kucharzy.............. ⑰

and of polonium in 1903 and 1911. The house is now the **Marie Skłodowska-Curie Museum** ★ (☼ open Tue 8.30am–4pm, Wed–Fri 9.30am–4pm, Sat 10am–4pm, Sun 10am–3pm; ✆10 PLN; ☎022 831 80 92; http://muzeum.if.pw.edu.pl) dedicated to the life and work of the great physicist.

The Warsaw Mermaid

Once upon a time two sister mermaids lived on the shores of the Baltic. One day, they got lost while swimming; the first one, who was stranded in the Danish straits, now sits at the entrance to Copenhagen's harbour. The second swam up the Wisła and, on her way, met two lovers, Wars and Sawa; she asked them to found the town and to give it their combined firstnames. Promising to stay and come to the rescue of Warsaw's inhabitants whenever they were in danger, the little mermaid, armed with a sword and shield, became the emblem of the town.

New Town Square B1

Freta Street leads to the New Town Square, as peaceful as the Old Town Square is buzzing. On the east side, the **Baroque Church of the Holy Sacrament** (Kościół Sakramentek) contains the funerary chapel of the Sobieski dynasty. The **Church of the Visitation** (Kościół Wizytek), built in Gothic style at the beginning of the 15C, is famous for its bell tower used as a landmark from the opposite bank of the Wisła.

Krasiński Square
(Plac Krasińskich) A1

At the foot of the glass building housing the Supreme Court stands the controversial **Uprising Monument** (Pomnik Powstania Warszawskiego). Erected on the spot where AK (National Army) troops launched their assault against the Nazis on 1 Aug 1944, this imposing metal sculpture represents armed insurgents coming out of their underground hiding places to attack the Germans but also their desperate retreat into the city's sewers. The **Krasiński Palace** (Pałac Krasińskich), designed by Tylman von Gameren at the end of the 18C, houses the special collections of the National Library and closes off the square. The building isn't open to

visitors but one can stroll through the gardens at the back of the palace. In the 19C, these gardens were the meeting place of Warsaw's high society.

Długa Street A2-B1

The Długa Street exit gives direct access to the **Archaeological Museum** (Muzeum Archeologiczne; Ul. Długa52; ⏰ open Mon–Thu 9am–4pm, Sat 9am–4pm, Sun 10am–4pm; ⬢8 PLN; ☏ 022 831 15 37; www.pma.pl), housed in a 17C arsenal, which displays archaeological collections of Polish prehistory.

Opposite and housed in the **Radziwiłł Palace** is the **Museum of Independence** (Muzeum Niepodłegiości, Al. Solidarności 62; ⏰ open Tue–Fri 10am–5pm, Sat–Sun 10am–4pm; ⬢5 PLN; Sun free; www.muzeumniepodleglosci.art.pl) offering an interesting analysis of the national history by recounting Poland's incessant struggle against her hostile and powerful neighbours.

Miodowa Street B2

Miodowa Street, exclusively lined with 18C Baroque and Neoclassical palaces, the most prestigious being the **Borch Palace (no. 13)**, now the residence of the Primate of the Catholic Church, and the **Pac Palace (no. 15)**, with its distinctive mouldings over the main entrance (original row of Empire-style curved arcades), which houses the Ministry of Health. Along this road, you will also find the **Basilian Church** (Kościół Bazylianów, at **no. 16**), Warsaw's only Uniate church, as well as the **Capuchin Church** (Kościół Kapucynów), repository of the heart of Jan III Sobieski.

Northern Town Centre

These elegant districts are accessible via Senatorska Street.

Eryk Lipiński Museum of Caricature
(Muzeum Karykatury im. Eryk) B2

Ul. Kozia 11. ⏰Open Tue–Sun 11am–5pm (Thu 6pm). ⬢5 PLN, Sat free. www.muzeumkarykatury.pl.

This tiny yet amusing museum stages temporary exhibitions devoted to Polish and foreign caricaturists; the collection holds 15,000 works.

Theatre Square
(Plac Teatralny) B2

Erected during the 1820s by Corazzi, the **Grand Theatre**★ (Teatr Wielki) features a fine classicist façade decorated with Greek sculptures and its interior rotunda is well worth a look. Rebuilt and extended after the war, the Grand Theatre combines the Opera and the National Theatre as well as a small museum occasionally hosting temporary exhibitions about the history of Polish drama.

▷ *Senatorska Street continues towards the bustling Bankowy Square.*

Bank Square★
(Plac Bankowy) B2

Warsaw's Town Hall, on the west side, is an imposing complex of 19C buildings designed by Corazzi, in front of which stands the statue of the famous poet Juliusz Słowacki. Next door, the **Museum of John-Paul II's Collections** (Muzeum Kolekcji im.Jana Pawła II; ⏱open Apr–Sept Tue–Sun 10am–5pm; Oct–Mar Tue–Sun 10am–4pm; ✆7 PLN; www.muzeummalarstwa.pl) houses a collection of around 400 paintings on religious themes.

Saxon Gardens★
(Ogród Saski) A-B3

On the way south to the town centre, one crosses the magnificent Saxon Gardens, with over 100 species of tree. Laid out by Tylman von Gameren for August II at the beginning of the 17C, these gardens escaped destruction during World War II. The main alleyway, featuring a 19C fountain, the town's first water tower and a sundial, ends with a group of elegant Baroque statues symbolising the Virtues, Science and the Elements.

▷ *Exit on Piłsudskiego Square.*

Piłsudskiego Square B3

Situated just behind the park's statues, the **Tomb of the Unknown Soldier** (Grób Nieznanego Żołnierza) was erected in 1925 to commemorate the anonymous heroes who died while fighting for Poland's independence; it contains the ashes of an unknown soldier who defended Lwów *(now L'viv in Ukraine)*, mixed with earth from the battlefields of World War I. It is located under the arcades of the old Saski Palace, which is all that remains of the Saxon kings' former residence destroyed during the war.

Its strong symbolic meaning makes it the obvious rallying point for important gatherings and, indeed, it is here that the demonstrations organised by Solidarity in the 1980s were launched and that, more recently, thousands of Warsaw residents watched the broadcast of John-Paul II's funeral. This vast, most of the time deserted square is an unusual mix of various architectural styles. Opposite the Stalinist bunker of the **Victoria Hotel**, is the **glass Metropolitan Building** business centre built by **Norman Foster**.

Zachęta National Gallery of Art★
(Zachęta Narodowa Galeria Sztuki)

B3 Plac Małachowskiego 3, on the corner of Piłsudskiego Square and Mazowiecka Street. ⏱Open Tue–Sun noon–8pm. ✆10 PLN, Thu free. ✆022 827 58 54. www.zacheta.art.pl.

The museum houses many of Poland's most important works of contemporary art; President Narutowicz was assassinated in the exhibition halls in 1922.

▷ *From Małachowskiego Square, follow Mazowiecka Street.*

HEADING FOR THE TOWN CENTRE

A short detour via Kredytowa Street will enable you to see the 18C Lutheran church (Ewangelicko-Augsburgski) and admire its huge dome, Warsaw's largest. Chopin gave his first concert here at the age of 14 and the church, renowned for its excellent acoustics, still holds regular choral and chamber-music concerts.

Facing the church across the street, the **Ethnographic Museum** (Muzeum Etnograficzne; ⏱open Tue–Thu 10am–6pm, Fri 10am–4pm, Sat–Sun 10am–5pm; ✆10 PLN, Wed free; ✆022 827 76 41; http://ethnomuseum.website.pl) will impress with its collection of traditional folk costumes from all over Poland.

2 THE ROYAL WAY
MAP II-MAP III

The Royal Way, Warsaw's most famous tourist trail, owes its name to the fact that it links the various residences of Polish kings. Stretching 4km from the Old Town's Plac Zamkowy, where the kings had their main residence, to the Wilanów Palace where they retired in summer, via the Ujazdów hunting palace and the imposing Łazienki Park. All the sights lining the Royal Way cannot be visited in the space of one day.

Krakowskie Przedmieście

As early as 1596, many aristocrats wanted to establish their residence along this street to be near the king, who had recently settled in the Old Town. Today, Krakowskie Przedmieście is one of Warsaw's main thoroughfares, lined with the President's residence, University buildings, cafés, boutiques as well as several historic churches and houses from the 17C and 18C. In 2008, the street was given a thorough overhaul: pavements were widened, reproductions of 18C paintings by Canaletto depicting Warsaw were placed periodically along the street to show how the street appeared back then, and most importantly, traffic is now limited to buses and taxis. On summer weekends it becomes a pedestrian mall.

St Anne's Church★
(Kościół Św. Anny) MAP II B2

Located at the beginning of the street is the church where royal princes used to swear homage and loyalty to the king. Founded in 1454 by Princess Anne of Masovia for the Bernardine Order, it was destroyed by the Swedes in 1656, then rebuilt in Baroque style during the course of the next century. The only remaining parts of the initial edifice are the brick-built Gothic presbytery adjoining the nave and the dome of the chapel. The church also features a sumptuous "crystal vault" and an original organ. From the northern side of the courtyard, you can climb to the top of the belfry (◷ open daily 10am–8pm; 4 PLN; ✆ 022 826 89 10) for a fabulous view of the river banks.

Before continuing, make a detour down to the small **Mariensztat District**, whose paved streets, lined with old houses and small cafés, are a haven of peace *(there and back via Bednarska Street)*. Immediately past the **Mickiewicz Monument** (one of the many of its kind dedicated to the poet throughout the country), you will see a church, slightly recessed from the street.

Carmelite Church★
(Kościół Karmelitów) MAP II B3

This is one of the rare edifices in Warsaw to have escaped unscathed when the town was destroyed at the end of World War II. Built by Schroeger in the 17C, it is one of the first examples of true Classi-

The Royal Way

B. Brillion / MICHELIN

cal style in Poland, featuring a delicately carved façade crowned by an unusual globe, while the Baroque interior contains a monumental 18C high altar by Tylman von Gameren.

Potocki-Czartoryski Palace
MAP II B3

The palace where Napoleon is said to have met Maria Walewska now houses the Ministry of Culture.

Radziwiłł Presidential Palace
(Pałac Radziwiłłów) **MAP II C3**
℘695 13 23.

It is here that the Warsaw Pact was signed in 1955 and that **Round Table Talks** between the Communist authorities and the leaders of Solidarity were held in 1989.

Walk past the art deco building of the **Bristol Hotel** and the adjoining gardens.

Warsaw University★
(Uniwersytet Warszawski)
MAP II C3

The extended university buildings occupy the whole second half of Krakowskie Przedmieście. Founded in 1818, the Warsaw University was closed by the tsar in 1832 in reprisal for the 1830 insurrection and it was only reopened in 1915. During the Nazi occupation, studies were forbidden and thousands of clandestine teachers and students were murdered.

As in most large cities throughout Poland, particularly in Kraków, a clandestine university was introduced; this tradition of a "moving university" continued during the communist era, when eminent opposition personalities gave regular lectures in public, each time in a different venue. The university campus still boasts magnificent monuments.

The **Kazimierz Palace** (Pałac Kazimierzowski), located on the main campus courtyard, was a royal summer residence before being Frédéric Chopin's home until 1827; it is now the home of the rector of the university.

The **Czapski Palace** *(opposite, across the street)*, was also inhabited by Chopin from 1827 to 1830; this fine Baro-

que edifice now houses the Academy of Fine Arts.

Holy Cross Church★
(Kościół Św. Krzyża) **MAP II C3**

This fine Baroque church, flanked by two towers, witnessed regular confrontations between students and the communist authorities. The statue of Christ at the entrance, carrying the Cross on his back, remains a symbol of the martyred city. This church is particularly special because it contains Chopin's heart (entombed in the pillar on the north side of the nave).

Staszic Palace
(Pałac Staszica) **MAP III B1**

This palace, which is the headquarters of the Polish Academy of Science, closes off Krakowskie Przedmieście, whereas, facing it, the statue of Copernicus (Pomnik Mikołaja Kopernika) symbolically opens New World Street (Nowy Świat).

NOWY ŚWIAT

This upmarket section of the Royal Way, dating from the middle of the 17C, lined with boutiques, cafés and restaurants, has had a number of personalities from the Polish art and literary world as residents, among them Joseph Conrad (1857–1924), at no. 45.

Frédéric Chopin Museum★
(Muzeum Fryderyka Chopina)
MAP III C1

Ul. Okolnik1. ⊙Open Tue–Sun 12am–8pm. ⊜22 PLN. ℘022 826 59 35. *http://pl.chopin.nifc.pl.*

Housed in the late 16C **Ostrogski Palace**, the museum houses over 5 000 items associated with Chopin, including the last piano on which he played (*see Żelazowa Wola [WARSAW]*).

▷ *Return to Nowy Świat via Foksal Street.*

Zamoyski Palace★ **MAP III C2**

This neo-Renaissance palace was, in 1863, the scene of an attempt to assassinate the tsarist governor. In reprisal, the building was confiscated after being ransacked by Cossacks who went as far as to throw one of Chopin's pianos out the window; the instrument belonged to the composer's sister who lived in the palace at the time.

Today, it houses the **Polish Architects' Association** and an **architectural centre (SARP)**, a pleasant café-restaurant with a terrace and the famous **Foksal Gallery**, one of the finest galleries of contemporary art in town (◑*open Mon–Fri noon–5pm (Thu 7pm); free; ℘022 827 62 43*). The gallery has been a cult place for contemporary and avant-garde artists since the beginning of the 1960s.

The 19C Branicki Palace is on Nowy Swiat 18/20 and parts of it can be seen if you enter the pharmacy built in 1851. The Palace was the HQ for the British Embassy between the World Wars.

▶ *Nowy Świat leads to the Charles de Gaulle Roundabout.*

Charles de Gaulle Roundabout★
(Rondo de Gaulle'a) MAP III C2

At the junction of the Royal Way and Jerozolimskie Avenue, this roundabout is one of the busiest in town. The imposing block-like edifice which once housed the headquarters of the **Polish Communist Party** (Budynek KC) and became the city's Stock Exchange until it moved to adjoining premises, houses private businesses. An amusing feature standing in the centre of the traffic circle is the fake 15m-high palm tree. The tree was the idea of artist Joanna Rajkowska. in Polish, **palm tree** *(palma)* is a figurative expression qualifying something absurd, a description which, according to the artist, well applies to Warsaw.

Three Crosses Square★
(Plac Trzech Krzyży Square)
MAP III C3

The Royal Way itinerary continues to Trzech Krzyży Square, in the middle of which stands **St Alexander's Church★** (Kościół Św. Aleksandra). Built in 1818 in honour of Tsar Alexander I of Russia, who was also King of Poland, the church was modelled on the Pantheon in Rome before being transformed into

a cathedral. Following its destruction during the war, the original church alone was rebuilt and its charm makes it a sought-after venue for weddings. Wiejska Street, heading south from the square, leads to the buildings of the **Polish Parliament** *(Sejm)*, erected in the 1920s after independence in 1918.

THE MODERN CENTRE MAP III

With the **Palace of Culture and Science** as its focal point, Warsaw's commercial and business centre is laid out on a grid plan with two main thoroughfares travelled by a fleet of colourful and

A

MIRÓN · HALA GWARDII · PAŁAC LUBOMIRSKICH · Marszałkowska · Saxo Garde · Granicza · Królewska · Pl. Dąbrowsk · Grzybowska · Ester Rachel Kamińska Jewish Theatre · Zielna · Próżna · Nożyk · Grzybowski Square · Bagno · Świętokrzys

Twarda · Świętokrzyska · Rondo ONZ · DOM MEBLOWY «EMILIA» · Śliska · Palace of Culture and Science · Sienna · Sosnowa · Emilii Plater · De · WARSAW TOWERS · ZŁOTE TARASY · Złota · Chmielna · WARSZAWA ŚRÓDMIEŚCIE · Central Station · 8

WHERTE TO STAY	WHERE TO EAT
Boutique Bed & Breakfast.............. ②	Bambino (Bar).......... ②
Diana (Résidence)..... ④	GAR...................... ⑥
Harenda...................... ⑥	Nowy Świat (Café).. ⑧
Mariott (Hotel)........... ⑧	Orchidea................. ⑩
Mazowiecki.............. ⑩	Sphinx................... ⑫
Oki Doki.................... ⑫	Zgoda.................... ⑭

A

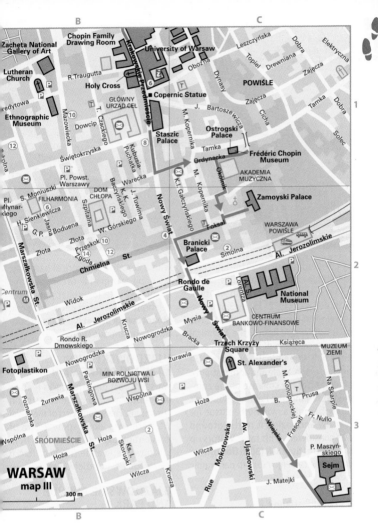

WARSAW
map III
300 m

often crammed trams. **Jerozolimskie Avenue** runs through Warsaw from east to west over several kilometres. **Warszawa Centralna** (Central Station) is opposite the Palace and, currently undergoing renovation *(until 2012)* is in striking contrast to the adjoining ultra-modern commercial centre **Złote Tarasy**. **Marszałkowska Avenue** is the main northsouth axis. Starting behind the shopping precinct (Galeria Centrum) extending along the east side of the avenue, **Chmielna Street**, a pedestrian shopping street of smaller proportions, leads straight to the Royal Way.

Palace of Culture and Science★★★
(Pałac Kultury i Nauki) **A2**
Palace of Culture and Science (PKIN) – 1 Plac Defilad (main entrance and parking in Marzsałkowska Ave.) – Viewing terrace ⏰open daily 9am–8pm (May–Sept "Palace at Night" Fri–Sat 11.45pm). 🎟20 PLN (15 PLN at night"). 📞022 656 76 00. www.pkin.pl.
A "Present from the Soviet nation to the Polish nation", the Palace of Culture and Science has become, ironically, a notable landmark and symbol of Warsaw. Commissioned by Stalin and designed

Palace of Culture and Science

by Lew Rudnyew, the 231m-high edifice, visible within a 30km radius, boasts 3,288 rooms on 42 floors and was built in three years (1952–55) by 3,500 Russian workers cooped up in isolation. The Palace of Culture houses the Technical Museum, Museum of Evolution, a congress hall, three theatre companies, a cinema, a club, a café and administrative offices. After the collapse of the communist regime, the Palace of Culture's future became a major urban issue for Warsaw and razing it to the ground was considered. A lift takes visitors up to the top of the **PKIN (30th floor)**, from where one can enjoy superb panoramic views of Warsaw.

♣♟ Fotoplastikon★ B3

Al.Jerozolimskie 51. ⏰*Open Tue–Sun 10am–6pm.* ⮞*4 PLN/2 PLN.* ☏*022 629 60 78. http://fotoplastikonwarszawski.pl.* The last display of its kind in Europe. Fotoplastikon allows people to glimpse life throughout 20C Warsaw via a selection of 3D images. During both wars it was fully operational, acting as contact point for the Polish underground during Nazi occupation and providing images of a happier, earlier time.

From Rondo R. Dmowskiego, head south along Marszałkowska Avenue, which leads to **Constitution Square★** (Plac Konstytucji) – referring to the constitution of 3 May 1791– a fine example of Socialist-realist architecture imbued

with a certain symmetrical harmony, featuring cold, grandiose constructions decorated with low-relief sculptures celebrating the Polish people at work. **Mokotowska Street** is lined with boutiques and antique shops.

UJAZDOWSKI AND ŁAZIENKI PARKS MAP I

Warsaw's vast peaceful parks feature undoubtedly among the city's main attractions. The second part of the Royal Way stretches along some 2.5km of uninterrupted green open spaces from Ujazdowskie Avenue *(south of Trzech Krzyży Square)* to Łazienki Park.

UJAZDOWSKIE AVENUE AND PARK B3

Ujazdowskie Avenue is one of the capital's most elegant avenues, lined mainly with 19C villas boasting beautifully carved façades (most of which are now occupied by embassies).

The Ujazdów Esplanade goes back in time further than Warsaw's history. This hamlet, whose origins go back to the 12C, was in fact the favourite resting place of Masovian princes until they decided to settle on the hill where the Old Town stands. However, the site remained a princely hunting ground until Anna Jagiellonka, the wife of King Stefan Barory, decided at the end of the 16C to have a royal residence built; this formed the initial structure of **Ujazdowski Zamek (Ujazdowski Castle)**★. Although the basic structure features the Renaissance style, the enlarged entrance, the curved roofline and the decorative turrets are in typical Polish Baroque style, otherwise known as Vasa style. The two large curved staircases linking the castle to the canal, built along the axis of the entrance, date from the first half of the 18C.

The Zamek is now an active **contemporary art centre** (Zamek Ujazdowski; ○ open Tue–Sun noon–7pm (Fri 9pm); ○12 PLN; ☎022 628 12 71; www.csw.art.pl) regularly hosting national and international exhibitions of painting and photography, performances, jazz and experimental music concerts. This temple of contemporary art also houses a trendy restaurant **(Quchnia Artystyczna)**, a café, a cinema showing art films, as well as a boutique and an art bookshop.

Łazienki Park★★
(Park Łazienkowski) B-C3

Łazienki Park is accessible either from Ujazdowski Park by crossing Agrykola Street, or through the main entrance, al. Ujazdowskie no. 106 (○open daily 8am–dusk, 4pm in winter).

A former hunting ground adjoining Ujazdowski Castle, Łazienki was bought in 1760 by King Stanisław August. Standing by the main entrance, the Chopin monument welcomes strollers who, when the weather is fine, flock to listen to the piano recitals of Chopin classics *(May–Sept, every Sun at noon and 4pm)*. The circular pond adds to the charm of these events.

Across the main path stands the elegant **Belvedere**★ (Belweder), initially owned by King Stanisław August, who set up a manufacture of ceramics inside. This Royal residence, built around 1660 and then redesigned in the 1820s for the benefit of Warsaw's governor, became the official residence of the leaders of the Polish State at the end of World War I; it was inhabited for ten years by General Jaruzelski, then by President Łech Wałęsa (before the presidential palace was transferred to *Krakowskie Przedmieście*); today, the Belvedere is still used for official receptions.

The Park's main monument, the **Łazienki Palace**★★ (Pałac Łazienkowski, ○ open Tue–Sun 9am–4pm ○closed major holidays; ○12 PLN; ☎022 506 01 83 ; www.lazienki-krolewskie.pl) is commonly known as the "palace on the water". Originally a Baroque Boathouse from the early 17C, the Palace was re-designed to achieve a Neoclassical look over 20 years starting in 1772. On the ground floor, the decorations at the base of the walls are a reminder that the palace was initially only a "bathhouse" (*łazienki* meaning "baths" in Polish), whereas the ballroom and the

Pałac Łazienkowski, the "Palace on the Water"

© Rognar/Dreamstime.com

painting gallery testify to the classical taste of King Stanisław. Upstairs, the king's private apartments boast, among others, a painting by Bellotto depicting the original bathhouse.

Facing the palace, the amphitheatre, featuring a décor of antique ruins set on an island and inhabited by peacocks, regularly hosts performances in summer. You can also take gondola rides in the lake (*7 PLN*).

A little further on is the **Jan Paderewski and Polish Expatriates Museum** (*open Tue–Sun 9am–4pm; *5 PLN*). Opposite stands the **Myśliwski Palace**, a present from the king to his nephew Józef Poniatowski. (*open Sun–Tue 9am–4pm; *3 PLN*). As you walk back towards the north side of the park, you will come across the **Orangery**★ (*Pomarańczarnia;*), one of the few remaining wooden theatres in Europe to feature its original 18C décor (1788); it now houses a sculpture gallery.

The **Botanical Gardens**★ (Ogród Botaniczny, *open Apr–Aug Mon–Fri 9am–8pm Sat–Sun 10am–8pm; Sept Mon–Fri 10am–6pm; Oct Mon–Fri 10am–4pm; *3 PLN*) provide a pleasant and/or romantic stroll through **Łazienki Park**. Laid out in 1818, and representing only part of Warsaw University's Botanical Gardens, take special note of the rose garden and the medicinal-herb garden.

The Royal Way continues south towards Wilanów via the residential district of Mokotów.

WILANÓW PALACE★★
(Pałac Wilanowski)
Access: Ul Stanisława Kostki-Potockiego 10/16 (free parking). By bus, from the town centre, nos 116, 117, 130, 139, 164, 180, 519, 522, 700, 710, E-2.
Open May–mid-Sept Sun–Mon, Wed 9am–6pm, Tue, Thu–Fri 9am–4pm, Sat 10am–4pm; early Feb–Apr and mid-Sept–mid-Dec Wed–Mon 9am–4pm (Sat 10am–4pm); last admission 1hr before closing.
*Closed major holidays. *20 PLN (Palace only), 25 PLN (includes park and Orangery fees), Sun free. *022 842 25 09. www.wilanow-palac.art.pl.*

History
South of Warsaw, Wilanów is a pleasant district surrounding the palace. Erected during the late 17C and extended by its successive owners, the palace is a typical example of Baroque country residence, "between courtyard and garden". Patron of the arts, Jan III Sobieski originally named his summer residence Vila Nova, which over the years became Wilanów. In 1799, it was acquired by Stanisław Potocki, author of many treatises on art and aesthetics and enlightened collector. He created in Wilanów one of the first public museums in the world.

Palace Tour
The sculptures and low-reliefs decorating the façade, inspired from Antiquity, are a tribute to the Sobieski dynasty and the king's military successes. The interior of the palace is a blend of three main architectural styles: original Baroque rooms of King Jan III Sobieski in the central part, 18C interiors in the south wing and in the pavilion adjoining the palace, and finally, 19C interiors in the north wing, the palace's most recent part, decorated and remodelled by the Potocki family.

The tour starts on the first floor with the portrait gallery, whose main interest lies in the numerous posthumous portraits placed on coffins, a specifically Polish custom. Beyond the Great Crimson Room and the Etruscan Study, you enter the oldest part of the palace. It was here that the Potocki Museum was set up; the marble slab bearing the inscription *"cunctis patet ingressus" (accessible to all)* recalls the precursor spirit which led to these works of art being shown to the public. The tour continues on the ground floor with Jan III Sobieski's apartments, the chapel designed by Henri Marconi and the Royal Library.

Gardens★
*Open daily 9am–dusk. *5 PLN (for Park only, Thu free).*
The gardens are at the back of the palace. They were laid out in the French

Wilanów Palace

C. Hervé-Bazin / MICHELIN

style on a dual-level terrace decorated with sculptures symbolising the four stages of love (reserve, the first kiss, indifference and the first quarrel). The original sundial is the work of the great Polish astronomer Jan Heweliusz, who invented the telescope.

Beyond the Orangery *(temporary exhibitions, same opening times as the palace)*, is an **English-style park**, adorned with sarcophagi, columns and obelisks. A Roman bridge, a Chinese kiosk and the pump room evoke Antiquity, Oriental Art and the Middle Ages.

Poster Museum★
(Muzeum plakatu)

Open Jun–Sept Mon noon–4pm, Tue–Fri 10am–4pm, Sat–Sun 10am–6pm. 10 PLN, Mon free. 022 842 48 48. www.postermuseum.pl.

This museum, next to the palace, is dedicated to an art form in which the Poles have always excelled: poster painting. Whether made for advertising, the cinema, the theatre, politics or tourism, the assortment consists of thousands of Polish and international posters that make it one of the world's largest collections.

MURANÓW AND MIRÓW (FORMER JEWISH GHETTO)
MAP II

Like other Polish towns such as Łódź, Białystok and Kraków, Warsaw had, for centuries, one of Europe's most important Jewish communities, estimated in 1939 at 370,000 persons, which represented a third of the population; in May 1945 that number was reduced to 300. Although Warsaw's prewar Jewish community was scattered throughout the whole town, not residing exclusively in any particular district, today the only traces of this community are located in and around the former ghetto, in the districts of Mirów and Muranów, and, to a lesser extent, in Praga, across the River Wisła. The extermination of the Jews is still generally a taboo subject in Poland; however, in Warsaw as in other Polish towns, above all in Kraków, the nucleus of a Jewish community is reappearing and with the support of the diaspora, they are actively endeavouring to keep alive the memory of the Shoah and to revive their ancestral culture.

Jewish Historical Institute★
(Żydowski Instytut Historyczny) A2

Ul. Tłomackie 3/5 *Open Mon–Fri 9am–4pm (Thu 11am–6pm).* 10/5 PLN. 827 92 21. www.jewish institute.org.pl.

The visit of the Institute is an excellent introduction to Warsaw's Jewish community. Founded in 1928, it hosts two permanent exhibitions: one of them is devoted to Jewish art (sacred and secular works of art) and the other to the Warsaw ghetto *(see the 35min film – in English, German, Hebrew and Polish)*.

The Institute also houses a research centre and a substantial stock of information about the history of Polish Jews since the 18C. Various books and guides relating to Jewish culture and history in Poland are available in the shop. On the site now occupied by the Błękitny Wieżowiec (Blue Skyscraper) once stood the **Great Synagogue** (Synagoga na Tlomackiem – the greatest synagogue in Poland). The synagogue was blown up by the Nazis in 1943. According to a story told by Warsaw Jews, a rabbi placed a curse that no other building would ever be built on the site of the synagogue. Which may be the reason why the construction of the Blue Skyscraper took more than 20 years. It was finished in the early 1990s.

The Path of Remembrance of Jewish Martyrdom and Struggle★★ MAP I A1

This "Path of Remembrance" starts from Bohaterów Getta Square featuring the **Ghetto Heroes Monument** (Pomnik Bohaterów Getta), unveiled among the ruins of the ghetto on 19 April 1948 for the 5th anniversary of the Ghetto Uprising. The sculpture "Struggle", carved on the west façade of the monument, represents the ghetto insurgents whereas the sculpture carved on the east façade symbolises the "March towards Extermination". The monument is covered with labrador slabs, originally ordered from Sweden by Hitler who, anticipating an early victory, intended to have a monument built in Warsaw to the glory of the Third Reich.

The plaque located next to the monument and bearing the inscription "Zegota 1942–45" commemorates the organisation intended to help the Jews at the time of the Holocaust. Of all the organisations active in Europe during World War II, this was the only one to be financed by a government, that of the exiled Polish Republic. On the empty square across from the monument a new museum is under construction: the Museum of the History of Polish Jews (set to open in 2012).

The Path of Remembrance continues along Zamenhofa Street, where there are **19 granite plaques** commemorating, in Polish and Hebrew, significant events and personalities of the ghetto: historian Emmanuel Ringenblum **(no. 5)**, ŻOB (Jewish Fighting Organisation) Commander in chief and leader of the Ghetto Uprising, Mordechai Anielewicz **(no. 10)**, Janusz Korczak **(no. 15)**.

Further up, on the **site of the former ŻOB Bunker** (Ul. Miła 18) stands an amazing and poignant monument: a heap of rubble, its height representing that of the rubble left after the destruction of the ghetto. Note, in the adjacent

Ghetto Heroes Monument

The Warsaw Ghetto

The Warsaw Ghetto was the largest "Jewish residential district" (according to the official terminology) in Nazi Europe: a 3m-high and 18km-long brick wall isolated 30 per cent of the population (around 50,000 people) on only 2.4 per cent of the town's area (400ha). The "Great Action" which, on 22 July 1942, saw the transfer of 265,000 Jews to the death camp at Treblinka, marked the beginning of a policy of massive extermination. Resistance within the ghetto began to get organised under the command of the ŻOB (Jewish Fighting Organisation), using arms smuggled into the ghetto. The Ghetto Uprising started on 19 April 1943; taken by surprise, the German army took a month to retaliate. A few thousand Jews only managed to escape, the others were shot on the spot or deported. The story of the Warsaw Ghetto, faithfully told in HW Szpilman's book *The Pianist*, which inspired Roman Polanski's film, remains one of the darkest episodes of the *Shoah (Hebrew term for Holocaust)*.

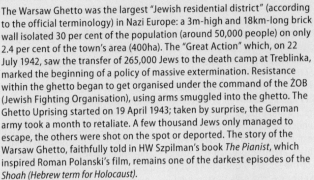

streets a number of houses built on the same level: pressed by the urgency of the situation and unable to cope with the extent of the damage and of the reconstruction work needed, the post-war communist authorities decided to erect new blocks of flats directly on the ruins of the ghetto.

The Path of Remembrance ends on the **Umschlagplatz** (*Ul. Stawki 10*) where, from July 1942, Warsaw Jews were systematically gathered and loaded into cattle wagons bound for Treblinka. The simple white-marble **monument** erected at the end of the 1980s and representing the cattle trucks used to transport the Jews is covered inside with 400 Jewish first names, symbolising the 300,000 Jews deported from Warsaw to the death camps. On the side wall, inscribed in Polish, Hebrew and Yiddish, one can read this verse from the Book of Job: *"O earth do not conceal my blood, let it cry out on my behalf"*. In 1988, a **stone** was also placed on the very spot where the trains started. It bears the following inscription: *"Through this path of suffering and death, during the years 1940–43, over 300,000 Jews went from the Warsaw ghetto to the death camps."* On the other side of the street stands one of the rare houses to have survived the destruction of the ghetto: it is the house occupied during the war by the SS officer supervising the Jews' departure from the Umschlagplatz (Warsaw Ghetto).

The Jewish Cemetery
(Cmentarz Żydowski) MAP I A1

▶ *Follow Stawki Street then turn left onto Okopowa and continue until you reach the main entrance to the cemetery, at no. 49/51 (☉open Mon–Thu 10am–5pm, Fri 9am–1pm, Sun 11am–4pm; ☎022 838 26 22; www.beisolam.jewish.org.pl).*
Established in 1806, it is one of the rare Jewish cemeteries still in use in Poland. Having miraculously escaped severe damage during the war, the cemetery contains some 250,000 graves, including those of some illustrious Polish Jews: the ophtalmologist and inventor of Esperanto, Ludwig Zamenhof, the writer D. H. Nomber, and Janusz Korczak. A guide of the graves is available from the caretaker at the entrance to the cemetery.

Around Grzybowski Square
MAP III A1/A2

The remaining memorial sites and places of Jewish worship and culture are grouped around Grzybowski Square, on the southeastern border of the Mirów district, near the Palace of Culture.

The most striking of these is undoubtedly the **fragment of the ghetto wall**★★ (*Ul. Sienna 55. Ring the entry-phone at no. 100 or wait for one of the building's residents to open the gate. The wall is in the courtyard on the left, beyond the porch.*) This tiny brick wall is all that remains of the 3m-high rampart which, from November 1940 to July 1942, sealed off Jewish Varsovians from the rest of the capital's Polish population. The commemorative plaque recalling the ghetto dates was placed here in 1992 by the Israeli president during the "inauguration" of the fragment of the wall; a second plaque mentions that two stones from the wall were transferred to the Holocaust Museum in Washington. Further up, on the corner of Grzybowski Square and Prozna Street, the only buildings that survived the destruction of the ghetto attest to Warsaw's prewar red-brick architecture. On the other side of the square stands the **Nożyk Synagogue★**, the only synagogue in Warsaw to have escaped total destruction because it was used for storage and as stables by the Nazis. Following complete restoration, it reopened in 1983 and features fine interior architecture *(Ul. Twarda 6, ⏰ open Sun–Thu 10am–7pm, Fri 10am–3.30pm; ☷6 PLN ☎022 620 43 24)*. Adjoining the synagogue, the **Ester Rachel Kamińska Jewish Theatre** *(Plac Grzybowski 2)* recreates popular shows given by the pre-war Jewish community. The building is also the headquarters of several Jewish associations.

PRAGA MAP I

Tram no. 4 Bankowy Square no. 22 from Jerozolimskie Avenue – stop at Wileńska.

The populous, working-class Praga district is still not appreciated by residents of the west bank of the Wisła. Yet, as the only district to have survived the war, it offers an authentic atmosphere and an interesting stroll away from the traditional tourist trail. Moreover, it contains Warsaw's oldest buildings, boasting façades scarred by gunfire during World War II. Beware thieves at night.

Orthodox Church of St Mary Magdalene★
(Cerkiew Św. Marii Magdaleny) C1
Ul. Solidarności 52. ⏰Open daily 11am–3pm. ☎022 619 84 67.

This fine ochre and gold edifice (1869), built for the benefit of the Russians living near and arriving at Wileńska Station, is one of the best examples of Russian influence in Warsaw: a large neo-Byzantine structure surmounted by several onion domes and an interior in perfect condition.

The artists' quarter (C1) extends over the northeast perimeter *(between Targowa, 11 Listopada and Konopacka streets)*. Drawn to abandoned factories and buildings in which they set up their studios, painters, sculptors and comedians are slowly bringing Praga back to life; the pioneers set themselves up in the now cult building standing at no. 3 Inżynierska Street. As for Ząbkowska Street, rightfully considered until recently as the capital's notorious crime centre, it has now been renovated and is becoming an area highly sought after by artists. Past no. 50 Targowa Street, the district's oldest building (1819), you will see the **Różyckiego Bazaar**, the longest-surviving bazaar in Warsaw. Established in 1902, it is now only a pale reflection of what it once was.

Praga also had an important concentration of Jews before the war as attested by the **Brodno Jewish Cemetery** *(on the corner of Ul. Odrowąża and Św. Wincentego, tram way no. 3 from Ul. Targowa)*, the oldest in town, founded in 1799.

👤👤 The Warsaw Zoo
(Miejski Ogród Zoologiczny) B1
Ul. Ratuszowa 1/3. ⏰Open daily 9am–7pm, last admission 1hr before closing. ☷16/11 PLN. ☎619 40 41. www.zoo.waw.pl.

Opened in 1928, and having completed massive renovation and upgrades to meet European Zoo standards, the zoo

Kazimierz Michałowski (1901–81)

Founder of the Polish school of Mediterranean Archaeology, this eminent archaeologist launched many excavation programmes in Egypt including those at Edfou (1936), Deir el Bahari (1961) and Faras.

houses elephants, cheetahs, rhinos, giraffes as well as a large colony of reptiles and birds.

MUSEUMS MAP I
The National Museum★★
(Muzeum Narodowe) B2
Al. Jerozolimskie3. ◑Open Permanent exhibitions Tue–Sun 10am–4pm. ✆12/7 PLN, Sat free. Temporary exhibitions Tue–Sun 10am–4pm (Thu–Fri 8pm). ✆17/10 PLN. ✆629 30 93. www.mnw.art.pl.

Construction on the current building began in 1926; Warsaw's National Museum contains valuable collections of medieval and ancient art, of Polish art from the 16C to the 20C , old maps and prints, decorative arts and a new gallery of Italian Painting.

The **Faras Gallery** (on the ground floor) presents frescoes and architectural elements from a Christian cathedral in the Sudan, along with a collection of Byzantine art. Today it is possible to admire, displayed in specially adapted rooms, approximately 60 frescoes dating from the 8C to the 14C, including the charming portrait of St Anne (8C) and Christ in Majesty (11C) with the symbols of the evangelists. The **gallery of medieval art** consists of seven rooms displaying splendid sculptures, altarpieces and paintings from all over Poland. Admire in particular the series of Gothic works, featuring a wealth of delicate details, from the region of Silesia and from Wrocław. The **painting galleries** (1st and 2nd floors) are rich in works from the various European schools of painting. However, the **Gallery of Polish Painting** (1st floor) deserves special attention. The huge canvas by Jan Matejko **"The Battle of Grunwald"** painted in 1878, depicts the defeat inflicted on the Teutonic Knights by the Polish army.

Warsaw Uprising Museum★★
(Muzeum Powstania Warszawskiego) A2
Ul. Grzybowska 79. ◑Open Wed–Sun 10am–6pm (Thu until 8pm). ✆7 PLN, Sun free. ✆539 79 05. www.1944.pl.

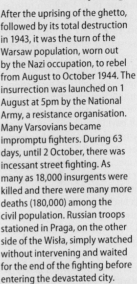

The Warsaw Uprising

After the uprising of the ghetto, followed by its total destruction in 1943, it was the turn of the Warsaw population, worn out by the Nazi occupation, to rebel from August to October 1944. The insurrection was launched on 1 August at 5pm by the National Army, a resistance organisation. Many Varsovians became impromptu fighters. During 63 days, until 2 October, there was incessant street fighting. As many as 18,000 insurgents were killed and there were many more deaths (180,000) among the civil population. Russian troops stationed in Praga, on the other side of the Wisła, simply watched without intervening and waited for the end of the fighting before entering the devastated city.

Opened in 2005, this museum was designed by architect Wojciech Obłutowicz in a brick building of a former tramway power station built in 1904. Using film, photos, life-size diorama, sound effects and various artefacts, the museum offers an evocative and informative experience to visitors to show what life was like during the resistance. Information plaques in both English and Polish feature prominently. The Polish resistance, with its resulting struggles and torment, is still painfully present in the collective memory.

EXCURSIONS
Kampinos National Park★★
(Kampinoski Park Narodowy) A1
20km from Warsaw Town Centre. By car: ◑ follow E30 towards Poznan and turn right at Paprotniat. Frequent bus services from Warszawa Zachodnia bus station.
A picturesque way to get to the park is by narrow-gauge railway from Sochaczew (◑May–Sept, departure every Sat 10am; round trip is 6hr including time to walk in the forest; ✆25/20 PLN; ✆46 862 59 75).

Kampinos is a rare example of a nature reserve (37,470ha) on the edge of a city with more than 1 million residents. Situated along the Wisła Valley, it offers splendidly varied landscapes of marshland, forests and sand dunes sheltering a remarkable fauna and flora. Since the 1950s the park has successfully carried out a policy of protection and reintroduction of endangered species: beavers, lynx, wild boars and elks, the latter having multiplied so much that they now migrate to other forested areas. Many birds (white storks, lapwings, kingfishers, etc.) have made their home among the 1,100 species of plant, the most famous of which is the black birch.

Excursions to Kampinos are made easier by the complex network of footpaths, cycle tracks and, in winter, cross-country skiing tracks. The classic itinerary from Truskaw to Palmiry *(5km)*, lined with small wooden houses whose inhabitants sell their honey, enables visitors to admire the beauty of the park. Another itinerary, leading deeper into the forest, stretches over 12km from Leszno to Kampinos, where there is a charming 18C **wooden church**. The ramble can be extended as far as the fascinating **Granica Museum**, devoted to the park's fauna and flora *(open Tue–Sun 9am–4pm; 4 PLN)*.

Pułtusk★
(Population 19,230)

62km north of Warsaw. Follow road 61 towards Suwałki. Bus services from Warszawa Zachodnia.

This charming market town through which flows the River Narew (a tributary of the Wisła) offers a relaxing setting. The town had its heyday in the 15C and 16C, when it became the official residence of the bishops of Płock. Its Jesuit College, founded at the beginning of the 16C, trained numerous Polish politicians and contributed to spreading education throughout the eastern part of the country, traditionally at a disadvantage. In 1806, Napoleon fought a battle against the Russians, which led to the Treaty of Tilsit founding the Duchy of Warsaw. Pułtusk hit the headlines again in 1868, when a mighty meteorite crashed to earth in the vicinity. Finally, during World War II, 85 per cent of the town was destroyed and half the population exterminated.

Pułtusk was rebuilt after the war with the help of late-18C illustrations. Today, one can admire the market square **(Rynek)**, reckoned to be the longest in Europe (400m), featuring in its centre the Gothic tower of the town hall which houses the **Regional Museum**. The rynek is closed off to the north by the Gothic collegiate church, remodelled in

Pułtusk

© Polish National Tourist Office

Żelazowa Wola, Chopin's house

R. Czerwinski/MICHELIN

Renaissance style in the 16C by Venetian architect Giovanni Battista. Renaissance frescoes were discovered inside.

The south side of the square is occupied by the huge horseshoe-shaped **castle**, which was once the residence of the bishops of Płock.

The castle was remodelled many times before being rebuilt in 1974 and given by the government to the association of the Polish diaspora; it then became the **Polish House** (Dom Polonii), a centre where Poles from all over the world meet. It was turned into a comfortable hotel for Poles from foreign countries but was open to all.

Żelazowa Wola★
(Dom Urodzenia Fryderyka Chopina w Żelazowej Woli)

▶ *54km west of Warsaw, on the edge of Kampinos National Park, near Sochaczew. Bus available either from the Warszawa Zachodnia PKS terminal or minibus arrangement from the Chopin Museum at Ostrogski Palace.* ℘*827 54 73.* ⏱*Open May–Sept Tue–Sun 9.30am–5.30pm; Oct–Apr Tue–Sun 10am–4pm.*⊕*23 PLN* ⏱*Closed major holidays.* ℘*(46) 863 33 00.*

The manor of Żelazowa Wola, the birthplace of **Frédéric Chopin** (1810–49), is now a museum. This fine residence originally formed part of the estate of Count Skarbek for whom the composer's father, Nicolas Chopin, a Frenchman, worked as a private tutor. The restored house, furnished in period style, and its surroundings are imbued with a very pleasant atmosphere, but unfortunately, there are few mementoes of Frédéric Chopin to be seen.

The charming adjoining **park** is the setting for open-air concerts given by music-school students (*May–Sept Tue–Sat noon*). On Sundays (*May–Sept noon and 3pm*) admirers from all over the world flock to listen to the concerts given by renowned soloists.

ADDRESSES

⌂STAY

Warsaw's range of accommodation has improved dramatically over the past five years. One is bound to find a type of hotel or hostel to suit one's needs. Prices vary quite a lot between weekdays, weekends and season but great deals can be had if you check the websites in advance.

IN AND AROUND THE OLD TOWN

⌂ **Kanonia** – *Ul. Jezuicka 2.* ℘*022 635 06 76. www.kanonia.pl. 42 rooms.*⧠. This quiet, well-kept youth hostel offers a roof in the most picturesque narrow street of the Old Town for a very modest price. No curfew and Internet access. Open year-round.

Castle Inn – *Ul. Świętojańska 2.*
022 425 01 00. www.castleinn.pl.
21 rooms. This boutique hotel is located right next to the castle in the Old Town. Rooms feature somewhat bizarre décor but the building and location are ideal. Reserve early.

Hotel Hetman – *Ul. Kłopotoskiego 36. 022 511 98 00. www.hotelhetman.pl. 68 rooms.* This hotel, boasting spacious rooms, simply painted in light sand colours, offers all the facilities of a three-star establishment for a slightly lower price. Located in a peaceful, tree-lined street in the Praga district, near the zoo and one tram stop from the Old Town. Internet access.

Duval – *Ul. Nowomiejska 10. 022 831 91 04. www.duval.net.pl. 4 apart.* This residence situated in the heart of the Old Town comprises four studio apartments, meticulously furnished in different styles (retro, Polish, Japanese and "classy"), all equipped with an Internet connection. Reservation advisable.

Le Royal Méridien Bristol – *Ul. Krakowskie Przedmieście 42/44. 551 10 00. www.lemeridien.pl. 205 rooms.* Ideally situated along the Royal Way, between the centre and the Old Town, the beautifuly renovated 19C building is a lovely place to stay. The hotel's *Marconi Restaurant* offers delicious weekend brunch.

Le Régina – *Ul. Kościelna 12. 022 531 60 00. http://.mamaison.com. 61 rooms.* Housed in an 18C restored palace in the heart of the New Town, this luxury hotel offers peace in the form of a beautiful coutyard garden. The walls of all the rooms are decorated with hand-painted frescoes. Swimming pool and gymnasium. Free WIFI Internet connection.

CENTRE

Oki Doki – *Plac Dąbrowskiego 3. 022 828 01 22. www.okidoki.pl. 30 rooms.* This youth hostel is undoubtedly one of the best moderately priced establishments in the town centre. Various sized rooms, individually decorated by local artists, very convivial staff, small shop, info on guided tours, bike rental. No curfew.

Free internet access. Reservation required.

Première Classe – *Ul. Towarowa 2. 022 624 08 00. www.premiereclasse. com.pl. 126 rooms.* Standard, yet bright and modern rooms, all fitted with individual bathrooms. Located along a dull avenue but at the crossroads of the main bus and tram lines.

Boutique Bed & Breakfast – *Smolna 14/7. 022 829 48 01. www.bed andbreakfast.pl. 4 apart.* Four apartments of a high standard, decorated with fresh flowers and equipped with wooden furniture, situated in a pleasant and peaceful street adjacent to the Royal Way; one can really feel at home. Free internet access, welcoming hosts.

Harenda – *Ul. Krakowskie Przedmieście 4/6 – 022 826 00 71. www.hotelharenda.com.pl. 43 rooms.* This hotel offers simple and clean rooms which are not up to the same standard as the elegant reception area; it is nevertheless recommended on account of its prime location and also of the attractive discounts applied at weekends. Bear in mind that there is a jazz nightclub in the basement. Entrance is off Krakowskie Przedmieście to the left.

Mazowiecki – *Ul. Mazowiecka 10. 022 827 23 65. www.hotelewam.pl. 56 rooms.* Halfway between the centre and the Old Town, this hotel's low prices and excellent location make up for the plain, slightly dated yet clean and neat rooms *(bathrooms are either individual or on the landing)*. Bear in mind that the street is very busy (ask for a room overlooking the courtyard).

Residence Diana – *Ul. Chmielna 13a. 022 505 91 00. www.mamaison.com. 46 apart.* Well appointed apartments boasting contemporary design, this residence is located in a fine inner courtyard, in a pedestrianised shopping area of the town centre. Apartments come in all sizes and prices.
The residence offers all the services of a 4-star hotel (internet access, plasma-screen TV, dry-cleaner's, Jacuzzi, etc.). A great find.

Hotel Rialto – *Ul. Wilcza 73* ℘*022 584 87 00. www.rialtowarsaw.com. 44 rooms.* Situated in a quiet spot and housed in a fine Art Deco building dating from 1906. The rooms boast a personalised décor with the latest modern conveniences.

Hotel Mariott – *Al. Jerozolimskie 65-79* ℘*022 630 63 06. www.marriott. com. 518 rooms.* Housed in a black skyscraper with beautiful views of the town. Directly across from the Central train station. Internet access and excellent fitness centre.

PUŁTUSK

Dom Polonii – *Zamek.* ℘*23 692 9000. www.dompolonii.pultusk.pl. 55 rooms.* A modernised hotel in the historic setting of a 15C Renaissance castle.

⌖ EAT

Warsaw offers a wide range of dining establishments, usually serving from noon to 10pm without a break.

OLD TOWN

Pierogarnia – *Ulica Bednarska 28/30.* ℘*022 828 03 92.* Homemade *pierogies*, sweet and savoury, along with soups and salads are ordered at the counter in a cosy low vaulted ceiling spot.

Kamienne Schodki – *Rynek 26.* ℘*022 831 08 22. www. kamienneschodki. pl.* Excellent value for money, serving traditional, tasty dishes.

Kompania Piwna – *Podwale 25.* ℘*022 635 63 14. www. podwale25.pl.* This vast, popular tavern offers good value for money in the Old Town. Traditional family-style dishes and generous helpings. The back room can get a bit rowdy, but there is also the optin of eating in the courtyard.

Na Prowincji – *Ul. Nowomiejska 10.* ℘*022 831 98 75.* This small Italian restaurant featuring stone walls and diffused lighting makes a welcome change from the traditional Polish restaurants in the Old Town.

Bazyliszek – *Rynek 1/3.* ℘*022 31 18 41. www. bazyliszek.com.pl.* This restaurant with a long-standing family tradition offers a wide choice of Polish specialities in a carefully preserved

historic décor: the hunter's room *(sala myśliwska)* and the knight's room *(sala rycerska)* are recommended.

U Fukiera – *Rynek 27.* ℘*022 831 10 13. www.ufukiera.pl. Reservations suggested.* This very famous Polish restaurant consists of three sumptuously decorated dining rooms lit by candlelight and a superb inner courtyard. Elaborate menu and impeccable service.

Fukiera restaurant in the Old Town

J. Malburet / MICHELIN

NEW TOWN

Antrakt – *Plac Piłsudskiego 9.* ℘*022 827 64 11. www. antraktcafe.waw.pl.* This small café-cum-restaurant housed inside the Grand Theatre offers simple good-quality food in a warm, friendly décor characteristic of literary cafés of the interwar period.

CENTRE

Bar Bambino – *Ul. Krucza 21.* ℘*022 625 16 95.* This milk bar exemplifies simple cooking and generous helpings; mixed clientele. The place is highly recommended as it provides an insight into the former canteens of the communist period.

Krokiecik – *Ul. Zgoda 1.* ℘*022 827 30 37.* A bright, clean, cafeteria-style eatery serving homecooked Polish dishes including a selection of soups and salads; almost like a milk bar but with style and friendlier staff.

Chłopskie Jadło – *Plac Konstytuji 1.* ℘*022 339 17 17. www.chlopskiejadlo.pl. Reservations suggested.* This "farmhouse kitchen" chain offers enormous helpings, accompanied by large loaves of fresh bread placed directly on the large wooden tables. All the dishes are delicious, starting with the *placki* (potato pancakes) and the *smalec* (streaky bacon lard, a speciality of the house). Service is quick and the atmosphere convivial.

Orchidea – *Ul. Szpitalna 3.* 𝄞*022 827 34 36. www.restauracjaorchidea.pl.* An excellent establishment offering a delicious Asian fusion-style cuisine. Charming staff.

Przygryź – *Ul. Mokatowska 52.* 𝄞*621 71 77.* On one of the most beautiful streets in Warsaw, this cosy café serves excellent *pierogi* and salads plus has amusing illustrations as part of the décor.

Qchnia Artystyczna – *Zamek Ujazdowskie (Ujazdowski Castle).* 𝄞*022 625 76 27. www.qchnia.pl.* Housed in the contemporary art centre, this restaurant is a refreshing and cool alternative to formal eateries.It proposes Polish and continental dishes, elegantly served in a pared-down décor renewed with each new exhibition hosted by the art centre. The potato-and-salmon pancakes *(placki z łososiem)* are a must. Wonderful outdoor terrace overlooking Ujadowski Park.

Restauracja Roma – *Ul. Grottgera 2.* 𝄞*022 841 01 33. www.restauracjaroma.pl.* Reservation advisable. Cosy atmosphere, with only eight tables, Roma serves homecooked Southern Italian dishes with soul.

U Aktorow – *Aleja Ujazdowskie 45.* 𝄞*022 628 65 50. www.uaktorow.com.pl.* Polish cuisine served in three spacious rooms, some of which are adorned with actors' glossies. Warm welcome.

Delicja Polska – *Ul. Koszykowa 54.* 𝄞*022 630 88 50. www.delicjapolska.pl.* Delicious dishes, a fairytale décor, efficient, discreet service. This restaurant is one of Warsaw's small gems. Try the house liquor *(nalewki kresowe)*, made from walnuts and bilberries.

Living Room – *Ul. Foksal18.* 𝄞*022 826 39 28. www.livingroom.pl.* Light and modern ambience with well-presented salads, pasta, fish and meat dishes. Delicious fruit cocktails available.

Venti-tre – *Ul. Belwederska 23.* 𝄞*022 558 10 94.* Located in the Hyatt Regency, the appeal of this Italian and

seafood establishment is not only the well-prepared food, but also the open-plan kitchen and wood-burning oven for well-fired pizzas.

PRAGA
Le Cèdre – *Al. Solidarności 61 (level with the Praski tram stop, just after crossing the Wisła)* 𝄞*022 670 11 66. www.new.lecedre.pl.* Excellent Lebanese food with an extensive menu; takeaway service. Water-pipes and belly dancing.

♟/CAFES / ♟ BARS
Most bars and cafés also serve meals throughout the day.

OLD TOWN AND NEW TOWN
To Lubię – *Ul. Freta 10.* 𝄞*022 635 90 23. www.tolubie.pl.* This bright, cosy café offers a large choice of teas and coffees as well as mouthwatering homemade cakes. Try their *miod pitny* (honey liquor) on a winter's day. A small drawing area is set aside upstairs for children. No smoking.

Same Fusy – *Ul. Nowomiesjska 10.* 𝄞*022 635 90 14. www. samefusy.pl.* Tea and coffee taken very seriously in this relaxing, candle-lit hideaway.

Stacja Rynek – *Rynek 15 (in the basement, on the corner of Świętojańska and Zapiecek streets).* 𝄞*022 635 76 82. www.stacjarynek.pl.* A subterranean haven to either relax in a big armchair and sip a drink, or have a snack while listening to chilled music. Garden available in summer.

CENTRE
Antykwariat – *Ul. Żurawia 45.* 𝄞*022 629 99 29.* Walls covered with old books, an indoor garden and an oriental room: this café is a must whatever the season and the time of day.

Café Karma – *Plac Zbawiciela 3/5.* 𝄞*022 875 87 09.* The ideal place to relax after a tour of the town or a shopping afternoon. Spacious and equipped with comfortable teak chairs spread around an ancient central fireplace, the café attracts a local clientele as well as the actors of the nearby theatre. Small exhibitions feature various local and international artists; Wi-Fi access.

Czuły Barbarzyńca – *Ul. Dobra 31.* 𝄞*022 828 95 58 . www.czuly.pl.* Bookshop and café, popular with all types of Varsovians, near the new university library.

Między Nami – *Ul. Bracka 20. ℰ022 828 54 17. www. miedzynamicafe.com.* A traditional and well-frequented haunt of Warsaw's cool and arty set, offers good food, coffee and the occasional intrguing exhibit hanging on the walls. Gay friendly and free internet access.

Wedel – *Ul. Szpitalna 8. ℰ022 827 29 16. www.wedelpijalnie.pl.* The temple of the famous Warsaw chocolate-maker serves the best hot chocolate in town (it's almost too rich) as well as copious and succulent breakfasts at reasonable prices. Non-smoking room.

ROYAL WAY

Café Blikle – *Ul. Nowy Świat 33. ℰ022 826 66 19. www.blikle.pl.* The ancestor of Warsaw's cafés (1869) offers delicious dishes and pastries (ice cream and rose-jam doughnuts, *pączki* are a speciality). Terrace in summer and non-smoking room.

Café Nowy Świat – *Ul. Nowy Świat 63. ℰ022 826 58 03.* Opened in 1883, this café is the legendary haunt of the Polish intelligentsia and is imbued with a unique atmosphere. Fine cuisine and excellent pastries. You can look at newspapers and magazines from all European countries and from the US as well. In summer, pleasant terrace located in the inner courtyard. Non-smoking room.

Vinoteka la Bodega – *Ul. Nowy Świat 5. ℰ022 745 46 10.* Excellent wine list, with the option of ordering cheeses and snacks to accompany your order. There is a bit of a romantic atmposhere, despite its being a shop as well! If you like a glass, you can buy the bottle.

PRAGA

Łysy Pingwin – *Ul. Ząbkowska 11. ℰ022 618 02 56.* Amusing, bohemian café crowded with local artists; the walls are covered with old film posters and vinyl LPs from the 1970s/80s, which are available to buy. Excellent sandwiches made to order.

NIGHTLIFE

Warsaw hosts bars and clubs ranging from ultra hip to local "drink bar". Trainers and jeans aren't often welcome in the trendy spots.

WHERE TO HAVE A DRINK

Clubs and cafés are concentrated in Ul. Foksal, Mazowiecka and Żurawia/Trzech Krzyży.

Paparazzi – *Ul. Mazowiecka 12. ℰ022 828 42 19. www.paparazzi.com.pl.* Slick atmosphere with excellent cocktails.

CASINOS

You can find casinos at a few of the big hotels, including the Marriott and the Hyatt. **Casinos Poland** in the Marriott Hotel (*ℰ022 584 96 50; www.casinospoland.pl)* offers a VIP room, several poker tables and slot machines. Jacket usually required and valid ID.

SHOWS AND ENTERTAINMENT

The Tourist Office produces a weekly updated list of cultural events taking place in the city. In addition, you can check the monthly publications mentioned in **useful magazines and brochures**. Warsaw hosts numerous places for cinema, music, dance and theatre. Below are a few notable venues:

Grand Theatre and National Opera (Teatr Wielki / Opera Narodowa) – *Plac Teatralny 1. ℰ022 692 02 00. www. teatrwielki.pl.*

National Philharmonia (Filharmonia Narodowa) – *Ul.Sienkiewicza 10. ℰ022 551 71 28. www.filharmonia.pl.*

Fabryka Trzciny – *Ul. Otwocka 14 (in the Praga district). ℰ022 619 05 13. www.fabrykatrzciny.pl.* A former factory converted into an elegant centre of art and culture, regularly hosting good-quality jazz, theatre and world music concerts.

SHOPPING

Take note that shops are often closed early on Sat afternoons, except in shopping centres.

POLISH TRADITIONAL HANDICRAFTS

Polish art and craft specialises in amber, ceramics, linen, folk costumes, glassware, and painted and carved wood.

Galeria Opera – *Ul. Freta 14. Open Tue–Sat 11am–6pm, Sun 11am–4pm. ℰ022 831 73 28. www.galeriaopera.com.* Glass, textiles and furniture.

Cepelia – *Ul. Chmielna 8. Open Mon–Fri 10am–7pm, Sat 10am–2pm.* ℘022 826 60 31.

Arex Folk Art Gallery – *Ul. Chopina 5b. Open Mon–Fri 9am–5pm (Fri 6pm), Sat 9am–2pm.* ℘022 629 66 24.

POSTERS AND CONTEMPORARY ART

Galeria Polskiego Plakatu – *Rynek Starego miasta 23. Open daily 10am–5pm.* ℘022 831 93 06. www.poster.com.pl. Polish poster painting and graphic art offering an impressive choice of film, theatre, opera and circus posters.

Galeria Plakatu Włodka Orła – *Ul. Dobra 56/66. Open daily 2pm–6pm.* ℘022 625 37 91. www.polskiplakat.link2.pl. This famous and unusual stall belongs to a passionate poster lover; low prices.

CLOTHES AND JEWELLERY

Metal Galeria – *Ul. Chmielna 32. Open Mon–Fri 11am–7pm, Sat 11am–3pm.* ℘022 827 45 09. Limited editions of original items made exclusively by Polish artists.

BOOKS

American Bookstore – *Ul. Koszykowa 55. Open Mon–Sat 10am–7pm (Sat 6pm).* ℘022 660 56 37. www.americanbook store.pl. A fine selection of classic and contemporary literature as well as guidebooks, maps, art, architecture and history.

GROCERY SHOPS

Skarby Smaku – *Ul. Hoża 43/49. Open Mon–Fri 9am–7pm, Sat 10am–2pm.* ℘022 622 43 00. www.skarbysmaku.pl. Organic food, along with traditional homemade cakes and regional dishes. Gift-baskets.

BAZAARS AND MARKETS

Two popular and picturesque flower, fruit and vegetable markets: **Hala Mirowska** *(Plac Mirowski; open Mon–Sat 7am–4pm)* and **Hala Banacha** *(Ul. Grójecka 95; open Mon–Sat 7am–2pm).*

SHOPPING CENTRES

Złote Tarasy   *Ul. Złota 59. Open daily 10am–10pm (Sun 8pm).* www.zlotetarasy.pl.

Arkadia – *Al. Jana Pawła 82. Open Mon–Sat 10am–10pm, Sun 10am–9pm.*

🚴 SPORTS AND RECREATION

Cycling isn't recommended within the city centre, but there are some great cycle paths along the Wisła: The Wisła Trail (37km) can start near Łazienki park and runs either north to Kampinos Forest or south to the Powsin Forest by Kabaty (last southern stop on the Metro). A shorter central path starts at Ludna and Solec Streets and finishes by the Gdański Bridge.

Boat Trips – Metropolitan Seafaring *(Żegluga Stołeczna;* ℘022 654 55 45; *www.zegluga-stoleczna.pl)* runs short trips along the Wisła. A fun diversion for both 2hr and 50min stints.

Ice rink – Torwar – *Ul. Łazienkowska 6a.* ℘502 666 981

🎭 FESTIVE EVENTS

International Beethoven Festival – International music festival dedicated to Beethoven, held during Holy Week. www.beethoven.org.pl.

Warsaw Summer Jazz Days – June–July at various venues.

The International Poster Biennale – Every two years in August. www.postermuseum.pl.

Jazz Jamboree Festival – *Annually in October* – The biggest international jazz Festival in Central Europe. www.jazz-jamboree.pl.

International Film Festival (Warszawa Film Fest) – Annually at the beginning of October. www.wff.pl.

Łódź★

Łódź (pronounced *"woodge"*), the country's third largest town (it lost its longstanding second place to Kraków in 2007) grew from a sleepy town into a powerhouse of Poland's industrial revolution in a matter of years. Prosperity began with the textile industry in the 19C, when it instantly became the "Promised Land", described in the novel by Władysław Reymont, laureate of the Nobel Prize in Literature *(adapted for the screen by Andrzej Wajda)*. Smoke from the slender brick chimneys once characterised the city's horizon, but today many people focus their sights on the city's famous Film School, the underground arts scene and the wealth of impressive architecture, undergoing a continuing programme of renovation.

A BIT OF HISTORY
Poland's Manchester

In 1820, tsarist Poland chose the small town of Łódź as the centre of its newly created textile industry. As early as 1823, the first working-class district was built at the instigation of Jewish manufacturers. Łódź rapidly became a "Promised Land" for thousands of farmers from the surrounding region and for Polish and foreign investors who flocked to the town. The suppression of trade barriers between Poland and Russia in 1850 led to a considerable increase in textile exports and during the second

- ▶ **Population:** 760,000.
- **Michelin Map:** Map of Poland A2 – Województwo of Łódź.
- **Info:** Ul. Piotrkowska 87. 42 638 59 55. www.cityoflodz.pl.
- **Location:** 120km southwest of Warsaw, 230km northwest of Kraków.
- **Parking:** Parking is available except along the pedestrianised part of Ul. Piotrkowska. Many areas are either metred or overseen by an attendant.
- **Don't Miss:** Piotrkowska Street, the Manufaktura mall and museum, the White Factory, the Modern Art Museum.
- **Timing:** Allow at least one day; two days to enjoy your visit to the full.
- **Also See:** Warsaw.

half of the 19C, Łódź became the world's top textile centre and a cosmopolitan metropolis. It was administered by Othodox Russians while the factories were run by Protestant German industrialists who, together with the Jews, founded the main factories employing Catholic Polish workers.

World War II broke just when the textile industry was beginning to decline. The town was occupied by the German army

GETTING AROUND

BY RAIL – Łodź Fabryczna PKP Railway Station – *Pl. Salinskiego 1.* All destinations to the north and east. *www.pkp.pl.*
Łodź Kaliska PKP Railway Station – *Al. Unii Lubelskiej 3/5.* Destinations to the south and west. 042 205 41 02.
BY BUS – PKS Bus Station – *Pl. Salińskiego 3.* Regular bus service to all the main towns and the surrounding areas.

PRACTICAL INFORMATION

Phone code – 042.
Postal code – 90-000.
Tourist Office – *Ul. Piotrkowska 87.* 42 638 59 56. http://en.cityoflodz. com. Open May–Sept Mon–Fri 8am–7pm, Sat–Sun 10am–4pm; Oct–Apr Mon–Fri 8am–6pm, Sat 10am–4pm.
Central post office – *Ul. Tuwima 38.*
24hr/day Internet café – *Ul. Narutowicza 41;* 42 631 91 57.

as early as September 1939. The Nazis set up Poland's first ghetto in the centre of Łódź, where 260,000 Jews were confined and starved before being sent to the death camps. The **Radogoszcz district** was partly turned into a transit camp, while other camps, exclusively intended for children and Gypsies were created.

Łódź is proud of its working-class history but has recently seen lean times due to a dearth of decent jobs. Such a backdrop is fertile ground for artistic expressions which can be seen in various galleries and clubs. Łódź is also known for its annual techno Love Parade.

SIGHTS

There is no historic castle, but **Piotrkowska Street**, the town's main thoroughfare, 4km long and predominantly pedestrianised, provides an excellent focal point. The 19C architecture draws its inspiration from the neo-Gothic, neo-Renaissance, neo-Baroque and Art Nouveau styles equally applied to the factories and to the industrialists' bourgeois residences.

Piotrkowska Street★

Starting from **Plac Wolności** featuring the former Neoclassical town hall (1827) and behind Kościuszko's statue stands a charming Uniate church. Piotrkowska and the streets perpendicular to it are lined with a series of magnificent bourgeois houses. The former residence of the printer Jan Pererilgy at no. 86 is quite impressive with its wealth of architectural details (including Poland's only statue of Gutenberg).

Take a detour via **Moniuszki Street**, lined with an uninterrupted row of fine neo-Renaissance houses, before returning to Piotrkowska Street and the splendid **Palace of Wilhem Schweikert (no. 282)**, headquarters of the Centre of European Studies.

Opposite and close to each other are two important churches. The neo-Gothic **St Stanisłas Cathedral★** (Archikatedra im Św. Stanisława Kostki) **at no. 273** features beautiful stained-glass windows and an interior with a particu-

larly spacious feel. The Lutheran **St Matthew's Church** (Kościół Św. Macieja) is the parish church of the descendants of the old German oligarchy; recitals are frequently given on the romantic-style organ, one of the finest of its kind in Poland.

*Note that the street finishes being pedestrianised when it intersects with al. **Piłsudskiego.** If you tire of walking you can always hire a ricksha.The **Kinderman Villa** (Ul. Wólczańska 31/33) is a brilliant example of Art Nouveau style introduced in Poland.

Jewish Cemetery
(Cmentarz Żydowski)

Ul. Bracka (entrance on Ul. Zmienna). ⏱️*Open Sun–Fri 9am–3pm.* 💰*4 PLN.*

Pre-World War II, the The Jewish community of Łódź was 30 per cent of the population. The synagogues and the old cemetery were razed to the ground, but the "New" Jewish cemetery founded in 1892 survived the war; with over 180 000 graves, it is, arguably, the largest in Europe. Its overgrown alleyways are conducive to meditation.

MUSEUMS
The Town's Historical Museum★
(Muzeum Historii Miasta)

Ul. Ogrodowa 15. ⏱️*Open Mon 10am–2pm, Tue and Thu 10am–4pm, Wed 2pm–6pm, Sat–Sun 11am–4pm.* 💰*8 PLN, Sun free.* 📞*42 654 03 23.* *www.poznanskipalace.muzeum-lodz.pl.*

Focusing on life in Łódź from the 19C to the outbreak of World War II, the museum offers the added interest of being housed in one of Europe's most elaborate manufacturing complexes of the Industrial Revolution, including the neo-Baroque Poznański Palace.Several rooms inside the museum are devoted to musician Arthur Rubinstein and other renowned Łódź natives. Next door, housed in the impressive former factory complex is the cultural, entertainment and shopping centre **Manufaktura**. In addition to the usual shopping and entertainment choices, this complex is also home to the fascinating **Museum**

Textile Museum

© Bogdan Kopania/iStockphoto

of the Factory (◷*open Tue–Sun 10am–7pm;* *6 PLN; www.muzeumfabryki.pl).*

Textile Museum★
(Muzeum Włókiennictwa)
Ul. Piotrkowska 282. ◷*Open Tue–Fri 9am–5pm (Thu 11am–7pm), Sat–Sun 11am–4pm.* *8 PLN, Sat free.* ✆*42 684 33 55. www.muzeumwlokiennictwa.pl.*
Located inside the Neoclassical building of the White Factory (Biała Fabryka), the first mill to be equipped with a steam engine (1838), the museum illustrates the saga of the textile industry in Łódź in an entertaining way by underlining its social implications. Impressive display of machinery and fabrics from the 16C to the 19C.

Modern Art Museum★★
(Muzeum Sztuki)
Ul. Więckowskiego 36. ◷*Open Tue 10am–6pm, Wed–Sun noon–8pm.* *8 PLN, Thu free.* ✆*42 674 96 98. www.muzeumsztuki.lodz.pl.*
Founded in 1929 and housed in another Renaissance Palace once owned by the Poznański family, this was one of the first avant-garde museums in the world. Created on the initiative of Władysław Strzemiński, an exponent of Polish Constructivism and a founder of the a.r. ("avant-garde du réel") group, the museum added its valuable contribution to the history of contemporary art in Poland. The collection includes abstract, constructivist, surrealist and figurative works by Polish avant-garde artists of the first half of the 20C: Kobro, Stażewski and Strzemiński.

The **Księży Młyn** complex *(Ul. Przędzalniana 72)* comprises the neo-Renaissance **Herbst Palace** and remnants of industrial and residential buildings built for the mill factory workers.

Cinema Museum★
(Muzeum Kinematografii)
Plac Zwycięstwa 1. ◷*Open Tue 10am–5pm, Wed and Fri 9am–4pm, Thu and Sat–Sun 11am–6pm.* *8 PLN, Tue free.* ✆*42 674 09 57. www.kinomuzeum.pl.*
Housed in the fortress-style palace of the Scheibler family, this museum acknowledges the fact that Łódź ranks among the top producers of filmmakers in Europe. Temporary exhibitions illustrating the history of Polish cinema, as well as the life and works of its most famous representatives, are housed here.

ADDRESSES

STAY
⊝ **Youth Hostel** – *Ul. Legionów 27.* ✆*42 630 66 80. www.yhlodz.pl. 30 rooms.* Neat, central and open year-round. 11pm curfew with exceptions if notification is given in advance.

⊝⊜ **Ibis** – *Al. Piłsudskiego 11.* ✆*42 638 67 00.* It may be part of a chain, but it's clean, modern, well located and serves business travellers well.

⊖⊜ **Polonia Palast Hotel** – *Ul. Narutowicza 38. ☎042 632 87 73. www.centrumhotele.pl. 167 rooms.* Basic and clean; excellent value for money. Halfway between the bus and railway stations and the town centre.

⊖⊜⊜ **Grand Hotel** –*Ul. Piotrkowska 72. ☎42 633 99 20. www.grandlodz.pl. 161 rooms.* Belle Époque establishment with a lot of history. It's not as "grand" as it once was, but it offers old-world style, a great location and a good international newsstand.

⍟/EAT
Piotrkowska street boasts a great many restaurants and cafés, offering a range from classic Polish dishes to pizza. Do not hesitate to step into the inner courtyards where there are very pleasant terrace-cafés in summer.

⊖ **Incentro** – *Ul. Piotrkowska 153. ☎42 636 99 92.* Best pizza in Łódź, offering various toppings, side salads and the option of eating al fresco. No-nonsense décor as it's all about the pizza.

⊖⊜ **Anatewka** – *Ul. 6 Sierpnia 2/4. ☎42 636 36 35. www.anatewka.pl.* A pleasure for the palette with authentic Jewish cuisine in an atmosphere reminiscent of the 19C.

⊖⊜⊜ **Restauracja Polska** – *Ul. Piotrkowska 12. ☎42 633 83 45.* Dedicated to serving tasty and traditional Polish cuisine in a mahogany hued space. A café is adjacent for light snacks and beverages.

⍟ NIGHTLIFE
The town's rich nightlife is concentrated along Piotrkowska Street, but try to get off the main strip to find cool spots in alleys and other streets.

Przechowalnia – *Ul. 6 Sierpnia 5. ☎42 630 21 41. www. przechowalnia.art.pl.* Basement haven for the artistic and the offbeat, full of nooks and mismatched furniture with art on the walls.

Łódź Kaliska – *Ul. Piotrkowska 102. ☎042 630 69 55. www.klub.lodzkaliska.pl.* Renowned nightspot filled with artwork, strong drinks, eclectic music, sometimes live, and a funky and occasionally frenetic vibe.

Kazimierz Dolny★

Having long thrived on trading and on its favourable situation on the banks of the Wisła, Kazimierz Dolny attracts both tourists and artists who continue to immortalise and capitalise on the picturesque qualities of the town. The history of Polish painting and that of Kazimierz Dolny have been closely linked since the 19C.

BACKGROUND
On the banks of the Wisła
According to legend, the founder of Kazimierz Dolny, King Kazimierz the Great, loved a beautiful Jewish maiden named Esther, who lived in the village of Bochotnica. In order to live their love in secret, the King had a 4km-long tunnel dug between the castle he had just had built and the village of his beloved.

▸ **Population:** 2,222.
◔ **Michelin Map:** Map of Poland A2 – Województwo of Lublin.
▤ **Info:** Rynek27. ☎081 881 00 46. www.kazimierz-news.com.pl.
▸ **Location:** 45km west of Lublin, near Puławy, on the banks of the Wisła.
▱ **Parking:** Several paying parking areas near the centre.
⌾ **Don't Miss:** A stroll along the Wisła, a walk up the Three Crosses Hill.
◷ **Timing:** Allow one day to stroll through the hilly countryside around the castle and the Rynek, to visit the museums and to cross the river to go and see Janowiec Castle.

Twin houses of the Przybyła Family

A. Galy / MICHELIN

The reality is less romantic. The castle was erected to fight the Tatar invasions and it later proved highly useful in defending the prosperous trading town. In the 17C, although it had barely over 2,000 inhabitants, Kazimierz Dolny ranked among the wealthiest towns in Poland.

Wheat granaries were dotted along the Wisła, cattle breeding and the timber and wine trades were thriving. This flourishing period was halted by Swedish invasions between 1655 and 1660 and by epidemics of cholera and plague.

A village of artists

At the end of the 19C, at the instigation of a few painters, including **Władysław Słewiński**, the village became the favourite haunt of generations of artists and their students armed with canvases and brushes. During a long stay in France, Słewiński became the student and friend of Gauguin, at a time when the latter was turning the Breton village of Pont-Aven into a temple of artistic and pictorial expression.

The upheavals and dramas of the 20C upset the harmony and creative output of this favoured environment, but the setting and the light found in Kazimierz Dolny continue to fascinate new generations of artists and the town boasts many studios and art galleries.

WALKING TOUR
Rynek★

This vast paved square has a lone well in its centre. In the 14C, it was surrounded by wooden houses followed, in the 17C, by fine residences built with the local limestone, such as the **twin houses of the Przybyła Family**★★(Kamienice Przybyłów) featuring low-relief sculptures depicting characters and animals. Situated on another side of the square is the Baroque **Gdańsk House**. These buildings attest to the wealth of the village merchants in the past.

The Rynek rises to the north up a hill, at the foot of which stands the **parish church** (Kościól Farny) famous for its organ built in 1620 by Szymon Liliusz and for its baptismal font dating from 1587.

The Good-Luck Dog

Sitting on the Rynek in Kazimierz Dolny, near the parish church, is a small bronze dog. If you touch his nose and make a wish, it should be granted. Children who are too small to reach his nose touch his paws instead. Originally, a dog from the village of Janowiec, on the other side of the Wisła, used to swim across to get little treats from tourists. He was replaced by this good-luck dog.

143

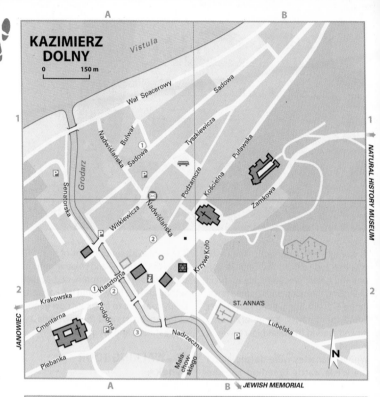

WHERE TO STAY		WHERE TO EAT	
Agharta (Pensjonat).. ①		Kwadrans (Restauracja).. ①	
Dom Architeka «SARP»................................... ②		Piekarnia Sarzński.. ②	
		Staropolska (Restauracja)... ③	

Gold- and Silverwork Museum
(Muzeum Sztuki Złotniczej)

Ul. Zamkowa2. ◑*Open May–Sept Tue–Sun 10am–5pm; Oct–Apr Tue–Sun 10am–3pm.* ◑*Closed major holidays.* ☏*7PLN.* ✆*081 881 00 80. www.muzeumnadwislanskie.pl.*
The museum displays gold- and silverwork made between 1650 and 1880, as well as contemporary jewellery designed by Polish artists since 1960.

▷ *Zamkowa Street leads up to the Castle ruins. You can make a detour by following the path on the right beyond the museum and climbing Three Crosses Hill★ (these crosses were erected during the plague and cholera epidemics). The magnificent views of the village and the Wisła are the main purpose of this ramble.*

Celejowski House Museum★
(Kamienica Celejowska)

Ul. Senatorska 11/13. ◑*Open May–Sept Tue–Fri 10am–5pm, Sat, Sun 10am–6pm; Oct–Apr Tue–Sun 10am–3pm.* ☏*7 PLN.* ✆*81 881 01 04.*
This remarkable **Renaissance residence** houses a museum devoted to the **history of Kazimierz's artist colony.**

▷ *A long path running beside the banks of the Wisła is particularly scenic.*

ADDITIONAL SIGHT
JANOWIEC★
Janowiec Castle
(Muzeum Zamek w Janowcu)

Ul. Lubelska 20. ◑*Open May–Aug Tue–Sun 10am–5pm; Sept Tue–Fri 10am–4pm, Sat, Sun10am–5pm; Oct–Apr Tue–Sun 10am–3pm.*

GETTING AROUND

BY BUS – Bus Station – *At the entrance to the town, on the road to Puławy, at the foot of Castle Hill.* Buses nos. 12 and 14 operate a regular service to Puławy (15min); from there it is easy to go to Warsaw and Lublin by bus or train.

BY CAR – Parking – You can't park on the street in the town centre and in the Rynek, but there are car parks at the entrance to the town, on the road to Puławy and along the River Wisła.

12 PLN. Free on Tue. 81 881 52 28. This Renaissance castle, now, mostly in ruins, is worth viewing for the panoramic views seen from the site. The museum provides maintenance and interpretation.

ADDRESSES

STAY

Pensjonat Agharta – *Ul. Krakowska 2. 81 882 04 21. www.agharta.com.pl. 5 rooms.* This splendid place, in a peaceful location at the foot of the monastery, is both an extremely comfortable guest house and an art gallery focusing on collectibles from the Far East.

Dom Architekta SARP – *Rynek 20. 081 883 55 44. 37 rooms.* In exchange for having the pleasure of sleeping in some of the Rynek's historic houses, one must make a few concessions about modern facilities. Large vaulted rooms and furniture from another era.

EAT

Restauracja Kwadrans – *Ul. Sadowa 7a. 81 882 11 11. www. restauracjakwadrans.pl.* Polish cuisine served on thick wooden tables among numerous clocks hanging on the walls.

Piekarnia Sarzyński – *Ul. Nadrzeczna6. 81 881 0643. www.sarzynski.com.pl.* Famous for their local baked rolls shaped like roosters, besides owning a bakery they also run a fine and atmospheric restaurant.

PRACTICAL INFORMATION

Phone code – *081.*
Postal code – 24-120.
Tourist Information – *Rynek 27. 081 881 00 46. www.kazimierzdolny. pl.* Open Mon–Fri 8am–5.30pm, Sat–Sun 10am–5.30pm.
Taxi – The taxi rank is in front of Rynek 2. *081 881 03 38.*
ATMs – In the Rynek, on the corner of Naswiślańka Street and the path leading up to the parish church.

Restauracja Staropolska – *Ul. Nadrzeczna14. 81 881 02 36. www.staropolska.kazimierz-dolny.pl.* This restaurant is dedicated to delicious Polish cuisine, served in a setting of dark murals and black-wood furniture.

CAFES

Kawiarnia "U Radka" – *Rynek 9. 81 881 05 16.* Café serving over 30 types of tea and a wide selection of alcoholic beverages. Sip your drink and enjoy lovely views of the rest of the main square or catch glimpses of well-known artists imbibing at nearby tables.

SHOPPING

There are many art galleries of varying quality. The main ones are around the Rynek and along Senatorska Street.
Galaria Lamus – *Ul. Plebanka daily noon–6pm.* This gallery specialises in romantic landscapes, ceramics, and antique furniture.

FESTIVE EVENTS

Festival of Folkgroups and Singers – During the last week in June. Songs and dances from all over Poland are performed.

Klezmer Music and Tradition Festival – A recent addition to the calendar in July, this Klezmer festival offers concerts and workshops in the music once heard regularly in many Polish villages.

Film and Art Festival – During August, outdoor and indoor film screenings are on offer. The festival aims to attract an international crowd and is recently opening up the medium to music, literature and visual arts.

Lublin★★

Lublin is well-known for its beautiful Old Town and Main Square (Rynek), which are incentive enough for any visit. Lublin's past is very much interwoven with that of its former Jewish population; landmarks found throughout the city evoke bittersweet memories of its cultural diversity and the events of the 20C. As with many other cities in Poland, Lublin's grand old buildings benefit today from a continuing program of renovation. Besides its rich architectural heritage, Lublin offers a thriving cultural life and a lively student population.

A BIT OF HISTORY
A Diverse History

Traders and travellers between Western Europe and Central Asia built a town which was granted a municipal charter in 1317 by **Prince Władysław Łokietek**. In 1569, the Union between Poland and Lithuania, known as the **Lublin Union**, was signed here, heralding the beginning of the town's prosperity. Taking advantage of its trading power and of its geopolitical role between Kraków and Vilnius, Lublin encouraged the various communities residing within its walls to express their differences and create a cultural mosaic. The first book in Polish was published in Lublin: *The Paradise*

▶ **Population:** 354,967.

⚲ **Michelin Map:**
Map of Poland A2 – Województwo of Lublin.

🛈 **Info:** Ul. Jezuicka 1/3.
☎81 532 44 12.
www.loit.lublin.pl.

◉ **Location:** 165km southeast of Warsaw.

🅿 **Parking:** Street parking during weekdays usually requires metred tickets until 6pm; private parking lots available.

◉ **Don't Miss:** Frescoes in the Holy Trinity Chapel, Kraków Gate, Grodzka Gate.

👪 **Kids:** The Lublin Open Air Museum.

🕐 **Timing:** Allow one day to visit the historic centre and the castle; half a day to go to the Majdanek concentration camp and to the *Skansen* on the outskirts of town.

⚲ **Also See:** Kazimierz Dolny.

of the Soul by **Biernat of Lublin**, who is considered as the"father of written Polish". Famous names of Polish music, such as Jan of Lublin who invented the organ tablature or Henryk Wieniawski after whom a famous violin competi-

Lublin Old Town

F. Sereau / MICHELIN

GETTING AROUND

BY RAIL – Railway Station –
Plac Dworcowy 1. About 2km from the town centre heading for Przemyśl. The extremely busy central station serves all the major cities: Warsaw, Kraków, Wrocław, Poznań and Gdynia.

BY BUS – Bus Station –
Al. Tysiąclecia 6. Located opposite Castle Square, across the avenue, the bus station is right in the town centre. There are frequent buses to Kazimierz Dolny, Sandomierz, Zamość and Warsaw.

PRACTICAL INFORMATION

Phone code – ✆*081.*
Postal code – 20.
Tourist Office – *Ul. Jezuika 1/3.* ✆*81 532 44 12. www.loit.lublin.pl.*
Open May–Sept Mon–Fri 9am–7pm, Sat 10am–5pm, Sun 10am–4pm; Oct–Apr Mon–Fri 9am–5pm, Sat 10am–3pm.
The Office, situated at the foot of the Kraków Gate, is well stocked with useful literature. It is a very pleasant place to draw up one's programme for visiting the town.

---

tion was named, are celebrated in Lublin. Later political upheavals did not interfere with the city's cultural life. Neither the invasion of the Union by Cossack or Swedish troops in the 17C, nor the repeated usurpation of power by the Habsburg Empire at the end of the 18C and then by the Russians at the beginning of the 19C, could destroy the town's cultural diversity. However, the first and second world wars succeeded in turning Lublin into a martyred town. The extermination of the Jews by the Nazis, symbolised by the **Majdanek** death camp, is a dark shadow hovering over the town that many residents of the historic centre are trying to dispel by promoting Jewish culture. Culture and art are once more Lublin's peaceful weapons.

☞ WALKING TOURS

FROM THE CASTLE TO THE DEPTAK★★

This itinerary goes through the Old Town (Stare Miasto) towards the main shopping street on the west side of the city (officially Krakowskie Przedmieście Avenue, but part of it is known as the *deptak* because it is pedestrianised).

Castle★

Situated on the hill, the castle was rebuilt in 1824 in neo-Gothic style to be used as a prison. It covers the remains of the castles erected in the Middle Ages and of the royal fortress built between the 14C and 16C. All that remains from the lat-

ter period are the chapel and the tower. Most of the castle is occupied by the **Lublin Museum**★(Muzeum Lubelskie, *Ul. Zamkowa 9;* ⏰*open Jun–Aug Tue–Sun 10am–5pm (Sun 6pm); Sept–May Tue–Sun 9am–4pm (Wed, Sun 5pm);* ☞*6.5 PLN;* ✆*081 532 50 01; www. zamek.lublin.pl)* and **Chapel of the Holy Trinity**★★ (Kaplica Św. Trójcy; *the chapel is in the courtyard of the castle, which can be reached via the museum; same opening times;* ☞*7.5 PLN).*

The museum is famous for Jan Matejko's painting, the "**Union of Lublin**". Matejko's other artistic and political work is a painting entitled *The admission of the Jews to Poland in 1096.* in addition, you will be able to see collections of archaeological and prehistoric items, medals and coins from the 14C to the 19C, weapons and various ethnographic objects.

The interior of the **Gothic Chapel** is entirely covered with **Russo-byzantine frescoes**★★. In perfect condition, these masterpieces, commissioned by King Władysław V Jagiello, were completed in 1418. They attest to the harmonious relations between different Christian cultures cohabiting in Poland in the 15C.

Castle Square
(Plac Zamkowy)

Situated at the foot of the steps leading to the castle gate. The curved houses surrounding it are facing the hill and the monument.

Grodzka Gate
(Brama Grodzka)

From Castle Square, a paved path leads to this gate opening onto the Old Town. Built in the 14C as part of a defensive wall and remodelled in 1785, the gate was a border between the Christian area on the hill and the Jewish district by the castle. The gate currently houses the **NN Theatre and Cultural Centre** that promotes the history and traditions of the former Jewish areas.

Walking along Grodzka Street, you will pass no. 5 housing a small **Pharmacy Museum** (🕐 *open Tue–Fri 11am–4pm;* 📞 *81 532 88 20;* 🎫 *free)*. A little further up, you will arrive at the Rynek.

Rynek★★

The centre is dominated by the **Royal Tribunal**, a building of excessive dimensions in comparison with those of the square. It is the former Town Hall built in 1578 and remodelled in Neoclassical style in 1781.

Surrounding the Rynek are a few **richly decorated houses**, sometimes featuring strange colours, enhanced by tasteful restoration work.

Klonowicz House at no. 2, was occupied in the 16C by the poet and mayor of Lublin, who gave it his name. The house was remodelled in Neoclassical style in the 18C. The medallions depicting poets or musicians only date from 1939.

At no. 8 is the **House of the Lubomelski family**, built in Renaissance style in 1540. The interior (o–▾) is decorated with polychrome paintings on the theme of Epicurian pleasures and love!

The **House of the Konopnic family**, at no. 12, erected in 1512, and later rebuilt, boasts splendid sculptures around the windows and on the façade. Male and female bodies, dragon heads and masks, as well as medallions featuring the owners are visible from the Rynek.

Kraków Gate★
(Brama Krakowska)

This Gothic architectural emblem of Lublin is a link between the city centre and the Old Town. The gate was altered

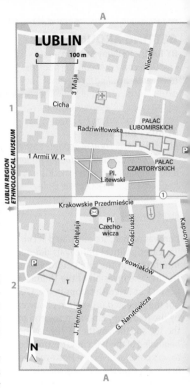

several times over the centuries: it was given a clock in the 16C and a Baroque roof in the 18C. The tower houses the **Museum of History of the Town of Lublin** (Muzeum Historii Miasta Lublina; 🕐 *open Wed–Sun 9am–4pm (Sun 5pm);* 🕐 *closed every first and third Sun in the month;* 🎫 *4.5 PLN;* 📞 *81 532 60 01;* *http://eng.zamek.lublin.pl; *note that this museum is a branch of the the Lublin Museum at the castle*).*

Containing maps, icons, portraits and archaeological exhibits, the museum is also worth visiting for the **panoramic view** from the top floor.

▷ *Follow Jesuit Street (Jezuicka), which starts from the Kraków Gate.*

Baroque Cathedral and Trinity Tower★

Ul. Krolewska 10.

The 40m-tall neo-Gothic tower houses the **Archdiocesan Museum of Sacral Art**.

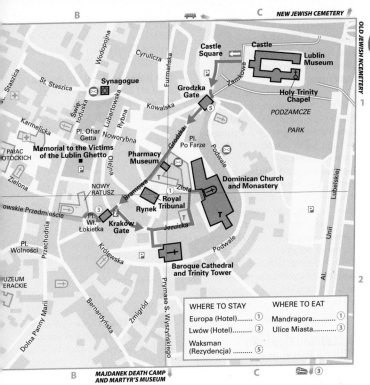

NEW JEWISH CEMETERY

OLD JEWISH NCEMETERY

Castle Square

Castle

Lublin Museum

Grodzka Gate

Holy Trinity Chapel

Synagogue

PODZAMCZE

PARK

Memorial to the Victims of the Lublin Ghetto

Pharmacy Museum

Pl. Po Farze

Dominican Church and Monastery

NOWY RATUSZ

Royal Tribunal

Rynek

Kraków Gate

Jezuicka

Baroque Cathedral and Trinity Tower

Podwale

WHERE TO STAY

Europa (Hotel)........ ①

Lwów (Hotel).......... ③

Waksman (Rezydencja) .... ⑤

WHERE TO EAT

Mandragora............ ①

Ulice Miasta............ ③

MAJDANEK DEATH CAMP AND MARTYR'S MUSEUM

Dominican Church and Monastery

Ul. Złota 9.

The construction of this ensemble began in 1342 and was completed in several stages. Originally built in Gothic style, it was remodelled after a big fire in 1575 in the Renaissance style.

IN THE FOOTSTEPS OF LUBLIN'S JEWS★

An itinerary signposted by panels bearing a blue star of David links the different sights connected with the history of the town's Jewish community. This itinerary starts from Castle Square, a vast esplanade which was once a lively built-up area reserved for the Jewish community. Having turned it into a ghetto in 1941, the Nazis destroyed it in 1943 and sent the Jewish community to the Majdanek concentration camp. Walk up towards the castle before following a panel pointing to the site of a **synagogue** destroyed in 1943, on Tysiąclecia Avenue.

At the junction of Kalinowszczyna and Sienna streets, there is an entrance to the **old Jewish Cemetery**★ with graves going back to 1541. Buried here are many rabbis and other influential members of the community.

The **new Jewish cemetery**, laid out in Walecznych Street in 1829, is still used by the Jewish community. It contains a monument commemorating the Holocaust and the graves of Jewish soldiers who served in the Polish army between 1944 and 1945.

The marked itinerary follows Lubartowska Avenue back to the historic district. Along this avenue, you will see the old University of Talmudic Studies, the former Jewish Hospital and the Cultural Centre. At no. 10 Lubartowska Avenue the town's only **synagogue** to have survived the war is located on the 1st floor. The **Monument to the Victims of the Lublin Ghetto** is temporarily on the corner of Radziwiłłowska and Niecała Streets, while its original location undergoes renovation.

EXCURSIONS

Majdanek Death Camp and Martyrs' Museum
(Muzeum Martyrologii na Majdanku)

▶ *4km southeast of Lublin.*
Ul. Męczenników Majdanka 67.
🕐*Open Tue–Sun Apr–Oct 9am–6pm;*
Nov–Mar 9am–4pm. 🕐*Closed major*
holidays. 🅿 *(*☞*10 PLN).* 📞*81 744 19 55.*
www.majdanek.pl.

Majdanek was established in October 1941 as a work camp under SS control. Polish and Russian prisoners of war and many Jews worked in weapons factories set up near the camp's electrified barbed-wire fences and watchtowers. Majdanek became a death camp in April 1942. The camp included 144 barracks and several gas chambers over an area of around 3sq km. Guides are available via reservation through the Lublin tourist office (*Ul. Jezuika 1/3*).

Lublin's Open-Air Village Museum★
(Muzeum Wsi Lubelskiej)

▶ *3km from the town centre.*
Ul. Warszawska 96. 🕐*Open Apr, Oct*
9am–5pm; May–Sept 9am–6pm; Nov–
late Dec Sat–Mon 9am–3pm. ☞*8/4 PLN.*
📞*81 533 85 13. www.skansen.lublin.pl.*
The *skansen* extends over 25ha of wooded countryside and features historic venues, workshops and guided tours (☞*90 PLN*). The *skansen* hosts many folk festivals and fun family events.

ADDRESSES

🛏 STAY

☞☞ **Europa Hotel** – *Ul. Krakowskie Przedmieście 29.* 📞*081 535 03 03. www. hoteleuropa.pl. 75 rooms.* Spacious and comfortable rooms in a neo-Renaissance building completed in 1867. Free internet access.

☞☞ **Lwów Hotel** – *Ul. Bronowicka 2.* 📞*081 745 57 09. www.lwow.lublin.pl. 19 rooms.* **Restaurant** ☞☞☞. Delicious Polish and Ukrainian cuisine served in simply decorated rustic atmosphere. Try the Veal roll with chanterelles. The hotel rooms are tastefully furnished and equipped to a three-star level of comfort. Choose from normal or attic rooms for a slightly reduced price.

☞☞ **Waksman Hotel** – *Ul. Grodzka 19.* 📞*081 532 54 54. www.waksman.pl. 6 rooms.* The rooms, furnished with character, in Louis XVI or Victorian style, overlook the royal castle. The ideal situation is another bonus, along with the hotel's retro feel, good prices and comfort.

🍽 EAT

☞☞ **Mandragora** – *Rynek 9.* 📞*081 536 20 20. www.mandragora.lublin. pl.* Located in a historic house, the three dining rooms are imbued with Jewish nostalgia and souvenirs. The establishment, which is both an art gallery and a reputable restaurant, offers a harmonious blend of culture and delicious flavours.

☞☞ **Ulica Miasta** – *Plac Łokieta 3.* 📞*081 534 05 92. www.ulicemiasta.pl.* Located right next to the Kraków Gate, this restaurant harks back to an Old Town feel of Lublin serving traditional Polish cuisine. Free children's menu on Sundays.

🍷 CAFES

Vanilla Cafe – *Ul. Krakowskie Przedmieście 12.* 📞*081 532 39 15.* Good coffee and cakes and perfect for a pitstop during a walk on the Deptak. Warm burgundy interior colours on the main floor and couches on the cellar level.

🍸 NIGHTLIFE

Restauracja Brama – *Ul. Grodzka 21.* 📞*81 534 99 33. www.regional.pl/zamek-ksiaz.* Located beneath Grodzka Gate, this convivial and cosy café-cum-restaurant is the favourite haunt of lovers of **klezmer** music – a rare form of Jewish folk music.

🛍 SHOPPING

Walk along the **deptak** (promenade) and side streets in the Old Town and you will find some interesting, independently run shops.

Zamość★★★

Zamość, known as the "Padua of the North," is a beautiful Renaissance town, where much of the layout has remained unchanged since the 16C. It remains relatively off the beaten track for foreigners, in spite of being recognised by UNESCO in 1992 as a World Heritage Site and attracting in-the-know visitors to annual summer events in the town centre.

A BIT OF HISTORY
One Man's Vision
Zamość is the result of **Jan Zamoyski's** (1542–1605) vision and ambition to make his mark in his country's history. Having studied at the Padua university in Italy, where he discovered the spirit of the Renaissance, he founded an entirely new town which reflected his taste and personality. The city's was officially established on 3 April 1580. Zamość was designed on a pentagonal plan, prolonged to the west by a rectangle enclosing the Zamoyski Palace and surrounded by fortifications. Jan Zamoyski commissioned the Venetian architect **Bernardo Morando** to carry out this idealistic project. The two men had a deep understanding of each other and Zamość was built within a few years. All the edifices were built with the same

- ▶ **Population:** 66,802.
- **Michelin Map:** Map of Poland A2 – Województwo of Lublin.
- **Info:** Ul. Rynek Wielki 13. ℘84 639 22 92. www.zamosc.pl.
- **Location:** 250km southeast of Warsaw, 130km from Lwow.
- **Parking:** Free parking found on Ul. Piłsudskiego and Ul. Partyzantów. Metered parking in the Old Town between 9am–6pm.
- **Don't Miss:** The Rynek Wielki, the tour of the ramparts and the Rotunda.
- **Timing:** One day to explore the town, another for the museums.
- **Also See:** Lublin.

enthusiasm, fully complying with the architectural criteria of the Renaissance: the Rynek Wielki and its bourgeois houses, the Town Hall, the fortifications, the academies and the residence of the Zamoyski family. Jan Zamoyski's wish, shared by his architect, was to separate the spiritual and religious part of the town from the districts occupied by

GETTING AROUND
BY RAIL – PKP Railway Station – *Ul. Szczebrzeska 11.* Railway station was closed in Sept 2009 and train service has been discontinued to and from Zamość.

BY BUS – PKS Bus Station – *Ul. Hrubieszowska 1. www.ppks-zamosc. com.pl.* Regular service to Warsaw, Lublín, Kraków, Łódz, Rzeszów and Przemyśl. Ask the tourist office about private mini-buses journeying to Lublin. This method is sometimes quicker than the regularly scheduled bus.

BY CAR – Taxi – Lux Taxi ℘84 196 24, Radio Taxi ℘84 191 91, Super Taxi ℘84 196 22.

Supervised car park– *Ul. Sadowa.* 24hr/day.

BY CYCLE – Bike hire – Atlanta – *Ul. Partyzantów 29.* ℘84 639 15 29.

PRACTICAL INFORMATION
Phone code – ℘084.
Postal code – 22-400.
Tourist Office – *Rynek Wielki 13 Open Mon–Fri 8am–6pm, Sat–Sun 9am–6pm.* ℘84 639 22 92. *www.zamosc.pl.* The office is located under the town-hall tower.
Post office – The Tourist Office sells stamps and a post box is at the disposal of visitors.

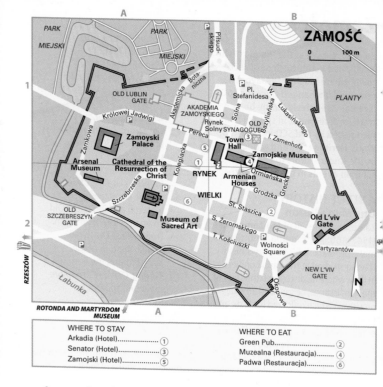

ZAMOŚĆ

0   100 m

WHERE TO STAY		WHERE TO EAT	
Arkadia (Hotel)	①	Green Pub	②
Senator (Hotel)	③	Muzealna (Restauracja)	④
Zamojski (Hotel)	⑤	Padwa (Restauracja)	⑥

craftsmen and merchants. On the whole, the religious and academic edifices stand outside the town centre, whereas the traders' houses together with the salt and water markets are gathered in the Rynek Wielki and along the adjacent streets. In spite of the Tatar, Swedish, Russian and Nazi invasions which took their toll on certain elements, the town in its entirety is breathtaking.

RYNEK WIELKI★★★

🕭 Any visit to Zamość should start with a visit to the Tourist Office inside the town hall in the Rynek Wiekli.

This perfect square with 100m sides, dominated by the 52m high **Town Hall Tower**, attracts visitors like a magnet. Unlike what can be seen in other towns dating from the same period, the **Town Hall**★★ does not stand in the centre of the square.

Jan Zamoyski did not want it to outshine his own palace and preferred to have the communal buildings integrated with the rest of the architecture. From the top

of the pink town-hall staircase, built a century later, one can see the whole structure of the square. The geometric uniformity of the arcades and of the straight streets reaching out to the remains of the red-brick ramparts, is impressive. Zymoyski dreamed of a corner of Italy and his wishes were granted. The Rynek Wielki boasts the pale yellow or blue of a Venetian or Florentine piazza. Pigeons, pizzerias and groups of tourists reinforce this impression of the "Padua of the North". In the morning, secondary school children and students walk across the square to their respective Academy or music schools. In the evening, the square becomes a vast football ground or a cabaret stage for buskers. Fortunately, the Rynek Wielki is by no means a museum district.

The **Armenian houses**★★ (🕭 see Zamojskie Museum), situated on the right of the town hall as you face it, differ from the Rynek's other bourgeois houses in their exuberant ornamentation added in the 17C to comply with the Oriental tastes of

Zamość Town Hall

A. Galy / MICHELIN

their owners, wealthy merchants from Armenia. **No. 30** in Ormiańska Street is the **Wilczkowska House** housing the **Zamojskie Regional Museum** (Muzeum Zamojskie) (*see Zamojskie Museum*). Next comes the **Bartoszewiczowska House** at **no. 26**, also known as the house "under the lion" or "under the angel", then the house "under the couple" at **no. 24** and finally a yellow house known as "under the Virgin" at **no. 22**. They are all surmounted by attics and painted in striking colours, often either ochre or purple. Walking round the square beneath the arcades, one discovers the decorative sculpted doors. By going through the corridors or down the staircases beneath the arcades with their painted ceilings, one soon reaches cellars which have been converted into bars or restaurants.

WALKING TOUR

Heading east on Grodzka Street leads to one of the town gates: the **Old Lwow Gate**. Go through the gate to find yourself outside the ramparts. It is possible to walk along the still intact bastions for a few hundred metres, then to re-enter the Old Town at the level of St Catherine's Church (Kościół Św. Katarzyny). Carry on along Akademicka Avenue as far as the **former Zamoyski Palace** and the **Cathedral**.

Façade in Zamość

A. Galy / MICHELIN

Cathedral of The Resurrection and St Thomas The Apostle★
(Katedra Wniebowstąpienia i Świętego Tomasza)
Ul. Kolegiacka.

Built between 1587 and 1598, under the supervision of Bernardo Morando, the collegiate church, now a cathedral, is one of the finest religious monuments from the Renaissance period in Poland, with its typical vaulting in Polish mannerist style. The artistic treasures it contains include the "Annunciation" painted by Carlo Dolci and the monumental Rococo-style silver tabernacle. The chancel houses four superb paintings representing the life of St Thomas, the patron saint of Zamość. The Zamoyski chapel houses the remains of the town's founder, his family, and of local dignitaries, artists and scholars. From the 18C **bell tower** (*open May–Sept 10am–*

4pm; ⬭2PLN) across from the cathedral entrance, there is a **panoramic view**★★ of the Old Town.

Museum of Sacred Art
(Muzeum Sakralne Kolegiaty Zamojskiej)
Ul. Kolegiacka 1A. ⓞ*Open May–Sept 10am–4pm, Sun 10am–1pm; Oct–Apr Sun 10am–1pm.* ⬭*4PLN.* ☎*84 639 26 14.*
Set up near the cathedral in the historic house, known as the *"Infułatka"*, of the mitred abbot *(name given to an abbot who had the same rank as a bishop)*, the Museum of Sacred Art is interesting for its collection of liturgical garments, bronze fonts and several items of gold- and silverwork.

▷ *From the cathedral, one can return to the Rynek Wielki along the western part of Grodzka Street.*

Old Synagogue
Ul. Zamenhofa 9.
Located on a back street, behind the Armenian houses, this is one of the best preserved synagogues in Poland, a late Renaissance structure with characteristic parapets lining the roof. A long "Revitilisation" project has transformed the synagogue into a centre for learning, cultural events, religious services and a multimedia museum dedicated to the Jews of the Zamość lands.

MUSEUMS AND GALLERIES
Zamojskie Museum – Regional Museum★★
(Muzeum Zamojskie)
Ul. Ormiańska 30. ⓞ*Open Tue–Sun 9am–5pm.* ⓞ*Closed holidays and the day after.* ⬭*6 PLN.* ☎*84 638 64 94. www.muzeum-zamojskie.pl*
The museum is housed inside the Armenian houses and contains several different collections of paintings, prints and ethnographic material. The selection includes old photographs of the Rynek Wielki, 16C Italian furniture inlaid with ivory, traditional 19C and 20C clothes, boots and scarves, and collections of cut stones dating from the Mesolithic and Palaeolithic periods.

Arsenal Museum★
(Muzeum Barwy i Oręża "Arsenał")
Ul. Zamkowa 2. ⓞ*Open as Zamojskie Museum.* ⬭*6 PLN.* ☎*84 638 40 76.*
Many of the collections in the Arsenal were damaged or plundered during foreign invasions. The building was remodelled in Neoclassical style in 1820 and a storey was added. Today it houses a **Military Museum** containing much 16C armour, 17C and 18C swords and sabres, as well as crossbows and French and Austrian rifles dating from 1820. There are also models of the town as it was in 1580 and 1825. Paintings and drawings, made by the soldiers themselves, illustrating life in the trenches and on the front line during the conflicts of 1915–16, and later during the 1930s, is very revealing. The **Open-Air Military Exhibit** *(*ⓞ*open Apr–Oct 9am–6pm)* shows World War II militaria.

Martyrs Museum, The Rotunda★★
(Muzeum Martyrologii "Rotunda")
Ul. Męczenników Rotundy. ⓞ*Open May –Sept 7am–8pm. Oct–Apr 7am–3pm.* ⬭*Free.*
The Rotunda is located beyond the Szczebrzeska Gate inside a wooded park. Built 500m from the Old Town and forming part of the fortifications, it was linked to the town by an underground passage. In 1939, Nazi troops used the Rotunda as a place of torture, execution and transit for those who were sent to the death camps, mainly Bełżec. Approximately 8,000 members of the Jewish community, local intellectuals, and Soviet soldiers were murdered within those walls, now treated as a memorial. There are explanations in various languages at the entrance and commemorative plaques and symbolic graves in each cell. Outside, the cemetery's tombstones feature "red stars" and "stars of David".

The Town-Hall Photo Gallery
(Galeria Fotografii "Ratusz")
Rynek Wielki 13. ⬭*Free.*
The premises of the Tourist Office host temporary photography exhibitions.

ADDRESSES

🛏 STAY

🛏 **Hotel Junior** – Ul. Gen. Sikorskiego6. *℘084 638 66 15. www.hoteljunior.pl. 30 Rooms.* 1.5km from the Rynek Wielki. This hotel offers basic, clean rooms at great prices.

🛏🛏 **Arkadia Hotelik** – *Rynek Wielki 9. ℘084 638 65 07. www.arkadia.zamosc.pl. 7 rooms.* The "mini" hotel is ideally situated inside one of the houses in the Rynek. The rooms, many which can accommodate 4 people, are neat and clean offering bathrooms and Satellite TV. The dining room overlooks the town hall. Enclosed free car park and billiard room.

🛏🛏🛏 **Senator Hotel** – *Ul. Rynek Solny 4. ℘084 638 99 90. www.senator hotel.pl. 23 rooms.* The hotel is located on a square behind the town hall, where the old salt market stands. It occupies an old house, entirely restored and modernised, the rooms are tastefully furnished and the service is friendly.

🍴 EAT

Most eateries are located around the Rynek. A few Polish restaurants are listed below, but if you wish to enhance your impression of the town's Italian atmosphere, you can also try one of the many **pizzerias** located under the arcades of the Rynek Wielki. They are called: Verona, Il Tempo, Italiana, la Cantina… You will be spoiled for choice!

🍽 **Corner Pub** – *Ul. Zeromskiego6. ℘084 627 06 94. www.corner.boo.pl.* Cosy atmosphere, with beers and food with a Polish flair. Poetry readings and Live music with a tendency towards Celtic folk is often on offer.

🍽 **Green Pub** – *Ul. Staszica 2. ℘084 627 03 36.* Situated near the Lwow Gate, this establishment is a disco Thu–Sat and yet is an easygoing place to enjoy generous servings of Polish cuisine with no pretense during the day.

🍽 **Muzealna** – *Ul. Ormiańska 30. ℘084 638 73 00. www.muzealna.com.pl.* This restaurant is housed in a cellar near the town hall. It specialises in traditional Polish cuisine. Ask for a table in the rooms at the back or in the garden.

🍽🍽 **Padwa** – *Ul. Staszica 23. ℘638 62 56. www.padwa.pl.* Located in the cellar of an old, tastefully restored house built in 1599. This restaurant/coffee house offers a wide choice of red wines and tasty traditional Polish cuisine. The goulash is remarkable.

🌙 NIGHTLIFE

Jazz Club Kosz –*Ul. Zamenhofa 3. www.kosz.zam.pl.* Jazz is very much appreciated in Poland and Zamość duly has its jazz temple. The Kosz Club is located in the former Jewish district, near the old synagogue. The concert hall is housed in the former baths. The Club brings jazz, blues and occasionally other kinds of music to life; it also hosts the "International Meeting of Jazz Vocalists" taking place every year at the end of September/ beginning of October, as well as several other mini music festivals (*see Jazz Festivals, below).* A charming place run by enthusiasts.

🛍 SHOPPING

The old *Hala Targowa* (market hall) in the city's fortifications has sadly closed. Construction of a larger, modern shopping mall, north of the Old Town on Ul. Kilińskiego is underway. *Set to open in mid-2011.*

🎉 FESTIVE EVENTS

Hetman Festival (Jarmark Hetmański) – A traditional fair (based on how it might have been in medieval times) featuring music, food, crafts and a celebration of past history in the heart of the Old Town. Takes place during the first weekend in June closest to 6 June.

International Folklore Festival – Every July. Folk culture presented in song, music and dance.

Jazz Festivals – Several festivals take place every year, including the *International Meeting of Jazz Vocalists* in September, *Jazz in the Borderland* in April and May, and a Jazz Festival in August.

In the Białowieża Forest
A. Galy / MICHELIN

The northeastern corner of Poland is the least urbanised part of the country, but it's still a fascinating area because of its cultural diversity and natural splendour. Unspoilt lakes abound, a paradise for water sports enthusiasts and bird watchers. Thick forests give shelter to the last of the European bison and boast places nearly untouched by man. All three of the regions in this part of Poland were truncated after World War II, land being handed over to Russia, Lithuania, and Belarus, though traces of these cultures, in addition to the German influence, can still be felt on the Polish side of the border.

Highlights

1 The pristine beauty of the **Białowieża Forest** (p161)

2 Canoeing through the marshes of the **Bierzba National Park** (p165)

3 Exploring the massive ruins of **Hitler's Wolf's Lair** (p179)

4 The **Teutonic castles** in **Lidzbark Warmiński** and **Olsztyn** (p180–81)

Lakes and Forests

Olsztyn is a pleasant city and the gateway to the Masurian Lakes district. It is also the second largest city after Białystok in northeast Poland and an important educational centre with more than 50,000 university students. As is typical for this region, the Teutonic Knights left behind some impressive Gothic structures: the church of St James and a castle.

Heading east from Olsztyn we enter Poland's Lake District, and encounter Lakes Śniardwy and Mamry, the two largest lakes in Poland, known as the "Masurian Seas". This is one of the most important holiday destinations in the country, attracting not only Poles, but many Germans as well, all in search of the old province of East Prussia.

The local forests also hide a more modern but sinister German artefact: the ruins of Adolf Hitler's first World War II military headquarters on the Eastern Front, known as the Wolf's Lair, or *Wolfsschanze* in German.

Further east and to the south, near the Belarusian border, is the city of Białystok. This is one of the more exotic cities in Poland, where onion-domed Orthodox churches are more common than elsewhere. Before the war Białystok was also an important centre of Jewish culture, but almost all the Jews perished; some 2,000 of the city's Jews were murdered when they were locked inside the Great Synagogue, which was then set ablaze by the Nazis.

Hitler's Wolf's Lair

Bison at Białowieża National Park

© Polish National Tourist Office

Bison Grass Vodka

Northeastern Poland is famous for its lakes and forests, and for the bison which live in the Białowieża National Park. These majestic creatures also bring to mind in every Pole the famous type of vodka called *Żubrówka* (*Żubr* means bison in Polish). *Żubrówka*, or bison-grass vodka, is made with rye grain and then infused with the flavour of "sweet grass" (or *Hierochloeodorata* in Latin), from the primeval Białowieża Forest, where the bison like to graze on this grass. This herbal concoction dates back at least to the 16C and started to become popular after the union between Poland and Lithuania in 1569 when Polish kings often stayed at hunting lodges in the forests in the northeastern part of their kingdom. The bison were nearly extinct by 1919 but were reintroduced to a special nature reserve in Białowieża at the end of the 1920s and are today one of Poland's national symbols.

Sweetgrass

© G. Nicolson/Dreamstime.com

The bison vodka is 40 per cent proof, greenish-yellow in colour and has a herbal, sweet taste. The flavor is a result of adding an infusion of bison grass to the distilled rye. Then a long blade of the grass is typically placed in each bottle for decorative purposes, but it is not the source of the flavour or colour, contrary to popular belief.

The most popular mixed drink containing bison-grass vodka is known in Poland as *szarlotka* or *tatanka*, available as a cocktail in the UK called *Frisky Bison*, or *Polish Kiss* in the US: it's one 50ml shot of vodka mixed with 150ml of apple juice and served over ice. The distinctive herbal flavour of the vodka in combination with the apple juice creates a pleasant and refreshing taste reminiscent of cinnamon apple pie! Be aware that although it makes a great gift or souvenir, you cannot pass through airport security with any bottles of liquid, so try *Żubrówka* while in Poland, purchase it at the airport's duty free shop (if you have a non-stop flight to your final destination), or pack it carefully into checked-in baggage.

Białowieża Forest★★

Puszcza Białowieska

Studied by scientists the world over, the Białowieża Forest is the last primeval forest in Europe and home to countless rare species of plant and animal life. With the Park's permission, visitors are allowed to walk about and observe areas in this isolated corner of Europe, once the private hunting grounds of the tsars. The tsars have vanished but luckily the magnificent bison have been successfully reintroduced to this forested haven.

A BIT OF HISTORY

Protected Wilderness Home to the European Bison

The powerful European bison, whose adult male weighs between 500 and 900kg and reaches a height of 1.8m, is the largest living mammal in Europe. It has practically no natural predators and was hunted by kings of Poland, and later by tsars of Russia, yet it was always a protected species.

In the 16C, bison hunters without permission from the king were condemned to death and, until the beginning of the 20C, a balance was maintained between hunting and the animal's reproduction cycle. During World War I, poachers and soldiers upset this balance so much that by 1919, there was not a single bison left in the Białowieża Forest.

In the 1920s, scientists studying the reintroduction of bison drew up a list of the natural resources of the forest and concluded protective action was needed for the forest environment as a whole. Today, the Białowieża Forest and its Belarusian equivalent are on UNESCO's World Heritage List. The Park, which covers part of the forest, is only accessible under very strict conditions, while scientists manage the herds of bison and oversee their reproduction. There are, at present, some 700 bison in the Polish-Belarusian controlled area.

♿ **Michelin Map:**
Map of Poland D2 – Województwo of Podlasie.

▤ **Info:** PTTK tourist office, Ul. Kolejowa17. ℘(85) 681 22 95. www.pttk.bialowieza.pl.

◗ **Location:** 100km southeast of Białystok; the forest extends across Poland and Belarus.

🅿 **Parking:** Paid parking next to the tourist office, free next to the post office.

◉ **Don't Miss:** The road which the tsars followed to reach Białowieża.

👫 **Kids:** A tour of the Bison Reserve gives the best opportunity for seeing bison up close.

🕐 **Timing:** Allow one day to explore the areas of the Park open to visitors. Outside the Park, the Forest is freely accessible. Allow half a day to discover the Tsars' Trail.

GETTING AROUND

BY BUS – Frequent buses link Białystok, Bielsk Podlaski or Hajnówka to Białowieża.

PRACTICAL INFORMATION

Phone code – ℘085.

Postal code – 17-230.

PTTK Tourist Office – *Kolejowa 17. ℘681 22 95. www.pttk.bialowieza.pl. Open daily 8am–4pm, 6pm in summer.* Located in a small yellow house hidden on a square next to the Hotel Żubrówka. It is possible to book a guide, hire a horse-drawn cart or a bike.

Białowieża Forest Park – *Park Pałacowy 11. ℘681 20 33. http:ll.bpn.com.pl.*

Guides' Office – *Park Pałacowy 5. ℘681 23 06.*

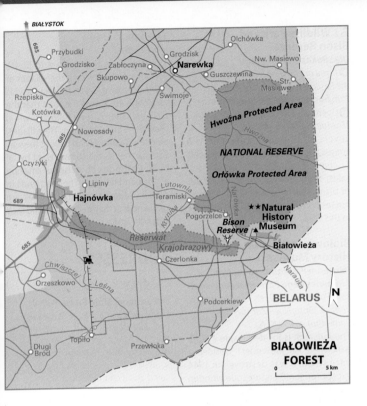

Przybudki
Grodzisko
Zabłoczyna
Skupowo
Rzepiska
Kotówka
Nowosady
Czyżyki
Lipiny
Hajnówka
Teramiski
Reserwat
Krajobrazowy
Chwiszczej
Orzeszkowo
Leśna
Długi Bród
Topiło
Przewłoka
Olchówka
Narewka
Grodzisk
Nw. Masiewo
Guszczewina
Str. Masiewo
Swimoje
Hwoźna Protected Area
Hwoźna
NATIONAL RESERVE
Orłówka Protected Area
Lutownia
Krynica
Pogorzelce
★★**Natural History Museum**
Bison Reserve
Czerlonka
Podcerkiew
Białowieża
Narew
Narewka
Narauka

BELARUS **N**

BIAŁOWIEŻA FOREST

0   5 km

BIAŁOWIEŻA FOREST PARK★★

All the tours start from the village of Białowieża, where information is available (&see Białowieża Forest Addresses on p162).

Orłówka Protected Area

Strictly protected.
Entry into this zone is through the Palace Park situated in the centre of Białowieża. The way into the park is via a road on the left of the red-brick Orthodox church.
One must be accompanied by an official guide.

The Orłówka protected area is described as a primeval forest because it has never been exploited by man. Bordered by the River Hwoźna in the north, the River Narewka in the west and Belarus in the east, this is the most strictly protected area of the Park. Unfortunately, visitors are barred from the major part of the 4,750ha.

The 7km itinerary, an easy walk of three hours across flat but often marshy terrain, offers an insight into the natural resources of the forest: 450-year-old oak trees soaring up to 40m, marshy areas covered with sturdy or uprooted spruce, pines once used as beehives by beekeepers who disregarded the ban on entering the area imposed by the tsar.

Hwoźna Protected Area

This area, located west of the River Narewka and north of the Hwoźna, covers over 50,000ha. As a result of past and present intrusion by man this is not truly a primeval forest but it is nevertheless a magnificent area for walking. Entry is via the village of **Narewka**.
It is criss-crossed by many marked tracks for hiking or cycling and for cross-country skiing in winter. This is allowed only in accordance with strict environmental protection guidelines.

♟♟ Wildlife Park and Bison Reserve
(Rez Pokazowy Zwierząt)

▶ *If you are arriving from Hajnówka, the Reserve is on the left of the road, 2km from the entrance to Białowieża.*

🕐 *Open Apr–Oct daily 9am–5pm; Nov–Mar Tue–Sun 8am–4pm.* 💿 *6 PLN/3PLN.*

Lovers of unspoilt nature and wild spaces might be disappointed, but this reserve undoubtedly offers the best and safest opportunity for getting a glimpse of bison, wolves or deer. Small Polish horses known as Tarpan Type also live in this area.

Białowieża Park Natural History Museum★★
(Muzeum Przyrodniczo Leśnym Białowieskiego Parku Narodowego)

Park Pałacowy. 🕐 *Open Apr–Oct daily 9am–4.30pm; Nov–Mar Tue–Sun 9am–4pm.* 💿 *12PLN.* ♿.

The museum is located inside a 50ha park where Tsar Alexander II's residence once stood. It was destroyed in 1944 except for some picturesque wooden pavilions and farm buildings now used by the Park's employees. The museum is a vast complex surmounted by a tower from the top of which is a panoramic view of the forest. Visitors gain a better understanding of the native animals found here through taxidermy exhibits and film screenings. The museum and exhibits also helps visitors to appreciate the work of scientists protecting the Park's delicate natural habitats.

EXCURSIONS
Narrow Gauge Tourist Train

(Jun–Sept) Tue, Thu, Sat at 10am. 📞 *(85) 682 26 89.* 💿 *20 PLN.*

A railway line links Hajnówka and the forest village of Topiło. The station is situated on the way out of Hajnówka, along the road to Białowieża, opposite the cemetery. Follow the signposts: "Kolejki Leśne w Puszczy Białowieskiej". This tourist train offers a different way of approaching the forest. There are scheduled stops along the way (11km) to enable you to discover the beauty of the forest up close.

The Tsars' Trail★
(about 30km)

The trail links Hajnówka and Bielsk Podlaski, going through the villages of Nowe Berezowo, Czyże, Łoknika, Pasynki and Widowo. This is the road that the tsars and their guests followed when they went bison hunting. The villages, whose inhabitants had to light the way with torches as the convoy went by, all boast **Orthodox churches** of amazing shapes and colours. The road ends in Bielsk Podlaski where churches are renowned for their decorations and their splendid icons.

ADDRESSES

🛏 STAY

🍽 **Pensjonat Sioło Budy**– *Budy 41 in Białowieża.* 📞*681 29 78. www.siolo budy.pl. 10 rooms.* Ideal for experiencing the local forests and folk culture in relative comfort. The hamlet of Budy is something between a *Skansen*, a scouts' camp and a country house.

🍽🍽🍽 **Best Western Hotel Żubrówka**– *Ul. Olgi Gabiec 6 in Białowieża.* 📞*681 23 03. www.hotel-zubrowka.pl.* 112 rooms. A luxurious option now managed by Best Western that features health spa, saunas, swimming pool. Top end rooms have jacuzzi and fireplaces.

🍴 EAT

🍽🍽🍽 **Restauracja Carska** – *Ul. Stacja Towarowa 4.* 📞*681 21 19. www.restauracjacarska.pl.*
The decoration and the cuisine are refined.Try the sturgeon or the game. French red wines are well represented.

Białystok★

Białystok is the capital of Podlasie and the largest city in NE Poland. Jews once made up the majority of the population and worshiped at the largest wooden synagogue in Poland. Today, ethnic diversity can still be seen among the city's sacred architecture at this crossroads of Catholicism and Orthodoxy, where Muslim descendants of Tatar horsemen settled centuries ago.

A BIT OF HISTORY
Birthplace of Esperanto
For centuries, Białystok has been a mosaic of cultures, religions and languages. In the 19C, the town had a population of 30 000 including 3 000 Poles, 18 000 Jews, 5 000 Germans and 4 000 Russians. These divisions were also present in the social and professional structures: although Russian was the official language, "intellectuals" spoke Polish, workers German, shopkeepers Hebrew and farmers White Russian, spoken today throughout Belarus. Communities and districts lived side by side without any real unity. Faced with this situation the young Jewish university student and idealist **Ludwik Zamenhof** undertook to create a common language. Born in Białystok in 1859, with a degree in ophthalmology from the University of Moscow, he invented Esperanto as a means to solve conflicts arising from language and communication barriers. Zamenhof went on to translate Shakespeare, Gogol and the Bible into his artificial language. He died in Warsaw in 1917. Today, some

> ▸ **Population:** 291,660.
> ⚅ **Michelin Map:**
> Map of Poland D2 – Województwo of Podlasie.
> 🄸 **Info:** Ul. Malmeda 6. ☏(85) 732 68 31. www.bialystok.pl.
> ◗ **Location:** 195km northeast of Warsaw, on the doorstep of Belarus. Lipowa Street runs through the centre of Białystok.
> 🄿 **Parking:** Plentiful paid parking in city centre, free in centre on weekends.
> ◈ **Don't Miss:** A walk throught the gardens of one Poland's best preserved Baroque residences, the Branicki Palace.
> ◕ **Timing:** Allow half a day to visit Białystok, and half a day to follow the Tatar Trail in the vicinity of the town.

150 universities throughout the world teach Esperanto.

SIGHTS
Cathedral of the Assumption★
The cathedral's 72.5m-high flamboyant towers loom above the western end of Lipowa Street. The neo-Gothic red-brick edifice, erected between 1900 and 1905 was designed as an annexe of the neighbouring Baroque church from 1627 to get around a Russian ban on constructing a "new" church.

GETTING AROUND
BY RAIL – Railway station – *Ul. Kolejowa 9.* Nine trains a day to Warsaw *(journey time: 2.5hr)*. Also, regular services to Kraków, Gdynia, Gliwice or Poznań.
BY BUS – Bus station – *Ul. Bohaterów Monte Cassino. 10.* Many buses leave Białystok bound for various destinations including Warsaw,

Wrocław, Gdańsk and Rzeszów. There are also buses bound for Belarus, Lithuania and W. Europe.

PRACTICAL INFORMATION
Phone code – ☏*085.*
Postal code – *15-000.*
Tourist Office – *Ul. Malmeda 6.* ☏*732 68 31. www.podlaskieit.pl. Open Mon–Fri 8am–5pm.*

Branicki Palace★

On the other side of Lipowa Street.

The original palace was destroyed during World War II and the building we see today has been entirely rebuilt. It is named after the family who gave this "Versailles of the North" its definitive appearance and style over the span of several generations. Completed during the 18C, the palace was a thriving centre of art and science which brought fame to Białystok. The kings of Poland and later the Austrian Emperor Josef II frequently stayed there. Today, it houses the Academy of Medicine, though it is possible to enter the place and admire a few rooms and the chapel (open Mon –Fri 3.30pm–5.30pm, Sat–Sun 9am–5pm). A vast park, alternating between the French and the English styles, leads to the **Planty** on the site of the old ramparts.

▶ *Follow Lipowa Street eastwards to the former Town Hall.*

Orthodox Church of "St Nicholas the Miracle Worker"★ *(Kościół Sw Mikołaja)*

Erected in 1843, this large domed church in Russian Neoclassical style is a reminder of the large Orthodox community in Białystok.

IN THE FOOTSTEPS OF MUSLIM TATARS★★

The first Tatars settled in Lithuanian and Polish territories at the beginning of the 15C. Having fought against Christian armies, some of them sought refuge in Lithuania. In 1679, Polish King Jan III Sobieski, who could no longer pay them, offered them land in Podlasie. Their descendants still live in Kruszyniany and Bohoniki, two tiny villages nestled among mosques and cemeteries. Before 1939, there were ten such villages. The mosques were subsequently burned down by the Nazis or the communists and the population expelled.

Sokółka

▶ *40km northeast of Białystok on road 19.*

The **Sokółka Regional Museum** (Muzeum Ziemi Sokólskiej; Ul. Grodzieńska; open Tue–Fri 8am– 4pm, Sat 9am–3pm; 4 PLN; ℘(85) 711 24 35). Although modest, offers additional background information on the origin of the Tatars in Podlasie.

Bohoniki

▶ *From Sokółka, follow road 674 towards Krynki for about 3km.*

The mosque built in 1900 was entirely restored in 2005. The cemetery is located on the way out of the village, on the left at the end of a tree-lined alleyway.

Kruszyniany

▶ *Drive to Krynki and continue south for about 10km.*

The wooden mosque erected at the end of the 19C is Poland's oldest. The cemetery, situated in the grove behind the mosque contains late 17C graves.

ADDRESSES

🏠 STAY

➁ **Villa Tradycja**– Ul. Włókiennicza 5. ℘652 65 20. www.villatradycja.pl. This hotel joins elegance, modernity and friendly atmosphere ensuring a relaxing stay.

➁➁➁ **Branicki Hotel** – Ul. Zamenhofa 25. ℘665 25 00. www.hotelbranicki.com. *32 rooms.* Charming high-class hotel *(sauna, cigar club, night-club and private car park)* located in a quiet street close to the centre.

🍴 EAT

➁ **Tatarska Jurta** – Kruszyniany 58. ℘749 4052. www.krusziany.pl. Dżenneta Bogdanowicz welcomes you into her own home, opposite the mosque. Simple and copious Tatar meals based on meat pies and soups are on the menu, along with the possibility of local sightseeing with a Tatar guide.

➁➁ **Chamelot** – Ul. Młynowa 24. ℘652 00 99. Open noon–10pm. International cuisine in this spacious, atmospheric restaurant with brick and timber interiors and a relaxing outdoor patio.

Biebrza National Park
Biebrzański Park Narodowy

The River Biebrza winds its way through myriad marshlands, often covered in the morning with cool mists. Elk and beaver flourish in the peaty bogs, while birds descend here in flocks during all seasons. The park is a birdwatchers' paradise and great for paddling in kayaks and canoes.

A BIT OF GEOGRAPHY
Largest Marshland Area in Central Europe

This "Polish Amazon", is one of the last living marshes in Europe. The **Biebrza National Park** was founded in 1994 and covers an area of 592sq km, which makes it the largest in Poland. Viewed from above, the park resembles an hourglass, and extends across the whole river basin after which it is named.

The Park can be divided into three zones: the first, in the north, is the least visited and hence the most serene. The second, covering the middle course of the river, essentially consists of humid forests of alders and several marshes including the **Red Marsh** (Czerwone Bagno). It is here that most of the elk population live. Reintroduced during the 1950s, elk have since then proliferated and now number around 500. The southern part of the basin consists mainly of marshes and quagmire. Birdwatchers will be in heaven as they can observe as many as 270 different species including great snipes, now rare, and numerous sedge warblers.

VISIT

In order to gain access to the Park, one must first go to the central information office, situated in the heart of the reserve, on the river bank facing the village of **Goniądz**, the starting point of our itineraries.

Open daily Oct–Apr 8am–3pm; May–Sept 8am–7pm. The Park itself is open from dawn till dusk. Brochures and maps are available here and you will be able to reserve the services of a guide

- **Michelin Map:** Map of Poland C2 – Województwo of Podlasie.
- **Info:** Biebrzański Park Narodowy, Osowiec-Twierdza 8, 19-110 Goniądz. (85) 738 30 35. www.biebrza.org.pl.
- **Location:** 60km northwest of Białystok, between Łomża and Augustów.
- **Kids:** A peaceful canoe trip down the River Biebrza.
- **Timing:** Allow two days for the park and half a day in Tykocin.

PRACTICAL INFORMATION
BIEBRZA - GONIĄDZ
Phone code – 085.
Postal code – 19-110.
National Park – Osowiec-Twierdza 8. 738 30 35. www.biebrza.org.pl.
TYKOCIN
Phone code – 085.
Postal code – 16-080.
Tourist Office – Ul. Złota 2. 718 16 27. www.tykocin.doc.pl. Open Mon–Fri 7.30am–3.30pm.

River Biebrza

© Polish National Tourist Office

or hire a canoe (5 PLN/hr, 30 PLN/day) or a kayak (4 PLN/hr, 20 PLN/day). Inside the Park, there are 500km of footpaths, three cycle tracks and 135km of waterways. ◉Admission charges to the Park: adults 5 PLN/day, children over 7, 2.5 PLN/day. There is a separate admission charge to itineraries within the Red Marsh (same as the Park). ◉Bear in mind that going through marshland in springtime can be tricky.

🏃 The North on Foot

Starting from Grzędy. As the crow flies, Grzędy lies 10km north of Goniądz. By road, it is best to skirt around the west side of the Park and to follow the road between Grajewo and Rajgród. The 18km hike takes about 8hr on foot. Follow the red markings. The track runs deep into forests of conifers and several hundred-year-old oaks. Rare, hot-climate plants grow on the Grzędy sand dunes. Elsewhere there are vast expanses of reeds. At the halfway point, there is an amazing view from the Wilcza Góra viewing tower overlooking the marshes.

🏃 The South on Foot

Starting from Gugny. This 10km hike (follow the red markings) takes four hours including a stop at each of the two viewing towers. The first tower is said to be ideal for watching elk and deer at sunset if you are lucky.

👫 Canoeing North to South

There are many options for canoeing down the Biebrza and its marshes at leisure. From north to south, villages with accommodation hiring facilities are Lipsk, Sztabin, Dolistowo, Goniądz, Osowiec and Brzostowo. Itineraries vary from 8 to 25km. Wizna is the southernmost village. Hiring a canoe in these villages is only possible after having acquired a boating permit from the Park authorities in Lipsk, Sztabin or Osowiec-Twierdza. Besides communing with nature, it's also possible to visit a late 19C Russian fortress at Osowiec known as the Russian Verdun because of the half-year battle there during World War I.

EXCURSIONS
Tykocin

▶ 30km southeast of the Biebrza Park, slightly north of the road linking Łomża and Białystok.

Tykocin is a sleepy Baroque village lying along the River Narew. The **Church of the Holy Trinity**, built between 1741 and 1750 by Jan Klemens Branicki, is fronted by a curved arcade topped by symetrical towers. Its renowned original organ is used for a series of special concerts.

Tykocin Regional Museum (Muzeum w Tykocinie)

Ul. Kozia 2. ◉Open Tue–Sun 10am–5pm. ◉10 PLN.

The most moving building in Tykocin is undoubtedly the former synagogue. Now a museum, this Baroque temple is one of the best preserved in Poland and showcases liturgical objects, a carved Torah ark and walls covered with painted fragments of Hebrew prayers.

ADDRESSES

🛏 STAY / 🍽 EAT

BIEBRZA - GONIĄDZ

◉◉ **Bartłowizna** – Ul. Nadbiebrzańska 32. ☎738 06 30. www.biebrza.com.pl. 36 rooms. This recent hotel complex offers a great variety of accommodation as well as the facilities of a traditional inn. All necessary information about hikes, canoe and guide hire are also provided. Regional food and home-smoked meats.

TYKOCIN

◉◉◉ **Dworek nad Łąkami** – Kiermusy 12. ☎718 74 44. www.kiermusy.com.pl. 13 rooms. ☞. Restaurant◉◉. Located in a delightful setting in the heart of the forest, this establishment is a blend of elegant hunting lodge, antiques gallery and 17C farmhouse. The retro look of the rooms is underlined by the absence of a telephone or a TV set. Here, everything is done to inspire nostalgia and to offer peace and quiet as well as top-quality service.

Suwałki

The Suwałki lakeland is one of the least known and explored areas in Poland, tucked away at the top of the Podlasie region in the northeast corner of the country. The wild, unspoilt, wooded landscape, is dotted with lakes, and is subject to severe winters reminiscent of the Arctic regions. The influence of nearby Russia, Lithuania and Belarus can sometimes be detected in the customs, cuisine and atmosphere of this northern area.

A BIT OF HISTORY

The glacial period which, at these latitudes, ended later, left a landscape marked by deep valleys and depressions today filled in by some 100 lakes among the deepest in Poland. Populated by Prussian and Lithuanian tribes in the past, the Suwałki region was often contested, occupied and subdued. In 1795, the third partition of Poland ceded it to Prussia. In 1807, Napoleon made it part of the duchy of Warsaw and it was returned to the kingdom of Poland 8 years later. Founded in the 17C by Camaldolese monks from Wigry Monastery, Suwałki reached its heyday in the 19C. Its location at the centre of a vast region of lakes makes it a perfect base for hikes around the magnificent landscapes.

- **Population:** 42,927.
- **Michelin Map:** Map of Poland D1 – Województwo of Podlasie.
- **Info:** PTTK-Suwałki, 16-400 Suwałki, Ul. T. Kościuszki 37. ℰ(87) 566 59 61. www.suwalki.pttk.pl
- **Location:** Suwałki is 280km northeast of Warsaw.
- **Parking:** Free parking is plentiful.
- **Don't Miss**: Hikes through nature parks, between lakes and forests.
- **Timing:** Because the region is so remote, it's advisable to devote at least two days to it. Bearing in mind that towns have little of interest to offer, staying in the scenic countryside is more pleasurable.

VISIT

Nestled inside a meander of the Czarna Hańcza River, which flows down from the Suwałki Landscape Park, the city gathers round the long main northsouth avenue.

The **small regional museum** (Muzeum Okręgowe w Suwałkach; *Ul. T. Kościuszki 81; open Tue–Fri 8am–4pm, Sat–Sun 9am–5pm; 5 PLN*) is interesting for

GETTING AROUND

BY RAIL – Railway station –
Suwałki: *Ul. Kolejowa 22.*
Augustów: *Ul. Kolejowa 1.*
BY BUS – Bus station –
Suwałki: *Ul. Utrata 1b.*
Augustów: *Rynek Zygmunta 18.*

PRACTICAL INFORMATION

Phone code – *℘087.*
Postal code – *16 400.*
Augustów Tourist Office – *Rynek Zygmunta Augusta 44. ℘643 28 83. www.suwalszczyzna.pl. Open May–Aug*

Mon–Fri 8am–5pm, Sat–Sun 10am–3pm; Sept–Apr Mon–Fri 8am–3pm. This office has the widest choice of information in the region. Free internet access.
Wigry National Park Information Centre – *Krzywe 82. ℘563 25 62. www.wigry.win.pl. Open Jul–Aug Mon–Fri, 7am–5pm, Sat–Sun 9am–2pm; Sept–Jun Mon–Fri 7am–3pm.* Wide choice of information, some in English, about hikes, activities, bike and boat hire points. Guides are available from dawn till dusk by prior arrangement.

its brief presentation of the Yotving-ians (also known as Suduvians), an extinct Baltic people, who left several necropolises in the area. Explanations are in Polish.

At the town's eastern end, along Bakałarzewska Street, several **cemeteries** testify to the various cultures that converged here over the centuries. The tiny Muslim area has no gravestones. The Jewish headstones that remained after the Germans ravaged the cemetery in 1942 form one central monument. The Orthodox area is dominated by the silhouette of a 19C wooden church.

EXCURSIONS
Wigry National Park★
(Wigierski Park Narodowy)
▶ *5km east of Suwałki.* ᴥ*3 PLN.*

The hilly terrain of this vast 15,000ha park was formed during the Ice Ages. Around 40 lakes, some of them no larger than a waterhole, are scattered among hills, peatbogs and forests. The nature reserve is named after the largest and most sinuous of these lakes, Lake Wigry. The Czarna Hańcza River flows through the park and then meanders southwards over a distance of 95km through the Augustów Forest, on its way to the Belarusian border; this is one of the finest courses for canoeing enthusiasts. Pines and firs grow on the shores of the lakes, together with oaks, alders and birches. It is a habitat of a rich fauna, including

beavers, the mascots of the Park. The reserve can be exmplored on foot or by bike along 130km of marked track.

The information centre located in the village of Krzywe, at the entrance to the Park, has a lot of informative literature in stock, some in English. The **Ethnographic Museum** housed in a former barn contains farming tools and machinery as well as objects of daily life. Next door, a small **Natural History Museum** introduces visitors to the diversity of the local flora and fauna, including the ubiquitous beaver.

Camaldolese Monastery★★
(Klasztor Kamedułów)

The monastery stands on a promontory which was once an island in Lake Wigry. In 1667, the land was ceded to the Camaldolese monks, an order close to the Benedictines, by the Polish king Jan Kazimierz. The monks soon built a Baroque church, a monastery and several small hermitages, not to mention outbuildings, from the smithy to the indispensable brewery. The influence of the monastery extended over a radius of 50km and the town of Suwałki was founded in the 17C. In 1800, the Camaldolese monks were expelled by the Prussians. The buildings suffered greatly during the two World Wars but were superbly restored and the place is once again serene. It is possible to stroll among the 15 houses once occupied

Camaldolese Monastery

by the monks. The isolated bell tower is a fine observatory, which provides a panoramic view of the region. Today the complex is a **hotel** charging very reasonable prices.

Boat trips on the lake.
Departure point at the foot of the monastery. Daily cruises May–Oct 10am–4pm. Trips last 1hr30min.

Suwałki Landscape Park★
(Suwalski Park Krajobrazowy)
⊙ *15km northwest of Suwałki.*
Founded in 1976, the Park covers 6,200 ha. It is one of the coldest spots in Poland. Formed by a glacier which retreated rather late, the deeply carved landscape looks most picturesque in winter under white snow cover. Over 100 lakes are scattered across the undulating Nordic-like terrain. Lake Hańcza, the deepest lake *(108m)*, in the Central European plain, is filled with water as clear as that of a mountain lake. The Cisowa Góra hill, the region's 256m-high symbolic summit, sometimes referred to as "Suwałki's Fujiyama", towers above the eastern shore of the lake.

The Park's Tourist Information Centre:
⊙ *7km west of Jeleniewo, in a place called Turtul.* 🕿 *569 18 01. www.spk. org.pl.* ⊙*Open Jul–Aug 8am–7pm, Sat 9am–5pm, winter Mon–Fri 8am–3pm, bike hire ⊗5PLN/hr).*

Augustów
(Population 29,713)
⊙ *33km south of Suwałki along road no. 8.*
Built on the edge of the forest by lakes Necko, Białe and Sajno, the town was founded in the 16C by King Sigismund August and named after him. The road linking Warsaw and St Petersburg and above all, the canal dug between 1824 and 1839, brought prosperity to the town in the 19C. During the 1920s and 1930s, it was a holiday resort sought after by the élite. During World War II the surrounding forests were used as a base for Polish partisans. Today it is a unattractive spa town and a base for watersports and sailing the famous local canal.

The Augustów Canal

What was Poland's largest investment in the 19C links the Wisła and Niemen basins to enable trading with the Baltic to take place. Spread along 110km (80 in Poland) are 18 locks (14 in Poland) negotiating a 50m difference in level. The canal crosses many lakes (Necko, Rospuda, Biale, Studziennicze...). Cruises organised by the **Żegluga Augustowska Company** (🕿 *643 28 81, www. zeglugaaugustowska.pl*) between May and September link Augustów with the Przewięż lock and Lake Studziennicze, both situated 7km east of the town *(tours last from 1 to 3hr).*

ADDRESSES

STAY

⊜⊜⊜ **Jaczno** – *In Smolniki, inside the Suwałki Landscape Park. Jaczno 3, 16-404 Jeleniewo.* 🕿 *568 35 90. www.jaczno.pl. 10 rooms.* The rooms are located in small log cabins gathered on a peninsula on the western shore of Lake Jaczno. A delightful place, all the more charming when surrounded by snow in winter.

⊜⊜ **Dom Pracy Tworczej w Wigrach** – *16–412 Stary Folwark.* 🕿 *563 70 00. www.wigry.org.* The unique chance to stay in monks' quarters, with a patio garden in a former monastery.

EAT

⊜ **Albatros** – *Ul. Mostowa 3 Augustów.* 🕿 *643 21 23.* Classic Polish cuisine, with copious helpings served in 1970s décor.

⊜ **Polski** – *Ul. Kościuszki 59 Suwałki.* 🕿 *565 01 93.* Tiny tavern offering popular specialities. Regular customers are a reassuring guarantee of quality.

⊜ **Pod Jelonkiem** – *Ul. Sportowa 7.* 🕿 *568 30 21. www.podjelonkiem.pl.* Small restaurant in the village of Jeleniewo, 12km north of Suwałki, where one can enjoy delicious regional dishes based on potatoes.

Masurian Lakes★

Situated in northeast Poland, Masuria is a tranquil paradise in summer, perfect for sailing, water sports, hiking and bird watching. Nature brilliantly outshines the comparatively dull towns in the region. Fifteen per cent of the area is covered by water, with canals, lochs, thick forests and isolated islets colonised by swans, cormorants and cranes; lake cruising offers a fascinating birdwatching adventure. Winter here is harsh; snow covers the post-glacial landscape for long stretches, but the ice and snow can be explored on skis, sleighs, or ice boats. Popular with locals as well as tourists, the tourist services are excellent.

A BIT OF GEOGRAPHY
Land of a Thousand Lakes

From the largest to the smallest, there are in fact, 4,000 lakes! The weight and slow to-and-fro motion of the glaciers, which covered the region over 10,000 years ago, gave shape to the hilly landscape with its peatbogs and basins. The string of lakes extends along a north-south axis. Lakes Śniardwy (110sq km) and Mamry (102sq km), Poland's largest, are in the centre of a vast waterway system formed of rivers and canals, which can reach a total of 200km. There is the

- ⚙ **Michelin Map:** Map of Poland C1 – Województwo of Warmia-Masuria.
- **Info:** Ul. Wyzwolenia2. ☎(87)428 52 65. www. gizycko.turystyka.pl.
- ▶ **Location:** 240km north of Warsaw and 65km east of Olsztyn.
- **Don't Miss:** Canoe trips down the rivers.
- **Kids** The organised lake cruises will delight them.
- 🕐 **Timing:** Allow three days.

dense pine Forest of Pisz (86,000ha) where one can encounter wolves, bisons and lynx. Some islets, such as those in Lakes Mamry and Dobsko, and remote lakes, like Lake Łukajno near Mikołajki, are real nature reserves. Swans, cormorants, herons, ducks and black-headed gulls live in total freedom, far from the threats of civilisation.

Border Region

Masuria's history was the logical consequence of its strategic position. The region was as much a melting pot of cultures: German, Russian and Lithuanian, as of religions: Catholic, Protestant and Orthodox. Prussian tribes from the Baltic were Christianised here, sometimes brutally, by the Teutonic Knights at the end of the 13C. Poles and Germans occupied the first towns and then after World

Masurian lake

GETTING AROUND

BY RAIL/BUS – Train timetables are available on the following website: www.rozklad.pkp.pl (in English). For bus timetables, visit www.pks.mragowo.pl.
Giżycko: Railway station – Pl. Dworcowy. Giżycko is situated on the line linking Olsztyn and Kętrzyn to Białystok, the region's busiest station. Bus station – next to train station.
Węgorzewo: Bus station – Ul. Armii Krajowej.
Mikołajkl: Railway station – Ul. Kolejowa. Bus station – Not a real bus station, just a simple bus stop Pl. Kościelny 1.
BY BOAT – The regular services provided by the **Masurian Sailing Company (Żegluga Mazurska)** (see Where to go, right) are a pleasant, if slower alternative to land transport.

PRACTICAL INFORMATION

Phone – ☎087. **Postal code** – 11500.
Giżycko Tourist Office – Ul. Wyzwolenia 2. ☎428 52 65. www.gizycko.turystyka.pl. Efficient, well-informed office.
Mikołajki Tourist Office – Plac Wolności 3. ☎421 68 50. www.mikolajki.pl. On the square, opposite the fountain with the fish.
Węgorzewo Tourist Office – Pl. Wolności 11. ☎427 40 09. www.wegorzewo.pl.

Navigation office – In Giżycko. ☎428 56 51. To be contacted in the event of a sailing accident.
Emergency Unit – ☎601 100 100. Medical help for sailing accidents.
Emergency Regional Centre – ☎112 (from a mobile phone). Medical help and rescue.

WHERE TO GO

Lake cruises – Off season, any boat trip with fewer than ten passengers is cancelled.
Masurian Sailing Company (Żegluga Mazurska) – In Giżycko – Ul. Kolejowa 9. ☎428 25 78, Mikołajki Office – ☎421 61 02, Węgorzewo Office – ☎428 25 78. Departure from the ports of Mikołajki, Giżycko, Węgorzewo, Ruciane-Nida. Tickets are sold on board or at the counters. Average price for the journey: Giżycko – Mikołajki (3hr) 50 PLN; Giżycko – Węgorzewo (2hr 30min) 40 PLN; Mikołajki – Ruciane-Nida (2hr 30min) 40 PLN; 2hr cruises on Lake Śniardwy 25 PLN.

Other trips to discover a lake or a nature reserve are also organised from every port. In spring and autumn, only few trips take place.
Some small companies offer thematic itineraries based on birdwatching or fishing. Enquire at tourist offices.

War II, the region became entirely Polish. The inhabitants of German descent were replaced by Polish farmers from Ukraine, which by then had been joined to the Soviet Union.

Poland's Green Lung

Protected from intensive industrialisation and urbanisation, the Masurian Lakes region fully deserves its nickname of "green lung of Poland". It is also the favourite destination of Warsaw's residents, who rush in as soon as they have a day's holiday. It is difficult to find accommodation in summer. Autumn and spring are less popular but offer more subtle aspects of nature: its awakening from April to June and the fireworks of colour from September to November. The climate is less predictable then and the sailing season limited to the period from June to September. However, the beauty of nature will delight hikers, anglers and hunters.

GIŻYCKO
(Population 30,000)

Situated on the isthmus (narrow strip of land) separating Lakes Kisajno and Niegocin, Giżycko is one of Masuria's largest towns and the capital of water leisure activities in Poland. Thanks to

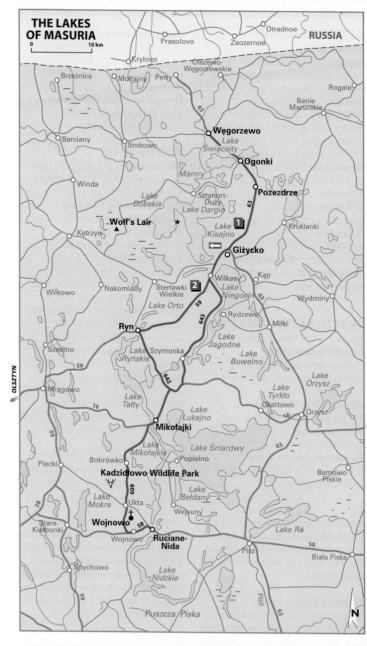

THE LAKES OF MASURIA

0   10 km

RUSSIA

Otradnoe
Prasolovo
Zaozernoe
Krylovo
Olszewo-Węgorzewskie
Brzeźnica
Mołtajny
Perty
Rogale
Banie Mazurskie
Barciany
Srokowo
Węgorzewo
Lake Święcajty
Winda
Ogonki
Mamry
Sztynort-Duzy
Pozezdrze
Lake Dobskie
Lake Dargim
63
Wolf's Lair
Kruklanki
Kętrzyn
Lake Kisajno
1
Giżycko
Wilkasy
Kąp
Wilkowo
Nakomiady
Sterławki Wielkie
2
Lake Niegobin
Wydminy
Lake Orto
59
643
Rydzewo
Miłki
Ryn
Szeszno
Lake Ryńskie
Szymonka
Lake Jagodne
Lake Buweino
Lake Orzysz
Mrągowo
59
16
642
Lake Tałty
Lake Łukajno
Lake Tyrkło
Okartowo
Orzysz
16
Mikołajki
Piecki
Bobrówko
Lake Mikołajkie
Popielno
Lake Śniardwy
63
Bemowo Piskie
Kadzidłowo Wildlife Park
Lake Bełdany
Lake Mokre
58
609
Ukta
Stare Kiełbonki
Wojnowo
Wejsuny
Lake Ró
Wojnowo
58
Ruciane-Nida
Spychowo
Pisz
Biała Piska
58
Lake Nidzkie
Piska
59
Puszcza Piska
63

OLSZTYN

N

its central location, it is the ideal starting point of a tour of the region, either to the north or the south. It gets very crowded in summer and visitors looking for peace and quiet will no doubt prefer to escape to the surrounding area.

Before being returned to Poland in 1946, the town was called Lötzen under the Prussian and German occupation. The **Gothic castle** (Zamek Pokrzyżacki), built by the Teutonic Knights in the 14C, has all but disappeared; all that remains is a wing remodelled in the 16C and 17C, and now allowed to fall into decay. It stands on the banks of the Łuczański canal, dug between 1756 and 1772 in order to link lakes Niegocin and Kisajno. It is spanned by a wooden **swing bridge** (Most Obrotowy), built between 1856 and 1860, and one of only two such specimens remaining in Europe.

Boyen Fortress
(Twierdza Boyen)
Ul. Turystyczna 1. ◐*Open daily 9am–dusk.* ◉*6 PLN.* ✆*428 83 93.* *www.boyen.gizycko.pl.*

Situated on the western edge of town, this huge star-shaped fortress was, for a whole century, the key to the lake region's defence. Intended to protect one of the rare isthmuses preceding the border with Russia, it was built between 1844 and 1848 at the instigation of the Prussian war minister, General Hermann von Boyen. Modernised at the end of the 19C, it played an essential role in the resistance put up against the Russian breakthrough in 1914 and became a military hospital between 1941 and 1944. It is now abandoned and overgrown apart from the moat, which has been turned into an open-air theatre and stages concerts and various performances.

A small **museum** (◐*open May–Sept*) is housed on the ground floor of one of the casemates. It illustrates the history of the fortress (fine scale model, which gives a good idea of the enormity of the structure) and contains souvenirs of World War II in Masuria as well as photographs of Giżycko in the past. The town's newest attraction is the red-brick 19C **Water Tower** (Wieża Ciśnień), recently opened for visitors *(viewing platform, museum)*. It boasts splendid views and a relaxing café to rejuvenate at after climbing the 129 steps (or taking the lift).

🚗 DRIVING TOURS

① NORTH OF GIŻYCKO
Several lakes lie north of Giżycko: Lakes Kisajno, Dargin and Dobskie, the latter

classified as a nature reserve. Next comes Lake Mamry. The surrounding area can be explored taking as a starting point the town of Węgorzewo, reached via road63.

Pozezdrze
First stop on the way to Węgorzewo, 12km from Giżycko. This village, dating from the 16C, was chosen by Heinrich Himmler, head of the SS, as his headquarters between 1940 and 1941. Half a dozen bunkers with over 2m thick concrete walls still remain. The best preserved is Himmler's private bunker, featuring double walls.

Węgorzewo
(Population 11,756)
▶ *20km south of Russia; 25km north of Giżycko.*

This small town on the shores of Lake Mamry once belonged to the Teutonic Knights, who left a massive and austere castle restored in 1980 *(private property)*. Wars and plagues decimated the town and it became a holiday resort during the 1920s. It was returned to Poland in 1946 when it was given its current name. The town has no monument of interest apart from a small museum combined with an **ethnographic park** (Muzeum Kultury Ludowej; *Ul. Portowa 1;* ◐*open Mon–Fri 8am–6pm, Sat–Sun 10am–3pm;* ◉*8 PLN)*. It displays a rustic kitchen from a bygone era and other objects of daily life, and comes to life during the workshops (pottery, weaving, lace-making and basket-making) organised by local craftsmen.

Węgorzewo is the ideal base for an excursion to the northeastern part of the lake region. Just 7km to the southeast, the large beach of the village of **Ogonki** overlooks Lake Święcajty, from where it is possible to reach the River Sapina by canoe.

② SOUTH OF GIŻYCKO
Two routes lead to Mikołajki. The first and undoubtedly the most pleasant skirts Lakes Niegocin and Jagodne (32km). Leave Giżycko along road 59 and as you exit the village of Wilkasy,

turn left onto road 643. The second route (40km) follows road 59 and then road 642, which makes a detour via **Ryn**, where you can see the **Gothic-style castle**, built in the 14C by the Teutonic Knights and then remodelled in the 19C, and the Dutch-style **windmill** standing on the edge of town.

Mikołajki
(Population 3,901)

Built on an isthmus separating Lakes Mikołajki and Tałty, this small resort with a population of 4,000 is one of the most pleasant in the whole lake region. It came into being in 1726 following the union of several villages on the site. Round the square, which boasts a fountain adorned with a crowned fish, a symbol of what the area owes to fishing, historic houses from the 18C and 19C recall this past. Invaded by pleasure-boat owners who bring life to bars and restaurants in the marina, the town sets its pace to the rhythm of its activities and concerts. One hour's walk leads to **Lake Łukajno**, east of the town, a nature reserve sheltering a colony of 1,000 mute swans.

Mikołajki

© Polish National Tourist Office

▷ *From Mikołajki, road 609 runs south towards Ruciane-Nida.*

Kadzidłowo Wildlife Park
(Park Dzikich Zwierząt w Kadzidłowie)

13km south of Mikołajki, a road turns right towards this 60ha park, home to deer, fallow deer, Tarpans (small Polish horses), as well as donkeys, goats, and even a bison. A kind of mini-zoo shelters specimens of all the animals living in the forest: beavers and lynx, as well as numerous birds, from storks to owls and waders. Nearby stands a **traditional house**★, splendidly restored in 2004 (Muzeum Chata Podcieniowa XIX; *www.kadzidlowo.pl*). Inside are the kitchen, living quarters with all the furniture and utensils, and a classroom which lacks only pupils and a teacher.

▷ *Rejoin road 609, continue south to the village of Ukta as far as a panel signalling the Orthodox monastery of Wojnowo on the right.*

Wojnowo Orthodox Monastery and Church
(Klasztor Staroobrzędowców w Wojnowie)

It is here that, in the 19C, Russian Orthodox monks known as the Old Believers, who rejected the 17C reform of Patriarch Nikon, sought refuge to practice their faith, opposing all changes and banning tobacco, vodka and tea. Settling on the shores of a lake, the members of the community organised their lives around a house of prayers and a church decorated with magnificent icons. A small wooded promontory shelters a tiny cemetery with many Orthodox crosses.

ADDRESSES

STAY

There are many hotels and B&Bs; tourist offices provide exhaustive lists. The closer to the lakes the accommodation is, the more expensive it is. Summer is the most expensive season, up to 50% more, and many establishments are closed from November to April.

GIŻYCKO

Europa Hotel – *Al. Wojska Polskiego 37. ✆429 30 01. www.hotel europa-gizycko.pl.* Perfect comfort awaits you in this simple, restful hotel, with rooms with a warm atmosphere. Ask for a lake view room.

Helena Hotel – *Al. Wojska Polskiego 58. ☎429 22 09. www.turysta. net.pl/hotele/helena. 50 rooms.* Large family hotel named after its owner. The rooms are small but attractive and the place is welcoming.

Zamek Hotel – *Ul. Moniuszki 1. ☎428 24 19. www.cmazur.pl. 12 rooms.* On the edge of a park, close to the canal and the ruins of the castle, this strange motel boasts a private garage under each of the rooms. The décor is dated but the place is pleasant and there are a few pitches for tents.

MIKOŁAJKI
Mazur Hotel – *Plac. Wolności 6. ☎421 69 41. www.hotelmazur.republika. com.pl. 30 rooms. Closed Oct–Apr.* A must in Mikołajki. This restored 19C residence with vast bedrooms is generally quiet except when the street livens up on summer nights. Choose a room overlooking the courtyard!

Amax Hotel – *Al. Spacerowa 7. ☎421 90 00. www.hotel-amax.pl – 16 rooms. Closed Dec–Apr.* On the other side of the lake, facing the lights of Mikołajki, this hotel probably offers more peace and quiet than any other. It may lack character but it fulfils its role of luxury establishment to perfection. Sauna and jacuzzi, swimming pool, beauty and fitness centre.

WĘGORZEWO
Nautic Hotel – *Ul. Słowackiego 14. ☎427 20 80. www.nautic.pl. 12 rooms.* Nice little hotel in the town centre, on the banks of the canal flowing into Lake Mamry. The rooms are small but neat and the hospitality warm. A fine terrace overlooks the canal, where one can have a meal or enjoy an ice cream.

Oberża pod Psem – *Kadzidłowo 1, 10km south of Mikołajki. ☎425 74 74. Restaurant.* Danuta and Krzysztof Worobiec's B&B consists of 5 rooms in two traditional houses. The coal-burning stove adds its contribution to the background heating, but you will not be sorry to have spent a night in an authentic Polish family home.

Vena Romantik Hotel – *20km west of Węgorzewo, at a place called Karłowo, north of the municipality of Srokowo. ☎427 62 44. www.venaromantik.com.*

25 rooms. Located on the heights overlooking Lake Rydzówka, which stretches eastwards, this hotel is a real paradise in the heart of nature, surrounded by pastureland. Wooden cottages with refined pastoral décor.

⏱/ EAT
GIŻYCKO
Karczma Pod Złotą Rybką – *Ul. Olsztyńska 15. ☎428 55 10.* This small unassuming restaurant specialises in fish from the lakes. Indulge in anything fishy you fancy from the menu: fish soup, fish by the weight, fried or served with a sauce, or a large dish of five different fish from the lakes including pike, perch and eel.

MIKOŁAJKI
Tawerna Pod Złamanym Pagajem – *Ul. Kowalska 3. ☎421 51 65.* In the marina. Even if the place is more of a snack bar than a restaurant, it has the atmosphere of a sailors' tavern. Specialities include *pierogi*, *kotlet schabowy* (breaded pork cutlet) and *bigos* (traditional stew).

Spiżarnia – *Pl. Handlowy 14. ☎(87) 421 52 18.* Great selection of fish dishes and more at this colourful place filled with shelves and cabinets containing jars of homemade indgredients that will end up on your plate.

WĘGORZEWO
Karczma – *Ul. Zamkowa 10. ☎427 32 23.* A small inn along the main road. Wooded surroundings and small terrace unfortunately overlooking the road and the traffic. However, the cuisine is good and the service attentive. This is the most commendable restaurant in town. Halina, the owner, offers sound advice for choosing a dish.

🛒 SHOPPING
Panels *(marked "Miód")* on the roadside signal the possibility of buying honey directly from the bee-keeper. Between Mikołajki and Ruciane-Nida, go up to Kadzidłowo *(see p174)*.

🏃 SPORTS AND RECREATION
SAILING
This is the best way to discover the lakes. In Giżycko, Węgorzewo, Sztynort, Mikołajki and Ruciane-Nida there are

boat-hire companies and marinas able to provide supplies and services. There are many hiring companies; the most important ones offer the best guarantees. The highest prices *(between 300 and 500 PLN per day)* are applied in July and during the first fortnight in August, as well as during bank holiday weekends. The lowest prices *(around 200 PLN per day)* are applied in May and September. *Allow around 500 PLN for the deposit and at least 100 PLN per day for the skipper.*

⚠**Beware:** insurance does not cover theft of an engine.

Allow 5 to 12 PLN for a night in a port and, in addition, 2 to 4 PLN per crew member.
Mooring: One can moor on the lakes for a night, but tying the boat to a tree is forbidden.

SAILING IN GIŻYCKO
Mazur Wind – *Ul. Klonowa 19 – in Wilkasy.* ☎428 01 72. *www.mazurwind.pl.* In a village south of Giżycko, on Lake Niegocin. With ten years' practice, the owner certainly knows his business and his boats are well looked after. Trips with or without skipper.

Marina Bełbot – *Ul. Smętka 20A in Wilkasy* – ☎428 03 85 – *www.marina. com.pl. Boat hire late Apr–late Sept.* On the shores of Lake Tajty. Appreciated within the profession, the company offers a wide choice of boats.

Almatur – *Ul. Moniuszki 24* – ☎428 59 71. *www.sail-almatur.pl.* Boat hire from late Apr to the first fortnight in Oct. On the shores of Lake Kisajno. At the western exit of Giżycko,turn right opposite the stadium. Also organise excursions for the disabled.

SAILING IN WĘGORZEWO
Port Keja – *Ul. Braci Ejsmontów 2.* ☎427 18 43. *www.keja.com.pl.* In Węgorzewo harbour. Several sizes of boat accommodating 4 to 8 persons. *Allow 140 to 450 PLN per day in high season, depending on the model chosen.*

CANOEING
Canoeing is an ideal means to explore rivers and small lakes, but it is not recommended to venture out to the middle of the lakes whose waters can be turbulent. There are many itineraries to choose from; enquire from the hiring company and tourist offices. Like pleasure-boats, canoes must carefully avoid the numerous bird sanctuaries. It is important to obtain all the necessary information. *Hiring a canoe costs between 25 and 50 PLN/ day.*

A few canoeing routes – The most famous follows the **River Krutynia** over a distance of 103km, from Ruciane-Nida to Sorkwity. It goes through Piska Forest in a northwest direction.

Starting from Gyżycko, another two-day course links **Lakes Niegocin and Śniardwy** via Lakes Tyrklo and Buwelno. It goes through a narrow valley, gouged out by glaciers and now flanked by wooded hills; one must organise the transport of the canoes over the 9km wide land strip separating the last two lakes. Starting from Węgorzewo, it takes 10hr to canoe down the **River Sapina** which leads to the village of Kruklanki, northwest of Giżycko.

BIKING
Eight marked itineraries, from 36 to 67km, criss-cross the region of Giżycko. The tourist office in Giżycko provides a brochure with detailed information about each one and signals bike-hire centres (including some hotels). *Allow 15 to 20 PLN/day.*

A 50km **loop circles Lake Mamry**, starting from Węgorzewo, and an 80km itinerary runs round Lake Śniardwy, starting from Mikołajki, via Lake Łukajno.

HIKING
All tourist offices provide a detailed map of the itineraries available.

In the Ruciane-Nida region, do not miss **Pisz Forest** (Puszcza Piska) covering an area of at least 86 000ha. Pines are the dominant species but there are also oaks and birches. It is possible to get a glimpse of some deer, roe deer, wild boars and tarpans, the small Polish breed of horses.

FISHING
In the clear water of the lakes in summer, through a hole in the ice in winter. Perch, tench and eel. *Permit: 15 PLN per day to 50 PLN per week.*

🎭FESTIVE EVENTS
International Folk Festival: In summer, there are **Festivals of Sea Shanties**. The most famous is mid-July's Giżycko Festival.

Kętrzyn

Kętrzyn is a pleasant historic town along the route to the Masurian Lakes region. Though less spectacular than other popular tourist areas, the town is a good base for visits to the diverse historic sites in the vicinity.

A BIT OF HISTORY
A base for Christianisation

In 1329, the Teutonic Knights erected a fortress on the banks of the River Guber, on the site of a Prussian village, Rast. The town, which became Rastenburg, was taken several times and fell again under the control of the order who founded St George's Church (Kościół Św. Jerzego), a massive, fortified edifice.

Walls soon surrounded the town, but that did not prevent it from being seized by the Prussians in 1454 and by the Russians in 1758. The closeness of Hitler's General Headquarters made it a choice target during World War II, at the end of which the town was handed back to Poland and given its current name.

CASTLE AND MUSEUM

Pl. Zamkowy 1. Open Mon 9am–3pm, *Tue–Sun 9am–4pm.* 6 PLN. *752 32 82.*

This fine building dating from the late 14C is the town's top attraction. Built on a square plan around a bailey, its typical red-brick structure features an attractive entrance gate and conical tower. Taken again and again, it was remodelled in the 18C and almost totally destroyed in 1945. The restoration work did not spoil its Gothic appearance, but do not expect to find any original historic interiors: you are more likely to think you've entered an administrative building from the communist period.

A **museum** illustrates the history of the town with a collection of postcards and municipal archives, in addition to sponsoring temporary exhibits and medieval festivals. **St George's Basilica** is also worth a visit for its well-preserved Gothic diamond vaulting dating from 1515, ten years before the church was

- ▶ **Population:** 28,619.
- **Michelin Map:** Map of Poland C1 – Województwo of Warmia-Podlasie.
- **Info:** Ul. Mickiewicza 1. (89) 751 47 65. www.ketrzyn.com.pl.
- **Location:** 250km north of Warsaw and 92km northeast of Olsztyn.
- **Parking:** Free along the town's streets.
- **Don't Miss:** Wandering among the ruins of Hitler's forest bunker.
- **Timing:** The four sites can be visited in the space of two days.
- **Also See:** Święta Lipka Monastery, Hitler's Wolf's Lair.

GETTING AROUND

BY RAIL – Railway station – *Ul. Dworcowa 10.*
BY BUS – Bus station – *Ul. Dworcowa 1.*

PRACTICAL INFORMATION

Phone code – *089.*
Postal code – *11 400.*
Kętrzyn Tourist Office – *Ul. Mickiewicza 1. 751 47 65. Open May–Aug daily 9am–9pm, Sept–Apr Mon–Fri 7.30am–3pm.* Located in a room of the town hall. Some literature in English.
Reszel Tourist Office – *755 00 97. Open Mon–Fri 10am–5pm, Sat 10am–3pm.* Housed in the town hall on the Rynek.

handed over to the local Protestants, whose church it remained until 1946.

EXCURSIONS
Reszel★
(Population 5,224)
▶ *18km southwest of Kętrzyn.*

The Legend of the Holy Lime Tree

At the beginning of the 14C, a man condemned to death was rotting in the dungeons of Kętrzyn Castle. The Virgin Mary answered his prayers and his repentance by sending him a piece of wood and a knife, asking him to carve a statuette of her, which he did in the space of a few hours, and with such talent that the judges, convinced this was a miracle, released the prisoner. On his way to Reszel, the man placed his work in the branches of the first lime tree he saw in order to comply with his saviour's wishes. Miracles and cures followed promptly.

This charming little town, lying in the heart of hilly countryside, occupies a strategic site on the edge of a steep plateau overlooking the River Izera. Built in the 13C by the Teutonic Knights on the site of a Prussian settlement, it has retained its characteristic grid plan centred on a tiny square. In 1808, the last witch in Europe was burned at the stake here.

In the centre of the **Rynek** stands the Classical-style **town hall**, rebuilt in 1815. The town offers a pleasant stroll along its narrow paved streets, now and then revealing the remains of the medieval ramparts or an 18C timber-framed barn (*Spichrzowa Street*).

The monumental **Church of SS Peter and Paul** (Kościół śś. Piotra i Pawła) stands in the southern part of town. Built in the 14C, it is dominated by a 65m-high massive square tower. The interior is a blend of Empire and Rococo styles. Nearby, in a field overgrown with wild grass, stands the former elegant presbytery, now unfortunately left to fall into decay.

The **two old 14C bridges**, the Fishermen's Bridge (Most Rybacki) and the Low Bridge (Most Niski), span the ravine dug by the river, which offers fine walks along its banks.

The **Gothic castle** (*3 Podzamcze Street, in the eastern part of town*) is the emblem of Reszel, with its towers soaring up to the sky from a height overlooking the river. Built from 1350 onwards, it was one of the key elements of Prussia's defence system. In the 16C, it lost some of its military importance and became for a few years the hunting lodge of the bishops of Warmia based in Lidzbark Warmiński. In 1795, the Prussian authorities turned it into a prison. In 1822, the refectory and the bishops' living quarters were transformed into an evangelical church to which was added a strange tower looking as if it were built of concrete. Today it is a **Museum of Modern Art** (◷ *open Tue–Sun 9am–5pm, ⊜3 PLN*) which stages temporary exhibitions. The castle surrounds a central courtyard, the south and east wings now housing a hotel. From the top of the tall keep, cylindrical over a square base, the **panoramic view** of the region is splendid.

Attempt on Hitler's Life

The attempt was undertaken by a handful of plotters gathered round Count Claus von Stauffenberg, an officer who had served in France, Poland, Russia and North Africa. The plot aimed at killing Hitler in order to end a war that many believed lost and thus to preserve what remained of Germany. On 20 July 1944, von Stauffenberg took part in a meeting of the High Command. Well known, trusted by Hitler, he easily avoided being checked and succeeded in placing his bomb in the room where the officers were. Nevertheless, the operation failed, Hitler, miraculously protected by part of the strong wooden table, was only wounded. Unmasked, the conspirators were pitilessly hunted down and punished. Marshall Rommel, who knew of the plot, was forced to commit suicide.

Święta Lipka Baroque Monastery★

> *10km southeast of Kętrzyn, 5km southeast of Reszel. Ul. Podzamcze 3.* Open daily 8am–6pm. P 3 PLN.

Located in a dale framed by two lakes, the "Baroque Pearl of Northern Poland" owes its name of Holy Lime Tree to a fine legend. A chapel was built on the site of the famous lime tree, then razed by the Protestants. The **Baroque monastery** was built between 1687 and 1693 at the instigation of the Jesuits. Today it is famous for the concerts given on its monumental organ, dating from 1721 and featuring mechanical statues.

On its **west front**, a Virgin in Majesty in the hollow of a tree recalls the legend. The interior, decorated with gold, contains a reproduction of the sacred lime tree adorned with ex-votos. Bright blue pillars framing the dark walnut-and-lime altar rise up to the vaulting covered with frescoes and portraits of kings. The **cloister**, featuring the Stations of the Cross, forms a square enclosure round the church. The four corners are adorned with the domes of Baroque chapels decorated with trompe-l'oeil Biblical scenes.

The Wolf's Lair★
(Wilczy Szaniec)

> *In Gierłoż, 9km northwest of Kętrzyn.* Open from dawn to dusk. Parking (12 PLN) and admission charge (8 PLN).

Invisible from the road running through the woods, this real fortress once housed the Eastern Front High Command. Built between 1940 and 1942 by the Todt Organisation, the Wolfschanz covers 18ha dotted with 80 buildings including 50 bunkers. The walls of several of them, in particular, Hitler's personal bunker and that of the highest Nazi dignitaries, are 8m thick. This small town produced its own electricity and had its own airfield, railway line and even a cinema. The ensemble, surrounded by barbed wire and minefields, was camouflaged under a huge net of artificial vegetation which was changed according to the season. Elite troops and an anti-aircraft system defended it.

Today it is a vast area covered with ruins, over which nature is regaining control. Held by the iron bars reinforcing the concrete, the remains of the bunkers blown up by the fleeing Germans in January 1945 seem to have been frozen on the spot by the explosion.

At the beginning of the path running through the ruins, a plaque marks the site of the building where the assassination attempt against Hitler took place on 20 July 1944.

ADDRESSES

STAY

KĘTRZYN

Zajazd Pod Zamkiem u Szwagrów – *Ul. Struga 3A.* 752 31 17. *www.zajazd.ketrzyn.pl – 4 rooms.* Situated at the foot of the castle, this pleasant inn which also has a **restaurant**, offers rooms with four beds, located under the eaves, perfect for families.

RESZEL

Zamek w Reszlu – *Ul. Podzamcze 3.* (089) 755 01 09. *www.zamek-reszel.com. 21 rooms. Restaurant* . The best address in the whole region. For a reasonable price, you can spend the night in the magnificent Reszel castle in the highly romantic setting of one of the vast rooms with stone walls. In addition, the Polish **restaurant** is excellent.

EAT

RESZEL

Pod Warkoczem – *Ul. Rynek 18.* This small homey bar with a piano and fine view of the town square is a local favourite offering simple Polish standards and even some fast food. Try the blueberry crêpes or *placki kartoflane* (potato pancakes).

Restauracja Rycerska – *Ul. Rynek 7* (089) 755 00 16. Located on the lovely town square, this local establishment offers traditional Polish cuisine in a large banquet-style hall. In summer, outdoor seating on the square.

Lidzbark Warmiński★

Lidzbark Warmiński was once a flourishing cultural centre that attracted famous scholars, such as Copernicus. The town's glory has faded but it does boast one of the best-preserved medieval castles in Poland, which has survived hundreds of years of war unscathed.

A BIT OF HISTORY

Mentioned as early as the 10C at the confluence of the Rivers Łyna and Symsarna, this is one of Warmia's oldest cities and a former regional capital.

Still visible are sections of the fortifications, including the **Main Gate** (Brama Wysoka), erected in the 13C by the Teutonic Knights to defend their military base. The bishops who ruled this powerful diocese between 1350 and 1795 were mainly Polish. Nicolaus Copernicus, the nephew of one of these bishops, Łukasz Watzenrode, lived in the town from 1503 to 1510.

CASTLE★
(Zamek)

Pl. Zamkowy 1. ⊙Open Tue–Sun May–Sept 9am–5pm; off season 10am–4pm. ℘767 21 11. ⊜8 PLN. Explanations in Polish, sometimes in English.

Lidzbark Warmiński Castle

W. Buss / MICHELIN

- ⛟ **Michelin Map:** Map of Poland C1 – Województwo of Warmia-Masuria.
- ℹ **Info:** ul. Wysokiej Bramy 2. ℘(89) 767 41 48.
- ▷ **Location:** 50km north of Olsztyn.
- P **Parking:** There is plenty of free parking along the town's streets
- ⊘ **Don't Miss:** The collection of Russian icons.
- ⊙ **Timing:** Allow around 1hr to visit the castle.

The impressive Gothic edifice, brick-built on a square plan with square corner towers, was the residence of the bishops of Warmia. A footbridge spanning the wide moat leads to the mound where it was erected in the 14C. The large Gothic doorway allows access to an inner courtyard from where one can see, on the first floor, a delicate arcaded gallery often compared to that of the royal castle in Kraków.

On the walls protected by the gallery are traces of vast frescoes, now severely damaged. The castle's cellars feature a series of vaulted rooms where ancient guns are displayed.

The different floors of the fortress now house the **Warmia Museum** (Muzeum Warmińskie), feature a succession of rooms covered with Gothic vaulting containing pictures of famous guests (such as Copernicus), period furniture and objects.

A few murals are sometimes visible under the whitewash covering the walls. They are particularly well preserved in the great hall of Ignacy Krasicki, known at the time as the poet-bishop.

The brick-paved Great Refectory, the finest hall in the fortress, contains a collection of 15C and 16C polychromes. The magnificent exhibition of **Russian icons** from the 17C to the 20C on the upper floors is the highlight of the castle's collection.

Olsztyn★

Lying halfway between Warsaw and Gdańsk, Olsztyn is surrounded by ten post-glacial lakes (to the west) and by vast forests, which make a visit to the capital of Warmia-Masuria particularly pleasant. The picturesque gorge of the River Łyna runs through the town and is dominated by the medieval Teutonic fortress. The small historic centre, meticulously restored, offers a pleasant surprise, even if there are few major monuments.

A BIT OF HISTORY

Mentioned for the first time in chronicles dating from 1348, the foundation of this town in the Warmia diocese seems to have coincided with the construction of the castle in the 14C. At first it came under the rule of the Teutonic Knights, who had conquered it, but it was integrated into Polish territory following the Treaty of Toruń in 1466. Having fallen under Prussian control and been renamed Allenstein after the first Partition of Poland in 1772, it continued to remain the heart of the Polish national and cultural movement in Warmia, despite the growing number of German immigrants who settled in the town during the second half of the 19C. Subjected to enforced Germanisation during World

▶ **Population:** 172,467.
◉ **Michelin Map:**
Map of Poland C1 –
Województwo of Warmia-
Masuria.
▤ **Info:** Ul. Staromiejska 1.
℘(89) 535 35 65.
www.mazury.travel.
◐ **Location:** 200km north
of Warsaw, 180km from
Gdańsk.
🅿 **Parking:** Ul. 11 Listopada,
just outside the city gate.
⊛ **Don't Miss**: The castle,
student bars in the
Old Town.
◔ **Timing:** Allow half a
day to visit the town.

War II, it became Polish again at the end of the conflict which left it partially in ruins (40 per cent of the town was destroyed) and practically drained of its inhabitants. The whole German population was then expelled and replaced by Poles arriving essentially from the eastern territories annexed by the Soviet Union, but also from Lithuania.

SIGHTS

The medium-size **Historic Centre** (Stare Miasto) is bound by the meanders of the River Łyna in the south and the fortifica-

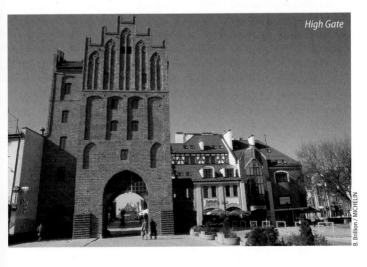
High Gate

B. Brillion / MICHELIN

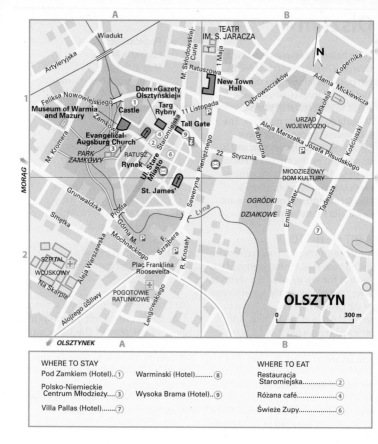

OLSZTYN

0 ——————— 300 m

WHERE TO STAY		WHERE TO EAT
Pod Zamkiem (Hotel)..①	Warminski (Hotel)..........⑧	Restauracja Staromiejska................②
Polsko-Niemieckie Centrum Młodzieży....③	Wysoka Brama (Hotel)..⑨	Różana café....................④
Villa Pallas (Hotel).......⑦		Świeże Zupy...................⑥

Floods of Tears at the Origin of the Town

Alina, the faithful wife of a Prussian tribal chief, made the mistake of rejecting the advances of a local witch's son. When the dangerous lover obtained from his mother the death in battle of the troublesome husband, Alina and her lady's maids cried so much that their floods of tears turned into a river which was named **Łyna** after the unfortunate wife.

The Prussian name of the town, **Allenstein**, is said to derive from that of the river... but some say it is more likely connected with the famous stone known as *Alue Status*, located inside the Lutheran church.

tions erected at the end of the 14C, formerly pierced by three gates, of which only the **High Gate** (Brama Wysoka) remains.

Rynek★

Small and steep, partially surrounded by arcaded Gothic houses, the main square is centred around the former town hall, now the municipal library.

St James' Cathedral
(Katedra Św. Jakuba)

Built from 1380 onwards against the former town walls, it is surmounted by a massive 63m-high tower, featuring fake arcades, erected between 1562 and 1596. The interior, covered with fine crystalline and netlike **vaulting**★★, resting on ten pillars, is bathed in a light conducive to meditation, diffused by modern multicolour stained-glass win-

Copernicus' statue stands guard over the castle bridge

B. Brillion / MICHELIN

dows. Note the **Gothic tabernacle** (*on the right of the high altar*) and the beautifully carved, painted and gilded 16C **triptych**★ of the Holy Cross, situated at the end of the north aisle, transferred from the church of the same name in 1802.

Castle★★

This attractive brick-built edifice, dating from the 14C, is surrounded by a large moat spanned by a stone bridge guarded by a statue of Copernicus. The castle was the head office of the Warmia Chapter's administration, whose treasure was kept here. Today it houses the **Museum of Warmia and Mazuri**.

Museum of Warmia and Masuri★★
(Muzeum Warmii i Mazur)

Ul. Zamkowa 2. ⏰Open Tue–Sun Jun–Sept 9am–5pm; Oct–May 10am–4pm. 👝9 PLN. ✆527 95 96. www.muzeum. olsztyn.pl.

The colourful ground-floor rooms house a fine portrait gallery. The first floor of the east wing features the *komnaty Kopernikowskie*, a series of rooms with splendid crystalline vaulting linked to the memory of Copernicus, who resided in the castle and was appointed administrator of the Chapter's Treasury between 1516–19 and 1520–21. In 1521, he took an active part in the city's defence against the attacks of the Teutonic Knights. The room at the end is devoted to Coperni-

cus and his work. The tour continues on the upper floor with an ethnographic exhibition about Warmia and Masuria, and with the visit of the castle tower. In the courtyard, next to the well, you will see a statue known as the Prussian Woman (*pruska baba*) found in Barciany, probably carved by Prussian pagan tribes from the Baltic, who once lived in the area. As you come out of the castle, note immediately after the bridge, the **evangelist church**, rebuilt in neo-Gothic style in 1899, which features under the high altar a sacrificial stone called *Alue Status*, probably a relic of an ancient pagan cult.

By the backway, you can reach the **Fish Market Square** (Targ Rybny), laid out on the site of the former medieval Mill Gate. On the square stands the building formerly occupied by the *Gazeta Olstyńska* newspaper, now an annexe of the museum.

Beyond the High Gate lies Upper District (Górne Przedmieście) centred around the **new neo-Baroque Town Hall**.

On the heights overlooking the town stand the **Planetarium** and housed in a former 19C water tower the **Astronomical Observatory**.

EXCURSIONS
Morąg
(Population 14,657)

❂ *Situated halfway between Elbląg and Olsztyn (50km from each of these towns).*

This small town of Prussian origin was the birthplace of philosopher and poet of the Age of Enlightenment **Johann Gottfried Herder** (1744–1803). Standing in the middle of the peaceful **Rynek** the elegant, Gothic-style, former **Town Hall** (Ratusz) now houses the Tourist Office (*open Mon–Fri 8am–4pm, Sat 10am–2pm. (89)757 38 26. www.morag. pl*). Between the square and the church is the monument erected to commemorate the local celebrity, opposite the house where he was born. Behind the Gothic church are the ruins of the old Teutonic castle, dating from the 13C.

J.G. Herder Museum★★
(Muzeum im. J. G. Herdera)
Ul. Dąbrowskiego54. Open Tue–Sun 9am–5pm. 7 PLN.
Do not miss this small but attractive museum housed inside the Pałac Dohnów, built between 1562 and 1571, then remodelled in the Baroque period. The right wing, devoted to Helder and his contemporaries, will be of great interest to amateurs of German culture. Born in Mohrungen (Morąg) in 1744, Herder died in Weimar in 1803, having spent the years between 1762 and 1769 in Königsberg and Riga. The left wing houses a collection of 18C portraits and 17C Dutch prints, a long gallery displaying 17C paintings from the Dutch School as well as several reconstructed rooms containing period furniture in Baroque, Second Empire, Art Nouveau and Biedermeier styles.

Olsztynek Ethnographic Park★
(Skansen – Muzeum Budownictwa Ludowego [Park Etnograficzny])
Ul. Sportowa 21, 11–015 Olsztynek (89) 519 21 64. mid–end Apr Tue–Sun 9am–3pm; May–Sept daily 9am–5.30pm; Sept Tue–Sun 9am–4.30pm, Oct Tue–Sun 9am–3.30pm. 10 PLN.
On presentation of your ticket, keepers will open locked buildings. Note also that there is a cheaper ticket allowing visitors to look at the buildings from the outside only. Allow 2hr for the visit. Literature in English (5 PLN), with a useful map of the site.

This *skansen*, originally set up in Królewiec (the former Königsberg and the present Kaliningrad in Russia), is Poland's oldest and largest open-air museum. Moved to Olsztynek between 1938 and 1942 to form with the Hindenburg Mausoleum a monumental ensemble named Tannenberg, devoted to east Prussian architecture in the past, it comprises some 50 reconstructed or original buildings from Warmia, Masuria, Podlasie *(eastern bank of the Lower Wisła)* and Lithuania, scattered in green surroundings. Some houses illustrate special themes: weaving, traditional costumes, painted furniture, domestic life. At no. 29, ask for the music box to be activated. Having admired the windmills, end your visit with a look at the fine painted-wood Protestant church and note the temptation scene depicting a particularly suggestive Eve.

ADDRESSES

STAY

Hotel Pod Zamkiem –
Ul. Nowowiejskiego 10. 535 12 87. www.hotel-olsztyn.com.pl. 15 rooms. Isolated within the castle park, this Secession-style villa – the town's former music school – offers simple, inexpensive accomodation.

Hotel Wysoka Brama–
Ul. Staromiejska 1. Between the TO and the gate of the same name. 527 36 75. www. hotelwysokabrama.olsztyn.pl. 25 rooms. Visitors on tight budgets will appreciate the basic, but neat rooms. There are also very inexpensive dormitory rooms.

Polsko-Niemieckie Centrum Młodzieży. *Ul. Okopowa 25. 534 07 80. www.pncm.olsztyn.pl. 22 rooms.* This Polish-German youth centre, ideally situated below the castle *(to the left of the amphitheatre)*, is no longer what its name implies. The initial customers have been replaced by business people and the **hotel-cum-restaurant** has adapted its standard accordingly.

Hotel "Villa Pallas" –
Ul. Żołnierska 4. 535 01 15. www.villa pallas.pl. 32 rooms. Comfortable rooms

housed in a huge villa full of staircases and corridors, situated on the heights overlooking the town. Elegant dining room with appetising à la carte menu.

🍽 Hotel Warmiński –
Ul. Kołobrzeska 1. ☏522 14 00. www.hotel-warminski.com.pl. 127 rooms. Don't judge this hotel by its unattractive concrete-block appearance; inside, the rooms are very pleasant and comfortable.

MORĄG
The owner of 🏰 **Dohnów Castle** lets the first-floor Renaissance apartment. *For 250 PLN, it accommodates up to five persons. Contact Anita Borlnicka on ☏(89) 757 42 98 and book two weeks in advance.*

🍴 EAT
🍽 Świeże Zupy –. *Ul. Św. Barbary 1. Open Sun–Thu 11am–10pm (Fri–Sat until midnight).* An establishment sought after by the locals who flock inside at any time of day to enjoy a mouthwatering bowl of homemade soup.

🍽 Restaurant Przystań –
Ul. Żeglarska 2. ☏523 77 73. Open daily noon–10pm. This restaurant, on the edge of a lake, is sought after for its setting and traditional cuisine. Drinks are served in the middle of the lake in summer.

🍽 Różana Café – *Ul. Targ Rybny 14.*
On the right before the bridge leading to the castle. ☏523 50 39. Open daily 11am–10pm. The best restaurant in the Old Town dedicated to the most fragrant of flowers, as can be guessed from the colour of the walls, the mural frieze and their presence on every table. The cost is not excessive for all that.

🍽 Staromiejska – *Ul. Stare Miasto 4/6 At the top of the Rynek. ☏527 58 83. Open daily 10am–10pm.* The locals' favourite place in the late afternoon for a chat and a beer or tea and biscuits. In the evening, it is an elegant old-world restaurant. Outside terrace.

🍷 BARS
Filmowy Bar Kawowy – *Stare Miasto 23. ☏527 28 27.* A bar dedicated to the cinema, where one can take a tea or coffee break. In the southwest corner of the Rynek. *Open daily 4–9pm.*

🎉 NIGHTLIFE
In the town centre, the riverside area is buzzing with life when the sun goes down. *Ul. Targ Rybny* has many bars.

Ostróda-Elbląg Canal★★
Kanał Ostródzko Elbląski

Dug between 1848 and 1876 on the basis of a project by Dutch engineer J.G. Steenke, the Ostróda-Elbląg canal, linking the Baltic and the south of Prussia, is a unique masterpiece of engineering. **80.4km long** *(including 40km of canal dug to link the six lakes)*, it forms the main section of a several-pronged system. Unfortunately, soon after the project was completed the canal system was rendered obsolete by the advent of the railway. It never had any real commercial value and is now only operated for tourists.

- 🧭 **Michelin Map:** Map of Poland C1 – Województwo of Warmia-Masuria.
- ℹ **Info:** Ul. Plac 1000-lecia PP 1A, Ostróda. ☏(89) 642 30 00.
- 📍 **Location:** Ostróda is 36km west of Olsztyn and Elbląg is 61km east of Gdańsk.
- 🅿 **Parking:** Parking is available in Ostróda by the castle, Ul. Zamkowa, close to the landing docks.
- 👁 **Don't Miss:** Taking a boat ride overland.
- 🕐 **Timing:** A full day is needed to sail the length of the canal.

Ostróda-Elbląg Canal

© Sławomir Pryc/Dreamstime.com

CANAL

The 9.6km situated between the villages of Całuny Nowe and Buczyniec, where the water level difference reaches 99.5m, form the most interesting stretch. In order to negotiate this level difference between Lakes Drweckie and Drużno, five successive slipways are used like ladders to link the various waterway levels. Once in front of a slipway, boats are hauled along rails by a system operated by hydraulic power. While one of the structures goes up on one side, the other goes down and the boats cross overland.

Cruises

*The company's main office is in **Ostróda** (Ul. Mickiewicza 9A; ⓘopen daily 7am–3pm, Jun–Aug 7am–6pm ℘(89) 646 38 71/0801 350 900) on the edge of Lake Drweckie. In **Elbląg**, the office is situated in a basement, 50m beyond the Vivaldi Hotel (Ul. Wieżowa 14; ℘(55) 232 43 07), but one can also call in the morning at the landing stage situated opposite St Nicholas' Church. ⓘA complete cruise costs 90 PLN (concessions 70 PLN, luggage 16 PLN, bike 32 PLN), a cruise as far as Buczyniec costs 70 PLN. www.zegluga.com.pl. Snacks available on board.*

A fleet of five boats provides daily service in July and August, and a less regular one in low season. Cruises go in both directions from Elbląg or Ostróda;

departure at 8am, arrival in the other town around 7pm. If this seems too drawn out, a good way to compromise is to do half the journey *(5hr)* from Elbląg to **Buczyniec**, the tiny village where there is the last and most spectacular slipway. In Buczyniec, a small **canal museum** (ⓘopen May–Sept daily 10am–6pm; ⓘ2 PLN; ℘(55) 249 80 85) illustrates the story of the canal project.

By Road

To watch boats going up the slipways, go to Buczyniec (diversion along the road beyond Pasłęk from Elbląg or at Morzewo from Ostróda) between12.30 and 2pm.

EXCURSION

Elbląg
(Population 128,016)

Seeing a few old photographs of Elbląg's former quays convince you that the town would have continued to compete with Gdańsk, had it been spared by the war. The old Protestant city of Elbing, daughter of the mythical old Prussian sea port of Truso and of the Hanseatic trading town founded by the Teutonic Order, is slowly rising from its ashes. It is possible to visit the **Galeria El w Elblągu** (Ul. Kuśniersko 6; ⓘopen Mon–Sat 10am–6pm, Sun 10am–5pm; ⓘ4PL), a Polish arts centre spectacularly housed since 1961 in the former Gothic St Mary's Church (Kościół Mariacki).

Frombork★★

This small sleepy town, perched above the Wisła estuary, is no doubt the most qualified for the coveted title of "Copernicus' city". Indeed, it is here that the illustrious astronomer spent the greatest part of his life and carried out most of his research, from 1509 to his death in 1543. The former Frauenburg *(Our Lady's town)*, which was for a long time the capital of the Warmia diocese, is still dominated by its charming fortified cathedral, picturesquely situated at the top of a cliff overlooking the town and sea. Copernicus was, for over 30 years, one of the cathedral's canons, which earned him the privilege of being buried inside it.

A BIT OF HISTORY

Initially established in Braniewo, the cathedral of the Warmia diocese, too exposed to the Prussian threat, was moved to Frombork at the end of the 13C while the bishops chose to reside in Lidzbark Warmiński. For a long time, Frombork remained under the influence of Braniewo and attempts to create a maritime trading port were repeatedly crushed by Braniewo and Elbląg. Having no fortifications, the town was often plundered – in particular by the Swedes in 1626 – and following the Prussian annexation in 1772, it only resumed its official role as residence of Warmia's bishops in 1837 and retained it until 1945.

TOWN

The only part of the town (80 per cent of which was destroyed) to have been spared the disasters of World War II is **Cathedral Hill**, where most of the sights are located. It can be reached on foot from the lower town via a stepped path, which skirts the walls *(to the left)* and enters the courtyard on the south side through the **Main Gate** (Brama Główna). *Admission to the courtyard is free, but there is an admission charge to the buildings (including the cathedral).*

- **Population:** 2,598.
- **Michelin Map:** Map of Poland C1 – Województwo of Warmia-Masuria.
- **Info**: Ul. Młynarska 5a. 244 06 77.
- **Location:** 94km east of Gdańsk and 32km northeast of Elbląg.
- **Parking:** Guarded parking on Ul. Dworcowa, by the train station.
- **Don't Miss:** The panorama from the cathedral's former bell tower.
- **Timing:** Allow 2 to 3h.

GETTING THERE

BY RAIL/BUS – Frombork can be reached by bus or train from Elbląg. There is also a less regular bus service between the town and Lidzbark Warmiński.

PRACTICAL INFORMATION

Phone code – 055.
Postal code – 14-530.
Tourist Office – Ul. Młynarska 5a. 244 06 77 or IT Globus, Ul. Elbląska 2. 243 7500.

Dominating the **Lower Town** and looking somewhat like a keep, the tower (14C–16C) adjoining the tourist office deserves its name of Water Tower *(wieża wodna)*. In 1571, it was fitted with a system enabling it to supply water to Cathedral Hill through a network of oak pipes. Today it houses a pleasant café, where one can sit at a table on one of the levels leading to the summit, which offers a fine **panoramic view** of the town (open May–Sept 8.30am–8.30pm; Oct–Apr 9am–4pm. 3 PLN). Note the burned-out roof of the massive St Nicholas' Church (Kościół Św. Mikołaja), now disused, one of the rare relics that were retained in the Lower Town.

187

Frombork Cathedral

© Maciekl/Dreamstime.com

CATHEDRAL HILL★★★
(Wzgórze Katedralne)
Information from the **Copernicus Museum** *(see below).*

Cathedral★★
(Katedra)
Open Mon–Sat 9.30am–5pm.
4 PLN.

Erected between 1329 and 1388 at the top of a cliff, on the site of a previous wooden cathedral built in 1280, it boasts a specific feature: it is surrounded by ramparts. Start by walking round the building and note that some elements were added to the Gothic structure, for instance St George's Chapel (15C) and St Saviour's Chapel (1732–35). Take time to admire the unusual **west front**, flanked by two octagonal turrets. The porch shelters a remarkable stone doorway decorated with a string of characters which runs on along the ribs of the vaulting. The interior, surmounted by fine star vaulting, contains some twenty Baroque altars, as many as 101 funerary plaques (essentially Warmian bishops and canons) and 19 epitaphs. One of these, located on the first pillar in the nave, immediately to the right of the chancel, was made in the 18C to commemorate Copernicus, since the great man's body is buried somewhere under a slab without anyone knowing exactly where. In 2010, Copernicus' exact burial spot was discovered and now there is a glass panel in front of the Holy Cross altar, where his tomb can be seen. The late-Baroque black-marble **high altar**, replaced in 1752 by the magnificent late-Gothic **polyptych** (1504), now in the north aisle. Note the **Baroque pulpit** (1785) and the fine **organ** (1684) renowned for its rich tone which, combined with the excellent accoustics of the place, offers the possibility of splendid concerts in summer *(on Sun from Jun–Aug)*. Also noteworthy is the Baroque Chapel of the Saviour, at the end of the south aisle, closed off by an imposing **wrought-iron railing** framed by a trompe-l'oeil painting.

Copernicus Museum★
(Muzeum Mikołaja Kopernika)
Ul. Katedralna 8. Open Tue–Sun 9am–4pm. 5 PLN. Explanations in Polish and German. 244 00 71.
www.frombork.art.pl.

Housed in the former Gothic Bishops' Palace remodelled during the Baroque period, the museum is essentially devoted to Nicolaus Copernicus (Mikołaj Kopernik) (1473–1543). Having visited the ground-floor exhibition of archaeological finds and fragments of stained glass from the late 19C and early 20C, originally in the cathedral, go to the first floor, where a room is entirely devoted to the great astronomer. Drawing inspiration from a famous three-quarter portrait, artists represented him in many different styles, using various techniques, including a masculine version of the Mona Lisa. Acting as canon of the Warmia Chapter during 30 years, Copernicus completed numerous missions in the course of his duties, as the exhibition shows. Having initiated a monetary reform, the author of the famous *De revolutionibus orbium coelstium*, published in Nuremberg and, as the story goes, seen by him for the first time on his death bed, was also asked in 1510 to draw up a map of the region. Several copies of the map are exhibited and will enable you to understand better the complicated history of Warmia. The last room presents a few telescopes.

Radziejowski Tower (belfry)
(Wieża Radziejowskiego)

🕐 *Open daily 9.30am–5pm.* 💳*6PLN.*
Situated in the southwest corner of the curtain wall, this former Gothic steeple, which rises 70m above the nearby sea, offers an exceptional panoramic view. Halfway up the tower, a **Foucault pendulum** confirms the earth's rotation. A spiral staircase then leads up to an outside gallery, level with the Baroque spire, from which the **panoramic view**★★★ of the Wisła's lagoon is breathtaking. In fine weather, one can even get a glimpse of the Russian town of Kaliningrad at the extremity of the bay. In the basement, a **planetarium** puts on four shows a day (💳*8 PLN;* ✆*244 00 83).*

Copernicus Tower
(Wieża Kopernika)

🕐 *Open Jul–Aug Mon–Sat 9am–5pm; rest of year call for hours.* 🕐*Closed 1, 11 Nov, 25–26 Dec.* 💳*5 PLN.* ✆*244 00 75.*
Built before 1400, destroyed and rebuilt several times *(the last time in 1965),* this square tower is the oldest part of the fortifications. It is thought to have been the scientist's study (those who say it was his home are wrong) and celestial observatory. The reconstruction of this Renaissance scientist's study is not exceptional and by no means a must-see attraction.

Hospital of the Holy Ghost and St Anne's Chapel★
(Szpital Św. Ducha i Kaplica Św. Anny)

Ul. Stara (on the left as you leave by the main door, then straight on). 🕐*Open Jul–Aug Tue–Sat 9am–5pm; rest of the year Tue–Sun 9am–4pm.* 💳*5 PLN.*

Situated outside the cathedral enclosure, this former medieval hospital from the late 14C, which was recently restored, houses a modest **Museum of Medicine** (Dzial Historii Medycyny). Past the entrance and the lovely paved floor, you will see the remains of a heating and waste-water disposal system. However, the main interest lies in the traces of **frescoes** painted on the walls of the chancel rotunda in the chapel. These naïve paintings, illustrating the Last Judgement in the form of sketches, feature a wealth of small devils fighting over the souls of the damned.

ADDRESSES

🛏 STAY

🛏 **Szkolne Schronisko Młodzieżowe COPERNICUS**– *Ul. Braniewska 11.* ✆*243 71 93. 9 rooms (50 beds), 2 private rooms.* Youth hostel east of the Cathedral Hill on the road to Braniewo.

🛏🛏 **Dom Familijny Rheticus**– *Ul. Kopernika 10.* ✆*243 78 00. www.dom familijny.pl. 10 rooms, 9 apart.* The place has the feel of a provincial railway station, with its somewhat austere exterior and far more convivial interior. This welcoming guest house, named after Copernicus' only disciple, offers spacious, rooms with high ceilings, each with its own kitchen.

🛏🛏 **Hotel Kopernik**–*Ul. Kościelna 2.* ✆*243 72 85. www.hotelkopernik.com. pl. 32 rooms. Restaurant*🛏🛏. This long, one-storey building, painted in yellow and red, contains standardised rooms with balconies, offering a pleasant view of the cathedral. Combined with a restaurant. Off-season discounts.

🍴 EAT
Not much choice really!
Several *Fish & Chips* located behind the Water Tower offer a quick-snack option. Otherwise, try 🛏🛏 **Don Roberto** *(Ul. Stara 1;* ✆*243 78 00).* Located down the hill past Ul. Katedralna they serve traditional Polish fare. The only real alternatives are the restaurant of Hotel Kopernik mentioned above, or **Restauracja "Pod Wzgórzem"***(Ul. Pocztowa 15)* a standard bar/pizzeria.

DISCOVERING POLAND
KRAKÓW

Tyniec's Benedictine abbey
© Riondt/Dreamstime.com

KRAKÓW AREA

Kraków is the essence of Poland; as the country's best-preserved historic city it boasts more monuments and symbols of the past than any other place in Poland. For centuries, the city and its surroundings have served as the spiritual heart of the nation. The tombs of kings stand as silent reminders of past glories: the oldest university in Poland, founded in the 14C, is a constant source of pride. Countless churches house the relics of saints and the monasteries and convents still shelter monks and nuns. The city also abounds with student cafés and jazz clubs often located in medieval cellars below the market square.

Highlights

1 Strolling around Europe's largest medieval town square, the **Rynek** (p197)

2 Listening to the **Hejnał** trumpet call from St Mary's Church (p198)

3 Exploring the underground chapels of the **Wieliczka Salt Mine** (p224)

4 The **Jewish Culture Festival** at the end of June and start of July (below and p231)

Old and New

Kraków used to be called "Little Rome" in Polish because of its number of churches, religious orders and sacred relics. The city centre does seem to have a church or cloister on every corner, and the city boasts Romanesque churches, massive red-brick Gothic structures, Renaissance mausoleums and many a Baroque façade.

Since the fall of Communism almost all of the churches and monasteries have been renovated after years of neglect. And the former palaces of noble families and the burgher town houses have also been restored and converted into cafés, clubs and restaurants.

Kraków also harbours many ancient traditions, like the trumpet call from St Mary's Church and the crafting of Christmas cribs. But the city government and tourism office have been making a great effort to promote Kraków as a cultural capital by launching many new festivals as well. Music can be enjoyed in many of the churches at Easter time and in August. May is photography month, when even crypts are used as exhibition spaces, and the streets of Kazimierz reverberate with music during Kraków's Jewish Culture Festival in late June and early July.

Craft stalls within the gothic Cloth Hall Sukiennice, Main Market Square, Krakow

Kraków★★★

Lying on the bank of the Upper Wisła (Vistula) River, Kraków is by far and away Poland's top attraction, equal in splendour to the finest European towns and included in UNESCO's very first World Heritage List (in 1978). This elegant cultural and university metropolis is an ancient royal capital, dear to the hearts of the Poles, who consider it to be the birthplace of their nation and culture. The remarkable Gothic and Renaissance complex in the town centre came through World War II virtually unscathed, whereas the Jewish community of the Kazimierz district was virtually annihilated, as portrayed in Stephen Spielberg's film *Schindler's List*. A symbol of "Old Poland" during the communist era, this provincial capital is brimming with cultural exploits, and is eminently young and dynamic, with nearly 130 000 students currently in residence.

▶ **Population:** 757,547.

Michelin Map: Map of Poland C4 – Województwo of Lesser Poland.

Info: Ul. Św. Jana2. ℘(12) 421 77 87. www.krakow.pl.

Location: 294km south of Warsaw, 114km southeast of Częstochowa, 536km southeast of Gdańsk, 220km southeast of Łódź, 100km north of Zakopane.

Parking: Don't bother in the Old Town; central on-street parking costs 3 PLN/hr.

Don't Miss: The Rynek, the altarpiece by Veit Stoss in St Mary's Church, Leonardo da Vinci's *Lady with an Ermine* in the Czartoryski Museum, stained-glass windows by S. Wyspiański in the Franciscan Church, Wawel Castle and Cathedral, the old Jewish district of Kazimierz, the Wieliczka Salt Mines, the atmosphere of the vaulted cellars of the Old Town's restaurants and cafés.

Timing: A minimum stay of three days will enable you to see the essentials, thanks to the relatively small size of the town, which makes it the ideal destination for a long weekend.

A BIT OF HISTORY
Foundation of the City

According to legend, Kraków was founded in the 7C by **Prince Krak**, or **Krakus**, who rid Wawel Hill of its dragon and whose daughter Wanda chose to drown herself in the Wisła rather than be forced to marry a German prince. Being the main settlement of the Vistulans (Wiślanie, from the Polish name of the River Wisła), Kraków, mentioned for the first time in 965, was incorporated into the kingdom of Poland by Prince Mieszko I. It was the first Christian centre in Poland and around AD 1000, it became a bishopric, then the capital of the Piast duchy and of the Polish kingdom during the reign of **Kazimierz The Restorer** (1038–58), who preferred the city to Gniezno. The 13C was marked by a series of Tatar invasions (1241, 1259–60 and 1287); the 1241 saw the timber-built city reduced to ashes.

Brick and stone replaced wood when it was rebuilt in 1257 during the reign of Bolesław V the Shy, according to the Magdeburg Law, and the grid pattern used at the time remains to this day; fortified during the following century, the town expanded considerably at the foot of the castle. In 1320, Władysław the Short was the first king to be crowned in Wawel Cathedral but it was during the reign of **Kazimierz The Great** (1333–70), the last sovereign of the Piast dynasty, that Kraków really flourished. He built the district, which was named after him, and in 1364 founded the first Polish university, modelled on Prague's:

The Tatars

Although the Tatar raids against the city took place in the 13C, Kraków never ceased to commemorate them. In addition to the **hejnał** tradition (&see p198), there is the **Lajkonik procession** which takes place every year in early June, eight days after Corpus Christi. The origin of this tradition, connected with the last Tatar raid in 1287, remains vague. Some say that members of the rafters' guild from Zwierzyniec prevented a horde of mongols from entering Kraków, then put on the Khan's clothes and proudly entered the city amid popular rejoicing. Nowadays, the procession still follows the ancient tradition, starting from the Premonstratensian Convent and heading for the *Rynek*. It is led by a richly clothed Khan (the costume was redesigned in 1904 by Wyspiański) parading well in front on his wooden horse *(lajkonik)* and followed by a band of musicians; donations collected from the crowd and shopkeepers gathered along the route are said to bring them good luck throughout the year.

the Kraków Academy, later known as the Jagiellonian University.

The Jagiellon Golden Age

Kraków's Golden Age was during the Renaissance period under the Jagiellon dynasty, founded by Prince Jagiello, Grand Duke of Lithuania, who was converted to Catholicism and baptised in the Polish city before becoming king of Poland under the name of Władysław, through his marriage with Jadwiga in 1386. However, it was essentially in the 16C, during the reigns of Sigismund I the Elder and his son Sigismund II August, that Kraków had its heyday and became one of Europe's most renowned artistic and scientific centres. The city's combined economic prosperity and artistic expansion were suddenly halted by King Sigismund III Vasa's decision in 1609 to transfer the capital to Warsaw. From then on, the town inexorably declined.

Neglect and Revival

Ransacked by the Swedes in 1655, the town was annexed by the Austrians in 1794 before becoming the free autonomous city of the Kraków Republic in 1815, a status it retained until 1846, when it once more formed part of the Austro-Hungarian Empir. However, from 1861 onwards, it enjoyed relative cultural and political freedom, attracting many artists who gave birth to the Młoda Polska movement, a Polish version of Art Nouveau. But in fact it was only in 1918, at the end of World War I, that Kraków became entirely Polish again. Proclaimed capital of the German General Government under Nazi occupation, it was shamelessly looted but completely spared any bombings or sieges. Proud of its rich heritage, Kraków now enjoys an enviable economic dynamism based on tourism, and has replaced Łódź as Poland's second most populous city.

Kraków Today

Seen from the sky, the Old Town looks like a huge pear narrowing round Wawel Castle. Behind the castle lies the medieval town whose ramparts were demolished in the 19C and replaced by the green belt of the Planty. In the north, Rynek Główny, the famous medieval market square, extends over 4ha. In the southeast, outside the medieval walls, the Jewish district of Kazimierz was a separate town until 1800, just like Podgórze situated on the opposite bank of the Wisła. During the socialist era, Kraków became the symbol of the middle-class "Old Poland" but this situation was redressed by the creation in 1949 of a modern satellite city, **Nowa-Huta** (the New Steel Works). This industrial workers' area situated some 10km from Wawel generated a considerable amount of pollution which proved detrimental to the old stones of the historic centre.

GETTING THERE

BY AIR – The **John Paul II Internationl Airport Kraków-Balice (Międzynarodowy Port Lotniczy im. Jana Pawła II Kraków-Balice)** is located 13km west of Kraków *(Ul. Kpt. M. Medweckiego 1, 32-083 Balice. www.krakowairport.pl. ☎ 295 58 00 information 24hr/day).*
From the airport to the town centre – By bus: bus no. 292. Bus stop near the Cracovia Hotel, by the Błonia field. Around 2 buses every hour from 4.30am to 10.30pm *(journey time: 35min)*. Normal urban ticket. Otherwise: bus no. 208 *(less frequent)* starting from Nowy Kleparz.

BY TAXI – the journey by taxi costs between 50 and 70 PLN.

BY RAIL – Railway station – The main railway station (**Dworzec PKP Kraków Główny**) is situated northeast of the Old Town, 5min from the Rynek. *Pl. Kolejowy 1. www.pkp.pl.* Frequent intercity trains to Warsaw *(2hr35min).*

BY BUS – Bus station – The new bus station (Dworzec Autobusowy PKS) is behind the railway station *(Ul. Bosacka 18. www.pks.krakow.pl).*

GETTING AROUND

MPK Public Transport *www.mpk. krakow.pl*). Bus or tram. Single tickets *(2.50 PLN)* available in kiosks, vending machines at major stops or from bus and tram drivers. A 15min ticket for 1.80 PLN is available for short rides.

BY CAR – The town centre is closed to motor cars except for driving into car parks in the Old Town: *Plac Biskupi, Ul. Powiśle, Ul. Karmelicka.* Parking costs between 3 and 5 PLN per hour.

Taxis – Mega Radio Taxi: *☎0800 200 200* Barbakan Taxi: *☎196-61*
Express Taxi: *☎196-29*
Radio Taxi: *☎191 91*
Wawel Taxi: *☎196-66.*

Car hire – Europcar, National, Budget, Avis and Hertz have a counter at Kraków Airport.

Joka. *Ul. Starowiślna 13 (Pałac Pugetów) ☎429 66 30.*

Avis. *Ul. Lubicz 23.*
☎629 61 08. www.avis.pl.
Europcar. *Ul. Szlak 2.*
☎633 77 73. www.europcar.com.pl.
Hertz. *Al. Focha 1 (Hotel Cracovia).*
☎429 62 62. www.hertz.com.pl.
Bike hire – Rent a Bike. *Ul. Św. Anny 4. ☎501 745 986. www.bikes-rental.pl.*

TOURING KRAKOW

Kraków Tourist Card (Krakowska Karta Turystyczna). Includes free admission to 30 museums and free travel on the whole MPK public transport network, as well as discounts from a selection of shops. Information at tourist offices, some hotels and travel agencies. *50 PLN for a 2-day pass, 65 PLN for a 3-day pass. www.krakowcard.com.*

Municipal Information Centre (Punkt Informacji Miejskiej). *Ul. Szpitalna 25. ☎432 01 10. Open daily May–Sept 9am–7pm; Oct–Apr 9am–5pm. www.krakow.pl.* This municipal Tourist Information Centre is not actually located in the street but in a kiosk standing in the middle of the Planty, halfway between the station *(straight on after the subway)* and the beginning of the Old Town *(behind the J Słowacki Theatre). Ul. Józefa 7. ☎422 04 71. Open Mon–Fri 9am–5pm.* This municipal Tourist Information Centre is situated in the Kazimierz district, near the crossroads of Józefa and Bozego Ciala Streets.

Małopolskie Tourist Information Centre (Małopolskie Centrum Informacji Turystycznej) – *Rynek Główny 1/3 (Sukiennice). ☎421 77 06. www.mcit.pl. Open Oct–Mar Mon–Fri 9am–6pm, Sat–Sun 10am–2pm; Apr–Sept Mon–Fri 9am–8pm, Sat–Sun 10am–4pm.* Located in the ground floor of the Cloth Hall, opposite St Mary's Church: this is the private information centre of the Małopolska region, combined with a shop and exchange office.

Cultural Information Centre (Centrum Informacji Kulturalnej) – *Ul. Św. Jana 2. ℘421 77 87. Open daily.* Comprehensive information about cultural activities. Located at the start of St John Street, starting from the middle of the north side of the Rynek.

Jordan Biuro Podróży (Jordan Travel Agency; *www.jordan.pl*) has several branches, which are open daily:

♦ Ul. Długa 9 (℘421 21 25) provides tourist information and a reasonably priced hotel on the same spot.

♦ Ul. Gęsia 8 (℘422 40 33), main branch.

♦ Bosacka (℘430 40 35) provides an accommodation service.

♦ Ul. Pawia 8 *(Centrum Informacji Turystycznej i Zakwaterowania opposite the station;℘422 60 91).*

Jarden Travel Agency. *Ul. Szeroka 2. ℘421 71 66. www.jarden.pl. Open daily.* This agency specialises in tours of the Jewish part of Kazimierz. Fine bookshop on the same theme (Jarden Bookshop).

Promotion and sale office of the Wieliczka Salt Mine (Biuro Promocji i Sprzedaży Kopalni Soli Wieliczka): *Ul. Wiślna 12a. ℘426 20 50. www.kopalnia.pl. Mon–Fri 9am–5pm.*

Tour Cracow – ℘500 807 358. *www.tourcracow.com.* The only native English-speaking licensed guide offering tours of Kraków.

Kraków's Royal Castle Educational Association (Castle Guides' Office). *Wawel 5. ℘422 09 04.*

℘*Welcome to Cracow* is a free monthly magazine that provides up-to-date information about the town. However, the best choice is the fortnightly English-language guide *Kraków In Your Pocket (5PLN)*, which includes a good selection of addresses and is available online: *www.inyourpocket.com.*

PRACTICAL INFORMATION

Phone code – ℘012.

Postal code – from 31-000.

Emergency service – ℘999 *(from a mobile, dial 112)*

Fire brigade – ℘998

Police – ℘997. Police station: *Rynek Główny 29;* ℘615 73 17 *(24hr a day).* Kazimierz: *Ul. Szeroka 35. ℘615 77 11.*

Post office – Urząd Pocztowy (Poczta Główna) *Ul. Westerplatte 20 31-045 Kraków 1. ℘421 03 48. Mon–Fri 8am–8pm, Sat 8am–2pm.* The main post office is located on the eastern outer edge of the Planty, on the corner of Westerplatte and Wielopole Streets. *Poste-restante* mail can be sent here and retrieved at counter no. 1. The other post office open on Sat until 8pm is located at Ul. Lubicz 4 *(in front of the railway station)*; mail posted there is dealt with 24hr/day. The post office located in Wawel *Castle is also open Sat and Sun, 9am–4pm.* Most other post offices are open Mon–Fri 8am–7pm and Sat morning until noon, 1pm or 2pm.

Banks and foreign exchange – There are many ATMs spread evenly throughout the Old Town. In most cases it is possible to select an interface in English. There are also numerous *kantors* (exchange offices) in the heart of the Old Town; their exchange rates are similar. The best place to change traveller's cheques is Pekao Bank *(Rynek Główny 31; open Mon–Fri 8am–6pm, Sat 10am–2.30pm)*, which takes a reasonable commission.

General Hospital – *Emergencies: Ul. Łazarza 14. ℘999*

Pharmacy open 24hr/day – Euro Apteka. *Ul. Karmelicka 23. ℘631 19 80. Apteka: Ul. Galla 26. ℘636 73 65.*

Internet Cafe. *Rynek Główny 23. Open daily 24hr/day. 15min: 1 PLN and 1hr: 3 PLN.*

Foreign newspapers – Empik *(Rynek Główny 5)*; PKP Central Station; Cracovia Hotel.

Rynek seen from a terrace under the arcades

R. Mattes / MICHELIN

THE RYNEK ★★★
(Rynek Główny) TOWN MAP II A-B2

A tour of the town invariably starts from the Main Market Square, the very heart of the city to which you will always be drawn as if by a magnet. The Rynek was, in medieval times, the centre of Kraków's religious, economic and political life and it remains today the heart of the city. This vast square with sides measuring 200m is a rare example of well-preserved medieval urban planning. Its layout dates from 1257 when the town was granted its charter by King Bolesław the Shy. The only exceptions to the symmetrical layout of the square are the small St Adalbert's Church and St Mary's Basilica, built before the square was laid out, as well as Grodzka Street, probably the town's oldest street, which starts from the southeast corner of the square and heads diagonally towards Wawel Castle, thus disrupting the regular layout. A good deal of the town's history lies behind the façades of the 47 houses surrounding the square. Most of them, originally built in the 14C and 15C, were considerably remodelled, particularly in the Neoclassical style, but the majority still boast original architectural features (ceilings with exposed beams, doorways, stucco and polychrome decorative elements).

An archaeological dig was recently completed under the eastern half of the market square and the Historical Museum of Kraków (*see p204*) is planning to open a new exhibit in these underground passageways that once served another market hall demolished in the 19C.

St Mary's Church ★★★
(Kosciół Mariacki) B2

The western half of the nave (entered through the porch) is freely accessible to worshippers. There is an admission charge to the chancel entered via Mariacki Square (south side). ○*Open Mon–Sat 11.30am–6pm, Sun and holidays 2-6pm.* ⊲*6 PLN.*

The lofty west front of Kraków's main parish church towers diagonally above the northeast corner of the Rynek. It is the third church dedicated to the Assumption of the Virgin to stand on this site. Rebuilt in Gothic style between 1355 and 1408, it represents the power of Kraków's middle class, who financed its construction.

Exterior

The austere **façade** features a late-Baroque **polygonal porch** (1750–52) designed by the Italian architect Francesco Placidi. The ground floor of the tower known as *hejnalica* (tower of the bugle call) houses **St Anthony's Chapel** also called "The Criminals' Chapel" *(capella captivorum)*; it was here that criminals spent the night preceding their execution in the company of their confessor. Opposite is the 17C **Częstochowa Virgin's Chapel**, which contains a copy of the famous icon from

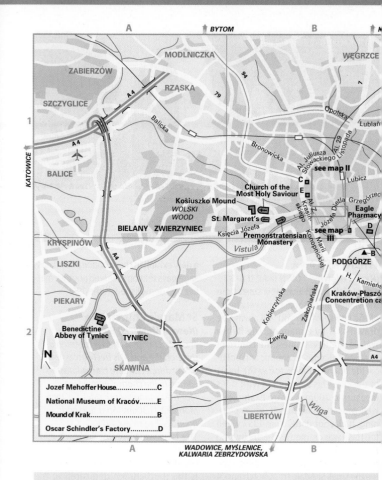

The Hejnał

Have you noticed the crowd that gathers every hour in front of St Mary's Church and looks up to the top of the higher tower? Have you heard a few anxious-sounding notes? Look up towards the last storey of the taller tower and you will get a glimpse of a trumpet playing a melody based on only five notes. In medieval times, a watchman used to signal the opening and closing of the town's gates and raised the alarm in case of fire or enemy attack. According to legend, during one of the Tatar raids, the watchman's warning of their approach was abruptly interrupted by an arrow which pierced his throat and the melody was cut short. In order to commemorate this event, the melody is still abruptly interrupted today. This custom, which dates back to at least the 14C, follows a strict ritual: on every hour, the signal is first sounded to the south towards the Wawel castle and then in turn to the other three cardinal directions. The ideal place from which to watch the **hejnał** is in front of St Barbara's Church, where the trumpeter in charge acknowledges the applause of the crowd with a friendly greeting. Should you ever forget the melody, bear in mind that the call *(Hejnał Mariacki)* is broadcast live every day at noon on the Polish national radio station and they have been broadcasting it since 1927, making it one of the world's longest-running musical programs on the radio.

KRAKÓW
map I

as a reminder that crime never pays. The taller tower *(on the right)*, or bell tower, was used as the town's belfry, whereas the tower on the left, which served as a watchtower, was surmounted in 1478 by a Gothic cupola comprising 16 pinnacles set round a high central spire. The tower is at the centre of one of Kraków's main legends and attractions: the **Hejnał**.

Interior

Its present appearance is the result of improvements made during the Baroque period (1753–54) by Placidi and followed by renovation work undertaken between 1889 and 1891 by the architect Tadeusz Stryjeński to restore the early Gothic appearance of the church. The painter Jan Matejko donated his designs for the **paintings** (1889–92) that cover the walls of the central nave and chancel when the city neglected to ask for his services. He was assisted by his students, Wyspiański and Mehoffer, who also helped in creating some stained-glass windows, including the one decorating the west front based on a design by Wyspiański (see *INTRODUCTION*).

Chancel

From the dark nave, one's eyes are drawn towards the depth of the chancel and the focus of attention becomes the high altar framed by Matejko's paintings against a background of sumptuous 14C **Gothic windows**★★.

The High Altar or Veit Stoss' Altarpiece★★★ *(the opening of the polyptych's panels takes place daily at 11.50am)*. The high altar is adorned with a huge five-panelled polyptych elaborately carved in limewood, painted and gilded. This dazzling jewel, which is the prize possession of the church, is the masterpiece of Veit Stoss (1438–1533), a sculptor from Nuremberg, whose name in Polish is Wit Stwosz. Made between 1477 and 1489, this vast 13m-high and 11m-wide altarpiece forms one of the largest Gothic high altars. Decorated with some 200 figures, it illustrates a cycle essentially dedicated to the life of the Virgin Mary.

the Jasna Góra sanctuary (although, according to a local legend, it is the original icon).

There are several anecdotes associated with the asymmetrical **towers**, the left tower *(81m)* soaring above the right one *(69m)*. According to one of these anecdotes, two brothers, both architects, competed in building the towers until one killed the other, thus halting the construction. Locked up inside St Anthony's Chapel (hence the tradition mentioned above), the fratricide was executed the next day but no architect ever agreed to complete the other tower stained by crime and the municipality was forced to top it with a dome. You might be more inclined to believe this story when you know that the murder weapon, an old rusty knife, hangs today under the arcades of Cloth Hall

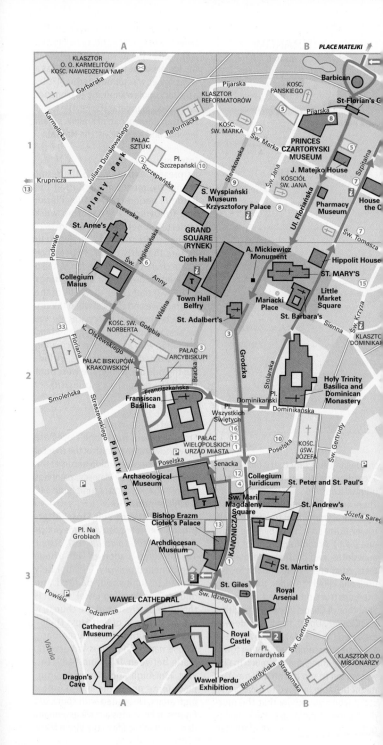

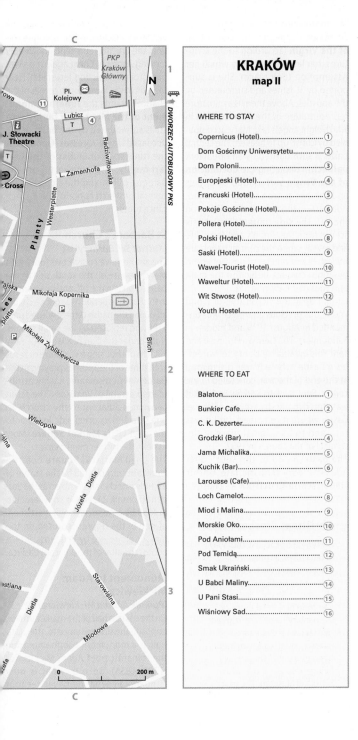

KRAKÓW
map II

WHERE TO STAY

Copernicus (Hotel).................................. ①
Dom Gościnny Uniwersytetu.............. ②
Dom Polonii.. ③
Europjeski (Hotel)................................ ④
Francuski (Hotel)................................. ⑤
Pokoje Gościnne (Hotel)..................... ⑥
Pollera (Hotel)..................................... ⑦
Polski (Hotel)....................................... ⑧
Saski (Hotel).. ⑨
Wawel-Tourist (Hotel)......................... ⑩
Waweltur (Hotel)................................. ⑪
Wit Stwosz (Hotel)............................. ⑫
Youth Hostel.. ⑬

WHERE TO EAT

Balaton... ①
Bunkier Cafe.. ②
C. K. Dezerter...................................... ③
Grodzki (Bar)....................................... ④
Jama Michalika..................................... ⑤
Kuchik (Bar)... ⑥
Larousse (Cafe).................................... ⑦
Loch Camelot....................................... ⑧
Miod i Malina....................................... ⑨
Morskie Oko... ⑩
Pod Aniołami.. ⑪
Pod Temidą.. ⑫
Smak Ukraiński.................................... ⑬
U Babci Maliny..................................... ⑭
U Pani Stasi... ⑮
Wiśniowy Sad....................................... ⑯

The **main scene** of the central panel when opened depicts the **Dormition of the Virgin** (according to the scriptures, her last sleep during which her Assumption took place). She is supported by St James and surrounded by the apostles. Above them is a miniature representation of the **Assumption** in which eight angels take Mary, accompanied by Christ, up to heaven. The central panel is surmounted by an openwork **baldachin** depicting the **Coronation of the Virgin** surrounded by angels and the two patron saints of Poland, Adalbert on the right and Stanisław on the left. The **side panels** illustrate six scenes from the Virgin's and Jesus' life and reveal, when the central panels are folded, 12 low-relief carvings, enhanced by bright colours, depicting the main episodes of the Virgin's life.

Caught up in the vicissitudes of World War II, this precious altarpiece was dismantled in August 1939 and hidden in Sandomierz. The Germans found it and sent this invaluable booty to Nuremberg Castle, where it was discovered at the end of the war, concealed in the cellars. Sent back to Kraków in 1946, it was stored in the stockrooms of Wawel Castle where it remained until it was returned to its original place in the chancel of the church in 1957.

The eastern end of the south aisle houses a very realistic late-Gothic (1496) **stone Crucifix**★★, charged with pathos, another masterpiece by Veit Stoss. Placed in a late-Baroque setting, the Crucifix represents the deeply moving agony of Christ against a silver background depicting Jerusalem. Near the exit, in the lower south corner of the chancel, stands the **funerary monument of the Montelupi family** with stalls surmounted by the busts of the deceased inside recesses. Opposite is the funerary monument of the **Cellari family**. Also noteworthy are the Baroque pulpit and the side chapels, several of which contain fine Renaissance tombs.

St Barbara's Church
(Kościół Św. Barbary) B2

This single-nave church overlooking St Mary's Square on the south side of the basilica, built in the 14C and redecorated in the Baroque period, was once a chapel adjoining the parish cemetery, used until 1796 and replaced by the small square. Note under the porch, a late 15C–early 16C chapel housing a sculpture of Jesus with three of the apostles praying in the Garden of Gethsemane, a work attributed to a pupil of Veit Stoss. The Jesuit convent is adjacent to the church on one side and its other side looks onto the quiet **Little Market Square** (Mały Rynek), the former meat market.

The small **Mariacki Square** boasts a **fountain** surmounted by the statue of a handsome character known as the Student (Pomnik Żaczka): a copy, erected in 1958 by an association of craftsmen, of one of the figures featured on the famous altarpiece by Veit Stoss, which adorns the altar of the adjacent basilica.

Monument to Adam Mickiewicz
(Pomnik Adama Mickiewicza) B2

On the eastern half of the market square, opposite the side entrance to the Cloth Hall, is a monument commemorating the romantic poet Adam Mickiewicz (1798–1855). Born in what is now Lithuania in 1798, he never set foot in Kraków during his lifetime. Having died near Constantinople in 1855, he had to wait another 35 years for his

Christmas Creches (szopki)

Every year on the first Thursday in December, a competition is organised at the foot of the Monument dedicated to Adam Mickiewicz. Shaped like castles and churches, the designs of the nativity scenes are inspired by Kraków's architecture. Prize-winning works are then honoured until February by being exhibited in the town's Historical Museum. The best are in the museum's permanent collection.

remains to be brought to Kraków with great pomp and laid to rest in the crypt of Wawel Cathedral on 4 July 1890. A favourite meeting point of Kraków's residents who gather at its foot in large numbers to wait for their dates, the statue is commonly referred to by the locals as "Pod Adasiem", an expression based on the nickname given to the poet and literally meaning "under Adaś". The poet stands on a high pedestal surrounded by four allegorical figures symbolising patriotism, poetry, education and heroism. Precisely because it represented a national hero, this monument was one of the first in Kraków to be taken down by the Nazi occupiers in 1939 and it was only in 1955, for the hundredth anniversary of the poet's death, that it was replaced by a replica.

The Cloth Hall★
(Sukiennice) A-B2

Standing in the middle of the market square, the imposing shape of the former Cloth Hall, famous for its crenellations decorated with lovely stone grotesques, contributes a great deal to the beautiful appearance of the square. Built at the end of the 14C and dedicated to the cloth trade, it was damaged by fire in 1555 and immediately rebuilt in Renaissance style by the Italian builder known as Padovano, who raised it by adding a splendid attic

The Knife

At the end of the passageway facing the Mickiewicz Monument you will see a strange metal knife hanging on the left. Two different versions are offered to explain this incongruous presence: the first maintains that it was meant to remind thieves that they would be punished by having their ears cut, the second is linked to a drama which occurred during the construction of the towers of St Mary's Church (see p199).

carved by Florentine artist Santi Gucci, designed to hide the steep gables. Spoilt later by the adjunction of many annexes, it was redesigned between 1875 and 1879 by Tomasz Pryliński who added the neo-Gothic side arcades. Devoted, like the arcades, to the tourist trade, the central gallery on the ground floor is today occupied by stalls selling Polish handicraft, while the first floor has, since 1883, housed the recently renovated Gallery of 19C Polish Painting (**Galeria Malarstwa Polskiego★**). A tour of the first floor of the Cloth Hall offers an introduction to the masters of 19C Polish painting, whose works have been exhibited here since 1883. Among the canvases in the collection, the symbolic, and once controversial, *Ecstasy* (a naked woman lying asleep over a horse's

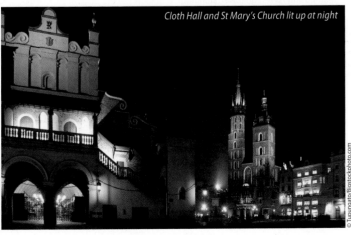

Cloth Hall and St Mary's Church lit up at night

neck) by Władysław Podkowiński made the headlines in 1894. On the east side, a whole room is devoted to the Polish Géricault, Piotr Michałowski (1800–55), who painted numerous horses and riders, as well as a number of portraits which are on display. The gallery on the right, devoted to historicist painters, offers the opportunity to admire Henryk Siemiradzki's great historical panoramas (Nero's Torch) and Jan Matejko's monumental works, including the overwhelming Prussian Tribute in 1525 (1882), a kind of group photo of the high society of that period, which occupies a whole wall of the gallery.

St Adalbert's Church
(Kościół Św. Wojciecha) A-B2
Standing alone in the southeast corner of the Rynek, just where Grodzka Street starts, and facing exactly the same way as St Mary's Basilica, this tiny edifice was the town's first church, built of wood in the 10C on the site where, according to tradition, St Adalbert delivered his evangelical sermons around the year 995. The original building was replaced in the 12C by a Romanesque stone structure, considerably remodelled between 1611 and 1618 to its current Baroque style.

Town Hall Belfry
(Wieża Ratuszowa) A-B2
Rynek Główny 31. ○Open Apr–Oct daily 10.30am–6pm. ⊗7 PLN.
This imposing 70m-high tower, standing in the southwest corner of the square, is all that remains of the former medieval town hall erected in the 14C and demolished in 1820. The very high steps of the narrow staircase lead up to the clock mechanism and from there, one enjoys a fine view of the town through the openings in the Baroque cupola, which replaced the Gothic spire in 1686. The vast cellars, where the former municipal jail, torture chambers and brothel were situated, today house the **Ludowy Theatre** (Teatr Ludowy; ℘68 02 112; www.ludowy.pl) and a café.

Krzysztofory Palace
(Pałac Krzysztofory) A1
Rynek 35. ○Open Wed–Sun 10am–5.30pm. ○Closed second Sun of month. ⊗Temporary exhibitions 7 PLN.
Boasting a fine arcaded courtyard with a well in its centre, this opulent 17C palace houses the **Historical Museum of Kraków**. It owes its name to the 14C statue of St Christopher, which used to decorate the façade. The first-floor apartments, featuring splendid ceilings decorated by the stucco specialist Baldassare Fontana, contain a wealth of documents and souvenirs related to the town's history (unfortunately, captions are in Polish only). The cellars house a famous art gallery connected with the avant-garde art movement, Grupa Krakowska (Kraków Group).

Hippoliti House
(Kamienica Hippolitów)
Pl. Mariacki 3. ○Open Wed–Sun 10am–5.30pm. ○Closed second Sun of every month. ⊗7 PLN, Wed free.
An annexe of the Historical Museum, this house is located on the left of St Mary's Church. The building is named after the family of merchants who came to live in this 14C house in 1599. More recently owned by the Zaleski family, it is sometimes referred to as the "Bourgeois House" because it presents the reconstruction of a middle-class Kraków interior.

⁀ WALKING TOURS

1 ROYAL WAY: FROM MATEJKO SQUARE TO WAWEL★★★
TOWN PLAN II B1 to A3
The Royal Way (Droga Królewska) was followed by the royal family and high dignitaries going to Wawel Castle.

Matejki Square B1
Lying outside the Planty (⬩see opposite), it occupies the site of the market square of the former medieval city of Kleparz, joined to Kraków in 1791. In the centre stands the imposing **Commemorative Monument of the**

Battle of Grunwald (Pomnik Grunwaldzki). The original monument, erected at the instigation of the pianist and politician Ignacy Jan Paderewski in 1910, for the 500th anniversary of the battle, was destroyed by the Nazis in 1939 and only replaced with a replica in 1976. The northeastern corner is marked by **Saint Florian's Church** (Kościół sw. Floriana). The first church on this site was Romanesque, but the style is now Baroque. It was built in 1184 as a mausoleum for the relics of St. Florian, the 3C Roman soldier and martyr. The church was a starting point for royal funeral processions to the Wawel Cathedral. John Paul II, then Father Wojtyła, was curate from 1949–51.

The Barbican★
(Barbakan) B1
🕐Open Apr–Oct 10.30am–6pm.
💰7 PLN (the ticket is also valid for the parapets of the city ramparts).

Built in 1499 in response to the Ottoman threat, as an outwork preceding the ramparts and the moats along the axis of the main towngate, this circular bastion, now standing isolated in the middle of the Planty, was originally linked by a passageway, known as "the neck", to the Florian Gate. This is one of Europe's rare examples of a perfectly well-preserved barbican, its high walls concealing an impressive system of machicolations and loopholes.

The Ramparts and the Planty★
A 4km-long system of fortifications was erected between 1285 – when the town was granted the privilege to surround itself with ramparts – and the mid-16C, when the municipal Arsenal was built. The ramparts, having become obsolete with the development of artillery, were demolished by the Austrians at the beginning of the 19C and the double moat filled in. The area they once covered was gradually replaced by the Planty modelled on the Viennese Ring. Kraków residents on their way from the city to the suburbs inevitably pass through this green oasis, which was relaid in 1988 and today features many statues, fountains and commemorative monuments as well as plaques marking the site of the former town gates.
Planty Park (Krakowskie Planty), an inspiration to artists, forms a green retreat around Kraków's Old Town.

Florian Gate
(Brama Floriańska) B1
This is the only remaining town gate out of the eight original ones that once pierced the medieval walls; it used to be the main entry point of the Royal Way into town. The 34.5m-high tower, stone-built in the 13C, was completed with red bricks at the end of the next century. Out of the 39 towers that once rose above the ramparts on both sides of the gate, only three bastions remain and Kraków's street artists now hang their paintings on the stones of the fortified wall.

Florian Street★
(Ul. Floriańska) B1
This main shopping street used to be the start of the Royal Way from the Florian Gate to the Rynek. It was lined with some of the finest houses in town, often featuring Renaissance or late-Gothic doorways.

Michalik's Den★★
(Jama Michalikowa)
Kraków's finest café at ul. Floriańska 45 boasts an interior décor worthy of a museum; during the Belle Epoque, it was the headquarters of the local bohemian population, gathered around the literary and artistic movement of Młoda Polska ("Young Poland"). In 1905, its members set up the Zielony Balonik ("Green Balloon") cabaret, famous for its puppet shows. Until 1921, it was under the management of Tadeusz Boy-Zelenski, an author who provided satiric texts for many of the performances.

Jan Matejko House
(Dom Jana Matejki)
Ul. Floriańska41. 🕐Open Tue–Sat 10am–6pm, Sun 10am–4.30pm. 💰8 PLN, Thu free.
Jan Matejko (1839–93), one of the most famous Polish painters, was born here

and spent his whole life in this house; some of his works are on display. Having set himself the task of illustrating Poland's history, he strove to create great historical panoramas, in particular reconstructed scenes of major battles. Highly interested in the town's history, he got involved in the preservation and restoration of many works and buildings, as can be seen from his preliminary sketches of the polychromes painted on the walls of St Mary's Church. Displayed on three levels are paintings, family memorabilia and fine antiques collected by the artist, including eastern and western weapons as well as costumes that he used as models.

Pharmacy Museum
(Muzeum Farmacji)
Ul. Floriańska 25. Open Tue noon–6.30pm, Wed–Sun 10am–2.30pm. *7 PLN.*

Founded in 1946, this museum, devoted to the history of pharmacy from the Middle Ages to the present, is considered by amateurs to be one of the most interesting of its kind.

In order to continue along the Royal Way towards Wawel Castle, walk across the Rynek until you reach Grodzka Street.

Grodzka Street★B2-3
This elegant street, forming the second section of the Royal Way leading to Wawel, runs south to **Św. Marii Magdaleny Square**, named after St Magdalene's Gothic church that used to stand here until 1811. The square links Grodzka and Kanonicza streets and is adorned with a statue of Father Piotr Skarga perched on top of a slender column. To the north, the former **Collegium Iuridicum (no. 53)**, featuring a small courtyard with tiered arcades reminiscent (on a reduced scale) of those of Wawel Castle, today houses the **Institute of Art History** (Instytut Historii Sztuki).

Church of SS Peter & Paul★
(Kościół Św. Piotra i Pawła) B2
Access to the crypt and transept. Open

Mon–Sat 9am–5pm, Sun 1–5pm (Jun–Sept until 5.45pm). *2,50 PLN.*

Built on the site of a Gothic sanctuary destroyed by fire in 1455, this church was the first Baroque building in Kraków. Its construction, begun in 1596, was based on the model of Roman Jesuit churches such as Il Gesù by Vignola; a series of mishaps delayed its completion until 1619. One's attention is first drawn to the elegant, well-proportioned **façade★★**, sheltering *(from left to right)* the statues of Stanisław Kostka, Ignatius Loyola, Francis Xavier and Aloysius Gonzaga, surmounted on the upper level by those of SS Sigismund and Ladisław. The church being set back from Grodzka Street along an axis at right angles with the street, the façade is preceded by a balustrade designed by Kacper Bazanka to correct the perspective of the church visually. The original monumental statues of the 12 Apostles (1723) by David Heel surmounting it were being corroded by pollution and were therefore replaced by replicas.

Interior – Particularly noteworthy is the **chancel★**, including the black-marble **high altar★** completed in 1735 by Bazanka (who also built the curved balustrade around the organ) and surmounted by a cupola with a semi-circular **stucco decoration★** (1633) by Giovanni Battista Falconi (who sculpted the statues of the four evangelists located in the cupola). The **crypt**, which is less interesting from an artistic point of view, houses the tombs of the fearsome Jesuit preacher and main architect of the counter reform, Piotr Skarga (1536–1612), of WSH Bieliński and of archbishop Andrzej Trzebicki, the latter boasting sumptuous Baroque decoration. Besides the concerts of classical music which take place regularly *(Mon, Tue, Thu 8pm)*, the other interesting feature of the church is its Foucault pendulum demonstrating the earth's rotation by oscillating from the top of the 46.5m-high dome.

St Andrew's Church★
(Kościół Św. Andrzeja) B3
One would never think – judging by the interior, completely remodelled

in Baroque style at the beginning of the 18C – that this church of the Poor Clares, dedicated to St Andrew and built between 1079 and 1098, is in fact one of Poland's best-preserved Romanesque edifices. The exterior, bearing numerous scars *(sealed-up windows and blocked-up main porch)*, features several narrow twin windows with a single central column which testify to the defensive purpose of the fortress-church. It was the only church in Kraków able to withstand the Tatar attack in 1241 and the population took refuge inside once again during a major fire in 1259. This defensive role is underlined by the beautiful yet austere limestone-and-sandstone **façade**★★ surmounted by two octagonal towers with square bases, topped in 1639 with Baroque belfries.

In striking contrast to the exterior Romanesque austerity, the opulent Baroque interior boasts a rich **stucco décor** and a fantastic rococo boat-shaped **pulpit** (St Andrew was a fisherman).

Continuing along Grodzka Street, you will walk past **St Martin's** Lutheran Church (Św. Marcina), dating from the 17C and rarely open to visitors, before reaching the former **Royal Arsenal** (Arsenał Królewski), located at the end of the street, opposite Wawel. It has been occupied since 1927 by the Jagiellonian University. This is the perfect place from which to look up towards the east wing of the castle and to observe the **Kurza Stopka**, an unusual Gothic pavilion, one of the rare parts of the medieval castle erected during the reign of Władisław II Jagiełło. Overlooking a small square, the unassuming single-naved Gothic **Church of St Giles** (Kościół Św. Idziego) has been run by Dominicans since 1595. In this former official place of worship of the Armenian community, Mass has been celebrated in English every Sunday at 10.30am since 1994 and concerts are often organised. Right in front of the building, a wooden cross commemorates the 50th anniversary of the Katyń Massacre (also known as the Katyń Forest Massacre) perpetrated in 1940 by the Soviet NKVD on some 20,000 Polish officers (long blamed on the Germans, it was only acknowledged by the Soviet authorities in 1990).

② WAWEL HILL★★★
(Wzgórze wawelskie)
TOWN MAP II A 3
The hill is freely accessible.
Open daily May–Sept 6am–8pm; Oct–Apr 6am–5pm (the castle's arcaded courtyard closes 1hr before). Closed 1 Jan, Easter, 1, 11 Nov, 24, 25, 31 Dec.
Wawel refers to the architectural ensemble standing at the top of a small limestone hill rising 25m above the River Wisła. Standing as a symbol of the glorious episodes of the nation's history, it

Wawel Hill from the Vistula River

© Grzegorz Japol/Dreamstime.com

has been the guardian of Polish national identity since the 11C, with the presence side by side of the Christian sanctuary and of the royal castle representing the close association of religious and secular powers. A place rendered even more symbolic by the fact that Polish kings were not only crowned in the cathedral but also buried there, together with many of the nation's illustrious families and famous sons. Having reached its heyday in the 16C, Wawel was abruptly abandoned in 1596 in favour of Warsaw by King Sigismund III Vasa, the king of alchemists, who, according to one legend, left Wawel following an unsuccessful alchemist experiment.

At the foot of the ramp leading to the castle, you will catch a glimpse of the imposing **equestrian statue of Tadeusz Kościuszko** standing at the top of one of the bastions built by the Austrians in 1852. Sculpted by Leonardo Marconi and inaugurated in 1921, it was destroyed by the Nazis in 1940 and only replaced by a copy in 1960. Along the ramp you will see plaques set into the brick wall inscribed with the names of the generous donors who took part in the castle's restoration during the interwar period. Go through the **Coat of Arms Gate** (Brama Herbowa), beyond which you will find one of the castle's two ticket offices, then through the **Vasa Gate** (Brama Wazów).

To the left of the Vasa Gate stands the cathedral and, slightly offset to the right, the Vicars' house, where you can buy tickets for the visit – inside the cathedral – of the Royal Crypt and of the Sigismund Tower.

Wawel Cathedral★★★
(Katedra Wawelska) A1
Open Mon–Sat 9am–5pm, Sun from 12.30pm. Free admission to cathedral; admission to the tower and crypt 12 PLN (ticket also valid for Cathedral Museum).
The present sanctuary is the third cathedral to be erected on this site; built in Gothic style at the beginning of the 14C, it replaced a Romanesque edifice of which all that remains today are St

Leonard's Crypt and the Silver Bells Tower (Srebrne Dzwony). The cathedral, of surprisingly modest proportions, was built during the reigns of King Władysław the Short and Kazimierz the Great and has not been greatly altered since it was dedicated to SS Stanisław and Wencesław in 1364. From 1320 to 1734, coronations took place in the cathedral, which was also the venue of royal funerals. At first buried in the nave (the oldest royal tomb is that of Władysław the Short, dating from the 14C), Polish monarchs and their families were laid to rest, from the 16C onwards, in the crypt (although a funerary monument in their honour continued to be erected in the various side chapels) which became a national pantheon in the 19C.

Exterior
Once through the **Baroque porch** (1619), your attention will no doubt be drawn to a collection of large **prehistoric bones** hanging on heavy iron chains, located to the left of the entrance. Their presence, said to keep evil forces at bay, is linked to a legend announcing the end of the world and of humanity. Framed with black marble, the magnificent wooden door (1636) is covered with an iron sheet stamped many times with King Kazimierz the Great's monogram, a "K" surmounted by a crown.

Interior
Standing in the middle of the central nave is the **Altar of St Stanisław★★**, Poland's main patron saint, whose relics are kept in a carved silver coffin, located under a Baroque black-and-pink marble baldachin. Made in Gdańsk between 1669 and 1671 by Peter van der Rennen, the reliquary is decorated with scenes illustrating the life of the bishop who became a martyr when he was killed by King Bolesław the Bold on 11 April 1079. Worshipped with particular fervour since its transfer to Wawel in 1254, the saint's tomb was considered as the altar of the nation (Ara Patriae), on which kings laid their war trophies. Surrounded by the four monuments of Kraków's bishops, the altar is preceded

along the nave by the sarcophagi of King **Władysław Jagiełło II**★ *(on the right)* and **Władysław Warnenczyk** *(left)*.

The Gothic **Holy Cross Chapel**★(Kaplica Świętokrzyska) is the only medieval chapel in the cathedral to have retained its original decoration, featuring fine **frescoes** inspired by Byzantine art, painted in 1470 by artists from the Russian School of Pskov. In the north-west corner, under a high baldachin supported by eight columns, lies the sarcophagus of King Kazimierz Jagiello made by Veit Stoss in 1492, the year of the King's death. Opposite the entrance, the imposing monument erected in 1790 depicting Bishop Kajetan Sołtyk standing on top of his own sarcophagus, from which a black eagle (the family's emblem) is escaping together with an arm holding a sabre, is noteworthy for its fantasy.

Along the right aisle are two royal chapels that perfectly complement each other: the **Vasa Chapel**★, named after one of the greatest 17C royal dynasties, is the perfect replica of the Sigismund Chapel; its Baroque ornamentation features a cupola decorated with stucco motifs. The doorway and bronze decoration of the doors are particularly interesting.

The **Sigismund Chapel**★★★ (Kaplica Zygmuntowska), the mausoleum of the Jagiellon dynasty, is a real masterpiece of Renaissance architecture in Poland. Commissioned by King Sigismund I the Elder, it was built between 1519 and 1533; designed by Bartolomeo Berecci on a square layout and surmounted by a dome, it was given a sumptuous decoration by Italian artists. The cupola was covered on the outside with gilded scales in 1591–92, at the request of Queen Anna Jagiellon. Facing the entrance, the **royal stall** in Hungarian red marble rests against the sarcophagus of Queen **Anna Jagiellon** (1523–96). On the right side, set within a two-tiered arcade, the funerary monument (remodelled by sculptor Santi Gucci in 1574–75) of **King Sigismund I the Elder** (1467–1548) stands on top while that of his son **Sigismund August** (1520–72) lies below. The coffered cupola is decorated with rosettes and surmounted by a lantern bearing the signature of the artist who designed the chapel. Facing the doorway of the chapel is the neo-Gothic (1902) **sarcophagus of Queen Jadwiga***(Hedwig)* (1373/4–99). Made of white Carrara marble, it was inspired by the tomb designed by Jacopo della Quercia for Ilaria del Carretto in the Duomo de Lucca in Tuscany.

Moving along the ambulatory, you will come across the **Olbracht Chapel**★★ which houses, under a fine Gothic vault, the **red-marble sarcophagus** of King John Olbracht (1459–1501), lying under a splendidly decorated triumphal arch. It was one of the first examples of Renaissance art in Poland. Opposite this chapel stands the **Gothic tomb of King Kazimierz the Great**★★ (1310–70).

Behind the **high altar** (1649) are the two exuberant late-Baroque **funerary monuments** (1760) of kings Michael Korybut Wiśniowiecki (1640–73) and John III Sobieski (1629–96). The chapel

---

A Sharp Wooden Tongue

Did you notice a **gagged head** among the carved heads of the Audience Hall ceiling? One day when Sigismund August presided the court hearing, a poor widow unjustly accused of shoplifting was brought before the King. He was about to condemn her when a powerful human voice, which appeared to come down from the ceiling, called out to him: *"August king, pronounce a just sentence."* This unexpected intervention by one of the heads was enough to convince the king that the woman was innocent but, for fear that this wooden head with a conscience should meddle in the affairs of the kingdom and contest his authority, the Monarch ordered the sculptor to cover with a patch the lips of the head which had spoken to prevent it from intervening again.

opposite houses the **mannerist funerary monument**★★ of **King Stephen Batory** (1533–86), delicately carved in 1595 by Santi Gucci. At the end of the east part of the ambulatory stands the **altar of the Crucified Lord Jesus**, where Queen Jadwiga is said to have had a vision. In the north part of the ambulatory, the recumbent figure of **King Władysław the Short** (1261–1333) was the first royal tomb built inside the cathedral.

In the left aisle, steps lead down to the **Crypt of the great national poets** which contains, among others, the sarcophagi of Adam Mickiewicz (1798–1855) and Juliusz Słowacki (1809–49), whose remains were brought back from France, where they lived in exile. The **Royal Crypt** (Groby Królewskie) has, since the 17C, housed the tombs of Polish kings and queens and also of some national heroes such as Tadeusz Kościuszko (1746–1817), Prince Józef Poniatowski (1763–1813), Marshall Józef Piłsudski (1867–1935) and General Władysław Sikorski. **St Leonard's Crypt**★, the only remnant of the Romanesque cathedral erected in the 11C and 12C, contains the most important series of tombs. It was here that in 1946, a young priest called Wojtyła celebrated his first mass.

Accessible via a staircase located in the sacristy (at the end on the left), the **Sigismund Tower**★★ (Zygmuntowska) offers a close-up view of the five bells of the cathedral reached through an impressive 16C timber staircase. The top bell, known as **Sigismund** (1520), is 2.6m in diameter and weighs 11 tonnes; it is the largest historic bell in Poland. Its powerful D major only rings across the city on the most important religious and national holidays and 12 men are needed to set the bell in motion.

Piłsudski's Crypt is the last crypt and can now be entered for free from outside the cathedral because this is where former President Lech Kaczyński and first lady Maria were laid to rest after the tragic plane crash of 10 April 2010 in Smoleńsk, Russia.

Cathedral Museum
(Muzeum Katedralne) A3

🕐Open Tue–Sun 10am–5pm. ☞12 PLN. (ticket also valid for the Cathedral crypt and bell tower).

The museum has been housed since 1978 in the chapter house of the cathedral. Its collection of sacred art includes liturgical vessels and clothes as well as historic items; for instance, St Maurice's spear, a present from Prussian Emperor Otto III to Bolesław the Brave in AD 1000, Stanisław August Poniatowski's coronation robe, diadems worn by Bolesław the Shy and his wife Kinga, and the reliquary containing St Stanisław's skull.

▶ *When leaving the cathedral, turn left to admire the south side. In front of you lies the magnificent Arcaded Courtyard (Dziedziniec) of the Royal Castle.*

The Royal Castle★★
(Zamek Królewski) B3

🕐Open May–Sept Mon–Sat 9am–6pm, Sun from 11am–6pm; rest of the year reduced hours. ☞22 PLN; child 14PLN, Sun free (ticket covers Grand and Royal Apartments; ☞guided tours 100 PLN). Seat and symbol of royal authority for six centuries, Wawel Castle is a blend of several architectural styles. Preceded by a palatium and later by a princely Romanesque residence, the first castle worthy of the name was erected at the beginning of the 11C by the Duke and future King Bolesław the Brave. During the 14C, Kazimierz III the Great, the last sovereign of the Piast dynasty, turned it into an imposing Gothic fortress destroyed by fire in 1499. The third castle was erected at the request of King Sigismund I the Elder who, during the first half of the 16C, commissioned the Italian architects Francesco Florentino and Bartolomeo Berecci to build the Renaissance palace, part of which we can admire today. In 1595, following a fire, the restoration of the north wing was entrusted to Italian architect Giovanni Trevano by Sigismund III Vasa, the same monarch who, a year later, transferred the capital to Warsaw, thus starting Wawel's decline. Abandoned from 1655 onwards to successive raids by the Swedes, the Russians and the Prussians, it was turned into barracks after being annexed by the Austrians in 1796 and the hill, which became a military training area, was surrounded by new brick-built fortifications. Ceded to the Poles in 1905, Wawel gave up its role of military garrison but its restoration only began when Poland regained her independence in 1918; Hans Frank, Kraków's Nazi Governor General, was the first to enjoy it when he moved in with his henchmen in 1939. Completed after the war, the full restoration of the edifice enabled it to regain part of its former glory.

Exterior

The vast inner courtyard, formed on three sides by three magnificent arcaded galleries featuring a combination of columns and arches, is a truly splendid sight, worthy of the most famous Italian Renaissance *palazzi*. Most remarkable is the upper gallery supported by very slender columns and covered with a steep tiled roof. The original frieze by Hans Dürer, which adorned the top part of the outside walls of the galleries, has recently been restored. In its heyday during the 16C, the castle was organised in the following way: the ground floor of the north wing contained the Crown Treasury and the administrative offices were housed in the east wing. The king's private apartments were situated on the first floor whereas the state apartments were located on the second floor, known as *piano nobile*. Today the galleries contain five main exhibitions displayed in over 70 rooms. The Lost Wawel exhibition cannot be accessed from this courtyard.

The Private Royal Apartments★★
(Prywatne Apartamenty Królewskie)
testify to the artistic taste of the Jagiellon dynasty. The main interest of these elaborately decorated rooms lies in the precious collection of Flemish tapestries hanging on the walls of King

Sigismund I the Elder's private apartments and of the State apartments located on the second floor. Only 136 out of the 360 16C tapestries (called *arrasy* after the manufacture situated in Arras, France) commissioned by the last monarch of the Jagiellon dynasty, have survived. Designed by painters Willem Tons and Michiel van Coxcie, known as the Flemish Raphaël, most of them illustrate stories from the Old Testament, such as Adam and Eve in the Garden of Eden, the story of Noah's Ark or the The Tower of Babel. Sent to Russia after The Third Partition of Poland in 1795, the precious tapestries only returned to Kraków during the 1920s. Removed to Canada by way of Romania, France, and England during World War II, the tapestries and other treasures from the castle were only returned to communist Poland in 1962.

The State Apartments★★★ (Komnaty Królewskie) are the castle's major attraction. Several rooms are named after the friezes running underneath the painted ceilings. Starting from the Audience Staircase in the middle of the east wing, you will see to your left a succession of rooms including the **Tournament Room** (from the frieze by Hans Dürer, Albrecht's brother, dating from 1535), the **Military Parade Room** (frieze by Anton Breslau dating from 1535), all decorated with paintings and furniture of Italian origin. At the end of this wing, you will find the **Audience Hall★★★** (Sala Poselska), undoubtedly the most spectacular room in the castle, once used for royal audience sessions and for debates by the Sejm, the Polish Parliament. Its specificity lies in its splendid décor of carved wooden heads literally springing from the coffered ceiling. This remarkable work was created between 1531 and 1535. Unfortunately, only 30 of the original 194 heads remain. The frieze on the theme of "The Life of Man", which decorates the hall is by Hans Dürer. The rooms located north of the staircase, such as the **Zodiac Room**, the **Planets Room** and the **Battle of Orsza Room**, also owe their name to the friezes made in the early

1930s. Another noteworthy room is the **Bird Room** (Sala pod Ptakami) featuring fine marble portals, situated at the beginning of the north wing, damaged by fire in 1595, remodelled in Baroque style by the Italian architect Trevano and decorated to suit the taste of the Vasa dynasty. Representative of this trend is the **Eagle Room** (Sala pod Orłem), the old royal court of justice, which houses a series of Dutch and Flemish pictures, including an **equestrian painting** of Prince Ladislas IV Vasa (1624) by Peter Paul Rubens. Finally, the Muses Room leads to the **Senators' Hall** (Sala Senatorska) with its fine Renaissance coffered ceiling. This hall, the largest in the castle, contains the most impressive group of Flemish tapestries illustrating scenes from Genesis. The exit is via the Senators' staircase which leads down to the northeast corner of the courtyard.

Housed in some fine Gothic chambers on the ground floor of the northeast corner of the castle, the **Crown Treasury** (Skarbiec Koronny) contains a profusion of precious objects connected with the Polish Crown and the kings' coronation (in spite of the fact that the original stock was looted several times, in particular by the Prussians). The prize exhibit is the kings' famous sword, called **Szczerbiec** (the jagged blade), a symbol of bravery used during coronations. The **Armoury** (Zbrojownia) exhibits a rich collection of Polish and European weapons and armours as well as war trophies. Also on display are copies of standards taken from the Teutonic enemy during the battle of Grunwald in 1410. Located in the northwest corner of the castle, the exhibition of **Oriental Art** (Sztuka Wschodu) consists of the spoils of war taken by King John III Sobieski after his victory over the Ottomans in Vienna in 1683, the showpiece being a precious ceremonial tent *(undergoing restoration work)*.

Lost Wawel Exhibition★
(Wawel Zaginiony) B3

Open Mon 9am–1.30pm, Tue–Fri 9.30am–5pm, Sat–Sun 11am–6pm. 8 PLN. Entrance from the Wawel exterior courtyard, near the cafeteria.
Housed on the ground floor and in the cellars of the building which closes the west side of the arcaded courtyard, this exhibition was designed to show what Wawel Hill looked like 1 000 years ago, the main attraction being the reconstructed foundations of the **Rotunda of the Virgin Mary** (or of SS Felix and Adauctus), the oldest stone church on the hill, built in the 10C or at the beginning of the 11C, and possibly Poland's first Christian church. Demolished by the Austrians at the beginning of the 19C, it was rediscovered during excavation work carried out in 1917.

End your tour of Wawel by walking towards the southwest part of the citadel. Behind the Thieves' keep (Baszta Złodziejska), one can admire a fine panorama of the meander formed below by the Wisła. Slightly to the left is the entrance to the Dragon's Cave (remember to visit the cave last, otherwise, having reached the exit of the cave, you would have to walk right round the citadel in order to go back up).

The Dragon's Cave
(Smocza Jama) A3

The cave is accessible from the summit of the citadel via a turret backing onto the fortified wall (an automatic machine dispenses tickets); a spiral staircase (135 steps) leads down into the bowels of the hill, to the deepest part of the cave.
Inside the cave shrouded in mystery, you will only explore 81m out of a total of 270m (so as not to disturb the dragon!). The tour is of no outstanding interest but offers a refreshing interlude in hot weather. The photogenic fire-breathing *(every 2min)* metal dragon (Smok Wawelski), waiting for you as you come out of the cave, was made in 1972 by sculptor Bronisław Chromy.

The Story of the Greedy Dragon

Once upon a time, according to legend, the peaceful life of Good King Krak's kingdom was threatened by the repeated disappearance of some of its inhabitants who ventured near the Wisła. A young man who narrowly escaped a similar fate revealed the nature of the danger: a horrible dragon had settled on Wawel. The King then offered half his kingdom and the hand of his daughter in marriage to whomever would deliver the town from the curse. Princes and knights tried in vain until a young cobbler claimed he knew how to kill the dragon – on condition that the King gave him his largest sheep. Having filled the animal's stomach with sulphur and tar, he placed it near the cave. At dawn, the town was woken by a huge explosion: the dragon had swallowed his prey but, feeling extremely thirsty, he had drunk so much water that his stomach had finally exploded! Good King Krak then fulfilled all his promises.

○ *Leave Wawel via the Bernardine Gate, along the second ramp leading to the castle; this will enable you to get a glimpse of several towers which are all that remain of the 15C fortifications. Having reached the Bernardine Church at the foot of Wawel, you could eventually tour the Kazimierz district by heading east.*

③ FROM WAWEL TO THE CHURCH OF THE HOLY CROSS A3 to C1

Kanonicza Street★★★ B3

Running parallel to Grodzka Street, this street has undoubtedly the most ecclesiastical and aristocratic atmosphere in all Kraków and it is also one of the most beautiful and picturesque streets in town. The medieval character of this slightly winding road has been remarkably well preserved. Façades are adorned with coats of arms, roofs surmounted by attics, splendid doorways and impressive carriage entrances *(do not hesitate to walk through)* conceal magnificent courtyards and sometimes beautiful gardens. It was traditionally the street of Wawel Cathedral's Canons, who had lived there since the 14C and after whom it was named (Kanonicza is derived from *canonicorum*). The 20 or so buildings lining it date from the 14C and 15C but many were remodelled later and show a great diversity of architectural styles. The first edifice to be erected at the foot of the castle was the 14C **House of Jan**

Długosz (at no. 25), featuring a fine Renaissance doorway surmounted by an inscription in Latin meaning "There is nothing higher in man than reason". The **Dean's House** (Dom Dziekański) at no. 21, rebuilt between 1582 and 1588 by Santi Gucci, the Italian architect of the Cloth Hall (*see p203*), is one of the most interesting buildings along the street. Behind its splendid **doorway**★ and **façade decorated with sgraffiti** lies a magnificent **Renaissance arcaded courtyard**★★ featuring an 18C statue of St Stanisław, bishop and patron saint of Poland, who is said to have lived here. The future Pope John Paul II lived in this traditional residence of Kraków's bishops from 1963 to 1967. The floors of the building are now linked to the adjoining Archdiocesan Museum.

Kanonicza Street

R. Mattes / MICHELIN

Facing the museum at **no. 16** is the **Hotel Copernicus**, a fine example of a successful restoration.

Bishop **Erazm Ciołek's Palace (no. 17)**, combining two Gothic houses, boasts a Renaissance doorway surmounted by a cartouche bearing the Royal eagle and the letter "S" referring to King Sigismund and by a fine Gothic window. The Palace was recently restored and now houses a museum of Polish sacred art and Orthodox icons.

The Three Crowns House (Pod Trzema Koronami) at **no. 7** boasts a pleasant summer garden. The Cricoteka Muzeum at **no. 5** is an information centre open to all those who wish to know more about the life and works of the incomparable Polish artist, Tadeusz Kantor (1915–90).

Archdiocesan Museum★
(Muzeum Archdiecezjalne) A3
Ul. Kanonicza 19-21. ◷*Open Tue–Fri 10am–4pm, Sat–Sun 10am–3pm.* ◉*5 PLN, Tue free.*

Karol Wojtyła lived in this house between 1952 and 1963 when he was only a priest, before being appointed bishop and moving into the apartments adjoining the Dean's House, where he remained until 1967. Many people turn up here out of curiosity to see the reconstruction of his bedroom-cum-study where his furniture, liturgical clothes and other personal memorabilia, such as a typewriter and even two pairs of skis are respectfully exhibited. However, the main interest of the museum lies in its collection of sacred art.

◔ *Having reached the top of Kanonicza Street, turn left onto the small Senacka Street; it is lined with an imposing building. Successively palace of the Tęczyński family, residence of the Benedictine abbots of Tyniec, municipal baths, Carmelite convent and finally Austrian prison in the 19C, this edifice now houses a large archaeological museum (public entrance is at no. 3 Poselska Street.*

Archaeological Museum★
(Muzeum Archeologiszne) A2
Ul. Poselska 3. ◷*Open Jul–Aug Mon, Wed, Fri 9am–2pm, Tue, Thu 2–6pm, Sun 10am–2pm; Sept–Jun Mon–Wed 9am–2pm, Thu 2–6pm, Fri, Sun 10am–2pm.* ◉*7 PLN, Sun free.*

This educational museum, ideal for arousing children's curiosity, features remarkable displays, such as the collection of Egyptian archaeology housed on the first floor, splendidly enhanced by subtle lighting. The section devoted to funerary rites, including a typological reconstruction of graves, boasts the museum's prize exhibit: an impressive stone **obelisk** from the 10C AD, known as Światowid Zbruczański and carved on four sides, which was discovered in the River Zbrucz in Podol (Ukraine) in 1848. Before leaving the museum, take a stroll round the adjacent garden with its magnificent display of roses.

Franciscan Basilica★★
(Bazylika Franciszkanów) A2
The construction of the Franciscan Church began in 1255, soon after members of the Order arrived in Kraków in 1237; the project was supported by Duke Bolesław the Shy and his sister the Blessed Salome, who chose to give up her princely status in order to become a Poor Clare and was buried in the chancel in 1269, the year the church was consecrated. Vandalised during the Swedish invasion then damaged by the great fire of 1850, the church lost its original Gothic décor during renovation, when it became a blend of neo-Romanesque and neo-Gothic styles, but acquired, at the turn of the 20C, some stained-glass windows and mural paintings by Stanisław Wyspiański, which are today its most famous and valuable assets. The splendid **frescoes**★★ covering the walls of the chancel and the transept combine floral, geometric and heraldic motifs with some figurative scenes. The sumptuous Art Nouveau **stained-glass windows**★★★, bathing the interior of the church with subtle light, are the artist's unquestionable masterpieces. Best admired in the morning light are

St Francis, the Blessed Salome and the Four Elements, located behind the high altar, while the monumental God the Father creating the world (1904), worthy of Michelangelo, reigns supreme in the middle of the west front *(glorious in late-afternoon light!)*.

The adjoining **cloister** houses damaged 15C **frescoes** as well as a **painting collection** started in the 16C, containing portraits of Kraków's bishops, including that of Piotr Tomicki by the famous artist-monk of Mogiła's Cistercian Abbey, Stanisław Samostrzelnik.

⊙ *From the square in front of the church, it is easy to make a detour towards the university district round the Collegium Maius building and the area of Św. Anny, Jagiellońska and Gołębia streets.*

Collegium Maius★★

Ul. Jagiellonska15. ⊙*Open Mon–Fri 10am–2.20pm (☞last guided tour); Apr–Oct until 5.20pm Tue and Thu; free Sat 10am–2.40pm (☞last guided tour).* ☞*Guided tours for groups (20 persons), duration 30min.* ☞*Main museum 12 PLN; main museum and scientific exhibition and Fine Arts collection (Mon–Fri 1pm, duration 1hr) 16 PLN. Tour in English.* ☎*633 15 21.*

The name "Great College" means this is the oldest and most prestigious building of the Kraków University, itself one of the oldest universities of central Europe, founded in 1364 by King Kazimierz the Great. Restored in 1400 by King Władysław Jagiello with the personal gifts made by his deceased wife Jadwiga, the Kraków Academy (Academia Cracoviensis), renamed Jagiellonian University in 1818, extended gradually by acquiring the neighbouring Gothic houses. Remodelled many times over the centuries, in particular in neo-Gothic style during the 19C, it was only restored to its original appearance between 1949 and 1964.

The beautiful arcaded **inner courtyard** is freely accessible, which enables visitors to witness the brief musical show perfomed everyday at 11am and 1pm

by the characters brought to life by the clock mechanism situated above the Golden Door. There are separate guided tours to the historical section on the first floor and the scientific section on the second. The tour shows off historic chambers of the medieval university, where professors once lived and lectured, and many valuables from the university treasury, including 15C royal sceptres which form the University emblem, and filmmaker Andrzej Wajda's Academy Award!

Five rooms on the second floor house the largest collection of scientific instruments in Poland.

St Anne's Church★
(Kościół Św. Anny) A1

Founded in 1689 by the teachers of the Jagiellonian University, this vast church, designed by Dutch architect Tylman van Gameren, is considered one of the finest Baroque buildings in Poland. Note the clever effect created on the **façade** by the overlapping of the three doorways in order to counteract the absence of perspective. Particularly noteworthy is the **stucco decoration**★★ adorning the nave by Italian artist Baldassare Fontana and the flamboyant high altar (1698) framing a picture of the Virgin with Child in the company of St Anne. The south transept houses a **sarcophagus**★ containing the relics of St Jan Kanty (1390–1473) supported by four allegorical figures symbolising the university's main faculties at the time: Philosophy,

Collegium Maius

R. Soberka / MICHELIN

Theology, Medicine and Law. The north transept contains the **monument** dedicated to Nicolaus Copernicus bearing the Latin inscription *sapere auso (know and dare)*, a likely allusion to the fact that Copernicus only revealed his shattering scientific theories at the end of his life. Renowned organ concerts take place regularly.

Facing St Anne's university church is the **Collegium Nowodworski**, the oldest grammar school in the country, where youngsters were supposed to prepare themselves to enter the prestigious university. With its twin-bannister staircase and arcaded courtyard, this building, erected between 1636 and 1643, forms one of the finest examples of Baroque secular architecture in Kraków.

At the end of Gołębia Street stands the main building of the modern Jagiellonian University, its façade overlooking the Planty. Built in neo-Gothic style, the **Collegium Novum** (1887) houses the University Headquarters and the local education authority. Among the nearby trees is a statue of Copernicus holding an astrolabe.

○ *Walk back towards the Franciscan Church.*

On the left, the Bishop's Palace was the residence of Karol Wojtiyła, the future John-Paul II, from 1967 to 1978 when he moved to the Vatican. Thousands of Kraków's residents gathered here, holding candles, on the day of his death (2 April 2005) and flowers and candles are still brought here by many Poles today to pay tribute.

○ *Continue straight on towards the Dominican Church.*

Holy Trinity Basilica and Dominican Monastery★★
(Bazylika Św. Trójcy i Klasztor Dominikanów) B2

The mother church of Poland's Dominican Order, founded by monks who arrived from Bologna in 1223 at the request of Bishop Iwo Odrowąż, is one of the largest and most important basilicas in Kraków. Erected on the site of a Romanesque church destroyed during the Tatar invasion in 1241, it was consecrated in 1249, then rebuilt several times, in particular in 1872, following the 1850 fire. The relatively well-preserved side chapels, added in the 17C by wealthy aristocratic families, are most interesting.

At the end of the right aisle is the **Myszkowski Chapel**★, erected in mannerist style between 1603 and 1614. It is topped with a dome featuring busts of family members *(made by Santi Gucci's workshop)* facing each other. Further on still, the Baroque **Rosary Chapel**, built to celebrate the victory of King Jan Sobieski over the Turks in Vienna (1683). Located on the other side, a staircase leads to **St Hyacinth's Chapel**★, named after the first Polish Dominican (*Jacek* in Polish), whose relics are kept in a marble coffin.

The buildings of the adjoining **monastery** are grouped around two courtyards, including a beautiful cloister with funerary monuments.

Church of the Holy Cross★
(Kościół Św. Krzyża)

This Gothic church, its slender red-brick structure offset against the green background of the Planty, is one of the most charming churches in Kraków. It served as the parish church of the Hospitallers of the Holy Spirit of Saxia which settled in Kraków in 1244. The present appearance of the edifice dates mainly from the 14C and 15C. The adjoining hospital, closed in the 19C, was demolished in 1891 to make room for the Słowacki Theatre. The almost square nave is surmounted by Gothic palm vaulting supported by a single central pillar featuring a tree-shaped capital; this symbol of the new tree of life represented by the Crucifix is chartacteristic of the Order and omnipresent inside the church.

Not far from the Church stands the imposing structure of the **Juliusz Słowacki Theatre**, erected between 1891 and 1893, remisniscent of the Opéra Garnier in Paris.

KAZIMIERZ★★ TOWN MAP III

Founded in 1335 as an independent town by King Kazimierz the Great and named after him, Kazimierz was surrounded by fortifications at the end of the 14C. The King offered hospitality and granted important privileges to the Jewish community who settled southwest of the Rynek before being resettled to Kazimierz following the pogrom of 1494, by King John Olbracht in the vicinity of the present Szeroka Street. At the beginning of the 16C, Jews who were being persecuted in other countries poured into Kazimierz. In 1791, the area officially became a district of Kraków. Nowadays, it includes a Catholic part (even if many Jews settled there in the 19C) in the southwest and a Jewish part to the northeast of an area which is has emerged from the dilapidated state it had been reduced to at the end of World War II. Interest for the Jewish Kazimierz was suddenly aroused in 1993, following the making of Steven Spielberg's film, *Schindler's List*.

The **Podgórze** district, on the south bank of the Wisła, includes several memorials linked with the holocaust of Kraków's Jews, which can be visited.

Pauline Church and Monastery in Skałka★
(Kościół Paulinów) A2

Built on the "rock" *(Na Skałka)* in the middle of a lovely park, the most pastoral of Kraków's churches is, like the Cathedral, a place of worship dedicated to the memory of Stanisław, the martyred bishop. The **idyllic setting**★ is enhanced by the presence of a strange four-sided pool (Sadzawka Św. Stanisława) with a statue of the patron saint of Poland emerging from its centre, dating from 1731. The present Baroque church (1733–42) is the third maybe even the fourth sanctuary built on this site. The main attraction, placed on the altar dedicated to it in the north aisle, is the tree trunk on which the martyred bishop is said to have been cut to pieces by Bolesław the Bold's henchmen on 11 April 1079, after the King cut off his head on this very spot. Every year on the

1st Sunday after 8 May, St Stanisław's feast day, a large procession wends its way from the cathedral to this church (which contained the saint's grave before its transfer to Wawel). Between 1877 and 1880, the **crypt** cut into the rock in 1792 *(accessible from the outside in the middle of the twin-bannister staircase)* was turned into a national Pantheon, in addition to that already existing in the Wawel crypt. Great creators in Polish culture, including the historian Długosz, the writers Siemieński and Kraszewski, artists Siemiradzki, Wyspiański and Malczewski, and the composer Szymanowski were laid to rest in sarcophagi. The latest to be admitted is the poet Czesław Miłosz, buried in great pomp on 27 August 2004.

St Catherine's Church★
(Kościół Św. Katarzyny)B2

This is one of the town's finest Gothic churches; founded in 1363 by King Kazimierz the Great to make amends, as the story goes, for the murder of a clergy member on the king's orders. Its history is marked by a succession of disasters: two earthquakes in 1443 and 1786, flooding around 1370 and three huge fires in 1556, 1604 and 1638; to top it all, it was turned into an arsenal by the Austrians during the first half of the 19C. This tragic succession of unfortunate events explains its extremely bare and austere interior in striking contrast with the monumental **high altar** (1634) miraculously spared, which frames a picture illustrating the mystical marriage of St Catherine. Outside stands the former 15C brick-and-timber belfry. Adjoining the north side of the church is the cloister of the Augustine Convent, which contains early 15C frescoes illustrating in particular the saint's martyrdom.

▷ *Walk up Skałeczna Street to Krakowska, then turn right towards Wolnica Square.*

Wolnica Square B2

Kazimierz's 15C **Town Hall** (Ratusz Kazimierski) stands on the former market place *(smaller now than it used to*

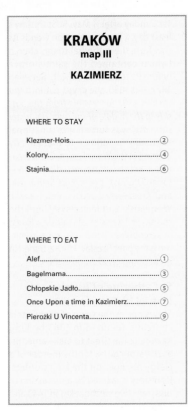

KRAKÓW
map III

KAZIMIERZ

WHERE TO STAY

Klezmer-Hois.................................②
Kolory...④
Stajnia..⑥

WHERE TO EAT

Alef...①
Bagelmama....................................③
Chłopskie Jadło..............................⑤
Once Upon a time in Kazimierz........⑦
Pierożki U Vincenta........................⑨

be). Topped on its west side by a fine crenellated attic and dominated by a 16C octagonal tower, it now houses the rich collections of the **Ethnographic Museum** (Muzeum Etnograficzne), including a large number of artefacts illustrating Polish traditional art and culture, in particular through reconstruction of rustic domestic interiors, mainly from the south of Poland. *Pl. Wolnica.* ○*Open Tue–Wed 11am–7pm, Thu 11am–9pm, Fri–Sat 11am–7pm, Sun 11am–3pm.* ○9 PLN. ○430 55 75.

Church of Corpus Christi★
(Kościół Bożego Ciała) B2
This was the first church in Kazimierz; built in 1340 by the king of the same name, it was completed in the middle of the 15C and remodelled several times. During the siege of Kraków by Swedish troops in the middle of the 17C, the church and its cloister were used as their

headquarters by King Carl Gustav and his troops. The church yard is still surrounded by old cemetery walls. The interior offers a striking contrast between the austere stone-and-brick architecture and the wealth of ornamentation of the carved Baroque altars. Don't miss the mannerist high altar, the stained-glass windows in the chancel, the fine stalls (1632) and the extravagant boat-shaped Baroque pulpit. The Wawel architect, Bartolomeo Berecci, who was murdered in 1537, is buried in St Anne's Chapel.

▷ *Continue towards the Jewish part of Kazimierz, via Józefa Street (the tourist office is at no. 7).*

The **High Synagogue (Bożnica Wysoka)**, at **no. 38**, was the third synagogue to be built in the town between 1556 and 1663. It owes its name to the situation of the prayer hall, "high" above street level.

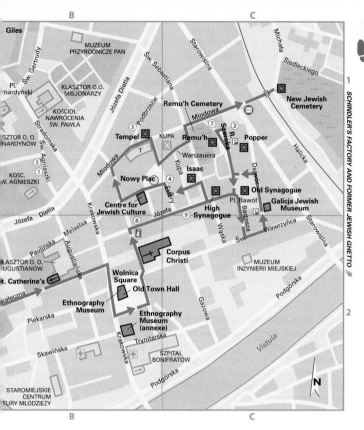

SCHINDLER'S FACTORY AND FORMER JEWISH GHETTO

It now houses a bookshop specialising in Jewish topics. **No 42** along the same street is a **prayer house** devoted to the study of the Torah *(Kowea Itim l'Tora)*, built in 1810 and restored in 1912. At the end of Józefa Street, you will come to the Old Synagogue, entered from the south side, which bars Szeroka Street.

◐ *Turn right onto Bartosza Street and join the parallel street.*

Galicja Jewish Muzeum★C1
Ul. Dajwór 18. ◑*Open daily 10am–6pm.* ◉*15 PLN.*

This museum, inaugurated in June 2004, is based on an interesting approach which consists in taking a fresh look at the Jewish past of Polish Galicia. The objective of the exhibition *Traces of Memory* is to bear witness, through a series of large photographs, to a civilisation which developed during almost 1,000 years and suddenly disappeared, practically obliterated from one day to the next. It is complemented by temporary exhibitions. Bookshop and cafeteria.

Szeroka Street★★C1
In spite of its name, this street looks very much like a square. Its present name meaning "Broad Street" is just as appropriate as its former name of "Main Street". It was the centre of commercial and religious life in the Jewish town from the 15C to the 19C and also assumed the role of market square. Its past bustling atmosphere having long disappeared, it is now the centre of tourist Kazimierz, full of visitors and cars, lined with hotels, galleries, bars and restaurants serving a traditional Jewish cuisine.

Tucked inside the courtyard of the Alef Restaurant is the former **Popper Synagogue** (Synagoga Poppera), founded in

1620 by a wealthy merchant and banker, Wolf Popper, known as The Stork. Vandalised during the war, in 1965 it was turned into a cultural centre open to visitors. The short southern side of the square is closed off by the Old Synagogue. On the opposite side stands the **Jordan Palace** (Pałac Jordanów), housing a fine Jewish bookshop.

Old Synagogue★

(Synagoga Stara or Bożnica Stara) C1

Ul. Szeroka24. ○*Open Mon 10am–2pm, Tue–Sun 9am–5pm.* ∞*8 PLN, Mon free.*
This is the oldest surviving Jewish building in Poland. The synagogue was built in Gothic style at the very beginning of the 15C, then remodelled in Renaissance style following the fire that devastated Kazimierz in 1557 by the Italian architect Mateo Gucci. During restoration work undertaken in the early 20C, the 16C level of the building was rediscovered, which explains why it is now below the present street level.

Surrounded by a fine wrought-iron railing decorated with the star of David, today the synagogue houses the Jewish section of the town's historical museum, devoted to the history of Kraków's Jewish community.

Remu'h Synagogue and Cemetery★★

(Bożnica Remuh i Cmentarz Remuh) C1

Ul. Szeroka 40. ○*Open Sun–Fri 9am–5pm.* ∞*5 PLN.* ☺*Men must wear a head covering.*
Sometimes called "The New Synagogue" as opposed to the Old Synagogue, it was founded by Israël Isserles Auerbach for his son Moses Isserles (1520–72) also known as Rabbi Remu'h, a scientist, philosopher and eminent Talmud specialist, and built between 1556 and 1558. It regained its religious role in 1945 and is now the only active Jewish synagogue in Kraków.

The visit of the synagogue is combined with a tour of the **cemetery**★★ *(here, too, it is compulsory for men to cover their heads)*, which is the oldest cemetery of Kraków's Jewish community and one

of Europe's oldest Jewish cemeteries. Situated behind the synagogue, it was created in the year 5331 *(1551 on the Christian calendar)* and remained the main necropolis in Kazimierz.

The most eminent members of the Jewish community were buried here until 1800, when it was closed by the Austrian authorities. Neglected from then on, it was vandalised by the Nazis during World War II and became more and more dilapidated until archaeological excavations carried out in 1959–60 revealed the presence of several layers of graves *(part of the cemetery which was not excavated still rises 5m above the rest)*. More than 700 tombs, including very valuable ones from an artistic point of view, were brought to light, restored and carefully replaced. Note that some eminent personalities had a second grave built after the war, when the original one was believed to have definitively disappeared.

The **grave** of Rabbi Remu'h, adjoining the western wall of the synagogue, was among the few tombstones spared by the Nazis, a kind of miracle interpreted by Orthodox Jews, who flock to the grave as one more sign of the Rabbi's holiness and supernatural powers. Fragments of old *matzevas* (Hebrew for "tombstones") were used to build a **memorial wall** against the enclosing wall overlooking Szeroka Street *(to the right of the entrance)*.

Isaac's Synagogue★

(Synagoga Izaaka) B1

Ul. Kupa18. ○*Open Sun–Fri 9am–7pm (Jul–Aug 9am–8pm).* ∞*7 PLN.*
The Italian architect Giovanni Battista Trevano and the stucco specialist Giovanni Battista Falconi worked on this imposing Baroque synagogue built between 1638 and 1644 for the wealthy merchant Izaak Jakubowicz. The outside staircase enabled women to reach the gallery reserved for them. The visit is rendered all the more interesting by the viewing of several archive films about the daily life of Kraków's Jewish community before the war and during the German occupation, including in par-

ticular, films of Nazi progaganda about the Podgórze Ghetto in 1941.

Head towards the **New Square** (Nowy Plac), known in the past as the Jewish Square; in its middle stands a circular covered market hall built in 1900. Between 1927 and the beginning of the war, it was used as a ritual poultry slaughterhouse. Today, the square is surrounded by a great number of trendy cafés which come to life at nightfall; a popular flea market takes place every Sunday morning.

In the corner of the square, along Meiselsa Street, the **Jewish Cultural Centre** (Centrum Kultury Żydowskiej) is the headquarters of the Fundacja Judaica *(Ul. Rabina Meiselsa 17;* ○*open Mon–Fri 10am–6pm, Sat–Sun 10am–2pm)*. Inaugurated in 1993, it is an exhibition centre and a concert venue. It is worthwhile going in to ask about the programme of events, or to enjoy the tearoom and take a break in the pleasant roof-garden.

▷ *Head for Miodowa Street*

Tempel Synagogue
(Synagoga Tempel) B1

Ul. Miodowa 24. ○*Variable opening times (more often in the afternoon from 1–3pm).* ○*5 PLN.*

Built in 1862 in neo-Romanesque style and given a Moorish-inspired decoration, it is the most recent synagogue in Kazimierz. Known to be a progressive *(postępowa)* synagogue, it was attended by a large number of Jewish intellectuals who called for equal rights, non-denominational education and objected to speaking Yiddish and wearing traditional clothes, thus opposing the precepts of strictly orthodox Jews and supporters of Hasidism.

▷ *Follow Miodowa Street towards the new cemetery situated on the other side of the railway line. A short detour via Estery Street will lead you to the Kupa Synagogue (Ul. Warszauera 8), very recently restored.*

Jewish cemetery

A. Galy / MICHELIN

New Jewish Cemetery★
(Nowy Cmentarz Zydowski) C1

Ul. Miodowa55. ○*Open summer Sun–Fri 8am–6pm; reduced hours in winter.* ○*Closed Jewish holidays.* ○*Free.* *www.jewishkrakow.net.*

Make a point of taking a stroll along the alleyways of this derelict, overgrown cemetery pervaded by a meditative atmosphere. Created in 1800, outside the Kazimierz district of that time, as a replacement of the Remu'h cemetery, it was vandalised by the Nazis who used the matzevas as building material. Bearing witness to the secularisation and cultural integration of a growing number of Kraków's Jews, some of the epitaphs inscribed on tombstones are in German or Polish.

PODGÓRZE

Follow Starowiślna Street towards the Vistula River and cross the bridge into the Podgórze neighborhood. Immediately on the right is Pl. Bohaterów Getta (Heroes of the Ghetto Square).

This is where the Nazis created a walled-in **ghetto** for the Jews of Kraków starting in March 1941. The ghetto existed for two years and was liquidated over a two day span, 13–14 March 1943 when those Jews considered fit for work were marched off to the Płaszów labour camp 3km south of here, while most of the old and sick were taken into various back yards and shot or sent to Auschwitz. The **square** is now covered with metal chairs that create an unusual memorial to the victims of the ghetto. Inspired by archival photos of Jewish schoolchildren carrying their chairs from Kazimierz into the ghetto in 1941, the chairs are aligned in special ways to point out different episodes in the tragic history of the ghetto. One preserved section of the old ghetto walls has been preserved on Ul. Lwowska, across from the square on the other side of the tram tracks about 300 meters further south.

Cross the busy road with tram tracks and follow Ul. Kącik until reaching elevated train tracks, from there take the tunnel under the tracks which leads to Ul. Lipowa. Another 200m further on is the former **Oskar Schindler Factory** (*Ul. Lipowa 4;* ○*open Tue–Sun 10am–6pm, Mon 10am–2pm, last admission 90min before closing;* ○*closed first Mon of the month;* ○*15PLN/13PLN, Mon free*). Oskar Schindler's former enamel ware factory has just recently been converted into a **museum** belonging the Kraków Historical Museum. In addition to documenting the history of Schindler's role in saving more than 1,000 Jewish workers during World War II, the museum exhibits are dedicated to the history of Kraków during the Nazi occupation (1939–1945).

MUSEUMS

Czartoryski Museum★★★
(Muzeum Książąt Czartoryskich)
TOWN MAP II B1

Ul. Św. Jana19. ○*Closed until 2012 for renovations.*

The Museum of the Czartoryski Princes, the direct descendants of the Jagiellon dynasty, is the pride of the city of Kraków. The initial stock collected by Izabela Czartoryska in her Puławy palace at the beginning of the 19C was sent to Paris to escape confiscation and was returned to Poland in 1876. Shamelessly plundered by the Nazis during the war, it was partially recovered then nationalized, thus forming part of the National Museum in 1949.

The prize exhibit is undoubtedly the delicate **Lady with an Ermine**, which was only authenticated and officially attributed to Leonardo da Vinci in 1992 when a set of his fingerprints were discovered under the first layer of paint. This marvellous work shares a room with another "painting" acquired in Venice in 1807, of which all that remains is the empty frame, symbolically hung on the wall; the painting itself, probably a self-portrait by Raphaël, was "borrowed" by the Nazis in 1939 and never recovered. Another major exhibit is Rembrandt's **Landscape with the Good Samaritan**, which looks out of place among the other Dutch paintings. Captions are in French, a likely consequence of the collection's long stay in Paris.

Stanisław Wyspiański Museum★★
(Muzeum Stanisława Wyspiańskiego) TOWN MAP II A3

Ul. Szczepańska11. ☎*422 70 21.* ○*Open Wed–Sat 10am–6pm, Sun 10am–4pm.* ○*8 PLN, Sun free.*

Recently housed in the 17C Szołayski House, this very pleasant museum contains works and souvenirs connected with the famous Art Nouveau artist, Stanisław Wyspiański (1869–1907). A leading member of the "Young Poland" movement, the Polish equivalent of Art Nouveau, this native of Kraków, who was very attached to his home town and to Polish national history, was a pupil of Matejko at the Fine Arts Academy. He was essentially a painter, but with more than one string to his bow, he was also a writer, a playwright and set-designer. The sumptuous stained-glass windows of the Franciscan Church were his masterpiece.

Kraków National Museum
(Muzeum Narodowe)

Al. 3 Maja1. ○*Open Tue–Sat 10am– 6pm, Sun 10am–4pm.* ○*8 PLN for permanent exhibitions, 16 PLN for temporary and permanent, Sun free.* *www.muzeum.krakow.pl.*

Situated in the heart of the new university district, this imposing modern edifice, begun in 1934, was only completed in 1989. The main building (Gmach Główny) of the museum contains the **Gallery of Polish Arms and Uniforms** *(ground floor)*, the **Gallery of Decorative Art** *(nine exhibition rooms, two annexes)*, the **Gallery of 20C Polish Art** *(extensive area)* and often stages excellent temporary exhibitions.

Józef Mehoffer House★
(Dom Józefa Mehoffera)
Ul. Krupnicza26. ⏰*Open Tue–Sat 10am–6pm, Sun 10am–4pm.* 🎟*6 PLN, Sun in winter free, Thu in summer free.*
Those who appreciate artists' houses should love the peaceful home *(and its pleasant adjoining garden)* of painter Józef Mehoffer (1869–1946), perfectly preserved in its original state.

Manggha Japanese Art Centre
(Centrum Sztuki i Techniki Japońskiej "Manggha") **A1**
Ul. Konopnickiej 26. ⏰*Open Tue–Sun 10am–6pm.* 🎟*15 PLN.*
This futuristic building with outside mirrors reflecting the view of the castle and the Wisła, was created on the initiative of film-maker and director Andrzej Wajda and his wife Krystyna Zachwatowicz. The construction of the building by Japanese architect Arata Isozaki was financed by the prize awarded in 1987 to the film-maker by the Inamori Foundation in Kyoto. The aim of this museum, inaugurated in 1994, is to familiarise the public with Japanese culture through beautiful exhibitions presenting, in rotation, the private collection of writer Feliks "Manggha" Jasieński, bequeathed to the Kraków National Museum in 1920.

EXCURSIONS
Zwierzyniec★★ TOWN MAP I B2
Head for the Salwator (The Saviour) district, at the end of tram lines nos. 1, 2 and 6. From there, you will have to climb another 1.6km to the summit of the Kościuszko Mound, alternatively directly accessible by bus no. 101 (infrequent service) starting from Grunwaldzki Bridge.

This walk through green areas west of Kraków, only a few minutes from the Rynek, will enable you to explore one of the town's most pleasant suburbs. The ascent of the Kościuszko Mound, the main attraction of this easy walk, will allow you to discover another aspect of the town and to enjoy the best possible view of Kraków.

Facing the end of the tram line, on the edge of the Wisła, stands the imposing **Premonstratensian Monastery** (Klasztor Norbertanek), founded in the 12C and remodelled many times. Every year, eight days after Corpus Christi, the Lajkonik parade, whose tradition goes back to the Tatar raid of 1287, starts from here and heads for the Rynek. Walk towards the mound along Św. Bronisławy Street until you reach, on the left, the 17C **wooden Church of St Margaret** (Kościół Św. Małgorzaty). Built on an octagonal plan, it is covered with shingles and surmounted by a lantern. People who died from the Plague during an epidemic were buried here. Slightly higher up, on the opposite side, the **Church of the Holy Saviour** (Kościół Najświętszego Salwatora) is one of the oldest in the city. Built in the 10C, it was destroyed during the Swedish occupation and rebuilt in the 17C. Note, just beyond the church, the estate comprising fine Art Nouveau houses. The street is prolonged by Washington Avenue with, on its left, the **Cemetery of the Saviour** (Cmentarz Salwatorski), occupying a superb position on the crest of the hill; it leads directly to the **Kościuszko Mound★★** (Kopiec Kościuszki). Erected between 1820 and 1823 as a tribute to the leader of the 1794 national insurrection, this manmade mound, 34m high and 80m in diameter sits on top of a hill (333m) known as Sikornik. In 1853, it was enclosed within a brick citadel built by the Austrians and today occupied by a hotel and the premises of the private RMF radio station. The top of the mound *(admission charge 🎟8 PLN)* is accessible from the back via the small neo-Gothic Chapel of St Bronisławy. Beneath the hill, you will see a vast meadow commonly called Błonia, which is the venue of great popular gatherings such as the grand papal masses celebrated by John-Paul II on his trips to Kraków.

Tyniec★★ TOWN MAP I A2

Accessible by bus no. 112 from the Grunwaldzki Roundabout (on the opposite bank of the Wisła, across the bridge of the same name), by taxi, or in summer by one of the river shuttles moored in front of Wawel.

Perched on a rocky promontory over-looking the south bank of the Wisła, 12km southwest of Kraków, **Tyniec's Benedictine abbey** (Opactwo Benedyktynów Tyńcu) is essentially a fortified church. Benedictine monks arrived from France in 1044 and founded the abbey at the beginning of the 11C. Originally Romanesque *(as the right side of the doorway shows)* but remodelled several times, the edifice today looks like a Baroque sanctuary with Gothic elements. The church, famous for its summer organ concerts, is the only part of the abbey open to visitors. However, the main asset of the place is its pastoral setting con-sisting of the **terrace-viewpoint**★★ offering a fine view of the meandering Wisła stretched out below.

The Wieliczka Salt Mine★★★
TOWN MAP I C2

10km southeast of Kraków – minibus (preferable to trains) stationed in Pawia Street, not far from the railway station, leave visitors near the entrance to the mine (this is not the end of the line). Ul. Daniłowicza10. **Ticket office** ◷ *open Apr–Oct daily 7.30am–7.30pm; Nov–Mar daily 8am–5pm.* ◷*Closed 1 Jan, Easter Sun, 1 Nov, 24, 25, 31 Dec.* ☞*Guided tours (3hr) in English (65 PLN) daily Oct–May 9am–5pm every hour; Jun–Sept 8.30am–6pm every 30min.* ✆*(12) 278 73 02.*

Some foreign tourists plan a trip to Poland with the sole aim of visiting Wieliczka *(pronounced Vielichka)*, a town situated on the outskirts of Kraków, renowned for its **rock-salt mine** (Kopalnia Soli), worked since the 10C and on UNESCO's World Heritage List since 1978. An incredible underground labyrinth dug from the 13C onwards in search of this "white gold" which for centuries represented a real godsend for the Polish kingdom's finances.

After a monotonous descent via a 53-flight staircase you will reach a depth of 64m. There is a permanent temperature of 14°C (*take appropriate clothing*). You will only tour the first three levels situated at depths of between 64m and 135m, but this vast pit spreads its network of galleries over nine levels

Wieliezka Salt Mines

R. Soberka / MICHELIN

The New Steelworks

Such is the evocative name of the new town whose establishment in Kraków's eastern suburbs was decreed by Stalin in 1949 to serve as a model of communist urban planning. A strictly political decision clearly aiming at symbolically punishing a city considered too intellectual, too conservative and a hotbed of anti-Communism. Presented as a gift from the Soviet nation to the Polish people, this modern town, dedicated to the working class and entirely centred on the huge steelworks complex, was also intended to change Kraków's social structure, dominated at the time by the middle class who, for the most part, had said "No" to the recent referendum seeking popular approval. This naïve ambition to create *ex nihilo* a perfect town that could rival Kraków enabled the historic centre of the latter to escape the whims of Socialist Realist architects.

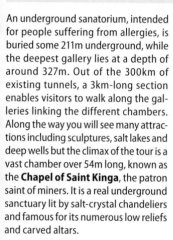

An underground sanatorium, intended for people suffering from allergies, is buried some 211m underground, while the deepest gallery lies at a depth of around 327m. Out of the 300km of existing tunnels, a 3km-long section enables visitors to walk along the galleries linking the different chambers. Along the way you will see many attractions including sculptures, salt lakes and deep wells but the climax of the tour is a vast chamber over 54m long, known as the **Chapel of Saint Kinga**, the patron saint of miners. It is a real underground sanctuary lit by salt-crystal chandeliers and famous for its numerous low reliefs and carved altars.

Nowa Huta TOWN MAP I C1

10km east of Kraków. Nowa Huta's main square (Plac Centralny) is accessible by tram nos. 4, 15 or 22 and bus nos. 502 or 522.

A prolonged stay in Kraków would be incomplete without a short but instructive excursion to Nowa Huta. A 2–3hr stroll through its wide streets will give you an overview of Socialist Realist architecture and an insight into the "Socialist reality", which was the Poles' daily diet during the 1960s. You will also be able to discover, drowned in this ocean of concrete, a few stone patches such as the famous Cistercian church of the old village of Mogiła.

Centralny Square – This central square, which lost its statue of Lenin in 1989, was ironically given "Ronald Reagan" as a second name. From this semi-octagonal,

sadly empty central space (some Poles would like Warsaw's Palace of Culture to be moved here), several avenues stretch out in various directions: Solidarity Avenue, General Anders Avenue and John Paul II Avenue (all of them notorious anti-Communists!), lined with endless monumental residential blocks, mostly grey and drab.

Compared to Kraków's charming old streets, these wide thoroughfares look somewhat sinister, even though the foliage of the now mature trees tends to soften the austere appearance of the façades. A good way to see the essential is to tour the town in a taxi and ask to be taken to all or some of the sights.

Situated on the eastern outskirts of the city, at the end of Solidarity Avenue, the industrial complex is entered through a very Socialist Realist gate of the **Sędzimir Steelworks** (Huta im. Sędzimira), owned today by the Indian steel tycoon Lakshmi Mittal. At the height of its production in 1977, the steelworks employed 38,000 workers with an annual production of 6.7 million tonnes of steel (today's production has stabilized around 1 million tonnes). Just as important was the pollution generated by the works, which not only endangered the health of the inhabitants but proved very damaging to the old stones of Kraków's historic monuments. The buildings standing on the left and right, known as "The Doges' Palace" on account of their crenellated attic, used to house the central administration of the former Lenin steelworks.

Church of Our Lady Queen of Poland, "the Ark"
(Kościół N.M.P. Królowej Polski "Arka") TOWN MAP I C1
Ul. Obrońców Krzyża 1.

A symbol of resistance to Communist power, this futuristic church, fervently wanted by Nowa Huta's residents, was only erected in the 1970s. Its long-awaited construction even sparked off famous riots after some Communists tried to bring down a cross erected by worshippers. Built in the very heart of enemy territory, ideologically speaking, on a foundation stone from St Peter's Basilica in Rome, sent in 1969 by Pope Paul VI, this church owes its construction to the inflexible will of the then arch-bishop of Kraków, Karol Wojtyła. Nick-named "Lord's Ark", due to its shape, the church is meant to be reminiscent of the boat built by Noah and run aground at the top of Mount Ararat; a hardly disguised metaphor illustrating the conviction that Christianity would be sure to outlive Communism.

The Wanda Mound
(Kopiec Wandy) TOWN MAP I C1
Ul. Ujastek.

Situated south of the Steelworks complex on the way to Mogiła, the Wanda Mound owes its name to one of the daughters of Prince Krak, who chose to throw herself into the Wisła rather than marry the German Prince Rytgier and thus became a symbol of national independence. Probably erected in the 8C, on the site of her grave, this 14m-tall mound is one of Kraków's oldest monuments.

The Cistercian Monastery of Mogiła★★ (Opactwo Cystersów)
Ul. Klasztorna11.

Looking like an island miraculously emerging from an ocean of concrete, this monastery is one of the rare relics of the old village of Mogiła. Founded by Kraków's Bishop Iwo Odrowąż, who presented it to the Cistercians when they arrived from Silesia in 1222, the monastery was named *Jasna Mogiła* (literally *"shining grave"*) on account of the assumed presence in the vicinity of Princess Wanda's grave. Behind a Baroque west front stands one of the oldest Gothic churches in Poland. The most interesting features of the basilica can be seen in and around the transept. Protected by a fine 17C ornamental railing and covered with ex-votos, the Chapel of the Holy Cross (Kaplica Krzyża Świętego), located at the extremity of the north transept, houses the highly venerated Mogiła Cross, miraculously saved from the 1447 fire: tradition requires that worshippers should proceed on their knees round the altar on which it stands. The transept and the chancel of the church (*as well as the library of the monastery*) have retained frescoes by Stanisław Samostrzelnik, an eminent artist-monk in the 16C.

Kalwaria Zebrzydowska
▶ *32km southwest of Kraków, along the road to Wadowice.*

Kalwaria (the Calvary) is known throughout Poland as a place of **pilgrimage**. Some 40 Baroque chapels suggesting the Golgotha were erected in the hills near the Bernardine monastery dating from 1600. Every Maundy Thursday and Good Friday, the **mystery of the Passion** is re-enacted by local people.

Wadowice
▶ *46km southwest of Kraków.*

This small industrial town nestled among rolling hills is renowned for being the birthplace of **Karol Wojtyła** (18 May 1920). Standing on the main square is the Basilica of the Presentation of the Virgin where he was baptised. His birthplace is in a street behind the square. **John Paul II's Birthplace** (Dom Rodzinny Świętego Jana Pawła I; *Ul. Kościelna 7;* ◷ *open Oct–Apr Tue–Sun 9am–noon, 1–4pm, May–Sept Tue–Sun 9am–1pm, 2–6pm;* ⊗*free*). Pilgrims flock to this place year-round and one may have to queue between 30min and 1hr30min. They all come to pay homage to the Pope's memory and to discover his photos, documents and personal objects as well as many of the garments he wore during his pontificate.

ADDRESSES

🏨 STAY

With over four million visitors a year, Kraków is one of the first tourist destinations in Central Europe and finding accommodation is not always an easy task. One positive factor is that most addresses are located within the Old Town or in the immediate vicinity. On the other hand, hotels outside the centre are often comfortable and offer good facilities, but rarely have the same charm as those in the Old Town.

In summer, there are several possibilities of finding seasonal accommodation, either in youth hostels, or in student hostels. In addition, there are now over 200 private hostels, many of which also offer a few private rooms. Tourist offices will provide all the necessary information. A downloadable brochure lists all types of budget accommodation in detail: *www.krakow.pl/en/turystyka/tanie_spanie/html/cheap_sleep_en.pdf.*

IN THE CENTRE

Waweltur – *Ul. Pawia 8.* ☎*422 19 21. www.waweltur.com.pl. Open Mon–Fri 8am–8pm (Nov–Jan 7pm), Sat 8am–2pm.* The town's tourist information and accommodation centre is a private agency situated opposite the station; it will find you a room in a private home *(107 PLN)* or an independent apartment with a kitchen *(200 to 250 PLN depending on the location)*, that would never be more than a 15min-walk from the Rynek.

⊜ **Youth Hostel** – *Ul. Oleandry 4.* ☎*633 88 22. www.smkrakow.pl/eng. 22–34 PLN/pers.* This is the largest *(360 beds)* of the town's permanent youth hostels *(2km from the station, near the Cracovia Hotel).*

⊜⊜ **Dom Gościnny Uniwersytetu Jagiellońskiego** – *Ul. Floriańska 49.* ☎*421 12 25. www.adm.uj.edu.pl. 23 rooms.* Situated in one of the major streets of the Old Town, the guest house of the university offers spacious rooms, most of them single, and intended not only for teachers. Fine staircase but no lift. There is also an annexe *(Bursa Pigonia)* of 33 rooms, situated close to the Planty, at no. 7a Garbarska Street *(☎422 30 08).*

⊜⊜ **Hotel Europejski** – *Ul. Lubicz 5.* ☎*423 25 10. www.he.pl. 36 rooms.* This huge fin-de-siècle hotel, standing on the left as you come out of the railway station, tries as best it can to conceal its 120 years of existence. Endless corridors lead to standardised rooms *(quieter at the back)* and to rooms without bathroom at more reasonable prices. Inner courtyard turned into a summer garden.

⊜⊜ **Hotel Pokoje Gościnne SHERP** – *Ul. Sławkoska 23.* ☎*429 17 78. www.sherp.com.pl. 6 rooms.* This is not strictly speaking a hotel but a boarding-house *(some services are not automatic: making the bed and supplying towels!)* well situated and managed by an association of Polish architects. It occupies the upper floors of a fine historic building: the former apartments comprise units of two rooms with shared bathroom and kitchen.

⊜⊜ **Dom Polonii** – *Rynek Główny 14,* ☎*422 61 58. www.swp.krakow.pl. 3 rooms, 1 apart.* It is difficult to find a more central place to stay: this apartment, located on the 3rd and top floor *(no lift)* of a fine building comprises three rooms, two of them overlooking the Rynek. A very sought-after apartment with a kitchen, two double rooms and a total of four beds; reserve well in advance.

⊜⊜ **Hotel Pollera** – *Ul. Szpitalna 30.* ☎*422 10 44. www.pollera.com.pl. 40 rooms.* Located near the Słowacki Theatre, opposite the House of the Cross, this hotel founded in 1834 by K Poller likes to remind its customers that it is one of Kraków's oldest hotels. Obviously resigned to being deprived of its past splendour, it does not, however, seem determined to completely erase the wear and tear caused by time and continues to maintain a fairly outdated style. The stained-glass windows in the staircase are the work of Wyspiański. The **restaurant** is as spacious as a ballroom.

⊜⊜ **Hotel Saski**. *Ul. Sławkowska 3.* ☎*421 42 22. www.hotelsaski.com.pl. 43 rooms.* Rather than dwell on the rooms themselves, one might prefer to enjoy everything that recalls the

Belle-Époque, the presence of a liveried doorman, a fine hall with an antique lift still in operation, and a profusion of long corridors. Even though it may not be such good value for money as some years ago *(one can always book a room without bathroom for a discount)*, the outdated style still prevails.

⊜⊜ **Hotel Wawel-Tourist**. *Ul. Poselska 22.* *℘424 13 00. www.wawel-tourist.com.pl.* *49 rooms.* Located in a quiet street southeast of the Rynek. Partially restored in 1995 in contemporary neo-Art Nouveau style, this hotel has retained very few original Secession-style features from past incarnations. Customers can choose between retro-style rooms and more modern but also more expensive ones, situated in the new part built onto the back of the hotel.

⊜⊜ **Hotel Wit Stwosz** – *Ul. Mikołajska 28. ℘429 60 26.* *www.wit-stwosz.com.pl. 17 rooms.* This 16C house belonging to St Mary's Church *(hence the name of the hotel)* is situated in a peaceful street east of the Mały Rynek; it provides a refined setting to the hotel's comfortable and elegant rooms. The fourth-floor rooms are slightly smaller and less expensive.

⊜⊜⊜ **Hotel Francuski** – *Ul. Pijarska 13.* *℘627 37 77. www.accorhotels.com.pl.* *42 rooms.* This hotel, jewel of the Orbis chain, was, when it was founded in 1912, one of the top luxury hotels in Europe. Completely brought up to modern standards of comfort in 1991, the French Hotel still retains its Belle-Époque palace atmosphere.

⊜⊜⊜ **Hotel Polski** – *Ul. Pijarska 17.* *℘422 11 44. www.podorlem.com.pl.* *54 rooms.* Established near the Florian Gate, inside three old houses recently returned to their former owners, the Czartoryski ducal family, who acquired them in 1913, the White Eagle Hotel is adjacent to the Museum-Palace of the same name. The communal parts are more attractive than the rooms, a little expensive and yet rather ordinary.

⊜⊜⊜⊜ **Hotel Copernicus** – *Ul. Kanonicza 16. ℘424 34 00. www.copernicus.hotel.com.pl. 29 rooms.* This luxury establishment, concealed behind an austere Gothic façade along Kraków's oldest street, is undoubtedly one of the finest hotels in town. The lovely atrium-style courtyard features wooden galleries leading to the rooms. The swimming pool inside the old Gothic vaulted cellars is a must. The bar on the roof terrace offers a fine view of the castle.

KAZIMIERZ

⊜⊜ **Hotel Alef** – *Ul. Św. Agnieszka 5.* *℘421 31 31. www.alef.pl. 39 rooms.* Located on a quiet side street next to the famous Chłopskie Jadło **restaurant**, this comfortable, modern hotel is ideally located to explore both Kazimierz and the Old Town.

⊜⊜ **Klezmer-Hois** – *Ul. Szeroka 6.* *℘411 12 45. www.klezmer.pl. 11 rooms.* At once hotel, **restaurant**, art gallery and concert venue, the Klezmer is housed in former Jewish ritual baths located in a fine building on the corner of the wide Szeroka Street. Lovely spacious rooms with a pleasant 1930s atmosphere. The restaurant is recommended, the terrace very peaceful.

✲/ EAT

The streets of the Old Town and of the suburbs boast many eateries of all kinds, each more appealing than the other. Most apply similar, generally affordable prices. One way of keeping one's budget under control is to have lunch in one of the popular canteens that still exist. These milk bars would bankrupt traditional restaurants if they didn't close so early *(before 8pm)*. For a modest price of between 10 and 20 PLN, you can have a simple meal – among Polish people – consisting of soup or a starter, a copious main dish and a traditional fruit compôte.

CENTRE

⊜ **Bar Grodzki** – *Ul. Grodzka 47. ℘422 68 07. Open Mon–Sat 9am–7pm, Sun 10am–7pm.*🖰. Slightly more exclusive than its rival in the same street, this milk bar – locally called *jadłodajnia* ("dish-of-the-day" restaurant) – is one of the reliable addresses in the district. Menu in English on the wall. Good traditional Polish cuisine including *placki (potato pancakes covered with goulash* *or mushrooms)*, which are particularly appreciated.

◉ **Bar Kuchcik** – *Ul. Jagiellońska 12. Open Mon–Fri 10am–6pm, Sat 10am–4pm.* 🍴. Close to the Collegium Maius of the Jagiellonian University, this establishment features a plain, unassuming white room which boasts the significant advantage for a milk bar of having a menu in English. And the food is excellent as the house logo suggests. It is also possible to have breakfast here.

◉ **Bar Mleczny Restauracja Pod Temidą** – *Ul. Grodzka 43. Open daily 9am–8pm.* 🍴. Undoubtedly the most sought-after self-service milk bar in town, the favourite haunt of students of the Art History Institute and of the Jagiellonian University's nearby Law Faculty. A meal consisting of a salad, a main dish and a compote will hardly ever cost more than 12 PLN.

◉ **Jadłodajnia U Pani Stasi** – *Ul. Mikołajska 18. Open Mon–Fri 12.30–5pm. Closed July.* 🍴. Located on the north side of the Mały Rynek, inside the courtyard *(accessible via the passageway adjoining the Cyclop Pizzeria)* of the "Pod Trzema Lipami" House. This very authentic Kraków eatery is housed in a small vaulted room crowded with regular customers at lunchtime. Sit down before ordering and pay on your way out. Menu in English with a wide choice of "special dishes of the day". *Pierogi* are popular; they go well with a glass of traditional fruit compôte. Prompt service *(past the queuing stage)* and extremely fresh food.

◉ **Kuchnia Staropolska U Babci Maliny** – *Ul. Sławkowska 17.* ☏*422 76 01. Open Mon–Fri 11am–9pm, Sat–Sun noon–9pm.* This folksy bar gets the top prize for decoration. Located in the cellars of the Polish Academy of Arts and Sciences, you have to go into the building and down the stairs into the inner courtyard. Great soups and enormous servings of Hungarian potato panckakes are just some of the highlights.

◉ **Gospoda C. K. Dezerter** – *Ul. Bracka6.* ☏*422 79 31. Open daily 9am–11pm.* For once you won't have to

go down into a cellar; this establishment located at street level consists of a succession of three long rooms: the yellow walls are decorated with discoloured photographs illustrating military themes of Austro-Hungarian inspiration.

◉◉ **Miód i Malina** – *Ul. Grodzka40.* ☏*430 04 11. Open daily noon–11pm.* This pleasant new restaurant caters for those wishing to try Polish cuisine (and for those who don't by offering Italian pasta and pizza). Somehow the combination works, and at weekends reservations are recommended.

◉◉ **Restauracja Balaton** – *Ul. Grodzka 37.* ☏*422 04 69. Open daily 9am–10pm.* A restaurant specialising in Polish-style Magyar cuisine. Opened in 1969, this gastronomic establishment (which refers to the large Hungarian lake of the same name) is, as always, a reliable address. The menu features copious helpings, the service is unrefined but very efficient. Inexpensive and nourishing. In addition, the restaurant offers its guests the possibility of enjoying Hungarian wine instead of Polish beer for a change.

◉◉ **Restauracja Morskie Oko** – *Pl. Szczepański 8.* ☏*431 24 23. Open daily noon–midnight.* From the street one gets the impression that the "Eye of the Sea" (a lake of the Tatras region) is totally empty. The action takes place in the basement, in a dozen successive vaulted cellars, where numerous customers sit at long rustic tables to enjoy the colours and flavours of the Tatras Mountains. Good to know: on Sundays and Mondays there is no live traditional music.

◉◉ **Restauracja Smak Ukraiński** – *Ul. Kanonicza 15.* ☏*421 92 94. Open daily noon–10pm.* Placed under the aegis of the adjoining Włodzimierza (Vladimir) Foundation, this restaurant housed in two lovely small cellars, plainly decorated, is mainly devoted to promoting Ukrainian cuisine. In summer one can enjoy the coolness of the indoor terrace.

◉◉ **Wiśniowy Sad** – *Ul. Grodzka 33.* ☏*430 21 11. Open daily noon–11pm.* The most "melancholic" of Kraków's cafés, in fact a Russian café-cum-restaurant, pervaded by an undeniable nostalgia. A single room where placemats, a *samovar (heated metal container for hot water)*, a piano, a mirror, an old column set in the wall and appropriate music are all it takes to recreate a Chekhovian atmosphere. This will hardly surprise you when you know that the translation of the name of the place suggests *The Cherry Orchard*. No smoking.

Restauracja Pod Aniołami – *Ul. Grodzka 35. 421 39 99. Open daily 1pm–midnight.* This restaurant, called "Under the Angels", is situated along the Royal Way in a 13C building which for 300 years housed goldsmiths and their workshops. The small cellars boasting an attractive blend of stone, brick and nice rustic furniture in light-coloured wood have more charm than the garden-courtyard despite the fact that it is decorated with a mosaic mural fountain. A large staff is employed to serve traditional Polish dishes, rather refined but also more expensive than elsewhere.

KAZIMIERZ

Ariel – *Ul. Szeroka 18. 421 79 20. Open daily 10am–midnight.* A favourite among groups visiting the former Jewish district. It occupies two buildings, one wing devoted to a private art gallery, the other, symmetrical, housing a café and a restaurant, where concerts of Yiddish music are given every evening from 8pm onwards. Good Jewish cooking.

Chłopskie Jadło – *Ul. Św. Agnieszki 1. 421 85 20. Open daily noon–midnight.* The wood-and-earth interior design creates the atmosphere of a mountain inn of the Tatras region. More than a restaurant, this is a real chain paradoxically advocating the authenticity of rural cuisine in mountain areas. This gastronomic institution, always filled with large tourist parties, now owns nine establishments in the country, including two more in Kraków's town centre, along Grodzka and Św. Jana Streets. Huge helpings, omnipresent background music, overwhelmed and not always attentive service.

Once Upon a Time in Kazimierz – *Ul. Szeroka 1. 421 07 76. Open daily noon–11pm.* One might reasonably hesitate before going into what looks like four old Jewish workshops from pre-war Kraków, each one with a sign bearing the name of its owner. Inside, the former shops – a general store, a joiner's, a tailor's and a grocer's – have been joined to form the dining area of a restaurant recreating the presumably typical atmosphere of Kazimierz in the past. In fact, the place is obviously intended for tourists yet is quite pleasant. The menu offers traditional Jewish dishes such as the excellent *Czulent* and the famous stuffed carp.

CAFÉS

Kawiarna Jama Michalika – *Ul. Floriańska 45. 422 15 61. Open daily 9am–11pm.* Undoubtedly the most famous café in town, if not in all Poland. An awe-inspiring café to be considered like a real museum on account of the numerous works of art decorating the walls. Vaulted rooms plunged in semi-darkness, which conceal the interior atmosphere from the street. Not a place that locals visit, but worth going to once for the old-fashioned atmosphere. Cloakroom compulsory. No smoking.

Loch Camelot – *Ul. Św. Tomasza 17. 421 01 23. Open daily 9am–midnight.* This lovely, somewhat Bohemian café, which attempts to perpetuate the cabaret spirit *(Loch Camelot)* in its own cellars, is mostly interesting for its large and pleasant terrace recessed on the side of the small St John's Church, whose position out of alignment with the axis of the road creates a fine perspective. Besides tea and coffee, it is also possible to have a snack, in particular salads and delicious crumbles *(szarlotka)*.

Café Larousse – *Ul. Św. Tomasza 22. Open Mon–Sat 9am–9pm, Sun 10am–9pm.* A tiny café with only four tables and walls decorated with yellowing plates from an illustrated French dictionary. Good coffee served with small homemade meringues.

Bunkier Cafe – *Pl. Szczepański 3a. 431 05 85.* When the weather is fine, the concrete Arts Bunker (Bunkier Sztuki) opens its greenhouse to the public; it is a pleasant urban observation post offering a front-seat view of the comings and goings along the green belt of the Planty. Amazing entirely blue café inside the art gallery.

Nowa Prowincja – *Ul. Bracka 3–5. Open daily 10am–midnight.* Located between the Rynek and the Franciscan Church, this café is popular among clients of all ages, high-school students to intellectuals to seniors. Try coffee with a slice of the homemade chocolate cake or if the smoke gets to you, escape to the hidden upstairs tearoom that is a non-smoking establishment.

℉ BARS

IN THE CENTRE

CK Browar – *Ul. Podwale 6-7. 429 25 05. Open daily 9am–last customers.* Beer lovers should not miss the large cellars of this "royal and imperial" *(CK)* brewer's, where four kinds of homemade piwo are available, either light or brown, from 11.5° to 14.5°. The establishment, which is sought after by young Kraków residents who have been meeting there in large numbers since 1996, is also a restaurant until 10pm.

Café Pauza – *Ul. Floriańska 18. Open Mon–Sat 10am–1am, Sun noon–midnight.* For once, you are not expected to bury yourself in a cellar but to climb the steps to Paradise *(take a look, it's written)* in order to get to the trendiest bar of the moment, where all the expatriates in town like to meet.

IN KAZIMIERZ

Les Couleurs café – *Ul. Estery 10 429 42 70. Open Mon–Fri 7am–2am, Sat 8am–2am, Sun 9am–2am.* Blue, white and red, these are the dominant colours in this bar, where everything is done to evoke France. Opens extra early for those in need of a caffeine fix.

Alchemia – *Plac Nowy. 421 22 00. www.alchemia.com.pl. Open daily 10pm –4am.* Strange atmosphere in this succession of four rooms, each more mysterious and obscure than the other *(the last one is a recreation of a peasant kitchen, left over from a film shoot)*. This extremely mysterious place, where electricity has been banned and modern facilities disregarded, is only lit by candlelight.

Café Singer – *Ul. Estery 20. Open daily 9am–3am.* Neither karaoke bar, nor tribute to the famous Yiddish writer, this café celebrates the famous American sewing machines fitted with a shelf, on which fabric was originally supposed to rest and is now convenient for holding glasses filled with beer or flavoured vodkas.

🛒 SHOPPING

Galeria Plakatu Kraków – *Ul. Stolarska 8/10. 421 26 40. www.cracowposter gallery.com. Mon–Fri 11am–6pm, Sat 11am–2pm.* Polish posters do not have a museum of their own *(only a gallery)*, worthy of this art form, in which the Poles excel. Unique postcards for the discerning tourist.

If you are fond of **handicrafts** you will enjoy walking among the stalls located in the central aisle of the Cloth Hall.

Do not leave town without having tasted an **obwarzanki**, a ring-shaped pretzel dotted with various kinds of seeds, sold in the street by hawkers.

🎭 FESTIVE EVENTS

Easter Fair on the Rynek and Emmaus Fair in Zwierzyniec on Easter Monday.
March: Rękawka Festivities, near Krakus Mound; Misteria Paschalia Baroque music festival.
April: International Jazz Festival.
May: Kraków Film Festival.
June: Town Festival; Lajkonik Parade; Festival of Jewish Culture; Short Film International Festival; The Great Dragon Parade; Festival of Jewish Culture *(Kazimierz)*.
July: Street Theatre International Festival; Summer Jazz Festival.
August: Music in Old Kraków Festival.
October: International Festival of Early Music.
November: Jazz in Kraków for All Saints; Andrzejki (St Andrew's Day). *Night of 29–30 November.*
December: Kraków Nativity Scene Competition.

Auschwitz Concentration Camp★★★

Oświęcim

No one could have foretold that the small provincial town of Oświęcim would become a place synonymous with Nazi atrocities and a symbol of the Holocaust. The town was incorporated into the Third Reich under the German name Auschwitz; two syllables that evoke the Nazis' final solution and the site where humanity's most extensive mass exterminations were carried out. Today, Auschwitz is more of a memorial than a museum and, with over 1 million visitors a year and over 30 million in all since its creation on 14 June 1947, it is one of the most-visited sites in Poland.

A BIT OF HISTORY
A Cemetery Without Graves

During the tour of the Nazi's largest concentration camp and the world's largest cemetery, one question comes to mind: how was the greatest crime in history against humanity ever allowed to take place?

The question finds no easy answer. What remains to be seen is how the people of today bear witness to the tragic events of the past, for the benefit of future generations. Along with the work of historians and the accounts of survivors – inevitably decreasing in number – new generations are dutybound to keep alive the memory of these events and to pass on a warning to others of what cruelty humanity is capable of, when left unchecked.

Most historians now agree that, between 1940 and 1945, the Nazis deported to Auschwitz at least 1,100,000 Jews, 150,000 Poles, 23,000 Roma, 15,000 Russian prisoners of war and 25,000 members of other nations; covering 28 different nationalities in all. There were Jews from many countries, but Hungarian Jews, believed to number

Michelin Map: Map of Poland C4 – Województwo of Lesser Poland.

Info: Ul. Więźniów Oświęcimia 20, 32-603 Oświęcim. ℰ48 (0)33 843 20 22. www.auschwitz.org.pl.

Location: 60km west of Kraków *(1hr by car)*. To get there by public transport from Kraków, it is better to take a bus *(about 15 PLN)* from the new regional bus station located behind the central train station, rather than the train, which stops a few km from the site *(journey time: 1hr30min)*. Buses depart nearly every 30min. A shuttle bus runs between both sites.

Parking: Guarded parking is available at museum *(7 PLN)*. Various car parks as Auschwitz I and Birkenau.

Timing: The two camps of Auschwitz and Birkenau are 3km apart and form one single museum. In order to appreciate it all, it is necessary to visit both sites. Allow *(depending on opening times)* a morning or an afternoon tour of Auschwitz I and then continue on to Birkenau, which does not include museum exhibits, and is shorter.

438 000, formed the largest group, followed by Polish Jews and French Jews: around 900,000 Jews in total, though the exact number is unknown since 70 to 75% of all deported Jews were led straight to the gas chambers and were never recorded. Only 400,000 prisoners were recorded (including 200,000 Jews) and 60,000 of them were still alive at the end of the war. As the Soviet Army approached, the prisoners who

were able to walk were taken on "death marches" deep inside the Reich. When the camp was liberated on 27 January 1945, the soldiers of the Red Army found only 7 000 survivors in a state of dire starvation.

State Museum Auschwitz II-Birkenau
(Państowe Muzeum Auschwitz-Birkenau w Oświęcimiu)

🕐*Open daily Dec–Feb 8am–3pm, Mar and Nov 8am–4pm; Apr and Oct 8am–5pm; May and Sept 8am–6pm, Jun–Aug 8am–7pm.* 🕐*Closed 1 Jan, 25 Dec, Easter Sun.* ✗. *http://en.auschwitz.org.pl/m. Admission to both sites is entirely free. However, there is a charge for the guide service – recommended for a better understanding of the functioning of the camp.* 😊 *Due to the large number of visitors, all persons are required to have a guide or join a tour from May–Oct between the hours of 10am–3pm. You can book a guide by phone ☎+48 (0)33 844 81 00, by fax +48 (0)33 843 22 27, by email dyspozytornia@pro.one.pl, or at the 🛈information desk of Auschwitz I Museum. Before your visit, it is advisable to endure the horrifying 15min documentary about the liberation of the camp by Soviet troops (depending on the days, the showings are at 11am, 1pm and 3pm in English; ⊚3.50 PLN).*

😊 A Bit of Advice 😊

Because Auschwitz is a memorial and an enormous cemetery, and not a typical tourist sight, strong emotions are aroused by a visit to the concentration camps. Bear this in mind if you intend to take children with you. Officially, visiting is not recommended for children under 13, and it is essential to prepare all youngsters for the visit.

The *Konzentrationslager Auschwitz* was at once a prison camp, a concentration camp, a work camp and a death camp where the Nazis locked up Jews, Roma, homosexuals, communists, members of the resistance, political prisoners, Russian prisoners of war, members of the Polish intellectual élite, priests, Jehovah's Witnesses, prostitutes and common criminals. At one time, Auschwitz comprised three main camps: Auschwitz I, Auschwitz II-Birkenau, Auschwitz III-Monowitz, as well as over 40 secondary camps scattered throughout the region. Today, the first two camps form the memorial-museum, set up as a State Museum in 1947, following a decision by the Polish parliament, and have been listed as one of UNESCO's Cultural and Natural World Heritage sites since 1979.

Prisoner photographs, State Museum Auschwitz II-Birkenau

© Paolo Cipriani/Dreamstime.com

AUSCHWITZ I

Established in former disused barracks of the Polish army, the base camp was built in April–May 1940 and received its first inmates, 728 Polish political prisoners transferred from Tarnów, in June 1940. It was here that in September 1941, the Nazis for the first time tested a pesticide gas on 850 Poles and Russians, which soon brought considerable wealth to its German manufacturer, Zyklon B. The number of prisoners, many incarcerated for political reasons, fluctuated between 12,000 and 16,000 with a peak of 20,000 in 1942 (the year that saw the arrival of women) and a total of 70,000 prisoners died here, some in the gas chamber and crematorium, which functioned in 1941 and 1942. The camp and barracks, essentially preserved in the state the Nazis left them in 1945, now house the main part of the exhibition.

The tour of the camp starts when you pass through the infamous **gate** surmounted by the cynical inscription *"Arbeit Macht Frei" (Work will make you free).* Standing among lines of poplars, surrounded by watchtowers and barbed wire, are the red-brick walls of **28 identical blocks** lining both sides of two central alleys. It would take you several hours to make a careful and exhaustive visit of all the accessible blocks. Start with those at the back, situated along the second alley and devoted to the **general exhibitions** (**Block 4**: Extermination, **Block 5**: Material proof of the crime, which houses the most haunting and horrifying exhibits, such as piles of women's hair, **Block 6**: The prisoners' daily life, **Block 7**: Accommodation and sanitary conditions).

On the right at the end of the alley stands the medical experiments and sterilisation block followed by the **Death Block (no. 11)**, no doubt the most sinister of them all, a section of the camp where prisoners were cruelly tortured. Between the two, in the courtyard was the Death Wall where thousands were executed after summary trials.

From there, return to the first alley with blocks devoted to **national exhibitions**.

Block no. 20 is dedicated to **France and Belgium**. The **Hungarian Block (no. 18)** takes you, during your visit, along particularly suggestive rail tracks. **Block no. 21** is for the **Dutch**, and located in the southwest corner, **Block no. 27** is devoted to **Jewish** martyrology and struggle. Finally, the itinerary leads to the end of the alley on the left, where the gas chamber and the crematorium, converted in 1943 into an anti-aircraft bunker, are located.

The gallows nearby was used in 1947 for the public hanging of Rudolf Höss, the first commandant of Auschwitz Concentration Camp.

AUSCHWITZ II–BIRKENAU

A free shuttle links the two camps every hour from 11.30am between 15 April and 31 November, and from 10.30am Jun–Aug.

Although Birkenau does not, for most people, have the same sinister ring to it as Auschwitz, it is nevertheless in this camp that the extermination first and foremost of the Jews but also the Roma was systematically carried out; a visit here creates an even stronger and more harrowing impression. Built from scratch in October 1941, 3km from the main camp, near the small Polish village of Brzezinka (Birkenau) meaning "small meadow with birch trees", it looks less like a concentration camp than a camp intended to implement the final solution.

Start by climbing to the top of the watchtower above the entrance gate to get an insight into the unbelievable extent of the camp (2 x 2.5km). Out of the 300 barracks which, in August 1944, housed over 90,000 prisoners, only 45 brick ones and 22 wooden have been preserved, along with the outlines and chimneys of demolished barracks. There is no museum here, just a deeply moving site for visitors to wander round.

Walk beside the very long unloading ramp to the monument to the dead. Inscribed in 21 languages, the commemorative plaque pleads against such barbarism ever being repeated. All around are the ruined remains of the crematoria and gas chambers, as well as the ponds into which human ashes were dumped. The creation of the four gas chambers and crematoria complexes began in 1942 and were fully operational until the SS dynamited them in 1944 as the Red Army was approaching, in order to erase all traces of their crimes.

Auschwitz Jewish Center
(Centrum Żydowskie w Oświęcimiu)
Plac Ks. Jana Skarbka 5 32-600 Oświęcim. Located north of the Rynek of the old town of Oświęcim, 3km from the camp. ○*Open Sun–Fri Mar–Oct 8.30am–8pm; Nov–Feb 8.30am–6pm.* ○*Closed Jewish Holidays. 5 PLN.* ♿ ☐ *♒(33) 844 70 02. www.ajcf.org.*
This museum, which counterbalances the emotional impact of the camps, aims to provide insight into the life of the former Jewish community of the town of Oświęcim. In 1939, Jews accounted for 7,000 of the 12,300 inhabitants of the town, nearly 60 per cent of the total population.

The museum is housed in the only remaining Jewish building in the town, the synagogue of the Society for the Study of the Mishnah (Chevra Lomdei Mishnayot), a centre of Talmudic studies and synagogue completed in 1930 and used as a place of worship until 1939 when the Nazis converted it into an arsenal. Only about 70 Jews survived the war and most of them left as soon as it ended in 1945.

As the last Jews have either died or emigrated, the Center *(supported by a foundation in NYC)* now makes a point of asserting the continuity of a Jewish presence in Oświęcim.

⌖ *Do not miss the short 14min documentary (in English), which presents the moving accounts given by Jewish emigrants evoking the Oshpitzin (Auschwitz in Yiddish) of their childhood.*

The Polish Jura★★
From Kraków to Częstochowa

This is a fairytale landscape of Jurassic limestone outcroppings topped by ruined castles that once guarded the approach to Kraków. At the southern end, Poland's smallest national park nestles within a deep, picturesque vale that features a restored Renaissance castle and bizarre rock formations.

A BIT OF HISTORY
The rugged limestone landscapes and eerie caves of the Polish Jura lend themselves to legends inspired by the extravagant rock formations that can easily be imagined as petrified armies or giants. This is also an area of craggy summits. When Poland was torn by wars in the 14C, the region became a border area which Kazimierz the Great fortified by building a series of castles which now forlornly lie in ruins.

- ♿ **Michelin Map:** Map of Poland C3 – Województwo of Lesser Poland.
- ℹ **Info:** *♒(12) 389 20 05. www.opn.pan.krakow.pl*
- ▷ **Location:** The Ojców Park is located less than 30km northwest of Kraków and the Polish Jura extends 80km further north to Częstochowa.
- ☐ **Parking:** 6.5–10 PLN.
- ⌖ **Don't Miss:** Rambles through the Ojców.
- ♟ **Kids:** The tour of the caves situated inside Ojców Park.
- ○ **Timing:** Count half a day to cross the Jura, stopping to visit a few castles along the way. Spend the night in the Ojców Park. There are delightful rambles to be made early in the morning.

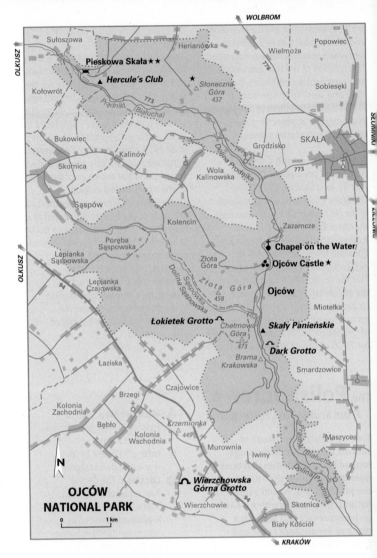

OJCÓW NATIONAL PARK★★
(Ojcowski Park Narodowy)

▶ *Some 20km northwest of Kraków. From Kraków, the park is easily accessible via road 778 as far as the village of Skała then along road 773, which runs through the Park.*

The Prądnik and Sąspówka rivers meet deep inside a valley offering a unique dreamlike landscape which lends itself to enjoyable rambles. Walking and biking are the best means of getting

around to explore this 21sq km park, the smallest in Poland. As you venture along paths, through the undergrowth and along river banks, you will discover a limestone landscape with no fewer than 400 caves and rock formations with mythical names such as Hercules' Club or the Kraków Gate. The microclimate here favours a rich variety of plants and wildlife, in particular bats, the emblem of the Park.

SOUTHERN PARK

It is possible to park in Ojców's vast parking area and from there to visit the main sights on foot via marked footpaths (map available).

Ojców Castle★
(Zamek w Ojcowie)

🕐*Open daily Apr–May and Sept 10am –4.45pm, Jun–Aug until 5.45pm; until Oct 3.45pm; Nov until 2.45pm.* 🎫*2.5 PLN.* 🅿️.

Built in the 14C by King Kazimierz the Great, this castle was the last defence structure before Kraków. The ruins stand on a rocky spur, which seems inaccessible. The fortified main gate, the first floor of which houses a model of the castle in its heyday, leads into the outer courtyard, where traces of the walls are visible.

▶ *Go through Ojców, where there are hotels, restaurants and shops.*

Chapel on the Water
(Kaplica na Wodzie)

Accessible via a footpath starting from the Ojców parking area; allow 10min on foot. 🕐*The chapel is open for Sunday mass at 8am, 10.30am and 4pm.*
It was built in 1901 across the River Prądnik following a law which forbade the construction of places of worship on Ojców land, but not on the water.

👥 Łokietek's Grotto
(Jaskinia Łokietka)

Via the footpath with blue markings (45min one way).
The path runs along the road then through the Kraków Gate (Brama Krakowska) and across the wooded hills. The cave (🕐*open daily Apr and Nov 9am–3.30pm, May–Aug until 6.30pm, Sept until 5.30pm, Oct until 4.30pm; 7 PLN;* ⚑*guided ours start every 20min)* is guarded by a railing with a spider web motif, recalling a local legend that the web of a spider hid the future king Władisław Łokietek here. The 320m-long cave consists of several chambers, each named after a room

GETTING AROUND

BY BUS – A minibus leaves Ul. Ogrodowa, across from the Galeria Krakowska. In summer, bus service also from regional bus station.
BY CAR – Please note that parking areas in the Park fill up very quickly at weekends and on public holidays.

PRACTICAL INFORMATION

Phone code – ✆*012.*
Information Centre – *Ojców 15.* ✆*389 20 89. www.ojcowianin.pl.* Above the grocer's shop *"Bazar Warszawski".*

of the cold *(7°C)* and damp residence of the exiled sovereign.

👥 Wierzchowska Górna
(Jaskinia Wierzchowska Górna)

▶ *Accessible by car; located a few km southwest of the Park and well-signposted from the E40.* 🕐*Open daily Apr and Septct 9am–4pm; May–Aug 9am–5pm; Nov 9am–3pm.* 🎫*14/12 PLN.* ⚑*Guided tours start every 20min.*
This is the most interesting cave in the area. Over a distance of 700m, the tour offers a chance to see chambers with evocative names such as the ballroom, the ossuary and the Gothic corridor.

NORTHERN PARK (BY CAR)

Hercules' Club★ (Maczuga Herkulesa) Owes its name to a sorcerer who is said to have challenged the devil to topple the rock. The challenge obviously remained unfulfilled. A cross is mounted atop the 25m-tall limestone formation to honour a Polish mountaineer who managed to climb the club-shaped rock in the 1930s, though today climbing is outlawed. The outline of the best-preserved castle in the Polish Jura can be glimpsed behind the rock.
Perched on a hillside at the northern extremity of the park, the 14C **Pieskowa Skała Castle**★★ (*Zamek Pieskowa Skała;* 🕐*open May–Sept Tue–Thu 9am–5pm, Fri 9am–1pm, Sat–Sun 10am–6pm; Apr and Oct Tue–Thu, Fri 10am–1pm, Sat–Sun*

Pieskowa Skała Castle

L. Gontier / MICHELIN

10am–4pm. 10 PLN; 🅿 ☏389 60 04. *www. pieskowaskala.eu*) was remodelled in Renaissance style in the 16C. From that period, it has retained a system of fortifications as well as a magnificent inner arcaded courtyard. It is now a museum with an impressive collection of European art from the Middle Ages to the 20C from the Wawel Castle collection in Kraków (🔆*see entry*).

THE EAGLES' NEST TRAIL
(Szlak Orlich Gniazd)

The Eagles' Nest Trail runs through the Polish Jura from Kraków to Częstochowa over a distance of some 100km.

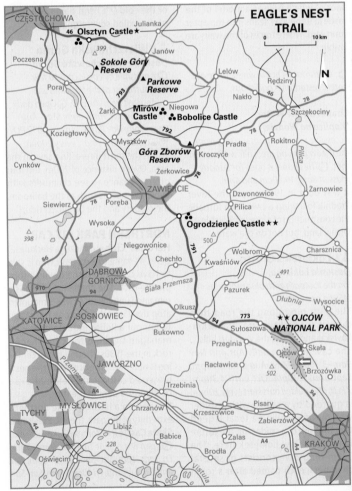

238

It owes its name to the fortresses erected in the 14C by King Kazimierz the Great to strengthen the kingdom of Kraków and to guard the trade route linking the capital (Kraków) and the rich region of Greater Poland. Over the centuries, the castles were looted by foreign armies and later abandoned. Built with local stone, the castles, or rather their ruins now blend well with the rest of the landscape.

There are at least 12 picturesquely situated ruins along the trail, some of which are popular with Polish filmmakers when shooting historical scenes. The trail also features the largest desert in central Europe, the Błędow desert, a 32sq km sandy expanse known as the Polish Sahara!

🔹 **A hiking footpath** links some 15 castles over a distance of almost 160km. *Detailed information is available from tourist offices in Częstochowa or Kraków.* The tour can also be done by car during the course of an afternoon.

FROM OJCÓW PARK TO CZĘSTOCHOWA

Beyond Ojców National Park, the Eagles' Nest Trail runs through hilly countryside where a few trees gather round outcrops and spectacular crags.

Ogrodzieniec Castle★★

⏱*Open daily Apr 11am–6pm; May–Aug 9am–8pm, Sept 9am–7pm; Oct 10am–6pm, Nov 10am–3pm.* 🎫*5.5 PLN.* 📞*673 22 85.*

Erected in the 14C on top of the highest hill in the area, was completely remodelled in Renaissance style in the middle of the 16C and destroyed by the Swedes in the 17C. It was partly rebuilt before being finally abandoned around 1810. Its spectacular ruins form a mass of tangled crenellated towers and curtain walls against the rugged landscape.

Just 5km southeast of Częstochowa, the relics and the characteristic round keep of **Olsztyn Castle**★ stand out above an isolated grass-covered hill. This residential palace was also destroyed by Swedish troops.

ADDRESSES

🛏 STAY

🛏 **Bazar Ojcowski** – *Ojców 20.* 📞*389 20 51.* Do not look for a shop, this place is a pleasant house located by the riverside, near Ojców's post office. Four rooms *(3 double)* in a private house with shared bathroom. Charming welcome.

🛏 **Agrotourism Glanowski**– *Ul. Podzamcze 2, Pieskowa Skała.* 📞*389 62 12.* Located near the Pieskowa Skała castle, this wooden house features 5 rooms, space for tents, home-cooked food and an area for grilling.

🛏 **Opalówki Guest Rooms** – *Ojców 3.* 📞*389 12 97.* A small guest house located in the heart of the Park offering three rooms with kitchen facilities plus a field for pitching tents.

🛏🛏 **Zajazd Zazamcze** – *Ojców 1.* 📞*389 20 83.* 🍴. In a large house between the river and the edge of the woods. 5 panelled attic rooms above this **restaurant** serving Polish cuisine.

🍽 EAT

In fine weather, improvised eating places spring up along the roads, offering *bigos*, sausages and country bread.

🍽🍽 **Zajazd na Złotej Górze** – *Ojców 8.* 📞*389 20 14. www.zlotagora.com.pl. Open mid-Apr–mid-Oct.* Restaurant offering traditional Polish food and places for pitching your tent as well.

🍽🍽 **Zajazd Krystyna**–*Bębło 165.* 📞*419 30 02.* Located outside of the Park, this spacious restaurant also provides accommodation and an outdoor patio restaurant from May–Oct.

🍷 BARS

Piwnica pod Nietoperzem – *Ojców.* The Bat, a small pub located in the basement of the Ojców post office, also has outdoor seating and grilled Polish specialities.

Częstochowa★

The spire of the Black Madonna Monastery rising above Jasna Góra Hill alerts travellers that they are approaching the Polish Lourdes. Nearly 5 million pilgrims flock here every year, 200,000 of them travelling on foot. The town itself may not be very attractive, but a visit to the sanctuary will immerse you in a unique atmosphere of piety and sincere religious fervour.

A BIT OF HISTORY

In the 13C the village of Częstochowa was involved in the iron industry and during the Communist period attempts were made to overshadow the spiritual heart of Poland by emphasising heavy industry, yet the fortified monastery and its holy image still serve as a beacon for visitors from around the world. The town and sanctuary are linked by the emblematic avenue of the Most Holy Virgin Mary (*Aleja Najświętszej Marii Panny, abbreviated to al. NMP*).

JASNA GÓRA MONASTERY

🕐*Open daily 5.30am–9.30pm. ⊗Free.*
In 1382, Ladisław, Duke of Opole, founded the monastery for the Pauline monks who, two years later, were given the icon of the Virgin that brought fame to Częstochowa. According to legend, the credit should go to St Luke, but in fact the icon was probably painted in Byzantium around the 6C. The monastery buildings, spread over 5ha on top of a limestone hill, were surrounded by fortifications to protect them from

- ▶ **Population:** 250,862.
- 🜨 **Michelin Map:** Map of Poland C3 – Województwo of Lesser Silesia.
- 🄸 **Info:** Al. NMP65. 🕿(34) 368 2250. www.info. czestochowa.pl.
- ◖ **Location:** 114km northwest of Kraków, 222km south-west of Warsaw.
- 🄿 **Parking:** Behind the monastery on Ul. Klasztorna, voluntary contribution.
- 🜨 **Don't Miss:** The view from the top of the bell tower.
- 🕓 **Timing:** Two hours for the visit to the sanctuary.

PRACTICAL INFORMATION

BY RAIL – Railway station –
Al. Wolności 21. 🕿366 47 89. www.pkp.pl.
BY BUS – Bus station – *Al. Wolności 45. 🕿379 11 49. www.pks-czestochowa.pl.*
Phone code – *🕿034.*
Postal code – 42 200.
Tourist office – *Al. NMP 65. Open Mon –Sat 9am–5pm.*
Jasna Góra Santuary Information Centre – *🕿365 38 88. Open daily May–mid-Oct 8am–7pm; mid-Oct–Apr 8am–5pm. Closed for religious festivals.*

plunderers. In 1655, the ramparts and, as tradition goes, the miraculous intervention of the Virgin, halted the Swedish invasion. Thus a myth was born and Mary was declared patron and queen of Poland. To enter the monastery one must pass the old fortifications and go through 4 successive gates. Inside, one can get an overall view from the top of the 106m-high **bell tower** (🕐*open Apr–Nov 8am–4pm*).

Chapel of the Miraculous Icon★

A dense reverent crowd continually flocks to this small Gothic chapel with walls covered with ex-votos. The icon

Icon of the Virgin

R. Soberka / MICHELIN

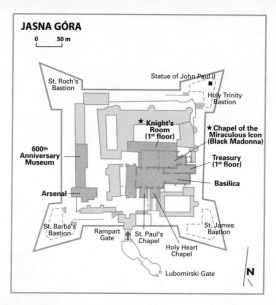

JASNA GÓRA

0   50 m

Statue of John Paul II

St. Roch's Bastion

Holy Trinity Bastion

★ Knight's Room (1st floor)

★ Chapel of the Miraculous Icon (Black Madonna)

600th Anniversary Museum

Treasury (1st floor)

Basilica

Arsenal

St. Barbe's Bastion

St. James Bastion

Rampart Gate

St. Paul's Chapel

Holy Heart Chapel

Lubomirski Gate

N

of the Virgin looks tiny, set within a Baroque ebony altar. Note the two gashes on the face, a souvenir from the Hussites dating back to 1430, and the jewel-encrusted fabrics offered by pilgrims.

The vast three-naved **Basilica** was built between the 15C and the 17C. Note the high altar in Italian Baroque style and the stucco-decorated vaulting. The **Knights' Hall**★ is a quiet place to admire a reproduction of the icon.

A set of nine paintings, hanging high up on the walls, illustrates the great episodes from the history of the sanctuary, including its foundation and the 1655 siege. The **600th Anniversary Museum** illustrates the history of the Pauline Order and of the cult of the icon and a fine collection of musical instruments. The **Arsenal** showcases weapons and armour, while oriental trophies recall the military history of the sanctuary and the sieges it successfully withstood over the centuries. The **Treasury** displays the most precious ex-votos deposited in the sanctuary. The **Ramparts** offer a fine view of the monumental Stations of the Cross laid out around the gardens. A monument to John Paul II was inaugurated in 1999. Leave the sanctuary via Barbary Street,

lined with souvenir shops: a mixture of plastic Virgins, portraits of the Pope and non-religious items.

ADDRESSES

🏠 STAY

🛏 **Camping Oleńka** – Ul. Oleńki 22/30. ☎360 60 66. 30 PLN for 2 persons with tent and car. 90 PLN for a bungalow for 3. Comfortable accomodation just a street away from the sanctuary. Reservation recommended.

🛏 **Hôtel Wenecki** – Ul. Berka Joselewicza 12. ☎324 33 03. 30 rooms. 🖥. A little far from the sanctuary, but very clean with a slight Italian touch. Bright rooms, new and very well-kept.

🍴 EAT

🍽 **Astoria** – ☎366 80 80. Open daily noon–11pm. Ul. Krakowska 45. The best restaurant in town, part of Sonex Hotel. Serves international cuisine and some Polish specialities, such as Żurek (sour rye soup).

🎭 FESTIVE EVENTS

3 May: Feast day of the Queen of Poland. **26 Aug:** Feast of the Częstochowa Virgin.

In the Zakopane region
R. Mattes / MICHELIN

Little Poland is full of bucolic pleasures; this mostly rural area is bordered on the south by the mighty Tatra Mountains, where Polish highlander culture is evident in everything from the language, cuisine, architecture, music and folklore. To the east are the gentler slopes of the Bieszczady, where traces of Orthodox Christianity and Judaism can be found in small towns and villages like Lesko and Sanok. UNESCO-listed timber churches are tucked away in small towns scattered throughout the region. Larger, historic towns such as Tarnów and Sandomierz boast preserved medieval town plans and masterpieces of Gothic and Renaissance architecture. The well-preserved castles in Łańcut and Krasiczyn display the former wealth and worldliness of Polish noble families, and the various mountain chains that run through the region offer ample opportunity for hiking or simply escaping into the wilderness after a day in town.

Highlights

1 A visit to one of Poland's best preserved castles in **Łańcut** (p258)

2 Taking in the relaxed atmosphere of **Przemyśl**, a quintessential border town (p259)

3 Exploring the largest Polish **skansen** (open-air museum) in Sanok (p266)

4 Hiking to the **Morskie Oko Lake** in the Tatra Mountains (p281)

Bucolic Pleasures

If you want to explore the mountainous regions of Poland, Zakopane is the natural starting point. Many hiking trails begin in or around the town, and the Tatra Mountains National Park headquarters are there. The Bieszczady Mountains are gentler and less dramatic, but offer less crowded trails and a sense of seclusion due to their position in the southeast corner of Poland. Sanok is the gateway to the Bieszczady and boasts what is perhaps the best *skansen* (open-air museum) in Poland, with some impressive timber Orthodox churches. The best towns for getting a feel of provincial Poland are Tarnów, Sandomierz and Przemyśl. Each feature some splendid architectural monuments, from Romanesque in Sandomierz to Late-Baroque in Przemyśł and a small town pace. For the health-conscious there are spas to experience: try the Bochnia salt mine in Bochnia or the waters at Krynica.

Typical Bieszczady landscape

A. Galy / MICHELIN

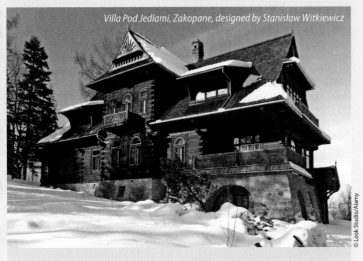

Villa Pod Jedlami, Zakopane, designed by Stanisław Witkiewicz

Stanisław Ignacy Witkiewicz "Witkacy"

Son of the art critic, painter and creator of the "Zakopane style" of architecture Stanisław Witkiewicz, Witkacy was, and is famous in Poland as an avant-garde painter, playwright and provocateur. Like his father, he was also associated with the mountain resort town of Zakopane, writing plays and painting portraits here in the 1920s and 30s while living in a guest house run by his mother. Some of Witkacy's bizarre paintings from his portrait studio hang in the first villa designed by his father in the Zakopane style *(now a museum)*. His portrait studio had strict rules: for example, clients were not allowed to comment or complain about their own portraits, nor could they demand that a portrait be destroyed if it didn't

Portrait of a Man (1924) by Witkacy

appeal to them! He is supposed to be buried in the splendidly picturesque Pęksowy Brzyzek cemetery on Kościeliska Street in Zakopane. Ever the prankster, Witkacy managed one last post-mortem prank: he fled Warsaw to the east in September 1939 after the Nazis invaded Poland, but after hearing on the radio about the Soviet invasion, Witkacy decided to commit suicide at the age of 54 on 18 September 1939 in what is now Ukraine. Buried in an unmarked grave, his remains were exhumed in 1988 and transferred to the Witkiewicz family plot in Zakopane. After the fall of Communism his remains were re-examined and they turned out to be the bones of a young woman who had died in her 20s! Ironically, one of his plays is about an old man transformed into a younger woman. His name is still inscribed on the cemetery grave marker, but don't let that fool you. Since the 1980s Zakopane has also been the home of the Witkacy Theater, founded by theater students from Kraków inspired by the dramatic works of Witkacy. *See Zakopane.*

Bochnia★

Bochnia is a small, peaceful town worth a visit for its interesting salt mine and a few nearby sights, including the historic castle of Nowy Wiśnicz and several wooden churches listed by UNESCO.

SALT MINE★

Close to the Rynek, Ul. Solna 2. ⊙*Open Mon–Fri 9.30am, 11.30am and 3.30pm, Sat–Sun 10.15am–4.15pm.* ⊛*30 PLN. www.kopalniasoli.pl.*

The Bochnia mine was first put into operation in 1248, thus making it the oldest continuously run industrial complex in Europe. The lift takes visitors right down into the rock salt seams, at a depth of between 170 and 290m. A small train then takes them to several chapels carved out of the salt and to educational reconstructions. Children will love going down the 140m-long wooden slide, sitting on a cushion and steering it like a toboggan. The slide leads directly to a working hall, which has been turned into a sports complex where one can play basketball or volleyball. Other rooms are furnished with bunk beds. This is explained by the fact that the mine is also used as a sanatorium because the air inside is beneficial to the bronchial tubes and the lungs. It is therefore possible to book a night here, as one would in a youth hostel. It is also possible to visit some parts of the mine in small boats and to have dinner

▶ **Population:** 29,376.

◔ **Michelin Map:** Map of Poland C4 – Województwo of Little Poland.

▤ **Info:** Ul. Solna 2, Bochnia. ☏(14) 615 36 36. www.kopalniasoli.pl.

▷ **Location:** 38km east of Kraków along the E40, between Kraków and Tarnów.

▣ **Parking:** Free at the salt mine.

▲▴ **Kids:** A ride on the underground wooden slides within the salt mine.

◔ **Timing:** Allow about 3hr for the visit of the salt mine, 1hr for the castle and around half a day for the tour of the wooden churches.

◔ **Also See:** Lipnica Murowana.

PRACTICAL INFORMATION

Phone code – ☏*014.*
Postal code – *32-700.*
Tourist office – *Ul. Bernardyńska 10.* ☏*612 27 62. http://bochnia.pttk.pl.*
Information on wooden churches and possibility of guided tours – *Tourist Information Centre at Ul. św Jana 2 in Kraków.* ☏*421 77 87.*

Nowy Wiśnicz Castle

A. Galy / MICHELIN

in the deepest underground restaurant in the world.

EXCURSIONS
Nowy Wiśnicz Castle★

From Bochnia, drive 6km south towards Nowy Wiśnicz then follow signs marked "zamek" (castle). Open May–Oct Mon–Fri 8am–6pm, Sat–Sun 10am–6pm; Nov–Apr 10am–2pm; last admission 1hr before closing. Guided tours in Polish; information in English at ticket office. 8PLN.

From the road, there is a fine view of the castle towering above the village and the wooded hills. The white mass of the Renaissance-style building looks like a trompe-l'oeil stage setting. This impression becomes stronger during the tour of the interior, for many rooms are completely empty and devoid of atmosphere. However, Nowy Wiśnicz Castle offers a precious account of the country's political and artistic history. The first building to stand on this site was erected during the Middle Ages, when the region lived on salt mining and trade between the East and the Baltic Sea, via Hungary.

Nowy Wiśnicz Castle had its cultural heyday during the lifetime of the grand marshal of the Crown, Piotr Kmita, who infused the castle with spirit of the Renaissance. When Kmita died, Nowy Wiśnicz was bought by the extremely wealthy Lubomirski family. Sebastian Lubomirski fortified the castle and gave the exterior the look it has today. Unfortunately, several Swedish invasions during the 17C and, above all, the 1831 fire deprived us of the sumptuous art collection recorded in the inventories, which included paintings by Raphaël, Titian, Veronese and Dürer, as well as a collection of manuscripts.

The timbered houses of the village surrounding the castle were destroyed by fire in 1850 and the last precious historical evidence disappeared with them. Bringing the glorious past back to life is not easy. Postwar restoration work spread over 30 years stabilised the building which contains mythological frescoes, models of the castle at different periods and an amazing collection of photographs illustrating the restoration of the castle. The terraces offer a panoramic view of the Carpathian foothills. It is worth noting that the main square – Rynek – in Nowy Wiśnicz is the ideal place to take a break and relax in one of the inviting outdoor cafés.

Wooden churches near Lipnica Murowana★★

Starting from Bochnia, drive 12km along the Limanova road to the village of Muchówka, then turn left towards Lipnica Murowana 5km further on.

In 2003, UNESCO included **St Leonard's Church in Lipnica Murowana** on its World Heritage list. The building stands next to an imposing lime tree, on the site of an older pagan temple dating from 1141 *(a wooden post that is supposed to portray the Slavic pagan deity Światowid is kept behind the main altar)*. The church, built of larch and oak wood, is famous for its 15C paintings and frescoes.

It is the ideal starting point for a discovery tour of wooden churches built between the 15C and the 18C. Ten of these are located near Lipnica Murowana. The churches of **Rajbrot** and **Iwkowa** to the south and those of **Pogwizdów** and **Sobolów** to the north as you drive back towards Bochnia are the best examples of 15C and 16C wooden architecture in the area.

ADDRESSES

STAY

Atlas Hotel – *Kopaliny, Stary Wiśnicz, 32-720 Nowy Wiśnicz. From the E40 linking Kraków and Tarnów, in Bochnia, turn south to Limanowa and drive for 3km. 612 91 25. 10 rooms.* Family hotel kept by a convivial polyglot. Spacious comfortable rooms, garden and terrace for long summer evenings.

EAT

Pub 19 Pizzeria – *Rynek 19, Nowy Wiśnicz.* On the vast village green. Good-quality pizzeria with a Wild West atmosphere.

Tarnów★

Tarnów looks back with nostalgia on its glorious past, when the town belonged to the powerful Tarnowski family and Jews, Gypsies, Ukrainians, Germans, and even Scots lived side by side in what was one of Poland's most diverse cities.

A BIT OF HISTORY
Renaissance Cultural Centre

Tarnów has stood since 1330 at the junction of trade routes between Russia and Western Europe and between Hungary and the Baltic States. The city became an important cultural and artistic centre in the 16C, thanks to Jan Tarnowski. In his capacity as governor of the Kraków region, this wealthy scholar called on Italian artists to embellish the town and cemented his authority through a tolerant policy towards the Jews and the many Ukrainian, Austrian, Czech and Scottish immigrants, who settled and prospered here. However, by the end of the century, wars, fires and the avarice of the local dignitaries had brought bustling Tarnów and its 2,000 inhabitants to a standstill. At the end of the 18C, Kraków restored Tarnów's influence by choosing it as the region's political centre, military headquarters and diocese. A century later, with over 20,000 inhabitants, Tarnów became the third town in Galicia behind Kraków and

▶ **Population:** 119,564.

& **Michelin Map:** Map of Poland C4 – Województwo of Little Poland.

Info: Rynek 7. ☎(14) 688 90 90. www.it.tarnow.pl.

▶ **Location:** 84km east of Kraków along the road to Rzeszów.

P **Parking:** Parking is plentiful in centre but you must buy a ticket from a local kiosk.

Don't Miss: A tour of the ethnographic museum for an insight into Roma history, culture and music.

Timing: Allow 2hr for visiting Tarnów and its museums.

& **Also See:** Dębno Castle.

L'viv (now in Ukraine). In 1939, almost half the town's 56,000-strong population was Jewish and Tarnów was one of the main centres of Jewish thought and culture. Many scientists, jurists, artists and businessmen contributed to the town's renown. The first 728 Polish inmates deported to Auschwitz (Oświęcim) on 14 June 1940 came from Tarnów. Today Tarnów is promoted locally as being the warmest spot in all of Poland, with the highest average temperature and longest growing season.

Tarnów Town Hall and Rynek

B. Brillion / MICHELIN

GETTING AROUND

BY BUS/RAIL – **Bus and railway stations** – *At the bottom of Ul. Krakowska, 10min on foot from the Old Town.* Trains link Tarnów to Kraków throughout the day and the journey lasts about 1hr.

PRACTICAL INFORMATION

Phone code – *℘014.*
Postal code – *33-100.*

Tourist office – *Rynek 7, ℘688 90 90. www.turystyka.tarnow.pl. Open May–Sept Mon–Fri8am–8pm, Sat–Sun 9am–5pm.*
Police – *℘997.*
Fire brigade – *℘998.*
Taxi – Express *℘9669* Euro *℘9625,* Viva *℘9626.*
Internet café – *The Tourist Office has free internet access and the entire area around the main square has Wi-Fi.*

SIGHTS

The main way into town is from the road to Kraków. Krakowska, one of the main shopping streets, leads gently up from the station to the historic district surrounding the Rynek.
The Old Town is oval in shape and can be best admired by walking along Ul. Wałowa, where the old fortifications once encircled this historic city.

Rynek

In the centre rises the imposing **Town Hall**★ *(Ratusz)* with the regional **museum** occupying the ground floor. This Gothic building, remodelled many times, wouldn't look out of place in Renaissance Italy. The square is lined all round with arcaded houses in the Renaissance style. **No 20**, built in 1565, was always a prominent place: in turn the residence of wealthy Scottish merchants, the seat of the Masonic Lodge, even a chapel, it is today an annexe of the regional museum.

Cathedral

Built in the 14C and remodelled in the 19C in the neo-Gothic style, the cathedral contains the magnificent Renaissance mural **graves** of the Tarnówski family and a set of Gothic stalls. Along the narrow street running behind the cathedral stands the Mikolajowski House, built in 1524 in the Gothic and Renaissance styles, now home to the **Diocesan Museum**.
Żydowska Street, which runs off the Rynek beyond **nos. 20 and 21**, leads to one of the former Jewish districts. All

that remains of the synagogue, built in 1661 and burned down by the Nazis in 1939, is the **Bimah**, where the Scriptures used to be read, now reduced to four stone columns. The Jewish cemetery, which contains numerous more or less well-maintained graves, lies outside the Old Town. Follow L'viv Street – Lwowska – then head north along the main thoroughfare known as Starodąbrowska. You will find the cemetery 200m further on, on your left.
The Catholic cemetery is situated south of the Old Town. There you will see a **wooden church** dating from 1440, typical of the Carpathian regional style. To reach it from the Rynek, you need to go down towards the ring road encircling the Old Town – *Targowa Bernardyńska* – and then follow Panny Marii Street as far a the church and the cemetery.

MUSEUMS

Regional Ethnographic Museum★
(Muzeum Etnograficzne)
Ul. Krakowska 10. ◷*Open Wed, Fri 9am –3pm, Tue, Thu 9am–5pm, Sat–Sun 10am–2pm*◌*5 PLN.*
In a fine rustic house, Tarnów's Regional Ethnographic Museum is essentially devoted to the history and traditions of Gypsies. Displays of costumes, photographs, paintings and musical instruments enable visitors to feel the atmosphere which characterises this nomadic people. You can follow their migration from India to Europe or the Middle East. Panels introduce the Roma language and its variations over the

centuries and successive migrations. Discrimination is not brushed aside. In addition to the repressive laws imposed in the 18C by throughout Europe, there is an uncompromising account of the Holocaust, which the Gypsy population suffered. Exhibits recall the 35,000 Polish gypsies exterminated in Treblinka and Auschwitz, together with 15,000 French Gypsies, 36,000 Romanian gypsies and 28,000 Hungarian gypsies. The cultural tour continues in the garden, where there are wooden caravans decorated with traditional Roma motifs. In summer, the garden is turned into a traditional Roma camp brought to life by the sound of the violins, cymbalums and singing of groups which sometimes perform there.

Town Hall Museum
(Muzeum Okręgowe)
In the centre of the Rynek. ⊚*4 PLN.*
The museum recounts the history of the town. Interesting collections of armour, coats of mail, firearms and bladed weapons are displayed on the ground floor. Upstairs, the great hall contains many portraits of the various *"Hetmans"* – commanders-in-chief – who reigned over the town from the 16C to the 18C. Note the engraving depicting Tarnów guarded by its ramparts in 1655 and a splendid etching of Dresden by Bernardo Belloto.

EXCURSION
Dębno Castle
❯ *22km west of Tarnów, on the road to Kraków, turn left onto a minor road signposted "zamek" (castle).* ◷*Open mid-Mar–Nov Tue, Thu 10am–4pm, Wed, Fri 9am–2pm, Sat–Sun 11am–3pm; last admission one hour before closing.* ⊚*8PLN.* ⌐*Guided tours in Polish; unaccompanied visits are not allowed.*
Dębno Castle is worth a detour for its surroundings and successful restoration, a model of its kind. Surrounded by trees and a dry moat, the castle overlooks an undulating landscape through which

flows the River Niedźwiedzia. From the time it was built for the Debiński family during the second half of the 15C, this fortified red-brick residence suffered wars, invasions and fires before being restored after World War II. A tour of the castle enables visitors to grasp the simplicity of its plan. Four two-storey buildings forming a rectangle are linked by four defensive towers.

The tour starts in the inner courtyard which, although relatively bare, successfully conveys the military yet elegant atmosphere. Inside, the wealth of furniture and paintings from the 16C to the 19C comes as a surprise. Note the the concert hall housing a piano used for occasional recitals and the pharmacy with its amazing inlaid furniture.

Every year in September, the castle becomes the setting for a tournament in which contestants, dressed as knights, fight their opponents with swords. The half-timbered **chapel** stands 100m above the castle.

ADDRESSES

⬡ STAY
⊖⊟⊟⊟ **Bristol Hotel** – *Ul. Krakowska 9.* ✆*621 22 79. http://hotelbristol.com.pl.* ⊡. *15 rooms.* ⊠. *20 PLN.* Five minutes from the Rynek, this hotel, boasting a fine façade overlooking the main shopping street, offers pleasant rooms in various shades of pink.

⊙/ EAT
⊖⊟ **Restauracja Impresja** – *Rynek 12.* ✆*621 53 33. Open 11am–10pm.* On the first floor of a building overlooking the Rynek; large attractive room, where one can enjoy a refined cuisine including unusual recipes: chicken with gambas, filet mignon with mushrooms.
⊖⊟ **Restauracja Tatrzańska** – *Ul. Krakowska 22.* ✆*622 46 36. Open 10am–10pm.* Refined Polish cuisine in a chic and convivial restaurant. Best ice cream in town!

Kielce★

Hilly Kielce may not be a top tourist destination, but the historic city does boast some fine architecture, including the Baroque Bishops' Palace. Kielce is also close to the undulating landscape of Świętokrzyski National Park, which offers a wide choice of hikes.

A BIT OF HISTORY
Cultural University Town

Over time, Kielce has gained a reputation as an enjoyable cultural city. The town could easily have become a dull insignificant centre, being far removed from the finest gems of Polish architecture. Instead, it thrives on the dynamism of its students and teachers, who account for 20 per cent of the population. Owing to this vitality, Kielce has become a highly artistic city with a cultural centre and houses devoted to music, the stage, photography and dance. The emblem of this success is no doubt Miles Davis, whose statue proudly stands in front of the cultural centre and attracts young skaters and bikers, who use him as a runway.

SIGHTS

The best way to explore Kielce is to aim for the top of the town. From the Rynek, walk up Mala Street, then cross Sienkiewicza Street to reach the **Cathedral** and the **Bishops' Palace**, now housing the **National Museum**.

Cathedral of the Assumption-of-the-Holy-Virgin

Founded in 1171 by Gideon, a Kraków bishop, it was remodelled and partly rebuilt in the 13C and 19C. Today, it looks like a Baroque church which has retained the simple plan of the original Romanesque edifice.

Walk across the garden laid out over the ruins of the former walls of the **fortress** and make your way over the hill. This green stretch, known as **the Planty**, features playgrounds and statues among the trees. The steep, open space reaches down to several expanses of water

▸ **Population:** 211,810.
♾ **Michelin Map:** Map of Poland C3 – Województwo of Little Poland.
Info: Ul. Sienkiewicza 29. ☏(41) 348 00 60. www.swietokrzyskie.travel.
▶ **Location:** Kielce is on the northern border of the Lesser Poland region – Małopolska. 120km north of Kraków, on the road to Warsaw.
P **Parking:** Ul Leśna- Secure multi-story parking *(2.5PLN)*.
☉ **Don't Miss:** A stroll along the Planty.
👪 **Kids:** Trains and planes at the Toy Museum.
⏱ **Timing:** Allow half a day for the town and its museums, half a day for the *skansen* in Tokarnia followed by the Sundial Museum in Jędrzejów, and half a day for wandering through the Świętokrzyski National Park.

Bishop's Palace, Kielce

J. Malburet/MICHELIN

GETTING AROUND

BY BUS/RAIL – Bus and railway station – *Plac Niepodległości.*
Buses and trains regularly link Kielce with Warsaw, Kraków, Wrocław, Lublin, Gdańsk and Zakopane. Buses also run to Sandomierz and the Świętokrzyski National Park.

BY CAR – It is difficult to drive into Kielce because the town is surrounded by a network of major roads and panels indicating *"Centrum"* are not always easy to spot. Once you have found the Rynek, park your car and continue on foot. Every sight of interest is easily accessible from this square. Tickets allowing you to park are on sale at the small booths located on the Rynek.

PRACTICAL INFORMATION

Phone code – ℘041.
Postal code – 25-000.

Geological Rambles

The town is famous for its karst topography. Paths running on the outskirts of town offer the opportunity to discover unusual landscapes and a few renowned karstic caves, including the Kadzielna nature reserve and the "Raj" cave.

where students and young parents like to spend their leisure time in a relaxed family atmosphere. From the bottom of the park, the extensive view of the city's architectural monuments comes as a surprise.

Palace and National Museum★★
(Pałac Biskupów Krakowskich)
Plac Zamkowy 1. &. ○*Open Tue–Sun 10am–6pm.* ⊜*10 PLN, Sat free.* ℘*344 40 14. www.muzeumkielce.net.*
The Kraków Bishops' Palace, built between 1637 and 1641 by Giovanni Battista Trevano and Tomasz Poncino, is a fine example of the architectural style of residences dating from the Vasa period. The façade and most of the rooms were not altered by the passing of time or rebuilding programmes. Since the 1970s, the building has housed the collections of the National Museum; the gallery of 19C and 20C Polish painting contains the most interesting and one of the richest collections in the country. Upstairs, numerous Gobelins tapestries hang on the walls and most of the ceilings are decorated with striking frescoes illustrating historic events, painted by the Venetian artist Tomasso Dolabelli in 1635. At the back of the Palace is a peaceful garden laid out in the Italian style with walking paths, benches and geometrically arranged plantings that make a perfect picnic spot among the greenery and apple blossoms.

Toy Museum★
(Muzeum Zabawkarstwa w Kielcach)
Pl. Wolności 2.www.muzeumzabawek.eu.
○*Open Tue–Sun 9am–5pm.*
⊜*8 PLN/4 PLN.*
The tour of the museum reveals a whole world of china dolls, some of them dating from the 18C, of scale models of planes, cars or trains offered to the museum by private collectors. In addition, there are models of prestigious sailing ships such as *The Mayflower*, *The Cutty Sark* or the trio formed by *The Nina*, *The Pinta* and *The Santa Maria*. The most famous Polish sailing ship, *Dar Młodzieży*, is also on display. Another room exhibits the work of naïve artist Tadeusz Żak, whose speciality was wooden horses and birds. Last but not least are the traditional representations of the witch Baba Jaga, known to all Polish children.

"Raj" Cave
▶ *On the road to Kraków, about 5km from the outskirts of Kielce.* ○*Open Mar–Nov Tue–Sun 10am–5pm.*⊜*16PLN.*
℘*(41) 346 55 18 (a tour of the cave with*

a guide should be reserved beforehand). An interesting cave with a profusion of stalagmites and stalactites, underground lakes and displays showing how Neanderthals lived.

EXCURSIONS
Tokarnia's Ethnographic Museum★★
(Park Etnograficzny w Tokarni)

▶ *From Kielce, drive 20km along the road to Kraków. The museum is located on the right side of the road as you leave the village of Tokarnia.* ◕*Open Apr–Sept 10am–5pm; Sept 10am–4pm; Oct–Mar Tue–Fri 10am–4pm.* 🎫*10PLN. Full visit: 2hr.*

Tokarnia's *skansen* offers a comprehensive display of traditional rural architecture, farms, houses and other edifices from the Kielce region, which once belonged to farmers, villagers or the local nobility. The 30 wooden buildings scattered around parkland covering some 80ha were moved from their original location during the 1970s. The group includes farm buildings, a windmill, a church, a school and an herbalist's shed. All of them date either from the 18C or the 19C. The vast reconstructed village gives the impression of being lived in. Men are working in the fields and in the gardens. Horses and fowls can be seen in the meadows and each plot of land is under the responsibility of a woman who looks after the garden and makes sure the houses are clean. Additional information in English is available for visitors with a keen interest. Three buildings are well worth looking at with particular attention:

The Pharmacy, situated at the entrance to the *skansen*. In the 19C, it served the village of Bieliny. Visitors can admire copper instruments, china jars, microscope and test tubes on display, and in addition, read amusing details about how this pharmacy once sold powders, plants and refreshing vodka!

The house of Jan Bernasiewicz, the naïve artist who died in 1984, leaving some charming works. His religious and pagan wooden statues are a powerful example of the importance folk art has played in Polish culture. Numerous photos of the artist are exhibited, in which he appears the ideal grandfather. They may give a false impression, but his works reveal his true nature.

Suchedniów Manor, one of the last places to be visited, stands in striking contrast to the farming world mainly represented in Tokarnia. It was built in 1812 by a local nobleman. Note the carefully assembled solid larch beams, the heating provided by splendid ceramic stoves and the furniture signed by the best craftsmen.

Świętokrzyski National Park★
(Świętokrzyski Park Narodowy)

▶ *About 35km from Kielce. Drive to Lublin; in Radlin, turn left towards Ciekoty.*

The two main villages of the Park are Święta Katarzyna and Nowa Słupia.

Nowa Słupia
Benedictine Abbey

From Nowa Słupia, the Abbey can be reached in two ways:

By car – *Follow the road skirting the south side of the Church towards Święty Krzyż. Drive 500m to the supervised car park (there is a charge for parking). Souvenir shops and snack bars are at your disposal near the car park and the summit.*

On foot – *Allow 2hr on foot there and back; allow additional time for the visit. The climb is sometimes steep but accessible to all.* 👟*Good walking shoes are recommended.*

The path carved out of the rock climbs through a forest and is sometimes steep but always manageable. The abbey and calvary at the top motivate elderly Poles to climb up and follow the Way of the Cross while praying.

Once you are on the plateau, you need to walk across a vast grass-covered area to reach the Abbey. The buildings are still occupied by Benedictine monks and Mass is celebrated in the church. The Abbey is accessible by road, but it would be a shame to choose the easy way! The smell of the forest and the birdsongs are an inspiration along the

Nowa Słupia Benedictine Abbey

hike. Once at the top, you can climb onto the telecommunications tower. From the level accessible to the public, the view extends over the whole area of the Świętokrzyski National Park.

Jędrzejów – Sundial Museum★★
(Muzeum Przypkowskich w Jędrzejowie)

▶ *38km from Kielce, on the road to Kraków. Pl Tadeusza Kościuszki 7/8.* ⏱*Tue–Sun Oct–Mar 8am–3pm; Apr–Sept 8am–4pm.* ⏱*Closed the day after public holidays.* ⊜*10 PLN.*

This place is fascinating, especially for fans of gnomonics (the art of using and constructing dials). The museum occupies the house of the Przypkowski family. Sundials, clocks, watches and globes have pride of place here. All the family members spent their life observing the stars, in particular the sun, and spoilt their eyesight through continually consulting ancient manuscripts as well as modern publications. This marvellous museum is the result of their determined and meticulous pursuit. Many rooms still retain the family furniture and one room alone contains nothing but glass cases entirely filled with miniature sundials. Most of them date from the 16C or the 17C and come from Prague, Madrid, Paris, Augsburg or London. Hundreds of sundials, made from the most precious materials, such as ivory, and elaborately decorated, form the third most important collection in the world. Before leaving, take the covered passageway to the small garden and stand as far back as possible from the building. You will then notice the astronomical observatory which the Przypkowski family had built on the roof of their house in 1906.

ADDRESSES

🛏 STAY

⊜ **Karczówka Hotel** –
Ul Karczówkowska 64. ☎*366 26 26.* *28 rooms.* Small, but comfortable and neat rooms. Varnished wood and lace give them a cosy look. Away from the town; guaranteed peace and quiet.

🍴/EAT

⊜ **Pałacyk Zielińskiego** – *Ul Zamkowa.* ☎*368 20 55. Open daily 10am–12am.* Zamkowa Street starts from the garden of the National Museum. At the Pałacyk Zielińskiego, traditional Polish dishes are served in a romantic setting. Piano recitals sometimes take place.

⊜ **Restauracja Bernasiówska** – *Pl Żwirki 1, Bodzentyn.* Located north of the Świętokrzyski National Park, this convivial family restaurant extends the warmest welcome to its customers.

🍴/CAFES

Wesoła Kawka–*Ul. Wesoła 50. Open Mon–Sat 9.30am–11pm, Sun 3pm–11pm.* The best coffee shop in town has a hushed and cosy atmosphere, with some tables hidden away in private nooks. Located on a quiet side street, just off the main pedestrian drag.

Sandomierz★★

Sandomierz is one of the gems of Lesser Poland, with an 800 year history. Once a lively trading port on the Wisła, this sleepy hill-top town features Romanesque, Gothic, and Renaissance architecture.

A BIT OF HISTORY

The history of Sandomierz is marked by the town's tolerant attitude. In 1367, the Jewish community was one of the first to be protected from discrimination by law. Two centuries later, in 1570, The "Sandomierz Agreement" sealed the desire for mutual respect expressed by Calvinists, Lutherans and Moravian Brothers. The city can be said to be the fruit of this harmony, since, as a result, it was only invaded by the Tatars and the Swedes. Still, one may wonder at the exceptional state of conservation of its picturesque heritage, which was neither damaged during World War II nor spoilt by the Soviet architects appetite for concrete. The only architectural problem Sandomierz has stems from its unstable subsoil, prone to landslides. During the 1960s, a tragedy was narrowly avoided and enormous quantities of concrete had to be injected into the foundations of buildings to consolidate the whole.

SIGHTS

Whether you arrive via the **Opatów Gate**★, which is all that remains of the fortress built by Kazimierz the Great in

- ▸ **Population:** 25,457
- **Michelin Map:** Map of Poland C3 – Województwo of Little Poland.
- **Info:** Rynek12. ✆(15) 832 23 05. www.pttk-sandomierz.pl.
- **Location:** In the most northern part of Little Poland, off road 74, linking Kielce and Lublin.
- P **Parking:** Paid parking is available just outside of the Opatowska Gate, Ul. Mickiewicza.
- **Don't Miss:** Ascending the city gate for a panorama of the town.
- ◷ **Timing:** Allow a whole day to visit the town and its museums. Spending an evening strolling around the Rynek is also highly recommended.
- **Also See:** Krzyżtopór Castle, Baranów Sandomierski Castle.

the 14C, or through the narrow cobbled streets climbing up from the castle, you will end up at the Rynek.

Rynek★★

The **Town Hall**★, dating from the 14C, stands in the centre of this vast sloping square, with sides exceeding 100m.

Town Hall

A. Galy / MICHELIN

GETTING AROUND

BY RAIL – Railway station –
Ul. Lwowska 35.
BY BUS – Bus station –
Ul. Listopadowa 22. There are regular bus and train services between Sandomierz and Lublin, Kielce, Rzeszów and Kraków.
BY CAR – Parking – The historic centre being a car-free zone, it is advisable to park in a car park.

PRACTICAL INFORMATION

Phone code – *℘015.*
Postal code – *27-600.*
Tourist office – *PTTK, Rynek 12.*
℘832 23 05. www.pttk-sandomierz.pl.
Open Mon–Sat 8am–4pm (until 6pm May–Aug, Sun 10am–5pm).

Built in the Gothic style, the edifice was simply raised by the addition of a Renaissance attic. The most characteristic town houses are the present post office, known as **Oleśnicki House**, at **no. 10**, the former Neoclassical guardhouse, now occupied by the PTTK tourist information office, and the houses at **nos. 23, 31** or **27**, today the Pod Ciżemką Hotel.

Underground Gallery
(Podziemna Trasa Turystyczna)
Ul. Oleśnickich. 🕐*Open daily 10am– 6pm.* 🎫*8 PLN. Entrance at the back of Oleśnicki House.*
This underground maze was intended to link the houses and shops of the Rynek, in order to protect the goods from pillage during the Tatar and Swedish invasions. The 500m long network of galleries, lined with red bricks, which extends beneath the square required a colossal amount of work. However, the passages are fairly bare and the visits are exclusively carried out in Polish.
In Zamkowa Street, near the Basztowy Hotel, You will find the **"eye of the needle"**, a tiny passageway linking the Old Town and the street leading to the castle.

Cathedral of Our Lady of the Nativity★
(Kościół katedralny)
🕐*Open Apr–Sept Tue–Sat 10am–5pm, Sun 1–2.30pm; Oct–Mar Tue–Sat 10am– 2pm, Sun 1–2.30pm.*
The Tatars and the Lithuanians made a thorough job of destroying the original Romanesque collegiate church, the former in the 13C, the latter in 1349; this prompted Kazimierz the Great to have the present edifice erected in 1360. The church is a fine example of monumental Gothic architecture and the interior is filled with interesting elements from various eras, including Byzantine frescoes from the 15C. The most curious paintings are the series of 12 scenes known as the **Kalendarium**★, which illustrate, in macabre detail, various possibilities of violent death, such as being impaled, cut to pieces or beheaded. The paintings and scenes are numbered to match each day of the year, find your birthday and find your death!

House of Jan Długosz★★ (Diocesan Museum)
(Dom Długosza – Muzeum Diecezjalne)
Ul. Długosza9. 🕐*Open Apr–Sept Tue– Sat 9am–4.30pm, Sun and public holidays 1.30–4.30pm; Oct–Mar Tue– Sat 9.30am–3pm, Sun and public holidays 1.30–3pm.* 🎫*6 PLN.*
This red-brick Gothic house, standing behind the cathedral, was built by Jan Długosz in 1476. On the north side, its windows offer a magnificent view of the Wisła. Since 1937, it has been occupied by the Diocesan Museum. Entrance is through a small garden, where trees are inhabited by carved-wood characters. The tortuous interior is noteworthy, even if you don't care for sacred art. Room V: the music you hear was recorded on a small 17C organ, kept in a glass case. Room VI: this contains a crib with characters in 18C dress. Room VII: an unusual library presents wooden books, their pages replaced by beetles, acorns or dried moss. The museum also displays splendid ceramics – 16C to 19C

– used to line stoves, richly decorated religious garments as well as numerous sculptures and religious paintings of the 15C and 16C, in particular the Three Saints, "Martha, Agnes and Clara", painted in 1518 by an unknown artist, or "Mary with the Child and St Catherine" by Łukasz Cranach.

Castle – Regional Museum★
(Zamek – Sandomierskiego Muzeum Okręgowego)
Open Apr–Sept Tue–Fri 10am–5pm, Sat–Sun 10am–6pm; Oct–Mar 9am–4pm, Sat 9am–3pm, Sun 10am–3pm. 7 PLN.

The West wing is all that remains of this Renaissance-style castle. The other three wings surrounding the arcaded courtyard were destroyed by the Swedish army in 1656. The castle houses a small regional museum presenting works of contemporary artists who use as their raw material 150-million-year-old sedimentary rocks, mainly from the Świętokrzyski region, and turn them into pieces of jewellery or miniature objects, as well as archaeological and ethnographic displays.

St James' Church
(Kościół Św. Jakuba)
Standing some 100m above the castle, this church built from 1226 onwards, is one of the oldest red-brick churches in Poland. Mainly Romanesque in style, the simple interior inspires peaceful contemplation, though there are later additions, such as the high altar dating from 1559.

DRIVING TOUR

Castles Tour
Round tour starting from Sandomierz – about 100km. Allow half a day.
One of them is a Baroque-style ruin, the other a Renaissance building turned into a luxury hotel situated in a lovely park.

▷ *Follow the Kielce road. In Lipnik, before Opatów, turn left towards Klimontów, then take the direction of Iwaniska. The ruined Krzyżtopór Castle is in the Ujazd municipality.*

Ujazd – Krzyżtopór Castle
(Zamek Krzyżtopór)
This 16C fortified palace, which once symbolised the greatness of the extremely wealthy Krzyżtopór family, is now open in all weather. The only sounds to be heard are the cry of the crows and the rattling of the corrugated-iron sheeting on the roof. Of the star-shaped fortress with five branches equipped with guns, only the skeleton remains. Of the palace, which the owners called "the palazzo", all that is left is the memory of magnificent festivities and collapsed windows.

▷ *Leave Ujazd and go back to Klimontów, where you can pick up the Rzeszów road. Turn right beyond the village of Łoniów. A signpost points to a ferry crossing the Wisła. About 1km further on, turn left at a T-junction without any signpost. Drive 4km along a road full of potholes. The 2min ferry crossing is free (two cars at a time). The village of Baranów lies on the opposite bank, a few hundred metres away. Turn right at the first junction, near the police station. The castle is at the village end.*

Baranów Sandomierski Castle
Situated away from the village, Baranów Castle shows how fashionable the Renaissance style was with Polish aristocrats in the late 16C. The Leszczyńskis asked the Italian architect Santi Gucci to design this elegant residence.

Nestled in a 14ha wooded park, with areas laid out in the French-style, the edifice lost its defensive character in favour of a more residential look. Four towers surmounted by a cupola – Falconi Tower – and four buildings surround an inner courtyard enhanced by a remarkable staircase leading to the Tylmanowska gallery with frescoes painted on the ceiling.

Inhabited until 1939 and hardly damaged during the war, this richly furnished architectural gem has been turned into a luxury hotel.

ADDRESSES

🛏 STAY

Królowej Jadwigi Motel – *Ul. Krakowska 24. ☎832 29 88. www. motel.go3.pl. 46 rooms.* This unique motel just below the castle is furnished like an antique shop. Inexpensive, yet excellent family cooking.

Basztowy Hotel – *Place Ks.J. Poniatowskiego 2. ☎833 34 50. www. hotelbasztowy.pl. 31 rooms.* Modern luxury hotel in the Old Town, with an austere façade but lively atmosphere.

Ciżemka Hotel – *Rynek 27. ☎832 05 50. www.hotelcizemka.pl. 9 rooms. Restaurant ☺☺.* Hotel housed in a listed building with windows overlooking the Rynek.

🍴 EAT

30-tka – *Rynek 30. ☎644 53 12.* The terrace overlooks the square and the view is pleasant. Plums and prunes are used in the preparation of most dishes.

Oriana – *Mariacka 5. ☎832 27 24.* Situated away from the hustle and bustle of the Rynek. Ask for a table in the inner courtyard.

Łańcut Castle★★★

Łańcut is famous for its vodka and even more for its castle, which belonged in turn to the illustrious and extremely wealthy Lubomirski, Czartoryski and Potocki families responsible for its successive alterations over the centuries. The castle is the setting for a music festival in May and classical music workshops in July.

A BIT OF HISTORY

In the 17C, Stanisław Lubomorski commissioned a Baroque residential palace from the Italian architect Matteo Trapola. This palace was surrounded by a five-pronged system of fortifications. During the 18C, Princess Izabella Lubimorska, a cultured woman and keen traveller who embodied the spirit of the Enlightenment, undertook the complete remodelling of the interior in the Rococo style. Then, at the end of the 19C, Roman Potocki called on the French architect Armand Beauqué and some of his Viennese and Italian colleagues to add a romantic touch to the castle and the park: the result was the orangery and the stables designed as wings of the palace. The last owner, the wealthy Alfred Potocki, sent furniture and objects abroad in 1944. The castle, now a national monument, contains furniture belonging to the State.

- 🕐 **Michelin Map:** Map of Poland D4 – Województwo of Sub-Carpathia.
- ℹ **Info:** www.zamek-lancut.pl. Information also at castle ticket office.
- 📍 **Location:** 20km west of Rzeszów, along the road to Przemyśl.
- 🅿 **Parking:** Available along main streets and by the park.
- 👁 **Don't Miss:** A walk through the park and a look at the interior of the synagogue.
- 🕐 **Timing:** It is worth spending a whole day on a thorough tour of the castle, the park and the museums.

VISIT

Tickets include admission to the castle, the park and the museums. ☞Visit by guided tour. Castle, Orangery, Stables and Carriage Museum have variations in their opening times; check at ticket office. ☞Variable, Mon free.

Castle and Orangery

The castle is a kind of museum of Polish interiors with numerous rooms: bright ones decorated with sculptures, music boxes, Chinese porcelain or elegant furniture, and dark ones containing massive furniture and glass cases full of weapons and armour. Because of the many bay windows and openings, the Park forms part of the décor as much as the furniture or display cases.

▶ *From the Orangery, walk out of the park and cross 3-Go Maja Street.*

Former Stables

Designed by the French architect Armand Beauqué, they now house the museums. **The Carriage Museum**★ presents the superb collection of 19C and 20C horse-drawn vehicles used for attending ceremonies or travelling, bequeathed by the Potocki family; they come from Paris, Vienna or London and also Warsaw and Kielce.

The Icon Museum contains a wealth of 16C and 17C Uniate art from the Przemyśl and Sanok regions and Slovakia.

The Park

A stroll along the alleyways lined with ancient beeches or chestnut trees leads visitors to the orchid house, the riding ring or the music school. In summer, music students practise under the trees.

The Synagogue

Just outside the Park, west of the Castle. ℰ*601 176 351.* ⏱*Open May–Aug Mon–Wed, Thu 11am–4pm, Fri 11am–6pm, Sun 2pm–6pm.*◉*6 PLN.(*☎*call to make an appointment from Sept–Apr).*

Built in 1761, this was the centre for many of the Lancut Jews, who during the 19C, represented 40 per cent of the total Lancut population. The colourful and decorative paintings and craftsmanship of the interior testify to the prosperity of the community at that time.

ADDRESSES

🍽 STAY

🛏🍽 **Pensjonat Pałacyk Hotel and Restaurant** –*Ul. Paderewskiego 18.* ℰ*(017) 225 20 43. www.palacyk-lancut.pl. 7 rooms. Restaurant*🍽🛏. A welcoming atmosphere in a gracious building with well-proportioned public rooms. The rooms are comfortable, with no special additions apart from TV, bottled water and clean, simple toilets/showers. Ensure you don't get an attic room during the summer as it will be too hot, but very cosy in winter.

Przemyśl★★

Considered for a thousand years to be a key town by military strategists, Przemyśl can at last enjoy relative peace. Once the largest fortress in the Austro-Hungarian Empire, it is now a sleepy border town picturesquely punctuated by hills and church spires.

A BIT OF HISTORY
1,000 years of Military History

From its very beginnings, Przemyśl was always a source of envy. Its geographical position put it on the invasion path, and at the centre of world conflicts and international tensions. Tatars, Cossaks, Transylvanians and, more recently, Austro-Hungarians, Russians, Nazis and Soviet occupying forces all tried to get

▸ **Population:** 67,955.

⌖ **Michelin Map:** Map of Poland D4 – Województwo of Sub-Carpathia.

🚩 **Info:** Ul. Grodzka 1. ℰ(16) 675 21 63. www.przemysl.pl

▶ **Location**: On the border with Ukraine, 265km east of Kraków, along the E40.

🅿 **Parking:** Plenty of parking on Ul. Mickiewicza by the train station.

🕐 **Timing**: Allow one day for strolling through the town and visiting the museums. Allow another day to explore the fortress and the surrounding area.

⌖ **Also See:** Krasiczyn Castle.

GETTING AROUND
BY BUS/RAIL – Bus and railway stations – *Ul. Czarnieckiego.* On the south bank, west of the Old Town. Regular services to Warsaw, Kraków, Radom, Lublin and Zakopane.

PRACTICAL INFORMATION
Phone code – ℘016.
Postal code – *33-700.*
Tourist office – *Ul. Grodzka.* ℘675 21 64. www.przemysl.pl. Open Mon–Fri 10am–6pm, Sat 10am–4pm.

control over this route linking Europe and the East.

It was only during the 16C and 17C that the city was able to develop its architectural heritage and economically prosper. The major part of the historic buildings we see today date from that period. The town's military heyday was during the reign of Emperor Franz-Joseph, who intended to make Przemyśl the "gateway to Hungary". The army high command decided to make it the most important fortress in the Empire. This involved creating a double network of small forts and underground galleries as well as arms depots all round the town, sometimes nearly 10km away. This plan was started in 1853 followed in 1855 by the construction of a railway line linking Galicia and Hungary. These two simultaneous projects triggered the town's economic development and a major increase in its population. There were 9,500 inhabitants in Przemyśl in 1850 and nearly 55,000 in 1910. At the beginning of the 20C, the Catholic, Orthodox, Graeco-Catholic and Jewish communities lived in harmony before the two World Wars revived interest in the town's strategic position, which once more in resulted decline and misery. 100,000 soldiers died inside the fortress during World War I.

☙ WALKING TOUR
The foaming River San flowing down from the Polish and Ukrainian Bieszczady separates the modern town from the historic city. Most of the sights of interest are located on the heights overlooking the south bank of the river. Start from the **Rynek** with its arcaded houses and walk up Kazimierza Wielklego, a pedestrian shopping street, as far as the Clock Tower.

The Bell and Pipe Museum
(Muzeum Dzwonów i Fajek)
Ul. Władycze 3. ⏱Open Tue, Thu,Fri 10.30am–5.30pm, Wed 10am–3pm, Sat 10am–4pm, Sun 11am–6pm. ✆4 PLN.
Housed inside the Baroque-style **Clock Tower**, this museum presents displays on seven levels devoted to two crafts that are still very much alive in Przemyśl: the manufacture of bells and pipes.

Bells: The collection covers the production of bells from the 17C to the 20C. Note in particular the former town hall bell dating from 1740, as well as items produced in the Gdańsk workshops and numerous ships' bells.

Pipes: Pipes manufactured in various workshops in town are either carved out of wood or made of porcelain. The oldest date from the 17C and 18C. Note in particular the pipe shaped like a horse's head, the property of a Ukrainian Cossack chief. From the terrace at the top of the tower, there is a panoramic view of the Old Town and the river.

▷ *Return to Rynek via Franciszkańska.*

Franciscan Church
The present church was built in the neo-Baroque style on the ruins of the town's first church erected in 1379 and destroyed in the 18C. Walk a few metres on Asnyka Street to the ensemble formed by the Graeco-Catholic cathedral, the national museum and, further up, the former Carmelite church of St Theresa.

Ukrainian Byzantine Cathedral
This former catholic cathedral was ceded to the Graeco-Catholics by Pope John-Paul II in 1991, which explains the presence of an iconostasis.

National Museum
(Muzeum Narodowe Ziemi Przemyskiej)

Plac Czackiego 3. ⏱ *Open Tue, Thu, Fri 10.30am–5.30pm, Wed and Sat 10am–3pm, Sun 10am–2pm.* 🎫 *8 PLN.*

Photos, drawings and objects illustrate the daily life and religious observance of the Jewish community in the 19C and early 20C. However, the prize exhibit is the collection of **16C and 17C icons**, due to the historic presence of Orthodox Christians and Graeco-Catholics. Most remarkable is the Passion (1703), one of the gems of the collection. On the second floor, documents and photos illustrate the military and economic role of the fortress, responsible for Przemyśl's prosperity before the World Wars.

▷ *The Catholic Cathedral boasts a 71m high Baroque tower. Katedralna and Zamkowa Streets lead to the castle.*

Still visible are traces of the first **castle** building, which archaeologists date from 992. The base of the castle goes back to 1340; the rest of the edifice was extensively remodelled. Largely destroyed, it serves as the setting for an outdoor café and the stage of a theatre.

▷ *To walk to the Rynek, follow Kmity Street then Grodzka Street (note the former Dominican monastery).*

Fortress *(Forty Twierdzy Przemyśl)*
Follow signs for tours on foot or by bike.
Przemyśl fortress is often compared with Verdun. Some 30 fortified sites form a 45km-long belt surrounding the town. Sometimes the structures closely follow the contours of the terrain, sometimes they are built underground, forming a line, or less frequently, an arc. The small forts were designed to hinder the advance of tanks, to shelter heavy guns or infantry troops and to protect command posts or telegraph stations. From a military point of view, the fortress seemed impregnable. However, on several occasions during the great 20C conflicts, attacking forces took advantage of an irremediable weakness, hunger!

EXCURSION
Krasiczyn Castle★★
▷ *Drive 8km towards Sanok.*
⏱ *Open Apr–Oct 9am–4pm, every hour; Nov–Mar reservation only.*
℘ *(16)671 83 21.* 🎫 *10 PLN.*

This Renaissance castle was named after Stanisław Krasicki, for whom it was built in 1580. The courtyard, decorated with frescoes depicting noble families, is enclosed by four towers.
The Pope's Tower, God's Tower housing a chapel and a crypt, The King's Tower with exhibitions of contemporary art on several levels and the Nobleman's Tower, offering from the terrace a panoramic view of the park planted with some remarkable trees.

ADDRESSES

🛏 STAY
🍽 **Farm holidays – Elżbieta Skrzyszowska** – *Leszczawa dolna 16, 37 740 Bircza.* ℘*672 61 23. 4 rooms. About 20km from Przemyśl on the way to Sanok.* Charming country house with all modern conveniences. Peace and quiet year-round.

🍽🍽 **Zamkowy w Krasiczynie Hotel** – *Inside Krasiczyn Castle.* ℘*671 83 21. www.krasiczyn.com.pl. 56 rooms.* The Renaissance setting of the castle makes this an exceptional place to stay. Luxury rooms and service. Waking up inside the castle surrounded by its park is an unforgettable experience.

🍴 EAT
🍽 **Mieszczańska** – *Rynek 9.* ℘*675 04 59.* In the cellars of the building of the National Museum on the Rynek. Inexpensive Polish standards like chicken broth and the best *pierogi* in town will warm up famished visitors.
🍽🍽 **Restauracja Jutrzenka – M. Tomaszewska** – *Pl. Konstytucji 3 Maja 6.* ℘*670 72 40. www.mtomaszewska.com.pl. Open noon–10pm.* Elegant setting reminiscent of the Austrian period. Excellent cuisine, photographs of old times and waltz-like atmosphere. Also boasts an ice cream shop and tea room *(open from 7am).*

The Bieszczady★★★

This wonderful mountainous area extends over Poland, Slovakia and Ukraine at the southern tip of the Podkarpackie region. Once sparsely populated due to its remoteness and recent political history, the Bieszczady are attracting increasing numbers of both domestic and international visitors, and are sought after by nature enthusiasts, keen walkers, cyclists and those with an interest in religious and Polish folk heritage. The landscape alternates between low, rounded mountains, covered with green pasture, and wooded valleys with mountain streams rushing through.

Although one passes through Sanok from the West first, Lesko is the official gateway from the West and Ostrzyki Dolne is a main entrance from the North and the East.

A BIT OF HISTORY

Since 1973, the **Bieszczady National Park** has been entrusted with the task of maintaining a balance between the development of tourism and the safe-guard of the environment. Botanists, geologists and zoologists share this ecological playground with ramblers, cyclists, skiers, sailing enthusiasts and various animals. As more people see the literal and figurative value in both the property and the natural resources

- 🕭 **Michelin Map:** Map of Poland D4 – Województwo of Sub-Carpathia.
- **Info:** Ul. Rynek, Lesko. ☎013 469 66 95. www.lesko.pl.
- **Location:** 80km south of Rzeszów, 186km southeast of Kraków and on the border with Ukraine and Slovakia.
- **Don't Miss:** The works of artist Zdzisław Beksiński, exhibited on the top floor of Sanok's Historical Museum, a boat trip on the Solina Lake and a walk in the hills.
- **Kids:** The Cisna-Majdan narrow gauge railway.
- 🕐 **Timing:** Allow at least three days to ramble through the Bieszczady, enjoy the boat trip on the Solina lake or the small mountain train. In Sanok, allow one day for the visit of the *skansen* and the museum.

of the area, it becomes more heavily trafficked and, as a result, more building takes place to accommodate the increasing numbers. The local councils in the area are working to

Połonina Wetlińska, Bieszczady

GETTING AROUND

Thanks to public transport and newly improved roads, access to Bieszczady is neither an obstacle to the growth of the region, nor, so far, a detriment to the environment.

BY BUS/RAIL – Bus and railway stations – They face each other, 10min walk south of the town centre in Sanok, on the road to Lesko. There are regular train services to Krosno, itself linked with the major towns in the south of Poland. Frequent bus services to Kraków and Rzeszów. Buses of all sizes link the Bieszczady villages.

PRACTICAL INFORMATION

Phone code – *013* for all villages.
Postal codes – *38-500 – 38-700.*

Tourist Info Centre Sanok – *Ul. Rynek14. Open Mon–Fri 9am–5pm, May–Oct Sat–Sun 9am–1pm.* *013 464 45 33. www.sanok.pl.*
Tourist Info Centre Ustrzyki Dolne – Ul. Rynek16. *Open Mon–Fri 8am–4pm, Sat 9am–1pm.* *013 471 11 30. www.cit.ustrzyki-dolne.pl.* You can get maps and suggestions for walks and trips throughout Bieszczady.
Tourist Info Centre Lesko – *Ul. Rynek* *013 469 66 95. www.lesko.pl.* Another office promoting both Lesko and Bieszczady.
Bieszczady National Park – *013 461 06 50. www.bdpn.pl.*
Police – *997*
Fire brigade – *998*
Mountain emergency – *013 463 22 04.*

---

promote the region while simultaneously stressing the importance of protecting the natural assets. EU money has helped improve most of the region's roads and legislation has helped protect the environment.

🚗 DRIVING TOURS

1 BIESZCZADY TOUR, FROM LESKO★★★

About 150km.
▶ *In Lesko, take road 893 towards Baligród, along the River Hoczewka.*

Baligród

This small town, created at the beginning of the 17C, is known for the quality of its spring water. The Jewish cemetery, in a wooded area on top of a hill *(follow signposts marked "Cmentarz Żydowski")*, and a ruined Graeco-Catholic church are all that remains of a period of tolerance.

👥 Cisna-Majdan Railway Line★★

(11km) Bieszczadzka Kolejka Leśna w Cisnej-Majdanie. 🕐*Open Jul–Aug daily; May–Jun and Sept Sat–Sun. Departures 10am and 1pm. Various routes ranging from 90min to 3hr.*

👝*10/8 PLN; 19/13 PLN.* *013 468 63 35. www.kolejka.bieszczady.pl.*

Cisna's main attraction is this renovated narrow gauge railway line because it travels through beautiful scenery at a slow pace so that many can enjoy the "ride on a piece of history". Children and adults can sit in the wooden carriages and appreciate the open-air feel as most of the carriages have no glass, just a covered roof with open sides so people can lean out and take photos. The line began construction in 1890 and opened in 1898. It was the most efficient means of transporting goods in the area due to the terrain and poor roads. At Majdan station *(walkable from Cisna)*, a small, unassuming museum presents a collection of various equipment used by railway workers, uniforms and numerous photos illustrating the construction and renovation of the line.

There are a few routes to choose from: the longer route to Przysłup climbs up a mountain providing great views; the shorter route to Balnica – on the border with Slovakia – runs through forest. All trips allow passengers to get off at a stop or two, depending on the route. When the train reaches the end of the line, the locomotive is detached and brought to

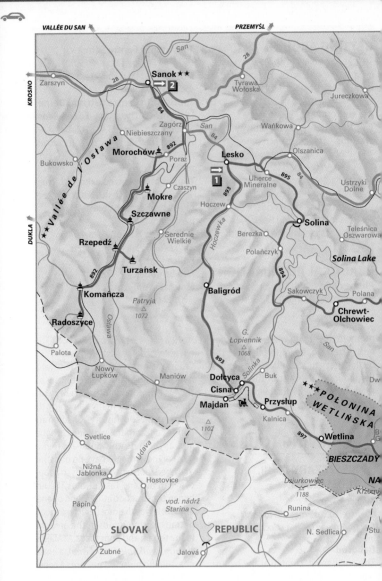

the "new" front of the train. Arrive at least half an hour before a departure as tickets sell out quickly.

Wetlina
Ramble through the Połonina Wetlińska★★★
Parking fee is charged on an hourly rate. Park 4/2 PLN.
Wetlina, lying at the foot of the Połonina Wetlińska mountains, is one of the many rendezvous points for ramblers. You can

also start to walk from Brzegi Górne, stop for a drink at Chatka Puchatka *(a no frills mountain hut with outhouse facilities)* and either walk back down or proceed along the ridge to Połonina Wetlińska.

Ridge walks are famous in Bieszczady and if the weather is good, you will be rewarded with outstanding views throughout the region. The walk is mostly easy to medium, but if you take the ridge walk give yourself at least

THE BIESZCZADY

ascent of the highest summit (1346) of the Polish Bieszczady, the Tarnica *(blue mark)*. The Bieszczady Park breeds Hucuł horses in Wołosate.

One of the finest wooden churches in the Bieszczady is located a few kilometres from Ustrzyki Górne. It stands just before the village of **Smolnik**★. Originally a Graeco-Catholic church, it is now used by the Roman Catholic community. Built in 1791, in typical Bojko style, it escaped the 1947 massive destruction.

Lutowiska

Lutowiska known as the "Polish Alaska", not on account of its climate but because of its sparse population and primarily wooded areas. It's a wonderful place to drive through due to its picturesque location and vantage point in the hills looking south.

▷ *On leaving Lutowiska, drive on to Czarna Górna, then turn left to Polana. A steep road running all the way to Solina offers magnificent views of what is sometimes called "the Bieszczady sea".*

Solina and its Lake

The "Bieszczady sea" is Poland's largest artificial lake, fed by the San and Solinka rivers. It extends over an area of 22sq km and has 150km of indented coastline, sometimes forming tiny fjords. This reservoir, which in parts reaches a depth of 60m, was created in the 1960s, following the construction of a dam over 650m long. Since then, Solina Lake has been a vast watersports area surrounded by forests where one can go mushroom or berry picking. The wide choice of sporting and leisure activities for the young, numerous bars, restaurants and discotheques, found both in Polańczyk and the town of Solina, make the area a unique recreation spot in the Bieszczady region.

If you like fish, be sure to order grilled trout (the local fish in the region). Be advised that the best way to appreciate the lake is to take a boat trip or rent some sort of water faring item to get onto the water as many parts of the shore are rocky and also muddy.

4.5hr to do a circuit. Sturdy footwear and windcheater needed.

Ustrzyki Górne

This small village attracts outdoor enthusiasts year-round and provides accommodation varying from hotels to camping sites. During the summer the village offers mini-festivals celebrating music and folk tradition. The village of Wołosate, signposted on the right of the road, is the starting point for a 2hr

Wildlife

Extending over 292sq km, the **Bieszczady National Park** only encompasses the highest part of the mountain range mostly covered with forests (80%). The fauna is particularly varied and plentiful. It is easy to see the numerous **storks** nesting on roofs or electricity poles. Most of the other species – bison, bears, wolves – are difficult to observe. Around 200 European **bison** were reintroduced in the area during the 1960s. In the 1970s and 80s, the males were hunted by the "communist elite", keen on taking trophies, and this greatly compromised their survival. There are also an estimated 90 **bears** who can reach a height of 2.5m and weigh 450kg. They roam around, especially in the forests surrounding Lake Solina and in the Słonne mountains southeast of Sanok. Should you accidentally come face to face with one of them, keep calm and make your retreat without hurrying.

Another legendary animal whose name alone scares people is the **wolf**! It is believed that about 210 of them live in small packs of between 5 and 8 animals. Again, you will only meet them by accident and they will disappear without any fuss. There are also 230 **beavers**, 120 **lynx** and numerous birds of prey including **golden eagles**. Because of their wingspan, which can extend to 2m, and the exceptional quality of their vision, they are formidable predators. Last but not least are the pacific **Huculs**, small, very sturdy horses, ideal for rambling. As natives of the Carpathian mountains, they are at home here. The Bieszczady Park and a private owner breed them and treat them like a species to be protected because they are so much a part of the region.

Mini-Cruise on the Lake★

There are several companies provide boat trips on the lake, operating mainly from Polańczyk and Solina. The docks are all easily sign-posted so you can choose. Boat trips can last 1–3hr and usually leave mid-morning to mid-afternoon.

▷ *Drive back towards Lesko.*

Sanok★★
(Population 41,261)

In 1366, Kazimierz the Great granted the status of township on Sanok. In 1417, the wedding of King Władysław Jagiełło and Elżbieta Granowska, celebrated in the Castle, established Sanok as a royal city, which led noble families to settle in the region. Sanok's political and economic role remained important until the end of the 19C, when the Beksiński and Lipiński families set up the coach and carriage industry, which was to become the region's economic driving force until coaches were replaced by motorised vehicles. Sanok's expansion in the 20C was due to heavy industries in rubber and mechanical engineering. With a fine cultural heritage, Sanok offers tourists the chance to visit churches, a wonderfully renovated Old Town Square *(Rynek)*, a superb *skansen*, an historical museum in town as well as summer festivals and an array of cafés and restaurants.

Ethnographic Open-Air Museum★★
(Park Etnograficzny/skansen)

Ul. Rybickiego 3. ⏱*Open daily May–Sept 8am–6pm; Oct 8am–4pm; Nov–Mar 9am–2pm; Apr 9am–4pm.*
💶*10/7 PLN (40 PLN for English-speaking guide).* ✆*013 463 16 72. www.skansen. mblsanok.pl.*

Located on the east bank of the River San, at the foot of the low Słonne mountains, Sanok's *skansen (part of the Museum of Folk Architecture)* enjoys an international renown and is the largest of its kind in Poland. The open-air museum opened to the public in 1958. Spread over 38ha, it provides a valuable insight into the architectural and artistic wealth of the four ethnic groups who lived in the area until 1947.

Museum of Folk Architecture, Sanok's skansen

C. Hervé-Bazin / MICHELIN

Most of the buildings erected by the Łemks (*Łemkowie*) and the Boyks (*Bojkowie*) stand on the wooded upper part of the museum. The houses and farms of the Pogórzanie and of the Dolinianie were reassembled in the lower part. The sites were selected according to the original settlements, some groups being essentially uplanders and others having mostly lived on the plains.

The museum presents over 100 buildings, many erected between the 17C and the 20C; they include houses, churches, windmills and several craftsman workshops. Paying extra for a guide is advisable as it allows you to enter certain buildings that wouldn't normally be open and the guide offers a more comprehensive interpretation.

Historical Museum★★
(Muzeum Historyczne)

Ul. Zamkowa 2. ◷*Open Jun–Oct Mon 8am–noon, Tue, Wed 9am–5pm, Thu–Sun 9am–3pm; Nov–May Tue–Sun 9am –3pm.* ⊛*10 PLN.* ✆*013 463 06 09. www.muzeum.sanok.pl.*

The museum is housed in Sanok's Renaissance manor house, built on the site of a former Ruthenian fortress. The contrasting atmosphere characterising the two main exhibitions is palpable. Displayed on several floors is a collection of icons enabling visitors to get a clear insight into the production of icons from the 15C to the 18C and to appreciate the true artistic and liturgical importance of icons in the Eastern Catholic religion. The top floor of the museum is devoted primarily to an exhibition of the

The Four Ethnic Groups

Four ethnic groups once occupied the region: the **Pogórzanie** around Gorlice, Jasło and Krosno; the **Dolinianie** around Sanok; the **Łemkowie** near the border with Slovakia; the **Bojkowie** in what is now the south of the Bieszczady on the confines of Ukraine and Slovakia.

Bojkowie and Łemkowie were the main victims of the massive deportations which began in 1947. There is little evidence left of Boyk culture apart from Sanok's *skansen* and the villages of Berehy Górne, Dwernik and Hulskie. The survivors of the clean-up operation now live in the Ukrainian part of the Carpathian region. As for the Łemk people who suffered the same fate, they lived along the River Osława, maintaining strong cultural exchanges with their Slovak brothers. The Łemkowie came back in greater numbers to live in the Bieszczady, thus enabling them to continue with their traditions.

works of Zdzisław Beksiński, the world-renowned artist and native of Sanok. His realism, sinister outlook, attention to detail and style have been seen in galleries throughout the world. The Osaka Museum in Japan devotes a permanent exhibition to Beksiński.

Zdzisław Beksiński was murdered in Warsaw in 2005. The museum also shows works of other contemporary artists on the lower level.

2 OSŁAWA VALLEY, THE ŁEMK CHURCHES TRAIL★★

▷ *Drive south towards Lesko as far as Zagórz, then turn right towards Komańcza.*

The Bieszczady and Sanok regions have several beautiful wooden churches worth seeing and it may make sense for you to decide what area you will be in and then plan which ones would be convenient to see. Most of the local tourist offices offer information sheets on where to find a *Cerkiew* (Uniat and/or Orthodox Church), local maps provide suggestions for *"Szlak Ikon"* (Icon trails) and it is possible to purchase a well produced booklet entitled *The Trail of Wooden Architecture*. If you have none of these aids, you will also spot signs on the road alerting drivers to an historical site and/or church. Usualy neighbouring houses or the priest have a key and you can always peak through the windows if no one is available to help. The exteriors are often as interesting as the interiors. Below are some suggestions of churches to view. The River Osława flows into the San at Zagórz. Along the road, which meanders over 40km through a wooded undulating landscape, there is a string of wooden churches built by the Łemks in the 19C.

▷ *On leaving Zagórz, turn right towards Poraż and Morochów.*

Morochów Church

Thanks to the priest living next door, one can gain access to the church.
A path starting from the road on the right-hand side leads to the building perched on a mound. Erected by the Graeco-Catholic community in 1837, it became an Orthodox church in 1961. The interior contains a remarkable 19C iconostasis.

Szczawne Church

The church of the Virgin Mary's Dormition, built in 1888 by Graeco-Catholics, is now used by local Orthodox Catholics. The iconostasis is a contemporary work but the polychrome murals date from 1925.

▷ *Continue towards Rzepedź.*

Rzepedź Church

Built in 1824 and restored in 1896, the iconostasis and the three-storey bell tower date from the construction of the church. The polychrome interior decoration dates from 1896. It was fully renovated in 2000.

In the village, turn left towards Turzańsk.

Turzańsk Church

The church of St Michael the Archangel was erected by Graeco-Catholics in 1803 but is now an Orthodox church. In addition to its late 19C iconostasis and two early 19C side altars, it boasts a bell tower built in 1817.

Also consider following the route along the River San towards Mrzygłód. The most typical churches are situated north of this small town, in the villages of **Hłomcza, Łodzina** *(off the road to the left),* **Dobra Szlachecka** and **Ulucz**.

ADDRESSES

STAY

USTRZYKI DOLNE

Villa Neve – *Ul. Fabryczna 9.* ℘013 461 46 46. www.villaneve.pl. *13 rooms.* A delightful and tastefully decorated guest house serving delicious buffet breakfasts and providing a warm welcome to families. Free internet.

SANOK

Sanvit Hotel – *Ul. Łazienna 1.* ℘013 465 50 88. www.sanvit.sanok.pl.

31 rooms. Situated in the very centre of Sanok, this hotel overlooks a wooded park and offers wheelchair-acessible rooms. The rooms are clean, but the highlights are the sauna, hydrotherapy room and salt chamber.

IN THE MOUNTAINS
Pensjonat Leśny Dwór – Wetlina 73. *013 468 46 54. http://lesny dwor.bieszczady.pl. 10 rooms.* Set amongst the hills, this large family house is very attractive and welcoming. Extras include a piano, library, weight room, sauna, mountain bikes and delicious cuisine. Super for winter and summer stays.

PTTK Hotel Górski – *Ustrzyki Górne 1 013 461 06 04. http://hotel-pttk.pl. 64 rooms.* There is a genuine rambling atmosphere in this place due to its location in the heart of the national park and close to several great walks. The hotel offers all meals, if needed, and special rates for those staying a week or more. Child friendly.

FARM HOLIDAYS
Ryszard Krzeszewski – *Chmiel 28 Lutowiska. 013 461 08 34. www.koniewbieszczadach.pl. 7 rooms.* Ryszard Krzeszewski is an important man in the riding world. Riders can hire Hucuł horses and go rambling in his company. His knowledge of the mountain and of horses, together with his interesting personality, make him one of the strong characters of the Bieszczady region.

EAT
SANOK
Gospoda pod Biała Gora – *Ul.Rybickiego 3 (by the skansen). Open daily 9am–10pm.* Delicious traditional food to enjoy, before or after a trip through the *skansen*. Specialities include the *hreczanyki*, which consist of buckwheat, meat and mushroom sauce; eat inside or outdoors.

USTRZYKI DOLNE
Restauracja "Bieszczadzka" – *Ul. Rynek 19. 013 461 10 74. www.bieszczadzka.com.* The décor might be stuck in the 1980s but the staff are friendly and the food is homecooked and delicious. The *pierogi* are some of the best in the region and people come far and

wide to buy them in the downstairs delicatessen. Other specialities include potato pancakes with *kasza* (buckwheat) and cottage cheese.

IN THE MOUNTAINS
Karczma Chata Wędrowca – *Wetlina. 013 468 46 21. www.chata wedrowca.pl.* Located by the roadside, this inn is housed in a large wooden building offering outdoor seating on the terrace. Inside are two dining areas exuding a sense of cosiness within a wooden décor reminiscent of a mountain hut, with walls full of trail maps. Generous portions are served, but quality isn't spared. They pride themselves on their "Big Blueberry Crêpe" *(naleśnik)*.

Solina/Polańczyk – make sure you find a simple "grill bar" that serves fresh-grilled trout *(pstrąg)*, a local speciality.

SHOPPING
Confident in the value of their traditions and folk art, the Bieszczady craftsmen formed an Association for the Promotion of Local Products. The range includes wooden objects, walking sticks, clothing with handmade embroidery, icons, honey, furniture, fabrics and cheese. Many of these items come with a specific "Bieszczady local product" seal of approval, which has the symbol of a bear pushing a wheel.

SPORTS AND RECREATION
Riding a Hucuł – Many riding farms organise riding tours using this small Carpathian horse. There is a breeding farm and accommodation facilities in the Bieszczady Park. The Park's Information Centre can also provide suitable addresses according to ability.

Hucuł Breeding centre: *Wołosate, 38-714 Ustrzyki Górne. 013 461 06 50.*

Biking across the Bieszczady – The Bieszczady Cycle Association: *Ul. 29 Listopada 51/1. Ustrzyki Dolne. 693 131 033. www.bieszczady-online.pl.*

TOURS
Grupa Eko-Karpaty *Ul. Rynek 19. 013 461 10 09. www.eko-karpaty.com.* Offering a selection of excursions in the area, with a roaring trade in day trips to Lwow in Ukraine that leave Ustrzyki Dolne at 5.30am.

Krynica and the East Beskid★★

*Beskides Sądecki –
Beskides Niski*

The East Beskid are split into two mountain ranges of medium height. The first, known as the Beskid Sądecki, follows a vertical line between Nowy Sącz and Krynica on the Slovak border. It is popular for the beneficial effect of its spas, as well as its colourful architecture and green undulating scenery.

The second, known as the Beskid Niski, is situated further east and covers an area extending from Nowy Sącz to Krosno in the north to the Slovak border via the Dukla pass. The Wooden Architecture Trail is a local highlight, along with the relaxing spa town Krynica, the "Pearl" of Polish health resorts.

- ◔ **Michelin Map:** Map of Poland C4 – Województwo of Lesser Poland and Sub-Carpathia.
- ▤ **Info:** Ul. Piłsudskiego 8. ℘471 61 05. www.krynica.pl.
- ▷ **Location:** 115km southeast of Kraków.
- ▯ **Parking:** Free along Ul. Piłsudskiego, 4 PLN by the post office on Ul. Zdrojowa.
- ⊛ **Don't Miss:** Oil Museum in Bóbrka, near Krosno.
- ◔ **Timing:** Allow half a day to visit Nowy Sącz and Stary Sącz; two days to make the most of Krynica, a charming spa town, and its surroundings, and spend half a day around Krosno.

KRYNICA

Krynica owes its charm to the cheerful, bright colours of its wooden houses, painted in light green, blue or yellow, and to the luxuriant vegetation of its parks and hillsides.

Promenade Nowotarskiego★★

You can reach this promenade from anywhere in Krynica. Also known as **"deptak"**, it prolongs Ul. Piłsudskiego, is lined with the town's main shops and is where most of the spa activity takes place. This large esplanade, skirted by the River Kryniczańska and flanked by ornate façades, is the place for strolling like a 19C aristocrat in search of a cure.

Springs

The main springs are located around the promenade in the Nowy Dom Zdrojowy, Pijalnia Główna and Stare Łazienki Mineralne. People can be seen walking about holding cups or oddly shaped

Krynica

mugs filled with foul-smelling water said to have healing powers!

Nikifor Museum
(Muzeum Nikifora)

Bulwary Dietla 19. ⏲Open Tue–Sun 10am–1pm, 2–5pm. 🎫6 PLN.

Nikifor (1893–1968) is considered to be Poland's greatest naïve painter. At the height of his career in the 1920s and 1930s, Nikifor distinguished himself by painting self-portraits and landscapes. The museum, located in his studio, displays about 100 works by the artist and devotes temporary exhibitions to other Polish painters.

NOWY SĄCZ AREA
Nowy Sącz
(Population 85,000)

▷ *35km north of Krynica.*

This is the largest town in the region. Founded in 1292, Nowy Sącz was ravaged by many fires throughout its history. Despite this, the town still features a spacious **Rynek**, renovated in 1895 in the neo-Renaissance and neo-Baroque styles, and an impressive **Town Hall**. It is worth visiting the Gothic House, also known as the **Canons' House** (Dom Kanoniczy; ⏲open Tue–Thu 10am–3pm), built at the beginning of the 16C. Displays illustrate the history of the monuments destroyed over the centuries. Nowy Sącz boasts a

GETTING AROUND

BY RAIL – Railway station – *Ul. Kolejowa.* Warsaw, Kraków, Gdynia, Budapest (Hungary) and Kosice (Slovakia) are linked to Nowy Sącz.

BY BUS – Bus station – *Situated on a square at the junction of Długosza and Wolności Streets.* Buses leave regularly for the spas and villages of the Beskid in the Nowy Sącz area. Nowy Sącz and Krynica are linked by many bus and minibus services. The journey lasts around 30min. There are bus services to all the large towns in southern and central Poland: Warsaw, Kraków, Zakopane, Lublin, as well as Bardejov in Slovakia.

PRACTICAL INFORMATION

Phone code – *☎018.*
Postal code (Krynica) – *33-380.*
Postal code (Nowy Sącz) – *33-300.*
Tourist office – Krynica: *Ul. Piłsudskiego 8. ☎471 61 05. www.krynica.pl. 10am–noon, 2-5pm. Located beneath the cinema.* Nowy Sącz: *Ul. Piotra Skargi 2. ☎444 24 22. www.cit.com.pl. Open Mon–Fri 8am–6pm, Sat 9am–2pm.*

Skansen (Sądecki Park Etnograficzy; *at the southern end of town, along the road to Stary Sącz;* ⏲*open Tue–Sun*

Water and Wood

The town has existed since 1547, but the beneficial effects of its mineral springs were only acknowledged at the end of the 18C. The fame of the resort and of its neighbours, Muszyna and Piwniczna, spread rapidly and many doctors set up treatment and fitness centres. In 1856, Józef Dietl, a famous doctor from Kraków University, launched a project for the creation of a spa. The number of baths, pump rooms and places to stay increased and there was an influx of the well-to-do and artists such as the writer Sienkeiwicz, the painters Matejko and Nikifor, or the musician Jan Kiepura, won over by the bucolic atmosphere and the wooden architecture. The building of a cable car, the creation of ski runs and the arrival of the railway only emphasised the fashion trend. After the World War II, instead of aristocrats the Polish Communist working class was invited to recharge its batteries in the numerous grey, post-war sanatoriums and guest houses, which spoilt part of the small town's charm. Fortunately, the current authorities understand how important the environment is for visitors and Krynica has now regained the assets that will ensure its success.

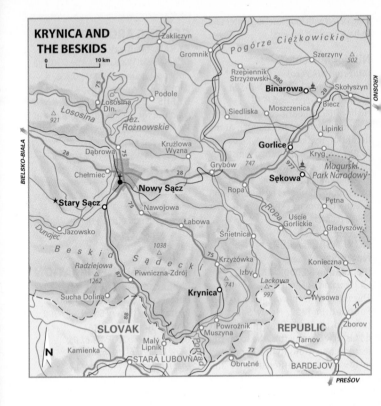

10am–6pm, ☞12PLN), showcasing the region's rich and varied culture, folklore and architectural heritage. Walk amid Orthodox churches, remnants of Gypsy camps, peasant cottages, plus a recreation of a Galician 19C town.

Stary Sącz★

▶ *From Nowy Sącz drive south along road 87 towards Piwniczna-Zdrój. Stary Sącz is on the right, 6km further on.*

During the Middle Ages, the town stood as an important centre at the junction of trade routes between Hungary and Northern Europe. Princess Kinga commissioned a convent to be built for the Poor Clares and became its first abbess on the death of her husband, Prince Bolesław the Chaste.

The chapels of this fortified monastery are decorated in glorious Baroque style. The treasury houses many relics concerning the princess. The small city

of Stary Sącz, like its more important neighbour, Nowy Sącz, was devastated by fire and wars. Today, the **Rynek** is a vast cobbled square, still surrounded by a few old houses such as **no. 6**, the "Na Dołkach" House, home to the **Regional Museum**.

UNESCO WORLD HERITAGE WOODEN CHURCHES★★
Gorlice Area
Sękowa

▶ *4km southeast of Gorlice, along road 977.*

St Philip and St James' Church (Kościół św. Filipa i św. Jakuba) dates from 1520. The nave is entirely covered with shingles and the square tower topped by an onion-shaped spire. Although the building was greatly damaged during World War I, the interior still retains a Gothic baptismal font dating from 1522 and polychrome decorations from 1888.

Binarowa

> From Gorlice, follow road 28 to Biecz then drive north along road 980 to Binarowa.

The **Church of St Michael the Archangel** was built around 1500, entirely from fir wood. The stencilled decorations on the ceiling and the Gothic sculptures date from the early 16C; as for the Baroque paintings, they are 17C works.

BÓBRKA

Oil Museum★
(Skansen Muzeum Przemysłu Naftowego)

> Drive to Krosno, 105km east of Nowy Sącz along road 28. In Krosno, head for Dukla along roads 28 and 9. After 8km, turn right towards Bóbrka and Chorkówka. Follow signposts to "Skansen Muzeum Przemysłu Naftowego" for about 5km.

Open Tue–Sun May–Sept 9am–5pm; Oct–Apr 9am–3pm. 9 PLN.

Lost in the middle of the Beskid, this open-air museum, covering an area of 20ha, offers an insight into a little-known aspect of 19C Polish economy: oil extraction, refining and transport. As early as the 15C, the chronicler Jan Długosz noted the presence of the precious liquid, but it was only in the 1850s that the "father" of the oil industry, Ignacy Łukasiewicz, formed the first company.

Traces of the oil industry can still be seen along this itinerary, but Bóbrka is without doubt the most informative collection. The museum, located on a former working site, displays a lot of the original equipment and various aspects of the industry are dealt with: technology, industrial development, working conditions.

ADDRESSES

STAY

KRYNICA

Nikifor Hotel – ul Świdzińskiego 20. 477 87 00. www.nikifor.pl. 32 rooms. The hotel is a real art gallery. Paintings, frescoes and sculptures are everywhere. The sauna and relaxation rooms appear to have been dug out of rock. In addition, there is an upstairs **restaurant** serving inventive dishes and a traditional inn on the ground floor. All in all, a charming place!

Pensjonat Małopolanka – Ul. Bulwary Dietla 13. 471 58 96. www.malopolanka.eu. 20 rooms. Conveniently situated close to the promenade, this "pensjonat" is ideal for people looking first and foremost for relaxation. Massage and sauna are highlights.

Pensjonat Willa Witoldówka – Ul. Bulwary Dietla 10. 471 55 77. www.witoldowka-krynica.pl. 40 rooms. Built in the heart of the spa, this large wooden building, characteristic of Krynica's architectural style, is one of the most famous "pensjonat". The quaint atmosphere complements the pleasure of staying in a comfortable historic monument.

EAT

KRYNICA

Kłynec – Ul. Świdzińskiego 20. 477 87 00. Open Mon–Fri 3pm–10pm, weekends 12pm–10pm. This traditional inn serves Lemko specialities, a small ethnic minority from this part of Poland. Huge wooden tables and open fires ensure a warm welcome.

NOWY SĄCZ

Restauracja Ratuszowa – Rynek 1. 443 56 15. Open daily 10am–10pm. Conveniently located under the Town Hall, this establishment features an unusual selection of *pierogi*, including *nettle pierogi*, plus well-renowned ice cream.

FESTIVE EVENTS

Jan Kiepura Festival. Kiepura (1902–66), the famous Polish opera singer used to come to Krynica regularly. Every year, his admirers, many orchestras and singers all gather for two weeks in mid-August for a series of concerts in his honour. *Information:* 471 29 17. *www.kiepurafestival.pl.*

Zakopane★★★

Zakopane is an attractive town, as much for its dramatic location as for its architectural style. Nestled at the foot of the spectacular Tatras Mountains, this relaxed resort town (alt. 838m) dominated by alpine peaks (culminating at almost 2,500m), proudly displays its mountain culture, as expressed in the local cuisine, dialect and music. The local highlanders have determinedly held onto their roots, which is just one of the many reasons why 19C aristocrats and city slickers adored the village and its environs, and why visitors continue to be enchanted by the town and its folklore.

▶ **Population:** 28,046.
Michelin Map: Map of Poland C4 – Województwo of Lesser Poland.
Info: Ul. Kościuszki 17. 201 22 11. www.zakopane.pl.
Location: 100km south of Kraków along the E77 then road95.
Parking: Free and paid parking on Al 3 Maja.
Don't Miss: Admiring the rustic charm of the Zakopane-style villas.
Kids: A visit to Aqua Park Zakopane.
Timing: Allow two days for visiting the museums and exploring on foot the long streets lined with wooden houses.

A BIT OF HISTORY
Evolution and Tradition

For the past 150 years, Zakopane has shown an extraordinary capacity for adaptation and transformation. Until the 19C, the village was known only for its population of rebellious shepherds, who loved freedom and were sometimes prone to commit robbery. It was then that Kraków's intelligentsia took control of the town's destiny. Doctors, scientists and artists were about to discover the beneficial mountain air and the area's tourist potential. Among them was Father Józef Stolarczyk who, as early as 1850, suggested to the members of his congregation that they should let rooms to visitors and then launched the idea of building guest houses. Tytus Chałubiński, a doctor and a botanist, established the therapeutic qualities of the Tatras in the fight against tuberculosis. This scholar understood that very soon the sick would not be the only ones to come on holiday and that it was necessary to provide facilities and entertainment for tourists. He initiated the creation of the Guides Company and invited musicians and dancers to come and provide evening entertainment in restaurants. According to legend, the "good doctor" laid the foundations of a true mountain resort. Last but not least was Stanisław Witkiewicz, the man who thought development of the resort could only be considered if the rules of traditional local architecture were observed. This painter, art critic and writer lived in Zakopane from 1890 to 1908. He was the promoter of the Zakopane Style, a real school of architecture rooted in the traditions of the Podhale region. Witkiewicz argued that it would have been damaging for the region had its architectural style been modified according to Swiss or Tyrolean models, as had happened in other mountain regions in Poland. Simultaneously, Witkiewicz was trying to promote a homegrown national style of architecture for patriotic reasons since Poland was under foreign control.

Most of the houses from the 19C consist of two buildings: the house and the farm. The house is split into two separate parts by an entrance hall: the black room is on the left, the white room on the right. Originally, only the black room was occupied by the family because it was heated, the smoke accounting for the colour of the walls and furniture. The white room's main

GETTING THERE

BY AIR – **Airport** – The nearest international airports are those of Kraków and Poprad in Slovakia.

GETTING AROUND

The bus and railway stations are adjacent and situated some 100m from the Tourist Office.

BY RAIL – **Railway station** – *Ul. Chramcówki 35. www.pkp.pl*

BY BUS – **Bus station** – *Ul. Kościuszki 23. www.pks.zakopane.pl* There are bus services to all the starting points of the walking tours through the Tatras and outlying districts of Zakopane.

Kraków is the destination with the most links to Zakopane. There are many bus and train services daily. The average journey time is 2hr by bus, 3hr by train.

PRACTICAL INFORMATION

Phone code – *0-18.*
Postal code – *34-500.*
Tourist office – *Ul. Kościuszki 17. 201 22 11. www.zakopane.pl. 9am–5pm.*
Main post office – *Ul. Krupówki 20.*
Police – *997.*
Fire brigade – *998.*
Mountain emergency – *Ul. Piłsudskiego 63a. 206 34 44.*

---

function was that of a reception room. It was here that festivities and ceremonies took place: weddings, wakes or religious feasts. Its decoration and furniture testified to the wealth and refinement of its owners. An exposed beam is engraved with a star within a circle, the year the house was built and the name of the family. The frames of the front door and windows are also adorned with folk motifs. Even if the interior has been remodelled, the outside appearance of modern houses is often in keeping with the criteria of the Zakopane style, which lends the town a harmonious appearance.

WALKING TOUR
ZAKOPANE-STYLE TRAIL★★

Zakopane is best explored on foot. It is important to note that houses illustrating the Zakopane style are mostly privately owned, so a certain etiquette should be observed. There are several possible itineraries. One of them starts from the bus and railway station.

Chramcówki Street

Walk along this street and don't hesitate to turn into the narrow pedestrian streets on the left. Note the **"Pyszna" Villa** at **no. 22a**, which shows that recent structures adhere to the traditional local rules of architecture. Also

admire the **Polonia House** at **no. 22** and the contemporary church on the right side of the street covered with a shingled roof. Up next is **Nowotarska Street**, lined on either side by a fine group of houses. When you reach the junction with Krupówki Street, continue towards Kościeliska Street.

Kościeliska Street

This very long street is Zakopane's architectural masterpiece. In addition to a wealth of houses, it offers the town's **oldest church**, dating from 1845, and the cemetery where a great many writers, artists and mountaineers who form part of the resort's legend are buried. The funeral monuments are often real works of art, sometimes adorned with **icons painted on glass** in true Podhale tradition. This is a picturesque cemetery. Further on, at **no. 18**, you will see the villa known as **"Koliba"**.
Built in 1893, from drawings by Stanisław Witkiewicz, it now houses the **Stanisław Witkiewicz Zakopane-style Museum**★★ (*open Wed–Sat 9am–5pm, Sun 9am–3pm; 7 PLN*). At the end of the 19C, Zygmunt Gnatowski, an ethnologist with a passion for the Tatras, wanted to have a summer residence built in Zakopane. Stanisław Witkiewicz succeeded in persuading him to let him have carte blanche so

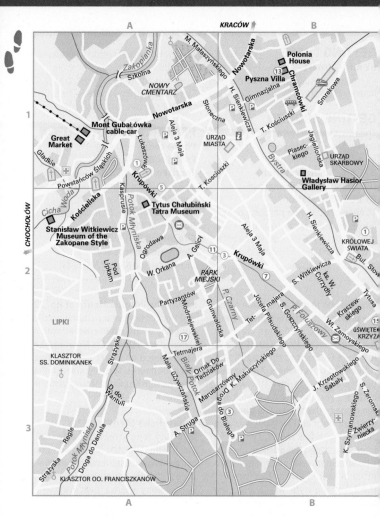

that he could put his architectural theories into practice. Therefore, when Villa "Koliba" was built in 1892, the Zakopane style was applied for the first time. Situated in a wooded area with a stream running alongside, it is now a museum presenting Zygmunt Gnatowski's personal collections of furniture and handicrafts.

It is the ideal place for visitors to understand the building criteria of the houses. From the decorations to the method used for insulation, from the objects of daily life to the furniture, everything seems to have sprung straight out of a charming fairytale. This was perhaps a means of masking the harshness of life in the Tatras at that time.

Definitely worth seeing are the bizarre portraits upstairs painted by the architect's son, the artist known as **Witkacy**. Note the strange codes scribbled on the paintings – they were the artist's shorthand for what drugs he was using at the time of producing the portraits!

The Witkiewicz Houses

Further away, east of the town centre, there are three buildings designed by Stanisław Witkiewicz: **Villa "Pod Jedlami"** at **no. 1 Koziniec Street**; Villa **"Witkiewiczówka"**, built during the 1930s on Antałówka Road, and further

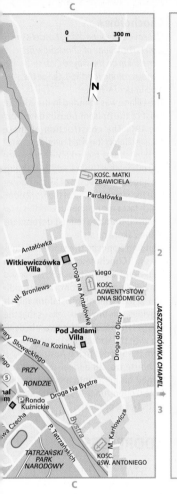

ZAKOPANE

on, the **Jaszczurówka Chapel** erected between 1904 and 1908 for the Uznański family.

◐ *To get there, follow signposts marked "Kaplica Jaszczurówka" on the way to the Łysa Polana border post between Poland and Slovakia.*

Krupówki Street★

This long pedestrian street runs through the town and is prolonged by the access path to the cable car leading to **Mount Gubałówka**. Although not the richest in terms of architectural heritage, this street is undoubtedly the most visited. Shops, restaurants, luxury hotels and street entertainment all vie for your attention.

No. 10 is home to the **Tytus Chałubiński's Tatra Museum**★ (Muzeum Tatrzańskie; ◐*open Tue–Sun 9am–5pm; ◎7 PLN*). Founded by Doctor Tytus Chałubiński and his faithful companion, mountain storyteller Jan Krzeptowski Sabała, this museum is housed in one of the rare Zakopane-style stone buildings. It traces the development of the shepherd village into a spa and resort. The ethnographic section is divided into two major parts: the first describes the layout of the houses, the second presents the Podhale region's economic activity: hunting, sheep raising and farming. The first floor is devoted to the geology of the Tatras and the Pieniny range, northeast of Zakopane. The museum also provides many informative displays illustrating the varied flora and fauna found in an alpine environment. Look out, chamois and marmots are watching you!

The Tatra Museum also runs the **Władysław Hasior Gallery** (*Ul. Jagiellońska 18B;* ◑*open Wed–Sat 11am–6pm, Sun 9am–3pm;* ⌖*7 PLN)* devoted to the works of this artist (1928–2000), who lived in Zakopane for many years and achieved celebrity in the 1960s. Władysław Hasior was in a class of his own, borrowing from Dadaïsm, Surrealism and Pop-Art to create works brought to life by the wind or placing side by side objects of daily life.

A short distance from the museum, horse-drawn carriages and their owners dressed in Podhale costumes await tourists keen on a ride through the most picturesque streets. At the lower end of the street, beyond the junction with Kościeliska Street, one enters Zakopane's **outdoor market**. Woollen clothes, wooden carvings, and famous **oscypek cheese** made from ewe's milk are on sale at all the stalls, right up to the entrance of the cable-car station.

👪 Aqua Park Zakopane

Just a few minutes' walk south of the train station. ul Jagielloska 31.
◑*Open daily 8am–10pm.* ✆*202 58 15. www.aquapark.zakopane.pl.*
Water slides for the kids, Jacuzzi and sauna for parents to relax those muscles after a long hike.

EXCURSIONS
Rambles around Zakopane★★★

◔*These are described in the next chapter entitled "The Tatras".*
In Zakopane itself *(southeast of the town)* you can visit the **Tatra Park Information Centre**, which houses a small museum devoted to fauna and flora.

Chochołów★

◐*Leave Zakopane along Kościeliska Street. The village of Chochołów lies some 15km on the way to Czarny Dunajec, along road 958.* ◔*See the map under TATRAS.*

The village was founded in the 16C but most of the present houses date from the 19C. The construction of these houses, lining the road over a distance of 1km, shows remarkable coherence and originality. The stacked fir-tree logs are huge and the eaves of all the houses face the street instead of the front door, which faces the neighbours. All this is far removed from the refined decorations of the Zakopane style.

Standing opposite the stone church is the small **Chochołów Museum** (◐*open Wed–Sun 10am–2pm;* ⌖*6 PLN),* housed in a building dating from 1798. In addition to the ethnographic information it provides, this tiny place tells us that the village is famous for its bravery in dealing with the various occupying forces, from the Swedes to the Austrians.

At house **no. 28** a local sculptor has turned his home into an open studio. A great opportunity to see authentic folk as it's being produced.

ADDRESSES

🛏 STAY

🍴 **Fian Hotel** – *Ul. Chałubińskiego38.* ✆*201 50 71. www.fian.pl. 38 rooms.*
Away from the town centre, this family hotel is modern and comfortable. It has struck the perfect compromise between services and price.

🍴 **Kasprowy Wierch Hotel** – *Ul. Krupówki 50B.* ✆*201 27 38. www.kasprowy.regle.pl. 30 rooms.*
Very friendy hotel boasting a large peaceful courtyard away from the hustle and bustle of the street.

🍴 **Pensjonat Antałówka** – *Ul. Wierchowa2.* ✆*201 32 71. www.anatalowka-zakopane.pl. 21 rooms.*
The facilities and decoration of this establishment are devoid of regional charm but perfectly adequate for a prolonged stay.

Pensjonat Lipowy Dwór – Jl H. Modrzejewskiej7. 206 67 96. www. mati.com.pl. 15 rooms. Situated 5min from the town centre, in a large wooden chalet-style house. Convivial welcome.

Pensjonat Renesens – Ul Chałubińskiego26. 206 62 02. www. renesans.pl. 23 rooms. This fine residence with character offers all the comfort one could wish for. Mountain songs and dances provide entertainment on some evenings and guides or leisure activities can be recommended.

Litwor Hotel – Ul. Krupówki40. 202 42 00. www.litwor.pl. 58 rooms. Most of the rooms are very bright and offer a panoramic view of the Tatras. The friendy welcome and the decoration create a warm atmosphere. Swimming pool, solarium, sauna...

Willa Pyszna Rooms – Ul Chramcówki22. 608 592 833. 1 apart: 6-8 pers. Experience the pleasure of staying in a modern and comfortable house in authentic traditional style.

Belvedere Hotel – Droga do Białego3. 202 02 11. – www.belvedere hotel.pl. 144 rooms. Restaurant . This central luxury establishment is fitted up in 1920s style with a regional touch. Fitness, beauty centre and gourmet cuisine are the key words.

/ EAT

Gazdowo Kuźnia – Ul. Krupówki1. 201 72 01. The dining room looks like an antique shop or a *skansen*! Foodwise, don't expect surprises, but look forward to traditional mountain dishes.

Mała Szwajcaria–Ul. Zamoysk-iego11. 201 20 76. 9am–10pm. Try Swiss mountain cuisine or fondue for a change at this restaurant located just up the hill from the main street.

Restauracja Sabała – Ul. Krupówki11. 201 50 92. 10am–11pm. The large, chalet-style house, which also includes a luxury hotel, dominates the street. Restorative dishes can be enjoyed while watching the incessant parade of passers-by and horses.

Karcma Zapiecek – Ul. Krupówki43. 201 56 99. http:// zapiecek.pl. Open 11am–11pm. Traditional Polish cuisine of the Tatra Mountains region. Definitely worth a try.

ART GALLERIES

Many artists now have their own studios and galleries in Zakopane. Most of them are painters, sculptors, photographers or graphic designers. Exhibitions are temporary, styles and materials varied. Check at the Tourist Office before venturing on a visit.

Miejska Galeria Sztuki – Ul. Krupówki41. 201 27 92.

Galeria Politechniki Krakowskiej "Stara Polana" – Ul. Nowotarska59. 206 40 15.

Galeria Sztuki im. W.i J. Kulczyckich – Ul. Koziniec8. 201 29 36.

Galeria "Seba" Ul. Tetmajera 7c. 600 809 813.

BARS

Cafe Piano – Ul. Krupówki63. Hidden off the main street. Relax on a swing at the bar or on a cosy couch but don't expect lounge music, just great vodka drinks at low prices!

SHOPPING

Shopping arcade (Elegancki pasaż handlowy) – Ul. Krupówki29. A variety of shops are housed in a contemporary wooden structure.

SPORTS AND RECREATION

Outdoor swimming and bowling Aqua Park – Ul. Jagiellońska31. 202 58 15.

Indoor swimming pool DW Sośnika – Ul. Modrzejewskiej7. 206 67 96.

Ice-skating rink, with speed-skating loop – Ul Br.Czecha1.

FESTIVE EVENTS

May: **Country Festival** (Majówka) This festival, which takes place in early May and sometimes in late April, consists of one week of festivities to celebrate the return of fine weather.

August: The Mountain Areas Folk Festival. During the last week in August, Polish and international groups meet in Zakopane to take part in impressive and colourful dance shows.

The Tatras★★★

Forming a natural border between Poland and Slovakia, the spectacular Tatras (Tatry) are the highest mountains in the western Carpathians. Some call them the "pocket-size mountains", for although they cover a relatively small area, they offer great diversity: Alpine peaks, crystal lakes, secluded caves, deep glens, dramatic vistas, and of course, refreshing mountain air. Zakopane is the gateway to the Tatras, opening the way to hiking, climbing and skiing.

A BIT OF HISTORY
The Birth of a Park

Before Zakopane developed economically and became a tourist destination, the mountains were occupied by shepherds, hunters, bears, chamois and marmots. In the 19C, hunting became widely practised as an aristocratic sport as well as an activity for subsistence and this upset the natural balance. The National Assembly in Lwów (now L'viv in Ukraine), which ran the affairs of Galicia, became aware of the danger and in 1869, banned the shooting of marmots and deer. However, this step proved insufficient and soon many scientists and lovers of the Tatra Mountains grew concerned about the destructive intrusions of man. As the years went by, due to the development of Zakopane's economy and tourist industry the local fauna had to share their environment

◔ **Michelin Map:** Map of Poland C4 – Województwo of Lesser Poland.

▣ **Info:** Ul. Chałubińskiego 42a. 34-500 Zakopane. ✆202 32 00. www.tpn.pl.

▶ **Location:** 100km from Kraków, the Tatra Mountains tower over Zakopane and mark the border with Slovakia.

P **Parking:** Park for a fee at most of the various Park entrances.

⊘ **Don't Miss:** The hike to the pristine Lake Morskie Oko.

◔ **Timing:** Allow two days if you are an occasional hiker, much more if you happen to be a mountain lover.

with the Sunday hikers and the chamois didn't stand a chance against trophy hunters. In 1873, scientists supported by the local authorities created the Tatra Association (Towarzystwo Tatrzańskie), intended to make the tourist welcome while safeguarding endangered animal and plant species. In 1885, the association launched an ambitious project to protect the forests surrounding Zakopane. The idea of creating a Park was slowly forming in the minds of the Association's members, but political and financial support was still lacking. At the beginning of the 20C, inevitably a clash broke out between those opposed to

Toponymic Facts

The Carpathians, which extend from Ukraine to Poland via Romania and Hungary, are a mountain range of moderate altitude except for the Tatra Mountains situated at their western extremity. Astride Poland and Slovakia, this range reaches altitudes of over 2,000m. The Rysy Peak, on the Polish side, culminates at 2 499m, while on the Slovak side, the Gierlach rises to 2,654m. The Polish Tatras are divided into three sections: to the east, Tatry Bielskie, a small area of 67sq km featuring many caves around Łysa Polana. Further south, the High Tatras (Tatry Wysokie), which extend over 335sq km and boast the highest summits (Gierlach, Rysy, Świnica). And last the Western Tatras (Tatry Zachodnie), covering some 400sq km and including the Kasprowy Wierch, the summit which attracts the most tourists.

the establishment of the tourist industry and those who wanted to cash in on it, whatever the cost to the environment. The two World Wars halted all argument but, in 1947, the project was once more considered and, finally in 1954 the Tatra National Park (Tatrzański Park Narodowy – TPN) was created. Today the Park's mission is to study and protect the natural resources of 21,164ha of forests, valleys and Alpine peaks. In addition to dealing with purely environmental matters, the TNP also advises on farming, cultural and architectural issues. This mission is carried out in close cooperation with the Park's Slovak equivalent (TANAP), which covers an area about five times the size of its Polish partner.

🚶 HIKING AROUND ZAKOPANE

There is a charge for admission to the Park and for parking. These relatively low charges (🔖4.40 PLN) go towards financing part of the cost of managing the TPN. No matter which itinerary hikers choose, they should bear in mind that mountains sometimes have surprises in store. 🔖Wear appropriate shoes and be prepared for sudden changes in the weather by taking warm, waterproof clothing. Every year, over 3 million tourists wander along the paths and tracks of the TPN. In order to preserve the Park's natural resources and to ensure the safety of visitors, it is essential for everyone to respect some elementary rules.

1 Mount Gubałówka★★

The ascent of Mount Gubałówka by cable car or on foot starts near the Zakopane handicrafts market. Allow 50min on foot and 5min by cable car. The Gubałówka culminates at an altitude of only 1,120m and its ascent is by no means a sporting achievement. It is nevertheless one of the favourite walks of tourists and locals alike. In addition to the restaurants and shops located near the cable car terminal, the summit offers a fabulous panoramic view south towards Zakopane and the Tatra mountain range and north towards the

PRACTICAL INFORMATION

Regional Tourist Office (Redykołka) – Ul. Kościeliska 1, 34-500 Zakopane. ✆(18) 201 20 04.
Tatra National Park (Tatrzański Park Narodowy) – Ul. Chałubińskiego 42a. 34-500 Zakopane. ✆202 32 00. www.tpn.pl.
The Pieniny National Park (Pieniński Park Narodowy) – Ul. Jagiellońska 107b, 34-450 Krościenko. ✆262 56 01. www.pieninypn.pl.
Tourist office – Ul. Drohojowskich 7. 34-440 Czorsztyn. ✆(18) 265 03 66. www.czorsztyn.com.pl.

Podhale region and the Beskid. Near the summit, several colourful farms and a small wooden chapel built in 1971 create an atmosphere straight out of an old postcard. The path leading from the Gubałówka to Butorowy Wierch in 40min is accessible to everyone and requires no special equipment.

2 Hike to Lake Morskie Oko★★ (Eye of the Sea)

▶ *Starting from Zakopane, drive east along the road to Łysa Polana. Leave the border post on the left of the road and drive on to the parking area at the entrance to the Park. Reckon on about 20km there and back including a tour of the lake. Difference in height: 450m. Minimum 6hr walk. There is no special difficulty as far as the lake. It is possible to call on a horse-drawn cart, which stops less than 2km from the lake. 🔖60 PLN, there and back.*

Several lakes throughout the world are nicknamed "eye of the sea" on account of the many legends linking mountain lakes and the sea. In this case Morskie Oko is supposed to be connected with the Adriatic.

Walkers climb towards Lake Morskie Oko along a car-free surfaced road cut through a forest of fir trees, following the River Białka, which marks the border between Poland and Slovakia. Some of the trees have been torn to shreds by

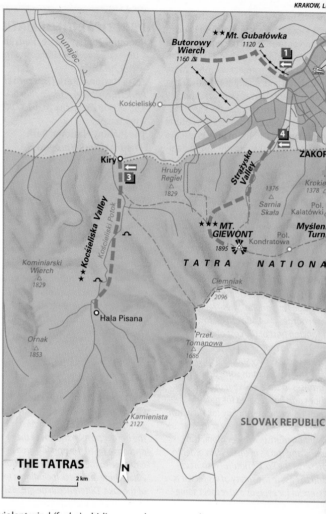

THE TATRAS

0 ———— 2 km

the violent wind *(foehn)* whirling round along the corridor formed by the valley. From the very beginning of the ascent, **Mount Gierlach** (2,564m), the highest summit of the Slovak Tatras, comes into view. Soon after, one reaches several waterfalls, among them the **Mickiewicz Falls**, named after the 19C poet. In winter the climb stops at this point because avalanches frequently occur beyond it. Further up, after walking for 6km, one reaches Polana Włosienica, a wide clearing, where carts drop off and pick up their customers. Part of the panorama known as Mięguszowieckie Szczyty unfolds before one's eyes. It encompasses the summits surrounding Lake Morskie Oko. After reaching the refuge overlooking the lake, one gets an overall view of the whole range, including the **Rysy** (2,499m), the **Czarny** (2,410m) and the **Wielki** (2,438m). Lake Morskie Oko extending over 35ha at an altitude of 1,395m is 50m deep, which makes it the most important trout reserve in the Polish Tatras. An easy path, with red markings, runs right round it and offers magnificent views of the various levels of mountain vegetation. Fir trees and beeches gradually give way to spruce which in turn disappears, until only scrub and dwarf pines remain.

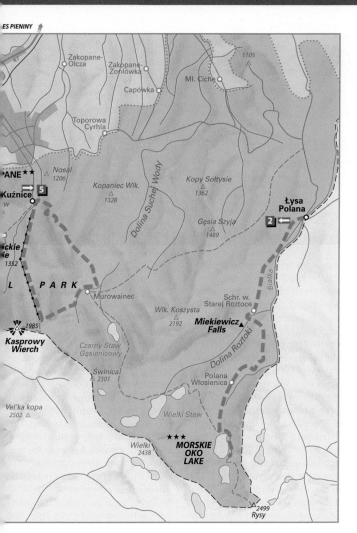

Then, above 1 800m, alpine pastures entirely cover the ground until they are replaced by arid rocks culminating at over 2,200m.

3 Walk through Kościeliska Valley★★ (Dolina Kóscieliska)

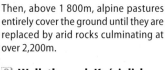

Leave Zakopane via Kościeliska Street and head for the village of Kiry 5km away. Buses link Zakopane and Kiry. Take the Zakopane – Ciche Górne line and get off at "Dolina Kóscieliska". Allow about 3hr on foot to cover the 6km and 180m difference in height. This walk offers no special difficulty and is not colour-coded. The track is wide enough to allow horse-drawn carts to take visitors to more distant junctions. The path runs along the Kościeliski Potoka, a tumultuous stream separating a vast expanse of grazing land from the forest. Beyond a forester's house, the path crosses a bridge over the Kościeliski Potok. *(To the left is the starting point of a longer itinerary which skirts the Slovak border, heading for the Czerwone Wierchy (4hr) and the Kasprowy Wierch (6hr). The path climbs above 2,000m and this hike is only suitable for experienced hikers. Note that it is possible to take a cable car (26 PLN) from the top of the Kasprowy Wierch to Zakopane-*

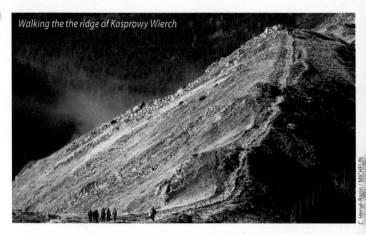

Walking the the ridge of Kasprowy Wierch

C Hervé-Razin / MICHELIN

Kuźnice. *A few hundred metres beyond the bridge, a path runs off to the right towards the Chochołów Valley (Dolina Chochołowska). Allow about 3hr to reach Polana Chochołowska, where the walk ends.)*

The path of the main itinerary leads to a wide valley offering a splendid panoramic view of the summits marking the Slovak border. A picturesque altar built long ago by miners looking for iron can be seen during the second part of the hike. There are many **caves** along the path, some of them open to visitors. There is an admission charge and visitors must take a guided tour. It is advisable to take warm clothing and a torch. The difference in level is usually negligible and the tours are open to all visitors. The caves which are most popular with Polish visitors are **Jaskinia Mroźna and Jaskinia Zimna**. They are tunnels several hundred metres long, with chambers covered with stalactites and stalagmites. The path continues towards Hala Pisana and its shelter, where the walk ends. Those who do not wish to retrace their steps can choose between several itineraries heading for Slovakia in the east or joining the Chochołów Valley to the west.

4 Walk through the Strążyska Valley and ascent of Mount Giewont ★★★

The hike starts in Zakopane. ▶ At the beginning of Kościeliska Street, turn left onto *Kasprusi Street which becomes Strążyska Street. The latter ends at a parking area and the entrance to the Park. Allow a total of 5hr on foot. It takes 45min for the first part of the hike, which has a difference in height of 250m, then over 2hr to cover the 600m difference in altitude to the top of Mount Giewont.*

During the first part of the itinerary, the stony path runs alongside a stream through a fairly dense forest, sometimes climbing steeply; however, the hike remains accessible to families. The path leads to a steep pasture where a **shepherd's house has been turned into a tearoom**. The setting is delightful and the products served by the establishment really taste homemade. A little higher up, in the thick of the forest, one can hear waterfalls, a very pleasant and refreshing sound in summer. Many Polish hikers make this convivial place the purpose of their outing. However, it is possible to go further along a more uneven and steeper path up to the top of the Giewont, one of the most famous summits of the Tatra Mountains. During the ascent, one climbs from the fir forest level to the sub-Alpine scrub level and finally to the stony ground of Alpine pastures. From the top of its 1 895m peak, the Giewont offers an overall view of the Zakopane Valley and of the small **Pieniny Mountains**, 50km further away. The summit of the Giewont is topped by a 17m-high metal cross, erected in 1901 by Zakopane's parishioners.

5 From Zakopane-Kuźnice to the summit of Mount Kasprowy Wierch★★

Kuźnice is situated 3km southwest of Zakopane. Access by car is not allowed, therefore one must walk there or take no. 59 bus. The Kasprowy Wierch rises to 1,959m. Its summit is accessible on foot or by cable car (one-way ticket 32 PLN). The journey by cable car takes 20min; on foot, allow 5hr there and back.

Ascent of the Kasprowy Wierch by cable car – The Kasprowy Wierch cable car was the first of its kind built in Poland. It was inaugurated in 1936 after a long debate posing members of the Union of Polish Skiers against those concerned with the protection of the environment. The total length is 4,000m with a difference in altitude of 936m. Each trip involves two cars carrying 36 persons travelling in opposite directions. The ascent is in two sections, separated by a halfway station, Myślenickie Turnie, clinging to the rock face at an altitude of 1,028m.

The first section reveals the Giewont and the Czerwone Wierchy. The 2,290m-long second section, at an angle of 30 degrees, offers **splendid panoramic views** of the valleys and the Zakopane ski area at Sucha Dolina Kasprowa. The summit of the Kasprowy Wierch, often windswept and shrouded by clouds, is equipped with a restaurant, souvenir shops and a meteorological station. It offers a spectacular panorama consisting of a **rocky barrier** rising to an average height of 2,200m (Świnica 2,301m; Krywań 2,495m). Slovakia extends beyond this barrier featuring snow-covered peaks in all seasons.

The descent to Kuźnice – Two paths lead down from the Kasprowy Wierch to Kuźnice. The first *(allow about 2hr30min)* follows the cable-car route. The second, more uneven *(allow 3hr30min)*, has yellow markings as far as Hala Gąsienicowa, then yellow or blue ones down to Kuźnice. Note that a footpath runs from Hala Gąsienicowa to Lake Morskie Oko. *Allow about 6hr on foot.*

EXPLORING THE PIENINY
The Pieniny and the raft trip down the Dunajec Gorge★★★

▶ *Starting from Zakopane, drive to Nowy Targ, then follow road 969 towards Krościenko. In Krośnica, turn right towards Sromowce Wyżne – Kąty. The pier is by the roadside. Follow the signposts marked: Polskie Stowarzyszenie Flisaków Pienińskich. Sromowce Wyżne – Kąty Pier. Open daily Apr 9am–4pm; May–Aug 8.30am–5pm; Sept 8.30am–4pm; Oct 9am–3pm. Closed Easter, Corpus Christi. 44 PLN. About 3hr. www.flisacy.com.pl.*

Pieniny National Park
(Pieniński Park Narodowy)

The Park includes the popular limestone summits **Trzy Korony** (982m) and **Wysoka** (1,050m). Famous for their varied flora (especially butterflies) and luxuriant vegetation, the Pieniny offer breathtaking scenary highlighted by jagged peaks, and rocky gorges. From their crests, one admires the sight of the Tatras along the horizon, beyond the expansive valley below. The River Dunajec flows down from the Tatras and cuts its way through steep ravines in the Pieniny before joining the Wisła northeast of Kraków. Rafting down the Dunajec Gorge is the most exhillarating way to admire the dramatic landscapes and is the region's major attraction.

Rafting down the Gorge

The trip is remarkably well organised and is absolutely safe, thanks to the cooperation between the Pieniny Park and the Association of Boatmen. The latter use all their expertise in navigating the tumultuous waters of this natural frontier between Poland and Slovakia for the benefit of tourists. On the banks of the river in Sromowce Wyżne – Kąty (men in regional costumes) help the would-be sailors into small, flat-bottomed boats, rendered perfectly watertight by branches of fir trees pressed between the planks. Each raft, steered by two men, takes about ten passengers. The trip starts at the foot of **Mount Macelowa** (802m). During the first few kilometres, the Dunajec is wide and calm. Very soon one catches sight of the high summits of the Tatras, then the boat sails past Slovak villages on the right bank and Polish ones on the left.The sheer cliffs are sometimes covered with vegetation, sometimes completely bare. As the crow flies, the Gorge is 3km long, but **seven wide loops** almost multiply this distance by three. The riverbed suddenly narrows to only 10m wide as the raft reaches a place called **The Bandit's Jump (Zbójnicki Skok)**. According to legend, while fighting against the oppression of a wealthy monarch, a famous bandit named Janosik escaped his pursuers by jumping over this narrow bend in the river. After a tumultuous stretch, it resumes its lazy course. According to another legend, the blessed who drink from the Slovak spring, which gushes forth in a spot known as *"Stuletnie Źródło"*, "the hundred-year spring", will live a century. The Dunajec flows on to the landing stage at **Szczawnica**. This bucolic, laid-back spa town has many inviting restaurants and 12 mineral-water springs to invigorate the weary tourist. *The bus terminal, for Sromowce Wyżne – Kąty, is situated below the bridge on the right. The minibuses leave when they are full.*

The road back affords an exceptional view of the valley and of the Tatras.

Note that **Szczawnica** is the starting point of several cycle tracks and footpaths giving access to the Pieniny Park and the highest summit, the Wysoka (1,100m) or to the Trzy Korony (the Three Crowns).

Around Czorsztyn Reservoir; Czorsztyn and Niedzica Castles

The Czorsztyn Lake was created as a result of the construction of a hydraulic dam on the River Dunajec. A few wooden structures, including several chapels, which would have found themselves on the lake bottom, were moved to a small *skansen* in Kluszkowce, a few kilometres northwest of Czorsztyn. The two local castles were spared due to their hilltop location and serenely cast shadows on the placid surface of the lake.

From road 969, in the village of Krośnica, head south towards Czorsztyn and then Niedzica.

Czorsztyn Castle

Open May–Sept 9am–6pm; Oct–Apr Tue–Sun 10am–3pm. Closed 1 Jan, 1 Nov, 25–26 Dec, Easter Sun. 4 PLN

The ruins of Czorsztyn Castle are worth a visit if only for the panoramic view of the lake, the Pieniny range and the Tatras. This small fortress, built in the 14C at the time of Kazimierz the Great for the Poor Clares of Stary Sącz, was struck by lightning in the 1790s and destroyed by fire. In the 19C the Austrians auctioned off what was left, hence the bare stone ruin we see today.

Niedzica Castle

Open May–Sept 9am–6pm; Oct–Apr Tue–Sun 10am–3pm. Closed 1 Jan, 1 Nov, 25–26 Dec, Easter Sun. 12 PLN

Niedzica Castle stands on the opposite shore of the lake. As the two castles face each other, they both offer spectacular views of the surrounding area. However, Niedzica Castle is historically more interesting than its neighbour and in much better condition. Built in the Gothic style in 1325, it guarded the frontier for centuries and alternately fell into Polish or Hungarian hands.

Dębno Church★★

Situated along road 969 between Nowy Targ and Krościenko. Open Mon–Fri 9am–noon, 2–4.30pm, Sat 9am–noon.

The first mention of this gem of sacred architecture, the Church of St Michael the Archangel in Dębno goes back to 1335. The current building was constructed without the use of a single nail, probably in the 15C, while the tower was added in 1601. The church boasts an exceptional interior decorated with beautiful Gothic furnishings. The highlight is the remarkably well-preserved medieval polychrome stencil paintings that cover the larch beam walls with medieval folk motifs. In 2003 the church was added to UNESCO's World Heritage List.

ADDRESSES

🛏 STAY

Most hotels are located in Zakopane or in the town's close surroundings.

🍽 **CHMIEL Jadwiga and Stanisław** – *Il. Ks. J. Kosibowicza41. 33 443 Sromowce Wyżne. ☎262 97 80. www.chmiel.pieniny. et. 4 rooms.* Fine rooms, a sauna and solarium in a house classified as "ecological accommodation", a stone's throw from the raft trips down the River Dunajec, with a view of Slovakia.

🍽 **Niedzica Castle** – *34-441 Niedzica. ☎(18) 262 9480. Up to 30 guests.* Not a hotel, but the castle does rent rooms in both modern and historic style for those seeking to lord over a castle.

🍴 EAT

🍽 **Dwór Polany Sosny** – *34-441 Niedzica, ś. Na Polanie Sosny. ☎(18) 262 94 03.* Enjoy huge servings of hearty Polish and Hungarian food in this 18C-style Polish manor house, which also rents rooms with views of the surrounding mountains and castles.

🏃 SPORTS AND RECREATION

Spelunking – Cave visits – Information available from the Tatra National Park.

Polish Mountain Guides Assoc. – *www.pspw.pl.*

Mountain Kayaking and Rafting School – *Ul. Maszyńskiego 28, 30-698 Kraków. ☎(18) 541 70 69. www.retendo. com.pl.*

Nowy Targ Flying Club and Parachuting School – Flights offering bird's-eye-views of the Tatras and of the Podhale region. *Ul. Lotników 1, 34-400 Nowy Targ. ☎(18) 264 66 16. www.aeroklub.nowy-targ.pl.*

Western Beskids★★

Beskid Żywiecki

Mount Babia Góra is known as the queen of the West Beskid mountains, towering over the rest of the range at an altitude of 1,725m and snow-capped much of the year. Listed by UNESCO as a World Biosphere Reserve, this region bordering Slovakia proudly retains the colourful folklore and traditions of its native ethnic groups, as witnessed by local wayside shrines, peasant cottages and shepherd costumes. Sucha Beskidzka and above all, Zawoja are the starting points for explorations off the beaten track.

A BIT OF HISTORY

The Babia Góra range is the second highest in Poland after the Tatra Mountains. The highest sections are known as the Witch's and Devil's Peaks due to local legends of pagan sabbaths that were held there, and on account of the

- ♿ **Michelin Map:** Map of Poland C4 – Województwo of Silesia.
- 🏴 **Info:** Babiogórski National Park. Zawoja 1403. ☎(33) 877 51 10. www.bgpn.pl.
- ◗ **Location:** 80km northwest of Zakopane and 80km southwest of Kraków, on the Slovak border.
- 🅿 **Parking:** Free parking in town, but for hikers paid parking at park entrances.
- 👁 **Don't Miss:** The hike to the top of the unpredictable Babia Góra.
- 🕐 **Timing:** Allow one day to discover the natural environment around the Babia Góra and Zawoja, and half a day to visit Sucha Beskidzka.

howling winds. The vegetation on its lower slopes, up to 1,400m, includes beeches, spruce, fir trees and a few white maples. Higher up, gnarled scrub

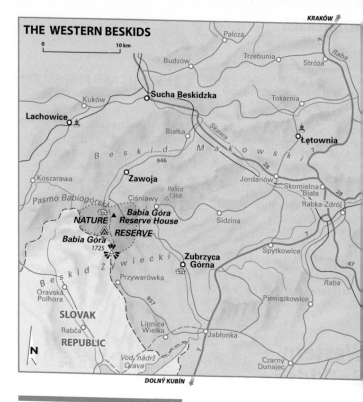

THE WESTERN BESKIDS

GETTING AROUND

BY BUS – There are many bus services from **Sucha Beskidzka** and **Zawoja** to **Kraków**.

PRACTICAL INFORMATION

Phone code – ✆*033.*
Postal code – *34-200.*
Postal code (Zawoja) – *34-223.*
Tourist office – *Babiogórski National Park. Zawoja 1403.* ✆*(33) 877 51 10. www.bgpn.pl.*
Tourist information services in Sucha Beskidzka and Zawoja can be contacted through *www.powiatsuski.pl.* Zawoja: *www.zawoja.pl.*

and wind-swept pastures cling to the rocky surfaces. Lynx, bears, wolves and grouse occupy the sparsely populated slopes, unaffected by industry. Sheep farming by nomadic shepherds, forestry and woodworking are the main economic activities, supported by the controlled development of tourism. In 1976, UNESCO decided to classify the Babia Góra region as a living laboratory for the study of the area's unique biosphere. This allows scientists to study and watch various parameters such as the impact of tourism on the environment, forest management, the quality of water and the survival of rare species, while encouraging economic growth.

BABIA GÓRA PARK
Zawoja

The Park's head office is in this village which stretches for several kilometres along road 957, at the foot of Mount Babia Góra. It's worth trying the locally grown blueberries and the ewe's cheese smoked in specially built shacks. In winter, the village becomes a family winter sports resort.

The wooden **St-Clement's Church**, situated in the village centre, on a mound overlooking the road, dates from 1759 but was rebuilt and restored on many occasions, the last time in 1888.

▶ *Drive south from Zawoja's centre towards Zubrzyca Górna and turn right in Zawoja-Widły towards the skansen and a place called Markowa.*

The Babia Góra Park Information Centre

🕐*Open May–Sept Tueun 9am–4.30pm; Oct–Apr Tue–Fri 9am–3pm.* 🚋*3.5 PLN.*
The exhibitions are devoted to the Park's natural environment and to the region's folk traditions. The small **Józef Żak Skansen** is situated a short distance from the Centre, along the road.

Hike to the top of the Babia Góra

From Markowa, drive about 500m to the "PTTK Markowa Szczawiny" shelter.
From there, allow at least 2 hours to reach the summit of the Babia Góra; from the top, the view extends over the Beskid, Slovakia and, further afield, the Tatra Mountains. The yellow-marked track offers no difficulty, so long as you wear adequate shoes and clothing.

Zubrzyca Górna – Skansen

▶ *Located 20km south of Zawoja along road 957.* 🕐*Open daily May–Sept 8.30am–5pm; Oct–Apr 8.30am–2.30pm.*🚋*11 PLN.*
The *skansen* illustrates the settlement of different communities of shepherds and farmers from Moldavia and from the northern part of Lesser Poland. The path runs through woods and vast meadows dotted with farms, windmills or weaving workshops. Note the fine collection of beehives. The group of buildings date from the late 18C and from the 19C. Most of the structures were transported here from nearby locations.

Sucha Beskidzka – The Castle

🕐*Open Tue–Fri 9am–5pm, Sat–Sun 10am–6pm.* 🚋*6 PLN.*
In 1614, Piotr Komorowski, a wealthy local scholar, had an extension added to a small fortified house built in 1554. The residence was transformed into a splendid Renaissance castle with an arcaded courtyard à la Wawel and it developed into a cultural centre. A library containing some 55,000 works collected by the owner and later by his descendants, paintings and drawings furnished the wings of the palace until the 1930s. The collections are now scattered in Poland's major museums yet despite this, the castle continues to perform its cultural mission by organising regular temporary exhibitions devoted to painting and sculpture. A stroll through the beautiful park leads visitors to the dilapidated orangery in English neo-Gothic style: it once contained 1,200 lemon and orange trees, which provided a decent income for the family of its initiator, Anna Konstancja Wielopolska. Further on, the **Gardener's House** is a small ethnographic museum illustrating the handicraft activity and spiritual life of the inhabitants of the Babia Góra region in the 19C.
Sucha Beskidzka also boasts some fine examples of religious architecture consisting of a monastery and several chapels dating from the 17C as part of the Church of the Annunciation complex. The overall design still shows signs of Gothic architecture, but the details are Renaissance and Baroque.
The **Roman Inn** (Karczma Rzym), built in the 18C, stands in the village centre. Although the building was restored in 1960, its traditional wooden architecture remains intact. The fact that the poet Adam Mickiewicz probably used it as the setting for one of his short stories only reinforces its status as a monument.

ADDRESSES

🏨 STAY

🛏 **Lajkonik Hotel** – *34-223 Zawoja 1550.* 🖉*874 51 00. www.hotellajkonik. com.pl. 17 rooms. Restaurant*🍴🛏.
On leaving Zawoja in the direction of Jabłonka. Located at the foot of Babia Góra, the hotel is housed in an atmospheric 1930s stone building.

Wrocław Town Hall
R. Mattès / MICHELIN

SILESIA AND THE SUDETEN

Silesia's turbulent past resulted in these lands changing hands countless times over the centuries, but the upheavals also brought about magnificent architectural achievements and industrial development. Wrocław is the region's cultural capital and one of the most exciting cities in Poland; it's also one of the most beautiful, featuring the second largest town square after Kraków, and many bridges and islands located in and around the Old Town. Most Polish cities turn away from their rivers, not so in Wrocław: part of the moat has been preserved and the Oder River picturesquely flows next to the cathedral island and its Gothic churches, the Baroque university district and the National Museum.

Highlights

1 An evening stoll around Cathedral Island in **Wrocław** (p303)

2 The Chapel of Skulls in **Czermna** (p311)

3 The amazing timber Peace Churches in **Świdnica** and **Jawor** (p315)

4 A hike to the top of **Mt. Śnieżka** in the Karkonosze National Park (p318)

Architectural achievement

Silesia's smaller towns boast wonderful town squares, Baroque burghers' homes, and diverse Protestant and Catholic churches that reflect the rich architectural heritage of the various Polish, German and Bohemian influences. The largest cathedral in Silesia can be found in Świdnica, a town that also boasts the UNESCO listed Peace Church and a fine town square enriched with Baroque fountains. The best preserved Gothic bridge in Poland, which shows Bohemian influences, can be admired in Kłodzko, along with a massive Prussian fortress that literally towers over the town.

Paczków is another good destination for fans of defensive architecture: the town's walls and bastions have been preserved and even the main church is a partially fortified structure. This is also a land of pleasantly attractive health spa towns nestled amongst foothills near the border with the Czech Republic. The Sudeten Mountains not only make a natural border for the area, but offer plentiful opportunities for hiking, mountain biking or just relaxing in the vibrant resort town of Karpacz.

Kłodzko, as seen from the Prussian fortress

© Saiori13/Dreamstime.com

Pszczyna

The name of this unassuming but lovely provincial town – known as "the pearl of Upper Silesia" – may be difficult to say, but Pszczyna is a pleasant oasis in a region known more for its smokestacks and mines. The town's castle features beautiful interiors, which make for memorable concerts, and an enchanting English-style landscaped park for romantic strolls.

A BIT OF HISTORY

Pszczyna, just like Silesia, has had a turbulent history. Annexed to Lesser Poland at the end of the 10C by the region's first duke, Mieszko I, it became a Silesian city in 1178 when it fell under the authority of the Piast Princes. Over the centuries Pszczyna changed ownership countless times and in 1846, the estate passed into the hands of the Counts Von Hochberg, one of the richest families in Europe, who imposed the Germanisation and industrialisation of Silesia. After World War I, the first of three Silesian uprisings took place in August 1919, and in the 1921 referendum 74 per cent of local voters opted for unification with Poland, returnin Pszczyna to its earliest roots.

SIGHTS
Rynek★

This attractive square, surrounded by a fine group of low 18C–19C burghers' houses, is dominated by the extremely wide neo-Baroque façade of the **Evangelical church** adjacent to the **town hall** (Ratusz). Erected in the early 17C, the town hall was remodelled in the neo-Renaissance style in 1931. In the northwest corner of the square stands the 17C guardhouse with its elegant **Gate of the Chosen** (Brama Wybrańców), the only way into the castle. This is also the location of the Tourist Office.

Castle Museum★
(Muzeum Zamkowe)

Ul. Brama Wybrańców1. ◐Open Nov–mid-Dec and Feb–Mar Tue 11am–3pm, Wed 9am–4pm, Thu–Fri 9am–3pm,

▶ **Population:** 26,830.
Michelin Map: Map of Poland C4 – Województwo of Silesia.
Info: Brama Wybrańców. ℰ(32) 212 99 99. www.pszczyna.info.pl.
Location: 28km from Auschwitz, 88km from Kraków.
Parking: Guarded parking next to the Old Town and River, Ul. Katowicka
Don't Miss: "The Telemann Evenings": a festival of Baroque music held inside the Castle in September and October (enquire at the Tourist Office).
Timing: Allow 3hr for exploring the town, castle and park.

GETTING AROUND
BY BUS/RAIL – Bus and train services link **Pszczyna** and **Kraków**. Allow 2hr30min to 3hr.

PRACTICAL INFORMATION
Phone code – ℰ032.
Postal code – 43-200.
Tourist office – Brama Wybrańców 1. To the left of the gate giving access to the castle. ℰ212 99 99. www.pszczyna. info.pl. Mon–Fri 8am–4pm; Sat–Sun 10am–4pm.

Sat 10am–3pm, Sun 10am–4pm; Apr–Jun and Septct Mon 11am–3pm, Tue 10am–3pm, Wed 9am–5pm, Thu–Fri 9am–4pm, Sat 10am–4pm, Sun 10am–5pm; Jul–Aug Mon 11am–3pm, Tue 10am–3pm, Wed–Fri 9am–5pm, Sat 10am–5pm, Sun 10am–6pm; last admission 1hr before closing. ⊜14 PLN. ℰ210 30 37. www.zamek-pszczyna.pl This 15C Gothic castle was rebuilt between 1870 and 1876 in the Neoclassical style by French architect Alexandre Destailleur when it was the property of

Castle Museum

W. Buss / MICHELIN

Count von Hochberg, who occupied it until it was nationalised in 1945. The members of this family, who originally came from the medieval castle of Książ in Lower Silesia, were allowed to keep the title of Princes von Pless. During World War I the German high command took over the castle and Emperor William made it his residence. One of the rare castles not to have been plundered during World War II – no doubt because of the German origins of its owners, it was turned into a museum in 1946.

The vast and sumptuous apartments were reconstructed to the last detail from old photographs. All the rooms were decorated in accordance with the principle of *horror vacui*, fear of empty spaces. For visitors, the absolute must is undoubtedly the prince's office. His "work" mainly consisted of hunting, judging by the impressive number of trophies on display.

Every September since 1979, the imposing Hall of Mirrors has been the setting of a **Festival of Baroque Music** (Sviatoslav Richter took part on several occasions) in honour of the composer Georg Philipp Telemann (1681-1767) who spent the summer months in the castle from 1704 to 1707. The castle is also famous for its 156ha English-style park (Zabyt-kowy Park Pszczyński), through which the Pszczynka River flows and which is criss-crossed by many footpaths and cycle tracks.

Regional Ethnographic Museum
(Zagroda wsi Pszczyńskiej)
In the eastern part of the castle's park.
Open May–Oct Mon–Fri 9am–5pm, Sat–Sun 10am–6pm. By appointment in winter. ℘604 508 718. 6 PLN.

This unpretentious yet charming *Skansen* (open-air museum) consists of timber houses and farm buildings located in the heart of the forest. Just before arriving, you will see a restaurant called Stary Młyn, housed in an old traditional wooden mill, similar to the buildings of the open-air museum.

ADDRESSES

STAY

Villa Retro – *Ul. Warowna 31.* ℘210 22 45. www.retro.pl. 20 rooms. This true family guest house close to the Rynek is very appropriately named and you will be able to appreciate the old-world charm of the rooms.

Hotel Zamkowy – *Rynek 20.* ℘449 17 20. www.hotelzamkowy.eu. 10 rooms. Restaurant Stara Piekarnia. New, elegant hotel in restored 18C town house combines a perfect location with subdued style.

EAT

Restauracja Frykówka – *Rynek 3.* ℘449 00 20. www.frykowka.pl. Open 10am–10pm. On the main square with outdoor patio. Traditional Polish food, including soups served in bread bowls.

Restauracja Kmieć – *Ul. Piekarska 10.* ℘210 36 38. www.kmiec.pna.pl. Open daily noon–9pm. Located in the Old Town, this establishment features good traditional Polish-Silesian cooking. Terrace in the inner courtyard.

Opole

Pleasantly located on an island in the Odra River, Opole is the region's capital. The city boasts a lovely Rynek and a Gothic burial chapel for the tombs of Polish princes. In addition to such ancient history, Opole is famous throughout the country for the festival of Polish song held here since 1963. Brzeg Castle is a short trip away.

BACKGROUND

Opole was founded in the 8C on a small island in the middle of the River Odra. Protected by its castle, of which all that remains is the 13C **Piast Tower** (Wieża Piastowska; ⓞ *open Tue–Sun 10am–1pm, 2–6pm; ⊜3 PLN*). From the 13C to 1532 it was the headquarters of the ruling Silesian Piasts. The town then fell under the control of the Habsburgs and later, the Hohenzollerns. Over the centuries, the town centre gradually moved to its present location on the east bank of the Odra.

SIGHTS

Rynek

The square is surrounded by Baroque and Renaissance houses, which were carefully restored after World War II. In the centre stands the massive **Town Hall**, built in 1936 in the style of the

- ▸ **Population:** 130,000.
- ⚙ **Michelin Map:** Map of Poland B3 – Województwo of Opole.
- ⓘ **Info:** Ul. Krakowska 15. ℘(77) 451 19 87. www.opole.pl.
- ▶ **Location:** 100km south-east of Wrocław and west of Częstochowa.
- Ⓟ **Parking:** Free parking in Old Town on Sun.
- ⊙ **Don't Miss:** Opole's peaceful Rynek, the Gothic churches.
- ⓧ **Timing:** Allow half a day to visit Opole, a few hours to see the churches scattered across the countryside and 2hr for a tour of Brzeg Castle.
- ⚙ **Also See:** Brzeg's Renaissance castle.

Palazzio Vecchio in Florence. All the sights are near the Rynek.

Franciscan Church
(Kościół Franciszkanów)
Ul. Zamkowa, south of the Rynek.
An atmosphere of deep meditation emanates from the nave and its ceilings decorated with an interlacing of foliage.

Rynek

© Polish National Tourist Office

GETTING AROUND

BY RAIL – Railway station –
Ul. Krakowska 48. www.pkp.com.pl.
BY BUS – Bus station – *Ul.1-go Maja 4.
www.pks.opole.pl.*

PRACTICAL INFORMATION

Phone code – *℘077.*
Postal code – *45 000.*
Tourist office – *Ul. Krakowska 15.
℘451 19 87.* Wide selection of
brochures in English.

The tiny **St Anne's Chapel**★ (Kaplica
Św. Anny) containing the mausoleum
of the Piasts, whose family tree is painted on the wall, has, since the 14C,
been housing the recumbent figures
of Bolko I, Bolko II, Bolko III and his wife
Anna of Oświęcim.
The Gothic ribbed vaulting is adorned
with oak leaves, angels and brightly
coloured coats of arms.

Opole's Silesian Museum
(Muzeum Śląska Opolskiego)
*Ul. Św. Wojciecha 13. ⏰Open Tue–Fri
9am–4pm, Sat 10am–3pm, Sun noon–
5pm. ∞5 PLN, Sat free.*
This interesting museum, housed in
a former Jesuit college, is devoted to
regional history. The town's history is
illustrated by archaeological finds, press
cuttings and 19C documents.
North of the Rynek stand the twin
towers of the **Cathedral of the Holy
Cross** (Katedra Św. Krzyża).

EXCURSIONS
Brzeg★
⯈ *45km northwest of Opole towards
Wrocław.*
The town boasts an interesting 16C
Renaissance town hall, designed by
two Italian architects, Francesco Parra
and André Walther, but the town's main
attraction is the **Museum of Silesian
Piasts**★ (Muzeum Piastów Śląskich;
⏰open Tue–Sun 10am–4pm; ∞8 PLN,
Sat free, explanations in Polish) located
in **Zamkowy Square**. It is housed in

the castle, one of the finest examples
of Renaissance architecture in Poland.
The Piasts occupied it until their dynasty
became extinct in 1675.
The richly carved façade is crowned by
the busts of members of this illustrious
family and the three arcaded storeys of
the inner courtyard are reminiscent of
Wawel in Kraków. The fine collections
are displayed in the beautifully restored
rooms, some of which have retained a
monumental portal or fireplace.

The Gothic Churches Trail★★
The small churches in **Małujowice,
Krzyżowice, Pogorzela, Strzelniki**
and **Łosiów**, near Brzeg, are well worth
a detour. Their frescoes, painted around
the 14C, were systematically plastered
over by the Protestants. This helped
to preserve them from the ravages of
time and today priceless polychromes
are being rediscovered. *Ask for the keys
next door.*

ADDRESSES

🛏 STAY
🛏 **Piast Hotel** – *Ul.Piastowska 1.
℘454 97 10. www.hotel-piast.com.
25 rooms.* Ideally situated near the
town centre, this luxury hotel overlooks
the River Odra. Spacious rooms.

🍽 EAT
🍽 **Starka** – *Ul. Ostrówek 19.
℘453 12 14.* Perched above the Odra,
this restaurant offers a wide choice of
beers and cocktails and serves refined
German and Polish dishes. A few
specialities on request including lamb
and Polish-style goose.

🍽🍽 **Restauracja Zagłoba** –
*Ul. Krakowska 39. ℘441 78 65. Open daily
noon–11pm.* Old-fashioned traditional
Polish cuisine served in historic vaulted
cellars. Mon–Sat lunch menu.

🎉 FESTIVE EVENTS
Festival of Polish Song: Late June.
An institution for over 40 years.

Wrocław★★★

The capital of Lower Silesia is a vibrant, multi-faceted city. The hustle and bustle of the Rynek, with its colourful façades, contrasts with the peace and quiet pervading the streets of Ostrów Tumski, the cathedral district. With 110 bridges over the Odra and dozens of islands, the Polish Venice is a continually changing student town, whose dynamism is reflected in its architectural innovations and countless festivals.

A BIT OF HISTORY

Wrocław was founded around the 9C on the island of Ostrów Tumski. In the year 1000, the Polish King Boleslas the Brave endowed the town with a cathedral and a bishop's palace. Wrocław then proudly resisted various raids and in 1138, became the capital of Silesia, a region soon to grow prosperous. The expansion of the town led to its centre being moved to the South bank of the Odra. In 1335, Poland lost control over the region which fell under Bohemian rule. The Habsburgs took over in the 16C but were replaced in 1741 by the Prussians who definitively acquired the town in 1763, at the end of the Seven Years War against the Austrians. They named it Breslau and turned it into a supposedly impregnable fortress. In the 19C, the city became one of Silesia's major industrial centres.

After World War II, the town was returned to Poland following the Potsdam agreement. The German population fled and a few thousand Poles were transferred from Lwów (now L'viv in Ukraine). They brought with them their lifestyle and part of their cultural heritage, including the statue of the writer Aleksander Fredro, the Racławice Panorama and the library collections of the Ossoliński Institute. The closeness of the German border explains the flood of German tourists who often undertake a nostalgic journey to the place of their childhood.

▶ **Population:** 630,000.
⚬ **Michelin Map:** Map of Poland B3 – Województwo of Lower Silesia.
ℹ **Info:** Rynek14. (71) 344 3111. http://wroclaw-info.pl.
▷ **Location:** 340km southeast of Warsaw, 270km northwest of Kraków.
🅿 **Parking:** 3-5 PLN for guarded parking throughout the city centre
⊚ **Don't Miss**: Night strolls through Ostrów Tumski, the panoramic view of the town from the cathedral tower.
👥 **Kids:** A visit to the zoo is a must.
🕑 **Timing:** Wrocław deserves two or three days of your time for you to appreciate its different facets to the full. Sights and museums are of real interest and the town is quite attractive by night.

WALKING TOUR

Rynek A-B2

This vast rectangle, measuring 173 x 208m, is the heart of the medieval city laid out in 1241 in a grid pattern. East of the town hall stands a copy of the stocks used for torture from the 15C onwards. On the west side stands the statue of comic author Aleksander Fredro, brought here from Lwów (now L'viv in Ukraine) after the war.

The original Gothic houses surrounding the Rynek were later remodelled in the Renaissance, Baroque or Classical style. Most of them were restored after 1945. The massive grey building in the southwest corner was supposed to prefigure a new Rynek – fortunately, the project never got off the ground. Note the **House of the Seven Electors (no. 8)**, the **House of the Golden Sun (no. 5)**, the **Griffin House (no. 2)** and, in the northwest corner, the two houses known as **Hansel and Gretel** (Jaś i

Present-day Wrocław

The Siege of Wrocław

One of the most hard-fought and destructive battles of World War II raged here over a three-month span in 1945 in the then German city of Breslau. When the war began, Breslau was the third largest city in Germany. Hitler declared Breslau a fortress to be defended at all costs in the autumn of 1944. Up until that time the city had suffered almost no damage as it was out of the range of Allied bombers. As the Red Army approached in January 1945 civilians were ordered to evacuate the city, but due to a shortage of trains and extremely cold temperatures as many as 90,000 of the German residents froze or starved to death during the desperate attempt to escape.

Many civilians (approx. 200,000) still remained in the city when the siege began on February 13 1945. During the three months of shelling and fighting most of the beautiful old town and cathedral island was destroyed, and other historic neighborhoods were demolished by the Nazis when they started to build an airfield in the heart of the city or when they razed whole streets to create huge piles of rubble as defensive barriers. Despite the long siege, continuous shelling, and horrific losses, the city continued to fight even after Berlin surrendered on May 2, 1945. The city finally capitulated on May 6, one day before the unconditional surrender of all German forces. As a result of the Potsdam Agreement, Breslau was handed over to Poland and given its old Polish name Wrocław while most Germans were expelled to be replaced by Poles relocated from Polish lands in the east which had by taken by the Soviet Union at the beginning of the war. Much of the Old Town and most of cathedral inland were reconstructed after the war and the city today has learned to embrace its pre-war German past as can witnessed by the many books and post cards documenting that bygone era.

Defensive barrier, 1945

GETTING THERE AND GETTING AROUND

BY AIR – **Airport** – *Ul. Skarżyńskiego 36. ☎358 13 81. www.airport.wroclaw.pl.* Some 12km northwest of the town centre. Journey time: 40 min by bus no. 406. Regular links with London; several flights daily, to and from Warsaw.

BY RAIL – **Railway station** – *Ul. Piłsudskiego 105. www.pkp.pl.* The main station is situated 1km south of the town centre. There are trains to Warsaw, Kraków and Poznań several times a day. *(The station is under renovation and set to reopen late 2011, temporary station entrance Ul. Sucha, behind the main station.)*

BY BUS – **Bus station**– *Ul. Sucha 1/11. www.polbus.pl.* Next door to the railway station.

BY CAR – Driving in the town centre criss-crossed by pedestrian streets is difficult. Opt for public transport. No fewer than 54 bus and 23 tram lines ensure a more than adequate service for a town of this size. Allow 26 PLN for a 7-day travel card, 8 PLN for a day ticket. **Taxis** – *☎9629/☎9626.*

PRACTICAL INFORMATION

Phone code – *☎071.*
Postal code – *50 000 – 53 000.*
Tourist office –*Rynek 14. ☎344 31 11. http://wroclaw-info.pl.*
Police: *☎997.*
Main post office: *Rynek 28.*
Pharmacy open 24hr/day – Apteka Katedralna – *Ul. H. Sienkiewicza 54/56.*
Internet Café – *W Sercu Miasta – Ul. Przejście Garncarskie 4. Open daily 10am–6pm. In the centre of the Rynek. 4 PLN/hr.*

WHERE TO GO

Wrocław In Your Pocket (www.inyourpocket.com/poland/wrocław) lists and comments on hotels, restaurants and nightlife places, while *The Visitor (monthly)* is more culturally orientated.

Małgosia). Standing in the middle of the square is the **Town Hall** next to a group of municipal buildings separated by a complex network of passageways; these buildings include the present town hall erected on the site of a cloth market. The glass fountain, which has pride of place in the western part of the Rynek, is one of the locals' favourite meeting places.

Town Hall★★★
(Ratusz) B2

This complex building, remodelled many times, is a real patchwork of styles, Late Gothic being predominant. The first wooden edifice, which stood here in the 13C, was replaced by a rectangular brick structure flanked by Renaissance corner turrets topped with conical roofs. It used to house the town's administrative offices and the basement was used as a beer cellar. The east façade boasts Flamboyant (late Gothic) ornamentation and features an astronomical clock from 1580. The south façade is richly decorated with carvings depicting medieval scenes and characters. The main entrance is on the west side. The elaborately decorated interior (⏰*open Wed–Sat 10am–5pm, Sun 10am–6pm;* 🎫*15 PLN*) comprises a succession of rooms where the city museum's collections are normally displayed but they are regularly replaced by temporary exhibitions. The most outstanding rooms are the small **Council Chamber** upstairs and the **Burghers' Hall** on the ground floor entered through a richly decorated wooden door with an intricately carved stone frame. Near the main door, a colour-coded map shows when the different parts of the edifice were built. The top of the tower features the oldest reproduction of the coat of arms adopted by the town in 1534.

Salt Square
(Plac Solny) A2

Laid out at the same time as the Rynek and accessed from the latter's southwest corner, the square is surrounded by chiefly Baroque and Classical houses.

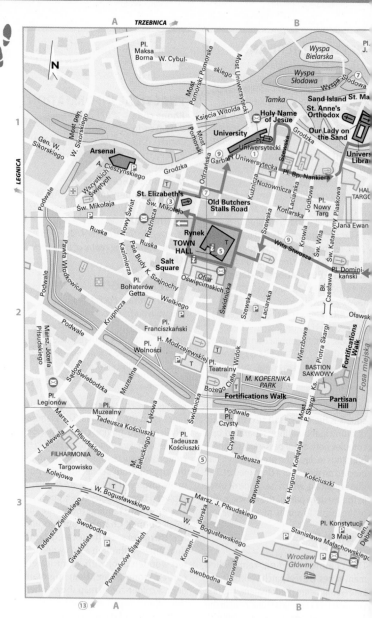

Note the "**Negro Sign" House** (Pod Murzynem) at **nos. 2/3** and, at **no. 16** on the south side, the old **Stock Exchange** (Starej Giełdy) dating from 1822.
Today, the square is occupied 24 hours a day by flower stalls surrounding a fountain and a modern sculpture.

St Elizabeth's Church
(Kościół Św. Elżbiety) A1

In the northwest corner of the Rynek.
The porch linking the Hansel and Gretel houses symbolically guards the entrance to the church. The layout of the paving stones recalls the path which once wound its way through gravestones up to the entrance of St Elizabeth's.

WROCŁAW

WHERE TO STAY

WHERE TO EAT

This church, dating from the 14C and 15C, was for a long time the town's main sanctuary; it remained a Protestant place of worship until the end of World War II. The interior has retained fine Renaissance, Baroque and Mannerist tombs. From the 83m high **tower** *(302 steps to the top)*, there is a splendid view of the town, sometimes extending as far as the mountains *(◐closed for renovation)*. Before the spire surmounting it was destroyed by fire, the tower was 128m high.

◐ *Walk along Kiełbaśnicza Street towards the River Odra. Turn right onto the tiny Stare Jatki Street.*

Old Butchers' Street
(Stare Jatki) A1

A timeless atmosphere lingers along this narrow paved street, which gives an idea of what Wrocław was like in the past. The former butchers' shops now house galleries belonging to artists and designers. At the end of the street, the sculpture of a pig and goat pays tribute to the animals slaughtered here since the 12C.

Kotlarska Street leads to Więzienna Street, where a former prison has been turned into a pub. Continue towards the University.

University★★
(Uniwersytet)

Pl. Uniwersytecki1. Open Mon, Tue, Thu 10am–3.30pm, Fri, Sun 10am–5pm, Sat 10am–6pm 10 PLN.
The town's largest monumental ensemble of Baroque architecture was erected by the Jesuits in 1670 on the site of the Piasts' ducal castle. The Austro-Prussian war turned the building into a military hospital. From 1811 onwards, the Prussian authorities took over the running of the university *(founded in 1702 by Emperor Leopold I)*. This Baroque edifice was erected between 1728 and 1742. The square tower of the observatory dominating the ensemble houses a collection of old astronomical instruments; it is crowned by four allegorical statues representing medicine, philosophy, law and theology, subjects once taught here. Located on the ground floor of the University is the **Oratorium Marianum**, where concerts still take place today. Upstairs, a heavy intricately carved wooden door leads into the **Leopoldine Hall** (Aula Leopoldina), an impressive 18C Baroque hall decorated with cherubs and gilded ornaments; all round the room are portraits of the founding fathers of the university. In front of the building adjacent to the **Church of the Blessed Name of Jesus** (Kościół Najświętszego Imienia Jezus) stands the statue of a naked swash-buckler which has stood there since 1904 and been the butt of facetious students. They regularly replace his foil with the oddest accessories. Nearby, at **no. 8 Kuźnicza Street** is a small university museum devoted to anthropology (*open afternoons Tue–Sat*).

Turn left past the Church of the Blessed Name of Jesus, then right onto the embankment. Walk up the narrow Szewska Street which skirts the library and turn right again onto Bp.Nankiera Street. Walk across Piaskowski Bridge (Most Piaskowy), the town's oldest bridge, mentioned as early as the 12C. It spans the river in front of the Market Hall (Hala Targowa), reminiscent of markets during the communist era, and leads to Sand Island.

Sand Island
(Wypa Pislowa) B1

The street, shared by trams and cars, is lined on the left by **St Anne's Orthodox Church** (Kościół Św. Anny) and on the right by the Baroque building of the University library, a former Augustinian convent. Next to it stands the Gothic **Church of Our Lady on the Sand** (Kościół NMP na Piasku). Inside, one of the chapels, dedicated to the deaf and the blind, is a nativity scene with moving mechanised figures which is popular throughout the year.

At the extremity of the island, turn right onto the metal bridge (Most Tumski) leading to the beginning of Cathedral Street (Ul. Katedralna). It is guarded by the statues of the patron saints of Silesia (St Hedwig) and Wrocław (St John the Baptist).

Ostrów Tumski C1

This is the oldest part of Wrocław. The town was founded here in the 9C, on an island joined to the river bank in 1810 when an arm of the Odra was filled in. The streets, where one can still see lamplighters at work when night falls, have retained a peaceful, serene, almost insular atmosphere. The island, fortified against invasions, was the seat of the ducal authority; in the 11C, a bishopric was established

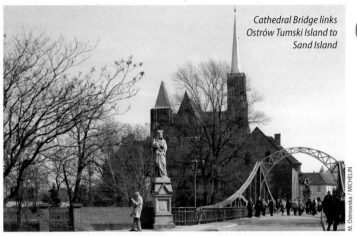

*Cathedral Bridge links
Ostrów Tumski Island to
Sand Island*

M. Ostrowska / MICHELIN

and, after the 13C, when the New Town developed on the south bank of the river, the island remained the seat of the Church authorities.

Church of the Holy Cross and St Bartholomew
(Kościół Św. Krzyża)C1

Built in the 13C and 14C, this Gothic edifice features a very unusual structure consisting of two churches, one on top of the other. The lower one is dedicated to St Bartholomew, the patron saint of the Piast dynasty.

Walking up Św. Marcina Street, one comes across the small **St Martin's Church** (Kościół Św. Marcina), the former castle chapel dating from the 13C, featuring a mixture of Romanesque and Gothic styles.

▶ *Return to Katedralna Street and continue until you reach the cathedral. The building is surrounded by the seat of the Archbishopric and the former Archbishop's Palace.*

Cathedral of St John the Baptist★
(Katedra Św. Jana Chrzciciela) C1

It stands on the site of the first Romanesque cathedral built around 1000, destroyed in 1037 by Bratislav, a Bohemian duke, rebuilt in the 12C and reduced to rubble once more by the Mongols in 1241. Work began almost immediately

on the present brick-built cathedral, the first to be erected in Poland. The foundation stone was laid in 1244, but the building was only completed two centuries later. In 1945, only 30 per cent of the edifice remained standing. The present state of the medieval stone doorway, where one can see, close to the ground, the statue of a lion from the original 12C sanctuary, testifies to the scale of the damage. At the end of the nave, the high altar is surmounted by a triptych, painted in Lublin in 1522, depicting the Dormition of the Virgin Mary. In the east end of the cathedral, note the two chapels on either side of the Lady Chapel, St Elizabeth's Chapel decorated with Italian sculptures, and the Corpus Christi Chapel. Note also, along the north wall, the oval-shaped Chapel of the Dead. Next to it, a door opens onto a narrow spiral staircase leading to the lift which takes visitors to the top of the North Tower (◷ *open Mon–Sat except during religious holidays 10am–6pm; ⌨4 PLN*). This viewpoint, surmounted like its twin by a 45m-spire in 1941, offers a panoramic view of the whole town.

▶ *Leave the cathedral and walk along the north side. Turn left under the arch on the corner of the small brick church dedicated to St Giles (Kościół Św. Idziego), undoubtedly Ostrów Tumski's oldest church. This leads to one of the entrances of the Botanical Gardens.*

Botanical Gardens★
(Ogród Botaniczny) C1

Entrance via Kanonicza Street and 23 Sienkiewicza Street. ⏰*Open Mar–Oct daily 8am–6pm; glasshouses open 10am–5pm.* 💲*7 PLN.*

Part of the town's fortifications, built alongside the arm of the Odra now filled in, used to stand on this site. Nature is cleverly given pride of place in this green oasis, which contains over 11,000 plant species spread around two vast expanses of water with ducks splashing about. This is the ideal place to escape the hustle and bustle of the town.

▷ *Return to the cathedral and eastwards to Katedralny Square.*

Archdiocesan Museum
(Muzeum Archidiecezjalne) C1

Pl. Katedralny 16. ⏰*Open Tue–Fri 10am–4pm, Sat–Sun 10am–3pm.* 💲*5 PLN. Captions and comments in English.*

This museum, one of the town's oldest, is devoted to religious art: chalices, clergical vestments, paintings and sculptures, including an awe-inspiring statue of the scourging of Christ. It also possesses a superb 13C–14C manuscript, Henrików's Book (Księga Henrykowska), which contains the first text written in Polish.

▷ *Walk around Katedralny Square, take Św. Józefa Street and return to the south bank of the Odra via Pokoju Bridge leading to the National Museum.*

National Museum★
(Muzeum Narodowe) C1

Pl. Powstańców Warszawy5. ⏰*Open Wed, Fri, Sun 10am–4pm, Thu 9am–4pm, Sat 10am–6pm.* 💲*15 PLN, Sat free.* ♿ ✗.

The museum is housed in a late 19C neo-Renaissance building. Each of the three levels is laid out around a huge central staircase. The first floor is devoted to Silesian art. The superb medieval collection includes polychrome wooden sculpture and a few paintings. Note in particular a very realistic 15C carved representation of the Flagellation and a Stations of the Cross with 11 life-size characters originally in St Mary Magdalene's Church in Wrocław. The rooms, devoted to the period stretching from the Renaissance to the 19C, contain mannerist and modernist painting and sculptures. The second floor presents Polish art from the 17C to the 19C. There is also an interesting collection of contemporary art.

Panorama of the Battle of Racławice★★
(Panorama Racławicka) C2

Ul. Purkyniego 11. ⏰*Open Oct–Mar Wed–Fri 10am–4pm Sat–Sun 9am–5pm; Apr–Sept Wed–Fri, Sun 10am–5pm, Sat 10am–6pm; also open last Tue of month year round 10am–5pm.* ⏰*Closed major holidays.* 💲*20 PLN (ticket also valid for the National Museum). Audioguides in English on loan.* ♿. *www.mnwr.art.pl.*

This vast panoramic painting measuring 120m x 15m is a real national monument. Its fame is such that it is essential to make a reservation if you wish to see it. The work gives a realistic rendering of the Battle of Racławice on 4 April 1794 which, following the Kościuskowska uprising, ended with the temporary victory of the Polish people led by General Tadeusz Kościuszko over the Russian occupiers.

▷ *Follow Jana Ewangelisty Purkyniego Street, then turn right onto Bernardyńska Street.*

Museum of Architecture
(Muzeum Architektury) C2

Ul. Bernardyńska5. ⏰*Open Tue, Fri–Sun 11am–5pm, Wed 10am–4pm, Thu noon–7pm.* 💲*10 PLN.*

The museum is housed in a former church and the adjoining cloister. Its moderately interesting collections consist of architectural elements from the 12C to the 20C, displayed in restored spaces. The collection contains some fine stained-glass windows and an unusual collection of ceramic stoves.

▷ *Return to the Rynek via J Słowackiego Avenue prolonged by Wita Stwosza Street.*

ARSENAL
(Arsenał) A1
Ul. Cieszyńskiego 9.
Situated northwest of the town centre, along the banks of the Odra, the former 15C arsenal houses the archaeological and military museums.

Archaeological Museum
(Muzeum Archeologiczne)
🕐*Open Wed–Sun 11am–5pm.*
🎟*7 PLN, Wed free.*
The museum has some interesting scenography and fine displays: funeral urns, fibulae, bronze axes and swords, even the grave of a horseman buried with his horse.

Military Museum
(Muzeum Arsenał)
🕐*Open Wed–Sat 11am–5pm, Sun 10am–6pm.* 🎟*7 PLN, Wed free.*
The first floor, devoted to firearms, presents an impressive variety of handguns and rifles, and above all, one of the most important collections of military helmets in Europe. The second floor houses a fine collection of Polish 19C–20C sabres.

FORTIFICATIONS
Promenade B2
Laid out at the beginning of the 19C, this promenade runs through greenery along the line of fortifications which once enclosed the south bank of the Odra. The moat is still intact. The most interesting section lies to the southeast of the town centre, on both sides of P Skargi Street. **Partisans' Hill** (Wzgórze Partyzantów), the site of a former bastion, was laid out in 1868 and it is still possible to reach the neo-Renaissance panoramic platforms, restored and transformed into an exclusive restaurant.

EXCURSIONS
The People's Hall
(Hala Ludowa)
Ul. Wystawowa1. 🕐*Open daily 9am–4pm.* 🎟*7 PLN.*
This vast circular building, in glass and reinforced concrete, is flanked by four apses and covered with a dome; 42m in height and 67m in diameter, it was

---

Hedwig, Patron Saint of Silesia

Born in 1178, Hedwig was the daughter of the Duke of Moravia. At age 12, her father sent her to the court in Wrocław. She was married at 18 to the Duke of Greater Poland, later to become known as Henry the Bearded *(in keeping with the vow he made to her to refrain from shaving)*. Hedwig cared for the poor, the sick, victims of war and those in prison. After the death of her son Henry the Pious at the Battle of Legnickie Pole, she retired to Trzebnica monastery where she died in 1243. After her death, her cult spread rapidly and pilgrims flocked to her grave in Trzebnica, not only from Silesia but also from Great Poland and Pomerania. She was canonised in 1267 and her feast-day established on 16 October.

---

designed by the modernist architect Max Berg and built in 1912–13 to commemorate the centenary of Napoleon's defeat at Leipzig. It is the venue for exhibitions, concerts and sporting events. In front of the building stands a 95m-high spire erected after the war by the communist authorities anxious to show their know-how and possibly outdo this masterpiece of German architecture.

🐾 Zoo
Ul. Wróblewskiego1. 🕐*Open daily Apr–Sept 9am–6pm.* 🎟*25/15 PLN.*
Founded in 1865, this is one of Europe's oldest zoos. Today the Zoo is home to kangaroos, giraffes, lions, elephants, antelopes, black panthers and tigers, as well as a reptile and amphibian house.

Jewish Cemetery
Ul. Ślężna 37/39. 🕐*Open daily Apr–Sept 8am–dusk; Oct–Mar 10am–6pm.*
🎟*7 PLN*
Situated in the southern part of town, the cemetery opened in 1856. With some 1 200 graves, it is one of Poland's best preserved Jewish cemeteries. Clo-

Interior of Lubiąż Abbey

sed in 1942, it was only reopened in 1991, following extensive restoration work. Today, it is regarded as an open-air museum of Jewish funerary art.

Lubiąż Abbey★★

▶ *55km west of Wrocław.* ◷*Open daily Apr–Sept 9am–6pm; Oct–Mar 10am–3pm.* ⊜*10 PLN. Visit with guide only.*

Situated in the middle of the country-side and rising above the east bank of the Odra, the impressive abbey complex has had a checkered history.

Benedictine monks, who occupied the site as early as 1150, were soon replaced by Cistercian monks. After a period of decline, the monastery prospered once more during the 17C. Extensive building work, carried out between 1690 and 1720, gave the complex its present appearance; the predominantly Baroque church nevertheless retained a few Gothic features. The Abbey was then one of Europe's largest monastic complexes, 223m long and 118m wide, with over 300 rooms. In 1810, it was abandoned and, for the next two centuries, it remained empty and stripped of its ornaments.

This imposing place, now being resto-red, conveys a somewhat ghostly impression. The breathtaking façade seems to crush visitors, who can only see a few rooms containing temporary exhibits.

ADDRESSES

⌂ STAY

⊜ **Savoy Hotel** – *Pl. Kościuszki 19.* ℘*344 30 71. 27 rooms.* Close to the station, very cheap and recently restored in true functional style, the Savoy should not be judged from its somewhat austere façade.

⊜⊜ **Dom Jana Pawła II** – *Ul. Św. Idziego 2.* ℘*327 14 00. www.pensjonat-jp2.pl. 60 rooms.* Located on Ostrów Tumski, between the cathedral and the botanical gardens, this new hotel boasts luxury facilities. The **restaurant** caters for communion and wedding receptions and gets crowded at teatime by people wanting to taste John Paul II's favourite cake.

⊜⊜ **Patio Hotel** – *Ul. Kiełbaśnicza 24.* ℘*375 04 00. www.hotelpatio.pl. 50 rooms.* 50m from the Rynek. The rooms are vast and very comfortable. Ask for one on the street side as it will be much brighter and more pleasant than any of those overlooking the tiny alleyway lined with flashy modern buildings.

⊜⊜ **Tumski Hotel** – *Wyspa Słodowa 10.* ℘*322 60 88. www.hotel-tumski.com. 58 rooms.* Situated on a small island between the town centre and Ostrów Tumski, this well-kept hotel suits all budgets. Apart from their more basic decoration and fittings, the cheap rooms on the ground floor are comparable to the more expensive ones on the floors above.

Zaułek Hotel – *Ul. Garbary 11. 341 00 46. www.hotel.uni.wroc.pl. 12 rooms.* The place has a quaint charm in spite of its favourable position in the university district, close to the hustle and bustle of the town centre; you won't find better value for money.

EAT

Bazylia – *Ul. Kuźnicza 42. Open daily 8am–8pm.* This university restaurant, open to everybody, serves a carefully prepared cuisine. Probably one of the most trendy establishments in town, it is situated on the ground floor of the new law faculty buildings, at the very hub of student life.

Kurna Chata – *Ul. Odrzańska 17. 341 06 68. Open Mon–Fri 11am–midnight, Sat–Sun noon–midnight.* Good traditional cooking at a reasonable price is served here, in a rustic decor. A young and not-so young eclectic clientele gathers round the few tables.

Paśnik – *Ul. Wita Stwosza 37. 342 57 18. Open daily 10am–midnight.* This café offering a classic menu is also the rendezvous of the town's chess players who take over the tables at any time of day. The atmosphere is unique and stylish.

Gospoda Wrocławska – *Ul. Sukiennice 6. 342 74 56. Open daily noon–midnight.* Situated in one of the passageways of the Rynek. The medieval-style decoration is slightly overdone but the menu offers all the classic dishes of Polish cuisine *(roast pig and special soup made with blood.).* In another room, fresh fish and seafood are served with just as much care.

Spiż – *Ul. Rynek Ratusz 2. 344 72 25. Open daily noon–midnight.* Housed in the vaulted cellars of the town hall, this restaurant offers a cosy, refined atmosphere and an eclectic cuisine. Tasty specialities, such as soup made with beer; that very beer, brewed on the premises, flows freely late into the night in the large brewery room.

TAKING A BREAK

K2 – *Ul. Kiełbaśnicza 2. Open daily 11am–11pm.* Perched up a narrow lane, at the top of a flight of steps, this tiny tearoom decorated in pastel colours offers a choice of pastries and teas in a friendly, cosy atmosphere. Also summer outdoor patio open till 10pm.

Pod Kalamburem – *Ul. Kuźnicza 29. 10am–11pm, Sun 3pm–midnight.* The Art Nouveau decoration and the large mirrors account for the unique cachet of this slightly bohemian student bistro, close to the university.

Mleczarnia – *Ul. Włodkowica 5. Open daily 10am–1am.* With its parquet flooring shiny with age, its old-fashioned photos covering the walls and wooden tables, this large café, extending inwards from the street, recalls the 1930s. Let yourself be tempted by its quiet daytime atmosphere and enjoy a delicious homemade cake.

ON THE TOWN

Bezsenność – *Ul. Ruska 51. Daily 6pm–late.* A popular local club with real style. Decorated like someone's living room with lots of comfy couches. Dance floor and venue also for concerts and DJs.

Graciarnia – *Ul. Kazimierza Wlk. 39. Mon–Fri noon–2am, Sat–Sun from 5pm.* Very atmospheric and romantic place for drinking and chatting, with even a spacious room for non-smokers. Wi-Fi access.

SHOPPING

Stare Jatki – *Ul. Stare Jatki.* No fewer than 20 boutiques belonging to artists and designers have taken over the old houses lining the former Butchers' Street. Stationery, artist's materials, linen clothes, framing, glasswork, painting, pottery, sculpture and costume jewellery.

FESTIVE EVENTS

Wrocław Jazz Festival: 3 days of jazz during this world-famous festival. April.

Wrocław Non-Stop: During this festival, live shows take over the sights and streets of the town. Late June.

Wratislavia Cantans: Early music both sacred and classical invades the city during this ten-day festival. September.

Kłodzko Region★★

This region, surrounded on three sides by the Czech Republic, was coveted and conquered many times over the centuries. Hilltop citadels and fortified towns testify to the military past while countless health spas reflect the area's rich mineral springs. The area has a fascinating series of underground labyrinths, caves and spectacular rock formations.

KŁODZKO

Kłodzko is a 1,000-year-old hillside city, once surrounded by ramparts, which, like other Silesian towns, successively belonged to the Poles, the Habsburgs and the Prussians before being returned to Poland in 1945.

Its steep, narrow, winding streets and flights of stairs greatly contribute to the charm of the city. The town hall, remodelled in the 19C, stands on the picturesque **Rynek** surrounded by elegant Baroque residences.

Gothic Bridge
(Most Gotycki)

The pride of the town, built in 1390, looking like a miniature of the St Charles' Bridge in Prague, spans the Młynówka canal; its parapets are adorned with six groups of statues representing various saints, erected in the 17C and 18C.

- ◔ **Michelin Map:** Map of Poland B3 – Województwo of Lower Silesia.
- 🛈 **Info:** Pl. Bolesława Chrobrego1.
  ℘(74) 865 46 89.
- ◖ **Location:** Kłodzko lies 80km south of Wrocław along the E67.
- 🅿 **Parking:** Free on the street or gaurded on Ul. Daszyńskiego16.
- ⊛ **Don't Miss:** Take time to explore the minor roads meandering through wooded hills dotted with isolated chapels and remote villages.
- 👪 **Kids:** The Erratic Boulders site.
- ◷ **Timing:** Ideally, you need to devote three days to this region to discover its monuments and caves, wander through the countryside and stroll through the towns.
- ◔ **Also See:** Chapel of Skulls.

Gothic Bridge with statues of saints

J. Gontier / MICHELIN

GETTING AROUND

BY RAIL – Railway station –
Kłodzko has two train stations. Main station: *Ul. Dworcowa 1* and town station: *Pl. Jedności, www.pkp.pl.* Kudowa Zdrój station: Ul. Główna.
BY BUS – Bus station – *Pl. Jednosci.* Buses link Kłodzko with various sights and towns throughout the region.
BY CAR – Parking is easy in the region's towns, except perhaps in the spa resorts during the high season. Many car parks in Kłodzko.

PRACTICAL INFORMATION

Phone code – ☎*074.*
Kłodzko's Tourist Office –
Pl. B. Chrobrego 1. ☎*(74) 865 46 89. www.klodzko.pl. Open Mon–Fri 8am–4pm, Sat 10am–4pm.* Well stocked with all kinds of guide books and maps (only a few are in English), this office centralizes all the information about the region.

Kudowa Zdrój Tourist Office –
Ul. Zdrojowa 44. ☎*(74) 866 13 87. www.kudowa.pl. Open Mon–Fri 10am–6pm, Sat 9am–5pm.* This office can provide all the necessary information about the Table Mountains as well as a few guide books and brochures *(some in English)* about the spa resorts.
Paczków Tourist Office –
Ul. Słowackiego 4. ☎*(77) 431 67 90. www.paczkow.pl. Open Mon–Fri 9am–5pm.* Convivial welcome, useful information. Free internet access.

WHERE TO GO

There are all kinds of maps of the Kłodzko region: road, sightseeing and rambling maps. There is also a detailed map of the Table Mountains, showing all the footpaths and the estimated time needed to walk along each of them.

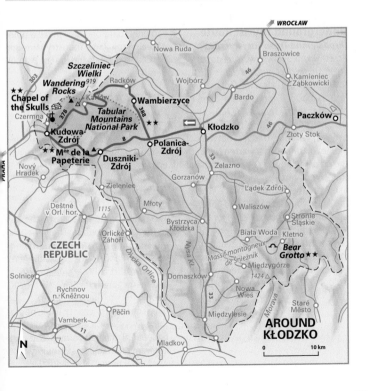

Church of the Assumption
(Kościół Wniebowzięcia NMP)

The church stands in the centre of a pleasant square, one street away from the Rynek. Built in the 14C, it has retained its Gothic appearance on the outside decorated with sculptures and gargoyles. The interior, entirely remodelled from the 17C onwards, boasts a wealth of Baroque ornamentation. The 16C Gothic vaulting over the central nave features stucco decorations from 1673. The Baroque altar dates from 1729.

Kłodzko Regional Museum
(Muzeum Ziemi Kłodzkiej)

Ul. Łukasiewicza 4. Open Wed–Fri 10am–4pm, Sat–Sun 11am–5pm. 6 PLN.

The museum's main interest lies in its impressive collection of clocks. Cuckoo clocks, wooden mechanisms, enamel, porcelain or carved-wood clock-faces are displayed throughout the second level. The museum also houses contemporary glassware dating from the 1950s and 1960s.

Underground Tourist Route
(Prodziemna Trasa Turystyczna)

Access via no. 3 Zawiszy Czarnego Street, under the Church of the Assumption and exit at the foot of the fortress. Open Apr–Oct 9am–5pm, Nov–Mar 10am–3pm. 7 PLN.

Discovered during the 1970s, after a series of cave-ins, this vast network of Medieval tunnels is a warren beneath the city, linking the cellars of some of the town's houses. Merchants once used them as storage space. Today the route consists of 600m of galleries (the rest having been filled in for safety reasons), which are nice and cool on hot summer days. The many cellars along the way often feature picturesque scenes and objects intended to create a gloomy and mysterious atmosphere.

Fortress

Open May–Oct 9am–6pm; Nov–Apr 9am–3pm. 7PLN. (74) 867 34 68.

Castles and forts have always stood on the strategic hill overlooking Kłodzko, which used to defend the buffer zone that this part of Silesia was in the past. The present fortress was built in the 18C by the Prussian authorities. Deep ditches and steep slopes were literally carved out of the terrain and high walls erected as reinforcements. The stronghold withstood 11 sieges without ever surrendering. An ingenious defence system, which prefigured mine fields, made it virtually impregnable. 45km of low, narrow and dark galleries run under the foundations and the idea was to blow up the sections located beneath enemy positions. Today, the tour includes 600m of these galleries, which form a real labyrinth.

WEST OF KŁODZKO

There are more worthwhile sights in this area than in the rest of the region. Don't hesitate to stop somewhere for the night. If, on the other hand, you can only spare one day, make a point of seeing the Paper Industry Museum, the Chapel of Skulls and the Erratic Boulders site.

THE SPA TOWNS ROAD
Polanica Zdrój

15km west of Kłodzko.

This very pleasant spa resort, nestled inside a valley, offers shaded promenades along the River Bystrzyca.

Duszniki Zdrój

23km west of Kłodzko.

This is the second spa town on the way to the Czech Republic. The beneficial effects of the region's mineral springs have been known since the Middle Ages, but the resort only became flourishing and internationally renowned in the 19C. Chopin took to the waters in 1826 and gave concerts for charity while he was there. Every year, a festival is held in his honour. This itinerary forms a loop starting from Kłodzko and extending westward as far as the Table Mountains.

Paper Industry Museum★★
(Muzeum Papiernictwa)

Ul. Kłodzka 42. ◑*Open May–Sept 9am–5pm; Oct–Apr 9am–3pm.* ◑*Closed holidays.* ◐*10 PLN.*

This fine museum is worth a detour for its superb presentation, handsome building and the activities on offer. The paper mill, powered by a paddle wheel, itself driven by the river current, was built in 1605. It is an elegant piece of Baroque architecture, with its wooden scrolls and panelled façade. Recently restored, the mill is operational once more. It produces paper using traditional techniques pleasantly presented in the museum and illustrated by paper samples and a collection of watermarks. Visitors can pitch in, if they wish.

Kudowa Zdrój
◉ *35km west of Kłodzko.*

The region's main resort lies at an altitude of 400m, only a few kilometres from the border with the Czech Republic. People come to the neo-Baroque pump room, situated in the middle of the English-style park surrounded by dales, to enjoy the waters from eight hot and cold mineral springs *(inhalations, baths and drinks from the public fountain).* It is also possible to visit a small but charming **Toy Museum** (Muzeum Zabawek; *Ul. Zdrojowa 46b).*

Chapel of Skulls★★
(Kaplica Czaszek)

In Czermna near Kudowa Zdrój Ul.Kościuszki. ◑*Open daily in summer 9.30am–5.30pm; rest of the year 10am–4pm.* ◐*4 PLN.*

Situated in a parish close comprising a 17C church, cemetery and tower, this tiny, unassuming chapel gives visitors no forewarning of the sight that awaits them when they enter. The interior is entirely lined with bones, some 3,000 skulls and shinbones representing the remains of victims of the Silesian and Seven Years' Wars and of the epidemics which marked the second half of the 18C. This unusual presentation was set up by the local priest, Wacław Tomaszek, between 1776 and 1804. The guide ends

the visit by lifting the trap door of the crypt, where another 20,000 bones are deposited.

Table Mountains National Park★★
(Park Norodowy Góry Stołowe)

◉ *30km west of Kołdzko. Access via the road linking Kudowa Zdrój and Radków.*

Taking advantage of the horizontal geological structure of the area – a unique occurrence in Poland – wind erosion imaginatively carved the spectacular landscape into the most bizarre shapes. The National Park, created in 1993, is covered with spruce forests providing a habitat for protected flora and fauna. The 20ha rock labyrinth 🚶🚶**Błędne Skały**★★ ("Erratic Boulders"; *alternate access from the road every 45min, 8am–6pm;* ◐*5 PLN)* is the most spectacular and also the most secluded site.

Dug into the sedimentary rocks, this labyrinth is up to 6–8m high and no wider than 20–30cm in places. It meanders between boulders polished by streaming water, which sometimes look as if they're about to topple over, creating a kind of petrified city.

From the village of Karłów, one can climb 665 steps hewn out of the rock *(1hr there and back)* to the **Szczeliniec Wielki**★★ **Reserve** where the mountains reach their highest point *(919m).* From this viewpoint covering an area of 50ha, the view extends eastwards to the Kłodzko region and westwards beyond the Czech border. Further on, between Radków and Wambierzyce, the wooded valleys of the **Petrified Mushrooms (Skalne Grzyby) Reserve** are criss-crossed by footpaths.

Wambierzyce
◉ *20km northwest of Kłodzko.*

Nestled at the foot of the Table Mountains, this Marian sanctuary, built in impressive Italian Baroque style, boasts an ochre façade preceded by a 56-step monumental staircase. The basilica contains a 40cm-tall wooden figure of Our Lady of Wambierzyce, who is said to have miraculous powers. Also of interest is the nativity scene, including no fewer than 800 moveable characters carved out of lime-tree wood by a local lock-smith, who started in 1882 and took 28 years to complete his masterpiece. On the hill facing the sanctuary, a giant Way of the Cross, including 29 Stations, has been attracting penitents and pilgrims since the end of the 18C.

SOUTHEAST OF KŁODZKO
Bear's Cave★★

◗ In Kletno, 30km southeast of Kłodzko. From the parking area, allow 20min on foot through woodland.
◷ Open 9am–4.40pm Feb–Nov Tues, Wed, Fri–Sun. Reservations essential ℘(074) 814 12 50. 18 PLN.
The tour lasts 45min. Come prepared: the temperature does not rise above 6°C and the extreme humidity creates slippery and misty conditions. Not recommended for young children.

The cave was discovered in 1966 during the quarrying of marble near the village of Kletno. It is undoubtedly one of Poland's finest. Extending over a distance of 2km are vast chambers (the largest is 60m long and 45m high), narrow passageways and forests of stalactites. The most delicate concretions suggest draperies while the most spectacular looks like an 8m-high calcite cascade. Remains of animals, such as lions and foxes, were found in the cave, together with the impressive skeleton of a bear dating from the Ice Age. The highlight of the tour is the total darkness and silence experienced by visitors when the guide switches off the lights.

Paczków

◗ 33km east of Kłodzko.
Situated in the Opole region, in an area bordering the former principality of the bishops of Wrocław, Paczków is known as Poland's Carcassonne. The comparison, although exaggerated, is based on the well-preserved **ramparts** surrounding the town, which have been protecting it since the 14C. There are 19 semi-circular towers dotted around the 1.2km long, 9m-high walls pierced by four entranceways flanked by towers. The town follows a medieval grid plan, in its centre is the small **Rynek** featuring a 16C **town hall** with a belfry reminiscent of northern Italy's Renaissance towers. From the **top of the belfry** (access daily 10am–5pm; 3 PLN), there is a fine overall view of the almost perfect oval ring of ramparts. The so-called **Wrocław Tower** (access Mon–Sat 7.30am–6pm, Sun 10am–5pm; 3 PLN, tickets on sale at the newspaper kiosk), closing off the ring to the northeast, also offers a fine panoramic view extending to the mountains marking the border with the Czech Republic. Southeast of the Rynek, the church of **St John the Evangelist** (Kościół Św. Jana Ewangelisty), a squat, almost cubic-shaped building crowned by defensive crenellations, is a typical example of a fortified church from the first half of the 14C. North of the ram-

Bear's Cave

parts, at **no. 6 Pocztowa Street**, a fine **museum** housed in former gasworks (Muzeum Gazownictwa, ○*open Mon–Fri 8am–2pm; ⊜4 PLN*) offers a fascinating presentation of the history of gas production and use in the town.

LEGNICA

Legnica is the most western town on our Polish itinerary. Life in this former capital of the Silesian Piasts is peaceful and revolves around the Rynek and the ducal castle. The village of Legnickie Pole, a few kilometres away, still remembers the dreadful battle in 1241, during which the Silesian army confronted the hordes of Tatar invaders.

A village defended by a fort already stood on the site of Legnica which really got off the ground after the Battle of Legnickle Pole. The Silesian Piasts made it one of their capitals, surrounded it with ramparts *(a few towers are still standing)* and built one of Poland's first stone fortresses before moving on to Brzeg in the 18C. The 1745 partition ceded it to Prussia, who renamed it Liegnitz. Badly damaged during World War II, it was returned to Poland in 1945.

Start from the **Rynek** lined with a few elegant edifices as well as less pleasing ones built of grey concrete to heal the wounds inflicted by war. The imposing buildings standing in the centre of the square are dominated by the belfry of the **Town Hall**, a fine Baroque structure backing onto the theatre. Behind is a row of eight arcaded houses: these arcades, once occupied by herring-mongers, lead to a **16C house**, its façade decorated with sgraffiti depicting hunting scenes. South of the square rise the two brick towers of the **Cathedral of St Peter and St Paul** (Katedra Św. Piotra i Pawła). Massive and almost square, they house the recumbent figures of Wacław 1, Duke of Legnica and his wife, Anna of Cieszyn. From the Rynek, Św Jana Street leads to a small **museum** (Muzeum Miedzi; *Ul. Partyzantów 3;* ○*open Wed–Mon 11am–5pm;* ⊜*6/3.5 PLN; www.muzeum-miedzi.art.pl*), which stages historical and contemporary exhibitions. Further on, the Baroque west front of **St John's**

Church (Kościół Św Jana) can be seen at the end of the street. Of the previous church built on this site, it only retained a chapel containing the mausoleum of the Silesian Piasts' dynasty, which died out in 1675 (○*open Mon–Fri 9am–3pm*). Walk along Partyzantów Street to the **Piasts' Castle** (⚷), an elongated edifice dominated by two Gothic red-brick towers that resemble minarets. Built in the 13C, the castle is a strange mixture of architectural styles. Note the superb Renaissance doorway designed in 1532 by George of Amberg. Extended in the 16C, the castle was then partially rebuilt in a romantic style during the 19C. A pavilion standing in the inner courtyard shelters the **remains of the Romanesque chapel** with an unusual 12-sided plan, built by Duke Henry the Bearded at the same time as the original 13C fortress (○*open Apr–Oct Tue–Sat 11am–6pm; ⊜2.5 PLN, Sat free; in winter months, the Muzeum Miedzi can arrange visits* ☏862 49 49).

ADDRESSES

🛏 STAY

Kłodzko's accommodation facilities are inadequate. The nearby spa towns have luxury hotels often providing fitness equipment. Enjoy ecotourism: the region has a wealth of B&Bs where comfort and country scenery compare favourably with what luxury hotels have to offer.

KŁODZKO

⊜⊜**Korona Hotel** – *Ul. Noworudzka 1.* ☏*(074) 867 37 37. www.hotel-korona.pl. 18 rooms.* Cheap prices and basic comfort combine to offer good value for money.

MIĘDZYGÓRZE

⊜**Słoneczna Willa** – *Ul. Śnieżna 27.* ☏*(74) 813 52 70. 22 rooms.* Beyond the village, the road meanders on and finally reaches this house, which looks like a hunting lodge. Plush family establishment. The mountains lie beyond.

⊜**Villa Millenium** – *Ul. Wojska Polskiego 9.* ☏*(74) 813 52 87. http://millenium.miedzygorze.pl. 11 rooms.*

At the entrance to the village. all the rooms are similar: neat, bright, some with a balcony. Cosy atmosphere and courteous welcome.

KUDOWA ZDRÓJ

Tadeusz and Agnieszka Jesionowscy's Place – *Ul. Kościuszki95. (74) 866 23 85.* As you leave town, in a wooded vale, 3km beyond the Chapel of Skulls. A few rooms available on two floors, the kitchen and living room are shared with the owners. Warm family welcome in this fine restored house dating from 1877.

POLANICA ZDRÓJ

Camping nr 169 – *Ul. Sportowa 7. (74) 868 12 10-30 PLN for two persons with a tent and a car.* North of the resort, near the road but far enough to offer peace and quiet. Nicely shaded with good grass-covered pitches.

Pod Rogaczem – *At "Studzienna", 15km northwest of Polanica Zdrój. (74) 868 17 97.* This B&B, located on the slopes of a vale, offers informal yet comfortable accommodation. It's ideal for those wishing to ramble through the region on the edge of the Table Mountains National Park. Riding and fishing available, consistent end-of-ramble snack on request. Accommodation in dormitory or double rooms.

LĄDEK ZDRÓJ

Cztery Kąty – *1.5km further along than Dom "Skowronki" (below). (74) 814 78 05. 4 rooms with bath. 15 PLN.* Four charming rooms, two of them with a balcony, in this restored house which has managed to retain its quaint charm. The place is peacefully located in the heart of a hamlet nestling in a vale. Communal kitchen and living room.

Dom "Skowronki" – *3km before the village when arriving from Kłodzko along road 392; follow signposts from the main road. www.domskowronki.emeteor.pl. (074) 814 78 02. 4 rooms with ensuite.* In a well-preserved 200-year-old house. Quality family welcome and service. The owner sometimes plays the accordion after meals. You won't want to leave. If you prefer to be more autonomous, you can rent (for the same price) the small adjoining house with its traditional interior and ceramic stove, which accommodates 5 persons.

EAT

KŁODZKO

W Ratuszu – *Pl. B. Chrobrego 3. (74) 865 81 45.* Housed in the town hall building; large room with dark woodwork and chairs covered with blue velvet. Refined inventive cuisine: pork with walnuts and grape sauce, or Portuguese-style beef (skewered meat with cheese). It's delicious and tastefully served.

Casa d'Oro – *Ul. Grottgera 7. (074) 867 02 16.* Undoubtedly the best restaurant in town. Cosy surroundings, excellent cuisine denoting Italian and Hungarian influences, very carefully served. Portions are huge and desserts are delicious.

POLANICA ZDRÓJ

This lively spa resort boasts many restaurants, particularly along Zdrojowa Street, shaded by chestnut trees.

Krokus – *Ul. Zdrojowa 3. (074) 869 08 90.* Tiny, very pleasant restaurant with a relaxed atmosphere. Classic meat and fish dishes as well as pizzas are served in the dining room or at the tables set out in the pedestrian street.

Swojska Chata – *Ul. Sienkiewicza24. (74) 868 30 12.* 3km north of the resort. This restaurant, featuring a friendly rustic setting, serves restorative Polish food. Pork and potatoes are featured. Fine terrace and games for children.

TAKING A BREAK

Two pleasant pubs have tables outside on Kłodzko's Rynek, but Polanica Zdrój remains by far the most pleasant town for a break at an outdoor café selling drinks or ice cream.

POLANICA ZDRÓJ

Zielony Domek – *Ul. Zdrojowa 8. (074) 868 21 45.* Excellent ice cream parlour in one of the spa resort's most pleasant pedestrian streets.

FESTIVE EVENTS

International Music Festival (Międzynarodowy Festiwal Moniuszkowski) – *In Kudowa Zdrój.* The festival, dedicated to the founder of Polish opera, Stanisław Moniuszko, takes place in August.

Dusznik Zdrój Chopin Festival – in August. *www.chopin.festival.pl.*

Świdnica and Jawor Churches★★

Nestling in the Silesian countryside, these half-timbered churches, now on UNESCO's World Heritage List, are both a technical feat and a symbol of religious resistance.

A BIT OF HISTORY
The Peace Churches
(*Kościół Pokoju*)

The Treaty of Westphalia, which put an end to the Thirty Years War in 1648, granted religious freedom to the Protestants living in Catholic Silesia No doubt to restrain religious practice, Protestant churches were submitted to certain conditions: they had to be built of wood, straw and clay, with no tower or sign revealing their religious function. Lastly, the edifice had to be built out of gun range from the town centre. Far from being discouraged, the Protestants performed a real act of faith by erecting the largest timber religious buildings in Europe, the austere appearance of their exterior contrasting with the splendour and exuberance of their Baroque interior. Three such churches were built but only those at Świdnica and Jawor, designed by the architect Albrecht von Saebisch, remain today.

SIGHTS
Świdnica Church★★

Ul. Pokoju6. ⏰*Open Apr–Oct Mon–Sat 9am–1pm, 3pm, Sun 3–5pm; in winter, call for reservations.* 📞*(74) 852 28 14.* ⚭*6 PLN.*

Built in the shape of a cross from 1656 onwards, the church is flanked on both sides by porches and chapels, which make it look to some extent like a Catholic church. It stands in the middle of an ancient cemetery and could hold 7,500 people, including 3,000 on the two-tiered galleries with balustrades decorated with epitaphs. Dedicated to the Holy Trinity, the church contains a high altar from 1752 and a Baroque pulpit.

ⓘ **Michelin Map:**
Map of Poland B3 and A3 – Województwo of Lower Silesia.

ℹ **Info:** Świdnica. Ul. Wewnętrzna 2 (Rynek). 📞(74) 852 02 90.

▶ **Location:** Świdnica and Jawor, 30km apart, are respectively situated 50km and 60km southwest of Wrocław.

🅿 **Parking:** On the streets of the Old Town, 1.50 PLN an hour Mon–Sat, free Sun.

⏰ **Timing:** Allow two hours to visit both churches.

Jawor Church★★

Park Pokoj. ⏰*Open daily Apr–Oct 10am–5pm. In winter, call for reservations.* 📞*(76) 870 32 73.* ⚭*6 PLN.*

Erected in 1654–55, the church could welcome a 6,000-strong congregation in the rectangular nave with its polychrome ceiling and in the four surrounding galleries. The balconies are decorated with scenes of the Old and New Testaments and enhanced by the donors' coats of arms. The church, dedicated to the Holy Spirit, later acquired a bell tower which, according to regulations, does not rise above the roof.

Interior of Jawor Church

© Polish National Tourist Office

Jelenia Góra★

This former border town, known as the pearl of the Karkonosze Mountains, occupies a strategic position in a hilly, wooded region and makes a relaxing base for exploring the local peaks or spas.

A BIT OF HISTORY
Deer Hill

Legend has it that in the 12C, during a hunting session King Bolesław the Wry-Mouthed followed a wounded deer to the top of this hill. Linen production in the 16C and the Industrial Revolution in the 19C brought prosperity, which can be attested by the lovely burghers' homes. The town changed hands several times over the centuries, ruled in turn by the neighbouring Czechs, the Austrians and the Germans before being finally returned to Poland in 1945 without serious war damage.

SIGHTS

Start from the supervised parking area next to the Tourist Office. Close by, a late-16C tower marks the western limit of the town's former fortifications flanked at this point by a gatehouse. From there, walk to the Rynek.

Rynek
(Plac Ratuszowy)

Steep and rather small, the square is surrounded by Baroque and Rococo

▶ **Population:** 95,000.
◔ **Michelin Map:** Map of Poland B3 – Województwo of Lower Silesia.
▤ **Info:** Ul. Bankowa 27. ℘(75) 767 69 25. www.jeleniagora.pl.
◖ **Location:** 125km southwest of Wrocław.
▣ **Parking:** Ul. Grodzka near the old city fortifications.
◉ **Don't Miss:** The view of the area from Szybowisko Hill.
◷ **Timing:** Spend one night in town. The surrounding area is rich in forests and rambling routes, as suggested by the Tourist Office.

GETTING AROUND

BY RAIL – Railway station – *Ul. 1 Maja 77. www.pkp.pl.*
BY BUS – Bus station – *Ul. Obrońców Pokoju 2. www.pks.pl.*

PRACTICAL INFORMATION

Phone code – ℘*075.*
Postal code – *58 500.*
Tourist Office – *Bankowa 27.* ℘*767 69 25. www.jeleniagora.pl. Open Mon–Fri 9am–6pm, Sat 10am–2pm, also Sun 10am–2pm in summer.*

Jelenia Góra Town Hall Square

arcaded houses from the 17C and 18C, painted in an array of pleasant colours from ochre to blue. This is the heart of the Old Town and one of the best-preserved ryneks in Lower Silesia. Behind a Baroque fountain overlooked by an effigy of Neptune stands the **Town Hall**, built in the 18C in a mixed Baroque and Classical style, on the site of a medieval edifice. It is prolonged by a group of buildings known as the **Seven Houses** (Siedem Domów). The town's main sights are located east of the Rynek, in the area around Konopnickiej Street and its continuation 1 Maja (1 May) Street.

St Erasmus and St Pancras' Church
(Kościół Św. Św. Erazma i Pankracego)

Away from Konopnickiej Street, this austere Gothic church dates from the 14C. The interior was modified during the Baroque period, as was the dome surmounting the bell tower.

1 Maja Street

It is possible to recognise the site of the former fortifications from the presence of the tiny **St Anne's Chapel** (Kaplica Św.Anny), which seems crushed by a tower that was originally part of these fortifications. Leaning against the chapel, the **Wojanowska Gate** (Brama Wojanowska) is all that remains of the medieval walls.

Holy Cross Church
(Kościół Świętego Krzyża)

Standing in the middle of a vast open space, the church *(shaped like a Greek cross)* was built between 1709 and 1718 by a Swedish architect who took his inspiration from one in Stockholm. A festival of organ music takes place every year. Tombstones, engraved with ornamental epitaphs, cover the outside walls; they were originally in the cemetery surrounding the church.

Karkonosze Museum★
(Muzeum Karkonoskie)

Ul. Matejki 28. Open Tue–Fri 9am–3.30pm, Sat-Sun 9am–4.30pm. 6 PLN.

The museum's impressive collection of glassware includes no fewer than 8,000 items. Other fine rooms are devoted to local painting, ethnography and archaeology.

EXCURSIONS
Góra Szybowisko★

▶ *5km north of Jelenia Góra.*
This hill offers a superb view of the surrounding area.

Cieplice Zdrój

5km southwest of Jelenia Góra.
The water springing up at a temperature of 86°C is recommended for the treatment of rheumatism and eye complaints. Already famous in the 12C for its curative properties, the resort was ceded to the Knights of St John in 1281. Shaded by the Baroque church is a very pleasant, if tiny, pedestrian centre, popular with people taking the waters. More pleasant still are walks through the two large wooded parks, one of which boasts a small **Natural History Museum** housed in a Norwegian-style pavilion.

Perched on a rocky spur, 3km southwest of the resort, the stately **Chojnik Castle** (Zamek Chojnik) is still an impressive fortress. From the top of the highest tower, there is a fine **view** of the surrounding area.

ADDRESSES

🛏 STAY

🍴🍴**Pałac Staniszów** – *Staniszów 100, 3km south of Jelenia Góra.* ☎755 84 45. Refined rooms and meals in an authentic manor set in an area of peaceful dales. Unforgettable.

🍴 EAT

🍴**Kurna Chata** – *Pl. Ratuszowy 23/24.* Cheap yet excellent Polish cuisine served under the arcades of the Rynek.

🍴🍴**Piwnice Rajców** – *In the Town Hall cellars.* ☎645 00 55. Open noon–10pm. A creative cuisine concentrating on meat and fish dishes is served in superb vaulted cellars.

Karkonosze National Park★★

Karkonoski Park Narodowy

Acting as a natural border between Poland and the Czech Republic, the Karkonosze Mountains rise abruptly beyond the hills of the Sudeten. The mountains are characterised by deep glacial hollows carved from the rocky slopes. Dense forests and high summits subjected to a harsh climate form the ideal environment for skiers in winter and for hikers in summer.

A BIT OF GEOGRAPHY
The Giants' Mountains

The name "Giants' Mountains" (Karkonosze in Polish) was given to this range as early as the Middle Ages. The park, covering 5 575ha of crystalline rocks, extends along a 35km northwest/southeast axis. Forests of spruce, maples and limes cover two thirds of the area, giving way as the altitude increases to pines, replaced higher up still by scrub and peat bogs. The summit of Mount Śnieżka which, with an altitude of 1 603m, towers 200m above the rest of the range, consists of barren stony expanses. On the mountain slopes, post-glacial hollows, waterfalls, mountain lakes and streams welcome visitors who are likely to meet Corsican mouflons (wild sheep) or boars during the course of their hike. There are spectacular granite rock formations such as the **Pilgrims** (Pielgrzymy), three twenty-metre high outcroppings, and the **Sunflower** (Słonecznik), a rock visible from the lowest part of the Jelenia Góra Valley. Tourism started in the 19C as a result of pilgrimages to the Baroque church of St Lawrence (Św. Wawrzyniec), patron saint of mountain guides, which stands at the top of Mount Śnieżka.

⚐ HIKING IN THE NATIONAL PARK
Access from Karpacz and Szklarska Poręba.

Admission⚅5 PLN, 3-day pass 8 PLN. The park is the paradise of hikers.

ⓖ **Michelin Map:** Map of Poland A3 – Województwo of Lower Silesia.

⊞ **Info:** Karpacz. Ul. Konstytucji 3 Maja 25. ℘(75) 761 86 05. www.karpacz.pl.

▷ **Location:** Karpacz: 125km southwest of Wrocław, 20km from Jelenia Góra.

🅿 **Parking:** Guarded parking by the Wang chapel and the chair lift, other wise free on the street.

⊘ **Don't Miss:** The ascent of Mount Śnieżka.

⚇ **Kids:** Alpine slide park.

⊙ **Timing:** 2hr are sufficient to catch the atmosphere of Karpacz but you need to spend at least a day wandering through the national park.

PRACTICAL INFORMATION
Karpacz Tourist Office –
Ul. Konstytucji 3 Maja 25.
℘(75) 761 86 05. www.karpacz.pl.
Open Mon–Sat. 9am–5pm.

🐾**Mount Śnieżka** – If you are short of time, take the chair lift (⊙*open daily 8.30am–4.30pm. 22 PLN, cheaper after 1pm)* linking Karpacz and Mount Kopa. Mount Śnieżka is then a 1hr walk away.

⚐ Other hiking trails

They all start from the upper part of Karpacz, next to the service station, where Konstytucji 3 Maja avenue becomes Karkonoska avenue, except for the blue trail which starts from the Wang chapel. Allow 4 to 5hr for each of the trails. All are moderately difficult.
The red trail leads to the **Łomniczka cirque** (Kocioł Łomniczki) and to **Mount Śnieżka**. Perched at the top like a stranded flying saucer, the **Meteorological Observatory** (Wysokogórskie Obserwatorium Meteoro-

Karkonosze National Park

M. Ostrowska / MICHELIN

logiczne; ⏱*open daily 10am–4pm),* houses a mountain refuge and now competes with St Lawrence's Chapel. In fine weather, the view extends as far as Wrocław. The blue, green and yellow trails lead to **Lake Wielki and Lake Mały** (Wielki Staw and Mały Staw) contained within impressive glacial hollows.

SIGHTS
Karpacz

Karpacz stretches along a road winding its way through the eastern part of the Karkonosze Mountains. Prospectors who, in the 14C, looked for gold and precious stones in the Łomniczka and Łomnica valleys, built the first village. Bohemia's Protestant community, fleeing religious persecution, joined them around 1622. The first tourists arrived in the 19C, attracted by the Wang Chapel and by the fact that the village is the gateway to the mountains.

Situated in the upper part of Karpacz is the **Wang Chapel**★★ (⏱*open mid-Apr–Oct Mon–Sat 9am–6pm, Sun 11.30am–5pm; Nov–mid-Apr Mon–Sat 9am–5pm, Sun 11am–5pm; service on Sun at 10am; ⏱6 PLN).* The 12C pine building assembled in northern Norway was bought by King Friedrich-Wilhelm IV of Prussia in 1841. Countess Frederika von Reden suggested he should present it to the Lutheran community in Karpacz. After a long voyage via Berlin, the reassembled or rather restored chapel was inaugurated on 28 July 1844. Among the original décor are the doorways and, inside, some capitals decorated with animals, floral motifs and interlacing. Note the elegant structure which combines the Viking and Romanesque styles, as well as the intricate timberwork put together with wooden pegs.

The **Gravity Hill** (Anomalia grawitacyjna) on Ul. Strażacka between Ul. Karkonoska and the waterfall is a local curiosity where cars, bottles and cans all appear to roll uphill due to an optical illusion created by the surrounding hills and trees.

👥 Alpine Slide Park
Ul. Parkowa 10. www.kolorowa.pl.
⏱*Open daily 9am–dusk.* 👶*Children younger than 8 must ride with an adult.* A summer recreation centre with alpine slides and carts.

ADDRESSES

🛏 STAY
🛌 **Villa Rosa** – *Ul. Okrzei 8 Karpacz. ☎(75) 761 95 50. www.rosa.karpacz.pl. 6 rooms with shared bathroom.* This guest house occupies a magnificent 17C house on the fringe of the forest. Some rooms have a verandah or balcony. Family atmosphere and large garden at guests' disposal. The Villa also offers an apartment for 4–6 persons in town.

Rynek, Toruń
B. Brillion / MICHELIN

GREATER POLAND

Greater Poland comprises the ancestral lands of the Polish nation. The creation of the Polish state started here in the 10C in a fertile land dotted with lakes and forests. Two ancient royal capitals, Poznań and Gniezno, can boast cathedrals that witnessed the coronations and burials of Polish kings before that right and privilege was transferred to Kraków. Poznań is the economic and cultural capital of the region, and is characterised by a businesslike, Prussian attitude. In addition to its famous trade fairs, the city has developed a wide variety of festivals that enliven the cultural calendar year round.

Highlights

1 **Poznań's Malta Festival** in June and the wonderful town hall all year round (p326, p329)

2 The Archeological Festival in **Biskupin** each September (p339)

3 Exploring **Toruń**'s narrow, river-side streets and sampling the local **gingerbread** (p345)

4 A visit to Teutonic **Chełmno** and its austere Gothic churches (p346)

Ancestral Lands

Kalisz may claim to be the oldest city in Poland, but if you want to see a truly ancient settlement, Biskupin evocatively displays how the people of this part of Europe lived before the Christianisation of the lands that are now Poland. From other archeological investigations in Poland it has been shown that the basic settlement layout and method of construction of houses and fortifications seen at Biskupin were typical for other early settlements up until the time of the first Polish kings.

Gniezno's importance as the cradle of the Polish nation is demonstrated by the legend associated with Lech Hill, the oldest part of the city, where the first Polish leader Lech is said to have seen a white eagle nesting at sunset *(hence the red and white of the Polish flag)* and so decided to found a city for his future fellow Poles.

Toruń, an impressive former Hanseatic town, boasts magnificent red-brick Gothic architecture, including the best preserved Gothic town hall in all of Poland, and little or no Baroque buildings. This is typical of the towns and cities associated with the Teutonic Knights, whose German settlers converted to Protestantism in the 16C. Along with the Chełmno, historically and culturally Toruń belongs more to Pomerania than Greater Poland.

Aerial view of Biskupin

Protesters surround a soviet tank, 28th June 1956

© Bettmann/Corbis

Poznań Uprising

The first major protest against the communist regime in Poland took place in Poznań on the morning of 28 June 1956, when workers from the Joseph Stalin Metal Works factory took to the streets to protest over the poor wages and overall low standard of living then typical for the People's Republic of Poland compared to before World War II. The striking metalworkers were soon spontaneously joined by other protesters and a crowd of 100,000 gathered outside the Imperial Castle, in whose vicinity the offices of the Communist party and police headquarters were located.

Monument to victims of Poznań

© Lukasz Tymszan/Dreamstime.com

Soon protesters started to remove red flags from government buildings, pulling down devices that jammed Western radio broadcasts and even freeing political prisoners from the local prison and raiding the arms depot. The rioters were labeled "provocateurs, counterrevolutionaries and Imperialist agents" by the Polish authorities and things turned violent after shots aimed at the crowd of protesters rang out from the Secret Police building. Then early in the afternoon tanks and armed troops entered the city on the orders of the Soviet commander of Polish defense who wanted to crush the uprising and prevent civil unrest from spreading to other parts of Poland.

Protests lasted until June 30th while the city was surrounded by more than 10,000 troops and hundreds were arrested. It is generally believed that between 60 and 100 persons were killed during the unrest and as many as 600 were injured. Sometime after the uprising the Communists realised that the workers were not "provocateurs" and that they had legitimate complaints so wages were increased and other concessions were made. During the communist era these events were covered up and could not be discussed. Now these first historic protests are commemorated with a day of remembrance every 28 June, and with a museum at the Imperial Castle in Poznań.

Kalisz

Kalisz prides itself on being Poland's oldest city. Even though the ravages of time and war (particularly World War I) somewhat altered its historic appearance, it still remains a pleasant town with a wealth of religious architecture and a picturesque main square.

A BIT OF HISTORY

The pride of Kalisz (*Calisia* in Latin) is the mention of its name on Ptolemy's famous 2C map. During the Roman period, and even well before that, it was a trading settlement on the Amber Route. In the 9C, a fortress guarded this strategic area and the small city to which Bolesław the Pious granted a charter in 1257. History has not been kind to the ancient city: a fire in 1792 and the Prussian occupation (until 1806) signalled the city's decline; it reached its lowest ebb in August 1914 when the Germans destroyed Kalisz. Returned to Poland in 1920, it was rebuilt with due respect to its medieval structure, but the Germans struck another blow in 1942 when they deported the entire Jewish population.

SIGHTS

Rynek

Bright and spacious, Kalisz is surrounded by fine houses and in the centre stands the town hall restored in 1920. From the top of the belfry (*open May–Aug Mon–Fri 9am–3pm*) there is a fine view of the local bell towers rising above the tiled roofs.

Franciscan Monastery
(*Zespół klasztorny Franciszkanów*)
Southeast of the Rynek, between Kazimierzowska, Sukiennicza and Rzeźnicza Streets.
The church, founded in 1257 but later decorated in the Renaissance style, houses a reliquary of St Jolanta as well as an unusual boat-shaped pulpit. The monastery buildings date from the 17C.

Return to the Rynek; Zamkowa and Kanonicka Streets to the cathedral.

▶ **Population:** 108,000.
⌖ **Michelin Map:** Map of Poland B3 – Województwo of Greater Poland.
🛈 **Info:** Ul. Zamkowa. ℘(62)598 27 31. http://osir.kalisz.pl/cit.
▶ **Location:** 140km northeast of Wrocław, 115km southeast of Poznań and 107km west of Łódź.
🅿 **Parking:** Parking in the Old Town requires buying a ticket from a local kiosk.
😊 **Don't Miss:** Walks through Gołuchów's parks.
🕑 **Timing:** One or two hours for strolling in town.

GETTING AROUND

BY RAIL – Railway station – *Ul. Dworcowa 1.* 2km southeast of the centre.
BY BUS – Bus station – *Ul. Górnośląska 82-84. www.pks.kalisz.pl.* Near the above. Buses leave for Wrocław and Poznań.

PRACTICAL INFORMATION

Phone code – ℘062.
Postal code – 62 800.
Tourist office – *Ul. Zamkowa.* ℘598 27 31. http://osir.kalisz.pl/cit. Open Mon –Fri 9am–5pm, Sat 10am–2pm.

St Nicholas' Cathedral
(*Katedra Św. Mikołaja*)
Erected in the 13C, the cathedral was often remodelled over the centuries. Beneath the Renaissance vaulting, the high altar is surmounted by a copy of the Descent from the Cross by Rubens. Outside, one can see the remains of the town's medieval walls, which once included 15 towers and two gates but were destroyed by the Prussians in the 19C.

Continue on Zamkowa Street; turn right on Chodyńkiego Street to reach Św.

*Exhibition of photographs on the
Old Town Market Square, Kalisz*

© Polish National Tourist Office

Józefa Square, where St Joseph's Church
and the Basilica stand.

Basilica of the Assumption
(Bazylika Wniebowzięcia NMP)
This Baroque edifice has retained a 14C
chancel, a fine Gothic polyptych and a
painting depicting the Holy Family said
to have miraculous powers. The bell
tower was erected in 1820.

EXCURSIONS
Gołuchów Castle
▶ *16km northeast of Kalisz.* ◷*Open
Tue–Sun 10am–4pm.* ◈*8 PLN, Sat free.*
Nestled among dales, ponds and forests,
this Renaissance manor, built in 1560,
now resembles a French château. Abandoned in the 17C, it was restored by Izabela Działyńska from 1872 onwards and
turned into a museum. The stocky castle,
flanked by polygonal towers, boasts fine
Neo-Gothic interiors, a plethora of art,
and is situated in a 19C English-style
romantic park.

Antonin's Palace
▶ *40km south of Kalisz.* ◷*Open daily
9am–8pm. Now a hotel and restaurant
that allows visitors, but may be closed
for special occasions so it's best to call
ahead.* ℘*(62) 734 83 00.*
When he was governor of the Grand
Duchy of Poznań, Prince Antoni Radziwłł,
had this elegant wooden hunting palace

built in the shape of a cross between
1822 and 1824. The centre is occupied
by a vast octagonal hall, surrounded
by two-tiered galleries and featuring
a huge central column decorated with
deer-hunting trophies.
A friend of the arts, the Prince invited
many artists who were no doubt fascinated by the romantic appeal of this
lakeside residence. Chopin stayed in
the Palace in 1827 and 1829. An annual
piano festival takes place in his honour.

ADDRESSES

🏠 STAY
⊖ **Europa Hotel** – *Al. Wolności 5.* ℘*767
20 31. www.hotel-europa.pl. 52 rooms.*
Entirely refurbished, the hotel offers
calm, well-equipped rooms near the
town centre.

⊖⊖ **Calisia Hotel** – *Al. Ul. Nowy Swiat
1-3.* ℘*767 91 00. www.hotel-calisia.pl.
80 rooms. Restaurant⊖.* Straightforward,
comfortable modern hotel, 1km south
of the Old Town. The restaurant of the
Calisia hotel is by far the best in town.

♀/EAT
⊖ **Piwnica u Roberta** – *Park Ludowy 2.*
℘*764 29 46.* Large restaurant in city park
serves Polish standards and features live
music on Fri and Sat.

Poznań★★

Poznań boasts a wealth of architectural and cultural heritage round one of the country's finest central market squares. The capital of Greater Poland is a dynamic city and perfectly manageable for a visit on foot; the narrow streets are ideal for strolling, while excursions into the surrounding area will take you to wonderful castles and forest hikes. Birthplace of the Polish State in the 10C, Poznań is now a lively student town, a trade fair centre and a perfect city break destination.

A BIT OF HISTORY
Birthplace of the Polish State

In the 10C, Mieszko I made this small settlement, on an island in the River Warta, one of the two capitals of his duchy. In 968, he established Poland's first bishopric in the town and soon had a cathedral built. Taking over where his father left off, Bolesław Chrobry (the Brave) became the first Polish king. Poznań developed and its position near the western borders of the kingdom made it an obvious target for restless neighbours. Although the capital was eventually moved to Kraków, the city felt cramped on its island and, in 1253, the new town centre situated on the west bank of the river was granted privileges which

▸ **Population:** 570,000.

⏣ **Michelin Map:** Map of Poland B2 – Województwo of Greater Poland.

▤ **Info:** Ul. Ratajczaka 44. ℘(61) 851 96 45.

◖ **Location:** 300km west of Warsaw, 147km south of Toruń, 170km north of Wrocław.

ⓟ **Parking:** Best bet is underground parking lot on Pl. Wolności, 5min from Rynek.

◉ **Don't Miss:** The narrow streets around the Rynek, the noon ceremony at the foot of the town hall.

▲▴ **Kids:** Malta Park, its choice of activities and tourist train, the zoos and the botanical garden.

◷ **Timing:** Allow a full day to visit the town and the main museums.

⏣ **Also See:** Rogalin Palace, Gniezno Cathedral.

stimulated the activity of the trade fairs. The town reached the peak of its power in the 16C, but its partial destruction by fire marked the beginning of a dark period. The decline brought about by

Poznań Town Hall

GETTING AROUND

BY AIR – **Ławica Airport** – *Ul. Bukowska 285.* ☎ *849 23 43.* *www.airport-poznan.com.pl.* 7km west of the town centre.

BY RAIL – *Ul. Dworcowa 1. www.pkp.pl.* The main railway station is situated 1km west of the Rynek. Links with Warsaw *(3hr)*, Kraków and Wrocław several times a day.

BY BUS – **Bus station** – *Ul. Towarowa 17. www.pks.pl.*

BY CAR – **Parking** – Driving in the vicinity of the Rynek is difficult because there are many one-way streets. Park your car in one of the numerous supervised car parks on the outskirts of town.

PRACTICAL INFORMATION

Phone code – ☎ *061.*
Postal code – *60 900.*
Tourist office – *Ul. Ratajczaka 44.* ☎ *851 96 45.* Open Mon–Fri 10am–7pm, Sat 10am–5pm. Excellent advice from English-speaking staff, selection of brochures, maps and books about Poznań and its region. A lot of free literature.

Glob-Tour – *Ul. Dworcowa 1.* ☎ *866 06 67.* Tourist Information CSentre at the station. Open 24hr/day.
Post office – In the Old Town: *Ul. Wodna 17.*
Pharmacy open 24h/day – *Galenica, Ul. Srzelecka 2/6.* ☎ *852 99 22.*
Internet Café – Klik – *Ul. Szkolna 15. daily 10am–midnight.* A few streets south of the Rynek.

WHERE TO GO

The three-monthly guide *Poznań In Your Pocket* is a mine of practical information about hotels, restaurants and out-on-the-town places as well as sights and museums.

PTTK office – *Stary Rynek 90.* ☎ *852 37 56. www.bort.pl (in English).* Access through the Londoner Pub. Guided tours of the town.

Poznańska Karta Miejska: A public transport pass with free admission to the main museums. Discounts in some restaurants and attractions. 30 PLN for one day, 40 PLN for two days and 45 PLN for three days.

---

the Swedish invasion in the 17C continued during the next century with the Prussian and Russian invasions, the Black Death and floods. The town finally fell under Prussian rule in 1793 and became Posen, the capital of the grand duchy of the same name. In December 1918, the rebellion of Greater Poland, launched in Poznań, led to the liberation of the region. This was short-lived since the province was annexed to Nazi Germany after 1939. Subsequently, over half the town was destroyed by bombings. It was here that the first uprising against the Communist regime took place on 28 June 1956. The terrible repression that followed resulted in 76 deaths.

Today, Poznań's activities revolve round its universities, trade fairs that go back to the Middle Ages, and the highly innovative Malta International Theatre Festival.

The Goats of Poznań

Legend has it that in 1511 the cook in charge of the town hall's inauguration banquet mistakenly let the meat burn. Two goats were brought in, but unwilling to finish up on the grill, they escaped to the top of the building and confronted each other in front of the dumbfounded crowd. The Governor took this to be a good omen and ordered that mechanical effigies of the goats be coupled to the clock so that the event could be celebrated daily. Since then, the mechanical goats have been replying to the twelve strokes of midday by butting their horns 12 times.

PARC NATIONAL DE GRANDE POLOGI

EXPLORING
Old Market Square★★★
(Stary Rynek) MAP II

The perfectly square paved Rynek is the heart of the city. It is surrounded by Gothic, Renaissance or Baroque houses, most of them destroyed in 1945 and splendidly restored after the war. Many of the townhouses boast stepped gable roofs and façades painted with warm pastel colours and decorated with paintings, for instance **nos. 58**, **66** and **73**. Note the façade of **nos. 78–79** with its pediment surmounted by sculptures from the **Działyński Palace** (Pałac Działyńskich) built in the Baroque style in the 18C, over which a pelican hovers, its wings spread. Often teeming with people, in fine weather the square is covered with tables and parasols.

The centre of the Rynek A1

In front of the town hall stand the **Baroque Proserpine Fountain** and a copy of the **1535 pillory** (*original kept in the town's history museum*). A nearby row of arcades marks the former **traders' houses**★ (Domki Budnicze). The coat of arms on **no. 17** with a herring is of the traders' guild, whose headquarters were once here. A narrow street leads to the **Bamberka Fountain**, a reminder that part of the population originally came from the German town of Bamberg. Standing behind it, the elegant **Weighing House** offsets the austere appearance and lack of charm of the building erected on its left during the communist era. Finally, the small 17C **Guardhouse** (Odwach), features a west-facing Classical colonnade.

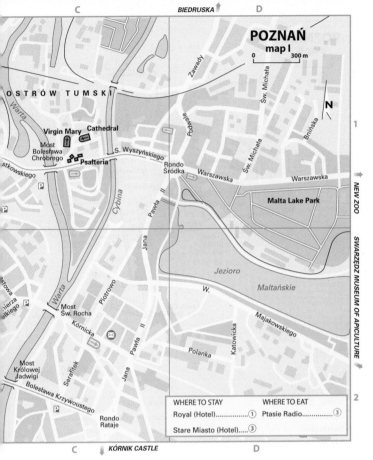

POZNAŃ
map I

0 ——— 300 m

N

OSTRÓW TUMSKI

Virgin Mary   Cathedral

Most
Bolesława
Chrobrego

Psalteria

S. Wyszyńskiego

Rondo
Śródka

Warszawska

Warszawska

Malta Lake Park

Jezioro
Maltańskie

W.

Majakowskiego

Katowicka

Polanka

Most
Św. Rocha

Piotrowo

Kórnicka

Pawła II

Most
Królowej
Jadwigi

Serafitek

Jana

Bolesława Krzywoustego

Rondo
Rataje

Zawady

Podwale

Św. Michała

Św. Michała

Bnińska

Cybina

Pawła II

Jana

Warta

Warta

C   BIEDRUSKA   D

C   KÓRNIK CASTLE   D

NEW ZOO
SWARZĘDZ MUSEUM OF APICULTURE

WHERE TO STAY	WHERE TO EAT
Royal (Hotel)...............①	Ptasie Radio...............③
Stare Miasto (Hotel).....③	

Town Hall ★★★
(Ratusz) B1

*Stary Rynek1. ⏱Open Tue–Thu 11am–
5pm, Fri noon–9pm, Sat–Sun 11am–
6pm. ⬤5.50 PLN, Sat free.*

Standing like a large cake in the middle of the Rynek and surmounted by a
high belfry, this is one of Poland's most
spectacular town halls. Destroyed by fire
in 1536, it was restored in the Renaissance style by Italian architect Giovanni
Battista Quadro. The façade featuring a
three-storey arcade is topped with three
pinnacles. At noon, all eyes converge on
the middle one to watch the two goats
of Poznań appear. Inside, the **Historical Museum of Poznań** (Muzeum Historii Miasta Poznania) is housed on the
two floors and in the Gothic cellars. It
illustrates the history of the town from

Rowhouses in Old Market Square

© Tim Becker/iStockphoto

329

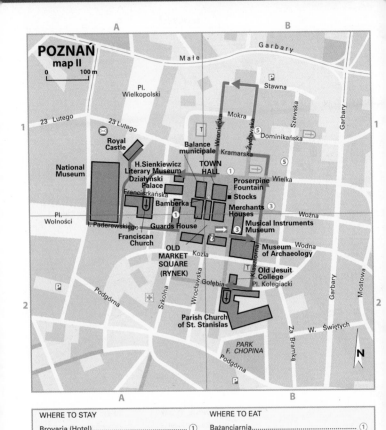

POZNAŃ
map II
0   100 m

the 10C to 1945: local archaeological discoveries, paintings, sculptures and an amazing exhibition of photographs showing what the town looked like at the end of the war, thus enabling visitors to appreciate the extent of the restoration work undertaken.

The highlight of the visit is the **Great Hall** (Wielka Sień). This Renaissance gem boasts a coffered ceiling from 1555, resting on two impressive columns and richly decorated with coats of arms, painted scenes and finely carved motifs.

Musical Instruments Museum★
(Muzeum Instrumentów Muzy-cznych) B2
Stary Rynek 45. ⊙Open Tue–Thu 11am–5pm, Fri noon–9pm Sat–Sun 11am–6pm.

⊜5.50 PLN, Sat free.

This interesting museum contains a unique collection of musical instruments. The ground floor presents unusual music boxes whose mechanisms, a cross between a barrel organ and a turntable, uses perforated discs, as well as harmoniums and wind instruments. The first floor contains string instruments and a large harpsichord decorated, like a Baroque altarpiece, with paintings and gilt motifs.

One room, dedicated to Chopin, displays his death mask, a cast of his right hand and a piano he played around 1820. The upper floor, reminiscent of an ethnographic museum, is devoted to ancient and traditional instruments from Poland, Asia, Africa, Oceania and America.

Henryk Sienkiewicz Literature Museum
(Muzeum Literackie Im. H. Sienkiewicza)

Stary Rynek 84. ○*Open Mon–Fri 10am –5pm.* ⊗*3 PLN.*

Fans of the author of *Quo Vadis* will be rewarded, others glad of this opportunity to visit one of the imposing residences around the Rynek. Mementoes of the 1905 Noble Prize winner include editions of his work in 39 languages, original manuscripts and his death mask.

⊷WALKING TOUR

The main sites being located close to the Rynek, the tour starts from the southeast corner of the square. Follow Wodna Street. Facing the arcades is the façade of the Górka Palace (Pałac Górka) which houses the Archaeological Museum.

Archaeological Museum★
(Muzeum Archeologiczne) B2

Ul. Wodna27. ○*Open Tue–Fri 10am–4pm, Sat 10am–6pm, Sun 10am–3pm.* ⊗*6 PLN, Sat free.*

A large room presents Greater Poland's Prehistory, from the Stone Age to the great migrations. Life-size reconstructions illustrate archaeological discoveries and recall the daily lives of hunters, gathers and farmers. However, the most interesting part deals with funerary art in ancient Egypt. The modest collection includes the mummy of a boy, those of a cat and of a crocodile, as well as funerary papyri and a "guide to the beyond".

▷ *Retrace your steps and turn left onto Świętosławska Street. The street dominated by the west front of the parish church forms an impressive picture, particularly when lit at night.*

St Stanislas Parish Church★★
(Kościół Farny Św. Stanisława) B2
Ul. Klasztorna11.

Erected for the Jesuits, this monumental Baroque church, boasting three naves supported by Corinthian columns, retains a certain stateliness in spite of its profuse ornamentation. Stuccoes, paintings, sculptures and a trompe-l'oeil dome frame the high altar made in 1727 by Pompeo Ferrari. Free concerts take place every day at 12.15pm and Thu at 8pm from June to September and on Saturdays during the rest of the year.

▷ *On leaving the church, turn right onto Gołębia Street. Through the railing of no. 8, one can get a glimpse of the arcaded courtyard of the former Jesuit school (Dawna Szkoła Jezuicka), now housing a ballet school. Further on stands the elegant belfry-doorway of the former Jesuit college.*

Old Jesuit College
(Kolegium Pojezuickie) B2
Pl. Kolegiacki17.

Today it houses the town's administrative offices. The refined outline of this elegant 18C building forms with the parish church a horseshoe-shaped ensemble. Napoleon stayed here in 1806. Across the street, on Kolegiacki Square, a bronze sculpture of two goats pays tribute to the town's mascots.

Follow Klasztorna Street, lined with restaurants and antique shops. Beyond a bend, it leads to Żydowska Street which, together with the parallel Wroniecka Street, marked the limits of the Jewish district.

At the end of the street stands the last of the three synagogues that once stood in the town; it has been a swimming pool ever since Nazi Occupation.

▷ *Return to the Rynek then follow Góra Przemysła Street to the Franciscan Church.*

Franciscan Church
(Kościoł Franciszkanów) A1
Ul. Franciszkańska2.

The church, reached via a flight of steps, was built between 1674 and 1728. This late-Baroque three-naved basilica is adorned with sculptures, stuccoes and paintings. Two chapels mark the end of the arms of the transept. In the north chapel, the delicate rendering of a tiny painting of the Virgin with Child outshines the huge black-wood altarpiece with gilded decorations in which it is set.

Walk up the street, then turn right towards the ruined ramparts and on to the esplanade to the Royal Castle.

Royal Castle
(Zamek Królewski) A1

Góra Przemysła1. ⊙*Open Tue–Thu 11am–5pm, Fri noon–9pm, Sat–Sun 11am–6pm.* ⬤*5.50 PLN, Sat free.*

Erected in the 13C, the remains of the hilltop castle tower above the town; it was once the residence of the governors of Greater Poland. Destroyed and remodelled many times *(plans exist to rebuild the castle in a historically faithful or modern style)*, it now devotes one floor to a small **Museum of Decorative Arts** (Muzeum Sztuk Użytkowych) featuring a collection of works from medieval times to the present. It is particularly interesting for fans of ornaments, furniture, ceramics and glassware. From the terrace is a fine view of the town.

Ludgardy St; Paderewskiego St.

Gallery of the National Museum of Painting and Sculpture★★
(Muzeum Narodowe Galeria Malarstwa i Rzeźby) A1

Al. Marcinkowskiego 9. ⊙*Open Tue–Thu 11am–6pm, Fri noon–9pm, Sat–Sun 11am–5pm,* ⬤*10 PLN, Sat free.*

© Andrea Seemann/iStockphoto

Poznań's Cathedral

The recently restored museum is housed in an austere early-20C building to which was added a modern extension providing vast exhibition areas for the contemporary collections of painting and sculpture. The old building houses Romanesque and Gothic works, together with a large collection of Italian painting from the 15C to the 18C, 16C Flemish art and Dutch works from the 18C. The museum also houses one of the most important collections of Spanish painting, including works by José Ribera and Francisco Zurbaran.

Return to the Rynek along Paderewskiego Street.

FURTHER OUT
Ostrów Tumski MAP I

This island, now away from the town centre, was the birthplace not only of Poznań, but also of the Polish State and Church. The town's oldest monuments are gathered here, shrouded in a slightly austere ecclesiastical atmosphere.

Cathedral★
(Katedra) C1

Poland's first cathedral was built in 968 and dedicated to St Peter and St Paul. Destroyed and remodelled several times, it is now a three-naved basilica with traces of Romanesque architecture. The two towers surmounted by Baroque cupolas rise above the main doorway featuring doors decorated with scenes of the lives of St Paul and St Peter. Some 15 chapels surround the nave, including the noteworthy **Golden Chapel**. Decorated in the Byzantine style in the 19C, it contains the sarcophagi and the statues of Mieszko I and his son King Bolesław Chrobry (the Brave). The crypt, symbolically just as important, houses the foundations of the early-Romanesque edifice as well as remains of the fonts and the original tombs of the two sovereigns.

St Mary's Church
(Kościół Najświętszej Marii Panny) C1

This slender brick-built Gothic church, featuring a very steep roof, stands opposite the cathedral. Erected during the first half of the 15C, it is in the process of being restored (o—). Excavations carried out beneath the church uncovered the foundations of a royal palace, the first seat of the Polish State.

Psałteria C1

Situated next to the church, this early-16C red-brick building used to be the residence of the cathedral's choristers.

WEST OF THE TOWN

The district lying at the end of Św. Marcin Street, near the station, livens up when one of the major trade fairs takes place in a vast centre **(Międzynarodowe Targi Poznańskie)** located on the other side of the railway track.

Imperial Castle
(Dawny Zamek Cesarski)
Ul. Św. Marcin 80/82.

This imposing edifice, stone-built in neo-Romanesque style at the beginning of the 20C and greatly damaged during World War II, today houses a cultural centre and a theatre. The beautiful park laid out behind the building offers a different view of the arcaded façade with its somewhat Moorish feel.

Next to it stand the huge intertwined crosses of the **28 June 1956 Memorial**, which pays tribute to the 76 protestors killed during confrontations with the police. The first Polish uprising against Communist domination rallied nearly 120,000 people.

PARKS AND GARDENS MAP I

Poznań boasts many open spaces. They make good places for a stroll or offer a choice of recreational activities, and your children will enjoy them.

Lake Malta Park D1

▶ *2km east of the town centre on the way to Warsaw.*

This vast artificial lake surrounded by open spaces is the favourite recreation area of Poznań's inhabitants. Activities on offer include swimming, rock-climbing and even skiing on a 150m-long artificial run. Regattas and other com-

petitions are organised. A **tourist train** *(daily May–Sept; ⊚5/3.5 PLN)* runs through the park from the western end (Zamenhofa Street) towards the **New Zoo** (Nowe Zoo; ⊕ *open daily 9am–6pm; ⊚14/8 PLN)*, which shelters nearly 2,000 animals in woodland watered by a stream. A pavilion is devoted to nocturnal species.

Old Zoo D1
Ul. Zwierzyniecka 19, 1km west of the town centre. ⊕*Open daily 9am–6pm.* ⊚ *3 PLN.*

Opened during the second half of the 19C, this venerable zoo covering 4.4ha is home to elephants, lions, dwarf hippopotami, giraffes and a few monkeys. An aquarium stands next to a reptile house and an aviary.

Botanical Gardens A1
▶ *3km west of the town centre.*
Ul.Dąbrowskiego 165. ⊕*Open May–Oct daily 9am–7pm.* ⊚*Free.*

Opened in 1925, these gardens belonging to the Adam Mickiewicz University and covering 22ha, contain nearly 8,000 species of plants from all over the world, representing various ecosystems, such as steppe, dunes and marshes.

Citadel Park *(Cytadela)* B1

Picnics, impromptu ball games on the vast lawns, students busy revising or couples relaxing in the shade of the trees, it is hard to imagine that the locals' favourite place for lazing around was once a powerful fortress. The terrain and a few remains are the only reminders of the citadel built by the Prussians, for which the German and Soviet armies fought in 1945. A cemetery recalls these events, as does a **Military Museum** (Muzeum Uzbrojenia; ⊕*open Tue–Sat 9am–4pm, Sun 10am–4pm; ⊚4 PLN, Fri free)*. Important collection of weapons and open-air exhibition of tanks, planes and military vehicles.

EXCURSIONS

It is possible to make a round tour and include the following sites. Allow a whole day, leaving Poznań early in the morning.

You won't need much time for the Rogalin site and even less for the Swarzędz site. Devote the afternoon to the National Park, if you intend to go on a hike.

Swarzędz Beekeeping Museum
(Skansen i Muzeum Pszczelarstwa)

▶ *In Swarzędz, 10km east of Poznań, alongside the E30.* ⏱*Open Nov–Mar Tue–Sun 9am–3pm; Apr–Oct 9am–5pm, Sat–Sun 9am–6pm; Dec–mid-Feb organised group tours only.* ⏱*Closed holidays.*🎟*10 PLN.*

Opened in 1963 by Professor Ryszard Kostecki, this small museum contains more than 200 exhibits, including an important open-air collection of beehives. Unusually impressive in size, theY are carved in the shape of characters or animals – for instance, a very life-like bear. The oldest beehive goes back to the 15C and most of them are still used to house bees.

Greater Poland National Park
(Wielkopolski Park Narodowy)

▶ *15km south of Poznań along road 430. The Poznań park is accessible by train or bus via Mosina and Puszczykowo on the east side and via Stęszew on the west side. The Mosina parking on the edge of the forest is close to the most interesting sites (Lake Góreckie, most picturesque valleys). The park is criss-crossed by 85km of hiking trails forming five itineraries of 10 to 14km each.*
A detailed map is available at the Tourist Office in Poznań (Ul. Ratajczaka 44):
Extending over an area of 7,584ha, this national park is the lungs of Poznań. The landscape, carved by glaciers, features 130m-high hills, a dozen or so lakes including six where swimming is possible, marshy areas and dense woods planted with conifers and oak trees which shelter deer, boar and other protected species.

Kórnik Castle

▶ *20km southeast of Poznań along road 11.* ⏱*Open Tue–Sun 10am–4pm.* ⏱*Closed mid-Dec–early Feb.* 🎟*13 PLN.*

The medieval fortress built on this mound surrounded by a moat, near the River Warta, was remodelled several times until in the 18C when it became a Baroque palace transformed in the 19C into a massive castle in English neo-Gothic style by Tytus Działyński, who made it his residence and furnished it with the impressive collections we see today. The ornaments, inlaid parquet flooring and period furniture displayed on two floors are just as interesting as the collections of paintings and weapons the former owner liked so much. Note on the first floor, the splendid Moorish room containing Hussars' armours. The castle over-

Rogalin Palace

© Karolina Paszkiewicz/iStockphoto

looks the oldest and largest botanical garden in Poland: a 30ha park housing 3,000 plant species from Europe, Asia and America. It is at the height of its splendour during the spring flowering period, when magnificent magnolias are in bloom.

Rogalin Palace★

◉ *10km west of Kórnik.* ◷*Open Tue–Sat 9.30am–4pm, Sun 9.30am–6pm.* ◷*Closed Easter Sunday.* ⊜ *8 PLN.*
The sumptuous Neoclassical residence of the Raczyński family was built on the banks of the River Warta by Kazimierz Raczyński, Greater Poland's governor, at the end of the 18C. A vast lawn lined with chestnut trees leads to a horse-shoe-shaped building; the right wing houses a reconstruction of the London study of the former Polish president in exile, Edward Raczyński; the left wing contains furniture and ornaments.
The outbuildings house an exhibition of modern Polish painting and a garage contains 19C carriages, carts and sleighs. Behind the Palace, a magnificent French-style garden leads to an English-style wooded park. Here, 945 oak trees, among the oldest in Europe, grow in this magical place near the river; the three most famous are named after the legendary brothers, Lech, Czech and Rus, who founded Poland, the Czech lands and Russia respectively★

ADDRESSES

🛏STAY

Most hotels are located around the Rynek and along Św. Marcin Avenue. Prices hit the roof when international fairs are on *(50 to 150% increases).*

⊜⊜ **Brovaria Hotel** – *Stary Rynek 73/74.* ✆*858 68 68. www.brovaria.pl. 19 rooms.* Ideally situated on top of the Rynek, this luxury hotel has a lot of character and brews its own beers, including a delicious one with honey. The bar and the **restaurant** are frequented by a trendy crowd.

⊜⊜ **Dom Polonii** – *Stary Rynek 51.* ✆*852 71 21. 2 rooms.* Two rooms under the roof; they are vast, in need of a fresh coat of paint but cheap and ideally situated on the top floor of a building overlooking the Rynek.

⊜⊜ **Rezydencja Solei** – *Ul. Szewska 2.* ✆*855 73 51. www.hotel-solei.pl. 11 rooms.* Tiny rooms in a hotel with a guest house feel, situated a few streets away from the Rynek. English spoken.

⊜⊜ **Royal Hotel** – *Ul. Św. Marcin 71.* ✆*858 23 00. www.hotel-royal.com.pl. 31 rooms.* Close to the station and slightly away from the Old Town, this charming hotel is attractive on account of its setting and quiet courtyard.

⊜⊜ **Stare Miasto Hotel** – *Ul. Rybaki 36.* ✆*663 62 42. www.hotelstaremiasto.pl. 23 rooms.* In spite of its name, this hotel lies some distance from the centre, 20min west of the Rynek. It is a fine establishment housed in a new building, with bright comfortable rooms.

🍴EAT

⊜ **Chimera** – *Ul. Dominikańska 7.* ✆*852 03 17. Open daily 10am–midnight.* A delightful **restaurant**-tea room decorated with pastel colours. Behind the counter, some 100 teas give off the most fascinating fragrances. Small menu offering carefully prepared dishes: roast camembert with sesame and salmon with green peppercorns.

⊜ **Cymes** – *Ul. Woźna 2/3.* ✆*851 66 38. Open Tue–Sun 1pm–midnight, Mon 4pm–midnight.* Tiny **restaurant** serving Jewish specialities; simple, generous and nicely decorated. The food, served on wooden tables, includes herring, gefilte fisch and a delicious Hungarian steak cooked with lard.

⊜ **Orfeusz** – *Ul. Świętosławska 12.* ✆*851 98 44. Open noon–midnight.* Good Polish cooking: bigos *(sauerkraut and meat)*, venison and seafood served in a refined décor with embroidered tablecloths; attentive staff.

⊜⊜ **Bażanciarnia** – *Stary Rynek 94.* ✆*855 33 58. Open daily noon–midnight.* This is an institution. A refined Polish cuisine is served in the dining room enhanced by fine woods and worthy of formal receptions: venison and game are served every day except Thursday, traditionally seafood delivery day.

🚂 TAKING A BREAK

There is a wide choice in the vicinity of the Rynek. Cafés lining the east side of the square (**Arvezo** and **Pub Columbus**) are ideal for an ice cream on summer afternoons.

Cacao Republika – *Ul. Zamkowa 7. Open Mon–Sat 10am–midnight, Sun 11am –11pm*. The temple of hot chocolate a stone's throw from the Rynek. A few tables on the ground floor, but more attractive are the sofas and thick cushions upstairs.

Cocorico – *Ul. Świętosławska 9. Open Mon–Thu, Sun 10am–midnight, Fri-Sat 10-1am*. The atmosphere of the two dining rooms with a Parisian feel is charming enough, but who could resist the coolness of the small flower-decked courtyard, where ice cream and drinks are served?

🍷 BARS

Lizard King – *Stary Rynek 86. www.lizardking.pl. Daily noon–2am*. Rock and blues concerts on Fridays around 10pm. As for the décor... cellos instead of columns and bar shaped like a saxophone!

Proletaryat – *Ul. Wrocławska 9. Open daily noon–1am*. Just a couple of blocks from the town square, you can't miss the bust of Lenin in the window. Beer at low prices and a museum of Socialist Realism to boot.

🛒 SHOPPING

Antyki – *Ul. Wodna, under the arcades. Open Mon–Fri 10am–6pm, Sat 10am–2pm*. A real three-room loft containing the most unusual objects, from stamps to old 78s, gramophones and ancient typewriters.

Antykwariat – *Ul. Klasztorna 1. Open Mon–Fri 11am–6pm, Sat 11am–2pm*. A small choice of objects carefully selected: ornaments, seals, a few rare books and documents as well as small pieces of furniture.

🎭 FESTIVE EVENTS

The calendar is mainly filled with the major trade fairs which take place throughout the year.

Malta Festival Poznań: June.

Midsummer: craftsmen and bric-a-brac traders invade the streets. 24 June.

Jazz Festival: March.

Masks: International Theatre Festival. November.

Feast of Św. Marcin Street: Feast of St Martin Street. November.

Gniezno

The cradle of the Polish State is a small, peaceful town built on a height overlooking a lake. Life flows on undisturbed in the shadows of the towers of the cathedral, which contains the relics of St Adalbert, patron saint of Poland.

A BIT OF HISTORY
The Cradle of the Polish state

According to legend, it was here that Lech, the Poles' legendary ancestor, said goodbye to his brothers Rus and Czech, and founded his tribe's first city. Duke Mieszko I introduced Christianity in 966 but chose to establish Poland's first bishopric in Poznań. His son Bolesław the Brave, Poland's first king, was crowned here and over the centuries, the tradition was perpetuated.

▶ **Population:** 70,200.

⚲ **Michelin Map:** Map of Poland B2 – Województwo of Greater Poland.

▤ **Info:** Ul. Rynek 14 ☏(61) 428 41 00. www. szlakpiastowski.com.pl.

◖ **Location:** 50km northwest of Poznań.

▣ **Parking:** Guarded parking available by the Cathedral.

⌖ **Don't Miss:** The panorama of the town from the cathedral towers.

◷ **Timing:** Allow two hours for exploring Gniezno.

Around the year 1000, Emperor Otto III made a pilgrimage to the grave of St Adalbert, acknowledged the newly founded

St Adalbert

Born in Bohemia in 956, the son of a Czech prince, Adalbert studied in Magdeburg, then became Bishop of Prague. From Rome, he went on missionary work throughout Italy, Germany and Hungary, then visited the court of Bolesław the Brave in Gniezno. He was murdered by pagans in 997 while on an evangelising mission on the shores of the Baltic, but his body was bought for its weight in gold by Bolesław, who had him buried in Gniezno. Stolen in 1039 but partly recovered, the saint's body was buried a second time in Prague.

Polish nation and crowned Bolesław the Brave as King.

SIGHTS

Cathedral★ *(Katedra)*

Erected at the end of the 14C, the cathedral was in fact the fourth sanctuary built on this site since the late 10C. The crypt contains part of the foundations of the pre-Romanesque edifice. This symbol of Polish Christianity houses the 17C silver tomb of the patron saint of Poland, Adalbert, who silently witnessed the coronation of Polish kings over the centuries. The Gothic interior features a Baroque nave surrounded by an ambulatory housing the tombstones of Archbishop Zbigniew Oleśnicki and Archbishop Ignacy Krasicki.

On the south side, a wooden door hides two monumental **bronze doors**★★★ (Ⓞopen Mon–Sat 9am–5.45pm, Sun between masses. ⊚2.5 PLN, Sun free, access from outside), dating from 1175. Eighteen scenes illustrate the life of St Adalbert. This masterpiece of medieval art justifies in itself a visit to the cathedral. Fine panoramic view from the top of the towers (same hours as doors; ⊚3 PLN).

Archdiocesan Museum
(Muzeum Archidiecezji)

Ul. Kolegiaty 2. Ⓞ Open May–Sept Mon–Sat 9am–5.30pm, Sun 9am–4pm; Oct–Apr Tue–Sat 9am–3pm. ⊚6 PLN.

16C wooden sculptures can be seen next to a large Entombment from 1430 and three superb Romanesque chalices from Trzemeszno Abbey.

One of them, made of gold and agate, dating from the 10C, is known as the St Adalbert chalice. Plus a fine collection

GETTING AROUND

BY RAIL – Railway station –
Ul. Dworcowa 13. www.pkp.com.pl.
BY BUS – Bus station – Ul. Dworcowa 15.
www.pks.gniezno.pl.

PRACTICAL INFORMATION

Phone code – ☎061.
Postal code – 62 200.
Tourist office – Ul. Rynek 14. ☎428 41 00. www.szlakpiastowski.com.pl. Open May–Sept Mon–Fri 8am–6pm, Sat 9am–3pm, Sun 10am–2pm; Sept–Apr Mon–Fri 8am–4pm.

of coffin portraits representing the deceased during their funeral, a tradition unique to Poland.

ADDRESSES

🛏 STAY

🛏 **Awo Hotel** – Ul. Warszawska 32. ☎426 11 97. www.hotel-awo.pl. 27 rooms. Situated inside a courtyard opening on a quiet street; small, with very cheap rooms.

🛏 **Pietrak Hotel** – Ul. Chrobrego 3. ☎426 14 97. www.hotel-pietrak.home.pl. 26 rooms. Luxury chain hotel located in the heart of the Old Town. Spacious, tastefully furnished rooms.

🍽 EAT

Many restaurants, particularly along Chrobrego Street, where you will find one after the other.

🍽 **Pod Piątką** – Ul. Tumska 5. Across from the Tourist Office. Homey and stylish, this place is at once a restaurant/bistro/café and offers genuine Polish cuisine.

Biskupin★★

Situated at the end of a peninsula jutting out into a marshy lake between Toruń and Poznań, Biskupin offers a major archaeological insight into Poland's prehistory. The phrase "Polish Pompei" has been used to convey the remarkable state of preservation of the remains and the total immersion in the past experienced by visitors during the fascinating tour of this archaeological park.

A BIT OF HISTORY

A chance discovery

During one of his walks in 1933, a local teacher made one of the most fascinating archaeological discoveries in Poland. He found fragments of fossilised wood once carved by man imbedded in the peat covering the ground of Lake Biskupin's peninsula. Excavations led by Professor Józef Kostrzewski of Poznań University started the following year. It turned out that the wooden remains were perfectly preserved in the marshy soil. Elements that were on the ground remained in place and, once the débris from the roofs and walls had been cleared, it was possible to piece together the structure of the buildings. Rows of logs forming streets became visible, as did the sites of houses and the oval line of 6m-high ramparts. A fortified gate guarded the entrance to the village and a moat used to separate the fortress from the shore. 1936 marked the beginning of the reconstruction of the site, half of which had been explored by 1939. The war interrupted the excavation work, though Heinrich Himmler ordered the sight to be investigated for propaganda purposes so as to prove that the German peoples had conquered the Slavs in prehistoric times as well. Legitimate research started again in 1946 and was completed in 1974.

A haven in the marshes

Built around 700 BC, the Biskupin site is linked to Lusatian culture. It is thought

▶ **Population:** 70,200.

◐ **Michelin Map:** Map of Poland B2 – Województwo of Kuyavia-Pomerania.

Info: Biskupin 17. ℘(52) 302 50 25. www.biskupin.pl. Access via the E261 to Żnin. From there, it is 15km south of Żnin by car or narrow-gauge tourist train to Biskupin *(40min, mid-Apr–Sept; ℘302 04 92; ⊜9 PLN)*. Museum: ℘(52) 302 54 20, (52)302 50 25. www.biskupin.pl. *◐Open daily 8am–6pm. ⊜8/6 PLN;* ℗✕. *Boat trips on the lake 15 Apr–Sept Tue–Sun 9am–5pm. ⊜7 PLN.*

▷ **Location:** 80km south-west of Toruń and 85km northeast of Poznań.

℗ **Parking:** 5 PLN at the large museum lot.

▲ **Kids:** The recreations during the September archaeology festivities.

◐ **Timing:** Two hours are sufficient to visit the site. Allow an afternoon to take in all the activities, particularly in September.

that the lake's level rose in the 6C BC forcing the inhabitants to abandon the village, which was soon repopulated. Around 1,000 people lived in it then, representing about 100 families occupying as many houses laid out in 13 parallel rows. The lake offered a certain amount of protection reinforced by stakes set below the ramparts. It also provided a supply of fish and water fowl, as well as reeds used on the roofs of houses. The surrounding area was cleared for use as arable land and for breeding cattle, sheep, goats and pigs. Horses, as a painting on a vase shows, were used for game hunting in the surrounding forests. Situated at the junction of east-west and north-south trade routes, the community exchanged

Biskupin Archaeological Site

L. Gontier / MICHELIN

pottery, furs, textiles and metal objects. Amber pearls and Egyptian objects were found during the excavations. Biskupin's decline seems to have been sudden. Various hypotheses were put forward: intensive farming could have made the soil barren, the lake's level may have risen as a result of climatic changes in the 5C BC or Scythian raiders may have destroyed the settlement. Whatever it was, the fact that Lusatian cemeteries disappeared proves that the population abandoned the area.

ARCHAEOLOGICAL SITE★★
(Muzeum Archeologiczne w Biskupinie)

From the vast parking area lined with stalls and snack bars, one reaches the entrance to the site on the other side of the tiny platform of the narrow-gauge tourist train linking Żnin and Biskupin. The archaeological park covers 28ha.

The Archaeological Museum stands next to a reconstructed 18C farm. Panels in Polish and English recall the discovery of the site and the different communities that inhabited the region, from the Palaeolithic to the Middle Ages. Life in Biskupin at the time of the Lusatians is illustrated by objects found during excavations. Floats made of bark, harpoons and hooks provide information about fishing techniques and pottery, and weaving-loom weights illustrate various crafts. Urns suggest the Lusatians'

funeral practice of cremation. A large model of the fortress shows the site in its heyday when the best use was made of the space within the enclosure.

Outside, a **wildlife park** shelters the different species that once lived in the area. Up on the hill, open-air **workshops** are set in a clearing. The place comes to life on the third weekend in September, during **Poland's Great Archaeological Festival** when visitors are treated to lectures, recreations, contests and concerts.

Camped on a peninsula, the **fortress** is accessible via two gates, one of which is the historic fortified gateway linked by a wooden floating bridge and protected by *chevaux de frise (defensive frames covered in spikes)*. Half the ramparts and two long buildings out of the 13 which made up the village were reconstructed; they now contain an exhibition of photographs illustrating the progress of the excavations, as well as two houses with their furniture, weaving loom and stone hearth. In summer, costumed extras recreate the atmosphere of centuries past. A marshy area which was never excavated shows what the site was like before the excavation work started.

Boat trips on the lake give visitors a different perspective on the site and more insight into its environment.

Toruń★★

A distinguished charm exudes from Toruń's massive Gothic red-brick churches, town squares, and streets winding among medieval fortifications and granaries. The city is Copernicus' birthplace and was once a Hanseatic port. Pleasant hotels, a variety of restaurants, numerous cafés and theatre performances add to the list of Toruń's assets, not forgetting of course, its glorious architectural heritage, which prompted UNESCO to include the city on its World Heritage List in 1997.

- ▶ **Population:** 200,000.
- **Michelin Map:** Map of Poland B2 – Województwo of Kuyavia-Pomerania.
- **Info:** Rynek Staromiejski 25. ℘(56) 621 09 31. www.it.torun.pl.
- ▶ **Location:** 200km northwest of Warsaw on the way to Gdańsk.
- **Parking:** Guarded parking on Ul. Dominikańska, just north of the Old Town.
- **Don't Miss:** The views of the town from the tower of the cathedral of SS John and from the belfry of the town hall.
- **Timing:** Allow one whole day to visit the city and its main sights, museums and monuments.

A BIT OF HISTORY
A wealthy trading city

In 1233, Hermann von Salza, the grand master of the Order of the Teutonic Knights, granted Toruń a foundation charter. In order to protect its construction, a castle was also erected along the river banks. The settlement grew rapidly. Commerce, stimulated in 1252 by tax exemptions, brought about the town's prosperity and markets were soon trading cloth, salt, spices, wood, fruit and fish. It became imperative to fortify the city and create a municipal council. In 1264, another charter established the eastern suburb as the New Town, where new inhabitants arriving from all over Europe settled. At the end of the 13C, Toruń, then called Thorn and known as the "Queen of the Wisła", joined the Hanseatic League. The town's expansion reached its climax in the 14C and 15C. Wooden buildings, considered unsafe, were replaced by brick ones. However, over the years, the city challenged the

political and economic power of the Teutonic Knights and in 1454, the population took over their fortress and chased them away. The open conflict ceased in 1466 when a second treaty was signed, returning to Poland territories stretching as far as Gdańsk. It is around that time that Copernicus was born. The town fell into decline in the 17C. The Swedish wars dealt a severe blow to Torún, and in 1793, following the partition of Poland, it fell under Prussian rule. In the 19C, it became a fortress surrounded in 1878 by a 22km long perimeter of forts. It returned to Poland after 1918, and got through World War II practically unscathed.

☙ WALKING TOUR
OLD TOWN

The Old Town lies within the remains of medieval fortifications and is prolonged eastwards by the New Town. The former, to the west, centres round the Rynek Staromiejski, the latter, to the east, surrounds the Rynek Nowomiejski (note that the New Town dates from the 13C!). In fact, the two districts are linked and we propose one itinerary for both.

The Town's Coat of Arms

Carried by an angel, it features a rampart with three towers and a gate. One door is ajar as a symbol that the town is open to outside influences which brought prosperity while the other is closed as a symbol of protection.

GETTING AROUND

BY RAIL – *Ul. Kujawska 1.* The main station is situated on the opposite river bank. Access by buses 22 and 27 from John Paul II Avenue. Warsaw–Toruń train journey 2hr30min, Poznań–Toruń 2hr30min.

BY BUS – Bus station – *Ul. Dąbrowskiego 26. www.pks.torun.com.*

Travel agency – PTTK – *Pl. Rapackiego 2. ✆622 49 26. Open Mon–Fri 9am–4pm, Sat 9am–2pm.*

BY CAR – A parking space in the street only costs a few złotys to be paid to a mobile parking attendant. Allow 30 PLN for a night in a car park.

PRACTICAL INFORMATION

Phone code – *✆056.*
Postal code – *87100.*

Tourist office – *Rynek Staromiejski 25. ✆621 09 31. www.it.torun.pl. Open Mon and Sat 9am–4pm, Tue–Fri 9am–6pm, Sun May–Aug 9am–1pm.* Well stocked with guides and maps, some in English. English-speaking staff.

Post offices: *Rynek Staromiejski 15 and Rynek Nowomiejski 25.*

Pharmacy open 24h/day – *Ul. Św. Faustyny 14A.*

Internet Café – *Jeremi. Rynek Staromiejski 33.* Wi-Fi available on main square.

WHERE TO GO

Boat trips along the Wisła: *Statek Pasażerski Wanda – ticket office ✆601 625 682.* 40min cruises. Departures every hour 9am–7pm, except in winter. 🚢14/10 PLN.

▷ *Start the tour from the Rynek, in front of the tourist office.*

The Rynek Staromiejski★★
B1-2

109m long and 104m wide, the Rynek Staromiejski is the historic centre of the city. The square is dominated by the Old Town Hall (Ratusz Staromiejski). On the west side stands the imposing neo-Gothic **post office** from 1881 next to the **Church of the Holy Spirit** (Kościół Św. Ducha) erected in 1756. In front, a **fountain** featuring a young fiddler charming an assembly of frogs represents the local version of the Pied Piper legend.

Old Town Hall★★
(Ratusz Staromiejski) B1

🕐*Open Tue–Sun mid-Apr–Jun 10am–4pm, Jul–Aug 10am–6pm; Sept–mid-Apr 10am–4pm.* 🚢10 PLN.

The Town Hall's red-brick outline dominates the centre of the Rynek. The hall built in the 13C was remodelled in 1393 in pure Gothic style, with two storeys surrounding an inner courtyard. In 1602–04, Dutch architect Anton van

Banks of the River Wisła near town

R. Mattes / MICHELIN

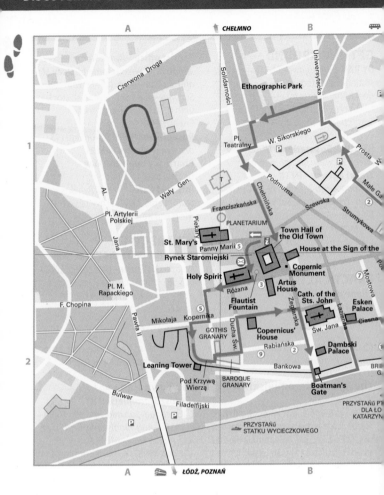

CHEŁMNO

A • B •

ŁÓDŹ, POZNAŃ

Obberghen added another storey, adorned it with stone sculptures and topped the angles with octagonal turrets in Dutch mannerist style. Burned down by the Swedes during the 1703 siege, the edifice was rebuilt between 1722 and 1738. Late-Baroque elements were added at the same time. Today, the conference hall is a concert venue.

The Regional Museum (Muzeum Okręgowe) was housed inside in 1958. Note, on the first floor, an imposing 19C painting celebrating the signing of the Treaty of Toruń in 1466. Further on, the Royal Bedroom, decorated with portraits of Polish monarchs, opens onto other rooms devoted to 18C, 19C and 20C Polish painters. The museum also houses collections of Gothic stained glass, painting and sculpture, as well as an exhibition of sacred art.

Do not miss the **panoramic view** of the town from the tower (🕐 open daily Apr–Sept 10am–8pm, Oct–Mar 10am–4pm; ⊚10 PLN).

Statue of Copernicus
(Pomnik Kopernika) B2

Erected in 1853, this bronze statue by Friedrich Tieck from Berlin is the favourite meeting place of the local population. The Latin inscription on the base reads: "Nicolaus Copernicus from Toruń stopped the sun and the sky and got the earth moving". This, of course, refers to the fact that Copernicus was the first to prove that the earth revolved round the sun and not the other way around.

House of Artus
(Dwór Artusa) B2

Built between 1889 and 1891, this large neo-Renaissance residence stands on the site of a building destroyed at the beginning of the 19C, where the Treaty of Toruń was signed in 1466, ending the conflict with the Teutonic Knights. Today, the building houses a cultural centre.

House at the Sign of the Star★★
(Kamienica pod Gwiazdą) B1-2

🕐 Open Tue–Sun 11am–5pm. ⊛7 PLN, Wed free.

In the late 15C, this elegant house was, the residence of Filippo Buonacorsi, the tutor of King Kazimierz Jagellon's sons. The Gothic building, restored at the end of the 17C, became the Italian-

Nicolaus Copernicus

(Toruń 19 Feb 1473 – Frombork 24 May 1543). A native of the town, Copernicus was not born, as was once believed, at no. 30 Kopernika. His astronomical observations led him to suppport the idea of heliocentrism, thus influencing Galileo Galilei.

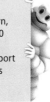

inspired Baroque edifice with a stucco-decorated façade that we see today. Its gable is topped with a golden star, to which it owes its name. It houses a small, but interesting museum of Far-Eastern art with collections of Chinese porcelain and painting, Japanese prints and ceramics and Indian sculptures, as well as bronzes going back to the 17C BC.

St Mary's Church
(Kościół NMP) A1
Ul. Panny Marii.
This massive brick-built hall church was erected by the Franciscans between 1343 and 1370. According to the rule of the order, three pinnacles replaced the usual bell tower. Inside, the church is adorned like a medieval manuscript; three naves soaring to a height of 27m contain large frescoes from the late 14C and star vaulting decorated with floral motifs. Note the 15C stalls, the high altar from 1731 featuring the Visitation and the Baroque mausoleum of the Swedish princess Anna Vasa, sister of King Sigismund III.

▷ *Starting from the Rynek, follow Różana Street, lined with arcades sheltering waffle sellers, then turn left onto Piekary Street. Pod Krzywą Wieżą Street skirts the ramparts and the Leaning Tower (Krzywa Wieża).*

Leaning Tower
(Krzywa Wieża) A2
This is one of the city's emblems. The 13C square tower was turned into a prison in the 18C before becoming a residence. It gave rise to a few legends and while its inclination (1.4m) may in reality be due to subsidence, some think it is a punishment inflicted upon

the town which was the birthplace of Copernicus, whose heretical theories displaced the Earth from the centre of the universe.

▷ *Rabiańska Street runs between two granaries, one Gothic and one Baroque, both due to be restored. Note the windows of the latter, on the right: their frames are shaped like wheat sacks. Turn left onto Ducha Św. Street then right onto Kopernika.*

Copernicus' House★
(Dom Kopernika) B2
Ul. Kopernika 15/17. ⊙*Open Tue–Sun Jan–Apr 10am–4pm; late May–Sept 10am–6pm; Oct–Dec 10am–4pm.* ⊜*10 PLN.*
These two 15C Gothic houses featuring elegant gables were restored in the early 1960s. The museum is housed in both buildings but Copernicus was born in **no. 17** on 19 February 1473. An exhibition on five levels recalls the astronomer's life and works through documents and objects. It shows how his unorthodox theories completely changed our idea of the universe. One room contains a model of the town in the 15C. The model is presented as part of an 18min sound and light presentation *(separate ticket ⊜12 PLN, or buy a combo ticket for 18 PLN)*. The building on the left displays the reconstructed interior of a Gothic house with its kitchen and money-changer's office. Other

Toruń's Rynek

rooms show portraits of Copernicus and facsimiles of his works.

Cathedral of SS John★
(Katedra śś. Janów) B2
Ul. Żeglarska 16.

Work began on the sanctuary dedicated to St John the Baptist and St John the Evangelist shortly after the foundation of the town. A 52m-high tower was added in 1433. It houses Poland's second-largest historic bell, the Tuba Dei *(God's Trumpet)*, cast in 1500. The brick building with Gothic frescoes on the walls was remodelled until the end of the 15C and Copernicus was probably christened inside. Around 1530, it was taken over by the Protestants, who whitewashed the walls to hide the frescoes and only one, depicting the Crucifixion, is visible today in the north part of the chancel. Returned to the Catholics in 1596, the church became the cathedral of Toruń's diocese in 1992.

Walking down Żeglarska Street towards the river, note, at **no. 8** on your right, the Baroque stucco decoration of the façade of the **Dąmbski Palace** erected in 1693 for the bishop of Kujawy, now occupied by the Fine Arts Department of the Copernicus University. The Banks of the River Wisła are reached through the **Boatmen's Gate** (Brama Żeglarska), once the official gateway for visitors arriving by way of the river and later turned into a prison. Walking along the banks of the Wisła, one gets an unobstructed view of the city's ramparts. This is where the merchant ships used to be moored and where, today, you will find a floating restaurant and boats inviting you for a trip on the river. *Walk up Łazienna Street.*

Esken Palace
(Pałac Eskenów) B2
Ul. Łazienna 16. ○Open Tue–Sun 11am–5pm. ◈7 PLN, Wed free.

This former medieval house, today known as the "red granary" belonged to the Esken family in about 1460. The edifice was modified at the end of the 16C into a Renaissance palace featuring a doorway carved by Willem van

Toruń's Gingerbread

Piernik Toruński: The recipe of this speciality, already mentioned in the 14C, remained a secret for a long time and was only revealed in 1725 in a medical publication. Honey and spices are the main ingredients. Made in different carefully sculpted shapes (characters, buildings), this gingerbread owes its taste and crispness to a long maturing process in a cellar. It is a prize gift, which was once traditionally included in dowries and offered to kings. Toruń has Europe's only museum dedicated to this tasty treat, in the Old Town on Ul. Rabiańska 9, where visitors can take part in gingerbread production (Muzeum Piernika).

den Blocke, a sculptor from Gdańsk. At the end of the 19C, it was turned into a granary, then into a warehouse for the Prussian army before finally being restored at the end of the 20C. It now houses the History and Archaeology Department of the Regional Museum.

◯ *Follow Ciasna Street and cross Mostowa Street at the end of which stands the Bridge Gate (Brama Mostowa), which used to be the starting point of ferries crossing the river. It owes its name to a bridge built around 1500, which was for a long time one of only two bridges to span the Wisła (the other was in Kraków), and disappeared in the 18C. Continue along the narrow Ciasna Street and walk across the ramparts to the castle of the Teutonic Knights.*

Teutonic Knights' Castle
(Zamek Krzyżacki) C2
Ul. Przedzamcze. ○Open daily 10am–6pm. ◈6 PLN.

Erected around 1235 to become the seat of the Teutonic authority and to protect the town's builders from Prussian raids, it originally stood in the southeast corner of the fortifications. On 8 February 1454, it was taken and destroyed by the population rising against the order's domination.

Today its ruins are spread over an open space, surrounded by the ramparts which separated the Old Town from the New Town and give a fair idea of what the austere fortress looked like. The best- preserved part, the Gdanisko Tower, reached via a suspended gallery, was originally used as latrines. The cellars now host concerts and cultural events.

⬤ *Pass through the fortified gate to reach Wielkie Garbary Street and walk towards the Rynek Nowomiejski along Ślusarska Street.*

The New Town Square
(Rynek Nowomiejski) C1

It marks the centre of the New Town erected from 1264 onwards, when the Old Town became too small to absorb the influx of new inhabitants. In the south corner stands the **Blue Apron Tavern** (Gospoda Pod Modrym Fartuchem), opened in 1489. The middle of the square is occupied by the Evangelical church built in the 19C on the site of the former Gothic town hall. It was until 1945, the city's Lutheran church. The lofty St James' Church rises in the eastern corner of the Rynek.

St James' Church
(Kościół Św. Jakuba) C1

Built from 1309 onwards to serve as the New Town's parish church, it was only completed in 1424. Its basilica plan, unique in Toruń, comprises a 21m-high central nave, twice as high as the two naves flanking it. The ensemble is dominated by an unusual tower with a double roof. The 14C pointed-arched doorway heralds the interior filled with Baroque altars and well-preserved Gothic wall paintings depicting scenes from the New Testament. Note, at the end of the south nave, a Gothic Crucifix known as "Christ and the Tree of Life".

⬤ *Walk to Małe Garbary Street via Król. Jadwigi Street and continue as far as Wały gen. Sikorskiego Avenue.*

Ethnographic Park B1

Ul. Wały gen. Sikorskiego 19. ⏱*Open mid-Apr–Jun Tue, Thu 9am–7pm, Wed, Fri 9am–4pm, Sat–Sun 10am–6pm; Jul–Aug Tue, Thu, Sat–Sun 10am–6pm, Wed, Fri 9am–4pm; Oct–mid-Apr Tue–Fri 9am–4pm, Sat–Sun 10am–4pm.* ⬤*9 PLN (Park only).*

A Prussian arsenal built in 1824 and a bastion from the 19C fortifications guard the entrance to this traditional village erected in the middle of town. Rural architecture from Toruń's surrounding area is represented by farms, watermills and windmills, a bread oven, a smithy and beehives, which all together, contain some 50,000 pieces of furniture, tools, implements and objects of daily life. The complex is at its most lively in summer when dozens of costumed extras and craftsmen bring past trades back to life.

⬤ *Cross the avenue towards the Theatre Square then return to the Rynek Staromiejski along the pedestrianised Chełmińska Street.*

EXCURSION
Chełmno★

⬤*45km northwest of Toruń.*

The "city of the nine hills" is built on a promontory overlooking the Wisła. As in Toruń, the Teutonic Knights left their stamp on this now-sleepy town and visitors have the chance to wander along the dusty streets of this remarkably well-preserved city that seems unaware of its architectural wonders.

Chełmno has retained its original grid plan and the centre boasts a vast **Rynek**, bright and open, dominated by a fine **Town Hall**★ housing a small museum. Built in Gothic style in 1298, the edifice now features an elegant Renaissance outline. Its southwest façade bears the standard metre, the unit of measure used by the town from medieval times.

Chełmno boasts six Gothic brick churches and monasteries. **The Parish Church of the Assumption** (Kościół Farny pw Wniebowzięcia NMP) is the most impressive. It houses the relics of St Valentine, the patron saint of lovers.

ADDRESSES

🛏 STAY

Most hotels are situated in the Old Town, in the vicinity of the Rynek.

Pod Orłem – *Ul. Mostowa 17. ☎622 50 25. www.hotel.torun.pl. 41 rooms.* A venerable institution, over a century old which gets rid of its quaint appearance a little more with each refurbishment. The rooms are clean but basic; pleasant family-style welcome.

Heban Hotel – *Ul. Małe Garbary 7. ☎652 15 55. www.hotel-heban.com.pl. 19 rooms.* This high-class establishment is housed in a former Renaissance residence refurbished in a modern style. The professional welcome and spotless rooms will satisfy the most demanding traveller. Wi-Fi in all rooms.

Petite Fleur – *Ul. Piekary 25. ☎621 51 00. www.petitefleur.pl. 22 rooms.* The hotel is as renowned as its **restaurant** serving good Franco-Polish cuisine at reasonable prices. Fine, tastefully decorated rooms; preference should be given to those in front, overlooking the street. Internet connection.

Retman Hotel – *Ul. Rabiańska 15. ☎657 44 60. www.hotelretman.pl. 29 rooms.* The rooms are plain but very comfortable in this high building situated between the Rynek and the Wisła. Very good value for money *(quality-service-price)*.

Spichrz Hotel – *Ul. Mostowa 1. ☎657 11 40. www.spichrz.pl. 19 rooms.* Backing onto the Mostowa Gate, this hotel is housed in a former granary built in 1719 and restored in 2003. The rooms have large windows; a décor of wood and natural fibres adds a distinctive warm touch to their comfort. Copious varied breakfast. Internet connection in all rooms.

🍽 EAT

Czarna Oberża – *Ul. Rabiańska 9. Open daily 11am–midnight.* Wooden décor and furniture give this self-service restaurant a rustic feel; good Polish cooking at unbeatable prices.

Manekin Union Pacific – *Stary Rynek 16. ☎621 05 04. Open Mon–Fri noon–11pm, Sat–Sun 10am–midnight.* This popular restaurant deserves its success. Crêpes are the stars of the menu, which lists no fewer than 40 different kinds of savoury and sweet ones. In summer, tables are set up on the square outside.

Leniwe – *Ul. Ślusarska 5. ☎477 54 03. Open daily 11am–9pm.* Very original choice of pierogi in a sleek, modern setting. Try the amazing plum-filled or gingerbread-flavoured dumplings. Wine and beer also available.

☕ TAKING A BREAK

Róze i Zen – *Ul. Podmurna 18. ☎621 05 21. Open Mon–Thu 11am–10pm, Fri–Sat 11am–11pm, Sun 11am–10pm.* A delightful unassuming place with an impressive menu offering a comprehensive choice of food and drink, in particular tea served in a very cosy 1930s-style room or in the courtyard set up like an open-air house with dressers, mirrors and paintings on the walls and stairs leading up to an imaginary first floor.

Kafeteria Artus – *Rynek Staromiejski 6. ☎621 11 43. Open daily 10am–midnight.* A very classy and slightly formal bar-tearoom located in the inner courtyard of the House of Artus. The glass-and-metal modern architecture blends well with the brick structure of the historic building.

🛍 SHOPPING

Pierniczek – *Ul. Żeglarska 24. Open daily 10am–8pm.* Gingerbread is the speciality here.

Emporium – *Ul. Piekary 28. ☎657 61 08. www.emporium.torun.com.pl. Open Mon–Fri 10am–6pm, Sat 10am–4pm, Jul–Aug Sun 10am–4pm.* Gingerbread and T-shirts on the theme of Copernicus and his theories.

🎭 FESTIVE EVENTS

Song of Songs Festival: International Ecumenical Festival of Christian Music. Early June.

Toruń's Feast: Celebrated on 24 June, the feast day of St John the Baptist, the patron saint of the town.

Toruń Muzyka i Architektura: Concerts given in outstanding monuments. July and August.

Jazz Od Nowa Festival: 2–3 days in Feb.

Toruński Festiwal Nauki i Sztuki: Art and science festival. Late April.

Kontakt: Theatre festival. May.

Old Medieval Crane, Gdańsk
© Polish National Tourist Office

POMERANIA

Pomerania is a land of austere beauty, centred around the Vistula River valley and river delta. Dense forests stretch to the west of the Vistula, and in the east begins Poland's lake district. Crowning the region at the mouth of the Vistula is proud and defiant Gdańsk, whose severe and imposing Gothic churches on the one hand are suitably Teutonic, but on the other, the city's municipal and merchant architecture seems transplanted directly from Flanders.

Highlights

1 **Gdańsk's Royal Way** and the riverside quay (p359–p362)

2 **Oliwa Cathedral** and its magnificent organ (p371)

3 Shifting sand dunes of **Słowiński National Park** (p379)

4 Europe's largest **Gothic castle** in **Malbork** (p381)

Baltic Coast

Heading north from Gdańsk you pass through its satellite cities of Sopot and Gdynia, the former built for pleasure, the latter for trade and transport. Then you reach the Hel peninsula, which delicately protrudes into the Baltic Sea and offers clean, sandy beaches and forests over its narrow length. Following the sea coast you arrive at Łeba, another haven for holidaymakers. But in addition to the beaches for swimming and the picturesque fishermen's boats, there are the unique shifting sand dunes of the Słowiński National Park. A rare opportunity to roam through a desert like environment in this part of Europe. South of Gdańsk are fertile lands and the former headquarters of the Teutonic Knights, Malbork Castle. This colossal castle, the largest Gothic structure still standing in Europe, dominates the entire surrounding landscape. Arriving by train at Malbork is an unforgettable experience as the rails pass through the outer reaches of the castle ramparts. Here not only do you feel the haunting presence of these Germanic crusaders, but in nearly every town a red-brick church or castle punctuates the landscape.

Neptune fountain, Gdańsk

© Polish National Tourist Office

Malbork Castle

Sopot Beach, on the Baltic sea

© Krzyssagit/Dreamstime.com

Baltic Amber

Amber was discovered on the Baltic coast at the mouth of the Vistula River in pre-historic times and became a precious material for jewellery and ornaments, and was highly sought after because of its supposed magical properties. For example, amber can acquire an electric charge when rubbed (this is also one way of testing the authenticity of amber jewellery) and the English word electricity comes from the Greek word for amber, *elektron*. Amber is considered a precious stone, but it is not a mineral; it's actually a preserved amorphous tree resin from ancient trees that grew tens of millions of years ago. Amber can be found in hundreds of shades and colours, from black to an off-white. It can provide a glimpse into the past because of the inclusion of leaves, hairs, and perfectly embalmed insects, as made famous by the acclaimed Steven Spielberg film, *Jurassic Park*.

Baltic amber was traded all over Europe, by land and by sea. Two of Poland's most important rivers, the Vistula and Oder, were essential parts of the Amber Road that led south to the Roman empire. During the Middle Ages, the city of Gdańsk was the main exporter and manufacturer of amber ornaments and the Teutonic Knights controlled and profited immensely from its trade. Fishermen caught keeping pieces of amber for themselves were sentenced to death and many coastal towns had gallows just for that purpose. The Protestant Reformation caused a downturn in the amber trade because, unlike Catholics, Protestants did not use rosaries, which at that time were often adorned with amber beads. Amber can still be found at the Baltic seaside and no one will hang you if you slip a piece into your pocket while strolling along the beach, but most amber for sale today comes from mines in Kaliningrad, Russia.

Ancient frog within baltic amber

© Galyna Andrushko/Dreamstime.com

Gdańsk★★★

The free city of Danzig, an old
Hanseatic town, hit the world's
headlines during the first few days
of September 1939 when Hitler
invaded Poland. Its return to Poland
was marked by a devastating fire
that left it a heap of smouldering
rubble. Although reduced to
ashes, the town was meticulously
reconstructed brick by brick, as if
nothing had happened: this says
a lot about the character of this
proud city. The architectural style
is reminiscent of Flanders and the
city is an inviting place for those
who love to stroll at leisure. The
birthplace of the "Solidarność"
trade union, it is also famous as
the capital of the amber trade.
Gdańsk celebrated its millennium
in 1997, and together with Gdynia
and Sopot, its sister cities on the
coast, it is part of the Trójmiasto
(Tri-City) conurbation extending
35km along the coast and home
to some 800,000 inhabitants. Each
town has its own well-defined role:
Gdańsk concentrates on historic and
cultural tourism, Sopot takes care of
seaside tourism and Gdynia fills the
economic role.

A BIT OF HISTORY
A troubled past
The missionary bishop Adalbert of Bohemia visited Gyddanyzc in 997, the year
it was granted its town charter. After
becoming the capital of the Dukes of
Pomerania in the 12C, the city fell into
the hands of the Teutonic Knights in
1308 and began life as a trading town
by joining the Hanseatic League in 1361.
It remained under the domination of
the Knights until 1454, when the Polish
population rebelled and destroyed
the fortress. During its heyday in the
16C–17C the city welcomed Renaissance influences, flourished and prospered. Twice besieged by the Swedes
in the 17C and by the Russians in 1734,
it fell under Prussian rule in 1793 following the second partition of Poland,

- **Population:** 461,653.
- **Michelin Map:** Map of Poland B1 – Województwo of Pomerania.
- **Info:** Ul. Długi Targ 28/29. ℘(58) 301 43 55. www.gdansk4u.pl.
- **Location:** 348km north-west of Warsaw, around Gdańsk Bay (*Zatoka Gdańska*), on the shores of the Baltic Sea.
- **Parking:** Guarded parking throughout the centre, 2 PLN an hour.
- **Don't Miss:** The Royal Way, Hans Memling's Last Judgement in the National Museum, the view from the tower of St Mary's Church, the boat trip to Westerplatte, organ concerts in Oliwa Cathedral, Sopot's pier.
- **Kids:** Sharks and other sea creatures at Gdynia Aquarium.
- **Timing:** Allow a minimum of two days to explore Gdańsk's Old Town, half a day for a tour of Westerplatte, another half a day to wander through the Oliwa district and a whole day to make the most of Sopot and Gdynia.
- **Also See:** Westerplatte, Oliwa, Hel.

was renamed Danzig and lost many of
its privileges. Between 1807 and 1815,
while the area was under French control, the western part of the coastal strip
including Sopot, was given to the free
city of Gdańsk while the eastern part
remained in Polish hands; an enclave
in Polish territory was thus created.
Returned to Prussia in 1815 following
the Congress of Vienna, on account of
its mainly German-speaking population, the town went through virtually
the same process at the end of World

GETTING THERE

BY AIR – Airport – Lech Walesa
Gdańsk-Trójmiasto Airport –
Ul. Słowakiego 200. ℘348 11 63.
www.airport.Gdańsk.pl. 10km west
of the centre. Flights to and from
Warsaw, London, Hamburg,
Copenhagen, Frankfurt and Munich.
210 bus to central station or no. 110
bus to Gdańsk Wrzeszcz Station.

GETTING AROUND

BY RAIL – Railway stations –
Gdańsk Główny Central Station
is a 10min walk from the town centre.
Kolejowa PKP *(Ul. Podwale Grodzkie 1).*
The **SKM Regional Network Station**
(towards Sopot and Gdynia) is
situated next door *(accessible via the
subway).* Trains every 10min from
platforms no. 3–6.
BY BUS – Bus station – PKS, *Ul. 3
Maja 12* . Behind the railway station via
the subway.
BY CAR – Car hire – Avis *(℘348 12 89),*
Budget *(www.budget.pl)* and
Hertz have a counter at the airport
(Ul. Słowackiego 200).
Avis – *Ul. Podwale Grodzkie 9.* ℘300
60 05. *www.avis.pl.* Open Mon–Fri
9am–5pm, Sat 9am–1pm.
Hertz –*Ul. Heweliusza 22.* ℘301 40 45.
www.hertz.com.pl. Open Mon–Fri
8am–5pm.
BY BOAT – Harbour station –
The ferry landing stage is in **Nowy
Port** *(Ul. Przemysłowa 1),* 7km north of
the town centre. Access by train from
Gdańsk Glowny Station. Get off at
Gdańsk-Brzeźno. The main shipping
lines are: **Polferries.** *Ul. Przemysłowa 1.*
℘343 18 87. *www.polferries.pl.*
Stena Line. *Ul. Kwiatkowskiego 60
(Gdynia).* ℘660 92 00. *www.stenaline.pl.*
Żegluga Gdańska. *Ul. Pończosników 2.*
℘301 74 26. *www.zegluga.pl.* This ferry
line has, since 1946, been providing a
shuttle service to Westerplatte, Sopot,
Gdynia and Hel. The ticket office is
located near the bridge, beyond the
Green Gate, set back from the lowered
quay. 50min one way to Westerplatte,
1hr 40min for the full tour.

PRACTICAL INFORMATION

Phone code – ℘*(0)58.*
Postal codes –
Gdańsk – *80-000 to 80-900.*
Sopot – *81-700 to 81-900.*
Gdynia – *81-300 to 81- 600* .

GDAŃSK
**Tourist Offices – Gdańska
Informacja Turystyczna PTTK –**
Ul. Długa 45. ℘301 91 51 *www.pttk-
Gdańsk.pl.* Open Mon–Fri 8am–6pm,
Sat–Sun 8.30am–4.30pm. Opposite the
Town Hall of the Main Town. The staff
speak English and some literature is
available in English. Central reservation
service for finding accommodation
in private rooms: the office provides
addresses and charges 5 PLN for
booking. Sale of maps, books, guides,
bus and ferry tickets.
Gdańska Tourist Organisation – .
Ul. Długi Targ 28/29. ℘301 43 55.
www.gdansk4u.pl. Open Jun–Aug
8.30am–6.30pm, Sept–May 9am–5pm.
At the end of the street near the
Green Gate. Has an annexe in a green
kiosk located opposite the main
station *(take the subway and come
up on the central island). Ul. Podwale
Grodzkie.* Open Mon–Fri 8am–4pm,
Sat–Sun 10am–2pm.
Centrum Kultury Gdańsk –
Ul. Korzenna 33/35. ℘301 10 51.
www.nck.org.pl. Open Mon–Fri 10am–
4pm. Here is your opportunity to visit
the former Town Hall of the Old Town,
which stages free exhibitions and
concerts. Bookshop.
Useful tips. – The fortnightly
brochure in English *Gdańsk In Your
Pocket (http://inyourpocket.com/
poland/gdansk)* is an excellent
handbook to carry around. The free
bi-monthly brochure *The Visitor* (Baltic
edition) also provides a wealth of
information about Gdańsk and Sopot.
Post Office – *Urząd Pocztowy.
Ul. Długa 23/28.* Open Mon–Fri 8am–
8pm, Sat 9am–3pm. A fine 19C
building. Telephone exchange on the
right of the entrance. Annexe inside
the building of the Postal Museum.

Guides Office – For information, contact the Tourist Office in Długa Street.
Police – ☎997 – Police station: Ul. Piwna 32/35 – ☎321 46 22.
Emergency – ☎999
Municipal police – ☎986
Fire brigade – ☎998
Pharmacy open 24hr/day – Apteka Dworcowa – Dworzec Główny (central station). ☎346 25 40.
Banks – A kantor is open 24hr/day inside the central station.

SOPOT
Tourist Office (Informacja Turystyczna Sopot IT) –
Ul. Dworcowa 4. ☎550 37 83.
www.sopot.pl. Open Jun–Sept daily 9am–8pm; Oct–May daily 10am–6pm.
On the left as you leave the station, behind the Rezydent Hotel as you go up Monte Cassino Street. Deals with accommodation in private rooms.
PTTK. Ul. Niepodległości 771. ☎551 06 18. www.sopot.pl/pttk. Open Mon–Fri 9am–5pm, Sat 10am–3pm.
Post Office – Ul. Kościuszki 2 (Sopot). www.poczta-polska.pl.

Pharmacy open 24hr/day – Apteka "Pod Orłem" – Ul. Boh. Monte Cassino. 37. ☎551 10 18.

GDYNIA
Tourist Office (Miejska Informacja Turystyczna IT Gdynia) –
Ul. 10 Lutego 24 . ☎622 37 66.
www.gdynia.pl – Mon–Fri 9am–6pm, Sat 10am–4pm – On the main street that leads from the Gdynia Główna railway to the water and aquarium.
Baltic Tourist Information Centre (Baltycki Punkt Informacji Turystycznej) – Al. Jana Pawła II. ☎620 77 11. May–Sept Mon–Fri 9am–6pm, Sat 10am–5pm, Sun 10am–4pm. A real lookout at the extremity of the long pier, on the right, beyond the aquarium.

WHERE TO GO
A combined ticket makes it possible, for 18 PLN (concessions 10 PLN), to visit the Central Maritime Museum, the Sołdek Ship, and the Wooden Crane. (Also includes the shuttle boat round-trip tkt.) Information from the ticket offices of these monuments.

War I when, in 1919, under the terms of the Treaty of Versailles, the territory of the free city of Danzig, under the authority of the League of Nations, was created between Poland and Germany. The accession to power of Hitler, who wanted to deprive Poland of an outlet to the sea and to annexe Danzig by linking it to Germany via a secure militarised strip, progressively undermined the foundations of the free city system.

On 1 September 1939, the battleship Schleswig-Holstein attacked the Polish garrison in Westerplatte and Hitler, intent on breaking through the Danzig corridor, invaded Poland, thus sparking off World War II. The heavy fighting, which led to the town's liberation by Russian troops in March 1945, left it in ruins. After the Allied victory, Gdańsk was returned to Poland, giving the country greater access to the sea.

A City in Ruins
When it was time to assess the damage in April 1945, about 90 per cent of the historic centre and 60 per cent of the periphery were found to be entirely

Gdańsk's Who's Who
Gdańsk has had several illustrious children, such as astronomer Johannes Hevelius (1611–87), Gabriel Daniel Fahrenheit (1686–1736), the inventor of the mercury thermometer, philosopher Arthur Schopenhauer (1788–1860) and German-speaking writer and winner of the Nobel Prize in Literature Günter Grass, born in 1927. The actor Klaus Kinski (1926–91) was born in Sopot.

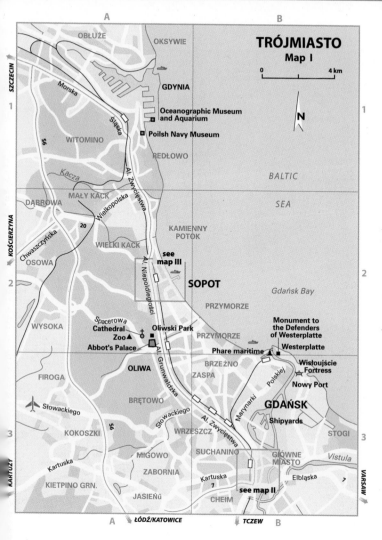

TRÓJMIASTO
Map I
0   4 km

destroyed. Some 6,000 buildings were completely wiped out, 1,300 partially. Three million cu m of rubble remained to be cleared. However, not only did the end of the war result in an assessment of the architectural heritage, it also meant significant demographic changes. The census conducted on 16 June 1945, recorded 8,000 Poles and 124 000 Germans who were forced to leave for Germany in 1946. Its German population having been expelled and nearly all its original inhabitants having disappeared, the newly Polish city was able to start afresh and plan its repopulation and reconstruction process. Between 1947–48, several thousand Polish families, originally from Galicia, who, when the new frontiers were established, found themselves in Soviet territory and were moved to Pomerania, Warmia and Masuria.

Even though the change in the population was such that today there is little chance of finding long-established inhabitants, it is immediately obvious that the will to preserve the soul of the town, without making a clean sweep of its past and erasing its German character forever, weighed heavily on the decision

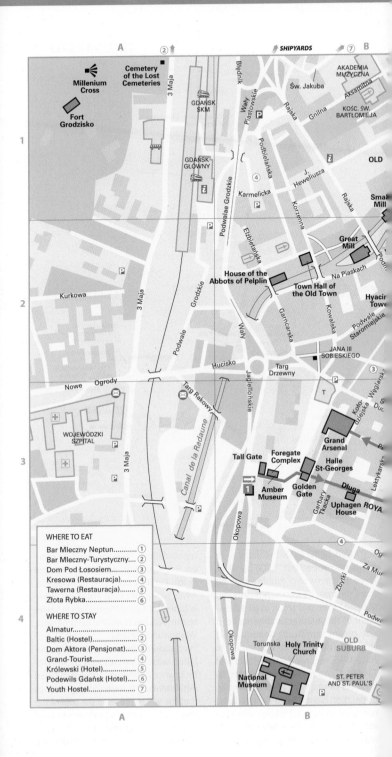

A · B

🚢 *SHIPYARDS*

Millenium Cross

Cemetery of the Lost Cemeteries

Fort Grodzisko

GDAŃSK SKM

GDAŃSK GŁÓWNY

AKADEMIA MUZYCZNA

Św. Jakuba

KOŚC. ŚW. BARTŁOMIEJA

OLD

Błędnik

Rajska

Gnilna

Podbielańska

Karmelicka

J. Hewieliusza

Korzenna

Rajska

Smal Mill

Elżbietańska

Kurkowa

3 Maja

Grodzkie

Podwale

House of the Abbots of Pelplin

Town Hall of the Old Town

Great Mill

Na Piaskach

Podi

Hyacir Towe

Garncarska

Kowalska

Podwale Staromiejskie

JANA III SOBIESKIEGO

Nowe Ogrody

Hucisko

Targ Drzewny

Jagiellonskie

Targ Rakowy

Canal de la Radaune

WOJEWÓDZKI SZPITAL

3 Maja

Tall Gate

Foregate Complex

Halle St-Georges

Grand Arsenal

Amber Museum

Golden Gate

Długa

Uphagen House

ROYA

Garbary Tkacka

Lektykars

Koło-dziejska Duc

Węglarsk

Okopowa

Okopowa

Torunska

Holy Trinity Church

National Museum

OLD SUBURB

ST. PETER AND ST. PAUL'S

Za Mur

Zbytki

Podwe

Og

WHERE TO EAT

Bar Mleczny Neptun...............①
Bar Mleczny-Turystyczny....②
Dom Pod Łososiem................③
Kresowa (Restauracja).........④
Tawerna (Restauracja)........⑤
Złota Rybka...........................⑥

WHERE TO STAY

Almatur..................................①
Baltic (Hostel).......................②
Dom Aktora (Pensjonat)......③
Grand-Tourist........................④
Królewski (Hotel)..................⑤
Podewils Gdańsk (Hotel).....⑥
Youth Hostel..........................⑦

A · B

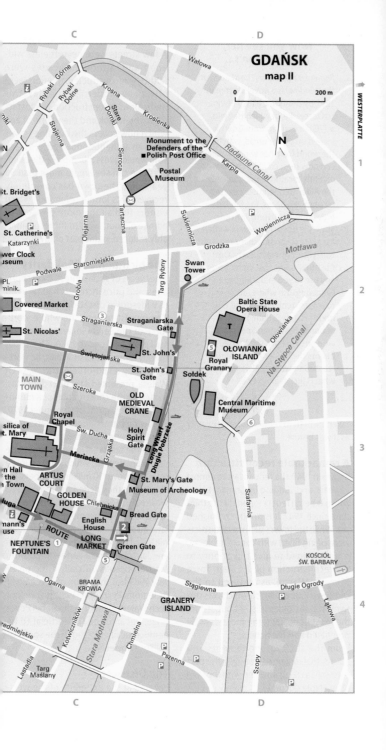

C   D

Wałowa

GDAŃSK
map II

0   200 m

WESTERPLATTE

N

Rybaki Górne

Rybaki Dolne

Krosna

Stare Domki

Stajenna

Krosienka

Radaune Canal

Karpia

1

Monument to the
Defenders of the
■ Polish Post Office

St. Bridget's

Sieroca

Postal
Museum

Tartaczna

Sukiennicza

Wapiennicza

St. Catherine's

Katarzynki

Olejarna

Grodzka

Motława

wer Clock
useum

Podwale

Staromiejskie

Grobla

Targ Rybny

Swan
Tower

2

Pl.
minik.

Covered Market

Straganiarska

Baltic State
Opera House

St. Nicolas'

Świętojańska

Straganiarska
Gate

T

Ołowianka

OŁOWIANKA
ISLAND

Na Stępce Canal

St. John's

Royal
Granary

MAIN
TOWN

Szeroka

St. John's
Gate

Sołdek

Royal
Chapel

Św. Ducha

Grząska

OLD
MEDIEVAL
CRANE

Central Maritime
Museum

silica of
t. Mary

Mariacka

Holy
Spirit
Gate

Long Wharf

Długie Pobrzeże

3

n Hall
the
n Town

ARTUS
COURT

St. Mary's Gate
Museum of Archeology

Szafarnia

GOLDEN
HOUSE

Chlebnicka

uga

English
House

Bread Gate

2

nann's
use

ROUTE

NEPTUNE'S
FOUNTAIN

LONG
MARKET

Green Gate

KOŚCIÓŁ
ŚW. BARBARY

Ogarna

BRAMA
KROWIA

Stągiewna

Długie Ogrody

Łąkowa

4

redmiejskie

Kotwiczników

Stara Motława

Chmielna

GRANERY
ISLAND

Szopy

Lastadia

Targ
Maślany

Pszenna

C   D

Now you see her, now you don't...

Panienka z Okienka (The Maiden at the Window) is a novel written in 1891 by Deotyma, alias Jadwiga Łuszczewska, in which Hedwig, a 17C fair maiden from Gdańsk locked up by her uncle, watches the world from her window. She can now be seen at her window, recently located in the gable of the Aldermen's House. Coveted by photographers, the fair lady only appears at 1pm, 3pm and 5pm *(she doesn't appear in winter)* for a few seconds... so make sure your camera is ready. On the other hand, that won't be any use to you in the adjoining Golden House where, according to a persistent legend, the ghost of Judyta Bahr, the wife of burgomaster Jan Speymann who once lived in the house, haunts the corridors whispering reassuring words: "Always do what is just, fear no one."

taken in 1948 to rebuild Gdańsk exactly as it was before.

A remarkable reconstruction

Begun in 1949, the rebuild lasted almost 20 years, and, judging by Granary Island which is being redeveloped for the third time since 1947, it is not quite finished yet. While the town's peripheral districts were being filled with concrete blocks, it was decided to give top priority to the reconstruction of the Main Town (Główne Miasto), as opposed to the Old Town (Stare Miasto), which was certainly not the oldest district but, in fact the most important, the most densely populated and the richest.

From the shells of monuments and houses that remained standing, this part of town was reconstructed with the help of available documents, mainly photos and souvenirs since most of the town's archives had gone up in smoke in 1945. Several houses, such as Steffens House,

were also reconstructed from the ornamental elements found in the rubble.

A few streets were nevertheless widened and, although façades were faithfully reconstructed, interiors were obviously modernised. Today, this meticulous reconstruction has lost its newly built look and the patina of age which now covers the buildings gives them an authentic appearance. In fact, who would guess that most of the buildings one can see are no more than 50 years old. The town has completely recovered its former splendour, which visitors find all the more pleasant to admire on foot, since traffic is considerably reduced in this part of town.

The birthplace of Solidarity

After years of social unrest, food shortages, and price increases had resulted in widespread dissatisfaction with the Communist regime, the whole workforce of the Lenin Shipyards went on strike on 14 August 1980. The strike quickly turned into a sit-in and the workers, led by a laid-off electrician, Lech Wałęsa, presented a list of 21 demands, including the construction of a monument to the victims of December 1970. Following bitter negotiation, an agreement was signed, allowing the foundation of the first legal independent trade union, *Solidarność*, which soon counted in its ranks over 10 million members; for 16 months they defied the regime and worried the Soviet Union. During the night of 12–13 December 1981, martial law was proclaimed by the Military Committee of National Defence led by General Jaruzelski and a curfew imposed. Martial law was officially lifted on 22 July 1983 but the union only regained its legitimacy in April 1989, just before Lech Wałęsa, winner of the Nobel Peace Prize, became the first official to be democratically elected in the soon-to-collapse Soviet Bloc.

The Districts

Located at the extremity of the western arm of the Wisła, known as the dead Wisła (Wisła Martwa), Gdańsk's historic town used to lie between the River

On the River Motława

C. Hervé–Bazin / MICHELIN

Motława and the Radunia Canal (Kanał Raduni). It formerly consisted of the **Old Town** (Stare Miasto) in the north, the **Main Town** (Główne Miasto), the **Old Suburb** (Stare Przedmieście), **Wheat Granary Island** (Wyspa Spichrzów) and the **Lower Town** (Dolne Miasto) in the south. Following the war damage, the Main Town was the only one to be reconstructed exactly as it was before and the Old Town only recovered some of its buildings and a few churches. Gdańsk's plan is that of a medieval port town with some of its streets running parallel to the quay while others are perpendicular to it.

① THE MAIN TOWN★★★
(Główne Miasto) PLAN II
ROYAL WAY★★★
(Trakt Królewski) B3

Running perpendicular to the River Motława between the Upland Gate and the Green Gate, it forms the town's main thoroughfare, on which the ceremonial parades of Polish kings who came on official visits to Gdańsk were staged. The Royal Way begins with Długa Street, literally the Long Street, which in fact extends only over a distance of 200m from the Golden Gate to the Town Hall, and continues with Długi Targ, once the market square and old Gdańsk's main square near the harbour.

Tall Gate
(Brama Wyższa) B3

The gate, which was the ceremonial entrance to the town and the starting point of the Royal Way, was erected in 1574–76 outside the existing walls, to reinforce the medieval fortifications. It was here that the king was given the keys to the city by the municipal authorities. The frieze decorating the west side features the coats of arms of Royal Prussia (with two unicorns), of Poland (with the arms of the "Ciołek") and of Gdańsk (with two lions). The coat of arms of the House of Hohenzollern was added to the east side in 1884. The following maxims in Latin are inscribed below the coat of arms: "Justice and Piety are the foundations of all kingdoms", "The citizens' most cherished possessions are peace, liberty and concord" and finally, "There can be no wiser deed than what is done for the community".

Just behind the Upland Gate stands the Gothic **Foregate** at the start of Długa (Zespół przedbramia ulicy Długiej), a barbican comprising the **Prison Tower** (Wieża Więzienna) linked to the **Torture House** (Katownia) B3, on the town side. The buildings now house a sleek, new amber museum.

(*Muzeum Bursztynu;* ◷*open Mon 11am –3pm, Tue–Sat 10am–6pm, Sun 11am– 6pm;* ⊜*10 PLN, Mon, free*).

Golden Gate★
(Złota Brama) B3

It was erected between 1612 and 1614 in Renaissance style; the eight ornamental sculptures surmounting the gate feature allegorical representations of civic virtues *(west side: Peace, Justice, Glory and Concord; opposite side: Prudence, Piety, Liberty and Unity)* were added in 1648.

St George's Court★
(Bractwo Św Jerzego) B3

Adjoining the left side of the gate, this Gothic brick building is topped with an imposing 16C lantern surmounted by a replica of the statue of St George and the Dragon (the 1556 original is in the National Museum). Built between 1487 and 1494 for a military brotherhood, the court is now the headquarters of the Polish Architects' Society.

Turn left onto Coal Market Square (Targ Węglowy) to see the silver **Millennium Tree** erected by blacksmiths in 1997 to commemorate the town's millennium.

Długa Street★ B3

The slight curve of the Long Street (Długa) reveals the slender outline of the Town Hall tower standing at its eastern end. The street is lined with tall, narrow mansions with splendid façades and elaborately decorated gables, dating from the 15C to the 20C and mostly rebuilt. Note in particular: at **no. 12**, the Rococo façade of the **Uphagens' House** (Dom Uphagena) is now a **museum** devoted to 18C bourgeois interiors *(⊙open Mon 11am–3pm, Tue–Sat 10am–6pm, Sun 11am–6pm; ⊛10 PLN, Mon free; ℘301 23 71).*

Behind the façade featuring large windows, the lofty entrance hall – typical of merchants' houses – boasts a fine staircase leading to the upper floor. The fairly bare rooms are almost exact reproductions of the original setting, judging by old photographs.

The late 19C mansions at **nos. 69 and 70** are among the rare buildings along the street to have survived the war and still be intact today.

At the east end of the street, on the right, stands the 16C **Kornets' House★** *(now the PTTK Tourist Office)*, one of the town's most elegant mansions; the Town Hall is on the left.

Town Hall of the Main Town★★
(Ratusz Głównego Miasta) C3

Built in 1379–81 by Henryk Ungeradin on the site of a previous edifice, mentioned in 1327, and damaged by the fire of October 1556, it was remodelled in Flemish Renaissance style.

Its slender tower is surmounted by a tall spire topped with a golden statue of Sigismund II August who looks down on the town from a height of 82m; a tribute paid by the population to the king who promulgated an edict granting the same rights to Catholics and Protestants. The building houses the **Historical Museum of Gdańsk★★**.

Długa Street

Historical Museum of Gdańsk★★
(Muzeum Historii Miasta Gdańska) C3

Ul. Długa 47, at the Town Hall. ◷*Open mid-Jun–early Sept Tue 10am–3pm, Wed-Sat 10am–6pm, Sun 11am–6pm, early Sept–mid-Jun Tue–Sat 10am–4pm, Sun 11am–4pm.* ✎*10 PLN.* ✆*767 91 00. The ticket office is on the left of the fine staircase, at the end of the passageway leading to the **Palowa Restaurant**, on the left.*

Housed on the upper floors of the Town Hall, which was completely destroyed at the end of March 1945, the museum is above all worth a visit for its ceremonial rooms, in particular the large **Council Chamber**★★★, also known as the Red or Summer Room, decorated in Dutch mannerist style in 1589–91 with remarkable sculptures by Szymon Herle and seven murals by the Dutch artist Hans Vredeman de Vries. The 25 mythological and biblical paintings on the ceiling are the work of another Dutchman Izaac van den Blocke, including the oval centrepiece, the famous **"Glorification of the Unity of Gdańsk with Poland"**★★★ (1608). It shows the city resting on top of a monumental triumphal arch, rising to the west behind its Upland Gate and its fortifications. God's right hand, coming through the clouds, holds the spire of the Town Hall tower, surrounded by an eagle, symbolising the divine presence embodied on earth by the municipal council. The source of the Wisła is linked by a divine rainbow with, on the right, the Tatras Mountains and a panorama of the royal castle on Wawel Hill in Kraków, Poland's capital at the time, and on the left, the place where the river flows into the Baltic, guarded by the Wisłoujście fortress.

The treasures contained in this room were fortunately dismantled and hidden during the war, which explains why they survived. The upper floor contains a fine display of ancient maps and interesting temporary exhibitions about the town's history. One of the last rooms is devoted to the chronology of the destruction suffered by the town during the last war from the first British bombing of July 1942 to the particularly devastating Soviet ones of 25 March 1945. Evocative photographs show the magnitude of the disaster. In summer, it is possible to climb to the top of the tower.

The Long Market★★★
(Długi Targ) C4

Lined with the town's most outstanding houses, each with its characteristic front steps, this square, formed by a widening of the Long Street, is the real heart of the town. The rich mansions were patiently rebuilt after the war.

In the top northeast corner stands the **Neptune Fountain**★★★ (Fontanna Neptuna), dating from 1633. An emblem of the town and a symbol of the proud city's wealth, this splendid fountain is surmounted by a bronze statue cast in 1615 by Peter Hussen. Neptune, the god of the sea and of navigation, represents the tight bond that exists between the town and the sea. Dismantled during the war, Neptune did not hold his trident again until 1954. Since then, the fountain has been the locals' favourite meeting point.

Behind the Neptune Fountain rises the sumptuous arcaded façade of **Artus' Court**★★★ (Dwór Artusa). Built between 1476 and 1481, this Gothic Court was the meeting place of six of the town's guilds. Its name suggest the Knights of the Round Table with whom the wealthy merchants identified for their democratic functioning. In 1616–17, the building was given a mannerist façade. Its royal doorway is decorated with two medallions of members of the Vasa dynasty, Sigismund III and his son Ladisław IV. Behind the façade, the only part to have been spared, the entirely rebuilt edifice houses a museum reached on the left through the adjoining **Old Jury House** (Stary Dom Ławy), but also linked from the inside to the adjacent house on the right, the **New Jury House**★ (Nowy Dom Ławy). Sometimes called the **Aldermen's House** or **Gdańsk's Hall** (Sień Gdańska), this building boasts a mainly Gothic façade with a fine Renaissance porch and its

What's to become of Granary Island?

This picturesque warehouse district facing the Main Town was built from the 13C onwards and, in the 14C, there were already 200 granaries on the island; their number kept on increasing and chronicles mention that the 1536 fire destroyed some 340 of them. In 1576, a canal (known as the New Motława) was dug to avoid the spreading of fires, thus forming a peninsula which was again ravaged by fires and the 200 or so granaries which escaped were laid waste by the 1945 bombings. The island is still in ruins today but, since the 1990s it has prompted endless projects. There are rumours about a hotel and marina. What will be will be...

gable, added in the 18C, has become the focus of attention on account of a local attraction: the "Maiden at the window" (&see sidebar).

Visit of Artus' Court

&767 91 80. ⊙Open mid-Jun–early Sept Mon 10am–3pm, Tue–Sat 10am– 6pm, Sun 11am–6pm; early Sept–mid Jun Tue–Sat 10am–4pm, Sun 11am– 4pm. ⊚10 PLN.

At the entrance to the great hall (450sq m) with its fine starred web **vaulting**★★ supported by four slender granite columns, visitors are greeted by a suspended ship fitted with tiny guns that used to fire a salute on special occasions. In the right-hand corner stands the prize exhibit, a large **ceramic stove**★★★, looking like a five-tier obelisk. Built in 1545 by master potter Georg Stelzener, this "king of stoves", 10.64m high and 2.5m wide at the base, is covered over with 520 painted tiles (including 437 original ones) portraying the most prominent figures of the early-16C Catholic and Lutheran world, in particular Charles V, his brother Ferdinand I and their respective spouses. The

top of the stove bears the coats of arms of Gdańsk, royal Prussia and Poland. It was filled with coal through an opening located in the north wall. The upper part was dismantled and hidden in 1943 but the base was damaged by fire and restoration work was only completed in 1995. Note, on the left, an expressive late-Gothic polychrome **low relief**★ by Hans Brandt depicting St George and the Dragon. The upper floor houses temporary exhibitions.

Golden House★★★
(Złota Kamieniczka) C3

Shifting one's attention two gables to the right of Artus' Court **(no. 41)**, one notices the wealth of ornamentation on the fine façade of this mansion. Built in 1609 for the then mayor, it features a blend of the three architectural orders, but is most noteworthy for its 12 carved friezes. These are separated, level with each cornice, by four busts, including those of Polish Kings Ladisław Jagellon and Sigismund III Vasa. At the top, the balustrade is surmounted by statues of well-known figures from Antiquity, Cleopatra, Oedipus, Achilles and Antigone.

Green Gate★
(Zielona Brama) C3

Closing off the Long Market in front of the banks of the Motława, this gate features four arches. It was erected between 1568 and 1571 on the site of a 14C defensive gate known as Koga, to serve as the King's residence. Apart from Marie Louise de Gonzague just before she married Ladisław IV in 1646, no Polish monarch ever stayed in it and today, the former President of the Polish Republic, Lech Wałęsa, has his office inside.

The local historical museum also organises temporary exhibits in the huge first floor hall that in the past hosted grand feasts and theatrical productions. Beyond the arcades, the axis of the Długi Targ is prolonged by the **Green Bridge** (Most Zielony) spanning the Motława to reach **Granary Island** (Wyspa Spichrzów); the **Long Quay** (Długie Pobrzeże), extending to the left along the river, leads to the famous wooden crane.

2 FROM THE MOTŁAWA BANKS TO THE OLD TOWN

THE LONG QUAY★★
(Długie Pobrzeże) C3

Before it was moved during the second half of the 19C to the "dead" Wisła and its side canals, the port of Gdańsk stretched along the Motława, at the foot of the town. All the perpendicular streets leading to the harbour opened onto the riverfront through fortified river gates that formed part of the medieval walls. In front of them, wooden landing-piers on stilts served as moorings for the ships. The increase in maritime traffic rendered these numerous jetties impractical and, at the beginning of the 17C, one long wooden quay was built for the loading and unloading of goods.

Today, the quay is a promenade lined with fine gabled houses reflecting in the still waters of the Motława and at intervals, with gates opening onto perpendicular streets. Beyond the Green Gate, the first and probably the oldest of these gates is the **Bread Gate** (Brama Chlebnicka), closing off the street of the same name. Built around 1450, it is surmounted by the town's oldest coat of arms: two crosses without a crown, which is the emblem of the Teutonic Knights. **No. 12** in Chlebnicka Street, known as the **Schlieff House**, was not reconstructed right down to the last detail because it was damaged during the war but because the Emperor of Prussia, Friedrich Wilhelm III, decided in 1820 to have it entirely taken apart and reassembled in Potsdam, Germany, where it still is. At **no. 16** stands the large gabled **English House**★ (Dom Angielski), also known as the "House Under the Angels" because of the angels decorating the façade. Built in 1569–70, it featured eight levels rising to a height of 30m and was the highest burgher's house in town. Owned by English merchants in the 17C, it later became a Masonic lodge and is now an annexe of the Fine Arts Academy.

No 26 along the quay is a tall, unusual-looking house of which only the façade was saved in 1945. It is topped with a turret used to keep watch over the ships before being turned into an astronomical observatory. Erected in 1598, in 1845 it became the House of the Naturalists' Society (attended by Humboldt); since 1962 it has been the home of the **Archaeological Museum** (Muzeum Archeologiczne; ☉open Jul–Aug Tue–Sun 10am–5pm; Septun Tue, Thu, Fri 9am–4pm, Wed 9am–5pm, Sat–Sun 10am–4pm; museum ⊜6 PLN, tower 2 PLN, museum alone free on Sat). This museum presents the region's heritage from the proto-Slav and Slav periods, and also devotes some space to Baltic amber, which has been at the root of an important trans-European trade since Antiquity. The top of the tower offers a fine panoramic view of the town and the River Motława.

Going right through the adjoining twin-turreted house, the Gothic **St Mary's Gate** (Brama Mariacka), surmounted by the town's coat of arms, leads to the

Gdańsk's "Drawing Rooms"

The *przedproża*, typical architectural features of Old Gdańsk, are those forecourts or perrons which stood in front of the smart mansions lining the street. While the terraces were turned into drawing rooms or summer dining rooms, the basements were used as shops, warehouses or workshops. Surrounded by balustrades and elaborately carved stone sculptures, these perrons were often ringed by gutters ending with splendid water outlets shaped like gargoyles.

Unlike the fine perrons along Mariacka Street which were reconstructed, those lining Długa Street were demolished in the 19C to make way for the tramway, now also vanished.

atmospheric street of the same name. Before entering, you can continue along the quay, passing the **Gate of the Holy Spirit** (Brama Św. Ducha), the **Gate of the Great Crane** (Brama Żuraw), **St John's Gate** (Brama Świętojańska) followed by the **Stall Gate** (Brama Straganiarska) and arrive at the **Old Fishmarket Square** (Targ Rybny), in front of the **Swan's Belfry** (Baszta Łabędź), which marked the northern end of the medieval fortifications. Beyond, the space extending between Grodzka and Na Dylach Streets was occupied by the **Teutonic Knights' Castle** (Zamczysko), built in 1340 and destroyed by the inhabitants in 1454, which has given its name to the district.

▷ *Retrace your steps.*

Old Medieval Crane★★★
(Stary Żuraw) C3
While strolling along the quay, you cannot miss the imposing and photogenic outline of this wooden crane once used for the loading and unloading of goods. The largest harbour-side lifting gear in medieval Europe, it was also one of the gates for entering the town of which it is still the emblem. Mentioned in 1367, it was rebuilt in 1444 following a fire. The upper crane, added in the 17C, was designed to hoist loads of up to two tonnes to a height of 27m but also to fit long masts onto ships. The winch was activated by two wooden drums – 6m and 6.5m in diameter – put in motion by men who, like tireless hamsters, climbed the steps lining the inside of the drums. Severely damaged during the war, the crane, restored between 1955 and 1962, forms part of the Central Maritme Museum whose main buildings are located on Lead Island opposite.

Granary Island and Lead Island★ D2-3
The splendid sailing ships of the Baltic are no longer moored in front of the island and the northern extremity of **Granary Island** (Wyspa Spichrzów) sometimes looks like a rubbish dump, yet the place offers a superb **panoramic view**★★★ of the Long Quay with the outline of Old Gdańsk in the background.

On **Lead Island**, facing the wooden crane across the River Motława, are three adjacent granaries: Oliwa (Oliwski), Copper (Miedź) and the Virgin (Panna), now housing the **Central Maritime Museum** which includes the **Sołdek Museum Ship**. Further along stands the equally proud and characteristic structure of the **Royal Granary**★ (Spichrz Królewski) erected between 1606 and 1608 at the town's expense to store goods produced by the royal estates and recently turned into a fine modern hotel.

▷ *The museum on Lead Island can be reached by taking the Motława River Shuttle(1 PLN) in front of the Old Crane or on foot (allow half an hour). Walk along Stągiewna Street, lined on the right with former granaries converted into offices, to the arm of the New Motława, preceded on the right by the Gothic Stągiewna Gate, which has retained former milk storage tanks formed by two adjoining towers. After crossing the bridge, turn left and walk by the marina before taking the first bridge to Lead Island.*

Mariacka Street★★C3
This emblem of Old Gdańsk is one of the town's most charming and most picturesque streets. Practically razed to the ground during the war, it was meticulously reconstructed in the 1970s with its façades, front steps, railings and

Mariacka Street

shop signs exactly as they were. Today the street is lined with most of the souvenir shops, in particular those selling amber jewellery, an ancient tradition to which Gdańsk owes its reputation as the capital of the amber trade.

St Mary's Basilica★★
(Bazylika Mariacka) C3
Free admission, contribution to the upkeep and restoration of the church (⬡3 PLN).

Known as "Gdańsk's Crown", this imposing basilica towering unchallenged above the town centre is the largest brick church ever built in Europe (105.5m x 66m). Covering an area of 4,900sq m, it can accommodate 20,000 people (that is to say, the town's entire population around 1450). It was often full to capacity during the martial law period when the inhabitants wanted to show their support for the members of the Solidarity trade union who took refuge inside. Work began in 1343, but the church was built in stages and only completed in 1502. Initially used by the Catholics, it passed to the Protestants in 1572, after the death of King Sigismund II August, before becoming a Catholic place of worship once more in 1945.

It was severely damaged during the war, its upper structure reduced to ashes, 40 per cent of its vaulting collapsed and all its frescoes were destroyed, yet 80 per cent of its artistic treasures were removed in time and saved. However, many of them are still not back in their original place; such is the case for the original of Hans Memling's triptych depicting The Last Judgement, which is now housed in Gdańsk's National Museum. The basilica's other gem is the magnificent **astronomical clock**★★ made by Hans Düringer between 1464 and 1470. Located in the north transept, it is 14m high and comprises three sections; it functioned until 1553, but was not put back in working order until 1993. The lowest part is the *calendarium* featuring two screens which show the hour and the date as well as the liturgical calendar. In the middle is the *planetarium* indicating the phases of the moon and

the signs of the zodiac. The upper part is a kind of theatre with a selection of biblical characters and a device allowing them to appear in rotation and on two levels (the 12 Apostles, the four Evangelists, the three Kings and Death holding a scythe) to strike the hours (noon is the most spectacular time). Right at the top, Adam and Eve standing on either side of the Tree of Knowledge, ring the bells. Also noteworthy are the **high altar**, a late Gothic polyptych by Master Michael of Augsburg dating from 1511–17, a lovely pietà (1410) by an anonymous master who also carved the beautiful **Madonna of Gdańsk**, situated in St Anne's Chapel *(north side)*, as well as the fine Baroque **organ**, entirely rebuilt after the war. If you have enough stamina, climb the 408 steps to the top of the only tower and enjoy the beautiful **panoramic view**★★ you get from the platform towering 82m above the town's roofs (◷*open Mon–Sat 9am–5pm, Sun 1–5pm;* ⬡*3PLN).*

Royal Chapel
(Kaplica Królewska) C3
The chapel, adjoining the presbytery, on the north side of the basilica, was commissioned by King John III Sobieski after the municipality refused, in 1677, to give the cathedral back to the Catholics. Designed by the Dutch architect Tillmann van Gameren, it was built between 1678 and 1683 in the shape of a Greek cross and surmounted by a dome topped with a lantern; it is the town's only Baroque church and the only evidence of the Counter Reformation (⚷).

Grand Arsenal★★
(Wielka Zbrojownia) B3
This elegant edifice barring the view at the end of Piwna Street (Beer Street) is the town's finest example of the influence of Flemish Renaissance on local architecture. Built between 1600 and 1605, it was used until the 19C. These days it houses a small supermarket and a shopping arcade, whereas the upper floors are occupied by the Fine Arts Academy.

FROM THE BASILICA
TO THE OLD TOWN

Return to the north side of the Basilica and follow the street successively named Globla (dyke) I to IV and turn right onto Świętojańska Street.

St Nicholas' Church★
(Kościół Św. Mikołaja) C2

Believed to be the town's oldest church, St Nicholas was probably a wooden church in the 12C before being rebuilt in brick by the Dominicans who settled in 1227; its present appearance goes back to the period between 1340 and 1380. The church was miraculously spared during World War II, suffering very little damage. Note the great organ from 1755 and the five-register altarpiece dating from 1643. The church always remained in Catholic hands and, in 1945, a religious community from Lwów *(now L'viv in Ukraine)* took charge of it.

Walk along Pańska Street to the octagonal **Hyacinthus' Tower** (Baszta Jacek) erected around 1400 on the site of the medieval fortifications which separated the Old Town from the Main Town. Known as the "Kitchen Window", it was used as a watchtower. Facing the tower is the fine 19C **Covered Market** (Hala Targowa), still in use.

OLD TOWN★★
(Stare Miasto)

Cross the Podwale Staromiejskie to enter the Old Town where today, paradoxically, only a few reconstructed buildings stand out against a modern background.

Monument to the Defenders of the Polish Postal Service

This monument was erected in 1979 in front of the Post Office **(Poczta Polska)** attacked by the Nazis at the same time as Westerplatte on the morning of 1 September 1939. Some fifty Polish post-office employees defended it for 14 hours. Four of them succeeded in escaping when they surrendered, the 35 who survived were shot on 5 October and their bodies were thrown into a pit in Wrzeszcz, which was only discovered in

1991. This episode is recalled by Günter Grass in his novel *The Tin Drum*, adapted for the screen by Volker Schlöndorff. The reconstructed building houses a small museum devoted to this tragic event, while also illustrating communication techniques (Muzeum Poczty Polskiej; ◷open Mon 10am–1pm, Tue–Fri 10am–4pm. ◉5 PLN; Mon free).

St Catherine's Church★
(Kościół Św. Katarzyny) C2

This is one of Gdańsk's oldest parish churches; founded at the end of the 12C, it was built in stages during the 14C and 15C. At one end of the church, a few photographs show the extent of the destruction *(collapsed vaulting)* that it suffered. During the restoration work undertaken from 1953 to 1957, fragments of frescoes were brought to light. Several panels provide some information about the astronomer Johannes Hevelius (1611–87) whose grave was recently discovered in the church together with his epitaph. *(The church was damaged by a fire in 2006 and some renovations continue, note the photos of fire damage.)* The high altar features a Crucifixion by Anton Möller (1610) and, occupying a prominent position under the organ loft on the left, is a huge painting by Bartolomeo Milwitz depicting Jesus Christ Entering Jerusalem (1590). A small door to the right of the porch gives access to the church tower and to the **Tower Clocks Museum** (Muzeum Zegarów Wieżowych) which contains a collection of clock mechanisms from the 15C to the 20C *(◷closed due to the fire; ✆305 64 92).*

The magnificent **carillon** *(normally activated every Friday at 11am, but inoperative due to the 2006 fire)* had a troubled history. The original dating from 1738 was destroyed by fire in 1905; it was replaced in 1910 by another one which the Germans took down during the war and transferred to Lübeck. It only came back from there in 1989, as part of the German-Polish reconciliation. The fourth octave, which increased the number of bells from 37 to 49 was installed in 1999.

St Bridget's Church
(Kościół Św. Brygidy) C2

Situated behind St Catherine's, St Bridget's Church was erected in 1396 to house the relics of the saint brought back from Rome and surmounted in the 17C by an unusual squat tower. Entirely destroyed during the war, it was rebuilt in the early 1970s and features contemporary furnishings including a monumental amber high altar. It became the sanctuary of the Solidarity trade union during the 1980s' strikes after a group of striking workers sought refuge inside and were welcomed by Henryk Jankowski, the controversial parish priest.

The Great Mill★
(Wielki Młyn) B2

Having reached the Raduna Canal, you will notice on your left the outline of this imposing mill which, from the time it was founded in 1350 by the Teutonic Knights until its destruction by fire in 1945, never stopped grinding nearly 200 tonnes of grain per day, thanks to its 18 hydraulic wheels. Rebuilt in 1962, this impressive Gothic edifice now houses a shopping centre. Almost facing it is the 14C **Small Mill** (Mały Młyn) spanning one arm of the canal.

▷ *Close to the mill, the tip of the island is occupied by a 17C house once owned by the Millers' Guild (Dwór Młyński) and now turned into a café-restaurant with a pleasant terrace at the back.*

Old Town Hall★★
(Ratusz Staromiejski) B2

The Old Town Hall stands facing a small park and a monument to Hevelius; its elegant façade, characteristic of Flemish mannerist architecture, surmounted by a slender turret. The edifice, built between 1587 and 1595, became the headquarters of the Soviet troops in 1945 but today you will find a room devoted to art exhibitions and a bookshop which forms **Gdańsk's Cultural Centre** (◑*open daily 10am–4pm;* ⊜*free*). It is worth going upstairs to see the richly decorated municipal council's great chamber: 17C paintings by Adolf Boy

and Herman Han, fine wooden spiral staircase, ceramic tiles from Delft and various 19C decorative elements from houses which were destroyed.

West of the Town Hall you will see the so-called **House of the Abbots of Pelplin** (Dom Opatów Pelplińskich) dating from 1612, one of the rare houses to come through the war unscathed; note the fine Renaissance **façade★**.

SHIPYARD

▷ *If you continue to follow the itinerary, you will reach the limits of the Old Town and eventually come to Solidarity Square (Pl. Solidarnośći) marking the entrance to Gdańsk's Shipyard (Stocznia Gdańska), known as the Lenin Shipyard until 1980.*

Monument to the Killed Shipyard Workers★
(Pomnik Poległych Stoczniowców)

Overlooking the square, it comprises a set of three 42m tall stainless-steel crosses weighing 133 tonnes, supporting crucified anchors, symbolising hope. It was inaugurated on 16 December 1980 to commemorate those who were killed or wounded ten years previously, during the workers' strikes of 16 and 17 December 1970. For the first time the authorities of a communist country recognised the victims of their own

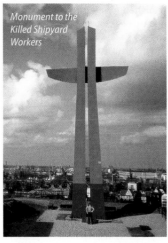

Monument to the Killed Shipyard Workers

B. Brillion / MICHELIN

regime and allowed a commemorative monument to be erected in their honour. Behind it, against the wall, is a series of commemorative plaques laid by trade unions from all over the world as a tribute to the victims of communism. Note the plaque and its expressive sculpture dedicated to the memory of Father Jerzy Popiełuszko, assassinated in 1984. A passageway, situated on the right of the entrance to the shipyard, leads to the historic "Sala BHP", which houses the exhibition of the Solidarity Museum: "The Road to Freedom".

"The Road to Freedom" Exhibition★★
(Wystawa "Drogi do Wolności")
Wały Piastowskie 24. ☎769 29 20.
🕓*Open Tue–Sun May–Sept Tue–Sun 10am–6pm; Oct–Apr 10am–5pm.*
👓*6 PLN (with leaflet).*
This multimedia exhibition situated at the entrance to the former Lenin Shipyard is intended to recount the history of the Solidarity *(Solidarność)* trade union which started the famous strike on 14 August 1980. A trail, starting from Solidarity Square, dotted with fragments of the Berlin Wall and of the Shipyard wall (which electrician Lech Wałęsa climbed over to get access to the establishment that had fired him for his trade union activities) leads, along the road to freedom, to the building now turned into a museum. One can see the famous **Work Hygiene and Safety** room where, on 31 August 1980, negotiations took place and a historic agreement was signed. An audiovisual presentation recalls the chronology of events *(with captions in English)* and, in the exact place where it all happened, an amazingly realistic reconstruction enables visitors to imagine the background to the negotiations.

Gdańsk's Heights
A nice way to end the itinerary is to climb from the back of the bus station up to the city's heights dominated by **Grodzisko Fort**, a group of military buildings connected with the siege of the town by the Russians in 1734 and

later with the intrusion of Napoleon's troops in 1807. The **Millennium Cross** (Kryż Milenijny) has been standing since 2000 at the top of the hill (64m), near the Jerusalem Bastion, offering a fine **view★** of the town and the shipyard and giving a good idea of the extent of the Tri-City and Gdańsk Bay. On the way down, you will catch a glimpse of the symbolic **Cemetery Monument of Non-Existent Cemeteries** *(near the Church of the Blessed Sacrament)*, intended to commemorate Gdańsk's populations, whose burying places have disappeared, wiped out by the passing of time or the furious assaults of history.

MUSEUMS
National Museum★★
(Muzeum Narodowe) B4
Ul. Toruńska1. ☎301 68 04. 🕓*Open Tue –Fri 9am–4pm, Sat–Sun 10am–5pm.*
👓*10 PLN, Fri free. www.muzeum. narodowe.gda.pl*
This fine museum is located in a former Franciscan convent in the **Old Suburb**; the cloister galleries and vaulted rooms on the ground floor house an interesting set of Gothic statues, religious gold and silverware, beautiful wrought-iron items, as well as the original statue of St George and the Dragon (1556) from the lantern of the Court of the Brotherhood of St George. One wing contains antique furniture including a kind of carved wardrobe, typical of Gdańsk and once famous throughout Europe. The upper floor is devoted to painting; immediately on the left is the unmissable **Altarpiece of the Last Judgement★★★**, Hans Memling's (c. 1433–94) most famous triptych, displayed in a glass case. The central panel depicts St Michael the Archangel among the Dead coming out of their graves; the right-hand panel shows the Chosen and the left-hand one the Damned. Walk round to see the magnificent portraits of the benefactors.
Start with the department on the left, devoted to 16C–18C local painting (Malarstwo Gdańskie); the first and most interesting room precedes a long portrait gallery. Proceed to the depart-

ment of Flemish and Dutch painting (Malarstwo Flamandzkie i Holenderskie), which has a few nice surprises in store for you and end the visit with the department of 19C–20C Polish painting (Malarstwo Polskie), where you will see, among others, works by Wyspiański, Malczewski and Pankiewicz.

Standing near the museum, the **Church of the Holy Trinity**★ (Kościół Św. Trójcy) boasts beautiful vaulting and elaborate interior decoration. Completed in 1514, it features an unusual east end separated from the nave by a wall adorned with fine late-Gothic polyptychs. Commissioned by King Kazimierz Jagellon for the benefit of the Catholic Polish population, **St Anne's Chapel** (1480–84) houses a pulpit from 1721 and a Baroque organ from 1710.

Central Maritime Museum★★
(Centralne Muzeum Morskie) D3
Ul. Ołowianka 9/13. ☎301 86 11. www.cmm.pl. ⏰Open Sept–mid-Jun Tue–Sun 10am–4pm; mid-Jun–Aug 10am–6pm. ⊕8 PLN (Granary); 8 PLN (Sołdek Museum Ship), 18 PLN (pass + ferry 2 PLN). The entrance is not easy to find; walk round the building to the right. Comprehensive informative booklets in English are available in each room. Tawerna Marina, a modest restaurant-cafeteria, enables visitors to have a snack on the premises. Allow at least two hours even for a selective visit. This museum is in several sections. The main one is housed in the three former wheat granaries rebuilt on Lead Island. It also comprises a tour of the *Sołdek* moored to the quay in front of the granaries. On the town side, there is another building linked to the wooden crane.

The Island's Granaries
The collections, displayed on several floors, illustrate river and harbour traffic in Gdańsk as well as seafaring along the Baltic coast from the origins to the present through paintings, documents, engravings, scale models and objects. The long succession of rooms offers an exhaustive account of all the aspects of maritime life, from

the naval battle against the Swedes, that took place in the Bay of Gdańsk on 28 November 1627 and is known as the Battle of Oliwa to the great discoveries. There is also a display about the Polish sailor, Józef Korzeniowski, better known under his name as an English writer, Joseph Conrad.

Sołdek Museum Ship
The visit continues with a thorough, signposted tour of the first ship to come out of the town's shipyards in 1948, named after her first captain, Stanisław Sołdek. For the Poles, this ship embodies their regained self-esteem and remains a symbol of national independence.

▷ *The visit ends with the ferry crossing of the Motława to the annexe of the museum partly located inside the medieval crane.*

Museum Annexe and Wooden Crane
Inside the annexe, one room in particular is devoted to traditional boats from all over the world; as for the crane, it was partly turned into a dwelling in the 17C and now houses several reconstructed scenes with dummies, illustrating traditional trades and crafts connected with the sea and fishing. The crane's lifting gear is also on show.

WESTERPLATTE★ MAP I B3
▷ *7km north of the historic town. Accessible by shuttle boat from Gdańsk's Long Quay (Apr–Oct). The ticket office is located near the bridge, beyond the Green Gate, set back from the lowered quay. 50min one way to Westerplatte (⊕30 PLN), 1hr40min for the full tour (⊕45 PLN). The landing-stage is situated between the monument and the fortress. From the central station, the journey by bus no. 106 takes visitors through an area of plots of land cultivated by the workers.*

Situated northeast of the town, mainly to the east of the Wisła estuary, the **shipyards** cover a considerable area. It is possible to visit, but one already gets a good glimpse of them during the boat trip to Westerplatte, at the eastern extremity of the harbour canal. A town within the town, this fascinating area, where everything seems to be rusting away, gives the paradoxical impression of being both abandoned and full of activity. The uninterrupted succession of large sheds and warehouses, all extremely dilapidated, and the forest of huge cranes standing out against the sky like ghostly figures, creates an awe-inspiring scene.

Monument to the Defenders of Westerplatte B2

Take the opportunity to breathe the invigorating Baltic air by going to this narrow peninsula where the Nazis began the first hostilities of World War II. On 1 September 1939 at 4.47 in the morning, the battleship *Schleswig-Hollstein* opened fire on the Polish garrison guarding the military transport depot created on this site in 1924 by decision of the League of Nations. In spite of the obvious disproportion between the opposing forces and their respective military equipment, the 182 soldiers led by major Henryk Sucharski only surrendered on 7 September after putting up a fierce resistance (which commanded the Germans' admiration and earned their heroic leader military honours during the surrender ceremony as well as the privilege of keeping his sword in prison). On 21 September, Hitler himself inspected the place where over 300 of his soldiers had died against just 15 Poles. One of the shelled buildings remains as it was then for memory's sake and a tiny **museum**, housed inside the former Guardhouse **(no. 1)**, to the left of the car park, recalls (in Polish) those terrible times (Oopen May–mid-Jun and Oct 9am–4pm; mid-Jun–Sept 9am–7pm; 3 PLN).

In order to commemorate this event symbolising Polish resistance, a 25m high monolithic **monument**, representing the hilt of a sword planted in the ground, was erected in 1968 at the top of a 22.5m-high artificial mound. Facing it on the opposite bank is the **latarnia morska** (lighthouse) of the **Nowy Port** (New Harbour) district. Built in 1893 and rising to a height of 90m, it has been reopened to the public (Oopen May–Sept daily 10am–7pm. 6 PLN).

Wisłoujście Fortress★★
(Twierdza Wisłoujście) B3

Designed to guard the entrance to the Wisła estuary (and at the same time to the whole of Poland!), which ships had to negotiate in order to reach the port of Gdańsk on the Motława, this fine fortress surrounded by water originally consisted of a Gothic lighthouse-tower (1482); in 1572, it was surrounded by a fort reinforced by bastions which was itself remodelled between 1584 and 1587. At that time, the sea was very close and now, although it looks fairly close from the Westerplatte landing-stage, it is a good twenty minutes' walk along the road (bus no. 106 stops near the junction where the path leading to it branches off). Abandoned for many years to the ravages of time, this ensemble is undergoing a thorough restoration which should last another few years.

OLIWA★★ MAPI A3

Oliwa is accessible by tram (nos. 5, 11 and 12; get off where the track runs round a roundabout) and by SKM regional train (get off at the Gdańsk Oliwa station and take the passageway on the left. As you come out of the station, take the first right then the first left. Cross a large avenue and walk to the right).

This peaceful district next to Sopot, at the foot of the wooded Pacholek hill, 5km northwest of Gdańsk, is famous for its park, featuring a formal French garden in the southwest and an English-style park in the north, and adjoining a former Cistercian abbey which became a cathedral in 1925, when it was incorporated into the city of Gdańsk. Walk to the east entrance of the **Oliwski Park**★ (Oopen 5am–6pm/8pm/11pm according to the season) and follow a small tree-lined canal until you reach a pool (main gate) then bear right towards the Abbot's Palace and the cathedral.

Abbot's Palace★
(Pałac Opatów) A2
Ul. Cystersów 15a. ◷*Open Tue–Fri 9am–4pm, Sat-Sun 10am–5pm; last admission 45min before closing.* 🎫*10 PLN, Fri free.* ✆*552 12 71.*
This fine Baroque edifice, built in 1754–56, now houses the much-ignored but restful **Department of Contemporary Art**★ (Oddział Sztuki Współczesnej), an annexe of Gdańsk's National Museum which offers a fine overview of 20C Polish art. A curious highlight are two works by Tadeusz Kantor.

▶ *Walk along the cloister wall to the cathedral entrance, next to the park.*

Oliwa Cathedral★★
(Katedra Oliwska) A2
**A troubled history
and many modifications**
Invited in 1186 by Sanbor I, Duke of Pomerania, Danish Cistercian monks settled here and founded their abbey in 1188. Erected in the 13C, the three-nave basilica was rebuilt in Gothic style after the 1350 fire. Next, it was burned down by Prussian pagans then again, on four occasions, by the Teutonic Knights and finally in 1577 by Gdańsk's Protestant population. Its reconstruction was completed in 1582. In 1626, the Swedes wrecked the church once more but in 1660, the **Treaty of Oliwa** was signed inside. In 1831, the Cistercian abbey

was definitively abolished by the King of Prussia. The church became a cathedral in 1925 and came through World War II relatively unscathed.
Bright and white, with a long, narrow nave and an extended chancel, the edifice is one of the three longest churches in Poland (107m). The undisputed jewel is the magnificent dark-wood **organ**★★★, elaborately carved and framing a stained-glass window representing the Virgin and Child. Designed on the initiative of the Abbot Józef Rybiński, it was made by a Cistercian monk, Jan Wulf of Orneta, who, during 25 years from 1763 to 1788, worked on his project, which was completed by organ master Friedrich R. Dalitz in 1791–93. The church is often crowded, particularly on Sundays, when the renowned demonstrations of the amazing instrument take place *(weekdays at 11am, noon, and 3pm, Sundays at 3pm*

Oliwa Cathedral

© Dariusz Kuzminski/iStockphoto

and 4pm. Jun–Aug additional performances on the hour. It is advisable to arrive
early as the doors are closed during the
demonstration). The nuns ask visitors
to stand up and invite them to say a
paternoster before the beginning of the
programme which includes a choice of
varied music. The 101 registers of the
instrument allow amazing sounds in
both quality and power to come out of
the 7,876 pipes.

The chancel boasts a **Baroque high
altar**★ (1688) featuring an impressive
black-marble colonnade in striking
contrast with the white-stucco vaulting
which suggests a cloudy sky dotted with
some 150 angels' heads. Before leaving,
look at the funeral monument (1620) of
the Kos family on the south side.

SOPOT MAP 1 A2
(Population 41,410)

*Sopot, situated 12km north of Gdańsk's
historic centre, is accessible by train
from platforms 1–5 of the SKM regional
network station. Trains every 10min,
journey time 25min, 9th stop (Sopot)
from Gdańsk Główny.*

Wedged between the two large towns
of Gdańsk and Gdynia on the one hand
and between the sea and the wooded
escarpment of the cliff on the other,
Sopot boasts no special monument
despite the fact that it is the country's
most upmarket seaside resort.

Given in the 13C to the monks of the Cistercian abbey of Oliwa, this former fishing village owed its real expansion to an
Alsatian, Georges Haffner, a former sur-
geon in Napoleon's army, who settled
there, had the first baths built in 1823
and the hydrotherapy establishment
the following year. After World War I, it
was included within the limits of the free
city of Gdańsk. It was soon the favourite destination of wealthy world travellers and had its heyday in the interwar
period (thanks, in particular, to its casino
founded in 1920) before becoming an
ordinary Polish town once more in 1945.
Today, it is a sought-after holiday destination, offering visitors a particularly
pleasant atmosphere in striking contrast
to the urban and densely historic feel

of its imposing neighbour. As the day
draws to an end, it becomes the paradise
of night-time revellers and of all those
who are looking for alternative restaurants and trendy bars.

Exploring Sopot

Walk down **Monte Cassino** Street, a
pedestrian mall which owes its name
to the battle and is called Monciak. It
leads from the railway line to the
beach. You can't miss the **façade of
no. 53** (Rezydent) looking as if it were
facing a distorting mirror, even if the
interior houses a score of uninspiring
cafés. At the very end, beyond Zdrojowy
Square, you will come to the wooden
pier★ (molo) which is the main attraction along the seafront (⊙*open Oct–Apri*

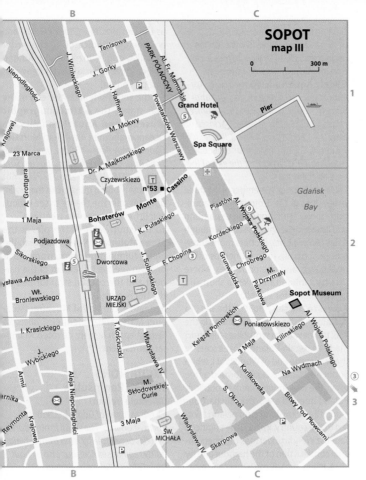

SOPOT
map III

0 · · · 300 m

Grand Hotel

Pier

Spa Square

Gdańsk Bay

n°53 ■ Cassino

Sopot Museum

Mon–Fri free; Sat-Sun and May–Sept Mon–Fri ◎ 3.40 PLN). Presented as Poland's longest pier, this 511m-long promenade will give you the impression of walking over the sea.

The fine-sand **beach** stretches on both sides. Near the beginning of the pier, it is possible to climb inside a **viewpoint-lighthouse** (◎4 PLN) to get a bird's-eye view of the surrounding area.

To the north, one can see the massive outline of the **Grand Hotel** where Adolph Hitler stayed in September 1939 while his troops were rushing towards Warsaw. If the beach is too hot, you can always walk north towards the forest, on the heights of the town, offering some fine walks. Built in 1909 and modernised in the early 1960s, the **open-air opera**

(Opera Leśna – meaning "Forest Opera"; Ul. Moniuszki 12) is an amphitheatre with some 5,000 seats (◎currently being enlarged and modernised, should re-open for 2011 season; www.operalesna.pl) nestled in the heart of the forest and protected by an impressive folding roof. In summer, it hosts a famous international song festival. A ski-lift takes visitors to the summit of the Bare Mountain (Łysa Góra), the highest point in the area.

GDYNIA A1
(Population 253,508)
Gdynia, situated 12km north of Gdańsk's historic centre, is accessible by train from platforms 1–5 of the SKM regional network station. Trains every 10min, journey time 40min, 14th stop (Gdynia

Główna Osobowa) from Gdańsk Główny. There is a tourist office on the main street, Ul. 10 Lutego 24 that leads from the Gdynia Główna railway to **Gydnia Aquarium** (🕐*open daily Apr–May and Sept 9am–7pm; Jun–Jul until 8pm; Oct–Mar 10am–5pm; ticket office closes 30min before closing;* 🕐*closed Mon Nov–Feb, 1 Jan, 4 Apr, 3 Jun, 1 Nov, 24–25, 31 Dec) and another one standing like a lookout at the end of the jetty on the right.*

This is the youngest member of the three sister cities in the Trójmiasto, an ambitious town, which goes on expanding and attracting many investors. Although it has fewer sights, it offers more entertainment thanks to its numerous cafés, restaurants and fine boutiques, where Gdańsk's inhabitants like to shop and families come for a stroll.

Access to the sea – Built on the site of a Kashubian fishing village founded in the 13C, this new town symbolises the effort made to regain Poland's lost access to the sea. At the end of World War I, when Sopot and Gdańsk again formed a free town, the new independent Republic of Poland needed a worthwhile harbour along the 72km-long strip of land allotted to the country. In 1921, the engineer, Tadeusz Wenda undertook the phenomenal construction of the harbour and by 1934, it was already the largest and most modern port in the Baltic. Severely damaged during World War II, the harbour was rebuilt and modernised and today, Gdynia is Poland's main commercial port.

Exploring Gdynia – There are no beaches and Gdynia's main attractions are located around Kościuszko Garden (Skwer Kościuszki) prolonged by a very wide pier. Two **museum ships** are moored along the north quay, the *Błyskawica (Lightning)*, a destroyer built in 1937, and the three-masted frigate *Dar Pomorza (Gift from Pomerania)*; they can be visited year-round. The latter, once used as a training ship, was replaced by the *Dar Młodzieży (Gift of Youth)* also moored nearby. Two commemorative monuments stand at the end of the jetty, a metal one known

as the *Gra Masztów (Play of Masts)* and a stone one dedicated to the writer of Polish origin, Józef Teodor Konrad Nałęcz Korzeniowski (better known as Joseph Conrad).

On the south side near the end of the pier stands the 🔱**Oceanographic Museum and Aquarium** (Muzeum Oceanograficzne i Akwarium Morskie ; 🕐*open daily 9am–4.30pm, until 7.30pm Jun–Aug;* 🕐*closed 1 Jan, Easter Sun, 1 Nov, 24–25, 31 Dec; 🎫16/12 PLN)*, not the most modern museum in the world, but does offer the chance to see various colourful and exotic sea creatures.

To the southwest of the pier is the **Stone Mountain** (Kamienna Góra), the area's culminating point, from which one can see the full extent of the harbour and the coastal strip formed by the Hel Peninsula.

Beneath is the **Naval Museum** (Muzeum Marynarki Wojennej; *Franciszka Sędzickiego 3)* largely devoted to military armament.

EXCURSIONS
The Hel Peninsula★
(Mierzeja Helska)

▶ *60km north of Gdańsk, 32km north of Gdynia. The small fishing port of Hel is accessible by train from Gdynia (fairly regular service), but also by boat from Gdańsk, Sopot or Gdynia mid-May–Sept.*

This narrow pine-covered peninsula, closing off Gdańsk's Bay, is 34km long with a width varying from 200m at the base to 2.9km at the tip. It is particularly sought after by windsurfers.

Seaside resorts (Chałupy, Kuźnica and Jurata) alternating with fishing villages (Władysławowo, Jastarnia and Hel) are dotted along the shore overlooking the bay, whereas the north shore, turned towards the open sea, is lined with fine sandy beaches. Situated at the tip of the peninsula, the small fishing port of **Hel** boasts a **Fishing Museum** housed in a former Gothic church as well as an aquarium for seals **(Fokarium)** and offers fine walks through the forest; you can get a beautiful view of the surrounding area from the top of the lighthouse.

ADDRESSES

🛏 STAY

GDAŃSK

Grand-Tourist – *Ul. Podwale Grodzkie 8. ℘301 17 27. www.gt.com.pl. Open Mon–Fri 10am–6pm, Sat 10am–4pm (Jul–Aug daily 8am–8pm).* Situated in the basement of the City Forum, the shopping mall of the Holiday Inn Hotel. From the station, take the subway, then turn right as you come out. Yellow sign and sliding door. This agency centralises private-room accommodation offered in the town centre. It has a stock of some 50 rooms *(100 PLN in the centre, 80 at the periphery)* and around 30 apartments *(1 room + kitchen + bathroom = 220 PLN).*✄. English spoken.

Almatur – *Ul. Długi Targ 11. ℘301 24 03. www.almatur.gda.pl. Open Mon–Fri 10am –5pm (Jun–Aug 6pm), Sat 10am–2pm.* This student travel agency deals with accommodation in university hostels during the months of June, July, August and September: about 10 sites in all, particularly near the University of Technology, situated between Gdańsk Politechnika and Gdańsk Wrzeszcz railway stations.

🛏 **Baltic Hostel** – *Ul. Wałowa 54. ℘721 96 57. www.baltichostel.com – 20 rooms.* Independent hostel located on the edge of the Old Town, not far from the shipyard's entrance and the Raduni Canal. Offers rooms suitable for one to 14 persons. 40 PLN in a dormitory and 60 PLN per person in a double room

🛏 **Youth Hostel** – *Ul. Wałowa 21. ℘301 23 13. www.ssm.gda.pl. 96 beds.* Located deep inside a small park, on the edge of the Old Town, not far from the shipyard's entrance, the most central of the three permanent youth hostels in town has rooms suitable for one to 10 persons. *(17 PLN in a dormitory and 50 PLN per person in a double room).*

🛏🍴 **Hotel Królewski** – *Ul. Ołowianka 1. ℘326 11 11. www.hotelkrolewski.pl. 30 rooms.* Discreet establishment with a fine but austere façade featuring characteristic windows; one of the rare 17C royal granaries still standing on Lead Island; restored in 2003 to house this handsome four-storey hotel. For the same price, you can have a room overlooking the quayside. Fine suites at the top of the building. Dining room service from 7 to 10pm.

🛏🍴 **Pensjonat Dom Aktora** – *Ul. Straganiarska 55/56. ℘301 59 01. www.domaktora.pl. 12 rooms.*✄. An exclusively female staff run this convivial guest house, well situated north of the Old Town, in a small, modern twin-gabled building. Fairly spacious rooms and fully equipped apartments for 2 to 4 persons.

🛏🍴🖥 **Hotel Podewils** – *Ul. Szafarnia 2. ℘300 95 60. www.podewils.pl. 10 rooms.* This small 5-star hotel, housed in one of the rare 18C buildings still standing, occupies a magnificent location opposite the famous crane, across the River Motława and near the marina. A bell-boy stands in front of the Baroque door. Discounts for last-minute bookings. Expensive but charming **restaurant** with peaceful terrace.

SOPOT

🛏🍴 **Hotel Zhong Hua** – *Al. Wojska Polskiego 1. ℘550 20 20. www.hotel chinski.pl. 49 rooms.* Situated by the beach in former baths transformed into pagodas, this hotel offers classic rooms as well as apartments with private terraces right on the beach. **Bike rental** *(5 PLN/hr or 25 PLN/day).* The north wing houses a **restaurant** *(🛏🍴, 1–11pm),* highly recommended and sought after by Polish people – boasting an oriental-style décor, which has the great advantage of facing the sea. The serving staff are Polish, as are the kitchen staff apparently, and the result is a selection of tasty and copious Chinese-style dishes.

🛏🍴🖥 **Pensjonat Irena** – *Ul. Chopina 36. ℘551 20 73. www.pensjonat-irena.gda.pl. 16 rooms (sleeps 36).* ✄. Note the discreet charm of this guest house occupying a large seaside villa on four levels and offering good value for money. Rooms on two floors round a vast entrance hall. Small but with high ceilings, they are all decorated with the same golden beige wallpaper. Very pleasant **dining room** *(🛏🍴, daily, lunch only)* where time seems to have stopped in 1925, and splendid Karczma pub on the ground floor: an amazing **restaurant** *(open daily 1pm–midnight)* serving traditional Polish cuisine from the time of King Jan III Sobieski's reign.

⊜⊜🗑 **Sofitel Grand Hotel** – *Ul. Powstańców Warszawy 12/14.* 📞*520 60 00. www.sofitel.com. 127 rooms.* This huge Art Nouveau building, erected in 1924–27, looks quite impressive both on the street side, with its colossal double ramp for cars, and on the beach side. Vast corridors on either side of the elegant central cupola lead to bright, high-ceilinged rooms. Rooms with a view of the Baltic are more expensive *(750-850 PLN)*. Elegant dining room.

🍴 EAT

After trying out Gdańsk's classic restaurants, you could try Sopot's more trendy restaurants and attractive cafés. Note also that all the hotels mentioned above have restaurants worth visiting.

GDAŃSK

⊜ **Bar Mleczno-Turystyczny** – *Ul. Szeroka 8/10. Open Mon–Fri 7am–6pm, Sat–Sun 9am–4pm.*🗀. The Poles flock to this establishment where it is possible to eat for a moderate price. Canary-yellow, budgie-green surroundings in this authentic milk bar – they were run as subsidised cafeterias under the former Communist régime – give it a nostalgic feel of times gone by.

⊜ **Bar Mleczny Neptun** – *Ul. Długa 33/34. Open Mon–Fri 7.30am–6pm, Sat–Sun 10am–5pm.* Inexpensive home-style Polish food served in a two-level cafeteria style milk bar. Fill up on potato pancakes. Ideal central location.

⊜ **Złota Rybka** – *Ul. Piwna 50/51.* 📞*301 39 24. Open Sun–Thu 11am–10pm, Fri–Sat 11am–midnight.* Situated on the ground floor of the Klub Yesterday this small snack bar boasts a convivial atmosphere in pleasant surroundings; note in particular the mezzanine with its ceiling lined with sea shells. The walls are decorated with local stars' autographs accompanied by their comments about the "Gold Fish".

⊜⊜ **Restauracja Kresowa** –*Ul. Ogarna 12.* 📞*301 66 53. Open daily 11am–10pm.* On a quiet street parallel to the main drag. This restaurant with a family-run atmosphere features many exotic dishes from Poland's neighbours, Ukraine, Lithuania, Russia – plus Jewish and Armenian delights.

⊜⊜🗑 **Dom Pod Łososiem** – *Ul. Szeroka 52/54.* 📞*301 76 52. Open daily noon–midnight.* The "Salmon" restaurant, which claims to have been opened in 1598, undoubtedly deserves to rank among the most elegant restaurants in town. Destroyed during the war, it only reopened in 1976. The speciality of the house is a mouthwatering roast duck with a crispy skin. Why not try the other local speciality: *Goldwasser*, a sweet drink made from herbs and... 22-carat gold (Catherine II's favourite alcoholic drink). This traditional German drink from Poznań was made here in the "Salmon"'s distillery (founded in 1598).

⊜⊜🗑 **Restauracja Tawerna** – *Ul. Powroźnicza 19/20.* 📞*301 41 14. daily 11am–2am (last orders 10.30pm).* Quite close to the quay, near the Green Gate, this high-class restaurant specialises in fish dishes, in spite of the fact that the menu mentions "specialities from Poland and French Limousin" *(reference to beef)*. Décor on a maritime theme enhanced by the long bar made of a splendid piece of wood with a dragon's head which you will find familiar (think of the gargoyles in Mariacki Street). Terrace in front and at the back.

SOPOT

⊜ **Bar Przystań** – *Al Wojska Polskiego11.* 📞*550 06 61. Open daily 11am–11pm.* Located to the south of the seaside promenade, this beach restaurant is a real local institution. The long beached ship, where one goes to place an order and eventually settle down, also offers a large terrace with a fine view of the sea and fishing boats. The menu *(in English)* offers "fast seafood."

⊜⊜🗑 **Klub Wieloryb** – *Ul. Podjazd 2.* 📞*551 57 22. Open daily 1pm–midnight.* An almost oppressive décor in which the greenish grey atmosphere is supposed to suggest the insides of a whale as the name implies. This very trendy restaurant, serving a French-inspired cuisine, may seem rather overdone, but it is at least surprising.

GDYNIA

⊜ **Bar Mleczny Słoneczny** – *Ul. Władysława IV. Open Mon–Fri 6.30am –7pm.* This milk bar occupies a vast room behind large white curtains with a floral motif. The rows of tables laid out close to one another, lead you to share your meal with strangers who come to spend as little as possible on dishes of invigorating Polish cooking.

🚃 TAKING A BREAK

GDAŃSK

Cafe π Kawa – *Ul. Piwna 5/6. ✆309 14 44. Open daily 10am–11pm.* This small, charming café, which always draws the crowds, offers a cosy environment for a teatime break.

Cup of tea – *Ul. Szeroka 119/120. ✆301 23 86. Open daily 11am–10pm.* Near St Nicholas' Church; a tiny place to visit for a tea, to read or to use their free WiFi.

SOPOT

Kawiarnia u Hrabiego – *Ul. Czyżewskiego 12. ✆550 19 97. Open daily 10am–10pm.* This very pleasant café-cum-tearoom-cum-art gallery occupies one of the oldest houses (200 years old) in Sopot. Forming part of the municipal heritage, this fine single-storey villa, now located right in the town centre, proposes a different exhibition every month and concerts every Thursday evening. Pleasant small summer garden.

Cafe Art Deco – *Ul. Boh. Monte Cassino 9 A. ✆555 01 60. Open daily 11am–10pm.* Situated at the very beginning of the unavoidable Monte Cassino Street, above the railway line, set back from the street, on the right. This tiny delightful café, boasting a literary atmosphere, is decorated with old photographs. Coffee made and served in Italian coffee pots. Excellent fresh cheese and grape cake.

GDYNIA

Café Cynamon – *Ul. Świętojańska 49. ✆781 31 31. Open Mon–Sat 9am–10pm, Sun 11am–10pm.* Truly excellent coffee and cakes in this modern, non-smoking establishment.

🎭 ON THE TOWN

GDAŃSK

Cafe Absinthe – *Ul. Św. Ducha 2. ✆320 37 84. www.cafeabsinthe.pl.* Relaxed during the day, but interesting events and wild parties after sunset at this club connected to the Teatr Wybrzeże.

Klub Yesterday – *Ul. Piwna 50/51. ✆301 39 24. Open Sun–Thu 6pm–2am, Fri–Sat 6pm–4am. The* alternative bar in the town centre, buried deep down in vast cellars near St Mary's Church. Current dance music chosen by a DJ who takes his role very seriously, even when the audience is down to three people!

SOPOT

Galeria Kiński – *Ul. Kościuszki10. ✆695 951 743. Open daily 4pm–3am.* This café is entirely devoted to the actor Klaus Kiński, alias Nikolaus Gunther Nakszyński. It's no surprise really since he was born in this house (built in 1898) in 1926.

Błękitny Pudel – *Ul. Boh. M. Cassino. 44. ✆551 16 72. Open daily 10am–1am.* Standing opposite the pretentious façade of the Centrum Rezydent, the unassuming but surprising Blue Poodle looks like a surrealist collage full of miscellaneous objects found in bric-à-brac shops.

Spatif – *Ul. Boh. Monte Cassino. 54. ✆550 26 83. Open 3pm–last customers.* Up a steep flight of stairs; you have to ring and prove you're acceptable if you wish to gain access to the vast room with its eccentric décor or to the attractive bar with its huge mirror.

🛒 SHOPPING

Known as the "Gold of the Baltic", amber is a great speciality of the city of Gdańsk. Workshops making and selling **amber handicrafts** are concentrated in Mariacka Street, the Długi Targ and the Długie Pobrzeże (quay).

Empik Megastore– *Ul. Podwale Grodzkie 8 (City Forum).* Offers the largest selection of books on the Tri City area in English, as well as magazines dedicated to cultural events.

🎭 FESTIVE EVENTS

Dominican Fair (since 1260)**:** During the first two weeks in August.

Gdynia's Polish Feature-length Film Festival: In September.

International Festival of Organ Music: in Oliwa's Cathedral from mid-June to the end of August. *www.filharmonia.gda.pl.*

Northern Peoples Folk Festival: mid-July. *www.nck.org.pl.*

"Baltic Sail": International yacht regatta during the 3rd week in July. *www.balticsail.pl.*

Street Theatre Festival: Mid-July. *www.feta.pl.*

Gdańsk Carillon Festival: End of July, beginning of August.

Shakespeare Festival: Beginning of August. www.teatr-szekspir.gda.pl.

Sopot's International Song Festival: (Open-air Opera), in August.

Słowiński National Park★★

Słowiński Park Narodowy

This coastal National Park boasts amazing shifting sand dunes *(ruchome wydmy)* on a scale unique in Europe. The Park gets its name from a small ancient tribe of Slav origin, the Slovincians, who settled permanently in this border area between Western and Eastern Pomerania. This desert landscape is broken by the presence of lakes and forests plus a small *skansen* devoted to traditional village architecture. The seaside resort of Łeba is the main gateway to the park.

A BIT OF GEOGRAPHY

Created in 1967, the Słowiński National Park was included in 1977 on UNESCO's List of World Biosphere Reserves. It extends along the 33km of coastline separating Łeba in the east and Rowy in the west, and its landscape combines beaches, dunes, marshes, moors and peat bogs. A quarter of its 186sq km total area is covered in forest, another quarter consists of a string of four lakes (Jezioro Łebsko, Jezioro Gardno, Jezioro Sarbsko, Jezioro Dołgie Wielkie), once bays progressively cut off from the sea by the formation of a sand bar.

With some 250 different bird species, both temporary and permanent inhabitants of the park, including the rare white-tailed eagle, the shores of the lake are a real paradise for ornithologists.

The most spectacular part of the Park is the narrow sand bank, covered with pines, which separates Lake Łebsko from the Baltic. This is where you will find the semi-circular shifting dunes, swept by the winds and constantly moving inland to the east.

The dunes which form a sand mountain covering some 5sq km, the highest topping 42m, advance at a speed of several metres a year *(up to 9m)* and one can observe the relentless process of the

- **Michelin Map:** Map of Poland B1 – Województwo of Pomerania.
- **Info:** Ul. 11 Listopada 5a, Łeba. ℰ(59) 866 16 23. www.lotleba.pl.
- **Location:** Łeba, situated in the eastern part of the Park, lies 110km from Gdańsk, 55km from Słupsk, 30km from Lębork.
- **Don't Miss:** A climb to the top of the shifting dunes, the fine beach at Łeba, a bike tour round Lake Łebsko returning to Łeba along the beach.
- **Timing:** Allow at least one whole day to enjoy the park, more if you wish to make the most of Łeba's seaside activities.

GETTING AROUND

BY BUS/RAIL – Train and bus – Access from **Gdynia station** *(4 trains/day)* to Lębork then bus *(1/hr)* to Łeba. **Bus** – Buses link **Gdynia** and **Łeba** *(94km)* 2 to 4 times a day.

BY BIKE – Bike hire on leaving Łeba towards the entrance to the park. Allow about 40 PLN for the day.

PRACTICAL INFORMATION

Phone code – ℰ(0)59.
Tourist Office – Informacja Turystyczna Łeba, *Ul. 11 Listopada 5a.* ℰ866 16 23. www.lotleba.pl.

sand burying the pine forest and creating a desolate but highly photogenic landscape.

At the beginning of World War II, General Rommel's Afrika Korps took over the dunes as their training ground and the site was also used to establish launching pads for the V1 and V2 rockets aimed at London, England and other European cities.

Dunes, Słowiński National Park

© Alexander Lorenz/iStockphoto

ŁEBA
(Population 3,892)

Framed by two lakes, the Baltic and a river of the same name, the peaceful little fishing port of Łeba (pronounced Weba) changes every summer into a seaside resort sought after by Polish holidaymakers. This Kashubian village founded in the 10C, lying west of the mouth of the River Łeba, was devastated by a terrible storm in 1558. The town was rebuilt on the opposite bank and the ruins of the former village disappeared under the sand. It was at the beginning of the 20C that the town set about developing its tourist industry, as shown by the former Kurhaus Hotel (now called **Neptun Hotel**), an impressive building erected on the seafront in 1903. The expressionist painter Max Pechstein, a member of the "Die Brücke" group, lived in Łeba between 1921 and 1945. Returned to Poland in 1945, the small town, which has no historic monuments, is worth a visit for its fine **beach**, which offers visitors a pleasant stay, even if the water temperature barely reaches 20°C in summer. It is above all the ideal gateway to the Słowiński National Park.

NATIONAL PARK★★

The Park's headquarters are located in Smołdzino (Ul. Bohaterów Warszawy 1a; ℘811 72 04), but information is available from the Tourist Office in Łeba. To enter the park, which can be explored on foot or by bike, there is a charge in high season of 4.60 PLN–0.50 PLN per bike. ⊙Open May–Sept 7am–9pm; Oct –Apr 8am–4pm. Cars and buses are not allowed beyond the Rąbka parking area situated 2.5km from Łeba.

The Góra Łącka Dune★★

From the Rąbka parking area, allow 3hr30min on foot return or 1hr by bike. This 42m-high dune, the highest of the shifting dunes, is easily accessible and, from the top, one can admire this strange, almost sahara-like landscape.

Bike Tour round Lake Łebsko

About 50km. Allow a whole day. Bike hire in Rąbka: 10 PLN/hr. Start from the southern part of the lake. After cycling 21km, you will reach Kluki, where the museum described below is situated; continue via Czołpino and return to Łeba by the "beach road" along the packed sand licked by the waves on the very edge of the Baltic.

Kluki
Slovincian Skansen (Muzeum Wsi Słowińskiej w Klukach)★

An annexe of Słupsk's Museum of Central Pomerania. If you are not cycling, Kluki's Skansen is accessible by car from Słupsk, 41km away. During the high season, a shuttle boat sails across the lake between Rąbka and Kluki. 76–214 Smołdzino. ℘846 30 20. ⊙Open mid-May–mid-Sept Tue–Sun 10am–6pm; mid-Sept–mid-May daily 9am–3pm. ⊚10 PLN. www.muzeum.slupsk.pl. Lying in a remote position southwest of Lake Łebsko, within the perimeter of the Słowiński National Park, the historic village of Kluki (*Klucken* in German) was turned into an ethnographic museum in 1963. This authentic village, comprising original houses (not ones that had been moved) was inhabited by Kashubians from western Pomerania called Słowińcy (Slovincians). Isolated by the massive germanisation forced on the region in the 19C, Slovincian traditions and culture survived longer in this micro-region and yet after the war there were only a few people left who still had vague notions of a dialect now lost.

Smołdzino

Not on the bike itinerary.
Allow 10km more there and back.
The National Park's headquarters are located here and Smołdzino also houses the **Park Museum**, which presents local flora and fauna. ⬆ 1km southwest of the village, a path leads (*in 15min*) to the summit of **Mount Rowokół** (114m). From the top of the observation tower, there is a superb view of the region.

Czołpino

From Czołpino (*furthest spot accessible by car*), you can climb (*10min*) up to the **lighthouse (Latarnia Morska)** standing at the top of the highest dune rising to an altitude of 55.1m above sea level (🕐 *open Jun–Aug 10am–7pm;* 🎫*3 PLN*).

KASHUBIA (KASZUBY)★★

Kashubian Switzerland (*Szwajcaria Kaszubska*) boasting fine landscapes dotted with lakes, forests and morainic hills is a region of picturesque folk traditions lying west of Gdańsk. Its 200,000-strong community does not speak a Polish dialect but an original language which mixes some German with archaic Slavic expressions. It was thanks to the Kashubians' deep attachment to Poland that, in 1918, the country obtained a 72km access to the sea.

Kartuzy

▶ *33km west of Gdańsk.*
This small town, which is the region's unofficial capital, gets its name from the Carthusian monks who founded a monastery at the end of the 14C.
The Carthusian monastery lies on the shores of Lake Klasztorne. There remains a Gothic collegiate church with an unusual Baroque roof designed to remind the monks of the shape of a coffin and therefore impending death. A surprising white angel of death, symbolically cutting down all new entrants into the church, and a *memento mor* placed at the top of the east end's buttresses add the finishing touch to this macabre setting.

Ethnographic Musuem

Ul.Kościerska1. 𝒫*681 14 42. www.muzeum-kaszubskie.gda.pl.* 🕐*Open May–Sept Tue–Fri 8am– 4pm, Sat 8am–3pm, Sun and public holidays 10am–2pm; Oct–Apr Tue–Fri 8am–4pm, Sat 8am–3pm.* 🎫*10 PLN.* The museum displays costumes, toys and objects illustrating the traditions of the Kashubian people.

ADDRESSES

🏨 STAY

Łeba offers many private rooms in addition to the hotels.

😊 **Arkun** – *Ul. Wróblewskiego 11.* 𝒫*866 24 19. www.arkun.ta.pl. 22 rooms.* This yellow-brick hotel near the canal with a corner tower offers plain and inexpensive year-round accommodation

😊😊💲😊 **Hotel Neptun** – *Ul. Sosnowa 1.* 𝒫*866 14 32. www.neptunhotel.pl. 32 rooms. Restaurant* 😊😊. Grand Hotel atmosphere (since 1903) in this fine building looking like a castle reigning supreme over the seafront. Compulsory half board in summer. Off season double room at 420 PLN.

🍽 EAT

Besides the hotel Neptun restaurant there's the **Karczma Kaszubianka** – *Ul. Kościuszki 19. Open 10am–last customer.* A large and rather loud establishment in the centre of Łeba, along the river. For a quick bite, they have a fish and chips stand.

Malbork Castle★★★

Formerly known as Marienburg (the Fortress of Mary), **Malbork Castle** was the residence of the grand masters of the Order of the Teutonic Knights and later the capital of that order from 1308 to 1457. It is Europe's largest medieval castle, an impressive red-brick fortress covering an area of 21 hectares, standing on the east bank of the River Nogat. Even though the patina of age may seem somewhat artificial, this castle, admired as a model of its kind by the romantic 19C, has been on UNESCO's World Heritage List since 1997.

A BIT OF HISTORY

In 1309, Hermann von Salza, the 4th Grand Master of the order of the **Teutonic Knights**, made Marienburg (Malbork) the capital of the order. The castle subsequently expanded throughout the 14C. In 1457, during the "Thirteen Years" war (1454–66) caused by the rebellion of the German middle class allied to the Polish nobility against the order, the Polish King, Kazimierz IV, seized the castle and the war ended with the knights' defeat. In 1525, when the Teutonic State was dissolved, Malbork became the regional administrative centre. Partially destroyed during the Swedish wars of 1655–60, the castle was turned into barracks by the Prussians after the first partition of Poland in 1772. A rebuilding programme, more romantic than medieval, was undertaken during the first half of the 19C; followed from 1882 onwards, by a more serious historic reconstruction. It is this replica, fairly true to the original castle (half destroyed in 1945), which was rebuilt.

TOUR

You will be amazed at the huge size of Malbork Castle as you get nearer to Malbork. The best way to appreciate it is to walk onto the footbridge leading to the opposite bank. The monumental

- **Michelin Map:** Map of Poland B1 – Województwo of Pomerania.
- **Info:** Ticket office on the esplanade, facing the castle entrance. ℰ(055) 647 09 78. www.zamek.malbork.pl. Open mid-Apr–mid-Sept Tue–Sun 9am–8pm (exhibitions until 7pm, ticket office until 7.30pm); mid–end Sept Tue–Sun 9am –5pm (courtyard until 7pm, ticket office until 6pm); Oct– mid-Apr Tue–Sun 10am– 5pm (exhibitions until 3pm, ticket office until 4pm). 35 PLN. Courtyard is the only part open on Mondays.
- **Location:** 58km from Gdańsk, 30km from Elbląg, 315km from Warsaw.
- **Don't Miss:** The overall view from the pedestrian bridge spanning the Nogat.

GETTING AROUND

BY RAIL – Railway station – Malbork station is a 15min walk from the castle. Several trains a day to **Warsaw**, Gdańsk and Olsztyn.

PRACTICAL INFORMATION

Phone code – ℰ0(55).
Postal code – 82-200.
Tourist Information Centre –
Ul. Kościuszki 54. ℰ647 47 47. Mon–Fri 8am–6pm, Sat–Sun 10am–2pm.

fortress, surrounded by a double ring of ramparts, consists of three castles: in the north is the Low Castle or Esplanade covering half the total area; in the centre is the MIddle Castle with the Grand Masters' Palace and in the south is the High Castle.

The Low Castle

(Zamek Niski) or **Esplanade (Przed-zamcze).** Dating mainly from the 14C,

The Teutonic Knights

Founded in 1190, during the Third Crusade to the Holy Land (1189–1192), the *Order of the Teutonic Knights of the Hospital of St Mary of Jerusalem* was a military and religious order. Established in Venice, the knights were called upon in 1226 to help the Polish Duke Konrad of Mazovia subdue the Prussians, a pagan tribe from the shores of the Baltic; having duly exterminated the Prussians and been rewarded with the gift of the stronghold of Chełmno, eventually they imposed their military strength and consolidated their power over the whole of Pomerania, then the Baltic coast and threatened the kingdom of Poland. At the same time as they moved eastwards, they settled in their path German colonies which contributed, through the expansion of trade, to accelerating the development of towns like Toruń, founded in 1233 by the Order, or Gdańsk, conquered in 1308.

One year later, the capital of the Order was transferred from Venice to Marienburg (Malbork). The knights' domination of the region lasted 146 years. Faced with a growing conflict with the Polish Crown to whom they denied access to the sea, the Order started to decline in 1410, after being defeated by the Polish-Lithuanian alliance at the battle of Grunwald-Tannenberg and, following the Treaty of Toruń signed in 1466, it had to give back to Poland "Royal Prussia" or Gdańsk's Pomerania. Dissolved in 1525, the Teutonic State became a Protestant duchy of eastern Prussia, with the Polish king as its overlord.

this freely accessible part comprises several annexes, such as the arsenal, the armoury or the bell foundry, as well as Gothic defences.

The Middle Castle★★
(Zamek Średni)

Ticket in hand, walk over the bridge spanning the large moat and enter the vast courtyard of the Middle Castle. To the west, on the river's side, stands the **Grand Masters' Palace**★★★(Pałac Wielkich Mistrzów), begun in the early 14C and completed between 1383 and 1393; note its fine façade, particularly at the third floor level. Open to the public following a lengthy restoration, this part comprises three different buildings. The **palace** itself, erected before 1305, containing the Grand Masters' living quarters, the tower known as the **"Winter Refectory"**, built between 1330 and 1340, and the main building housing the **"Summer Refectory"**, built between 1330 and 1390. These two refectories, situated on the third floor, feature splendid palm vaulting and traces of polychrome decorations. Adjoining the Grand Masters' Palace, along the whole length of the west wing, is the largest room in the castle *(450sq m)*, the

Knights' Hall (Sala Rycerska) or **Great Refectory** (Wielki Refektarz), boasting further palm vaulting. The building situated in the east wing, on the other side of the courtyard, contains a remarkable **collection of amber**★★ (Dzieje Bursztynu).

The High Castle★★★
(Zamek Wysoki)

The tour continues with the High Castle, the third and oldest part of the castle but also the best preserved of the three, where the order's treasure was kept. To get to it, cross the second drawbridge over the "Dry Moat" situated on the right of a group of sculptures representing four Grand Masters of the order. Note the ceramic low relief depicting a Teutonic knight above the doorway. Beyond the entrance is a courtyard framed by Gothic galleries with, in its centre, a covered well surmounted by a pelican nourishing its offspring. The cloister feel of the place comes from the fact that the construction of this quadrangle began in 1280, before the transfer of the order's seat to Malbork, and that it was therefore intended as a stronghold to house the soldier-monks.

After visiting the **kitchens** and **utility rooms** on the ground floor *(note* *there is no set direction to follow, so be inquisitive),* go up to the first floor to look at the dignitaries' **bedrooms** and the **dormitories**, then to the second floor, where you will find the **refectory**★ and the **Room with the two fireplaces** followed by the **Convention Communal Room**. On the way down, the north wing of the cloister leads to the **Chapter House**★★★ then to the famous **Golden Gate**★★★ (Złota Brama) marking the entrance to the **Church of Our Lady**★★★ *(accessible and interesting because it has not been restored yet).* This fine 13C carved doorway, covered with polychrome decorations, frames a rare oak door from the early 14C. From there, it is possible to reach the top of the **square tower** *(mid-Apr–mid-Sept; additional ⌗8 PLN),* affording a **view**★★★, which extends over the whole surrounding Żuławy. A walk along the terraces surrounding the castle will lead you to the **Crypt of St Anne**★, a funeral chapel with fine portals at the north and south entrances; the chapel houses the funeral stelae of three Grand Masters of the Order, dating from the 14C and 15C. A spiral staircase *(near the main door)* gives access via the "Dry Moat" to the outer defences.

EXCURSIONS
Gniew★
(Population 6,929)
33km south of Malbork.
This charming little town, situated on high ground on the north bank of the Wisła, is one of the oldest cities in Pomerania. Founded in 1297, Gniew *(Gnief,* which means anger in Polish) also has its own **Teutonic castle** built in 1282 and partly preserved 14C **ramparts** which account for it being sometimes called the "Polish Carcassonne". The outline of the castle hill (Wzgórze Zamkowe) offers from a distance an impressive view of this massive stronghold. The fortress, which is a real conservatory of medieval customs and traditions, houses the **medieval section of Gdańsk's Archaeological Museum** (◷ *open May–Oct Tue–Sun 9am–5pm; ⌗8 PLN)* and is the setting

of several festive events in summer. The small **medieval town** boasts a lovely gently sloping **Rynek** with a Gothic 14C town hall at its centre.

Pelplin Cathedral★★
▶ *14km northwest of Gniew.*
In spite of Pelplin being known as the "Pomeranian Athens", the small town's only treasure is its Gothic cathedral, the former church of a Cistercian abbey founded in 1274 by the Duke of Pomerania. The brick edifice, built between 1280 and 1320, features amazing dimensions and late-15C Gothic vaulting. The interior is sumptuously furnished: it has a monumental Renaissance high altar from 1623 framing a painting by Herman Han (1625) and 21 other altars.

ADDRESSES

ⵖ/EAT
⊜⊜ **Gothic Cafe** – Ul. Starościńska 1. ℘647 08 89. This excellent restaurant is located in the middle castle of Malbork.

🛏 STAY
GNIEW
⊜⊜ **Hotel Restauracja Pałac Marysieńki** – Pl. Zamkowy 3, 83-140 Gniew. ℘(58) 535 25 37. www.zamek-gniew.pl. 40 rooms. Fine view of the peaceful Wisła from some of the back rooms of this 17C palace, once the residence of Queen MK Sobieska, built by Jan III Sobieski. The **restaurant** linked to the hotel is less picturesque.

MALBORK
⊜⊜⊜ **Hotel Stary Malbork** – Ul. 17 Marca 26–27. ℘647 24 00. www.hotelstarymalbork.com.pl. 30 rooms. Decorated in various shades of pastel green, this Art Nouveau-style hotel offers convenient facilities in recently restored 19C twin houses.

⊜⊜⊜ **Hotel Zamek** – Ul. Starościńska 14. ℘272 84 00. www.hotelprodus.pl. 42 rooms. A little of the dark austere atmosphere of the castle pervades this hotel housed inside the former Teutonic hospital in the Low Castle.

INDEX

INDEX

INDEX

INDEX

INDEX

INDEX

🏠 STAY

🍴 EAT

MAPS AND PLANS

COMPANION PUBLICATIONS

MICHELIN MAP 720 POLAND
Large-format map providing detailed
road systems.
 ◆ Comprehensive city and town index
 ◆ Scale 1:700 000 (1cm = approx. 7km)
 ◆ Driving Time Chart

MICHELIN MAP 705 EUROPE
Main road map of Europe showing
major road networks and relief. The map
also includes driving information and
distance charts, ideal for route planning.
 ◆ Comprehensive index
 ◆ Scale 1:3 000 000

EUROPE ROAD MAP
This European main road atlas comes
with a full index, and includes 74
town and area plans, distances and
temperatures. Scales in:
Western Europe, 1:1 000 000
Eastern Europe, 1:3 000 000.

INTERNET
Michelin is pleased to offer a route-
planning service on the Internet:
www.ViaMichelin.com.
Choose the shortest route, a route
without tolls, or the Michelin
recommended route to your destination;
you can also access information about
hotels and restaurants from *The Michelin
Guide*, and tourists sights from *The Green
Guide*. There are a number of useful
maps and plans in the guide, listed
opposite.

MAP LEGEND

	Sight	Winter sports resort	Spa
Highly recommended	★★★	✵✵✵	♯♯♯
Recommended	★★	✵✵	♯♯
Interesting	★	✵	♯

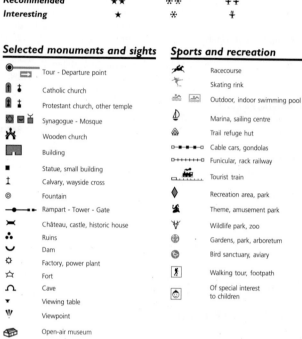

Selected monuments and sights

	Tour - Departure point
	Catholic church
	Protestant church, other temple
	Synagogue - Mosque
	Wooden church
	Building
	Statue, small building
	Calvary, wayside cross
	Fountain
	Rampart - Tower - Gate
	Château, castle, historic house
	Ruins
	Dam
	Factory, power plant
	Fort
	Cave
	Viewing table
	Viewpoint
	Open-air museum

Sports and recreation

	Racecourse
	Skating rink
	Outdoor, indoor swimming pool
	Marina, sailing centre
	Trail refuge hut
	Cable cars, gondolas
	Funicular, rack railway
	Tourist train
	Recreation area, park
	Theme, amusement park
	Wildlife park, zoo
	Gardens, park, arboretum
	Bird sanctuary, aviary
	Walking tour, footpath
	Of special interest to children

Abbreviations

A	Agricultural office (Chambre d'agriculture)	P	Local authority offices (Préfecture, sous-préfecture)
C	Chamber of Commerce (Chambre de commerce)	POL.	Police station (Police)
H	Town hall (Hôtel de ville)		Police station (Gendarmerie)
J	Law courts (Palais de justice)		Theatre (Théâtre)
M	Museum (Musée)	U	University (Université)

Additional symbols

	Tourist information		Post office
	Motorway or other primary route		Telephone
	Junction: complete, limited		Covered market
	Pedestrian street		Barracks
	Unsuitable for traffic, street subject to restrictions		Drawbridge
	Steps – Footpath		Quarry
	Train station – Auto-train station		Mine
	Coach (bus) station		Car ferry (river or lake)
	Tram		Ferry service: cars and passengers
	Metro, underground		Foot passengers only
	Park-and-Ride		Access route number common to Michelin maps and town plans
	Access for the disabled	Bert (R.)...	Main shopping street
		AZ B	Map co-ordinates

You know
the Green Guide

...Do you really
know MICHELIN?

● Data 31/12/2009

The world No.1 in tires
with 16.3% of the market

A business presence in over **170 countries**

A manufacturing footprint
at the heart of markets

In 2009 **72** industrial sites in **19** countries produced:

- **150** million tires
- **10** million maps and guides

Highly international **teams**

Over **109 200** employees* from all cultures on all continents

including **6 000** people employed in R&D centers

in Europe, the US and Asia.

*102 692 full-time equivalent staff

The Michelin Group
at a glance

Michelin
competes

At the end of 2009

- **Le Mans 24-hour race**
  12 consecutive years of victories

- **Endurance 2009**
  - 6 victories on 6 stages
  in Le Mans Series
  - 12 victories on 12 stages
  in American Le Mans Series

- **Paris-Dakar**
  Since the beginning of the event,
  the Michelin group has won
  in all categories

- **Moto endurance**
  2009 World Champion

- **Trial**
  Every World Champion title
  since 1981 (except 1992)

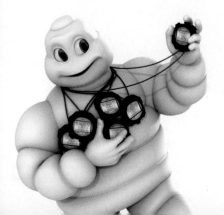

Michelin,
established close to its customers

○ **72 plants in 19 countries**

- Algeria
- Brazil
- Canada
- China
- Colombia
- France
- Germany
- Hungary
- Italy
- Japan
- Mexico
- Poland
- Romania
- Russia
- Serbia
- Spain
- Thailand
- UK
- USA

● **A Technology Center spread over 3 continents**

- Asia
- Europe
- North America

● **Natural rubber plantations**

- Brazil

Our mission

To make a sustainable contribution to progress in the mobility of goods and people by enhancing freedom of movement, safety, efficiency and the pleasure of travelling.

Michelin committed to environmental-friendliness

Michelin, world leader in low rolling resistance tires, actively reduces fuel consumption and vehicle gas emission.

For its products, Michelin develops state-of-the-art technologies in order to:
- Reduce fuel consumption, while improving overall tire performance.
- Increase life cycle to reduce the number of tires to be processed at the end of their useful lives;
- Use raw materials which have a low impact on the environment.

Furthermore, at the end of 2008, 99.5% of tire production in volume was carried out in ISO 14001* certified plants.

Michelin is committed to implementing recycling channels for end-of-life tires.

*environmental certification

**Passenger Car
Light Truck**

Truck

Michelin
a key mobility enabler

Earthmover

Aircraft

Agricultural

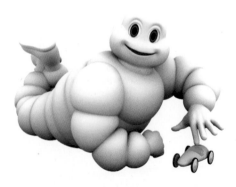

Two-wheel   **Distribution**

Partnered with vehicle manufacturers, in tune with users,
active in competition and in all the distribution channels,
Michelinis continually innovating to promote mobility today
and to invent that of tomorrow.

**Maps and   ViaMichelin,   Michelin
Guides   travel   Lifestyle,
                  assistance   for your travel
                  services   accessories**

MICHELIN
plays on balanced performance

- **Long tire life**
- **Fuel savings**
- ○ **Safety on the road**

... MICHELIN tires provide you with the best performance, without making a single sacrifice.

The MICHELIN tire
pure technology

1 Tread
A thick layer of rubber
provides contact with the ground.
It has to channel water away
and last as long as possible.

2 Crown plies
This double or triple reinforced belt
has both vertical flexibility
and high lateral rigidity.
It provides the steering capacity.

3 Sidewalls
These cover and protect the textile casing
whose role is to attach the tire tread
to the wheel rim.

4 Bead area for attachment to the rim
Its internal bead wire
clamps the tire firmly
against the wheel rim.

5 Inner liner
This makes the tire
almost totally impermeable
and maintains the correct inflation pressure.

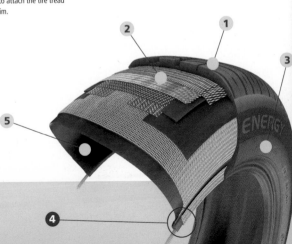

Heed
the MICHELIN Man's advice

To improve safety:

- I drive with the correct tire pressure
- I check the tire pressure every month
- I have my car regularly serviced
- I regularly check the appearance of my tires (wear, deformation)
- I am responsive behind the wheel
- I change my tires according to the season

www.michelin.com
www.michelin.(your country extension – e.g. .fr for France)

Michelin Apa Publications Ltd

A joint venture between Michelin and Langenscheidt

58 Borough High Street, London SE1 1XF, United Kingdom

No part of this publication may be reproduced in any form
without the prior permission of the publisher.

© 2011 Michelin Apa Publications Ltd
ISBN 978-1-907099-08-3
Printed: November 2010
Printed and bound in Germany